The Early Modern Englishwoman:
A Facsimile Library of Essential Works

Series I

Printed Writings, 1500–1640: Part 2

Volume 5

Elizabeth and Mary Tudor

Advisory Board:

Margaret J.M. Ezell
Texas A & M University

Elaine Hobby
Loughborough University

Suzanne W. Hull
The Huntington Library

Barbara K. Lewalski
Harvard University

Stephen Orgel
Stanford University

Ellen Rosand
Yale University

Mary Beth Rose
University of Illinois, Chicago

Hilda L. Smith
University of Cincinnati

Retha M. Warnicke
Arizona State University

Georgianna Ziegler
The Folger Shakespeare Library

The Early Modern Englishwoman: A Facsimile Library of Essential Works

Series I

Printed Writings, 1500–1640: Part 2

Volume 5

Elizabeth and Mary Tudor

Selected and Introduced by
Anne Lake Prescott

General Editors
Betty S. Travitsky and Patrick Cullen

Ashgate

Aldershot • Burlington USA • Singapore • Sydney

The Introductory Note copyright © Anne Lake Prescott 2001

All rights reserved. No part of this publication may be reproduced, stored in a retrieval system, or transmitted in any form or by any means, electronic, mechanical, photocopying, recording, or otherwise without the prior permission of the publisher.

Published by
Ashgate Publishing Limited
Gower House
Croft Road
Aldershot
Hants GU11 3HR
England

Ashgate Publishing Company
131 Main Street
Burlington, VT 05401-5600 USA

Ashgate website: http://www.ashgate.com

British Library Cataloguing-in-Publication Data
Tudor, Elizabeth
The early modern Englishwoman : a facsimile library of essential works. – 2nd ed.
Part 2: Printed writings, 1500–1640: Vol. 5
1. English literature – Early modern, 1500–1700 2. English literature – Women authors 3. Women – England – History – Renaissance, 1450–1600 – Sources 4. Women – England – History – Modern period, 1600– – Sources 5. Women – Literary collections
I. Title II.Tudor, Mary III. Travitsky, Betty S. IV. Cullen, Patrick Colborn V. Prescott, Anne Lake VI. Marguerite, Queen, consort of Henry II, King of Navarre, 1492–1549. Godly medytacyon of the christen sowle VII. Cancellar, John. E. R. godly meditations, or prayers, set forth after the order of the alphabet, of the Queen Maiesties name VIII. Erasmus, Desiderius, d. 1536. Paraphrase of the gospel of St. John
820.8'09287

Library of Congress Cataloging-in-Publication Data
The early modern Englishwoman: a facsimile library of essential works. Part 2. Printed Writings 1500–1640 / general editors, Betty S. Travitsky and Patrick Cullen.

See page vi for complete CIP Block 99–55937

The woodcut reproduced on the title page and on the case is from the title page of Margaret Roper's trans. of [Desiderius Erasmus] *A Devout Treatise upon the Pater Noster* (circa 1524).

ISBN 1 84014 218 9

Printed in Great Britain by Antony Rowe Ltd, Chippenham, Wiltshire

CONTENTS

Preface by the General Editors

Introductory Note

Elizabeth Tudor, trans.,
[Marguerite of Angoulême, Queen of Navarre]
A Godly Medytacyon of the christen sowle (1548)

Appendix: Selections from [John Cancellar] *E.R. Godly Meditations, or Prayers, set forth after the order of the Alphabet, of the Queenes Maiesties name* (1568)

Mary Tudor, trans.,
[Desiderius Erasmus]
The paraphrase of Erasmus upon the gospell of sainct John in *The first tome or volume of the Paraphrase of Erasmus upon the newe testament* (1548)

Library of Congress Cataloging-in-Publication Data
Elizabeth and Mary Tudor / selected and introduced by Anne Lake Prescott.
p. cm.– (The early modern Englishwoman. Printed writings, 1500–1640, Part 2 ; v. 5)
Includes bibliographical references.
Contents: A godly medytacyon of the christen sowle / Marguerite d' Angoulême ; translated by Elizabeth Tudor – Godly meditations, or prayers set forth after the order of the alphabet, of the queen maiesties name / John Cancellar – Paraphrase of the gospel of St. John / Desiderius Erasmus ; translated by Mary Tudor.
ISBN 1-84014-218-9
1. Bible. N.T. John – Paraphrases, English. 2. Spiritual life – Christianity – Poetry. 3. Christian Poetry, French – Translations into English. 4. Queens – Prayer-books and devotions – English. 5. Elizabeth I, Queen of England, 1533–1603. I. Elizabeth I, Queen of England, 1533–1603. II. Mary I, Queen of England, 1516–1558. III. Prescott, Anne Lake. IV. Marguerite, Queen, consort of Henry II, King of Navarre, 1492–1549. Miroir de l'âme pécheresse. English. V. Cancellar, James. Godly meditations, or prayers set forth after the order of the alphabet, of the queen maiesties name. VI. Erasmus, Desiderius, d. 1536. Paraphrasis in Evangelium secundum Joannem. English. VII. Series.

BS2617 .E713 2000
841'.--dc13

99–55937

PREFACE
BY THE GENERAL EDITORS

Until very recently, scholars of the early modern period have assumed that there were no Judith Shakespeares in early modern England. Much of the energy of the current generation of scholars has been devoted to constructing a history of early modern England that takes into account what women actually wrote, what women actually read, and what women actually did. In so doing the masculinist representation of early modern women, both in their own time and ours, is deconstructed. The study of early modern women has thus become one of the most important—indeed perhaps the most important—means for the rewriting of early modern history.

The Early Modern Englishwoman: A Facsimile Library of Essential Works is one of the developments of this energetic reappraisal of the period. As the names on our advisory board and our list of editors testify, it has been the beneficiary of scholarship in the field, and we hope it will also be an essential part of that scholarship's continuing momentum.

The Early Modern Englishwoman is designed to make available a comprehensive and focused collection of writings in English from 1500 to 1750, both by women and for and about them. The three series of *Printed Writings* (1500–1640, 1641–1700, and 1701–1750) provide a comprehensive if not entirely complete collection of the separately published writings by women. In reprinting these writings we intend to remedy one of the major obstacles to the advancement of feminist criticism of the early modern period, namely the limited availability of the very texts upon which the field is based. The volumes in the facsimile library reproduce carefully chosen copies of these texts, incorporating significant variants (usually in appendices). Each text is preceded by a short introduction providing an overview of the life and work of a writer along with a survey of important scholarship. These works, we strongly believe, deserve a large readership—of historians, literary critics, feminist critics, and non-specialist readers.

The Early Modern Englishwoman also includes separate facsimile series of *Essential Works for the Study of Early Modern Women* and of *Manuscript Writings*. These facsimile series are complemented by *The Early Modern Englishwoman 1500–1750: Contemporary Editions*. Also under our general editorship, this series will include both old-spelling and modernized editions of works by and about women and gender in early modern England.

New York City
2001

INTRODUCTORY NOTE

The two translators whose printed works are contained in this volume were half-sisters, daughters of the capricious Henry VIII of England; both became ruling queens. The older, Mary Tudor (1516–1558), daughter of Henry and his repudiated first wife, the Roman Catholic Catherine of Aragon, ruled England from 1553–1558; her attempts to stamp out heresy and return the country to the Catholic faith earned her the sobriquet 'Bloody Mary'. The second, Elizabeth (1533–1603), daughter of Henry and his beheaded second queen Anne Boleyn, ruled from 1558–1603. As children, both sisters suffered from their father's changes of wives and faiths, but after his marriage in 1543 to Katherine Parr (his sixth and surviving queen) both benefited from their new step-mother's kindness. Through her influence both daughters were brought back to court. In different ways, Katherine was involved in the production of the texts contained in this volume; they appear here according to the order in which they were first printed.

Elizabeth Tudor (1533–1603): ***A Godly Medytacyon of the christen sowle***

When Elizabeth was eleven someone – we do not know who, but perhaps one of her teachers or her step-mother Katherine Parr – suggested that she translate *Le Miroir de l'âme pécheresse* (1531), a verse meditation by Marguerite of Angoulême, sister of Francis I, King of France, and wife of Henry, King of Navarre. Elizabeth probably began during the second half of 1544. Working from a 1533 edition or perhaps its 1539 reprint, she printed her letters carefully on ruled paper, inserted neatly written corrections, and embroidered a pretty cover for the finished book (Salminen, 1979; Schell, 1993). She dedicated it to Katherine as a New Year's present in January, 1545. It is unlikely that so young a princess, whatever her piety or her love for an affectionate step-mother, decided on her own to take on this task, though it is possible she was also exercising her own taste, for she had a life-long interest in foreign languages (Marcus et al., 2000, p. xv). The enterprise, moreover, may have had a diplomatic aim: England was negotiating peace with the French, Marguerite was a leader of a pro-English faction, and there was talk of marrying Elizabeth to a French prince (Prescott, 1985; Vose, 1985).

The *Miroir* had apparently disturbed some conservatives in France. Although Marguerite seems to have thought of herself as Catholic, those who cherished orthodox theology and Church traditions suspected her of being not just reformist and evangelical but Lutheran. Her poem speaks fervently of her nothingness before God and the inadequacy of her will, doing so in terms of family relationships: she is God's sinful wife, daughter, sister, mother. But the poem also celebrates the Lord's loving forgiveness as the sinner's husband, father, brother, and son. To express religious passion through a paradoxical tangle of familial relationships has ample biblical precedent even if treating God as a brother is fairly unusual and, granted the queen's political and emotional closeness to her own brother, psychologically resonant (Snyder, 1997). The same Lord, for Christians, is Mary's father and son; Christ is the Bridegroom married to his Church or to the individual – often feminized – human soul. And if we are all siblings, then Jesus must be our brother. Still, it is hard to find another poem that plays so forcefully in such a concentrated way with these relationships. More worrisome to traditionalists was Marguerite's stress on the Bible: her poem is a web of scriptural quotation with little room for saints, purgatory, or sacraments.

Whatever the impetus for the translation, the gesture was delicately positioned: the *Miroir* was not heretical enough to disturb Francis and his court, where Marguerite was in good favour, but it could be read as evangelical and even anti-papist in its scriptural emphasis and its insistence that only God, not human willpower, has saving force. Indeed, in the fall of 1533 the Sorbonne's theological faculty was trying to have

Miroir censored until Francis, who had been out of town, put a stop to such efforts (Salminen, 1985, pp. 21–30). Some in England, moreover, still hoped against hope that Francis would lead the French Church out of Rome's orbit. In its small way, the translation may have been meant to promote such a move. At any rate, news of it might please Francis I. It would also, of course, please Katherine, whose attitudes in many ways would prove to parallel Marguerite's. Whether it would have pleased Henry VIII is another matter. Marguerite tells God gratefully that he forgives his unfaithful 'wife', whereas human kings would send them to be executed. Such a thought might well upset the King who had Elizabeth's mother, Anne Boleyn, and step-mother, Katherine Howard, beheaded for adultery. The translation was printed only after Henry's death.

In April 1548, John Bale, once a monk but converted into an eager Protestant hoping to return to England now that Edward VI was king, published Elizabeth's translation as *A Godly Medytacyon of the christen sowle*. It is Bale's edition that is reprinted in this volume from the copy of The Huntington Library with the last page supplemented by the title page of the copy at the Folger Shakespeare Library. (On editions, see Hughey, 1935.) Whether Bale worked from Elizabeth's holograph (which long remained in the Parr family's possession before being acquired by Oxford's Bodleian Library) or whether he had someone else's copy is unknown. The text has been revised, if not thoroughly, with a few corrections, paragraphing, and a somewhat different set of marginal citations of Scripture. Bale says that Elizabeth also sent along, in her own hand, some verses from Ecclesiasticus and some 'sentences' based on Psalm 13 ('The fool hath said in his heart there is no God') translated into several languages. He includes these in the printed text. Perhaps, then, the princess was involved in this publishing venture, at least indirectly. The full metrical translation of Psalm 13, though, is probably Bale's own; at least he does not credit it to Elizabeth. His opening epistle scourges Catholic corruption in a style typical of Reformation polemic, while his Conclusion once more praises the translator's wisdom and anticipates yet greater things when her 'dyscressyon and years shall be more rype and auncyent'. That Bale thinks she made her translation when she was fourteen, though, shows ignorance of her work's history.

Bale, and whoever sent him his manuscript, had an agenda in publishing this work: keeping England on a Reformed path. Bale celebrates not only Edward VI, that young idol-smasher and new Josiah (righteous son of the idol-worshipping Judean king, Amon, who had been slain by his servants [2 Kings 21, 23, 30]) but also female rulers and female experts on religious matters (Kesselring, 1998). Such praise implicitly supports such Protestant leaders as the dowager Queen, Katherine Parr, who despite her sex would have influence over her step-son, the boy king (Bale could not have known that she was soon to die). The *Medytacyon* is a work of contemplative piety, but printing it in 1548 had political meaning: a Protestant princess had translated a work disliked by the ultra-Catholic and presented it to a Protestant king's Reform-minded step-mother now more than ever in a position to help guide the religious direction of the realm. Perhaps Bale wanted also to help ensure that Elizabeth, not her Catholic sister, Mary, would be next in line for the throne should Edward leave no heir. Bale's roll calls of impressive women, whatever doubts he possibly harboured in his male heart, are generally relevant to early modern pro-feminist discourse; they also had an immediate political point and should be read in light of circumstances at the English court: the King's illness-ridden youth, the fragility of the Reformation in England, the role of Katherine and other great Protestant ladies.

Bale's comments kept their pertinence in 1558 when Elizabeth succeeded to the throne and some said openly what many whispered: God never intended women to govern. (In theory, Bale's arguments would also support the dead Mary Tudor's rights, but as a Catholic she was not the sort of godly queen he had in mind.) The next time the *Medytacyon* saw print (*STC* 17320.5, probably 1568), however, it had shed Bale's apparatus. Why? Anti-Catholic polemics like his were still being written, although his praise of Edward VI would have looked dated. Perhaps the printer, H. Denham, simply lacked legal rights to Bale's version. In any case, a new preface, the omission of the humble dedication to Katherine Parr and epistle to the reader, a set of prayers by James Cancellar designed to be said by Elizabeth, and the passing of twenty years or so all make this a very different text. The translation itself is basically the same, although the phrasing can vary a little. For example, whereas the opening paragraph of Bale's edition (*STC* 17320) says of the speaker's sins 'I perfyghtly fele that their roote is in me', *STC* 17320.5 has 'I perfitely feele also, that the roote of sinne is so graffed in me'. More striking, though, are a splendid image of the royal coat of arms and an acrostic on 'Elizabeth Regina' spelling out imperatives ('Embrace Vertue, Love perfectlye, Imitate Christ', etc.) that could be taken as an admonition to the Queen or as her own rules for herself; the typography stresses that the prayers' first letters also spell ELIZABETH REGINA. This is no devout girl's present but a queen's performance – although it is unclear who is stage-manager and whether Elizabeth helped with the production.

The one extant copy, now in The British Library and reprinted here with their permission, lacks a title-page and date. Since Denham entered it in the Stationers' Register in 1567/8, scholars assign it to 1568, which makes sense. Yet Cancellar's prayers, imagining for the Queen a scripture-citing humility in fact characteristic of her, yet perhaps irritating as a mere subject's implied admonitions, would gain resonance if the true date were several years later. One prayer, for example, reminds God that 'Thou didst promise unto Abraham, a Sonne when he was aged: thou fulfilledst thy promise in olde and barren Sara' (Genesis 15), a reference all too relevant to a queen at least thirty-five years old and childless, and then quotes Psalm 131 on how God promised David an heir: 'of the fruite of thy body, will I set upon thy regall throne' (sig. F3^{v}). There are also several allusions to health, such as the prayer to be released from bodily oppressions (sig. F6^{v}). In 1568 such petitions and reminders would be reasonable. In the early 1570s, when Elizabeth was conducting marriage negotiations and had been severely ill, they would have had (or taken on) added weight – whatever the force with which Elizabeth had told Parliament that any decision to marry was hers alone.

There were to be three more editions of the *Medytacyon*: one, *STC* 17321, likewise by Denham, was reprinted in Thomas Bentley's sumptuous collection of women's writings, *The Monument of Matrones* (1582, *STC* 1892), as its second 'lamp' (a term alluding to Jesus' parable about the wise virgins who keep their lamps trimmed while waiting for the divine Bridegroom). Bentley adds a dedicatory preface noting the Queen's 'owne Honourable works', 'perpetuall virginitie', and example to other women, praying that she have a 'heroicall spirit' and guard her realm's peace so well that 'manie thousand virgins in England and elsewhere' may joyfully sing 'the sweet songs of Sion in their owne land'. Now Elizabeth, not Edward VI, is 'our good Josias'. Bentley's exhortation to the reader explains that the work was originally by 'the vertuous Ladie Margaret Queene of Navar' and 'verie exactlie and faithfullie translated by our most gratious sovereigne', who has won 'great renowme' by it. Now hard to come by, he says, it deserves to be made available. Bentley retains Cancellar's prayers, separating them from the translation by some pages, empties the margins of scriptural citations, and adds prayers he says Elizabeth wrote while imprisoned in the Tower and after her coronation. And, like Cancellar, he admonishes his queen under cover of religious rhetoric, constructing a prayer and soliloquy for her made of phrases from David's psalms as interpreted by the Huguenot scholar Theodore Beza.

Last came a reprint of Bale by R. Ward (1590, *STC* 17322.5). It includes Bale's preface and conclusion but not Cancellar's prayers, which presumably were Denham's property. The unimpressive volume looks like a printer's business venture built on hopes that even an older version of the Queen's work might sell. Unlike Denham's and Bentley's productions, it does not radiate royal glory. Nor do we know what the Queen thought of this revival of her childhood piety in its nearly original form. There were no more editions during her reign. At some point after 1603, however, Thomas Blunville carefully copied out Bentley's version for Katherine Paget; the manuscript is at the Houghton Library, Harvard University (MS Eng 942).

Mary Tudor (1516–1558): *The paraphrase ... upon the gospell of sainct John*

About the same time that Elizabeth translated Marguerite of Angoulême, Queen of Navarre, her older half-sister, Mary (1516–1558), was likewise helping her step-mother, Katherine Parr, reform Tudor devotional life through scripture-based scholarship, literature, and translation (King, 1985; McConica, 1965). Since the Queen was trying to give her new family an atmosphere of warmth and harmony, it must have seemed doubly right to ask the Princess to join a group, headed by the scholar Nicholas Udall, involved in translating the influential *Paraphrases in Novum Testamentum* (1517–1524) by the great humanist Desiderius Erasmus, a set of paraphrases of the New Testament excluding Revelation. Or so many have assumed, although a letter asking that the finished manuscript be delivered soon, while certainly by Katherine, is in Elizabeth's careful script, a fact that complicates the question of the translation's authorship (Mueller). If the texts of the paraphrases of the Gospels and Acts were ready by the fall of 1545, on the other hand, it would seem more likely that Mary, not her much younger sister, was indeed the translator of this long Latin text (Devereux, p. 147). And one could postulate that Elizabeth wrote out a letter to Mary on Katherine's behalf for any of a variety of reasons. Again according to tradition, and indeed according to the prefatory letter to this portion of the publication addressed to Katherine by Nicholas Udall, Mary was only part way through the section on the Gospel of John when illness required her to turn the rest over to her chaplain, Francis Malet.

Intelligent and educated, Mary was well-equipped for the task, and it is probably not merely affection, flattery, or hope of patronage that led some to praise her capacities (Loades, 1989). In his prologue to two texts on the Virgin Mary, for example, the learned Henry Parker, Lord Morley, referred glowingly to the accuracy of a translation she did of a Latin prayer by Thomas Aquinas (cited by McConica, pp. 156–57, from Royal MS. 17 C.xvi). Her translation of Erasmus, too, is fairly close by Renaissance standards. That is to say, Mary does not merely paraphrase Erasmus' line of thought but follows him with some fidelity. On the other hand, her syntax, whatever her individual phrases' sinewy strength, shows a typical mid-Tudor looseness quite unlike the original's taut Latin. Her longer sentences, even when they incorporate subordinations and lexical clues that suggest a tight logical structure, can meander, so modern readers might want to keep handy the recent translation by Jane E. Phillips (1991).

The translations, including Mary's contribution, began to see print under the general editorship of Richard Grafton in 1548, by which time Edward VI was king and the project's noble patronage was about to pass from Katherine Parr to Anne Seymour, Duchess of Suffolk (Devereux, 1983). The Government enjoined all parishes to acquire copies, so that together with various English Bibles and the Book of Common Prayer (first published in 1549) the *Paraphrases* long helped shape England's religious life, bringing what Erasmus thought the best of patristic and modern learning to bear on scripture. The next year the remainder was printed. Because the work was so important, requiring huge press runs and occasional revisions, the bibliographical situation is very tangled. We reprint the entire section on John's gospel from a copy of the 1548 edition at The Huntington Library (*STC* 2854), including Erasmus' preface to the Archduke Ferdinand of Austria and the epistle by Nicholas Udall to Katherine Parr, who was soon to die. The letter, which credits the translation to Mary, is significant for its praise of such admirable women as the learned Cornelia (mother of the Gracchi) or Cicero's eloquent daughter Hortensia, and for its account – doubtless idealized – of scholarly and pious young women in aristocratic Tudor households. Some of what Udall says needs to be taken with a grain of salt. His exclamation that Mary, that 'pierlesse floure of virginitee', prefers her 'maydenlye studies' to 'Courtly delices' (sig. Aaa2), for example, does not square with the evidence (although it admirably suits the persona Elizabeth adopted during those years). As Mary's unhappy reign was to show, she could be deadly serious about religious matters, but she was capable of secular pleasure and as a princess had been faulted by the sobersided for gambling, dancing, and love of fancy clothes and jewels (Loades, p. 119).

No one knows how much of the translation is Mary's and how much her chaplain's. Nor can we be quite sure that illness was the only reason she stopped work. She was, after all, a steadfast Catholic, and by the mid-1540s more than old enough to know that some Catholics thought Erasmus no sound guide to religious life or the Bible. Doubtless he thought himself a good enough Catholic, and his refusal to join the Reformation saddened the more militant Protestants. Still, many believed the saying: 'Erasmus laid the egg that Luther hatched', and Mary may have become uneasy at participating in an enterprise expanding his influence. For example, when Jesus thrice tells Peter to 'Feed my sheep' (John 21.15–17), Erasmus stresses that the apostle's *love* for his master is the source of his elevation (McConica, p. 244). Some might hear in this a rebuke, typical of Erasmus, directed at popes he thought more power-hungry than charitable. Mary's devoutly Catholic mother, Katherine of Aragon, had encouraged humanist studies, but Henry VIII's break with Rome involved a divorce that had brought both women misery, including the bastardization of Mary and, at times, Henry's requirement that mother and daughter not see each other. Even if she experienced no particular theological scruples, Mary may have felt that translating Erasmus was in some way a betrayal of her mother and her supporters, whatever Erasmus' prowess as a scholar and whatever her own chaplain's willingness to carry on; John King (1985, p. 48) says that Mary stopped 'possibly out of disagreement with her step-mother's

Reformist sympathies'. This must remain speculation, of course. Stephen Gardiner, a future leader of 'Bloody' Mary's campaign against 'heresy', denounced the project, but it is unclear if during her reign the *Paraphrases* were removed from English churches (Devereux p. 150). As translation of the *Paraphrases* had neared completion under Edward VI's government, it had become a more obviously Protestant enterprise; on the other hand, Mary may have taken pleasure in the thought of her own learning so widely distributed throughout the kingdom.

References

STC 17320; 17320.5 [Elizabeth]; *STC* 2854 [Mary]

Devereux, E.J. (1983), *Renaissance English Translations of Erasmus: A Bibliography to 1700*, Toronto: University of Toronto Press

Elizabeth I, Queen of England, *Collected Works*, Leah S. Marcus, Janel Mueller, and Mary Beth Rose (eds.) (2000), Chicago: University of Chicago Press

Erasmus, Desiderius, *Collected Works* 46, Toronto: University of Toronto Press, 1974–; 1991

Hughey, Ruth (1935), 'A Note on Queen Elizabeth's "Godly Meditation"', *The Library*, 4th ser. 15, 237–40

Jourda, Pierre (1930, 1978), *Marguerite d'Anqoulême, Duchesse d'Alençon, Reine de Navarre (1492–1549). Etude biographique et littéraire*, 2 vols., Paris; Geneva: Slatkine Reprints

Kesselring, Krista (1998), 'Representations of Women in Tudor Historiography: John Bale and the Rhetoric of Exemplarity', *Renaissance and Reformation* 22, 41–61

King, John N. (1985), 'Patronage and Piety: The Influence of Catherine Parr', in Margaret Hannay (ed.), *Silent but for the Word: Tudor Women as Patrons, Translators, and Writers of Religious Works*, Kent, Ohio: Kent State University Press, 43–60

Klein, Lisa (1997), 'Your Humble Handmaid: Elizabethan Gifts of Needlework', *Renaissance Quarterly* 50, 459–93

Loades, David (1989), *Mary Tudor: A Life*, Oxford: Blackwell

Marguerite, Queen of Navarre, *Le Miroir de l'âme pécheresse*, J.L. Allaire (ed.), 1972 Munich

McConica, James Kelsey McConica (1965), *English Humanists and Reformation Politics under Henry VIII and Edward VI*, Oxford: Clarendon Press

Mueller, Janel (forthcoming), *Queen Katherine Parr: Letters and Documents*

Prescott, Anne Lake (1985), 'The Pearl of the Valois and Elizabeth I: Marguerite de Navarre's *Miroir* and Tudor England', in Margaret Hannay (ed.), *Silent But for the Word: Tudor Women as Patrons, Translators, and Writers of Religious Works*, Kent, Ohio: Kent State University Press, 61–76

Salminen, Renja (1979), *Marguerite de Navarre: Le Miroir de l'âme pécheresse* (Helsinki: Suomalainen Tiedeakatemia; Annales Academiae Scientiarum Fennicae, Dissertationes Humanarum Litterarum 22), with a diplomatic transcription of the manuscript, a bibliographical study and a stylistic analysis

Shell, Marc (1993), *Elizabeth's Glass with 'The Glass of the Sinful Soul' (1544) by Elizabeth I and 'Epistle Dedicatory' & 'Conclusion' (1548) by John Bale*, Lincoln and London: University of Nebraska Press

Snyder, Susan (1997), 'Guilty Sisters: Marguerite de Navarre, Elizabeth of England, and the *Miroir de l'âme pécheresse*', *Renaissance Quarterly* 50, 443–58

Vose, Heather M. (1985), 'Marguerite of Navarre: that "Right English Woman"', *Sixteenth Century Journal* 16, 315–33

ANNE LAKE PRESCOTT

A Godly Medytacyon of the christen sowle (*STC* 17320) reproduced by permission of The Huntington Library (RB 219031). The text block of the original is 60 × 115 mm.

The missing last page of this copy has been supplied by the copy at The Folger Shakespeare Library.

A Godly Medytacyon of the chriſten ſowle, concerninge a loue towardes God and hys Chriſte, compyled in frenche by lady Margarete quene of Nauerre, and aptely tranſlated into Englyſh by the ryght vertuouſe lady Elyzabeth doughter to our late ſouerayne Kynge Henri the. viij.

Inclita filia, ſereniſſimi olim Anglorum Regis Henrici octaui Elizabeta, tam Græce quam latine fœliciter in Christo erudita.

To the ryght vertu=ouse and christenly lerned yonge lady Elizabeth, the noble doughter of our late souerayne kynge Henry the. viii. Johan Bale wysheth helth with dayly increace of Godly knowledge.

Dyuerse and many (most gracyouse lady) haue the opynyons bene amonge the prophane philoso=phers and christen dyuy=nes, concernynge ryght Nobylyte, and no fewar stryues and con=tencyons for the same. Some autours ha=ue vaynely boasted it to take orygynall of the olde Goddes of the Gentyles, as eue=ry lāde hath had hys peculyar Saturne, Jupiter, & Hercules. yea our Englāde here and all. Some hath fatt it from the foure generall monarchyes of the As=syrianes, Perseanes, Grekes, and Roma=nes. Some haue attrybuted it, to the bol=de battayles and bloudshedynges, in Ni=nus of Babylon the first inuētour of poly=cyes in warre. in our great Albion the Chamesene, whych first in thys regyon

Nobylyte

Albion

supres

ſuppreſſed the poſterite of Japhet, vſur-
pynge therin the firſt monarchy. in [illegible]e
that more than ſix hondred yeares after
defaced of hym the tyrannouſe yſſue. in
Ebrãck and Dunwallo. in Brenne and
Belyne, in great Conſtantyne, Artoure,
Cadwalader, Engiſt, Egbert, Alphrede
wyllyam cõquerour & ſoch other, for lyke
cõqueſtes of the Romanes, Grekes. Gal-
les, pyctes, Brytaynes, Saxons, Danes
Iryſhens and Englyſhens.

Note.

The hawty Romanes ſet not yet a
lyttle by themſelues, that they haue ryſẽ
of Aeneas & Romulus, of whom the one
moſt ſhamefully betrayed hys owne na-
tyue kyndred and contraye, and the other
moſt vnnaturally ſlewe hys owne brother
for worldly domynyõ. Lyke as our walſhe-
men here in Englande, aduaũcynge their
ſucceſſyon or progeny aboue the Englyſh
wyll nedes come of Dardanus & Brute, a
fondacyõ not all vnlyke to the other. Theſe gloryouſe champyons for thys farre fat-
ched grõde of their Nobylyte, accõpte all
other nacyons and peoples, ignoble, profane, and barbarouſe, as is to be ſeane in
the monumẽtes of their writers. But in
the meane ſeaſon, they are not aware that

Romani.

Gwalli.

they

they vndyscretely prefarre cursed Cham to blessed Japhet, by whose posteryte the Iles of the Gentyles were first sorted out in to speches, kyndredes, and nacyons, Gene. 10. and not by Chams ofsprynge, of whome the Troianes and Romanes had their noble begynnynge. That the Chamesenes had in those Iles, was by cruell vsurpacyon & tyrany, as testyfyeth Berosus the Caldeane and therfor that grou͂de of Nobylyte is not all the best. Ouer and besydes all thys, some haue applyed it to renomed byrth or successyon of bloude, some to the habu͂dau͂ce of pleasures worldly some to the mayntenau͂ce of great famylyes, some to the su͂ptuousnesse of notable buyldynges, some to the hygh stomake & stature of persone, some to valeau͂tnesse in marcyall feates, some to semely maners of courtesye, some to lyberalyte of rewardes and gyftes, some to the auncyentnesse of longe coutynuaunce, some to wysdome lernynge & stody for a co͂me͂ welth with soch lyke. And these are not all to be dysalowed, for we fynde them in Abraham, & Dauid with other iust fathers.

Japhet.

kyndes of Nobylyte

But now foloweth, a monstruouse, or whether ye wyll, a prestygyouse nobylyte

The Romysh clergye ymagenynge to exalte themselues aboue the lewde layte (as they shame not yet to call the worldly powers) haue geuen it in a farre other kynde, to mytars, masses, Cardynall hattes, crosers, cappes, shauen crownes, oyled thombes, syde gownes, furred amyses, mõkes cowles, and fryres lowsy coates, becõmynge therby põtyfycall lordes, spiryruall sirs, and ghostly fathers. Thys kynde of Nobylyte dygged out of the dongehyll, haue I seane gorgyously garnyshed with the retoryckes of Porphyry, Aristotle, Duns, and Raymundus decretals, in the bokes of Johan Stanbery byshopp of herforde, De superioritate ecclesiastica, De discrimine iurisdictionum, and De potestate põtificia. In the bokes also of Walter hũte an ordynary reader sũtyme in Oxforde, De precellẽtia Petri, & De autoritate ecclesie. Yea, and amõge thẽselues they haue moch contended both by disputacyon & writynges, whych of their sectes myght other excell in the nobylnesse of christen perfection. The monkes in publyque scoles, by a dystynccyon of the actyue and contemplatyue lyfe, haue aduaunced their ydell mõkery aboue the

Clergy.

Stãbery

Hunte.

Fryres.

offyce of a byshopp, and the fryres their scalde crauynge beggery. aboue the degrees of the Both. As is largely seane in the brawlynge workes of Rycharde Maydeston, Thomas walden, Wyllyam Byntre & other whych haue written Contra wicleuistas, & Pro mēdicatione fratrū,

Myluerton.

In the dayes of kynge Edwarde the fourt, Johan Mylucrton prouyncyall of the Carmelytes, was full thre yeares, a prysoner in the castell of Angell at Rome at the sute of the byshoppes of Englande for the same, and lost so the byshopryck of saynt Dauids, wherunto he was a lyttle afore elected. Thys matter haue I hearde, vndre the tyttle of Euangelyck perfeccyon, most depely reasoned in their ordynary dysputacions at their concourses cōuocacyons, aud chapters (as they than called them) yea by those whome I knewe most corrupt lyuers. Herūto for fournyshynge out the same, the graye fryres added. S. frances paynted woūdes, the, blacke fryres. S. Domynyckes bolde dysputynge with heretykes, the whyte fryres our ladyes fraternyte, and the Augustyne fryres the great doctryne of their patrone. In the vnyuersytees afte moch

4. orders.

 to and

Prestes to and fro, hath it bene concluded, that the order of a prest haue farre excelled in dygnyte the order of a byshopp. And thys haue they left behynde them for a most graue and depe reason therupon. Marke their more than lucyferyne presumpcyon therin. Soch power hath a prest (saye they) as hath neyther Angell nor yet Man, be he of neuer so great autoryte scyence, or vertu. For a prest by worde maye make hym agayne, that by worde made heauen & earth. A prest maye euery daye both byget hym and beare hym, where as hys mother Marye bygate hym (beare hym they wolde saye) but ones. These are their very wordes in a boke entytled. De origine Nobilitatis. ca. 5. with moch more cyrcumstaunce of matter. O blasphemouse bellybeastes, & most ydell wytted sorcerers. How ydolatrously exalte they themselues aboue the eternall lyuynge God & hys Christ?

O Deuils Incarnate

Nobylyte

Johan Chrisostome a man taught and brought vp in the christen philosophy, defyneth the true Nobylyte after a farre other sort, than ded the prophane writers. He calleth it not with Aristotle, a worthynesse of progeny, neyther yet with

Varro a opulēcy of ryches, but a famouse renome obtayned by lōge exercysed vertu. He is pusaunt, hygh, ād valeaunt (sayth he) and hath Nobylyte in right course, that dysdayneth to geue place to vyces and abhorreth to be ouercomen of them. Doctryne greatly adourneth a mā hyghly borne, but a godly indeuoure of christyanyte bewtyfyeth hym most of all. By nō other wayes haue the Apostles and Martyrs obtayned a noble report, than by the valeaunt force of pure doctryne and fayth. A gētyll hart (sayth Seneca) or a stomake that ys noble, moueth, prouoketh, and sturreth, only to thynges honest. No man whych hath a noble wytte, delyteth in thynges of small value, moch lesse in matters of fylthynesse or supperstycyon. Chefely apperteyneth it to men and women of syncere Nobylyte, to regarde the pure doctryne and faythe. vnto soch hath God promysed in the scriptures, habundaunce of tēporall thynges, longe lyfe, fortunate chyldren, a kyngedome durable, with soch other, Deut. 28.

Apostles.

Faythe.

A most worthy conquerour is Gedeon noted in the scriptures, for destroyenge false relygyō & renuynge the kyngedome

Gedeon.

of fayth

Asa rex. of faythe. Judi. vj. So is kynge Asa, for remouynge the male stues from the prelates abhorrynge marryage, & for puttynge downe ydolles whych hys forefathers maynteyned. 3. Reg. 15 So is kynge Josa-
Josaphat phat, for beynge couragyouse in the wayes of God, and for puttynge downe the hyll aulters & their sacrifices. 2. parali.
Jehu. 17. So is kynge Jehu, for sleynge the ydolatrouse Prestes, and for breakynge and burnynge their great God Baal, and for
Ezechias makynge, a Jakes of their holy churche 4. Reg. 10 So is kynge Ezechias for clensynge the house of the lorde from all fylthynesse, afore hys tyme therin occupyed 2. Parali. 29. and for breakynge downe the brasen serpent and ydolatrouse ymages with their aulters and sanctuaryes. 4. Reg. 18 So is kynge Josias, for suppres-
Josias. synge relygyouse persones and aulter prestes, for cosumynge their iewels & ornamētes, & for ouerthrowynge their buggery chambers in the howse of the lorde 4. Reg. 23. Thys noble kīge also destroyed all theyr carued ymages, he strewed the dust of thē vpon their graues that had
Prestes. offered to them, and brent the prestes bones vpō their aulters, restorynge agayne

the lawes

the lawes of the lorde. 2. parali. 34. Jesus
Syrach reporteth of hym fynally, that he
whollye dyrected hys hart to the lorde, &
toke awaye all abhomynacyons of the vn
godly. Eccle. 49, Besydes that is spoken
of kynge Dauid and kynge Salomon.

Ecclesi. 49.

Not J only, but many thousandes more
whych wyll not from hens fourth bowe
any more to Baal, are in full & perfyght
hope, that all these most hyghly notable
and pryncely actes, wyll reuyue & lyuely
florysh in your most noble and worthy
brother kynge Edwarde the sixt. Most
excellent & godly are hys begynnynges
reported of the very foren nacyõs callynge
hym for hys vertuouse, lerned, and godly
prudent youthes sake, the seconde Josias.
Those hys wonderfull pryncyples in the
eyes of the worlde, and no lesse gloryouse
afore God thus beynge to hys honoure,
that eternall lyuynge God contynue and
prospere to the ende, that he maye haue
of them, as had these worthy kinges afore
rehearced, a ryght noble and famouse re
port. Nobylyte sought by wycked enter-
pryses and obtayned by the same (as in
many afore our dayes, and in some now
of late) is not els but a publyque and

Edwarde vj. rex.

Ignoble

notable infamye, and in the ende eternall dapnacyon. Nobylyte wonne by the ernest sekynge of Gods hygh honour, is soch a precyouse crowne of glory as wyll neuer perysh here nor yet in the worlde to come.

Tyrantes

Cain after a worldly maner, or amonge the vngracyouse sort, is holden noble for slayinge hys brother Judas of the prelates (for he receyued of the, a noble rewarde) for betrayenge Christ, Herode of the Jewes for murtherynge the innocetes. And what is there more worthy reproche, dyshonour, and shame, than are these execrable factes. The nature of true Nobylyte (as I haue sayd afore) is not to ryse of vyce but of vertu, though many men there seke it. Of the most excellet kinde of Nobylyte is he sure (most vertuouse and lerned lady) whych truly beleueth and seketh to do the wyll of the eternall father. for therby is he brought forewarde, and promoted into that heauenly kyndred Joa. 1. By that meanes becometh he the deare brother, syster, & mother of Christ Math. 12. a cytizen of heauen with the Apostles and Prophetes, Ephe. 2. yea the chylde of adopcyon and heyre togyther wyth Christ in the heauenly inherytaunce

Nobylyte

O Noble kyndred.

Roma. 8. No soch chyldren left Socrates behynde hym, neyther yet Demosthenes Plato, nor Cicero, with all their plesant wysdome and eloquēce. No soch heretage coulde great Alexander the Macedonean, byqueth to hys posteryte neyther yet noble Charles, Artoure, nor Dauid.

Alexander.

Of thys Nobylyte, haue I no doubt (lady most faythfully studyouse) but that yow are, with many other noble women & maydēs more in thys blessed age. If questyon were axt me, how I knowe it? my answere wolde be thys. By your godly frute, as the fertyle tre is non other wyse than therby knowne, luce. vj. I receyued your noble boke, ryght frutefully of yow translated out of the frenche tunge into Englysh. I receyued also your golden sentences out of the sacred scriptures, with no lesse grace than lernynge in foure noble lāguages, Latyne, Greke, Frenche, & Italyane, most ornately, fynely, & purely writtē with your owne hande. Wonderfully ioyouse were the lerned men of our cytie, Murseus, Buscoducius, Bomelius Lithodius & Imānus, as I shewed vnto them the seyd sentences, in beholdynge (as they than reported) so moch vertu.

Frutes.

4. tūges.

Men lerned.

faythe

faythe, scyence, & experyẽce of lãguages & letters, specyally in noble youth & femynyte. Through whych occasyon there be of thẽ (I knowe) that cannot withholde their lerned handes frõ the publyshynge therof, to the hygh prayse of God the geuer, neyther yet from wrytynge to your worthy grace for studyouse contynuaunce in the same. Your seyd sẽtẽces, (they saye farre passeth the Apohthegmes of Plutarchus, the Aphorismes of Theognis, the Stratagemes of Isocrates, the graue golden cõnsels of Cato & the manyfolde morals of Johan Goldeston the great allegoryser, with soche other lyke.

Sẽtẽces.

Your first written clauses in .iiij. speches latyne, frenche & Italyane, out of the xiiij. Psalme of noble Dauid, mẽcyoneth that the vnfaythfull reckeneth folyshly in their hartes, there is no God. Wherupõ so corrupt they are in their vayne coniectures, and so abhomynable in their dayly doynges, that not one of their generacyõ is godly. By thys do your grace vnto vs sygnyfye, that the barẽ doctryne & good workes without fayth of the hypocrytes, whych in their vncõmaunded latyne ceremonyes serue their bellyes & not Christ,

The first clause.

Hypocrytes.

in ored-

in gredyly deuourynge the patrymony of poor wydowes & orphanes, are both execrable in themselues, and abhomynable afore God for though those paynted sepulchres haue the name of the lorde in their mouthes, & greatly boast the good workes of the lawe, yet knowe they not what belongeth to hys true honoure, but hate in their wycked hartes both hys gloryouse name and worde. The true doctryne of faythe, and the feare of God, wyll that wycked sort (whome thys psalme wryngeth) not heare, but styll tormet the conscyences of myserable wretched ydyotes for aduauntage of Masses and momblynges. Happy are they of thys latter age, that in the Gospell haue receyued the sauynge helth out of Syon (as your grace hath done) beynge clere from the stynge of those vyperouse wormes. Blessed be those faythfull tuters & teachers whych by their most godly instruccyons haue thus fashyoned your tender youth unto the ryght ymage of Christ and not Antichrist. Yea most blessed be those godly gouernours and magistrates, whych haue traueled and yet laboryously trauayle with worthy Moses, to brynge

Hate.

Happye.

Tuters.

Rulers.

Gods people clerely out of their mo[st]
wretched captyuyte.

Your latter clause in the Greke, incy-
teth vs to the ryght worshyppynges of
God in sprete and veryte Ioã.4. to honou[r]
ringe of our parẽtes in the semely offyce[s]
of naturall chyldren. Ephe. vj. and to th[e]
reuerent vsynge of our christen equalle[s]
in the due mynystracyons of loue. 1. pet[er]
2. Neyther Benedyct nor Bruno, Domy-
nyck nor Frances (whych haue of long[e]
yeares bene boasted for the pryncypall
patrones of relygyon) euer gaue to thei[r]
superstycyouse bretherne, so pure preceptes of syncere christyanyte. Neyther yet
Peter lombarde in hys. iiij. bokes of sent[en-]
ces, with whose smokye dyuynyte, the lo[u-]
sy locustes monkes, chanons, prestes, and
fryres, haue these. iiij. hondred yeare[s]
darkened the clere sunne, whych is the v[e-]
ryte of God, Apoca. 9. If godly wyse me[n]
wolde do nomore but conferre thys lernynge of yours and of other noble women
i these dayes, with the doctryne of Rober[t]
Kylwarby archebyshopp of Canterbur[y]
and Cardynall, whych the vnyuersytees o[f]
Oxforde & Parys were sworne to, for ma[yn-]
tenaunce of that christyanyte in th[e]
yeare of

The latter clause

Monachi

[Lom]bardus.

Robert. Kylwarby.

yeare of our lorde. 1276, by the consent of all masters regentes & non regentes, I doubt it not but they shulde fynde iust cause to holde vp both their handes and prayse their lorde God for changynge that helle into thys heauen. An vnsauery gust therof shall they fynde, adioyned of the Paryseanes as necessary dyuynyte, to the foresayd sentẽces of Peter lombarde.

A change

The boke

In your forenamed boke, cōposed first of all by the ryght vertuouse lady Margarete, syster sūtyme to the frenche kynge Frances, and quene of Nauerre, And by your noble grace most dylygently and exactly translated into Englysh, fynde I most precyouse treasure concernynge the sowle. Wherfor I haue added therunto the tytle of a Godly medytacyon of the sowle, concernynge a loue towardes God and hys Christ. Most lyuely in these and soch other excellent factes, expresse ye the naturall emphasy of your noble name Elischabeth in the hebrue, is as moch to saye in the latyne, as Dei mei requies, in Englysh, the rest of my God. Who can thynke God not to rest in that harte whych sendeth fourth soch godly frutes? I thynke nō that hath ryght dyscressyon

Elizabeth

Your pẽne hath here plenteouslye vttered [An hart.] the habundãce of a Godly occupyed harte, lyke as ded the vyrgynall lyppes of Christes most blessed mother, whan she sayd with heauenly reioyce, My sowle magnyfyeth the lorde and my sprete reioyceth in God my sauer, luce. i. Many noble women of fresh literature haue bene afore tyme in thys regyon, whose nomẽclature or rehearsall of names I intende [Noble womẽ lerned] to shewe in the ende of thys boke, but non of thẽ were euer yet lyke to those whych are in our age. No, neyther Cambra, Marcia, Constantia, Agasia, Vodicia, Bundunica, Claudia, Helena. vrsula. hilda, nor soch other lyke. Thys one coppye of yours haue I brought into a nombre. to thintẽt that many hungry sowles by the inestymable treasure contayned therin, maye [Cõclusio.] be swetely refreshed. The sprete of the eternall sonne of God Jesus Christ, be alwayes to your excellent grace assystent that ye maye sende fourth more soch wholsome frutes of sowle, and become a noryshynge mother to hys dere congregacyon to their confort and hys hygh glorye Amen.

Your bounde oratour
Johan Bale

A Godly Medytacyon of the christen sowle, concerninge a loue towardes God and hys Christe, compyled in frenche by lady Margarete quene of Nauerre, and aptely translated into Englysh by the ryght vertuouse lady Elyzabeth doughter to our late souerayne Kynge Henry the. viij.

The preface.

If thu do throughly reade thys worke (dere frynde in the lorde) marke rather the matter than the homely speache therof, consyderynge it is the stodye of a woman, whych hath in her neyther cōnynge nor scyence, but a feruent desyre that yche one maye se, what the gifte of God the creatour doth whan it pleaseth hym to iustyfye a hart. For what is the hart of a Man, concernynge hys owne strēgth, before he hath receyued the gift of faythe? Therby only hath he knowledge of the goodnesse, wysedome, and power of God. And as sone as he through that faythe, knoweth pythely the truthe hys hart is anon full of charyte and loue

Math. 9

Hebre. 11

So that by the feruentnesse therof he excludeth all fleshly feare, & fyrmely trusteth in God vnfaynedly. for certaynely the gifte, whych God the creatour geueth frely at the begynnynge, doth neuer cease tyll it hath made hym godly, whych putteth hys full trust in God. — 1. Joã. 4.

O happy and fortunate gifte. whych causeth a Man to possesse a grace so desyred Alas no man coulde thys vnderstande, onles by soch gyfte God had geuen it hym. And great cause he hath to doubte of it, õles God hath made hym to feale it in hys harte. Therfor gẽtyll reader, with a godly mynde I besyche the pacyently thys worke to peruse, whych is but small in quantyte, and taste nothynge but the frute therof. Prayenge to God full of all goodnesse, that in thy harte he wyll plãte the lyuely faythe. Amen. — Joan. 6.

finit præfatio.

liber incipit

WHere is the helle, full of trauayle, payne, myschefe, and torment? Where is the pytte of cursednesse, out of whych doth sprynge all desperacyon? Is there — Job. 7.

anyhelle

any helle so profounde, that is suffycyent to ponnysh the tenth part of my synnes. whych are so many in nombre, that the infynyte swarme of them so shaddoweth my darkened sences that I cannot accompte them neyther yet wele se them: I am farre entered in amongest them, and (that moch wors is) I haue not the power to obtayne the true knowledge of the depe daũgers of them. I perfyghtly fele, that their roote is in me. And outwardly I se non other effecte but all is eyther brãche leafe, or els frute that it bryngeth fourth all aboute me. If I thynke to loke for better, a brãche cõmeth and closeth myne eyes, and in my mouthe doth fall whan I wolde speake, the frute so bytter to swalowe downe. If my sprete be sturred for to harken, than a great multytude of leaues doth entre in myne eares, and my nose is all stopped with flowers.

Roma. 7.

Psal. 9

Now beholde how in paynes cryenge & wepynge, my poore sowle, a slaue and prysoner, doth lye without lyghte, hauynge her fete bounde through her concupyscẽce & also both her armes through euyll vse, yet the power to remedy it, doth not lye in me, neyther haue I power to crye for

2. Cor.

 helpe

helpe. Agayne, so farfourth as I can perceyue, I haue no hope of socour, but through the grace of God that I can not deserue, whych maye rayse euery one from deathe. By hys bryghtnesse he geueth lyght to darkenesse. And hys power examynynge my faulte, doth breake all the vayle of ignoraunce, and geueth me clere vnderstādynge, not only that thys cometh of me, but also what thynge abydeth in me. Where I am and wherfor I do laboure. Who he is whom I haue offended, to whom I ded obeye so seldome. Therfor it is cōuenyent that my pryde be suppressyd

Job. 12.

And humbly with wepynge harte, I do confesse that I am moch lesse thā nothynge, before my byrth myer, after a dungehyll, a body prompte to all euyll not wyllynge other stodye, also subiect to care, sorowe, and payne. A short lyfe, and thende vncertayne. The whych vndre synne by Adam is solde, and by the lawe iudged to be damnyd. For I had neuer the power to obserue one only cōmaundemente of God, I do fele the strength of synne in me, therfor is my synne no whyt the lesse to be hydden. And the more he is dyssembled outwardly, so moche the more he encreasyth

Job. 14.

creasyth within the harte. That whych God wyll, I can not wyll, and what he wolde not, I ofte tymes desyre to perfourme. Whych thynge doth constrayne me by importable sorowe, to wyshe thende of thys myserable bodye through desyred death, bycause of my werye & ragynge life

Sapi. 9.

Who shall be he than, that shall delyuer and recouer suche good for me? Alas it can not be a mortall man, for hys power and strength is not suche, but it shall be the only good grace of the almyghty God whych is neuer slacke to preuent vs with hys mercye O what a master is that, with out deseruynge any goodnesse of hym: I serued hym slouthfully, and without ceasynge offended hym euery daye, yet is he not slacke in helpynge me. He doth se the euyll that I haue, what and how moche it is, and that of my selfe I can do nothynge that good is, but with hart and body so enclyned am I to the contrarye, that I feale no strength in me onles it be for to do euyll. He doth not tarry tyll I humbly praye hym, or that (seynge my helle & dāpnacyon) I do crye vpō hym. For with hys sprete he maketh a waylynge in my harte greatter than I can declare, whych

Roma. 7.

Gene. 6.

asketh the gyfte wherof the vertu is vnknowen to my lytele power.

Psal. 37.

And thys the same vnknowne syghte doth brynge me a newe desyre, shewynge the good that I haue lost by my synne, & gyuē me agayne through hys grace & boūtye, that whych hath ouercomē all synne O my lorde what grace and goodnesse is thys, whych doth put out so manye synnes Now maye we se that thu art full of all godly loue to make me of a synner, thy seruaūt & chyelde. Alas my God, I ded not seke the but I fled & rāne awaye frō the. And here beneth thu camyst to me whych am nothynge but a worme of the earthe, all naked. What do I saye, worme? I do hym wrōge, that am so naughtye, & swarme so full of pryde, deceyte, malyce & treason. The promyse whych my fryndes made whā I was baptysed is such, that I alwayes through faythe in thy passyō shuld fele the mortyfycacyō of my fleshe & dwelle alwayes with the i the crosse where thu wert fast nayled (as I beleue) and yelded Death dead as I also shuld yelde all synne

Luce. 19.

Collo. 3.

Thys haue I often tymes taken downe agayne, vntyed, and set at large, I haue broken, denyed, and falsyfyed my promyse

and

& through pryde, I haue lyfte vp my wyll in suche a maner, that through slouth. my dewtye towardes the was forgoten. And that moche more is, as wele the profyte or value of thy promyse, whych I had of the in the daye of my baptysme, as also thy sauynge loue and promyses folowynge, I haue all alyke neglected. What shall I saye more? Albeit that often tymes thu perceyuynge me wretched and vnhappye hast geuē me so many warnynges in fayth and in sacramētes, admonyshynge me by preachynges, and confortynge me by the recayuynge of thy worthye bodye and sacred bloude, promysynge also to put me in the nombre of them that are now adourned with perfyght innocencye. Yet haue I all these hygh benefyghtes, throwne into forgetfullnesse,

Mat. 16.

Joan. 6.

Often tymes haue I with the broken couenaunte. And partly for that my poore sowle was to moche fed with euyll breade or dāpnable doctryne of hypocrytes, I despysed such socoure and ghostly physyck in Gods worde, as wolde haue holpe me And if I had bene wyllynge to loke for it yet knewe I at that tyme no teachers cōuenyent. For there is neyther man, saynte,

Hiere. 7

dor Angell, for whome the harte of a synner without thy sprete wyll change. Alas good Jesus, thu beholdynge my blyndenesse, and that at my neade I coulde haue no socour of men, dedyst open the waye of my saluacyon. O how great is the goodnesse, and how inestymable the swetnesse whych thu hast shewed therin? Is there any father so naturall to the daughter or brother to the syster, whych wolde euer haue done as he hath done? For he came into the helle to socour my sowle, where agaynst hys wyll she was, intendynge to haue peryshed, because she ded not loue

Psal 118.

Alas swete lorde thu hast loued her yea, to the very outshedynge of thy most precyouse bloude. O charyte feruent and incōparable. Not slacke art thū in loue that so louest euery synner, yea, and also thyne enemyes, not only in forgeuynge their offences, but also in geuynge thy selfe for their saluacyon, lybertie, and delyueraunce, to the death, crosse, trauayle payne and sufferaunce. Whan I cast in mynde, what shulde be the occasyō of thy loue towardes me. I can se nothynge els but a loue wonderfull, whych moueth the to geue me that I can not deserue. Than

1. Joā. 3.

Joā. 5.

my God

my God as farre fourth as I can se, I ought to geue no thãkes for my saluacyon but only vnto the, to whome I owe the prayse therof, as to hym whych is my sauyour & creatoure. What a thynge is it that thu hast done so moche for me? Thu art not only contented to haue forgyuen me my synnes, but also hast gyuẽ vnto me the ryght fortunate gifte of grace. Ephe. 3.

For it shulde suffyse me, I cõmynge out of suche a daunger, to be lyke a straũger vsed. But thu dost handle my sowle, (if I durst so saye it) as a mother, daughter, syster and wyfe. I lorde, I am the trespaser whych am not worthy to come nere the dore of thy ryght hygh place to aske breade, where thy dwellynge is. O what grace is thys, that so sodenly thu vouchesauyst to drawe my sowle in to suche hyghnesse, that she felyth herselfe ruler of my bodye. She poore, ignoraunte and lame, doth fynde her selfe wyth the, ryche, wyse, and stronge, because thu hast written in her harte the roote of thy sprete, & holy worde, geuynge her true fayth for to receyue it. Whych thynge made her to conceyue thy sonne, in beleuynge hym to be man, God, sauyour, and also the true Roma. 8

remyttes

remytter of synnes. Therfor dost thu assure her, that she is mother to thy sonne of whom thu art the only faither.

Math. 12

And farthermore, O my father here is a great loue, for thu art not wery of wele doynge syth that thy sonne full of dyuynyte hath taken the bodye of a man, & ded myngle hymselfe with our ashes, whych thynge a man can not vnderstāde vnlesse he hath a true faythe. It hath pleased the to put hym so neare vs, that he ded ioyne hymselfe vnto our fleshe. Than we seynge hym to be called man, we are bolde to call hym syster and brother. Now the sowle whych maye saye of her selfe, that she is the syster of God, ought to haue her harte assured. After thys dost thu declare with greate loue, how her creacyon is only of the good wyll, whych it pleaseth the alwayes to haue towardes her, geuynge assuraunce that before her first daye, or tyme of beynge prouyded for her, thu bestowedest thy loue on her, & how through loue thu hast made her (as alone of power thu cannyst wele do it) and also how thu dedyst put her within thys body, not for to sleape with slouth, but that both of them shulde haue non other exercyse, but only to thynke

Phil. 2.

Gene. 1.

to thynke how to do some seruyce vnto the

Than the truthe maketh her to feale that there is in the, true paternyte. O what honoure. what swetnesse, and what glory hath the sowle, whych doth alwayes remember that she is thy daughter, & in callynge the fayther, she doth thy commaundement? What is there more? Is that all? No, It doth please the to gyue her an other name, to call her thy wyfe, & that she agayne do call the husbande, declarynge how thu hast frely manyfested the marryage of her. By the baptysme thu hast made a promes, to gyue her thy goodes and ryches, and thu agayne to take her synnes, for she hath nothynge els by herytage of her first father Adam. All her treasures, that she hath of nature, are nothynge els but synnes, whych thu hast tyed vpon the, and payed all her whole debte with thy goodes and. landes

Tren. 2.

Colos. 2.

Thu hast made her so ryche, and with so great a ioynter endued her, that she knowynge her selfe to be thy woyd wyfe, doth beleue to be quytt of all that she oweth, estemynge very lytel that she hath here beneth. She forsaketh her olde father, & all the goodes that he gyueth, for her

Roma. 5.

husbandes

husbandes sake. Surely (o my God) my sowle is sore hurte to be fedde with suche good, and agayne releued in leauynge the pleasure of thys worlde for that whych is eternall, where peace is without warre. I maruayle that she, thys remembrynge, doth not lese her witt, cōtenaunce, and speache. Father, father, alas what ought I to thynke. Shall my sprete be so bolde as to take vpon hym to call the father? yea, and also onr Father, for so hast thu taught in the Pater noster. But to call the daughter, hast thu so sayd? I besyche the, tell me. Alas yea, whan with great swetnesse, thu saydest daughter, lend me thy harte.

2. Joa. 5.

Prouer, 23.

O my God, in stede of lendynge, he is ready to geue hym selfe wholly vnto the Receyue hym than, & do not permyt that any creature put hym from the, so that for euer with faythfull stedefastnesse he maye loue the with a daughterly loue. Now my lorde if thu be my father, maye I thynke that I can be thy mother? In dede I can not wele preceyue, how I shulde conceyue the that createdyst me. But thu dedyst in thys matter satisfye my doubte, whan in preachynge and in

Apoca 13

streatchynge

streatchynge fourth thy hãdes dedyst saye Those that shall do the wyll of my father they are my bretherne, also my syster and mother. I beleue than, that hearynge & readynge the wordes whych thu hast taught & vttered by thy holy prophetes. the same also whych through thy true preachers, thu dost dayly declare vnto mẽ in beleuynge it and stedefastly desyerynge to fulfyll, I cõceyue the & beare the by loue.

Luce. 11.

Therfor without ãye feare, wyll I take vpõ me the name of a mother. What mother of God? O swete vyrgyne Marye, I besyche the, be not angry that I take vp suche a tytle. I do neyther stele, nor vsurpe any thynge vpon thy pryuylege. For thu only hast aboue all wemẽ receyued of hym so great honoure, that no mã can in hym selfe comprehende how he hath bene wyllynge to take in the our fleshe. For thu arte mother and perfyght vyrgyne before and after, and in hys holy byrth. In thy blessyd wombe thu dedyst beare hym and norysh hym. Thu dedyst folowe hym in hys trybulacyons, and also in hys teachynges. Now breuely to conclude. Thu hast with God founde suche grace, as the enemye through malyce and deceyte,

Math. 1.

had caused

had caused Adam & hys posteryte to lose

1. Cor. 15. By Eue and hym we had lost it, & by thy sonne hath it bene yelded vnto vs agayne

Therfor hast thu bene ryghteously cal-

Luce. 1. led full of grace. For thu lackedyst ney- ther grace nor vertu, sith that he whych is the best amonge them that be good, also the sprynge of all goodnesse and power whych hath created in the so pure innoce- cye that thu arte the example of all vertu- es) hath buylded in the hys dwellynge & temple. He through loue ded conforme hymselfe with the, and thu arte transfour- med in hym. Therfor if any man shulde thynke to geue the greatter prayse than God hymselfe hath done, it were a fule

Luce. 1. blasphemye. For there is no suche prayse, as is the same whych commeth from God Thu also hast had faythe so fyrme and cõ- staunt, that (by grace) she had the power to make the godly. Wherfor I wyll not ta- ke vpon me, to geue the greatter prayse than the hououre whych thy souerayne

Acto. 1. lorde hath geuen vnto the. For thu arte hys corporall mother, and also thruogh fayth hys spyrytuall mother.

And I folowynge thy fayth with hum- blenesse, am hys spirytuall mother also

Alas

Alas my God the brotherlynesse that thu hast towardes me through thy humblenesse, in callynge me syster, is great. Sedyst thu euer saye it any thynge afore? Alas yea. For thu hast broken the kyndred of my olde father, callynge me doughter by adopcyon. Well than, seynge that we haue both but one father, I wyll not feare to call the my brother. For so hast thu reported it by Salomon in hys ballet, saynge, My syster and spouse thu hast wounded my harte with the swete loke of one of thyne eyes, and with one cheyne of thy necke. Alas my brother, I wyshe for nothynge els, but that in woundynge the, I myght fynde my selfe wounded with thy loue, To that wolde I geue ouer my selfe And lyke wyse thu dost call me wyfe in that place, shewynge largely that thu louyst me, saynge by these wordes amorouse

Roma. 8.

Canti. 4.

Aryse my dere doue, and come hytherwarde my dylectable spouse. Therfor shal I saye with louynge fayth, thu arte myne and I am thyne. Thu dost call me thy loue & fayre spouse. If it be so, suche hast thu made me. Alas, doth it please the, to gyue me suche names? They are truly able to breake a mannys harte, and cause it to

Canti. 2.

burne through loue vnspeakeable, wha[t]
he thynketh vpon the honoure that thu
dost vnto hym, whych is moche greatter
than he hath deserued. A mother, a mo
Luce. 8. ther? Alas but of what chylde is it? Truly
of suche a sonne, that my harte doth brea
ke for loue. My God, my sonne? O Jesus
what speache thys is. mother, daughter,
O happy kynrede. O what swetnesse doth
proceade out of that paternyte. But what
doughterly and reuerent feare ought I
to haue towardes hym, my father, yea &
my creatour, my protectour and sauer? To
be thy syster, alas here is a great loue.
Canti. 8. Now dost thu breake my harte i the myd
dest to make rowme for the same so swete
a brother. So that no other name be wri
te in the same, but only my brother Jesus
the sonne of God. Non other man wyll I
Acto. 4. geue place to, for all the scourgynge and
beatynge, that they cā do vnto me. Kepe
my harte then, my brother and frynde, &
lete not thy enemy entre in to it. O my father, chylde, brother, and spouse, with ha[n]
des ioyned, humbly vpon my knees I yelde the thankes and prayses, that it plea
seth the to turne thy face towardes me
conuertynge my harte, and coueryng me
with

with suche grace, that thu dost se nomore my euyls & synnes. So wele hast thu hydden them, that it semeth, thu hast put thē in forgetfulnesse, Yea, & also they seme to be forgoten of me, whych haue cōmytted them, For fayth and loue causeth me to forget them, puttynge wholly my trust in the alone,

Ezech 33

Than my father, in whom lyeth vnfayned loue, wherof can I haue feare in my harte? I confesse that I haue done all the euyll that one creature can do, and that of my selfe I am nought. Also that I haue offended the as the prodygall chylde ded, folowynge the folysh trade of the fleshe, wherewith I haue spente all my substāce, and the habundaūce of goodes whych I had receyued of the. For pouerte had wetheryd me awaye euen as heye and yelded my sprete dead for hunger, sekynge to eate the releafe of swyne. But I founde very lytle sauoure in suche meates. Than I seynge my lyfe to be so myserable, I ded returne vnto the my father agayne, sayenge. Alas I haue synned in heauen and before the. I am not worthy (I tell it before euerybodye) to be called thy chylde. But O bountyfull father, do no

Psal. 31.

Luce. 15.

Ezech 18.

worse to me, than to one of thy howshol de seruauntes.

Alas what loue and zele is thys? for thu woldest not tarry my commynge and prayer but stretchynge out thy hãde receyuedyst me, whan I ded thynke that thu woldest not loke vpon me. And in stede to haue ponnyshed, thu dedyst assure me of my saluacyon. Where is he thẽ that shall ponnysh me, whan my father shall denye hym my synne? There is no iudge that can condẽpne anye creature, vnlesse God hymselfe wolde dampne hym. I feare not the want of goodnesse, syth I haue my God for my father. My enemye shall do me no harme, for my father shall take all hys strength awaye. If I owe anye thynge, he shall paye it all for me, If I haue deserued death, he (as a kynge) shall pardõ me, & delyuer me frõ pryson & hãgynge.

Luce. 15.

Esa. 27.

But here is the worst. What maner of mother haue I bene? For after that I by fayth, had receyued the name of a true mother, I became very rude vnto the, by cause that after I had conceyued and brought the fourth, I left reason, And beynge subiect to my wyll, not takynge heade vnto the, I fell a slepe and gaue

Roma. 7.

place to

place to my great enemye, The whych ithe nyght of ignoraunce, I beynge a sleape ded steale the from me craftely, and in thy place, she ded put her chylde whych was dead. So ded I lese the, whych is an harde sorowe and remorce for me. Now haue I lost the by myne owe faulte (my sonne) bycause I toke no hede to kepe the. Sensualyte my neyghbour (I beynge in my beastly sleape) ded steale the from me, & gaue me, an other chylde whych had no lyfe in hym, named synne, whom I wyll not haue, for I do vtterly forsake hym.

3. Reg. 3.

She affirmed that he was myne owne but I knewe hym to be hers. For as sone as I came to the lyght of grace, whych thu haddest gyuē me, thā I knewe my glory to be changed, whan I sawe the dead chylde not to be myne. For the same whych was alyue (whom she had taken awaye) was myne owne. Betwene Jesus & synne is the chaunge so apparant. But here is a straunge thynge. Thys olde woman causeth me to kepe hym whych is dead, whom she reporteth to be myne, and so she wyll mayntene. O Salomō, a full true iudge, thu hast hearde thys lamentable processe and ordayned to cōtent the partyes, that

1. Cor. 6.

the chylde shulde be deuyded in two partes. The false woman agreyth, it shulde
be so. But I remembrynge hym to be myne owne sonne, was rather contente to
lese hym, than to se hys bodye parted in
two peces. For true and pefyght loue is
neuer contente with one halfe of that it
doth loue.

3. Reg. 3

I had rather to wepe for my whole
losse, than to recouer but one halfe. My
mynde coulde not be satysfyed. if I had
recouered one halfe without lyfe. Alas
gyue her rather the chylde whych is alyue
Better it is for me to dye, than to se Jesus
Christ dyuyded. But O my lorde, thu dedyst loke better to it than I. For thu seynge the anguysh that I ded suffer, & how
I ded rather forsake my ryght, than to
beholde suche cruelnesse Thu saydest, thys
is the true mother and so caused them to
gyue me my chylde agayne, for whom my
harte was so sorowfull. O swete Jesus, I
founde the after, to haue proued me if I
ded loue the. Yea, I whych had lost the
yet dedyst thu returne unto me, Alas dost
thu vouchesaue to come agayne to her,
whych beynge lett with synne coulde not
kepe the, my swete chylde, my sonne, my

I. Cor. 4.

Sapi. 3.

helper

helper, my norysher, of whome I am a ryght humble creature. Do not permytt that euer I do leaue the agayne, for I do repent my selfe of the tyme passed. Gene. 6.

Now come my sensualyte with synnes of all qualytees, for thu hast no power to make me receyue the chylde whych is dead. The same that I haue is stronge ynough for to defende me, & he shall not permyt that thu take hym awaye from me, He is alredy more stronge than anye man is. Therfor I maye sleape and take rest neare hym. For all thynges wele consydered, he shall kepe me moche better than I coulde hym. Then as I thynke I maye take rest. O swete rest of the mother & the sonne togyther, my swete chylde. O my God, honoure & prayse be vnto the only; so that euery creature maye se how it hath pleased the to call me a mother, lesse than nothynge. The more that the thynge is straunge and harde to be done, the more ought thy goodnesse to haue prayse for it. And also I fynde my selfe more bounde vnto the than euer I ded for thys, that it pleaseth the to haue retayned me for thy syster. Esa 132. Psal 118

I am syster vnto the but so naughty a

syster, that better it were for me, that I were without the name, for I forgate the honoure of adopcyon in so noble a kyndred, & also thy so good & brotherly behauer towardes me. I with pryde ded ryse agaynst the and (not remembrynge my faultes, but goynge a straye from the, ded agree with my brother Aaron, beynge in wyll to geue iudgment agaynst thy workes. Priuely I grudged agaynst the also, whych thynge causeth me to haue a great remorce in my conscyence. Alas ryght bountyfull God, brother and true Moses. whych doist all with goodnesse and Justyce. I haue estemed thy workes to be euen synne, beynge so bolde to speake euyn rashely, saynge. Wherfor hast thu marryed a straunge woman? Thu gyuest vs a lawe, and ponnyshemente if we do not fulfyll it. And thu woldest not be bounde to it, forbyddynge vs the thynge whych thu thy selfe doist.

Nume. 12.

Nume. 12

Deute. 5.

For thu doist forbyd vs to kylle anye man, and thu doist kylle and sparist non of thre thousande whych thu causydest to be slayne. Also God gaue vs in commaundemente by the, that we shulde not marry the doughter of a straunger. Yet

Exo. 32.

Exo. 34.

thu tokest thy wyfe amonge them. Alas my dere brother, with a great meany of soche wordes (whom I knowe to be folyshe) with Aaron (whych is my owne wytte) I imbrayded the, Wherof I do repente. For the lyuely voyce of God, rebukyngly toke me vp, before I wente out of the place. What woldest thu than of my synne? Alas my brother thu woldest not haue me ponnyshed. but rather woldest my saluacyon and helthe, in askynge for me, thys great benefyght, that it shulde please God to mytygate hys iudgemente The whych thynge thu couldest not obtayne. For I became a lazar, so that whan any body shulde loke vpõ me, they myght wele se that I had not bene wyse. And so was I put ont from the tentes and tabernacles of the people, bycause that a sycke bodye maye infecte thẽ whych be in helthe

Ezech.18

Nume 12

Oh, a sowle can not haue a greatter Põnyshement, than to be bannyshed out of the cumpanye of them whych are holye, and good: But what dedyst thu seynge my repentaunce? Thu prouydedyst that ny penaunce was sone at an ende, and with trne loue dedyst make meanes for me, wherupon I ded returne. O what

Ezech 33

1. Joã. 2.

C [illegible] brother

brother wolde, in stede to ponnyshe hys folysh syster, so naturally cleaue vnto her? For iniurye, grudge, & great offēce, thu geuyst her grace & loue in recōpēce. Alas my brother, how excedynge is thys thy loue? Moch more is it, than brotherhede is bounde to geue to so poore & wretched a woman as I am. I haue done the euyll, and thu geuyst me good for it, I am thyne, and thu sayest, thu arte myne. Euē so I am, and wyll be so for euer. I feare nomore the great folyshenesse of Aaron, for nomā maye separat me frō the. Now that we are brother & syster togyther, I care very lytle for all other men. Thy landes are myne owne inherytaunce.

Psal. 50.

Lete vs than kepe (if it please the) but one howsholde. Syth it haue pleased the to humble thy selfe so moche, as to ioyne thy hart with myne, in makynge thy selfe a leuely mā, I do ryght hartely thāke the And as to do it as I ought, it lyeth not in my small power. Take my meanynge than, and excuse my ignoraunce, seynge I am of so great a kyndred as to be thy syster. O my God, I haue good cause, to loue, to prayse, & to serue the vnfaynedly and not to feare, nor to desyre any thynge saue the

Phil. 2.

haue the only. Kepe me wele than, for I Hester. [illegible]
aske no other brother nor frynde. If anye
father haue had anye pytie vpon hys chyl
de. If anye mother haue take anye care
for her sonne. If anye brother haue hyd
the synne of hys syster, it is thu. I neuer
sawe (or els it was kepte wōders secrete)
that euer husbande wolde througly for
gyue hys wyfe, after she had hym ones
offended, and ded returne vnto hym.

There haue bene ynough of thē whych
for to auēge their wronges. haue caused
the iudges to put them to deathe. Other Here.
beholdynge their synnes, ded not spare
their owne hādes, sodenly to kylle them.
Other also seynge their faultes to apere,
ded sende thē home agayne to their owne
fryndes. Some perceyuynge their euyll
dysposycyons, haue shut them vp faste in
a pryson. Now breuely to conclude vpon
their dyuerse complexyons, The ende of
their pretence is ponnyshment, and the
least harme that euer I coulde perceyue
in pōnyshynge thē. is thys, that they wol Deut. 24.
de neuer se thē agayne. Thu shuldest rather make the skye to turne thā, so to forsa
ke thy wyfe for her mysdoynge. Wherfor
my God, I can fynde no mā to be cōpared
vnto thē. For of loue thu arte the perfect

example. Now my God, more than euer I ded, I confesse that I haue broken my othe and promyse.

Alas thu haddyst chosen me for thy wyfe, and dedyst set me vp in great state & honoure. For what greatter honoure maye one haue, than to be in the place of thy wyfe, whych swetely taketh her rest so nere the. Of all thy goodes quene, mastres, and lady, and also in suretie both of body and sowle. Of great fauoure is it, that I so vyle a creature, am so ennoblyshed by the. Now to speake it breuely. I haue more, & better than any man mortall can desyre. Wherfor my harte hath cause to sygh alwayes, and with habundaunce of teares, myne eyes to come out of my heade. My mouthe can not make to many exclamacyons. For there is neyther newe nor auncyent writynges, that can shewe so pytiefull a case, as the same is whych I wyll tell now. Shall, or dare I tell it? Maye I pronounce it without shame? Alas yea. For my confusyon is it not to shewe the great loue of my husbāde. Ther for I care not, if for hys worshyp I do declare my faulte.

Joan. 15.
Luce. 6.
Psal. 50.

O my sauer, whych dyed & was crucyfyed on

fyed on the crosse for my synnes. Thys dede is not suche, as a father to leaue hys sonne, or as a chylde to offẽde hys mother or els as a syster to grudge & chyde. Alas thys is worse. For the offence is greatter where more loue & knowledge is. For the more famylyaryte we haue with God & the more benefytes we receyue of hym the greatter is our offẽce whan we with hym dyssemble. Specyally that I shuld so do, whych am called hys spouse, and loued of the as thyne owne sowle. Shall I tell the truthe? Yea. I haue lefte the, forgoten the, & ranne awaye from the. I ded leaue the for to go at my vayne pleasure. I forsoke the and chose other. Yea. I refused the, the welspringe of all goodnesse and faythfull promyse. I ded leaue the. But whyther went I? Into a place where nothynge was but cursednesse.

Esa. I.

Iob. 18.

I haue lefte the my trusty fryndé and louer, worthy to be loued aboue all other I haue put the asyde. o welspringe of all helthesomnesse, by myne owne wretched wyll. Yea, I haue forsaken the, full of bewtie, goodnesse, wysdom, and power, & sought to withdrawe me from thy loue. I haue accepted thy great enemyes, that is the deuyll, the worlde, and the fleshe, agaynst whõe thu faughtest so sore on the crosse, to ouercome for my sake, to set me at lyberte, whych was by thẽ of lõge tyme a prysoner slaue. And so bounde, that no man coulde cause me to humble my selfe And as for the loue & charyte that I shulde haue had towardes the, they ded quẽche it so that the name of Jesus my husbãde, whych before I had founde so swete, was to me tedyouse & hatefull. So that often tymes I ded iest at it. And if any man (I hearynge a sermon) had sayd vnto me, the preacher sayth wele, I wolde afferme it but the worde went awaye from me, as a fether doth in the wynde.

Hebr. 12

Luce. 8.

I went neuer yet to the preachynge, but for maner only. All my dedes were playne hypocresye, for my mynde was in other places. I was anoyed whan I hearde speake of the, for I was more wyllynge to go at my pleasure. Now breuely to conclude, All that thu dedyst forbyd me, I fulfylled & all that thu cõmaũdedyst me to do, I ded eschewe. And thys was the cause (my God) I ded not loue the. But yet lorde, for all thys that I ded hate the and forsake the, ranne awaye from the, &

Iere. 2.

betrayed

betrayed the, shulde I geue thy place to an other? Or hast thu suffered that I shulde be mocked, eyther yet beate or kylled? Hast thu put me in darke pryson, or bannysshed me for euer, settynge nought by me? Hast thu taken awaye thy gyftes agayne from me, and precyouse iewels, to ponnysh me for my vnfaythfull [f]rutes? Haue I lost my ioynter whych thu promysedyst me, through my offece agaynst the? Am I accused by the afore the eternall father, for a naughty woman? Yea, hast thu forbyd me thy presēce (as I deserued) & that I shulde neuer apere in thy howse?

Math.25

O most true husbāde, & pure perfyght frynde, the most louynge yet amonge all good louers. Alas thu hast done otherwyse: For thu soughtest for me dylygenly, when I was goynge into the most depe place of helle, where all the euyls are done. Whan I was fardest from the both in harte and mynde, & clerlye out of the true waye. Than dedyst thu louyngly call me backe, saynge. My dere doughter harken, and se, and bowe thy hearynge towardes me. Forget that straunge nacyon to whom thu dedyst ronne awaye and also the house of thyne olde father

Luce.15

Psal.44

olde father, where thu hast dwelled so
longe Than shall the kynge full of all
faythfulnesse, desyre thy bewtie. But
whan thu sawest that thy swete & gracy
ouse callynge, ded not profyte me. than be
gannyst thu to crye lowder. Come vnto me
all yow whych are wearyly loaden with
laboure. for I am he that shall plenteous
ly refreshe yow and feade yow with my
breade of lyfe. Alas vnto all these swete
wordes wolde I not harken.

Math. 11

For I doubted whether it were thu, or
els a fabyllouse writynge that so sayde.
For I was so folyshe, that without loue
I ded reade thy worde. I consydered not
wele the comparyson of the vyneyearde
whych brought fourth thornes & bryers
in stede of good frute, that it sygnyfyed
me whych had so done. I knowe it wele
ynough, that whan thu dedyst call the
baren wyfe, sayinge. Returne Sulamyte.
All thys dedyst thu speake that I shulde
forsake my synne. And of all these wordes
ded I, as though I had vnderstande neuer a whytt. But whan I ded peruse Hie
remy the prophete, I confesse that I had
in the readynge therof, feare in my harte
and bashefulnesse in my face. I wyll

Esa. 5.

Canti. 6.

tell in

tell it, yea with teares in myne eyes, and all for thy honoure, and to ſuppreſſe my pryde. Thu haſt ſayde by that holy prophete, if a woman hath offended her huſbande, and is ſo left of hym for goynge a ſtraye with other. Namely if he therupō refuſeth her for euer, is ſhe not to be eſtemed poluted and of no value?

Hiere. 3.

The lawe doth conſente to put her in the hādes of iuſtyce, or to dryue her awaye & ſo neuer to ſe her or to take her agayne. Thu haſt made the ſepracyon from my bedde (ſayth he vnto me) & placed ſtraūge louers in my roume, commyttynge with them fornycacyon. Yet for all thys thu mayſt returne vnto me agayne. For I wyll not alwayes be āgrye agaynſt the. Lyfte vp thyne eyes, & loke aboute the on euery ſyde. Thā ſhalte thu wele ſe, into what place thy ſynne hath led the, & how thou lyeſt downe in the earthe. O poore ſowle, loke where thy ſynne hath put the. Euen vpon the hygh wayes, where thu dedyſt wayte, and tarrye for to begyle thē that came by, euen as a theſe doth whych is hydden in the wyldeneſſe: Therfor thu in fulfyllynge thy wycked pleaſure, haſt with fornycacyon infected all the earthe

Ezech. 16

Hiere. 3.

whych was aboute the. Thyne eye, thy fore heade, and thy face haue loste all their honest good maner. For they were suche as an harlot hath, and yet thu haddest no shame of thy synne.

And the surplus that Hieremy sayth, constrayneth me to knowe my wretched lyfe, & to wyshe with sorowfull syghes, the houre, the daye, the moneth, the tyme and the yeare, that I ded leaue it, yeldynge my selfe condempned, and worthy to be for euer in the euerlastynge fyre. The same feare whych doth not of me but of the procede, and exceadeth many of thy other gyftes, put me rather in hope than dyspayre, as often as I ded remembre my synne. For as sone as thu knewest my wyll bowynge vndre thy obedyence, than puttynge in me a lyuely fayth, thu dedyst vse great clemencye. So that after I knewe the to be that lorde, master, and kynge whom I ought to haue feared. Than founde I my feare not quenched, but mixed with loue, beleuynge that thu wert so gracyouse, gentyll, and swete, & so pytiefull an husbande, that I whych shulde rather haue hydde me, than to haue shewed my selfe, was not than in feare to go fourth and to

Job. 10.

Hebre. 11

and to loke for the. And in so sekynge I founde the.

But what dedyst thu than? Hast thu refused me? Alas my God, no, but rather hast excused me. Hast thu turned thy face from me? No, for thyne eye so swete ded penetrate my harte, woūdynge it almost to the deathe, and geuynge me remorse of my synnes. Thu hast not put me backe with thy hāde, but with both thy armes and with a swete, and mā́ly harte thu dedyst mete with me by the waye, and not ones reprouynge my faultes, enbrasydest me. I coulde not se in beholdynge thy cōtenaunce, that euer thu dedyst ones perceyue myne offence. For thu hast done as moche for me, as though I had beue good and honest. For thu dedyst hyde my faulte from euery body, in geuynge me agayne the parte of thy bedde, and also in shewynge that the multitude of my synnes are so hyddē & ouercome by thy great vyctorye that thu wylte neuer remembre thē. So that now thu seyst nothynge in me, but the graces, gyftes and vertues whych it hath pleased thy fre goodnesse to gyue me.

Psal. 9.

Canti 4.

Roma. 8.

O charyte most precyouse. I do se wele that thy goodnesse doth consume

my lewdenesse, & maketh me a newe god
ly and bewtyfull creature. The euyll that
was myne, thu hast destroyed, and made
me so perfyght a creature, that all the
good whych a husbande can do vnto hys
wyfe thu hast done it to me, in geuynge
me, a faythfull Hope in thy promyses.
Now haue I through thy good grace re=
couered the place of thy wyfe. O happye
& desyered place, gracyouse bedde, trone
Math.11 ryght honourable, seate of peace, rest from
all warre, hygh steppe of honoure, separa
te from the earthe. Doist thu receyue
thys vnworthy creature, geuynge her the
scepture and crowne of thy empyre and
gloryouse realme? who ded euer heare
speake of suche a storye? as to rayse vp one
so hygh, whych of her selfe was nothynge
& maketh of great value, that of it selfe
was naught.

Alas what is thys? for I castynge myne
Joan.3. eyes on hygh, ded se thy goodnesse, so vn=
knowne grace, & loue so incomprehẽsyble
that my syght is wonderfull. Than am I
constrayned to loke downe, & in so lokyn
ge downewarde, I do se what I am, and
what I was wyllynge to be. Alas I do
se in it the lewdenesse, darkenesse, and

extreme depenesse of my euyll, My deathe whych by hublenesse closeth myne eye
The admyrable goodnesse of the, & the
vnspeakeable euyll whych is in me, Thy
ryght hyghnes & pure maiestie, my ryght Sapi. 14.
fragyle and mortall nature, Thy gyftes,
goodes, & beatytude, my malyce & great
vnkyndnesse. O how good thu arte vnto
me, and how vnkynde am I to the. Thys
that thu wylte, and thys that I pursue.
Whych thynges consydered, causeth me
to maruele, how it pleasyth the to ioyne
thy selfe to me, seynge there is no compa
ryson betwene vs both.

Thu arte my God, and I am thy
worke, thu my creator, and I thy creature
Now to speake breuely, though I can not Esa. 64.
defyne what it is to be of the, yet knowe
I my selfe to be the least thynge that
maye be compared vnto the. O loue thu
madyst thys agrement, whan thu dedyst
ioyne lyfe, and deathe togyther. But the
vnyon hath made alyue deathe. Lyfe dyen
ge, and lyfe without ende, haue made our
deathe a lyfe. Deathe hath geuen vnto
lyfe a quyckenesse, Through suche deathe
I beynge dead, receyued lyfe, and by dea Colos. 3.
the I am rauyshed with hym whych is

alyue. I lyue in the, and as for me, of my selfe I am dead. And as cōcernynge the bodyly deathe, it is nothynge els vnto me, but a cōmynge out of pryson. Deathe is lyfe vnto me. For through deathe. I am alyue. Thys mortall lyfe fylleth me full of care, and sorowe, and deathe yeldeth me content.

Apoca 14 O what a goodly thynge it is to dye, whych causeth my sowle to lyue. In delyueryng her frō thys mortall deathe, it exēpteth her frō the deathe myserable, & matcheth her with a most myghty louer. & vnlesse she thus dyeth, she lāguyssheth alwayes. Is not thā the sowle blameles, whych wolde fayne dye for to haue suche lyfe? Yes trulye, & she ought to call deathe her welbeloued frynde, O swete deathe, plesaunt sorowe, myghty keye delyuerynge from all wyckednesse. Those Roma. 8 whych trusted in the (o lorde) and in thy deathe, were mortyfyed, because they ded trust in the, and in thy passyon. For with a swete slepe thu dedyst put them oute of that deathe whych causeth manye to lamente. O how happye is the same slepe vnto hym, whych whan he awaketh, doth fynde through thy deathe, the lyfe euerlastynge.

lastynge. For the deathe is no other thynge to a christen man, but a lyberte or delyueraunce from hys mortall bande.

And the deathe whych is fearfull to the wycked, is plesaunt and acceptable to them that are good. Than is deathe through thy deathe destroyed. Therfor my God, if I were ryghtly taught, I shulde call the deathe lyfe, and thys lyfe deathe, ende of laboure, and begynnynge of euerlastynge ioye. For I knowe that the lõge lyfe doth lett me from thy syght. O deathe, come, and breake the same obstacle of lyfe. Or els loue, do a myracle now, syth that I can not yet se my spouse Transfourme me with hym both bodye & sowle, and than shall I the better tarry for the cummynge of deathe. Lete me dye that I maye lyue with hym. For there is nõ that can helpe me, onles it be thu only. O my sauer, through faythe I am planted, and ioyned with the. O what vnyon is thys, syth that through faythe I am sure of the. And I maye call the, father brother, sonne, and husbande. O what giftes thu dost gyue, by the goodenesse of those names.

Roma. 7.

Psal. 35.

Joan. 15.

O my father, what paternyte, O my

brother what fraternyte, O my chylde what dylectyon, O my spouse, what coniunctyon is thys? Father full of humylyte

Apoca 12

Brother hauynge our symylytude, Sõne engendered through faythe. & loue, Husbande louynge, and releuynge in all extremyte. But whom doist thu loue? Alas it is she whom thu hast withdrawen from the snare, wherin, through malyce she was bounde, and put her in place, name and offyce of a doughter, syster, mother, and wyfe. O my sauer, the same is a great sauoure of swetnesse, ryght plesaũt, and dylectable, whan a man, after the hearynge of thy worde, shall call the without feare, hys father, brother, chylde, & spouse. I in hearynge that worde, do perceyue my selfe to be called there thy mother, syster, doughter, & spouse. Alas the sowle whych doth fynde suche swetnesse, maye consume, and burne for loue.

Luce. 8.

Is there any loue, onles it be thys, but it hath some euyll condycyon? Is there anye pleasure to be herto estemed? Is there any honoure, but maye be accompted shame, to thys compared? yea, is there any profyte equall to thys? More ouer to conclude it breuely. Is there any thynge

Joan. 14

that I

that I coulde more ernestly loue? Alas no. For he that vnfaynedly loueth God, reputeth all these thynges worldly, of lesse value than the dũge hylle. Pleasure profyte, honoure of thys worlde, are all but vayne tryfles vnto hym whych hath founde God. Suche loue is so profytable honourable, & abundaunt, that (I dare saye) she only suffyseth the harte of a godly man, and yeldeth hym so content, that he neuer desyreth or wolde haue other. For who so euer hath God, as we ought to haue hym, accounteth all other thynges superfluouse or vayne.

2. Cor. 3.

Now thanked by the lorde, through faythe haue I gotẽ the same loue, wherfor I ought to be satysfyed and content. Now haue I the my father, for defence of my longe youth from wanton folyshnesse. Now haue I the my brother, for to socoure my sorowes wherin I fynde non ende. Now haue I the my sonne, for my feble age as an only staye. Now haue I the a true, & faythfull husbande, for the satisfyenge of my whole harte. Now syth that I haue the, I do forsake all them that are in the worlde. Syth I holde the, thu shalte escape me no more. Seynge

Phil. 2.

that I se the, I wyll loke vpon non other thynge that myght kepe me backe from the beholdynge of thy dyuynyte. Seynge that I do heare the, I wyll heare nothynge that letteth me frō the fruycyō of thy voyce. Syth that I maye frely talke with the, I wyll cōmen with non other. Seynge it pleaseth the to put me so nere the, I wyll rather dye than to touche any other Seynge that I serue the, I wyll serue non other master.

Esa. 55.
Joā. 10.

Seynge that thu hast ioyned thy harte with myne, if he depart from thyne, lete hym be ponnyshed for euer. For the departynge from thy loue is harder, than is any dampnacyon. I do not feare the payne of ten thousande helles, so moche as I do feare the ones losynge of the. Alas my God, my father, and creator, do not suffer that the enemy, inuentor of all synne, haue suche power, that he make me to lese thy presence. For who so euer hath ones felte the losse of thy loue, he shall saye that he wolde rather be bounde for euer in helle, than to feale the payne that one shall haue by the losse of the same thy loue one momente of tyme. O my sauer, do not permytt that euer I departe from the. But

2. thes. 2.
Ro. 15.

if it

If it please the, put me in suche a place, that my sowle through wantonnesse of synne be neuer separated from thy loue.

In thys worlde I can not haue perfyghtly thys my desyre. Whych thynge consydered maketh me feruently & with all my harte, to desyre the departynge from thys bodye of synne, not fearynge the deathe nor yet any of her instrumentes. For what feare ought I to haue of my God, whych through loue offered hymselfe and suffered deathe, not of dett or dewtye, but because he wolde for my only sake undo the power that mortall deathe had. Now is Jesus dead, in whom we are all dead, and through hys deathe he causeth euery man to lyue agayne. I meane those whych through faythe are partakers of hys Passyon. For euen as the deathe before the great mystery of the crosse, was harde to euery bodye, and there was no mā but was feared therwith, consyderynge the copulacyon of the bodye & the sowle, their order, loue, and agrement, so were their sorowes extreme in the departynge of the one from the other.

Roma. 7

Hebre. 9

Eccle. 4

But sens it hath pleased the swete lamded offer hymselfe vpon the crosse, hys great loue hath kyndeled a fyre within the harte so vehement, that euery true beleuer estemeth the passage of deathe but a playe or pastyme, and so prouoketh Sapi. 3. other constauntly in hys truthe to dye. And eue as the feare of deathe ded retarde vs, so ought loue to gyue vs a desyre to dye. For if true loue be vnfaynedly within the harte of a man, he can fele non other thynge, because that loue is so stronge of it selfe, that she kepith all the roume, and putteth out all other desyres, not sufferyn 1. Joa. 4. ge any thynge there but God only. For wher soeuer true and perfyght loue is, we do neyther remebre feare nor yet sorowe

If our owne pryde for to attayne honoure, maketh vs to seke deathe so manye strau nge wayes. As if for to haue a folysh pleasure, a man putteth hym selfe in ieopardye of lyfe. If a merchaūte to obtayne ryches, doth daunger hymselfe, somtyme for the value of a shyllynge. If the first cōceyuynge of robery or murther, crueltie Deute. 16 or deceyte, doth so blynde a man, that he doubteth nothynge the daunger of deathe, neyther yet mysfortune whan he seketh to auēge hymselfe or doth any other euyll. If the fury of syckenesse or the ran-

kenesse

kenesse of Malancholy causeth a creature scarcely to wyshe for deathe, & oft tymes to drowne, hãge, or kylle thẽselues. For suche euyls are somtymes so great that they cause their payned pacyentes to chose deathe for lyberte. If it so be than that these paynes full of euyll, and imperfectyons, causeth them not to feare the hasarde of deathe, but rather to thynke that deathe tarryeth to longe.

Eccle. 1.

Alas what ought true and laudable loue to do? What ought the loue of the eternall creatour to wyshe? Shulde she sturre a harte suche wyse, that he beynge transported with suche affectyon, shulde fele non other thynge in hym? Alas yea. For deathe is a plesaunt thynge to the sowle, whych is in loue with God, and estemeth the passage easye, through the whych she commyth out of pryson. For the harde waye, wherthrough she commeth, can not wearye her for to enbrace her husbande. O my sauer, how good is the same deathe, through whom we shall haue the ende of all sorowes? By whom I shall enioye thy syght without impedyment, and be transfourmed into the lykenesse of thy maieste?

Roma. 8.

2. Cor. 3.

O dyathe

O deathe, through thy dede I trust to haue suche honour, as vpon my knees with cryenge and wepynge I do dayly desyre. Therfor come quyckely, and make an ende of my sorowes. O happy doughters, ryght holy sowles ioyned to the cytie hierusalem, open your eyes and with pytye loke vpon my desolacyon. I beseche yow that in my name ye do shewe vnto my bestbeloue, my God, frynde & kynge, how at euerye houre of the daye, I do languysh for hys loue. O swete deathe, through suche loue come vnto me, and with loue brynge me vnto my lorde God. O deathe where is thy stynge and darte Alas they are bannyshed from myne eyes, for rygour is changed into swetnesse seynge that my frynde ded suffre deathe vpon the crosse for my sake. Hys deathe doth so incourage my harte, that thu wert wonders gentyll to me, if I myght folowe hym.

Canti. 5.

I. Cor. 15.

O deathe, I beseche the come to put the frynde with hys loue, Now syth that deathe is so plesaunt a lyfe, that she pleasith me more than feareth me, than ought I to feare nothynge but the ryght iudgement of God, All my synnes with hys iust

Iob. 1.

balaūce

balaũce shall be wayed & shewed opẽly. Apoca 20
Thys that I haue done. also my thought
and worde shall be better knowne, than
if they were written in a rolle. And we
maye not thynke that charyte wolde offẽ
de iustyce & truthe. For whoso euer doth
lyue vnfaythfully, shall be ponnyshed in
euerlastynge payne. God is iust and hys
iudgemẽt is ryghteouse. All that he doth Psal. 118
is perfyght in all thynges. Alas what
am I consyderynge my ryghtousnesse, I
wretched and poore creature?

I knowe that all the workes of iust mẽ
are so full of imperfectyon, that afore God
they are more fylthye than myer or any Esa. 64
other vylenesse. What wyll it be than cõ
cernynge the synnes whych I do cõmyt,
wherof I feale the burden importable?
I can saye nothynge els but that I haue
wonne by them dampnacyon. Is thys the
ende? Shall dyspayre than be the confor
te of my greate ignorauñce? Alas my God
no. For the inuysyble faythe causeth me Hebre. 11
to beleue, that all thynges whych are im
possyble to men, are possyble vnto the. So Luce. 18
that thu do converte my worke, whych is
nothynge, into some good worke of thyne
in me, whych is specyally faythe. Than my Ioan. 6

lorde, who shall condempne me, & what iudge wyll dāpne me, syth that he whych is geuen me for a iudge, is my spouse, my father, and refuge? Alas what father? Suche as doth neuer condempne hys chylde, but alwayes doth excuse and defende hym.

Than I perceyue to haue non other accuser but Jesus Christ, whych is my redemer, whose deathe hath restored vs our lost inherytaunce. For he made hym selfe our man of lawe, shewynge hys so worthye merytes afore God, wherwith my great debte is so habundauntly recōpenced, that in iudgement it is accompted for nothynge. O redemer, here is a great loue? We fynde but fewe suche mē of lawe. Swete Jesus Christ, it is vnto the that I am a detter, yet dost thu both praye, and speake for me. And moreouer whan thu dost se that I am poore, with the abūdaūce of thy goodes thu dost paye my debte O incomprehensyble see of all goodnesse. O my father, dost thu vouchesaue to be my iudge, not wyllynge the deathe of a synner? O Jesus Christ, true fysher, and sauer of the sowle, frynde aboue all fryndes, Fo thu beynge my man of lawe dedyst excuse

1. Joā. 2.

Math. 18

dyſt excuſe and ſpeake for me, where thu couldeſt iuſtly haue accuſed me. (Colo.)

I feare nomore to be vndone by any man for the lawe is ſatiſfyed by the for all. My ſwete ſpouſe hath made the payment ſo habundaunt, that the lawe can aſke nothynge of me but is payed of hym. For as I beleue, he hath taken all my ſynnes vpō hym, and hath geuē me in place of them, hys owne goodes in habundaunce. O my sauer, preſentynge thy vertues, thu doſt content the lawe. Whan ſhe wyll reproche me of my ſynnes, thu doſt ſhewe her how willyngly in thyne owne fleſhe, thu haſt taken the dyſcharge of thē, through the coniunctyon of our marryage. Alſo vpon the croſſe through thy paſſyon, thu haſt made ſatiſfactyon for it. Moreouer thy only charyte hath geuē me thys, that thu haſt for me deſerued. Therfor ſeynge thy meryte to be myne, the lawe can aſke nothynge of me. Than wyll I feare nomore the iudgement, but with deſyre rather than parforce, I do tarry for the tyme that I ſhall ſe my iudge, and heare a iuſt iudgemente of hym. (Eſa. 53.) (1. Pet. 2.) (1. Ioã. 4.)

Yet I knowe that thy iudgemēte is ſo iuſt, that there is no faulte therin, & (Pſal. 118) that my infydelyte is worthye to suffer the cruelnesse of helle. For if I do only consydre my deseruynge, I can se nothynge in it that can keape me from the fyre of helle. True it is, that the torment of helle was neuer prepared but for the deuyll, and not for reasonable men. Neuer thelesse if any man haue set in hys mynde to be lyke to the deuyll, than ought he as the deuyll to be payed with a lyke rewarde. But if a man through cōtemplacyon of the sowle, do holde of the, hys Angell of coūsell, vertue, goodnesse & perfectyō, he is sure to obtayne heauen, whych is a place of thy deseruynge for hym. Than shall the vycyouse be ponnyshed with the same, to whom they ioyned themselues. For sith that they folowed Sathan, they must holde suche place as is for hym and hys angels prepared.

Math. 25

Luce. 13

Now I consyderynge the dyuersyte of both the sortes, am lytle conforted in spret by thys. For I can not denye but I am more lyke the deuyll than the Angell of lyght, wherfor I feare and tremble. For the lyfe of the Angell is so pure & myne so vnpure, that I am nothynge lyke vnto hym, thys do I confesse, But to the other

Hebre. 1.

I am

I am so lyke in my doynges, and so accu
stomed in hys wayes, that of hys payne
& tormente I ought to be partaker. For
the cruell synne whych hath bounde me
in helle, is so great and hys force so stronge, that it leteth nothynge to come from
it, neyther feareth it the cōtrary assaulte
of any man. But he whych is in thys kyn- Luce. 11.
de stronge, knoweth not how hys strength
goth awaye, whan a stronger than he cōmyth. Synne is stronge whych bryngeth
vs to helle.

And I coulde neuer yet se, that anye
man by meryte or payne takynge, coulde
euer yet vanquyshe that helle, saue only
he whych ded the great assaulte through
hys vnspeakable charyte, whan he hum- Phil. 2.
bled hym selfe to the crosse. Wherby he 1. Cor. 15
hath ouercomen hys enemye, broken helle
and hys power so that it hath no farther
strength to keape anye sowle prysoner,
that hath put her trust in God. Than be
leuynge in the great strength that he
hath, I do not set by helle and synne, No
not so moche as a strawe. So that synne
can neuer haue holde of me, vnlesse it be
for to shewe how my God is mercyfull,
stronge, myghtie, & a pusaūt vanquysher Roma. 8
 of all

of all the euyls whych were within my harte. If my synne forgyuē, is the glorye of my most louynge sauer, I ought also to beleue, that my glorye is encreased therwith, seynge that I am planted or engrafted in hym.

Hys honoure only doth honoure all hys, and hys ryches doth replenysh euery one of hys with hys goodes. Than deathe helle and synne are ouercome by hym. O glottonouse helle, where is thy defence? Thu cruell vyllayne synne, where is thy tyrannouse power? O deathe where is thy stynge & vyctorye, whych are so moche spoken of? In steade of deathe, thu deathe geuyst vs lyfe, and so dost thu contrary to thy wyll. Also thu synne which couetyst to drawe yche creature to dāpnacyon thu geuest vs a ladder to reache therby that goodly cytie Hierusalem. Yet woldest thu of thy cursed nature that our eternall maker shulde lose hys creature. But through hys loue and grace, the sorye remēbraunce of thy vncomelynesse, doth cause her by repentaunce to come agayne, and submyt her selfe vnto God more than euer she dyd. Hys inestymable goodnesse causeth the to lose the whole

Apoca. 5.
1. Cor. 15.
Apoca. 21.

labour whych thu takest all the weke.

Therfor helle hath not had all the nomber that he did pretende to haue. bicause that the solacyouse shaddowe & power of hys passyon, is suche a myghtye protectyon to the sowle, that she therby nedeth neyther to doubte deathe, synne, nor helle Is there anye thynge can pull me backe if God be wyllynge through hys gyfte of faythe to drawe me to hym? I meane suche faythe as we must nedes haue to obtayne the hygh graces from aboue, & also suche faythe as through charyte doth ioyne the humble seruaunt to hys maker. I beynge ioyned vnto hym, ought to haue no feare of trauayle, payne, nor sorowe, For who so euer doth wyllyngly suffer anye maner of deathe or sorowe for the truthe, as ded Christ, he doth feale in suche torment great consolacyon for hys sowle, knowynge that as for my selfe, I am weake, and with God I am ryght stronge.

Osee. 13.

Joan. 6.

Math. 10

Through hys confort I maye do all thynges. For hys loue is so cōstaūt & permanet that it varyeth not for anye worldly thynge. Who can thā withdrawe me from hys grace? Surely the great heyth

Roma. 8. of heauen, nor the deapenesse of helle, nor the breadeth of the whole earthe, neyther deathe nor synne, whych doth warre euery daye agaynst me, can separate me one mynute from the great loue & charyte, that my heauenly father through Jesus Christ hath vnto me. Hys goodnesse is suche, that he loueth me whych haue not at all tymes loued hym. And if J now loue hym, than shall J feale hys loue to increase in me.
1. Joā. 4. But bycause that my loue is not worthy to loue hym, J desyre hys loue to be myne the whych J feale suche as though it were myne owne, Hys desyre is to loue, and through hys loue he causith my harte to be inflamyd with loue.

And through suche loue he fyndeth hym selfe so welbeloued, that hys owne dede yeldeth hym wele content, & not my loue Joan. 13. or strengthe. Contentynge hys selfe, hys loue doth increase more in me, than J can of hym desyre, O true louer, fountayne, or welspringe of all charyte, and only purse of the heauēly treasure. Ought J to thynke, or dare J saye what thu art? Maye J write it, or can anye mortall man comprehende thys goodnesse & loue? And if thu prēte in anye mānys harte, cā he expresse it? No it? No surely. For the capacyte of no man can comprehende the vnmesurable goodnesses whych are in the. for naturall reasō doth shewe vs how there is no cōparyson betwyne an eternall & a mortall thynge. But whan through loue the mortall is ioyned with the eternall, the mortall thynge is so fulfylled with the eternall, that it can not fynde the ende therof. For it hath in it more good therby, than it can contayne or holde.

Roma. 11

Ephe. 3.

Therfor doth a man thynke, whych hath the loue of God, that he hath all the goodes in the worlde therwith. Euen as we se the sūne with one only sparcle of hys lyght doth blynde the eye, and yet doth she witholde her great lyghte. But aske the eye what he hath seane, and he wyll saye that he hath beholden the whole bryghtnesse of the sunne. But that is a great lye. For he beynge dymmed with a lytle sparcle, coulde not se the whole cleartye therof. And neuertheles he is so contente, that it semith vnto hym as though he had so moche lyght as the sunne contayneth. Yet if he had more than the seyde sparcle, he were not able to suffer it. Euen so the sowle whych through

Roma. 8.

Ecco. 12.

faythe doth fele one sparcle of the loue of God, doth fynde therwith the heate so great and maruelouse, so swete and delycyouse, that it is impossyble to her to declare what thynge the same loue is.

Psal. 118

For a lytle threof that she hath felte doth yelde her mynde satisfyed & desyerynge of more wherof she hath ynough. So doth she lyue languyshynge & syghynge. The harte doth fele wele, that he hath receyued to moche, but he hath cōceyued suche desyre in thys to moche, that he alwayes desyerith to receyue the thynge whych he can not haue, neyther is he worthye to receyue it. He knowith the good that he hath alredy to be vnspeakeable, and yet wolde he haue more of that wherof he can not skylle. Truly he can not fele or thynke the good whych is in hym. Then lyeth it not in my power, to tell what thynge the loue of God is, sith that I haue no knowlege of the feruentnesse therof. He that thynketh to haue all thys loue withyn hys harte, can not truly declare what thynge it is. Happye is he wych hath suche abundaūce of thys loue, that he maye saye, My God, I haue ynough of it.

Phil. 1.

1 Ioā. 4.

He whych hath thys loue within hym, dare not moche boaste therof, least in moche speakynge he lose it, vnles it be to edyfye hys neybour vnto saluacyon. The impossybylyte than of the declaracyon of thys loue shall make me to holde my peace, For there is no Saynte so perfyght, if he wyll speake of the loue of the hygh God, of hys goodnesse, swetnesse, graces, and of all thynges els whych pertayneth to hym, but lokynge a lowe shall fynde hymselfe vnworthye, and so stoppe hys mouthe. I than a worme of the earthe, lesse than nothynge, ought to cease and not to speake of the incomparable hyghnesse of thys loue. Yet were it to moch vnkyndenesse to be noted in me, if I had writen nothynge, hauynge that done vnto me whych wolde satisfye a moche better wytte than myne is. For he that wolde hyde the goodnesse of God, so good a mastre, shulde commytt a synne worthye to be ponnyshed with the euerlastynge payne.

Therfor come. O happye Paule, whych hast tasted so moche of the same swete honye, beynge blynded for the space of thre dayes, & rapte vp vnto the thirde hauē. Now I besech the, satisfye my ignorāce

Jaco. 3.

Apoc. 3.

Math. 25

2. Cor. 12.

& faulte, & tel me what in suche vysyon thu hast seane. Harke thã what he sayth.

Roma. 11 O the vnspeakeable hyghnesse of the abũdaunt ryches or treasure both of the wysdome & knowledge of God. How incomprehẽsyble are hys iudgemẽtes & how vnsearchable hys wayes vnto our weake wittes? O holye Paule, thy wordes causeth vs moche to maruayle, that thu hauynge knowledge of so heauẽly secretes, woldest speake no further in them At the least yet tell vs, what thynge we maye hope to haue one daye through suche godly loue. Geue eare and ponder the wordes that he sayth.

Sapi. 17

1. Cor. 2. Neyther hath the eye seane, nor yet the eare hearde, neyther yet hath it euer entred into the harte of anye man, what God hath prepared for them that loue hym. And wolde he speake it no farther? No truly. yet all thys that he sayeth here, is for non other purpose, but to prouoke vs ernestly to loue. He wylleth vs also therin to esteme, that he neyther can declare nor yet name it, & so to geue forth our hartes to pacyẽce & hope of that thynge whych neuer mã yet coulde se, neyther yet dyscerne, what though many through loue for it hath dyed. O excellent gyfte of faythe

Esa. 64.

Roma. 8.

wherof ſo moche good cōmyth, that it cau
ſith man to poſſede the thynge whych he
can not cōprehende. Faythe ioyned with
the truthe, bryngeth fourth hope, wherby
perfyght charyte is engēdered, And charyte is God, as thu knowiſt. If we haue 1. Ioā. 4
charyte, thā we haue alſo God therwith.

Than is God in vs, and we are in hym
And all thys cometh through the benefy
te of faythe. For he dwellith in all men
whych haue true fayhe. Thus haue we a Ioā. 14
greatter treaſure thā we cā tell of, or yet
anye man expreſſe vnto vs. Now to cōclu
de. Syth that ſo great an Apoſtle as ſa-
ynt Paule is, wyll ſpeake no further of
God & hys ineſtymable loue, accordynge Roma. 12
to hys ryghtouſe exāple and doctryne, I
wyll holde my peace & be ſtylle, folowynge neuertheleſſe hys teachynges. Not
withſtādynge yet though herin I acknowledge my ſelfe but earthe and duſte, yet
maye I not fayle to yelde thankes vnto my
eternall lyuynge God, for ſuche great gra
ces, and benefytes, as it hath pleaſed
hym to gyue me. Vnto that euerlaſtynge 1. Timo. 1
kynge of heauen immortall, inuyſyble
incōprehenſyble, myghty, and wyſe only,
be all honoure, prayſe, glorye, magnyfy-
cence, and loue for euer & euer. Amen.

Textes of the scripture.

These.iiii.clauses of the sacred scripture added my lady Elisabeth vnto the begynnynge and ende of her boke, and therfor I haue here regestred thē in the ende.

Eccle. 25.

There is not a more wycked heade, than the heade of the serpente, And there is no wrathe aboue the wrathe of a womā.

Eccle. 25.

But he that hath goten a vertuouse woman, hath goten a goodly possessyon. She is vnto hym an helpe and pyller, wherupon he restith.

Eccle. 25.

It were better to dwelle with a lyon and dragon, than to kepe howse with a wycked wyfe.

Eccle. 7.

Yet depart not from a dyscrete and good woman, that is fallen vnto the for thy porcyon in the feare of the lorde, For the gifte of her honestie, is aboue golde.

CErtayne, & sure am I (most gentyll reader) that all they whych shall peruse thys godlye boke, shall not therwith be pleased. For amonge readers are alwayes sondry appetytes, and in great assemblyes of people, dyuerse, and varyaunt iudgementes. As the saynge is, so many heades, so many wyttes. Neyther fyne paynted speche, wysdome of thys worlde, nor yet relygyouse hypocresye (whych for pryuate commodyte many men seketh) are herin to be loked for. And a reason why, For he that is here famylyarly commoned with, regardeth no curyosyte, but playnesse and truthe. He refuseth no synner, but is wele contented at all tymes to heare hys hombly tale. Hyde not thy selfe from me (sayth he) whan thu hast done amys, but come boldely face to face, and commen the matter with me. If thy synnes be so redde as scarlet, I shall make the whyter than snowe. And though thy factes be as the purple, yet shall they apere so whyte as the wolle. Esa. 1. For as truly as I lyue (sayth he) no pleasure haue I in the deathe of ỹ synner, but wyll moch rather that he turne

Appetytes.

Synner.

The lorde

turne and be saued. Eze. 33.

If the hombly speche here do to moche offēde, cōsydreit to be the worke of a woman, as she in the bygynnynge therof, hath most mekely desyered. And yet of nō other woman, than was most godly mynded Marke Dauid in the psalter, whych was a man both wyse and lerned, and ye shall fynde hys maner in speakynge not all vnlyke to thys. Faythe (saynt Paule sayth) standeth not in floryshynge eloquence, neyther yet in mannys polytyque wysdome, but in the grace and power of God. 1. Cor. 2. If the ofte repetynge of some one sentence, engendereth a tedyousse werynesse to the reader, lete hym wele peruse the holy workes of S. Iohan the Euāgelyst, & I doubt it not but he shall fynde there the same maner of writynge And hys occasyon is (as all the chefe writers afferme) the necessary markynge of the preceptes of helthe, or of matter chefely concernynge the sowles saluacyon. For a thynge twyse or thryse spoken, entereth moche more depely into the remēbraunce than that is vttered but ones.

Dauid.

S. Iohā

And as touchynge the porcyon that my ladye Helisabeth, the kynges most noble

noble syster hath therin, whych is her translacyon. Chefely haue she done it for her
owne exercyse in the frenche tunge, besydes the spirytuall exercyse of her innar
sowle with God. As a dylygent & profytable bee, haue she gathered of thys flow
re swetnesse both wayes, and of thys boke
consolacyon in sprete. And thynkynge
that other myght do the same, of a most
fre christen harte. she maketh it here cōmen vnto them, not beynge a nigarde
ouer the treasure of God. Math, 25. The
first frute is it of her yonge, tender, and
innocent labours. For I thynke she was
not full oute .xiiii. yeares of age, at the
fynyshynge therof. She haue not done
herin, as ded the relygyouse and anoyn
ted hypocrytes in monasteryes, couētes
and colleges, in spearynge their lybraryes
from men studyouse, and in reseruynge
the treasure contayned in their bokes, to
most vyle dust and wormes. But lyke as
God hath gracyously geuen it, so do she
agayne most frely dystrybute it,

Soch noble begynnynges are neyther
to be reckened chyldysh nor babysh, though she were a babe in yeares, that hath
here geuē them. Seldome fynde we them

Lady helisabeth.

Her first frute.

Lybraryes

The age

that in

The aged that in the closynge vp of their wythered age, do mynystre lyke frutes of vertu. An infynyte swarme beholde we of olde dotynge bawdes and beastes, that with cōscyences loaden with synne (as S. Paule reporteth them) taketh euery paynted stocke & stone for their God, besydes the small breades that their lechrouse chaplaynes hath blowen vpon. They shall not be vnwyse, that shall marke herin, what commodyte it is, or what profyght myght growe to a christen cōmen welthe if youth were thus brought vp in vertu & good letters. If soch frutes come forewarde in chyldehode, what wyll folowe and apere whan dyscressyon and yeares shall be more rype and auncyent? A most manyfest sygne of Godlynesse is it in the fryndes, where youth is thus instytute, and a token of wonderfully faythfull dylygence, in the studyouse teachers, tuters, and dayly lokers on.

Youth.

Tuters.

Nobylyte whych she hath gotē of bloude in the hyghest degre, hauynge a most vyctoryouse kynge to her father, & a most vertuouse, & lerned kynge agayne to her brother, is not in the earely sprynge dystayned with wanton ignorauūce, neyther

yet

yet blemyshed with the commen vyces of dyssolute youth. But mest plenteously adourned with all kyndes of languages, lernynges, and vertues, to holde it styll in ryght course. The translacyon of thys worke, were euydence stronge yneugh, if I had not els to laye for the matter. But marke yet an other moch more effectuall and cleare, at the whych not a fewe lerned men in Germany haue wondered. In. iiij. noble languages, Latyne, Greke Frenche, and Italyane, wrote she vnto me these clauses folowynge. Whych I haue added to thys boke, not only in commendacyon of her lerned youth, but also as an example to be folowed of other noble men and wemen, cōcernynge their chyldren. The written clauses are these, whych she wrote first with her owne hande, moch more fynely than I coulde with anye prentynge letter set thē fourth.

Lerned.

Clauses added.

Stultus dixit in corde suo, non est Deus. Illi corrupti sunt, & abhominabiles in sua impietate, nullus est qui aliquid boni facit.

Latyne.

Le fol disoit en sō cœur, il n'a nul Dieu. Ils sont corumpus & sont abhomi-

French.

nables en leur impiete, il n'a nul qui faict bien.

Italiane. Is stulto disse uel suo core, non v' e alcuno Dio. Corrutti sono & abhominabile nella loro impietà, nissuno è buono.

Greke. Ton theon phobou, tous de goneis tima, tous de Philous aeschynou.

The first clause in thre lãguages, latyne, Frenche, and Italyane, comprehẽdeth thys only sentence, as I shewed afore in the Epystle dedycatory.

Antichrist hys clergy. The fole sayth in hys harte, there is no God. Corupt they are, and abhominable in their wyckednesse (or blasphemyes agaynst God) not one of them doth good.

The Greke clause is thus to be Englyshed.

Christiane. Feare God, honoure thy parentes, and reuerence thy fryndes.

Thus haue she geuen vs coũsell, both to go and to come, to leaue and to take. To

declyne

derlyne from the euyll, and to do that is
good Psal. 36. To flee from the Antichrist
& hys great body of synne or blasphemouse cruell clergy, & to returne to God by a
perfyght feare, honoure, and loue. So lyuely Apothegmes, or breue and quycck sē-
tences, respectynge christyanyte, haue sel-
dom come from women. I haue serched
Plutarchus, Boccatius, Bergomas, Tex-
tor, & Lander of Bonony, whych all wrote
of the vertues and worthy actes of womē.
But amonge them all haue I founde no
counsels so necessary to the cōmen welthe
of our christyanyte. I denye it not, but excellent thynges they vttered, and matters
of wysdome wonderfull, concernynge mo-
rall vertues. But these most hyghly respec
teth the kyngedome of fayth and regymēt
of the sowle, whych Jesus Christ the eternall sonne of God, from heauen by hys doctryne and death so busyly sought to clere.
Many graue sentences had they concernynge pryuate causes. But vnyuersally
these are for all sortes of people, hygh, lowe, hayle, sycke, ryche, poore, lerned, & vnlerned, that myndeth to haue fredome by
Christes deadly sufferynges, or to be delyuered frō helle, synne, deathe, & the deuyll

The pope

Writers

Women

All sorte

by the pryce of hys precyouse bloude.

No realme vndre the skye hath had more noble women, nor of more excellent graces, than haue thys realme of Englande, both in the dayes of the Brytaynes, and sens the Englysh Saxons obtayned it by valeaunt conquest. Guendolena the wyfe of Locrinus the seconde kynge of Brytayne, beynge vnlaufully dyuorced from hym for the pleasure of an whore, whom he longe afore had kepte, tryed it with hym by dynte of the swerde, had the vyctory, and reigned after hym as kynge the space of .xv. yeares, tyll her sonne Maddan come to laufull age. Cordilla the doughter of kynge Leyer, and least of all her systers, as her father was deposed, & exyled out of hys lande, she receyued, conforted, and restored hym agayne to hys princely honoure, and reigned alone after hys deathe, for the space of .v. yeares Cambra the doughter of kynge Belyne, and wyfe to Antenor than kynge of France, ded not only excede in bewtie, but also in wysdome. In so moch that she first instructed the noble men how to buylde cyties, castels, and other stronge holdes, the cōmē people more comely maners, and the womē a most semely

Guendolena.

Cordilla.

Cambra.

mely deckynge of their heades. She made their cyuyle lawes, whych vpon her name were called. Leges Sycambrorum. She taught them to sowe flaxe and hempe, to watter it, drye it, dresse it, spynne it, weaue it, whyten it, and fasshyon it, to all maner of vse for the bodye.

Lawes.

Martia the wyfe of kynge Guythelyne, a lady excedyngly fayre, wyse, & lerned in all the lyberall scyences, inuented thynges wonderfull by the hygh practyse of her wytt. After the death of her husbāde she reigned .vij. yeares as kynge, tyll Sicilius her sonne came to age. She reredressed the commen welthe, refourmed the grosse maners of the people, and made most honest lawes/ called of her name, Leges Martiane. So delyghted the Frenche kynge Nicanor in the wysdome, lernynge, and comely maners of hys wyfe Constantia, the doughter of kynge Eliodorus, that he not only holpe her brother Geruntius in see battayle agaynst the kynge of Orchades, but also sent hys most dere sonne Priamus into Brytayne to haue the same selfe bryngynge vp. The Scottysh kynge Finnanus thought hys pryncely honour most gloryously increased, as he had obtayned

Martia.

Constantia.

Agasia.

Agasia the doughter of kynge Blegabri=
dus, to be coupled in maryage with Gor=
stus hys sonne, for the manyfolde graces
that he behelde in her. What though the
seyd vngracyouse Gorstus, in spyght of the
Brytaynes, ded afterwarde vse her most
wyckedly. Bundwyca a woman both hygh
of stature, and stomacke, also of myst no=
ble lynage amonge the Brytaynes, percey=
uynge the hauoke whych the Romanes
dayly made in the lande, with great pu=
saunce of worthy warryours she inuaded
them, slewe them, hynge vp their captay=
nes, and folowed the remnaunt of them to
the very Alpes of Italy. Where at the lat=
tre by reason of dayly labours, she syckened
and so dyed, euen the very glory of women.
sayth Ponticus Virunnius.

Būdwy=ca.

Voada the first wyfe of kynge Aruira
gus, a woman of wonderfull force & hart
strongly armed her selfe, her.ij. doughters,
and.v. thousande women more of the Bri=
tannysh bloude / in battayle agaynst the
furyouse fearce Romanes, to suppresse the=
ir tyranny and execrable fylthynesse in
abusynge maydes, wyues, and wydowes.
But as she behelde the vyctory vpon their
sydes bycause she wolde not come vndre

Voada.

their

their captyuyte, she poysened her selfe, & so dyed. Voadicia her yonger doughter, afterwarde escapynge the handes of the seyd Romanes, with a myghty power of the Brytanes entered into the yle of Mane, and in a nyght battayle, there slewe thē in a wonderfull nombre, destroyenge their fortalyces, and holdes. Notwithstandynge at the lattre beynge taken, she was byheaded, her eldar syster beynge maryed to kynge Marius. Athildis the doughter of the seyd kynge Marius, was also a most noble woman, whom the Frenche kynge Marcomerus marryed for the only naturall gyftes and scyences whych she had aboue other women, and had .vii. sonnes by her. Claudia Rufina, a noble Brytayne, wyttye and lerned both in Greke and Latyne, hauynge to husbande one Aulus Rufus a lerned knyght, a poete of Bonony & a phylosopher of the Stoycall sort, is moch cōmēded of Martialis the poete, for the Epygrammes and poemes whych she than compyled in both those tunges.

Voadicia

Athildis

Claudia Rufina.

Emerita the syster of kynge Lucius, whych is called the first christened kynge, a lady most vertuouse and faythfull, for cōstauntly affermynge the veryte of Christ,

Emerita

 suffe-

suffered most tyrannouse death and was brent in the fyre. Helena Faluia, the doughter of kynge Coelus, and mother to great Constantyne the Emprour, was a woman of incomparable bewtie and lernynge. Non coulde be founde lyke her in the artes lyberall, neyther yet in the fyne handelynge of all instrumentes of musyke. She excelled all other in the dyuerse speches of nacyons, specyally in the Latyne, Greke, and Hebrue. She made a boke of the prouydence of God, an other of the immortalyte of the sowle, with serten Greke poemes, epystles, and dyuerse other treatyses. Constantia her doughter, was also a woman of most excellent giftes, had she not in the ende declyned to the detestable secte of the Arryanes, by serten hypocrytysh prestes. Vrsula Cynosura, the floryshynge douter of Dionothus the duke of Cornewale, was so nobylly brougt vp in all lyberall dyscyplyne, that Conanus the kynge of lytle Brytayne desyred her to wyfe, and as she went thydrewarde with .xi. thousande Brytaynes wyues more, by chaũce of wether and vyolence of see rouers both she and they peryshed by the waye.

Anna the syster of Aurelius Ambrosius whych.

Helena Flauia.

Cõstãtia.

Vrsula.

nne due

whych was afterwarde marryed to Lotho the kynge of Pyctes, & Anna the twynne syster of kynge Arthure, are of writers magnyfyed for their dyuerse and excellent graces. Morganis a woman of incomparable loue towardes her parentes, and contraye, so secretly and wysely conuayed the body of kynge Arthure, the most worthy gouernour of the Brytaynes, that the Englysh Saxons coulde neuer come to it, to do their vyolẽce theron. Hermelinda, rysynge of the Englysh Saxons bloude, for her excellent bewtie and noble behauer became the wyfe of Cunibertus the kynge of Lombardy. Hylda, a noble woman, both godly, wyse, and lerned, not only dysputed in the open Synode at Streneshalce in the North contraye agaynst the prelates, concernynge their newly founde out celebracyon of Eastre, and their crowne shauynge, with other ceremonyes, but also wrote a treatyse agaynst byshopp Agilbert a Frencheman, the busyest amonge them. The thre doughters of kynge Alphrede, Elfleda, Elfritha, and Ethelgora, were wonderfully experte in the lyberall scyences. Alenor the wyfe of kynge Henry the seconde, was lerned also, & wrote dyuerse

Morganis.

Hermelinda.

Hylda.

Tres filiæ.

Alenora.

epystles to pope Celestyne the thirde, & also to kynge Johan her yongest sonne.

Joana. Joāna the yongest doughter of the seyd kynge Henry, so moch delyghted in good letters, that before she shulde be marryed to kynge wyllyam of Cycyll, she caused her father to sende ouer. ij. lerned men of Englande. walther and Rycharde with a French doctour called Petrus Blesensis to instruct hym in them, specyally in the arte of versyfyenge. And at her cōmynge thydre, the one of those Englysh men was made archebyshop of Panorme, & the other byshop of Siracusa, in recompēce of their labours. Margareta. Margarete the noble mother of kynge Henry the. vij. so plenteously mynded the preferment of scyences & goynge forewarde of lernynges, that she buylded in Cambryge for the same porpose, the colleges of Christ & of S. Johan the Euāgelyst, and gaue landes for their mayntenaunce, as quene Helisabeth ded afore, to the quenes college there. Elisabeth. Longe were it to rehearce the excedynge nombre of noble women, whych in thys lande of Brytayne or realme of Englande, haue excelled in bewtie, wytte, wysdome, scyence, lāguages, lyberalyte, polycyes, heroycall force, and ce, and soch other notable vertues, and by reason of them done feates wonderfull. Eyther yet to sort out their Names and regestre them one by one, whych haue bene marryed out of the same, to Emprours, kynges, dukes, earles, worthy captaynes, Phylosophers, phesycyanes, astronomers, poetes, & other of renomed fame and letters, only for their most rare graces and gyftes.

Names.

Though non in thys lande haue yet done as ded amonge the Grekes Plutarchus, & amonge the Latynes Boccatius with other authours afore named, that is to saye, left behynde them Cataloges or Nomenclatures of famouse and honorable women, yet haue it not at any tyme bene barrayne of them. No, not in the dayes of most popysh darkenesse. As apereth by Alenor Cobham, the wyfe of good duke Umfrey of Glocestre, brother to kynge Henry the fift. Whom Antichristes grande captaynes, the byshoppes than of Englande, in hate of her name and beleue, accused of sorcerouse inchauntmentes and experymentes of Necromancy agaynst their holy horned whorysh churche. And at the last slewe her noble husbande in a false parlement

Writers.

Alenora Cobham.

lement at Bury, by their owne hyred sla-ughter man Pole, as they neuer are with-out soch. If they were worthy prayse, whych had these aforenamed vertues syn-gle, or after a bodyly sort only, we must of congruence graunt them worthy double honoure, whych haue them most plēteously doubled. As now sens Christes Gospell hath rysen, we haue beholden them, & yet se them styll to thys daye in many noble wo men, not rysynge of flesh and bloude as in the other, but of that myghty lyuynge spre te of hys, whych vanquyshed deathe, helle, and the deuyll.

Double honoure.

Consydre yet how strongly that sprete in Anne Askewe, set them all at nought with all their artyllery and mynysters of myschefe both vpon the racke and also in the fyre. Whose memory is now in bene-dyccyon (as Jesus Syrach reporteth of Moses) and shall neuer be forgotten of the ryghteouse. She as Christes myghty membre, hath strongly troden downe the head of the serpent, and gone hence with most noble vyctory ouer the pestyferouse seede of that vyperouse worme of Rome, the gates of helle not preuaylynge aga-ynst her. What other noble women haue,

Anne Askewe.

Noble.

it doth now, and wyll yet herafter apere more largely by their godly doctryne and dedes of fayth. Marke thys present boke for one, whose translacyon was the worke of her. whych was but a babe at the doynge therof. Marke also the graue sentences, whych she geueth fourth to the worlde & laude that lyuynge father of our lorde Jesus Christ, whych hath thus taken hys heauenly wysdome from the great graue senyours, that only are wyse in their owne consaytes, and geuen it so largely to chyldrẽ, Math. 11. That heauenly lorde grãut her and other noble women longe contynnaũce in the same to hys hygh pleasure. That lyke as they are become gloryouse to the worlde by the stody of good letters, so maye they also apere gloryouse i hys syght by dayle exercyse in hys dyuyne scriptures, Whose nature is in processe of tyme to kyndle their myndes and inflame their hartes in the loue of Christ their eternall spouse, as thys present boke requyreth, So be it.

Women

Prayer.

Thus endeth thys godly Medytacyon of the christen sowle concernynge a loue towardes God and hys Christ, aptely translated into Englysh by the ryght vertuouse lady Elyzabeth doughter to our late souerayne Kynge Henry the. viii.

The conclusyon.

¶ The .xiii. Psalme of Dauid, called, *Dixit insipiens*. touched afore of my lady Elizabeth.

Fooles that true fayth, yet neuer hod,
Sayth in their hartes, there is no God.
Fylthy they are, in their practyse,
Of them not one, is godly wyse.
From heauen the lorde, on man ded loke,
The knowe what wayes, he vndertoke.
All they were vayne, and went a straye,
Not one he founde, in the ryght waye.
In harts and tunge, haue they deceyte,
Their lyppes throwe fourth, a poysened beyte.
Their myndes are mad, their mouthes are wode.
And swyft they be, in shedynge blode.
So blynde they are, no truth they knowe,
No feare of God, in them wyll growe.
How can that cruell sort be good?
Of Gods dere folcke, whych sucke the blood?
On hym ryghtly, shall they not call,
Dyspayre wyll so, their hartes appall.

The Conclusyon.

At all tymes God.is with the iust/
Bycause they put,in hym their trust.
Who shall therfor, from Syon geue,
That helthe whych hãgeth.in our beleue?
Whan God shall take,frõ hys the smart,
Than wyll Jacob,reioyce in hart.

Prayse to God.

Imprented in the yeare of our lorde
1548. in Apryll.

[John Cancellar] *E.R. Godly Meditations, or Prayers, set forth after the order of the Alphabet, of the Queenes Maiesties name* (*STC* 17320.5) is reproduced by permission of The British Library (C.134.a.23). The text block of the original is 60 × 115 mm.

L	*Loue perfectlye.*	B	*Be mercifull.*
I	*Imitate Christ.*	E	*Expell vice.*
Z	*Zelouslie praye.*	T	*Trust not flatterie.*
A	*Aske heauenly gifts.*	H	*Hate worldly vanitie.*
R	*Rule prudentlie.*	I	*Incline to humilitie.*
E	*Execute iustlie.*	N	*Nourish friendly amitie.*
G	*Giue bountifullie.*	A	*Aduaunce ciuill policie.*

MUSEUM

E. R.

Godly Meditations, *or Prayers, set forth after the* order of the Alphabet, of the Queenes Maiesties name.

ELIZABETH.

ENter not into iudgement wyth thy seruant, O Lord, for no flesh is righteous in thy sight. *Psal. 143.*

¶ O God which dwellest in light, that no man can attaine. O God which art hid, and canst not be seene with bodylie eies, nor comprehended with anye vnderstanding, neither expressed with the tongue of men or angelles. O my God, what is it to be righteous in thy sight? It is, that we should bee without sinne before thee, which no man euer was since the fall of Adam. For which cause the holye Prophet Dauid sayde in this wise: Enter not into iudgement with thy seruaunt, O Lorde, for no flesh is righteous in thy sight.

If then no flesh be righteous in thy sight:

O

O vnhappie that I am, loden, and burdened with sinne, who shall haue pitty or compassion on mee, or whether shall I go? My sinnes are euer before me, my vnrighteousnesse condemneth mee. What shall I doe? Shall I dispaire. God forbid: for mercifull meeke, and louing is my sauiour: My refuge therefore shall be in my God, for certaine I am, he will not forsake his owne ymage, neyther will he forsake the worke of his owne hands.

h.14.

Wherfore most meeke, louing, & mercifull father, to thee come I all sad and sorrowfull. But what shall I say vnto thee? I will say: Enter not into iudgement wyth thy seruant (O Lorde) for no fleshe is righteous in thy sight. And agayne, I will with the Prophet poure out before thee, the words of sorrowe: I will heartily beseeche thee saying. Haue mercie on mee (O God:) haue mercye on mee, according to thy great mercye. Not after the mercie of men, but after thy great mercie, which is incomprehensible, which is vnmeasurable, and which passeth all sinnes without comparison.

Psal.51.

According therefore vnto that thy great

mercie : by the which thou hast so loued the worlde, that thou gauest thy sonne for it; by the which thou hast taken awaye all our sinnes : by the which thorow his crosse, hast lightned all men : by the which also thou hast restored all things in heauen, and in earth; wash me I say O Lorde, wash me in his blood, restore mee in his resurrection, and iustify me by thy grace & fauour, and the redemption which is in Christ.

John.3.

Rom.a.3.

L

LOrde, looke thou no more on my sinnes : but according to the multitude of thy compassions, wype away all mine iniquities.

Psal.51.

¶ Thy mercie O Lorde, is the abundance of pittie. Thy compassions, are the workes and processe of thy mercie. By the one thou lookest gently on the poore, and wretched: by the other þ forgiuest the multitude of sinnes O sweete, and mercifull Sauiour Jesus Christ, the sorrowfull and penitent sinner,

Marie Magdalen, came prostrate before thy feet, she washed them wt hir bitter teares, she wiped them with ye heares of hir head, & forgauest al hir sinnes, & sent hir away in peace this was, good Lord, one of thy compassions.

Peter thrise denied thee, and forsooke thee wt an othe, thou mercifully lookedst on him, and he beholding thee, bitterly wept, & thou Lorde forgauest him, which was another of thy compassions.

The theefe on the Crosse was saued with one worde: Paule in the furious madnesse of persecution was called, and by and by, was filled with the holy ghost, these al Lord are thy pittifull compassions.

Sith therfore, that thou art the same our God, with whome is no alteration, neither shadowe of chaunge, and sith there is but one Mediator, & atonement betweene God, and man, that is Christ Iesus, which endureth for euer. Why doest thou not poure out thy plenteous compassions vpon vs, as well as thou diddest vpon our forefathers? Why standest thou so farre, O Lorde, and hidest thy face in the needefull time of trouble? Hast thou forsaken vs, or are all thy

mer-

Luc.22.

Math.25.

mercies spent, and none left.

O Lorde my God, I hartily beseech thee and most humbly pray thee, that thou wilt, according to the multitude of thy compassions, wype awaye all my iniquities, that as thou hast drawne and receiued innumerable sinners to thee, and hast made them righteous in thy sight, euen so thou wilt vouchsafe to draw and take me, and also to make mee righteous, thorowe thy grace, and so to clense and purifie my hart, that after al mine iniquities, and vncleanesse put out, it may be as a cleane table, in the which thy finger, O God maye wryte the lawe of thy loue and charitie. Amen.

I

IN the day of trouble, I wil cal on thee (O Lorde) bicause thou hast saide. In what howre soeuer a sinner doth repent him of his sinnes, I will no more remember his iniquitie.

Psal. 50.

Eze. 18.

¶ Beholde good Lord now are the dayes of sorowe, nowe are the daies of calamitie,

and

and nowe is the time wherein I must call on thee: for now feele I mine olde canckred and festred sores of sinne, readie to breake forth in me, to my utter confusion.

Beholde good Lorde, all my desires, all my lamentable and sorrowfull sighes, I poure them all before thee: crying and saying, O Lorde clense mee from my sinnes, for I am uncleane and filthy before thee. Increase therfore thy light in me, that I maye be a vessell of thy grace, kindle my hart with thy loue, put out all feare, for perfite loue expelleth feare.

Iob.3.

1.Iohn.4.

Let the loue of the worlde, the loue of the flesh, the loue of vaine glorie, and the loue of my self, utterly depart from me, that I may (through thy mercie) be clensed from myne iniquitie, by the which I haue offended thee.

Clense me therfore, O Lord, with the water of thy gracious fauour, of which water he that drinketh shall no more thirst, but it shall be made in him, a fountaine of liuing water, running and flowing into eternall life.

Clense me I say (O Lord) with the water of my weeping teares. Clense me wyth the

the comfortable waters of the sacred Scriptures: that I may be numbred among them, *Iohn.15.* vnto whome thou saydest. Now are ye cleane thorowe the wordes, which I haue spoken to you.

Z

ZAche was a perfit man, and thou Lord *Luke.19.* saydest vnto him (when he was in the Figge tree) Zache come down, for to day I will come into thy house, and he came downe, and ioyfully receiued thee.

¶ O Mercifull GOD, how many sinnes haue I done in thy sight, which I would in no wise haue done before mortall mē: I feared men more thā thée, bicause I was blind, & loued blindnesse. I had only eies of fleshe, therefore did I onely feare and looke on men which are flesh.

O my God, beholde, I stande before thy face, that I might finde mercie, I stande before thy goodnesse and benignitie, looking for thy fauourable answere; haue mercy therefore on me.

Thou

Thou saydest to Zache, this day I will abide in thy house: and he ioyfully receyuing thee, sayde, Lorde the halfe of my goodes I giue to the poore: and if I haue done anye man wrong, I will restore him foure folde.

But Lorde Iesu, I will not part halfe that I haue, but I bequeath my selfe wholye vnto thee, reseruing nothing from thee, promising to serue thee for euer, with a clene and pure hart.

O sweete Lorde Iesus, what sawest thou in Zache: euen thine own image, for he had cast off the image of the deuill, which before was on him, & had put on him thy image.

If then thou didst see in Zache, by putting frō him the image of ẏ deuil, that which did drawe thee to his house, take then from mee swete Iesu all my sinnes, and wickednesse, all I praye thee that none remaine in mee, which may keepe thee from mee, that I may put off as Zache did that euill which is in mee, that thou mayst see in mee, which thou sawest in Zache, that when thou shalt call mee out of the Figge tree of thys miserable worlde, ẏ mayest say vnto me, come downe for this day I will abyde with thee.

A pure

A

A Pure hart create in me, O God, and a right spirite renue within me. *Psal. 51.*

¶ Alas my Lorde and Sauiour, my hart hath forsaken thee, it is turned from thee, and is gone astraye. It is wandred into straunge countries, and ensueth vanities. Hir eies are in ẏ vttermost part of ẏ world! It is lost, gone, and solde vnder sinne. It is stonie, ye harder than the Flint or Adamant stone, which relented & yelded at thy sonnes death.

What nowe Lorde, what shall I say? A pure hart, create in mee: a fleshy hart, a mollified hart, an humble hart, a penitent hart, a mercifull hart, a deuout hart: yea, & suche a hart, as will loue thee aboue all things.

Create therefore good Lord such a hart in mee, that it may be of such efficacie, thorow thy grace, as nature is not able to make it.

Giue me also a right spirite, that I maye loue, and worship thee, which art the chiefe and principall spirite, for thou art a spirite: and wilt be worshiped in spirit and verity. *Iohn. 4.*

My soule (good Lord) is also a spirite, and

so made of thée, that of it selfe it is right, for of hir owne nature shée loueth thée aboue hir selfe, and desireth al things for thy glory, so that hir owne naturall loue is right, bicause it commeth of thée.

Make stedfast therefore in me (O Lorde) thorowe thy gracious fauour, this spirite, that it may (according to his owne nature) leade and kéepe mée in the waye of thy commaundements, and that by it, my hart may be so enflamed with heauenly loue: that it may cause me to sigth vnto thée, to embrace thée continually, and neuer to forsake thée, but alwayes to be firme, and constaunt in thée. Giue me therefore, an vpright spirite, not séeking hir owne glorye, but thy will and glorie: renewe it in mée, I praye thée good Lord: renew it I say, for my sinnes haue quenched the first that thou gauest me.

B

Psal. 51.

BEholde Lorde, agaynst thee only haue I sinned, and haue done euill in thy sight:

ſight: that thou mayſt be iuſtified in thy words, and mayeſt ouercome when thou art iudged.

To thee onely (O God) it it is proper to forgiue, and to bee mercifull, for thorowe mercie and forgiueneſſe, thou doeſt declare thine almightineſſe.

I graunt therefore Lord & confeſſe, that againſt thee only haue I offended: and haue done that, which is euill in thy ſight.

Haue mercie therefore on me (O Lorde) haue mercie: and expreſſe and ſhowe forth thy omnipotencie in mee, that thou mayeſt be iuſtified in thy wordes: For it is written, thou cameſt not to call the righteous, but ſinners to repentaunce. *Math.9.*

Graft in mee therfore good Lord a true repentant hart, and iuſtifie mee according to thy wordes: call me, receiue me, and giue me thy grace, ſo that thereby I may doe the workes of repentaunce.

Thou ſaydeſt, when I am lifted vp from the earth, I will drawe all vnto my ſelfe. *Iohn.3.* Verifie, Lorde thy wordes on me, draw mee after thee, and let me runne with thee in the ſweeteneſſe of thine oyntments. *Canti.1.*

Againe, thou saidest: come unto me all ye that labor, and art loden, and I will ease you. Behold my Lord, and my God, I a sinner do come unto thee, all loden with sinnes daye and night, labouring in the sorrowe of my hart for thy grace and mercye: Refreshe and ease me therefore good Lorde, that thou mayest be iustified and proued, when thou art iudged: for there are many which saye, there is no helpe for him in his GOD. Ouercome Lorde these persons, when thou art thus iudged of them, and forsake not me at anye time, but giue to me thy creature, thy mercye and perdon: and then are they vanquished, which say, there is no helpe for him in his God.

Psal. 3.

E

Psal. 51. Establish me (O Lord) wyth a free and principall spirite, and restore vnto me the ioy of thy sauing helth.

¶ It is a great thinge, O heauenly Father, that I desire of thee, seing thou art a great Lorde and King aboue all Gods. Hee doth

Psal. 94.

doth thee iniurie which asketh of thee small things, and he which asketh of thee bodily things, asketh but vaine tryfles: He therefore that desireth spirituall thinges, desireth great thinges: but hee that desireth thy sauing helth, desireth the greatest thing that thou hast to giue.

What is thy sauing health: but Jesus Christ thy onely sonne, which is very God, and euerlasting lyfe. And for so muche as thou hast beene so louing and liberall a Father as to giue him to the death of the Crosse, and there offered him for mee, why shoulde I be ashamed to aske him of thee whome thou hast giuen for me: giue mee therefore thy principall spirite, that I may reioyce in thy sauing helth.

And forsomuch as in thy holy worde thou biddest mee aske and knock euen till I seeme importunate: and what can I aske that shoulde be more holesome to mee, than that thou shouldst make mee reioyce in thy sonne our sauing helth: I will therefore continually crye to thee saying, make me againe to reioyce in thy sauing helth: and restore to me againe the thing, which my sinnes haue lost:

Luke.18

 lost:

last: Restore to me that which thorow my fault, is perished in mée. Restore mée, I besêech thée, for his merites sake, that euer sitteth on thy right hand, and maketh intercession for me, that by thy gracious fauor, I may at my last ende enioye the fruitfull benefite, of thy sauing helth.

T

Psal.51. THou euer O Lorde, hast loued truth, and the vnknowne things of thy wisdome hast thou reuealed vnto me.

¶ What meaneth it to saye, thou louest truth, but that of thy gracious mercie, thou makest vs promises, and fulfillest them for thy truthes sake.

Thou didst promise vnto Abraham, a *Gene.15.* Sonne when he was aged: thou fulfilledst thy promise in olde and barren Sara, bicause thou louest truth.

Psal.131. Thou madest promise vnto Dauid thy seruant, saying, of the fruite of thy body, will I set vpon thy regall throne: and it came to passe, bicause thou louest truth.

Thou

Thou hast promised vnto sinners, which will come vnto thée, forgiuenesse and fauor, and thou hast neuer defrauded any man, for thou louest truth. *Luke.15.*

There are other innumerable promises, in the which thou hast euer bene faithfull, bicause thou louest truth. Loue therfore (O Father of mercies) this truth in me, which with repentant hart turneth to thee: behold therfore thy creature, in whome thou mayst kéepe it, and to whome thou mayst forgiue many sinnes.

Spare good Lord, spare thy seruaunt, and commaunde mée to be of the number of thy Babes, that the vnknowne things of thy wisdome, which thou hast opened vnto me, may leade me vnto the fountaine of wisedome which is on hie, that thou mayest be praysed in the workes of thy mercie, which thou doest exercise towarde thy seruant (O Lorde) which neuer forsakest them that trust in thée. Amen.

E. R.

H

Psal.51. HAddest thou (O Lorde) desired sacrifice, I would haue giuen it thee: but thou delightest not in burnt offerings.

¶ My mouth Lorde, shall shewe forth thy glorious fame, for I knowe it to be most acceptable before thee, seing thou hast declared it by the mouth of the Prophet, saying, *Psal.48.* The sacrifice of praise shall glorifie mee, by which meane, sayth the Lord, I shall be entised to shew him my sauing helth. Therfore will I offer praise vnto thee for my sinnes, euen the praise of Infants and Sucklings.

And why? shall I offer prayse for my sinnes, rather than sacrifice? bicause thou delightest not in burnt sacrifice, for if thou hadst desired sacrifice, I had surelye offered them, but thou delightest not in them.

Ose.6. And againe, thou saidst, I require mercie, and not sacrifice. Therefore my mouth shall shew forth thy praise, bicause thereby I doe shewe forth thy honour, and it sheweth me *Math.9.* through thy grace, the waye to my sauing health.

(O Lord) thou madest the body for the spi-

rit,

rit, therefore seekest thou spirituall things, and not bodilye things: for thou sayest my Sonne, giue thy hart vnto mee: Which is the sacrifice that pleaseth thee. Let me therfore offer vnto thee (O Lorde) a hart repenting & sorrowing for my sinnes, and inflame it with a desired loue of heauenly thinges, and then wilt thou desire no more of me: for with such sacrifice wilt thou O Lord be pleased.

Prouer.23.

REGINA.

REbuke mee not (O Lorde) in thine anger, neither chasten thou mee in thy heauye displeasure: but haue thou mercy on me, for I am weake and in miserye.

Psal.6.

¶ My sinnes, O Lord, are so manye, that the burthen of them hath weakened mee. My bones are so brused, my sinewes are so shrunken, my strength so fayleth me, the rod of thy displeasure hath so chastined me, that

I féele no helpe in my selfe.

Luke.15. I appeale therfore (O Lord) to thy mercie, crying out with the prodigall and vnthriftie sonne, saying, O father, I haue sinned against heauen and before thée: haue mercie (therefore) haue mercye on mée, not bicause I haue deserued thy mercie, but bicause thou art mercifull.

Sith therefore thou art merciful, what art thou but euen the verie mercie it selfe: and what am I but verie miserie? beholde therfore O God, which art mercy, behold misery is before thée.

What shalt thou doe, O Mercie? trulye thy worke: canst thou goe backe from thy nature? and what is thy nature? verily to take away miserie. Haue mercie therfore on me (O God) God which art mercie, take away my misery: for the depth of miserie requireth the depth of mercie.

The depth of sinne requireth the depth of grace and fauour, Greater is the depth of mercie, than the depth of miserie: let therefore good Lord, the one depth swallow vp the other. Let the bottomlesse depth of mercy, swallow vp the depth of misery.

Except

EXcept Lorde, the prayer of thy seruaunt, as thou diddest the prayer of Cornelius: and cast me not cōfused from thy presence.

¶ O sweete Jesus, who euer came to thée with a pure and stedfast fayth, and went awaye confused? or who euer desired thy fauour, and went without it? Surelye thou passest in thine aboundant pittie, both the deseruings, and also the desires of them, that praye vnto thée: for thou giuest more than man can desire.

The Woman of Cananée followed thée, she cried and made a pitteous noyse, she moued thy disciples vnto compassiō, & worshipt thée, and sayd: Lord helpe me, but yet wouldest thou not aunswere: yet she trusting in thy mercie, prayed againe, saying: Lorde helpe me. Unto whose importunitie, thou didst aunswere, saying, it is not good to take the childrens bread and cast it vnto dogges. Math. 15.

Oh Lord, who would not haue bene confounded, and haue gotten him awaye, at these thy wordes? and yet did this Woman con-

continue still in prayer, and sayd: it is truth Lord that thou sayest. It is not meete to cast the childrens breade vnto dogges: but yet Lorde the dogges doe eate of the crummes which fall from the childrens table. And thou Lord reioysing in hir great constancie, didst say: O woman great is thy faith, be it vnto thee as thou desyrest.

Now therfore, sweete and mercifull Lord Jesu, as thou diddest vouchsafe to accept and heare the Prayers of Cornelius, and of this woman of Canane, so I hartily beseech thee to heare my humble prayers, which I make day and night before thee, not onelye that thou shouldest deliuer me from bodily oppressions, but also from the spirituall power of the deuill, that after this mortall lyfe I may come to thy blessed presence in the euerlasting kingdome, where thou raignest God with the Father, and the holy Ghost.

G

Giue eare (O Lorde) and let all my sorrowfull complayntes, which goeth forth of vnfeined lips, come before thee that my mouth maye shewe foorth the worthy prayse of thy name. *Psal.17.*

¶ Thy prayse is a great thing (O Lorde) for it procedeth out of thy fountaine, wherof no sinners drinketh: there is no glorious praise in the mouth of a sinner, deliuer me therefore O Lord, from the waye of sinners, and my tongue shall magnifie thy righteousnesse: and my lips and my mouth shall shewe forth thy praise. *Eccle.15.*

Thou hast the key of Dauid, which shuttest and no man openeth, and openest and no man shutteth: Therefore open thou my lips, as thou hast opened the mouthes of infants, out of whose mouthes thou hast established thy praise. *Esay.22.* *Psal.8.*

Truely the Prophets and Apostles, and all other thy Saintes, praised thee and despised themselues. The sucklings extoll thy fame and glory, which they knowe, through thy heauenly and celestiall grace. *Act.2.3.*

Thy

Thy friendes which spreading thy glory, haue conuerted innumerable soules from sinne vnto vertue and true felicitie. Thy beloued haue openlye preached thy bounteous gentilnesse and mercifull fauor, which thou shewedst in thy deere sonne vnto al ÿ world. Nowe therefore mercifull God, giue mee true humilitie, that thou mayest stablish thy praise by my mouth. Make mee as one of the Infantes and Sucklings, that I maye euer hang on the pappes of thy wisedome, for thy pappes (O Lorde) are better than Wine, and thy wisedome better than riches. Make me as one of thy friends, or beloued, that I may constantly abide in thee, that my mouth and voice may among the sucklings extoll and set foorth thy prayse, saying and singing, Ozanna in the hiest.

Cant.1.

I

Psal.15.

I Am filthye and vncleane before thee (O Lorde) if thou therefore sprinckle me with Isope, I shall be cleane: if thou wash me, I shall be whiter than Snowe.

¶Isope,

¶ Isope, Lorde is a lowe herbe, it is hote and of a good sauour, which signifieth nothing else, but thy only sonne, Jesus Christ, which humbled himself vnto death, euen vnto ye death of the crosse, which with the heat of his feruent loue, loued vs, and washed vs from our sinnes in his bloud: which also with the redolent and swete sauour of his beneuolent and righteousnesse hath replenished the worlde.

Phi. 2.

Therefore with this Isope shalt thou, O holy Father, sprinckle me, when thou shalt poure vpon me the vertue and bloude of thy deare Sonne Christ, when he through faith shall dwell in me. When thorowe loue, I am ioyned with him, when I shall imitate and followe his humilitie and passion, then shall I be clensed from all myne vncleannesse.

Then shalt thou washe me wyth my owne teares, which floweth out of the loue of thy Sonne Christ. Then shall I sigth til I be wery, then shall I water my bed euery night with my teares, so that it shall swim in them: and then Lorde shalt thou washe me, and I shall be whiter than snow.

Not

E R.

N

Math.7. NOt euerye one, that sayeth to mee Lorde, Lorde, shall enter the kingdome of heauen, but he that doeth the will of my Father, which is in heauen.

Iohn.11. ¶ Thy will is (O heauenly Father) that we doe beleeue in thy beloued sonne, whom thou hast sent. Thy will is, that we beleeue, that he whom thou hast sent, is come in the fleshe: and thy will is, that we imitate and keepe his saying.

Thy will is (also) that we shoulde heare him: for thou spakest from heauen saying, Roma.4. this is my welbeloued Sonne, in whome I delight, heare him.

Giue me therefore (O heauenly Father) a stedfast fayth, a strong fayth, yea, such a fayth, that no tribulation, that no vexation, that no persecution maye cause me to denie thy Sonne, whome thou hast sent, but that I may with a pure and constant fayth, confesse him to be come in the fleshe, for the redemption of the worlde: and that I may so imitate & follow him, that I may keepe his Math.17. saying, who was deliuered for my sinnes,

and

and was raysed againe for my iustification.

Giue me also (O holy Father) a perfite hearing, and not a corrupt hearing, but that I maye throughe the teaching of the holye ghost heare thée, out of the Prophets, out of the Apostles, out of the penne of the Euangelist, and out of the mouth of thy Spouse the Catholike Church: to whom thou saydest, I will send you a comforter, euen my spirite, which shall leade you into all truth. *Ephe. 3.* *Iohn. 14.*

Graunt me (O Lorde) this spirite, for there is none that can saye Iesus is the Lorde, but by this thy holy spirite.

A

A Sacrifice to God, is a troubled spirite: a contrite and humble hart, O God, shalt thou not despise. *Psal. 51.*

¶ A broken and troubled spirite, and not broken and troubled fleshe pleaseth thée, O Lord: for the fleshe is broken and vexed bicause it hath not the carnall things that it desireth, or else féeleth in it selfe thinges which it hateth.

The spirite is broken and unquieted for his faulte, bicause it hath offended against God whome it loueth: he sorroweth that he hath sinned against his Maker and Redeemer, and that he hath not regarded such a good and louing Father.

This broken and sorrowing spirit, is unto thee, O Lorde, a sacrifice of most sweete sauour, which notwithstanding, hath hys confection of most bitter spices, euen of the remembrance of his sinnes: for when our sinnes are gathered togither into the morter of the heart, and beaten with the Pestell of compunction, and made into powder, and moysted with the water of teares, thereof is made an Oyntment, and Sacrifice moste sweete, which being offred to thee, O Lord, thou wilt not despise.

Marye Magdalene, which was a great sinner, made suche an Oyntment, and put it into the Alablaster Boxe of hir hart, shee feared not to enter into ỹ Pharisies house, & there humbling hir selfe at thy feete sweet Lord, washed them with hir teares, wiped them with hir heare, and annointed them with most precious Oyntment, and ceased not

Luke.7.

not to kisse them, surely Lorde hir sacrifice was right, acceptable, and pleased thée, so that thou preferredst it aboue the Pharisey, which in his owne sight was righteous.

O Lorde, great is thy power, great is thy might, which declareth it selfe most chiefly, in sparing and hauing compassion on sinners: shewing to vs, that a contrite and humble hart thou wilt not despise.

Accept therefore, swéete Lorde Jesu, this my sacrifice of prayse, procéeding out of a broken and sorrowfull heart, and if it be vnperfit amend thou the fault mercifull Lord, which onelye art of power to doe it, that it may bée an holy and acceptable sacrifice, inflamed with the feruent heate of thy bounteous charitie, that it may be acceptable vnto thée, or at the least that thou despise it not: for if thou despise it not, I know well that I shall finde fauour in thy sight, and that hereafter none of thy Saints either in Heauen or in earth shall despise me.

Accomplish therfore in me euen now, O Lorde, that which I so oft doe craue of thée, which is, that thou wilt haue compassion on me, according to thy great mercye, and that

 also,

E. R.

also, thou wilt receiue me, for a sacrifice of righteousnesse: for a holye oblation, for a burnt sacrifice of good liuing, and for a calfe to be affered vpon thine Aultar or Crosse, by the which I may passe this vale of miserie, vnto that ioye which thou hast prepared for them that loue thee. A-men.

FINIS.

BRITISH
14 FE 1924
MUSEUM

The paraphrase of Erasmus upon the gospell of sainct John in *The first tome or volume of the Paraphrase of Erasmus upon the newe testament* (*STC* 2854) is reproduced by permission of The Huntington Library (RB 60448). The text block of the original is 134 × 225 mm.

13

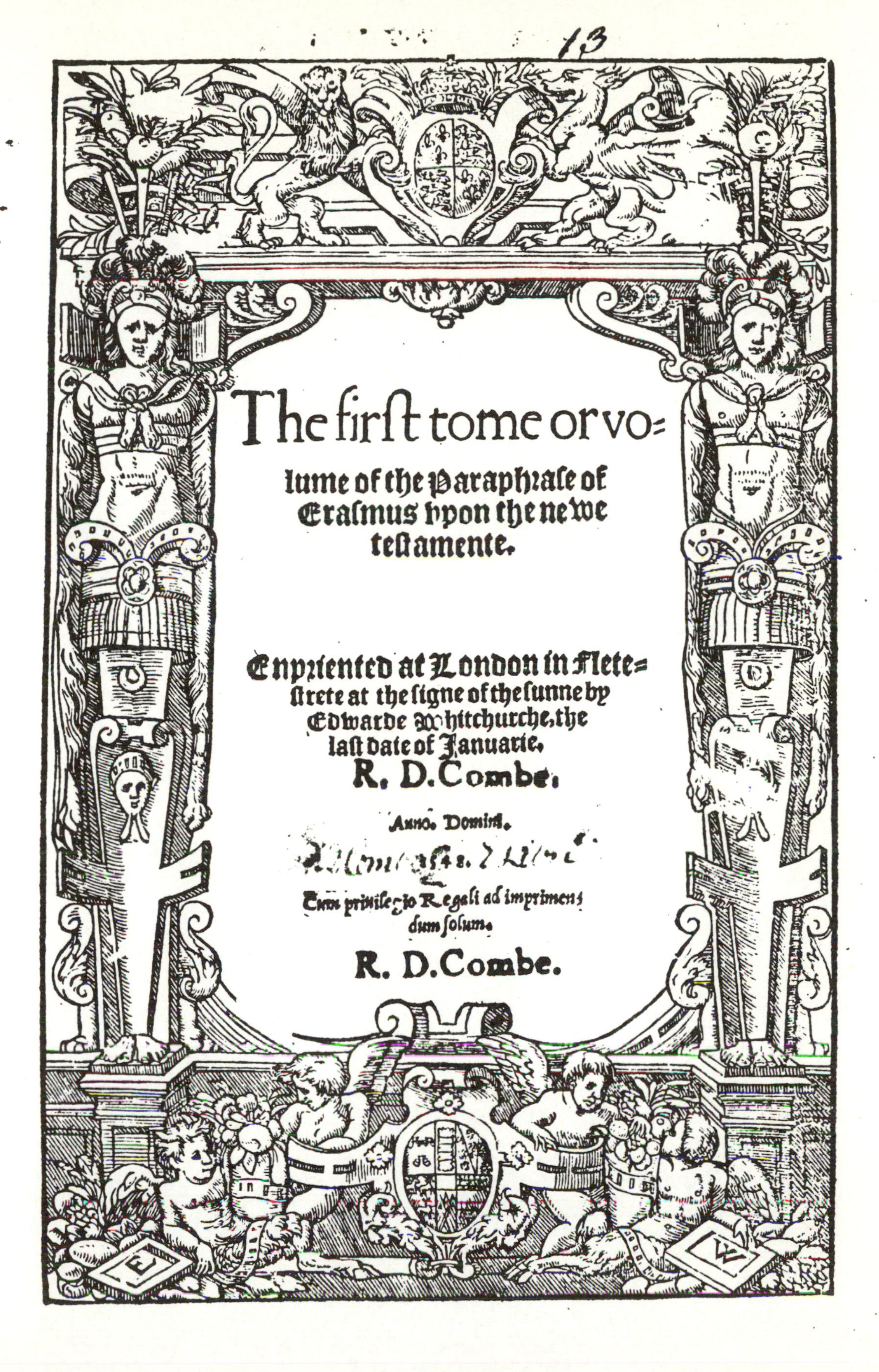

The first tome or volume of the Paraphrase of Erasmus vpon the newe testamente.

Enprented at London in Fletestrete at the signe of the sunne by Edwarde Whitchurche, the last date of Januarie.

R. D. Combe.

Anno. Domini.

1548.

Cum priuilegio Regali ad imprimendum solum.

R. D. Combe.

To the moste vertuous Ladie and moste gracious Quene Katherine late wife to the moste noble kyng Henry the eight of moste famous memorie deceassed, Nicolas Udall your highnesse moste humble seruaūt wissheth health, and all prosperitee in Christ.

When I cōsider, most gracious Quene Katerine, the greate noumbre of noble weomen in this our time and countreye of Englande, not onelye geuen to the studie of humaine sciences and of straunge tongues, but also so throughlye experte in holy scriptures, that they are hable to compare wyth the beste wryters aswell in endictynge and pennynge of godlye and fruitfull treatises to the enstruccion and edifiynge of whole realmes in the knowleage of god, as also in translating good bokes out of Latine or Greke into Englishe for the vse and commoditie of suche as are rude and ignoraunte of the sayd toungues, I cannot but thynke and esteme the famous learned Antiquitee so ferre behynde these tymes, that there cannot iustelye bee made any comparison betwene them. Cornelia a noble matrone of Rome through the longe conuersacion and continuaunce with her learned housebande, was in processe of tyme so wel learned & so eloquent, that hirself was the chiefe & principall instructrice and bryngen vp of hir two sonnes Caius Gracchus, and Tyberius Gracchus in all their learning, and made the same at lengthe so fyne, that they yet to this daye remayne registred in the noumbre of the absolute and perfecte Oratours of olde tyme. We reade of one Amesia in Rome a woman so well spoken & so fine of toungue, that beynge on a time indicted and arrained of a grieuous offēce, she so wittily, so piththily, and wich suche grace made answer for hirself: that all the whole benche & Cōurte than presente, iudged her, for ye mere respecte of her eloquence and witte in that present perill and ieoperdie there shewed, worthy by theyr whole cōsentes & sentences, to be quit and discharged of the law for that crime. Hortensia the daughter of Quintus Hortensius, & brought vp continually frō hir cradle and tendre infancye in the house and companye of suche a noble Oratour, came at lengthe so nere to the perfect eloquēce of her father, that she was hable in publique hearing to make oracions, and the same of so piththye a sorte, that where the noble weomen of Rome were on a time sore taxed to departe with their golde, & iewels toward certayne necessarie charges of that cōmon weale: Hortensia came before the cōmissioners to speake in the behalfe of the matrones, & with her exquisite talke obteined a mitigacion almoste of the wholle taxe whiche the sessours had afore agreed vpon, and appointed vnto the weomen to contribute.

These exaumples of eloquence in weomen, lyke as they are but verye fewe in noumbre, so are they thynges of no suche highe excellencie to be meruailed at. For what great matier of woondre is it that emong so many thousādes three or fower should be founde hable to speake before a iudge in open audience? or what straūge case is it to be reputed, if some one or two weomē haue ben foūd wittie or learned in the Latine toungue beeynge their owne natiue language which euerie carter and handicraftes man than spake, though not al thinge so finely as the learned men and Oratours dyd: what high matier of praise and commendacion is it, if a few weomen being either wiues or daughters to excellent fine Latine men, could in continuaunce of a greate manye yeares speake Latine well: yet are these weomen specialy chronicled in histories as notable, yea and syngulare exaumples worthy perpetuall fame and memorye for their wytte, learnyng, and eloquence. After these heathens, Hierome in his Epistles writeth speciall high praises and commendacions of Eustochium the mother, Paula the daughter, and Blesilla the daughters daughter: of whiche euerye one were passyng well sene not onely in holy scryptures, but also in Latyne, Greke and Hebrewe: whiche toungues they learned exactely in a veray shorte tyme, & excelled in the same. The like testymony he geueth of Marcella a veray noble woman in Rome, whome he reporteth to had in his time so well profyted in the knowleage of holy scriptures, that after his departure from Rome, yf there were any doubtefull question or any poynte of difficultee concernyng scripture: all folkes woulde resorte to hir as to a iudge hable and also sufficient to decise any matier of controuersie or ambiguitee that happened emonge them. But this knowleage extended no ferther then to the priuate edifyinge of theyr owne selues with a very fewe others, and the same in suche places where Latine was their mother toungue and their natiue language. But nowe in this gracious and blissefull time of knoweleage, in which it hath pleased almighty god to reuele and shewe abrode the lighte of his most holy ghospell: what a noumbre is there of noble weomen (especially here in this realme of Englande,) yea and howe many in the yeares of tender virginitie, not onely aswell sene and as familiarlye traded in the Latine and Greke tongues, as in their owne mother language: but also bothe in all kyndes of prophane litterature, and liberall artes, exactly studyed and exercised, and in the holy scriptures and Theologie so ripe, that they are able aptely, cunnyngly, and with muche grace eyther to endicte or translate into the vulgare toungue for the publique instruccio̅ and edifying of the vnlearned multitude. Neyther is it nowe any straunge thing to heare ientle weomen in stede of moste vaine communicacion aboute the moone shynyng in the water, to vse graue and substanciall talke in Greke or Latine with their housebandes of godly matters. It is now no newes in Englande to see young damysels in nobles houses and in the Courtes of princes, in stede of cardes and other instrumentes of idle trifleing, to haue continually in theyr handes eyther Psalmes, Omelies, and other deuoute meditacions, or els Paules epistles, or some booke of holy Scripture matiers, and as familiarlye both to reade or reason therof in Greke, Latine, Frenche, or Italian, as in Englishe. It is nowe a common thing to see young virgins so nouzeled and trained in the studie of letters, yͭ they willingly set all other vayne pastimes at naught for learninges sake. It is nowe no newes at all to see Quenes and Ladies of moste highe estate and progenie, in stede of Courtly daliaunce, to embrace vertuous exercises of readyng and wrytyng, & with moste earneste studie both erely and late to applye themselues to the acquiring of knowlage, aswell in all other liberall artes and disciplines, as also moste specially of God and his moste holy worde, wherunto all christen folkes, (of what estate or degree so euer they be,) ought to the vttermoste of their possible powers, moste principally and moste earnestly themselues to geue & dedicate. But what a great cause of publique reioycyng (o lorde) maye it be, yͭ in this time of Christes haruest, euerie good bodye moste busily applyinge the

worke

worke of his vocaciō towardes the inning of the lordes corne, some by instructyng the youth, some by teachyng scholes, some by preachyng to their simple flockes, some by godly inducing of their familles, some by wrytyng good and godly treatises for the edifying of suche as are willing to reade, and some by translating good bokes out of straunge toūgues into our vulgare language for the helpe of the vnlearned: the most noble weomen of bloude and estate royall, are no lesse diligent trauaillours then the best, (in any of the aboue named offices mete for their sexe,) ne take any manier skorne or disdeigne in ẏ labour of drawing this haruest home, to bee ioyned as yokefelowes with inferiour persons of moste lowe degre and condicion. Howe happie art thou, o England, for whose behoufe and edifying in Christe, Quenes and Princesses spare not neceasse with all earnest endeuour and sedulitee to spende their tyme, their wittes, their substaunce, and also their bodyes. And in this behalfe lyke as to your highnesse, moste noble Quene Katerine, aswel for composyng and setting foorth many goodly psalmes and diuerse other contemplatiue meditacions, as also for causyng these paraphrases of the moste famous clerke and moste godly writer Erasmus of Roterodam to bee translated into oure vulgare language, Englande can neuer bee able to render thankes sufficiente: so may it neuer bee able (as her desertes require) enough to praise & magnifye the moste noble, the moste vertuous, the moste wittye, and the mooste studious Ladye Maries Grace, daughter of the late moste puissaunte and moste victorious Kyng Henry the eyght of moste famous memorie, and moste derely beloued systur to the king our soueraigne lorde that now is, it maye neuer bee able (I saye) enough to prayse and magnifie hir Grace for takyng suche great studie, peine and trauaill, in translatyng this paraphrase of the said Erasmus vpon the gospel of John at your hyghnesse speciall contemplacion, as a noumbre of right well learned men woulde bothe haue made courtesie at, and also would haue brought to wurse frame in the doyng. O how greatly maie we all glory in suche a pierlesse floure of virginitee as her Grace is: who in the middes of Courtly delices, and emiddes the enticementes of worldly vanities, hathe by her owne choice and eleccion so vertuously, and so fruictefully passed her tendre youth, that to the publique comforte and gladfull reioycing whiche at her byrth she brought to all Englande: she doeth nowe also conferre vnto the same the vnestimable benefite of fertheryng bothe vs and our posteritee in the knowleage of Goddes worde, and to the more clere vnderstandyng of Christes gospell. O royal exercise in dede of virginly educacion. O vnestimable and precious fruite of maydenly studies. O noble successe of princely spending the tyme, especially in a womā. O zele of prouokyng Gods glory worthy immortalitee of fame and renoume. For what coulde be a more manifeste argumente of myndyng the publique benefite of her countrey, what coulde bee a more euident profe of her will and desyre to dooe good to her fathers moste derebeloued subiectes, what could be a more plaine declaraciō of her most constaunt purpose to promote Goddes worde, and the free grace of his gospell: then so effectually to prosecute the woorke of translatyng whiche she had begoonne, that whan she had with ouer peynfull studie and labour of wrytyng, cast her weake body in a grieuous and long syckenesse, yet to the intent the diligent Englishe people shoulde not bee defrauded of the benefite entended and ment vnto them: she committed the same woorke to Maister Fraunceise

Malet doctour in the facultee of diuinitee with all celeritee and expedicion to be finished and made complete. That in case the kynges maiesties moste royall commaundemente by his moste godly iniunccions expressed, declared, and pu-blished, (that the sayed Paraphrases shoulde within certaine monethes bee sette foorthe to the Curates and people of this Realme of Englande) hadde not so preuented her grace, but that she might eftsones haue put her style to the poolishing thereof: where it is nowe alreadie veraye absolute and perfeict, it woulde than emong the rude and homely dooinges of me and suche as I am, none otherwise haue glyttered, then clothe of golde enpowdred emōg pat-ches of canuesse, or Perles and Diamoundes emong peoblestones. But in the meane tyme, to what learned man maye not the sedulitee of suche a noble princesse bee a spurre and prouocacion to employe the talente of his learnyng and knowlage to the publique vse and commoditee of his countrey? To whō maye not this moste notable exaumple of so vertuous a Lady, be an occasion to shake of all sluggishenesse, and to yeld vnto the common weale of Englande some condigne fruicte of his studie and learning? To what idle loiterer maye not this moost excellent acte of a kynges daughter and the same a kynges sistur bee a shame, and reproche of negligence? To what persones (be they ne-uer so ignoraunt or vnlearned) maie not this moost earnest zele of a princesse of suche highe estate, bee an effectuall prouocacion and encouragyng to haue good mynde and wyll to reade, heare, and enbrace this deuout and catholyke Paraphrase so plainly and sensibly translated, and so graciously by her offred, and (as ye would saie) put in all folkes handes to be made familiar vnto them? Besechyng therfore almighty god that it maie in the hartes of all good En-glishe people take no lesse place, ne worke any other effect of godly knowleage and innocent liuing, then your highnesse in procuryng these trāslacions, and the said Ladie Maries grace on her partie also haue ment it: I shall sembleablye be a continuall peticioner to his diuine Maiestee, longe yeres to preserue bothe your estates: you to the procuring of many such good translacions for the edi-fying of simple people in Christes discipline, and her to the doing of many lyke actes for the publique vtilitee of vs al, wherby ye maye bothe of you atteygne in this worlde condigne fame and renoume with per-petuall memorie emong men, and after this lyfe a croune of immortall glorye and blisse in heauen eternally there to raigne with Christ and his holy Aun-gelles. Amen.

To the moste renoumed Prince, Ferdinando Archeduke of Austriege, and brother to Charles the fift, the Emperour of the Romaynes. Erasmus of Roterodam wysheth health.

He laste yere, moste gracious prince Ferdinando, I tooke on hande to write a paraphrase vpon the gospell of saincte Mathewe, more at the vrgente request of the moste reuerende Lorde Mathewe, Cardinall of Hedune, then of myne owne mynde, partly because the greate excellencie of the woorke by a certayne reuerente feare withdrewe my minde from medlinge therwithall, partlye also forasmuche as there was besides this, many and sundry difficulties, the whiche mighte abashe my weakenesse (whiche did acknowleage his owne inhabilitie) from medlyng with a treatise so farre aboue my power, so that me thought I was vtterlye dispatched of all suche kinde of wrytyng: yet all this notwithstandyng I am compelled (I cannot tell how) after the same sorte to declare the ghospell of sainte John, partely by the successe of my former bolde enterprise, partly by the auctoritie of certayne noble personages, whose desire, if I should not satisfie, I might be thought very vnkynde, and wicked also yf I should disobey their commaūdementes: yet was it not vnknowen vnto me how muche more full of godly maiestie this present gospell was, the whiche for the moste parte doeth trauaile in the declaracion of suche secrete misteries, as vnto the nature of God doeth appertaine, and the wonderfull copulacion of the sayed nature vnto ours by his incarnacion. For what is he that canne by very imaginaciō, comprise how that God the father, beyng without beginning, doeth continually beget God the sonne: in to whom the begetter doeth so wholy powre out him self, that yet thereby he is nothyng diminished, of whō also the sayed sonne is after suche wyse borne, that yet thereby he is nothyng secluded: againe how that from them bothe, the holy ghoste doeth so procede, that there continueth a perfit copulacion of one nature emōgst them, without any confusion of the distincte proprietie in persons. Who can by witte atteyne to knowe by what coniunccion the omnipotente and vnspeakeable nature by incarnacion, did couple mannes nature vnto hys: so that the selfesame whiche euermore had bene very God of the lyuyng God begotten, was also very man borne of the virgin Marie. In the declaracion of suche matters, in the whiche oftentymes, the bare transposing of one woorde is an haynous offence, what lybertie can a Paraphrase haue. Aboue all this I did perceyue that I muste go, if I did prosecute my purpose, ouer places incumbred with many and sundry difficulties: hedged and diched, parted and diuided with fluddes, and gulfes, ouer the whiche it should not be possible to passe by reason of thickets, and standynge moates. For there is none of all the gospels that hath eyther mo, or more harde questions to be solued, either in whom more vehement studie hath been bestowed of the old and excellent autours: finallye in whose exposicion the interpreters do more varry and discent, the whiche verilye I doe not thinke mete to be imputed to their dulnesse or lacke of learnyng, but either to the obscuritie of the stile or elles to the diffusenes of thinges conteyned therin. There were besides these, other peculiar difficulties in the sayed matter, because that all the wordes which the Euangelist doeth attribute vnto Christ, are intricate with enigmaticall questions, the whiche if a man shoulde expresse in wyse of a paraphrase, suche thinges will not agree with their answer, ỳ did not perceiue to what purpose Christ did speake so. For many thynges be spoken of Christ, after suche a sorte, that he knewe well that they neither coulde, neither woulde he that they should be perceyued vntill the conclusion of the thyng dyd declare his sayinge: Furthermore in asmuche as it is the office of a Paraphrase to expresse that thing that is breefely spokē, and in fewe wordes couched, with more copy ⁊ plēty of wordes, I could not obserue ỳ due measure of time. For wher as it is read that our lorde did kepe his maundy vpon the night time with his disciples, ⁊ at the saied time to haue washed their feete, yet after thesame maūdy he had so long cōmunicatiō with his disciples, that it maye be thoughte a wonder that he had time to speake so manye wordes, namelye seynge that the woordes of the other Euangelistes do declare that manye other thynges also wer bothe saied and doene by hym thesame nighte: wherfore dewe measure in tyme could not be obserued of me, whiche should declare at large all the sayed thynges with more copy ⁊ plenty of wordes. Finallye this Euangelist hath a certaine peculiar kynde of stile of his own. For he doth knit his stile as though it wer ring ⁊ ringe ioyned ⁊ linked togither, sumtime with contrary mēbres, sumtime with like, sumtime with one selfe thynge sūdry tymes repeted, so that a paraphrase is not able to expresse suche pleasaunte elegance of his stile: I meane syche places as this: *In principio erat verbum, & verbum erat apud deum, & deus erat verbum.* In the beginning was the worde, and the worde was with God: ⁊ God was the worde. In these.iii. places worde after worde, ⁊ God after God is pleasaūtly repeted. And byanby repetyng agayne the beginning, he concludeth the sentence. *Hoc erat in principio apud Deum.* Thesame was in the beginninge with God: ⁊ again: *Omnia per ipsum facta sunt, & sine ipso factum est nihil.* All thynges wer made by thesame, ⁊ without thesame was nothing made ỳ was made. *Quod factum est in ipso vita erat, & vita erat lux hominum, & lux in tenebris lucet, & tenebre eam non comprehenderunt.* In him was the life, ⁊ the life was ỳ light of men, and the lighte shineth in derkenes, and the derkenes did not cōprehend it. In these it doeth appeare how that euery membre of the sentence doeth alwaye repete the former, so that the ende of the former beginneth the latter: ⁊ suche a lyke thyng may be perceiued here, as the Greke Eccho is wōt to represent: but as touchynge these thinges, sumthyng haue I spoken in the argumentes of the Euāgelistes gospels and Epistles. This peculiar grace and elegancie of speche, I perceiued well could haue no place in my paraphrase. Therfore although I did perceiue these and many other like difficulties, yet I toke vpon me this busye piece of worke, seyng that so many and noble men did by theyr exhortacion, encourage me thereto, ⁊ by auctoritie enforce me: specially because the good successe of my former dewtie and obedience, rather than any presumpcion, dyd bolden me to thesame. For I had not onely good successe forasmuche as the gentyll reader for my trauayle and paines doeth thanke me, but also forasmuche as Charles (of al Emperours ỳ for this eight hundreth yeres hath reigned in this world, doth of moste puissance, if we beholde his large dominion, and also the moste vertuous, if we consider besides his other very imperiall qualities, his feruent

affeccion

affeccion and zeale towardes religion and godlynes)hath this my paynes(for vnto him J did dedicate it)not only by countenaunce and wordes, but also by letters both full honorably and louingly wrytten, certified me that it was most thankfully accepted of his grace, wherupõ me thought it conuenient that seing Mathew was to the Emperour Charles dedicate and presẽted : John should be vnto Ferdinando, the other and second Charles, dedicate. And plainly good hope doeth greatly comfort my minde, promising me that it shal come to passe, that like as my former labour by Charles good fauour did wel procede, & had good successe, so shal this my present endeuour by the gracious fauour of Ferdinando, procede & haue lucky successe. These be two names in our tyme moste fortunate, a couple of brethren in these daies moste lucky. Neyther is it to be doubted, thinke J, but ẏ the fauour of God wil prosperously set forth the godly purpose of suche so godly disposed princes. For a man maye(as J thynke)haue a good opinion in them, in whom beeyng yet of tender age, the excellente fruite of vertue doeth satisfy ẏ great expectacion, the whiche(if J might so call it)the blading tendre age did put vs in comfort of. For in your very chyldage, there appered in you a certayne straunge and meruelous towardenes of suche prudencie, moderacion, mekenes, integritie, deuocion and godlines, that euery mã did hope that your grace woulde be a wonderfull excellent prince in euery condicion perfite and absolute. And now as touchyng the publike hope, that al the whole world hath cõceyued of you, like as hitherto you haue not frustrated it, so haue you brought to passe that nowe when you be come to the age of more discrecion, it doeth appere that you will not onely contente and fullfill the sayde hope and expectacion, but also the desire of all men to the vttermoste. My litle treatise of a Christian Prince, suche as it was, for many dayes agoe when ye were a young man, you caused all studious persons to lyke, in asmuche as ye dyd vouchesafe to reade it. And this present worke dedicate vnto your graces name, you shall likewise cause to be lyked, seing that of all yoũg mẽ in our time you be the floure, and for manyfold consideracions vnto all the worlde moste derely beloued, neyther shall ye so do eyther to aduaunce your glorye and renoume, eyther to procure me any benefit or commoditie, for neyther your noble estate, neyther suche a sober and moderate nature doeth couet or looke for the prayse or commendacion of man, neyther my minde or fantasie doeth seke any thyng els, then the fauour of Christe, but that those for whose furtheraunce these paines were taken(and for all men in generall is my paine bestowed)more plentifully might haue cõmoditie ther by. For suche as be of their owne nature commendable, haue then especiall profite and singuler commoditie, when they ouercum all malice, and be thought worthie the fauour and commendacion of all men. To this present purpose maye your grace muche helpe, if you declare this my present worke compiled by my payne and studie, for to haue bene not reiected of your graces maiestie. For it is not to be feared, J truste, leste your graces wysdome geue credence vnto them, the whiche peraduenture will saye when they shal vnderstande a paraphrase vpon the ghospell to be dedicate vnto prince Ferdinando, what should a laye prince and a younge manne do with the gospell? And wil make cauillacion & saye ẏ J geue frogges wine, as the Greke prouerbe speaketh. As though it wer to be thought that only suche do presente princes wᵗ mete giftes, ẏ which bryng vnto them bokes written in barbarous tõgue, conteyning matters of huntyng, kepyng of dogges, and horses, of in-

gines for warre, yea & mafortune of disyng & carding. Uerily I am in a contrary opinio: for I deame that where the euangelical and heauenlye philosophie
is thought to be to all, of the hyghest, lowest, and myddle estate, wonderfull
profitable, yet it is to none more necessarie, then to the supreme heades & powers of the worlde. For the more weight, charge, & burden, that they susteyne,
the more daungerous the storme is, that apperteineth vnto them for to caulme
and assuage, the more manyfold occasions they haue whereby good wyttes
well inclined by nature, and well instructed by education, maye be marred and
corrupted, so muche the more it is semyng that they shoulde be instructed and
armed more diligently then the reste, with the moste godly and infallible preceptes of holy doctrine: for suche cannot offende withoute the great dammage
of the whole world. It is the peculiar office of the prelates to nourishe ẏ people
with plentifull and abundant foode of the euangelicall doctrine. For the which
cause they be called pastours and herdes in scripture. I graunte all these to bee
true. Yet the poete Homer of the most cōmendable christian auctors is commēded, & not vnworthily, because he calleth a kyng, a herd ouer his people: howe
muche more then it is mete ẏ this name & title agre with euery christiā prince.
A prince doeth not preache & teache the gospell, but he doeth obserue, practise,
& fulfill it, & yet doeth he after a sort teache it, whosoeuer doeth kepe & obserue
it. But how can he fulfil it if he knowe it not. how shall he know it, excepte by
diligente and frequent readyng he peruse it, except with a great studie he profoundly print it in his memorie. whom behoueth more stedfastlye to beleue ẏ
the celestial king is gouernour of this world, vnto whō nothing is vnknowen,
whose ies no man can deceiue, whose power no man can resiste, who shal
iudge euery man accordyng to his merites, then the supreme powers, whiche
by reason of their power do dreade no man, and can if they list easilye deceyue
whome they list: whiche if they trespasse any thyng, bee not cited to appere at
any mortall mans consistory, but be commended also oftymes for their misde-
des. In whose mindes ought it to be more depely grauen that after this present lyfe (wherof the kynges thēselues haue no assuraunce, no not asmuche as
of an houre and whiche no man can enioye long) there is to come another lyfe,
that neuer shall haue ende: in the whiche indifferentlye without respecte of e-
state, or dignitie, (sauing that the strayter iudgement shallbe to them, straiter
accōpt shal they make, ẏ which in this world hath surmounted other in roume
office, and auctoritie) euery man shall by the sentence of the moste righteous &
iust iudge (whose iudgemēt no man shall escape) reape ẏ croppe of that, which
he hath sowen in this presēt life, neither shall anye scape but that either for his
good dedes he shall receyue the crowne of eternal glory and blisse, or els for his
offences be committed to euerlastyng fier: In whose myndes (I say) is it more
necessarie this thyng to be depely infixed, then theirs, whom al kynd of prosperitie and flatterye of man, doeth prouoke both to set their affiaunce in thinges
present, & to forget what is hereafter to come. In whose memorie is it requisite more depely to be printed, that Christ hath plainlye threatened vs in these
wordes, (wo be to ẏ riche, & the high powers of this world, which hath their
comfort in this world) than in theirs whiche haue plentie, and store of all suche
thinges, wherby mans minde is corrupt & degenerate. In whose eares is it
more cōueniēt diligently to be beate that euery man ought warely to bestowe
his talent which the lorde hath committed vnto him, in the waye of vsurie, for
the

the lordes auauntage, and wil cal euerye man to make accoumpte thereof, then theirs whiche by reason of their power committed vnto them by God, may at their pleasure, either profit most, or disprofit most in this world. Who ought more, assuredly to beleue that all men be they neuer so puissant & in high aucto-ritie, can of themselues do nothyng, & that all thynges that be good & commē-dable, do come of God, of whom al thinges ought to be desired, that maye by christian peticion lawefully be desired, and that vnto him the whole glory and prayse of all that we prosperously do in our affaires ought only to be attribu-ted and ascribed, then they whom the world doeth commēde and magnifie by reason they haue suche thinges as Christ taught should be despised. whō be-cause of certaine vaine and fantastical apparent shadowes of thinges ẏ seme cōmendable, ẏ base sorte doeth in maner regard and wurship as goddes. who ought more thorowly be perswaded ẏ sternnes is hated of God, that iniurie ought not to be reuenged by iniury, ẏ nothing is more commendable thē peace nothing more acceptable to God then meaknes & clemencie, then suche whome so muche busynes dayly doeth prouoke to vnquietnes, to warre, & reuengyng of displeasures. In whose minde oughte it more depely be printed, ẏ neyther for desire of life, neither feare of death, it is lawfull to swarue from honesty ẏ in this present life no man oughte to loke for to be rewarded for his merites & desertes, seyng that in the nexte world no man shall be defrauded of his dewe rewarde, then in the mindes of princes, whom so manye prouocaciōs, so much troublesome busines, so many occasions doeth oft and many tymes entise & al-lure to dishonestie. Verely such a minde vpon which ẏ general felicitie or mise-rie of the whole world doeth depend, ought with weightie & profoūd persua-siōs of philosophy be armed: whereby it maye vprightly & nothing shrinking, perseuer againste all policies and engines of this worlde: but suche doctrine whiche doeth so peyse the minde that it be not tossed by the waues and surges of fortune, and worldly busines, no otherwyse then the balans dothe staye the shippes in tyme of tempest, can neither more conueniently, neither of more cer-tayne veritie, neyther yet of more efficacie and power be collected out of any o-ther worke, then the ghospel of God. If ẏ profane princes, forasmuch as thei must commonly trauaile in worldly affaires, & maintenaunce of publique trā-quillite and reste, cannot alwayes obserue suche thynges as they perceiue, and iudge to be most conuenient to be kepte & obserued yet at the least if the euan-gelical doctrine be profoundly rooted in them, they shal be able to do this, that forasmuche as lieth in them to do, they shall alwaye endeuoure themselfes to approche nigh vnto ẏ performaunce of Christes preceptes, & litle or nothing swarue from theyr marke. This thing as we desire that it may appeare in all such as be gouernours of this worlde, so most gracious Prince Ferdinando, we greatly hope to se it in you, whome we haue knowen from your childeage hitherto, to haue been marueilously geuē to the readinge of the gospell for you were not wont, whyle the priest is at seruice, to spende your tyme either in su-persticious kind of praiers, eyther vnfruitful iāgling as the moste parte of no-bilite doth, but to opē the testamēt, & reuerently to se what the epistle & gospel of that day doeth instructe & exhorte you to do. Neyther do we doubt but that this example of your childage, you haue muche encreased by encrease of age. Neyther do we mystrust but that in tyme to come in euery place, many other will folowe this your exaumple. For like as an infeccion of vice taken at the

example

example of men of estate, doeth spedely crepe vnto many: euen so the example of vertue, if it haue his beginning of renoumed persons, wil soone be well lyked of all men. In what estimacion the worde of God was had in old time, may euidently appere by those rites and ceremonies as yet be vsed in the churche, lefte vnto vs of old antiquitie. The boke is adorned truly with gold, iuery, & precious stones, reserued & laied vp deuoutly emõgst ÿ iewels. It is not broughte forth ne caried in without greate reuerence. The gospeller desireth the licence of hym that doeth execute, that he maye rede and pronounce it. After that, ther is caused an holy perfume by censing of frankincense, of stacten, the droppyng of mirrha, of mirrha it selfe, and of the powder of the herbe galbanum. The forehead and brest hath the signe of the crosse made vpon them, glorye is geuen to the lorde downe to the ground, euery man ariseth and standeth bolte vpright, the heades be bare, the eares attentife, the iyes full of reuerence. At the name of Jesus as oft as it is mencioned, the knees be bowed downe to the ground, after all this with great reuerence he holdeth the boke before his brest, and carieth it about, euery man doeth kisse it, and at the laste it is reuerently layd vp emongest ÿ reliques. What other thyng doeth these ceremonies meane, or put vs in remembraunce of, than ÿ nothing ought of christian men to be more regarded, more dertly beloued, more reuerently handled, then that celestiall doctrine whiche Christ hath preached vnto all persones: the whiche for so manye hundreth yeres ago, the consent of the whole world hath allowed, the whiche against this worlde, and the prince therof, maketh vs to preuaile? but like as wurthely the vain and misordred deuocion of the Jewes is reproued, whiche Jewes doe greate reuerence vnto the booke of their lawe the olde testamente, in laying pure and cleane clothes vnder it, knelyng downe to it, and wurshipping it, not once touchyng it, but with cleane and vndefiled handes, (where as such thinges as their lawe doeth chiefly teache them, they wickedly contemne and despyse) so it is to be perceyued of vs, that we be not as vndeuoute in keping and fulfylling the ghospel, as we be superstitious and scrupulous obseruers of the rites and ceremonyes. For what doeth it auayle to haue the booke adourned with Juorye, siluer, golde, and sylke, if our lyuing bee polluted and infected with such vice as the ghospell doeth so straytely forbid? if our soule bee decked with no vertue accordyng to the ghospell? what can the booke auayle vs borne before our hert, if the doctrine of it be not in our herte and mynde? what seruice doeth the perfume and odour caused by censyng, if that his doctrine bee contemned, if our lyuyng haue a dayly pestilent sauer? what the better be we to bowe downe our necke to the booke, if our lustes obstinately and with stiffe neckes repine at his preceptes? what doeth it profit and auayle vs to rise vp, and to stand bare headed, if al our whole life be suche that it declare openly that we despise the doctrine of the ghospell? howe dare ye be so bolde as to kisse the boke that the ghospell is in, the whiche beeyng subiect to lecherye, to auaryce, to ambicion, to sensualitie, and yre, do defile and dishonest the admonicions of the ghospell? howe dare he kysse the booke that teacheth nothyng but peace, but mekenesse, and charitie, the whiche despysyng Christes doctrine is wholy consumed with enuie, replenished with hatred, boyleth in anger, inflamed with desyre to bee reuenged, furious and madde against his neyghbour, the whiche also (so his mynde maye bee satisfied) forceth not by wood battayle to set all the world by the eares together? howe

howe dare he be so impudent as to embrace and wurshippe this holye booke, the whiche in all kinde of liuing and conuersacion is vtterly geuen and married vnto this worlde, whiche as a mortall enemy, the doctrine of the gospell doeth detestate and abhorre? with cleane handes and verye reuerentlye we vse to touche the holy boke of the gospell, and with filthy myndes doe we despise the preceptes of the gospel: why doe we not rather lay thẽ to our hert? why doe we not kisse them with mind and pure affeccion? why do we not here bee we down our neckes? Certain there be that hath hanging about their necke, and carie the about with them a part of S. Johns gospell, as a remedie againste diseases, and suche other heuy missfortunes. Why doe not we rather beare aboute with vs the doctrine of the gospell in our mynde, the whiche maye remedy al disease of synne and vice? I doe not discommend any ceremonies, I doe not raile vpon the deuocion of the simple people: but plainly, thā will these said thinges profit vs, if we put in practyse that thynge whiche the visible signes putteth vs in remembraunce of. If we be true christien men, that is to saye, yf we vnfainedly professe the doctrine of the gospell, let vs inwardlye in our myndes practise all suche thynges as in these signes is outwardly represented vnto vs. I haue heard saye that it is a fashion in some places that the prince shall at the ghospell tyme stande holdyng a naked sweard in his hand, the rest laying their handes vpon the hyltes. Howe shall he defende the ghospell with the swearde, whose mynde doethe hate the gospell, whiche is wholy affeccionate vnto the vanities of this worlde, in whose opinion nothyng is lesse regarded then the excellente precious perle of the ghospell, of whome nothynge is more hated, then that whiche Christe taughte onely to be coueted? He that pouleth the people, that oppresseth the poore, that by warre defaceth all both good and badde, he that is the occasion of manyfolde calamities, for whose vaine glorye so muche mannes bloudde is shedde, doeth he, I saye, drawe his swearde to defende Christes gospell withall? let him first be made at one with the gospell, lette him cutte awaye his vicious and naughtie appetites out of his mynde with the swearde of the gospell, and then yf he lyste, lette hym drawe his swearde against the ennemies of the ghospell. But these thynges haue I spoken, moste renowmed Prynce, in the waye of aduertisement, without reproche of any person. I open the matter onelye. I reprehende no person: and the more boldelye vnto your grace I wryte thus, because no kynde of suspicion at al, of any suche faulte or enormitee, can be suspected to be in you. There bee none, Byshoppes except, that of congruence ought to liue more after the gospell then Princes. But they oftentymes by simplicitie vnder an assemblaunce of deuocion be deceyued. For by the perswasion of suche whiche be thoughte the perfite professours of religion, they ofttymes esteme it a poynt of great perfeccion, if they daily saie ouer their praiers the which they call their mattens, if they see a masse euery daye once. The whiche thinges as in a lay prince and a young man also, I graunt is a certaine token & signe of a well disposed mind, yet be there many other thinges ye which do more straitly appertayn to a christẽ princes office thẽ these. For if he foresee that no storme of warre arise, that the publike libertie be not diminished ne violated, that the poore comminaltie bee not compelled to famishe, that no naughty officers be made and permitted, in my opinion he shall do a more acceptable seruice to God, then yf he should saye these praieres. vi. yeres together. yet do I commende the said thinges if that whiche is more

principall

principall bee coupled and ioyned therto. But and if a prince do suppose that he lacketh no porcion of godly perfeccion, putting his confidence in the obseruacion of those thinges, settyng a part suche thinges whiche do peculiarly appertain unto a kynges office and dutie, plainly that is the confusion of all religiō, that is the subuersion of the common welth: and they that geue suche councel do neither geue profitable nor holsome councell for the prince, neither yet for his subiectes. It is a good dede to heare seruice, if thei be pure ẏ do it: but how can I cum in pure life unto the sacrifice doen in remembraunce of the true and highest prince, the which for to redeme his seruauntes bestowed his own life, if through my fury, my vainglory, and negligence, so many thousande men bee eyther vexed or vtterlye perishe. I thinke it not nedefull to shewe that for the most part princes be neuer at more leisure, neither lesse carefull, then when thei be at diuine seruice. What great thyng is it, if a prince saye those praiers at an houre prescribed therfore, whiche cannot haue sufficiente tyme and leisure to order and dispose thaffayres of a common wealth. A prince shall pray inough at full, if he saye daily and recite from his hearte, the notable prayer of the wyse kyng Salomon. Lorde geue me wisdome and knowledge how to behaue my selfe unto thy people. Or the other praier muche lyke unto the same, the whiche the wyse man, as I remember, reciteth in the boke of wisdome. Geue me wisdome whiche is euer about thy seate, that she maie be with me, and labour wt me, that I may knowe what is acceptable in thy sighte, for she knoweth and understandethe all thinges, and she shall leade me sobrely in my workes, and preserue me in her power: So shall my workes be acceptable, and then shall I gouerne thy people righteously, & be worthy to sitte in my fathers seate: who can haue knowledge of thy understandynge and meanynge, except thou geue wisdome, and sende thy holy ghost from aboue, that the waies of them which are upon earth, maye be refourmed, that men may learne the thinges that are pleasaunt unto the. This wisdome that this most wise young mā desireth to haue, may a man chiefly fynde in the holy scripture, if a mā list unfainedly and with a godly curiositie seke to haue it. Otherwise, howe is it cū to passe that christen mens behauiour and maners partely bee decayed into a conuersacion wurse then the Gentiles or Ethnickes were, partly degenerated into a certaine Iudaical superstition, but by reason that the doctrine of the ghospell hath not been had in regarde. Notwithstandyng to saye the very trueth, in all tymes there hath been euer sum, of whome the gospell hath beene hadde in due honoure and reuerence, yet neuerthelesse for this fower hundred yeres past, the liuely heate and feruencie therof, hath been greatlye abated with the most part. Wherfore the more we ought to the vttermoste of our power, endeuour our selfe that euery man for his parte do reuiue thissame sparkle of heauenly fire again, the whiche the eternall veritie Iesus Christe our Lorde hath sent down into the earth, wishyng nothyng els but that it maye be feruentlye kyndled, and in great circuite to spreade it selfe abrode, and be set all on fyer.
In this our tyme when mans condicions be so corrupted and of so great dissencions in opinions, wherby at this houre all thinges be confounded & out of order, whither shall we rather flee to haue redresse, then as S. Hilarie doeth well admonishe vs, unto the most pure fountaine and well spring of holy scripture, wherof the moste pure and undefiled part be ẏ gospels. Neyther oughte the gospel to be mislyked of the supreme powers for this cause, as though it
did

dyd as sum saye, cause suche to be sedicious and disobedient, whose parte and duetie is to bee obedient vnto their princes: nay it rather profiteth princes in this pointe, insomuche as it doeth teache them to execute the true offices of princes, and not to be tirauntes, and causeth the people more gladlye to obey euery good prince, and more quietly to tollerate and beare with the bad. Finally the gospell is not to be blamed, if any man do not vse all of the best, that thing whiche of his nature is moste excellent, and the very best. It is called the gospel of peace: reconcilyng god and vs to vnitie, and secondlye couplyng mutuall loue and amitie betwene eche of vs together. If any man stumble at this stone, let him blame hymselfe and not the gospell. There is no power that man hath, no policy, no cōspiracy or coniuracion together, that is able to vanquishe & oppresse the veritie of the gospel, whiche moste mightily setteth furth it self, when it is most greuously persecuted. But as touchyng these matters I feare me I haue heretofore spoken inough and to muche. Now that this paraphrase may with the more fruite bee red, after I haue spoken a worde or two of the euangelistes entent and purpose, I wyll make an ende. After that the lyfe and doctrine of our Lord Jesus Christ by thapostles preachyng and the other Euangelistes wrytinges was spred at large ouer all the world, the Euangelist S. John whome Christ so notably loued, after all the other toke on hande to write this present gospell, not so muche for thentent to compile the historie of the gospel, as to make rehersall of certaine thinges omitted by the other euangelistes, because they semed not vnworthy to be knowen. But the especiall cause why that he wrote this gospel, men suppose was to set forth & confirme the godhead of Christ against the heresye, whiche euen in those daies (as euill weedes emongest good corne) begun to spring, and namely against the heresye of the Cerinthians, and Ebronites, the whiche besyde other erroniouse doctrine, preached that Christ was nothing els but man only: nether that he was in any wise before he was borne of ŷ virgin Marie. Now it was very necessarie that the worlde shoulde knowe and beleue Christe to be bothe very god, & very mā: of which twoo, the former article doeth principally helpe to inflame the loue of man toward him: for the better we knowe a thing, with the better wil we do loue it: secōdarily it doth cause vs to haue more feruēt courage to folowe the steps of him. For who will attēpt to folow & cōuterfait ŷ thing which is doen of an aungell by a vision & apperaunce only & not in very dede: furthermore like as it is hard to obserue ŷ thinges which he cōmaundeth, euē so the thinges be excedyng excellēt that he promiseth: it was therfore requisite also, that his godhed should not be vnknowen, to thentent ŷ we might haue cōfydence ŷ he vndoubtedly would helpe his seruaūtes whō he after such sort did loue, neither will defraude them of his promise, ŷ which is able wt a becke to do what him list. The Euāgelistes ŷ wrote before S. John, made in maner no mencion of the diuinitee of Christe. For I thynke this to bee the wysedome which s. Paul vsed to speake emōgst ŷ perfit, emōgst the rest professing himself to know nothing els but Jesus Christe & him to be crucified. Ma fortune as then ŷ time did not suffer so inexplycable a misterie to be put in wryting to al mens knowledge, lest it should be had in derisiō of ŷ wicked, because they could neither beleue it, neither vnderstand it. For in other matters also the olde aūcient auctours as oft as they make mēcion of heauēly thinges, doe vse to speake both very seldome and very reuerently therof, beyng more copious in suche

thinges

thynges as doe more profite and appertaine to godly lyuing. The Apostle S. John was constrayned therfore by the vndiscrete boldenes of the heretikes, more plainly & euidently to affirme both the natures to be in Christe, like as by the bolde presumpcion of the Arians, the catholyke fathers were inforced more precisely to discusse certaine thinges as touching the same matters wher as they would rather not haue medled with the diffinicion of suche matters, whiche both dorth greatly passe the capacitie of mannes wittes, and cannot be determined without great daunger and perill. But as for this matter not without consideracion it was reserued for S. John so wel beloued of Christ, and so well worthy, whome as he that is the well of all wysedome dyd loue aboue the reste more feruently, so is it to be beleued that the same did more plentifully reuele and open certain secretes and misteries vnto hym (if I maye so cal him) his so wel beloued dearlyng. Him therfore so derely beloued of Christ, let vs all profoundly and groundely vnderstand, that we for our part may be the louers of Christ. Well of this one thing and no more, I will put the reader to acknowleage, that in this present Paraphrase I folowe the mynde of moste allowed olde autours, but not in euery place, neyther in euery thing: for they themselues do often disent emong themselues, yet do I alway sincerely and faithfully, declare and bring forth that, the which me thinketh is the most true sence & meaning, for as muche as I dyd perceiue that the olde auctours contendyng against the opinion of heretikes, haue wrested some places something violently to their purpose, yet it is not my mynde that any manne geue more credence to this my Paraphrase, then he would geue to a commentarye, if I had wrytten one vpon it, notwithstandyng a Paraphrase is a kynde of a commentarie. As for allegories in the whiche I perceiue the olde auctours to haue been very scrupulously and supersticiously diligente, haue I not medled withal, but very seldome, neyther more copiously then me thought conuenient. Farewell redoubted prince, & with all your endeuour, fauour and sette foorth the glory of the gospell, so almightie Christ of his part graciously assist you in all your desyres.

Yeuen at Basile, the yere of our Lord. M.D.xxiii. the .v. daye of Januarye.

¶ Saint Johns lyfe wrytten by Saynt Jerome.

Ohn the Apostle whom Jesus loued right well, beyng the sonne of Zebedeus, and James the Apostles brother, whom after the Lordes deathe Herode had beheaded, wrote his ghospel last of all ye rest, being desired therto by the byshops of Asia, both agaynst Cerinthus, and diuers other Heretickes, but principally agaynste the opinion of the Ebeonites, whiche euen than arose, which Ebeonites auouche that Christe was not before Marie: by reason wherof he was enforced to shew euen his diuine natiuitie. They saye that besydes this, there was an other cause of his wrytyng, because that whan he had red the volumes of Matthewe, Marke, and Luke, he well allowed the texte of the story, and affirmed that they had sayd the trueth, but had only made their story of one yeres actes, in whiche after the imprisonmente of John, Christe suffered. Wherfore omittyng that yeres actes, whiche were sufficiently entreated of all three, he shewed such thynges as were doen before John was imprisoned. Whiche thyng may euidently appeare to suche, as shall diligently reade the volumes of the fower gospels: the whiche thing also doeth take awaye the disagreyng that semeth to be betwene John and the rest. He wrote besides the premisses one Epistle, which beginneth thus. That which was from the beginnyng, which we haue heard, which we haue sene with our yes. &c. The other two which begin. The elder to the welbeloued Lady and her chyldren. &c. And the elder to the best beloued Caius, whom I loue in the trueth. &c, are affirmed to haue been written of John the priest, whose funerall toumbe is at this daye to be sene at Ephesus, and many suppose that there are two memorials of this same John the Euangelist, of whiche matter we will entreate, after we shall by order come to the lyfe of Papias his scholler. In the fowertenth yere than, at what tyme Domicianus after Nero styred vp the seconde persecucion, John being banished into the Ile of Pathmos, wrote ye Reuelacion, which is entitled the Apocalipsis, which Justine the martir, and Hireneus doe make commentaries vpon. But after Domitian was slayne, and all his actes reuoked by the Senate, because of his ouermuche crueltie, he returned to Ephesus, in the tyme of prince Nerua: and continuyng there vntill the tyme of the Emperour Traiane, he instituted and gouerned all the churches of Asia, and there continued tyll he was impotente for age. He dyed the three score and eight yere after the passion of the Lorde Jesu, and was buried a lytle besyde the same Citie.

The paraphrase of Erasmus

vpon the gospell of saint John.

¶ The first Chapiter.

Because the nature of God doeth passe beyond measure the weaknesse of mans wit, although in other thinges it be right good and of quicke sight, yet that diuine nature can neither be perceiued with our senses, as it is in dede, ne conceyued in mynde, imagyned nor expressed with woordes. And although in thinges create, certain apparaūce of godly power, wisdome, and goodnesse is shewed, and so it commeth to passe that the similitudes brought foorthe of those thinges, whiche we dooe sumwhat perceyue with our senses and witte, maye bringe vs into summe small and shadowelyke knowlage of incomprehensible thinges, that we may behold theim as it wer in a dreame and a cloude, yet that not withstanding no similitude maye bee taken out of any thinges create, whether ye behold the Aungels, the woorkemanship of the heauens, or els these inferiour bodies, whiche although they bee familiare to our senses, neuerthelesse we cannot fully perceiue theim: no similitude I say, canne bee broughte foorth of any of these forsaied thinges, whiche maye in all poynctes agree to the reason and nature of those thinges, of the whiche for to attaine the knowelage, those comparisons are brought in place. Therfore it behoueth manne to apply all the study of his minde to this, that he may rather loue the goodnesse of God, then meruail at, or comprehende his highnesse, whiche neither Cherubin or Seraphin dooeth fully attayne to. And although God cannot but bee meruaylous in all his workes, yet he had rather be beloued of vs for his goodnesse, then to be meruayled at for his excellēcy. But the more full knowlage of the diuine nature is reserued in the worlde to come for theym, whiche haue purged the iyes of their herte here, through godlynesse of innocent lyfe. No man knoweth the father as he is in dede but the sonne, and suche as the sonne will manifeste him vnto. Therfore to serche the knowlage of Goddes nature with mans reason, is presumptuous boldenesse: to speake of those thinges that cannot bee expressed with wordes, is madnesse, to geue iudgemente therof, is wickednesse. If we haue grace in the meane while to beholde any parte therof, it is more truely comprehended with pure faith, then with the helpe of mans wisedome. And in the meane tyme it is enough for to attayne eternall saluacion, to beleue those thinges of God, whiche he did openly sette furth of himselfe in holy scripture, by men chosen for that purpose, whiche were inspired with his spirite: and suche thinges as he hymselfe afterwarde being conuersaunt in yerth, opened to his disciples: and last of all hath vouchsaued to declare manifestly by the holy gost to the same disciples chosen for that entent. To beleue these thinges simply and truly, is christen wisedome, to reuerence these thinges with a pure hert, is true religion: By these thynges to goe forewarde vnto the meditacion of an heauenly lyfe, is godlynesse: to continue and perseuer in these thinges, is victorye: to haue had the victorie by these thinges, is the whole summe of felicitie. But for man to serche of godly causes with mans reasons ferther then these thinges, is a certaine perilous and wicked boldnes. And although it semed to be enough ŷ was bothe trulye preached and set furthe in writinge of the other Euangelistes, whiche declaring in order the natiuitie of Jesu Christe as concerning his manhed, life, & deathe, did affirme him to haue the true nature of man: and farthermore by declaringe his sermones, rehersinge his miracles, and resurrection from death, did so declare his godly nature as that time required: speaking nothynge all that while of his diuine natiuitie, by the whiche he was borne by an vnspeakable waye of his father without beginninge: and refreynynge also to call him manifestly by the name of God, to thintente that neyther the trueth should be hidden from those that were godly disposed and easy to be taughte, neither occasion should be geuen to the weake and vntaught Jewes to go backe frõ the doctrine of the ghospell, whiche had vtterly perswaded themselfes by the tradicion of their elders, and also out of Moyses holy bookes, that the name of God coulde not bee rightfullye attributed but onelye to God the father, whom they had alwaies wurshipped. And besides that also leste the gentiles, whiche did wurshippe innumerable goddes, yea goddes made of men, should haue taken occasion to continue in their peruerse errour; if they had perceiued that in the ghospell the name of god had beene made common to many, which thinge the eares of the Jewes not hable to receiue this mistery (as thinkinge that name to bee appropriate but to one) at the firste could by no meanes haue borne. And the minde of the Gentiles beynge broughte vp in the opinion of many goddes, coulde not at the firste bee perfectly taughte, that there were thre deuided in proprietie of persones, of the whiche thre euerye one was very God: and yet thre was but one God, by the occasion of one godly nature, whiche was common to all thre equally. Yet thus it hath pleased God that to thintente the faith of the ghospell shoulde bee the more stablished, he woulde haue it declared to mankinde by litle and litle, as shoulde beste serue the time and mans capacitie. So the nacion of the Jewes did wurshyppe God the father deuoutly many hundrethe yeres, being ignorannte bothe of the sonne & the holy goste. And the sonne of God himselfe whan he was here in yerthe a very man, and (as we can witnes) did hungre, thirste, slepe, sorowe, wepe, was displeased, & had compassion, longe suffred to be reputed for none other but manne, yea euen of his owne disciples. Also after his resurrection he would haue them ignoraunt in some thinges. In so muche that by the holy goste he did not open all thynges to them, but those thinges onelye, whiche helped forwarde the perswasion and beliefe of the euangelical doctrine and saluacion of mankinde. For considering that the nature of godly thinges is incomprehensible, yea to the highest wittes of men or Angels, and the profession of the gospel pertainethe indifferently to all men, the heauenlye father hath opened vnto vs so muche of godly thinges by his sonne, as he hath willed to be sufficiente for the obtaininge of our saluacion. Therefore it comethe of a certaine perilous presumpcion to affirme any thyng of the godly nature more then that whiche either Christ himselfe, or the holy goste haue opened vnto vs.

The texte.

¶ In the beginning was the worde, and the worde was with God, and God was the worde.

But because in these daies, as the wheate of gods worde hath growen in the

the

the hertes of good folkes, so also the cockle of the wicked hath ouergrowen, whose cursed presumpcion hath braste out so far, that some hath not ben afraide to take from Jesu Christe his manhed, bringing in stede of man, a vain vision & similitude of man: Some contrariwise woulde take from him his godhed, falsely saying that his beginning was but then, whan he was borne of the virgin Mary: because they being blinded with yerthly affeccions, coulde not attain the mystery of Gods counsaill, howe very God toke vpon hym to bee very man, that one person shoulde bee both, that in the meane while nothing should be withdrawen from the immutable nature of god, and yet the perfectnesse of his manhed shoulde still remain: I shall therfore set forth sum thinges more plainly in the ghospell, so much as the spirit of Christ hath vouchsaued to open vnto me, and asmuche as he had thoughte sufficiente to obtein saluacion by, thorow the faith of the ghospell. But as I began to say, forasmuche as there is nothing any where emonges all the thinges that euer God made, wherof we may make comparison whiche can throughly agree with the truth of the godhed, I must (though improprely) vse the termes of thinges that our vnderstādyng is acquainted with, to thintent that I may geue some knowlage to other, of thinges whiche passeth all mens vnderstanding and vtteraunce. Therfore as holy scripture calleth God that most excellent minde, whiche mind is both greatter & better then all thinges that can be imagined: euen so it calleth his onely sonne, the woord of that minde. For although the sonne bee not the same that the father is, yet he is so very lyke the father, that a man may see the one in the other, that is to say, the father in the sonne, and the sonne in the father. But the resemblaunce of the father, & the sonne, whiche in mans generacion is many waies vnperfit, is moste perfit in God the father and his sonne. And there is nothinge which dooeth more fully and euidently expresse the very secretye of the minde, then the true declarynge of it by woorde, for that is the very loking glasse of the minde, whiche cannot be sene with bodely iyes. And if we couete to haue any man knowe the will of our minde, that thinge is broughte to passe by no meanes more certainly or quickely, then by speache: whiche beinge fetched out of the inward priuities of the minde conueiethe by a certaine secrete efficacie, the minde of the speaker into the minde, of the hearer, through the eares of the hearer. Neither is there any thynge amonges men more effectuall to stire vp euerye mocion of their mindes, then to vtter it by speaking. For & if we haue auctoritie, we maye shortly appoynte with our woorde what we will haue done. Therfore he is called the sonne, because being equal in al other thinges with his father, he is distincte, and differeth in onely proprietie of person. He is called the word, because god, whiche in his own proper nature can no waies be comprehended, woulde be knowen to vs by him: neither was his pleasure to be knowen for any other cause, but to thintente we mighte attain euerlastinge felicitie by the knowlage of him. This birthe is not tēporal or during but for a time, ne yet this woorde is like to mans woorde. There is no corporall thing in God, nothing that passeth with time, or can be conteined in place, neither is there in him any thynge at all subiect to beginninge, proceding, age, or any mutabilitie, he is alwaye one, whole, and altogether in himselfe, and the sonne is continually begotten of him euen such an one as he is himselfe: eternall, of him that is eternall, almightie, of him that is almightie, most good of him ẏ is best: in conclusion God of God: neither later in time, nor inferior to hys father: the euerlastinge worde of the euerlasting mind, by the which the father speaketh to himselfe al waies as it were by a secret thought, yea before the world was made, being knowen to no body, but only to himselfe and his sonne. He did euermore & shall begette the sonne in himselfe, and in like wise did euermore bringe foorthe his almighty woorde, he had no nede of any thinge that is create, to whose felicitie nothinge can be added: but of his naturall goodnesse he hath made this whole ingine of the world, and set therin euangelicall mindes, and mankinde as in the meane betwene aungels & beastes, to thintent he might gather of thinges wonderfully create, and also of himselfe, the power, the loue, and goodnes of the maker therof. And as if there were a greate mighty king, whatsoeuer he commaunded to be doen shoulde be doen by and by: euen so the veraye almightye father hath made all thinges by his sonne and woorde. And firste by this way he shewed furth his woord by whom he woulde be knowen, as though he had spoken vnto vs himselfe. And beinge so knowē by the wonderfulnes of his moste fayre workemanship, might wind himselfe into our inward mocions. Therefore they do erre and go very far frō the trueth, whiche thinke the worde of god to be so after him in time, from whom it procedeth, as emonges vs the mind goethe before the speache. And so they also whiche take the worde of God (by the whiche God the father hath made all thinges,) to bee numbred emonges thinges create. But their errour is more rude & grosse, whiche do suppose the sonne and woord of God than to haue begun and neuer before, whan he was borne bodily of the virgin Mary. What thinge soeuer is create hath his beginning in time, but the sonne of God was twise borne, once of his father before time, or rather with out time, very God of him that is verily God: Again he was borne of the virgin Mary in time appointed thereto eternally of the euerlastynge father, very man of mankynde. For it hath pleased God after this sorte to bringe furthe agayne to vs hys woorde, that is to saye his sonne, to thintente he mighte be knowen after a more plaine waye, or more familiarly. That person therfore is wicked which maketh argumente that Jesus Christ was nothinge els but manne, or that contendethe him to haue beene create emonges other creatures. The father did beget him that was bothe his sonne and his woorde, & yet all one, after soundry waies, once in time, as touchinge his manhed, and alwaye without all time, as touchinge his godhed. For before there was this vniuersall creacion of thinges, both yearthly and heauenly, the eternall woorde was alredy with the euerlastinge father. And this woorde did so procede from the father, that yet it remained still with the father. He was of suche an inseperable nature with the father, that by proprietie of person he was with the father: And yet he did not cleue to the father, as the accidente doeth to the substaunce: But he was god of god, he was god in God, and he was God with God, by reason that they both had but one diuine nature common to both. They twaine were so bothe one that nothing made difference betwene theim sauing onely the proprietie of person of the father and the sonne, of the speaker and the worde that was spoken: like as he was the onely begotten sonne of his onely father, so he was the onely woorde of the said father, being therof the onely speaker.

The woord was with god. &c.

An accident is a thing that may be or not be without corrupcion of ye wherin it is, as for example: one may take awaye the whightnes of a wal yet the substaunce doeth stil remayne.

The texte. ¶ The same was in the beginning with god: al thinges were by it, and without it was made nothing that was made.

And albeit this woorde was God, being almighty of him that was almightie, yet differing in proprietie of person, not by vnlikenes of nature, he was with

with god þ father, not brought furth in time, but before all tymes: so alwayes procedyng from the fatherly mind, that neuertheles he neuer departed from the same. Neyther was he create of the father, but the father made all thynges that be create both visible & inuisible, by this his worde, beyng lykewyse eternall as he is himselfe. By the same woord he gouerneth all thinges, & by the same he hath restored all thinges, not vsyng it as an instrument or minister, but as a sonne, of the selfe same nature and vertue, that he is of: to thinent that all maner of thynges should come from the father, as the excellent auctour and maker of the same, but by the sonne, whome he had eternally begotten, and shall beget without ende, like to himselfe in all thinges.

All thinges were by it. &c.

The texte.

¶ In it was lyfe, and life was the light of men, and the light shineth in darkenes, and the darkenesse comprehended it not.

And this woorde of god had might & power not only to make all thinges in generall both visible and inuisible at his will & pleasure, as it were with a becke, but also in that worde was the life & strength of all thinges that were create, that by the same euery thyng should haue his naturall strength and force: and by the might whiche was once geuen to them, saue themselfes in their kynde, by continuall generacion. For there is nothing idle or without vse emonges so great a multitude of thinges. Euery herbe and tree hath his strengthe put into it, and euery beast hath a certain wit in his kynde. But as by his prouidence he hath framed al thinges, whiche he hath create by a certain power naturally graffed in theim, euery thing to worke his propertie, and to the continuaunce of his kinde, so he hath not lefte the moste faire workemanship of this worlde without light. For as he is to all folkes the fountain of lyfe, so is he also the fountain of lyght, by reason that his father powreth into hym the fulnes of the diuine nature, by an euerlasting natiuitie. So that he only restoreth lyfe, yea euen to the dead, and by his light putteth awaye the darkenes of mens myndes be they neuer so darke. Therefore the woorde of God, whiche is Christ Jesus, is to mens myndes the selfe thing, that the yearthly sunne is to bodily iyes, whose myndes after they were fallen thorowe synne into most depe darkenes and death, he labored to helpe with his vnspeakable charitie. For before that tyme men dyd lyue in ignoraunce, and abyding in the darkenes of synnes, worshippyng dumme ydoles, in stede of the true God, beyng synfully drowned in blind desyres of theyr myndes, lacked the iyes of the hert, wherwith eternall truthe is perceyued. God had sprinkled into mens myndes some litle sparke of a quicke perceyuing wit, but bodily affeccions and darkenes of synnes had blinded the same. And the darkenes of this worlde was so very great, that neyther mans wisedome and philosophie, neyther the religion of Moses lawe, nor yet the lyght of the Prophetes, coulde put it clerly awaye. But at the last came that our eternall moste bright sunne, to whose inuincible light all darkenes geueth place, and he came to restore lyfe to all men, not only to the Jewes but to all nacions of the worlde. And by putting away the darkenes of synnes to geue syght to all people, that thorowe the lyght of faith they might acknowlege God the father only to bee worshipped and loued, and his onely sonne Jesus Christe. This bodily sunne doth not geue lyght to all men at once, for it hath his soondrye courses: but this other spirituall lyghte by his naturall power, dooeth shyne, yea euen in the moste thicke darknesse of the worlde, offeryng it selfe to all menne to thentente they maye haue lyfe again, and see the waye of eternall saluacion, whiche is open

The lyght shineth in darkenes. &c.

to euery body through the faith of the ghospell. And although the world being blinded with the filthines of synne, and the cloude of synfull desyres, woulde not beholde this lyght, yet could it bee blemished with no darkenes of this worlde, how greate soeuer it were. For he onely was pure from all impurenes of synne, neyther was he any other thyng but light: all manier waies pure and vncorrupted. For the darkenes of this worlde doeth cōtinually striue against the lyght, wiche the worlde hateth as the bewrayer of his workes, and that darkenes doth eyther quenche or darken the beames of many, but against this lyuely and eternal lyghte it coulde nothyng preuayle. The Jewes haue striuen against this lyght, the Philosophers, the great men of the world, and all those whiche hath dedicate themselfes wholly to transitory thinges, but this light hath had the victory: it shineth still in the middes of the darkenes of the worlde, and euer shall shine, making all men partakers therof, so they will apply themselfes to bee apt to receyue it. But what should a man doe to them whiche wittingly and willingly repell the lyght, whan it is offred vnto them, whiche whan they bee allured and called to the lyght, of purpose shut theyr iyes because they wyll not see it? Truely the sonne of God dyd leaue nothyng vndone, wherby any man should lacke his lyght.

The texte.

¶ There was sent from God a man, whose name was John, the same came as a witnes to beare witnes of the lyght, that all men through hym might beleue: he was not the lyght, but was sent to beare witnes of the lyght.

The same came as a witnes.

For he dyd not preace hymselfe sodainly into mens sight, lest he shoulde the more haue blinded them by reason of their incredulytie and lacke of beliefe. For who woulde haue beleued a thing so muche to bee meruayled at, excepte lytell by lytel, he had prepared mens mindes by many wayes to belyefe? Therefore he not being satisfyed to haue declared to all men by this wunderfull creation of the worlde, both his almightye power, wisedom, excedyng great goodnes, and excellent charitie towardes mankind, neyther yet contented as it were to sygnifie his cumming before hand by so many prophecies of the prophetes, and so many shadowes and figures of the olde lawe, in conclusion he sente a man more excellent then all the Prophetes, wose name was John, who although he deserued the chiefe prayse of holynes emonge all men that were borne vntil his time, and was called an Aungel for the dignitie of his office being greater then any Prophetes office, yet he was none other but man, very largely endued with many giftes of God. But all those came of Goddes liberalitie, and not of his owne nature, that was geuen hym at the firste, yet he was chosen and sente of God for this purpose, that accordyng to the prophecie that was prophecied of hym before, he myght beare witnes of that godly lyght: whiche being couered with his manhed, was conuersaunt in the worlde, not (as who say) that he whiche was God, and so declared before by the voice of the father, shoulde nede mannes witnes: but to thintent he might by all manier of meanes cause hymselfe to bee had in credit with the people, he woulde that John shoulde bee the goer before the lyghte: as the day sterre appearing before, sheweth the rysyng of the sunne to the worlde. And also that by his preachyng, he shoulde prepare mennes mindes to receyue that lyght, whiche shoulde immediatly come after. And because synne is the let wherby the heauenly lyght is not admitted and receyued, John dyd allure and call all people to penaunce, proclaming openly that the kyngdome of heauen was at hande: for the firste degree or step to the lyghte is that men shoulde hate their owne darkenes. And this John was of so great

auctoritie

auctoritie emonge the Jewes for the excellente holines of his liuinge, that many toke him for Christe himselfe, whereby Christ would the rather bee commended to the Jewes by his witnes, as that time required: to thintente that litle by litle (as men do commonly vse) he might crepe into the mindes of the people, for otherwise the meaner person is alwaye wount to bee commended by the witnes of the greater: And Esay had promised that at Christes cumming, there shoulde a certaine excellente lighte arise and springe vp to theym whiche did liue in darkenes, and in the shadowe of deathe: and for that cause before that Christe was notable by his miracles, many suspected John to haue been the light whiche was promised of the Prophete. But John was onelye the publisher before of the true lighte, and not the light it selfe. Therefore Christe, as the oportunitie of that time serued, did, as ye woulde saye, abuse both the errour of the Jewes, and the auctoritie of John, to prepare the mindes of all men to the faithe of the gospell. Truely John was a certaine light, that is to saye, a burninge candle, and geuinge lighte feruently: burninge in godlines, and geuing light by holynes of life, neuertheles he was not the lighte whiche should bring life to the whole worlde: but the woord of God, whereof wee doe speake at this presente was that true light, euer proceding from God the father, the fountaine of all light: from whence, what soeuer is lightsome in heauen and earth, boroweth his lighte: what sparke of witte, what knowlage of trueth, what light of faith soeuer there be, either emong men or Angels, all the same cummeth from this fountaine.

He was not the light.

¶ That lyght was the true light, which lighteth euery man that cummeth into the worlde.

The texte.

As this worlde is blind without the sunne, so all thinges are darke without this light. The worlde also was full of darkenes on euery syde, because sinne and abhominable errours did reigne in euery place. And in the tyme of this darkenes there did often tymes shine foorth men excellent in holynes of lyfe, as a lytell sterre in the moste darkest nightes, and gaue some lyght as it were thorow a cloud, howbeit they dyd it but to the Jewes only or to the borderers of Jewry, but this true light geueth lyght, not onely to one nacion, but to all men that come into the darkenes of this worlde. The Jewes went about to challenge this lyght seuerally to themselues, because they thought it to be promised to theim onely, for asmuche (as touchyng the fleshe) it dyd spring of theim, and emonge theim: but that light came to geue lyght to the hertes of all nacions, of the whole world, thorow the faith of the gospel. Neither Scithian, Jewe, Spaniard, Gothian, Englisheman, kynges, nor bondmen, be excluded from this lyght. The lyght came to geue light to al men asmuche as lay in it: but if any continue in their darkenes, the faute is not in the lyght, but in hym that frowardely loueth darkenes and abhorreth the lyght. For the lyght shineth to al mē, because none might pretend any excuse, when willingly, & wittingly he perisheth thorow his owne faute. As if a man shoulde get a knocke at noone daies, because he woulde not lyfte vp his iyes.

Whiche lighteth euery man.

¶ He was in the world, and the world was made by hym, and the world knew hym not.

The texte.

This woord of God was alwaies in the worlde, not (as who say) that he whiche is without measure, can bee contayned in any circuite of place, but he was so in the world, as the deuise of the workeman is in his woorke, and as the ruler is in that thing he ruleth. Also at that tyme this lyght dyd shine in the worlde, sumwhat opening the godly power, wisedom and goodnes thereof, by these thinges which were wunderfully creat by it, and by this meanes it did then, after a sorte, speake to mankinde. But many putting their felicitie in the visible thinges of this worlde (whome for that cause of good righte our lorde Jesus did accustome to cal by the name of the worlde) when he taughte them eternall thinges, they beinge blinded with earthly affeccions, did not acknowleage their maker. The darkenes of mindes was so greate, that the worlde knewe not the maker thereof, but did wurship serpentes, oxen, goates lekes, oynions, yea & that whiche is more vile then all these, stockes, & stones, dispising him, of whome they had receiued both that themselfes were, and all that they had.

The texte. ¶ He came emong his owne, and his owne receiued him not.

They being accustomed to darkenes, did abhorre the light, and being blinded with sinne did enbrace deathe in stede of life: yea and whan he did shewe himselfe more familiarly to the worlde being conuersaunt & liuing in his manhed emonges men, he was not knowen of them whiche had dedicate themselfes wholy to this worlde. Neither is it any meruail though the gentiles beynge woorshippers of ydols, & measuring all thinges by the commodities of this life, being also ignoraunt of the prophetes, and the lawe, did not acknowleage him, whiles he liued here in the shape of a man. This is more to be meruayled at, that when he came specially to his owne people, to whome Messias had ben promised by so many prophecies of the prophetes, to whom he had bene shadowed with so many figures, of whom he had ben loked for so many hundreth yeares before, which saw him do miracles & heard his teaching, yet they wer so far from receiuing of him, that with fierce mindes they wente about his destruccion, whiche came specially to saue them. And procured that innocentes death, who frely brought life to his enemies. They sawe & did not see, heard and did not heare, & hauing intelligence did not vnderstand: whiche thorow a froward study of the lawe, did rise against him whom the law had promised. Therfore by their malice it came to passe ẏ the light whiche brought eternall lyfe to the beleuers therof, was to them occasion of greater blyndnes. But their frowardnes could not hinder the health of theym that beleued in it, but rather the blindnes of the Jewes made open way for the Gentiles to the lyght of the ghospel. They which vnto that time were taken for the people of God, which onely did boaste theimselues in the wurshipping of the true God, in the religion of the lawe, in the kynred of the fathers, and in the promises of Gods testament, turned theimselues from the sonne of god, when he came to theim. And therefore the Jewes being righteously caste out as rebels to the ghospell, the grace of the ghospell remoued thence to the Gentiles: that the course of thinges being altered, they whiche before swelled in pride thorowe the false colour of religion, shoulde openly declare their wickednes, rejecting the sonne of him, whom they wurshipped for God. And on the other parte, they which before were vtterly contrary to true religion and dyd wurship beastes, and stockes for their goddes, shoulde enbrace the holynes of the ghospell by faith: howebeit vpon this occasion the Gentyles were so admitted to bee saued by the ghospell, that neyther the Jewes nor any other nacions at all, shoulde be excluded from hauing entry therunto, so they woulde put away their stubbernes, and shewe theymselues obediente to faith, which is the principall and onely gate to eternall saluacion.

The texte, But as many as receyued hym, to theim gaue he power to be the sonnes of God, euen them that beleued on his name.

And albeit many both of the Jewes and the Gentiles whiche loued the worlde more then God, withdrewe themselfes from this lighte, yet the cunning thereof was not in vayne. Firste of all, it did manifeste their infelicitie, whiche thorowe their owne faulte did depriue themselues of so greate goodnes frely offered vnto them: Neyther coulde any man doubte, but that by the iuste iudgemente of God they shoulde be reserued to eternall deathe. Furthermore it caused that of the contrary parte it shoulde more euidently appeare, howe notable the liberalitie of God was to them which with a simple & redy faith would receiue the woord of the gospel. And for that cause, he that was bothe the sonne of God and God, did humble himselfe to our lowe estate, to thintente y thorowe faith he might exalte vs to his highnes. Therfore he toke vpon him the rebukefull misery of our mortalitie, to make vs partakers of his godly glory. Therefore also he woulde be borne a corporal man of the virgin, to thintente we should be borne again spiritual of God: and for that purpose he came downe into the earth to carry vs vp into heauen. The stately scribes and pharisees, the proud kinges and powers of the worlde, the stoute and hault philosophers, were reiected because they woulde not beleue. But to this high dignitie were admitted men of lowe degre, of litle estimacion, without renoume, vnlearned persons, bondemen, barbarous men, and sinners, whom the worlde hath in no estimacion at all, of whom nothing is required but pure faithe, neither cunninge, nor noblenes of bloode, nor yet the professyon of Moses lawe: but all that did receyue this worde, of what nacion or condicion soeuer they were, of his behalfe, he gaue to theim this dignitie, that they beinge graffed in Christ thorow faith and baptisme, and hauing professed his name, should be made euen the children of God, that they mighte bee made by adopcion the same thinge, whiche Christe was by nature. And what can bee higher then this honour, that they whiche before were the children of the deuill & inheritours of hell, shoulde thorowe faithe onely be made the children of God, the brethren of Jesu Christe, and coinheritours of the kingdome of heauen. As touching the flesh we were all borne the children of wrath of our firste father Adam, but by the worde of God we be released from that sinfull kinred: & touching the spirite, we be happily borne again of God by Jesu Christ.

Which were borne not of blood, nor of the will of the fleshe, nor yet of the will of man, but of God. — The texte.

For finally God taketh for his children, not suche as bee borne the children of Abraham by mans sede, or actuall luste in generacion, but those that be borne of God by faith. Our first father Adam had begotten vs after an vnfortunate and miserable sorte, for he begate vs to deathe and hell. Moreouer they whiche are borne touchinge the carnal birthe, bee not all borne to one estate, for some be borne to a kingdome, & some to bondage: But Christe Jesus the auctor of our newe generacion doth regenerate al men without difference to like dignitie, that the bondage of sinne and the misery of mortalitie put awaye thorow faith and grace, they may be made children of the lyuyng God.

And the same woorde became fleshe and dwelt emong vs. — The texte

Neyther is it any meruaill though man be transformed after a sorte, into the felowship of the godly nature, seyng the woord of God did submit it selfe for this cause to take our fleshe, that is to say a mortall body of the virgine, ioynyng together in himselfe two thynges moste vnlyke, God and manne: what thing is more frayle or more vile then mans fleash: and what thing is more mighty or more excellente then God? Neuer meruaill that these thinges were knit togither. It was God that did it. Neither mistrust that men may be made the children of God, seyng he loued vs so, that for our sake he himselfe would be made the sonne of man: doubtles he toke vpon him no fantasticall body, for who coulde loue a vain vision, or a disceitful illusion? but truely he toke vpon him the body of a manne, that is to say, the full and perfect nature of man, abhorring not so muche as that parte, wherby we be subiect to death, and dooe very litel differ from the kinde of brute beastes. And he became not man for a small time redy by and by to put awaye that thinge, whiche he had taken: but to proue assuredly that he toke his manhed not deceitfully or vnder a colour, he was long conuersaunt in earth, he was hungrie, thirstie, diuers waies punished, suffred death, was seen with iyes, hearde with eares, and touched with handes. And to thintent this dignitie should alwaye remaine with mankinde, the godhed, hauing the manhed with it, and in it being glorified, sittinge on the righte hande of the father allmighty, dooeth stil dwell in vs.

The texte, And we sawe the glory of it, as the glory of the onely begotten sonne of the father, full of grace and trueth.

Neuertheles he lacked not his godly maiestie, when he in his manhed walked here in earth: for we whiche liued familiarlye with him, are witnes, that he was both God and man: we haue seen him hungry, athirst, slepinge, wepinge, vexed and dyinge. We haue hearde him speake with the voice of a man, we haue touched him with our handes, and by all profes, and tokenes we haue founde him to be very man: yea and also we haue seen his godly glory in very dede mete for the onely sonne of God, the like whereof was neuer shewed to any of the angels, Prophetes, or Patriarches, but it was suche as God the father woulde haue his onely sonne to be honoured with. And this glory we haue seen in the workinge of his miracles, in the vttringe of his heauenly doctrine, and in the vision vpon the mounte Thabor, when he was transfigured before our iyes, when also the very voice of his father cumming downe from heauen, professed him to be his dearly beloued sonne, as the saied father did notably set him furth in his baptisme, both with his voice and with the holy goste, vnder the figure and similitude of a dooue. And againe when the sonne before his death desired hym to glorifye hym with that glorye whiche he had before the worlde was made, a voyce came downe from heauen and knowledged him to bee his sonne, saying: Bothe I haue and will glorifye the. In conclusion we haue seen hym in his resurreccion, both when he already beeyng risen from death to lyfe, did shewe furthe to vs his body, whiche we mighte touche and handle, but yet was it subiecte to no euill, and also when before oure iyes he was carried vp into heauen. And his glory did appeare and shine vnto vs not onely by these thinges, but also his very death did aproue his godly power and strengthe, when as the vaile of the temple was deuided, the earth quaked, the stones braste in sounder, the graues and monumentes did open, the dead bodies did rise againe, the sunne losinge his lighte, broughte sodaine darkenes into the worlde: And whiles immediatly after a vehement crie, he yelded vp his goste, as who sayeth he forsoke his life wyllyngly and not for lacke of strengthe. By thys so wunderfull a death he did so glorify the father, that both the thefe whiche did hange by him, and also the Centurion, did acknowledge him to bee the

sonne

sonne of God. And albeit when he was conuersaunt here in earth, and went about the busines of our saluacion, he had leauer shewe vs exaumple of sobrenes, mekenes and obedience, then to boast his owne greatnes, yet all his communicacion, all his dedes, yea his very behauiour and countenaunce did declare hym to bee full of all godly giftes, full of eternall, and suche trueth as cannot bee confounded. For although God dorth geue to other holy men also large giftes of his grace & trueth, yet he did powre into him as into his onely sonne the whole fountaine of heauenly giftes, to thintent that in hym alone might be so muche as shoulde suffice all men. And we did thorowly see him to be suche one euen vntill his ascencion.

¶ John beareth witnes of hym, and crieth, saying: This was he, of whom I spake, whiche though he came after me, went before me: for he was before me.

The texte.

Let vs now procede and declare how he was first knowen vnto the worlde, wheras vntil this time not so muche as his owne brethren beleued hym to be any other but man, for he woulde be knowen lytle by lytle, lest so straunge a thing shoulde not haue been beleued emonges men, if it had risen sodainly. And truly many thinges went before, whiche might some maner of way haue prepared mens mindes to faithfull beliefe: as the auctoritie of the prophetes, the shadowes of the lawe, the agreable song of the Angels at his natiuitie, the godly deuocion of the shephardes, the guiding starre, the deuout behauiour of the three wise men, the vnquietnes of kyng Herode with all Jerusalem for the birth of this new kyng, the prophecies of Simeon and Anna, and also certain thinges that he did, beyond the reche & course of mans nature, wherat his mother and Joseph meruailed with theim selfe what those thinges should meane: yet neuertheles, when the tyme was come, wherin it was decreed eternally that he should openly take in hande the busynes of preaching the kingdome of heauen, it pleased hym (as I sayd before) to be commended and set furth by the witnes of John also for a tyme: not that he neded mans witnes, but because so it was expedient, eyther to allure the Jewes to beleue, of whom euery one had John in hye estimacion, or els to rebuke the vnbeliefe of the wicked, when they woulde not beleue, no not hym bearing witnes of Christ, to whom in other thinges they did attribute so much, that they toke him to be Messias, which was promysed by the prophecies of the prophetes to deliuer the people of Israell. Therfore when John preaching ye kyngdom of God to bee at hand, had alredy gathered together many disciples, dyd dayly baptise many & was had in great auctoritie emong al men (but in very dede men had an ill opinion of Jesu) the said John doth openly beate into the heades of the multitude, and efsons reherseth that thing whiche diuers times before he had witnessed of him: And accordyng to Esaies prophecy whiche dyd tell before hand that he shoulde in wildernes say with a loud voice, make redy the way of the lorde, he nowe not priuely vnto his owne disciples, but to all people indifferenly, which euery day resorted to him accustomably because of his baptisme and doctrine, yea and came purposely to heare the very certaintie what opinion so notable a man had of Jesu, he, I say, spake out with a plain and a cleare voice, saying: This is he of whom heretofore I haue often spoken vnto you, before whome thorow errour you do prefer me, when that I tolde you there shoulde be one which should folowe me in age and time of preaching, and shoulde also be rekened inferiour to me in the opinion of the multitude, he hath nowe ouertaken me: and whereas he semed to bee after me, he hath begun to be before

By his witnes he vnderstande his disciples.

be before me. And no meruaile, seing that euen then also he did excell me in all giftes, although in the iudgemente of men he semed inferiour vnto me.

The texte.

¶ And of his fulnes haue all we receiued, euen grace for grace: for the law was giuen by Moses, but grace and trueth came by Jesus Christe.

He is the fountain of all truth and grace. All we whom ye haue in so great admyracion bee nothing els but as it were litle brookes or furth cumming streames: for the litle that we haue euery man according to his porcion, is drawen furth out of the fulnes of this fountain, frō whence, whatsoeuer appertemeth to euerlasting saluacion springeth vnto all men. All the vertue that was in the patriarkes, in the prophetes, and in Moses, dyd come from this fountain. I am nothing els but the goer before of hym that is cumming, he is both the very publisher, and also the auctour of the grace of the ghospell, whiche geueth true and euerlastyng saluacion to all men thorow faithe. We are bounde to thanke hym for that by the voyce of the Prophetes we haue been enstructed to godlinesse: by the prescript and appointmente of the lawe we haue been forbidden to dooe euill, and for that we haue receiued as it were the shadowe of true religion. Nowe doeth euen very he offre to all men more plenteous grace, who thorowe the faythe of the ghospell, pardoneth freely all synnes, and geueth euerlasting life to theim that deserued death. For Moses whose auctoritie is had emong you as a thing halowed or consecrate, is no maner of waye to bee compared to hym. Moses was onely the pronouncer and setter furth of the lawe but not the auctor, and he brought a lawe vneffectuall, sharpe, and hard, the whiche with figures and shadowes might bee, as it were a preparacion to the light of the ghospell, that should come after: and the said Moses lawe, should rather make synnes to bee knowen, then take them awaye: yea and to say trueth, shoulde rather make a way to health then geue health, or allure vs with promises. But nowe in steade of the straytnesse of the lawe, grace is geuen by Jesu Christe, whiche thorowe faith of the ghospell, frely and wholy forgeueth all men their synnes. He hath geuen the lawe of trueth in steade of shadowes, wherof he hymselfe is not onely the declarer, but also the auctor, as he vnto whom God the father hath geuen all power.

The lawe was geuen by Moses.

But grace and trueth came by Jesus Christ.

The texte,

No man hath seen God at any time: the onely begotten sonne, whiche is in the bosome of the father, he hath declared him.

And truely these be the secretes of God the father, these bee the hidde counsailes of the diuine mynde, by the whiche it hath pleased hym that god shoulde become a manne, and after a sorte to make menne Godlike, to mixe moste highe thinges with the lowest, and to exalt the lowest vnto the hiest. He dyd neuer fully open these thinges to any of our forefathers, although he dyd sometyme shewe furth to theim certain lytel sparkes of his lyght, by Angels, by dreames, and by visions. For no mortall man (were he neuer so great) did euer see God as he is in dede: but couertly as it were in a shadowe. And although he dyd open in some parte to Moses, to the Patriarkes and Prophetes a litell porcion of his secretes, yet none but his onely begotten sonne dyd receyue this fulnes of grace and trueth: who beyng made man, did so come down to vs, that neuerthelesse by his godly nature he doeth alway remaine in the bosome of God the father, and as touchyng all thinges that pertayne to the obteyning of euerlastyng saluacion, he hath declared vnto vs more familiarly and plainly, without wrappyng, or coueryng the thyng whiche he dyd signify to the other but partely, or vnder a cloud, and as it were in a slepe.

The texte.

¶ And this is the recorde of John: When the Jewes sente priestes and leuites from Hierusalem to aske him, what art thou? And he confessed and denied not, and saied plainly: I am not Christe.

When John had often times priuely commended Christe by this maner of witnes, then did he openly declare, what maner of man he was, doing the duetie of a pure honeste seruaunte, whiche neither woulde wrongfully take vpon him the honour of his maister, whē the Jewes woulde haue geuen it to him, neither yet woulde depriue his saied maister thereof, althoughe he knewe well inough that he shoulde not onely by that meanes leese the estimacion and auctoritie, which alredy he had emong the Jewes, but also it shoulde cause them to enuy him muche, because they had rather haue geuen that auctoritie to John, whose birthe also was famous & notable emonge the Jewes, who for the dignitie that his father was of, beinge a head prieste, was the more highly estemed of them: who for the straungenes of his diet, his wearinge of Camell skinnes, his beinge in wildernes, his baptisme, and the greate numbre of his disciples, caused ẏ people to haue him in admiracion, whereas Christe for the basenes of his kinred, & by reason of his trade of liuing and apparell, nothinge differing from the cōmon vse of people, at that time was litel set by: therefore seing that poore Christ himselfe did not contente the proud Pharisees, yea and they began sumwhat to enuy John, only because he had commended Christe in his preaching, the said Pharisees sent from Jerusalem priestes and leuites being men of great auctoritie, to enquire of John before the multitude who he was, of whom the iudgemente of the people did so muche vary: For some said that he was Christ that shoulde deliuer the whole nacion of the Jewes from seruitude. Some supposed him to be Helye, whom according to Malachies prophecie, they thought was come again to be ẏ goer before of Messias to come. As touching Christe very fewe regarded hym, because both his parentes, & himselfe liued barely and poorely, yet neuertheles some began to enuy hym. And so the crafte of the Pharisees did then goe aboute this thyng to thintent they might frame Christ to their euill desires. Whiche thing they thought shoulde be brought to passe, if he had not been alowed but by theyr auctoritie & profe: for if he had taught thinges repugnaunte to theyr affeccions and vices, they woulde haue disalowed and taken away his auctoritie emong the people, whose doctrine they had perceyued shoulde hinder theyr commodities. This is the foliche policie of worldely wisedom. But Christe whose doctrine is all heauenly, woulde not haue any part of theyr humain auctoritie to be mixt with his euangelicall doctrine. Some of the Jewes also did trust it should come to passe, that John although he wer not Christ, yet would accept so honorable a name that was willingly offred him. They being bondmen most addict & geuen to glory, did know wel inough that moste holye men be soone deceiued with this pestilence of vaingloyre: they were not ignoraunt how muche all that nacion woulde haue reioyced, if John woulde haue taken vpon him the name of Messias, which already a good part of the Jewes did willingly attribute to him. If he had taken it vpon him emonge the people, they had occasion wherby they might exclude Christe, whom they hated for his poore estate: if he had not taken it vpon him they woulde furthwith haue falsely accused him. Therefore they aske John before the people by the auctoritie they had of ẏ Priestes & Phariseis, saying: Who art thou?

When the Jewes sent priestes.

Who arte thou?

for

for alredy they had begunne both to be greued with his auctoritie, and sumwhat to enuy his good renoume. He beinge well assured that they asked him these questions for the hatred they had to Christ, did not byanby open vnto them his owne opinion as concerning Christ, but did repell the false suspicion that they had touchinge himselfe, whiche mighte haue hindred the glory of Christ among the people: & boldly contemning the glory of an vnrighteful title, did confesse that he was not Messias (as many thought he had ben) neither did he deny himselfe to bee that thinge he was in dede, beinge redy to declare who he was, to whom the glory of that name was due. Of whiche two aunswers, the one, that is to saye the confessing what he was himself, endaungered him to lose his owne estimacion: & the other (whiche declared him redy to confesse Christe) put him in ieopardy to be hated of the Pharisees. But the manne being perfeicte without corrupcion passing nothing of either of bothe these daungers, did openly confesse that he was not Messias, whiche was promised by the prophecies of the Prophetes, and by the voyce of Moses: not denying Messias to be alredi come, but I am not he (saith he). He shewed thē that this surname was due to an other that excelled him, who neuerthelesse was lesse regarded after their opinion. And so this maliciouse diligent serche of the Pharisees came to none other effecte, but to stablishe the faythe of the gospell.

I am not he

The texte.

¶ And they asked him, what then? Arte thou Helias? And he saieth: I am not. Arte thou that Prophet? And he aunswered, no.

Therfore after they wer disapointed in this first question, they did procede to demaunde further, sayinge: If thou be not the chiefest of all, and that which many attribute vnto the, seing thou doest vsurpe a new dignitie wythout the auctoritie of the Scribes & Pharisees, & causeste the people wonderfully to fauour the, not without ẏ decay of the common auctoritie of the priestes & Phariseës, at the leaste thou muste be one very nie vnto Messias, & not much vnder him. And we reade in the prophet Malachie that before Messias cummeth, Elias the Thesbite shal cum: who shall repaire again all thinges. Art not thou therfore that Elias? John denied that he was Elias, not but that he was Elias in sum respecte, because he was the goer before Christe in the spirite of Ely, but that he was not that Elias the Thesbite whiche was rapte & sodainly caried vp into the aier in a fiery chariot, whom the Prophet iudged to be reserued for this purpose, that he maye be the goer before of the second cumminge of Jesu Christe. The Jewes had read the prophecy, but they vnderstood it not, neither were thei wurthy to learne this mistery, for so much as they enquired it of an hatefull minde, and because they knewe that Moses had promised, that a certaine Prophete shoulde come of the Jewes kinred, whom he commaunded thei should geue eare vnto. And some of them knewe right well that this Prophete shoulde be Messias himselfe, moreouer some other bruited abrode, that one of the auncient Prophetes was rysen agayne, and they suspected John to bee the same: therfore they asked him whether he was that Prophete promised of Moses, or at leaste some other of the Prophetes, whiche beeynge rysen from deathe to lyfe, shoulde take vpon him that auctoritie. He did frankely and playnly confesse, that he was no suche thynge as many toke him to be.

Art thou Elias?

He answered, no.

The texte.

¶ Then sayed they vnto him: What art thou, that we may geue an aunswere to them that sente vs, what saiest thou of thy selfe? He sayed: I am the voyce of a cryer in the wildernes

dernes, make streight the way of the lorde, as sayed the prophete Esaias. The texte.

But now when they had no more matier to question with hym of, seeing mens conjectures touching John, were at a full pointe, they moued hym ernestly to tell openly what he hymselfe was: and because he shoulde no longer make any delay or excuse, they prouoked him by the auctoritie of the priestes to thintent that euen for very feare of power, he should confesse who he was. We do perceyue (say they) that thou takest vpon thee more then the Pharisees, priestes, and scribes do. We can no ferther diuine or conjecture therof, and yet we must bring some aunswer to them which haue sent vs hither: If all the people bee deceiued in their so diuers and soundrie opinions of thee, tell thou thyselfe who thou art: for vndoubtedly thou arte knowen to thyselfe wel ynough. Therfore whom doest thou professe thy selfe to bee? Here now John because he spake to them that were learned in the lawe, lest he shoulde seme to take vpon him of mans presumpcion that thing whiche he was in dede, he taught them out of the very prophecie of Esay, whiche was righte well knowen to the Pharisees, both howe he was none other but the goer before Christe, and that the lorde hymselfe was already come, whom they ought to receyue with cleane hertes, whom also they being blinded with enuie, ambiciō, and pride, shoulde crucifie. I (sayeth he) am neyther Messias, nor Elias, nor any of the prophetes reised vp agayne to this lyfe, neyther yet haue I taken vpon me this office by myne owne autoritie, forasmuche as many yeres heretofore, I was appointed to the busynes of this office, by the auctoritie of God. For I am euen he of whom Esay did write. The voice of the criar in desert, make right the way of the Lorde. You see the deserte, you heare the voice of the crier: nowe there lacketh no more, but that you cast away worldely desire, and prepare your mindes against his cumming, that he maye come to you a very sauiour. Moses did set him furth vnto you as it wer in a shadowe and the Prophetes did long agone prophecy that he shoulde come: But I doe shew him vnto you nowe already cumming.

What arte thou?

I am the voice of a crier in wildernes, &c.

And they, whiche were sent, were of the Pharisees. The texte.

And you shall vnderstande that they which were sent to John, were of the Pharisees secte, for the Pharisees in those daies did excell all other bothe in knowlege of the lawe, in opinion of holines, and also in auctoritie. And they were not farre of from the doctrine of the gospel, forsomuch as they did beleue the immortalitie of soules, and that there was an other life to cum after this. But ambicion, couetousenes, and enuy, had corrupted their mindes. Howbeit at that time their malice as yet was not so farre inflamed, that they woulde openly shewe themselfes aduersaries to Christ, but within a while after when they perceiued his doctrine to bee contrary to their renowme, aduantage, and autoritie, being vtterly caste into an extreme rage, they went about to crucify their Messias, whom they had promised to the people by the prophecies, and in the knowlege of whom they had muche bosted themselfe. So hurtful and pestilent a thing it is, yea the knowlege euen of holy scripture, excepte a mans minde be free & voide from yearthly desires. But the prudence of God being far wiser then mans inuencions, can clerely turne the malice of the wicked men to the welth of the good. For this so enuious and so craftie enquiring of the Pharisees hath stablished our beliefe.

The texte.

And they asked him, and saied vnto him: Why baptisest thou then, yf thou be not Christ nor Helyes, neyther that Prophet? John aunswered theim, saying: I baptise with water, but there standeth one among you, whom ye know not.

Therefore

Therefore they nowe being more stired and prouoked, and not onely enuiyng Christe, whom alway they had in contempte, but also John whom heretofore they had in reuerence, goe aboute further to charge hym, and fynde faulte with him, sayinge: What is the cause, that thou takeste vpon thee, the power to baptise the people if thou be neither Christe, who (as the prophecies do declare) shal put away the sinnes of the people, nor Elias the goer before Messias, nor that notable Prophete, whom Moses did promise, neither yet any other of all the Prophetes, whie then dooeste thou enterprise to putte awaye sinnes by thyne owne auctoritie, whiche thou neither hast of God, nor by any decree of the Priestes, whose auctoritie thou darkeneste with thy newe customes? To this slaunderous demaunde John did aunswere mekelye: but yet in suche sorte, that he did both frely knowlage his owne lowe estate, and did openly declare the dignitie of Christe. My baptisme (saieth he) is euen suche like as my preaching is. For as my preaching is not perfit but onely prepareth your mindes to the wisedom of the gospel, so my baptisme whiche consisteth onely in the water doth not washe a way the filthynesse of mindes, but in a certaine resemblaunce of true baptisme, frameth the ignoraunte: that they being prepared with repentaunce of their former life, maye bee hable to receyue that baptisme by the whiche Messias thorow his spirite shall washe away all at once, the vniuersall vnclennes and vices of all theim that shall credite his heauenly doctrine. And now he is not farre hence, but is alredy present in this same great noumbre of people, and as one of the multitude is conuersaunte euen in the middest of you. And he is therfore either despised, or not knowen of you, because after the worldes estimacion he is but poore and of small regarde, vaunting himselfe with no pompe of those thinges, by the whiche they that honour the worlde doe esteeme a manne. It hath not pleased him as yet to put furth his power and greatnesse, but in veraye dede he is an other maner of persone, then you take hym to bee.

I baptise with water. &c.

The texte. ¶ He it is whiche though he came after me, was before me: whose shooe latchet I am not wurthie to vnlose.

I who in the peoples iudgement seme to bee sumwhat notable, in comparison of his highnes am nothing at all. This is veray he of whome I tolde you before that men toke him to be mine inferiour, and to come after me, but in dignitie he did preuent and excel me, to whose wurthines I am so vnwurthy to be compared, that I know my selfe vnwurthy to serue him as a bondman in the lowest kind of seruice, yea to leuse the buckles of his shoes.

The texte. ¶ These thinges wer doen in Bethabara beyonde Jordan, where John did baptise.

John did pronounce this so full and so honorable witnes of Christe to the Phariseis, Priestes and Leuites, in the presence of a great noumbre of people, and that in a famous place, that is to saye, in Bethabara, which is not farre from Jerusalem beyond Jordane a place very conueniente for him that was a baptiser and preacher of penaunce, by reason that plentie of water was nigh to it, and also the deserte, to whiche place a great preace of people out of diuerse coastes of Jurie, did resort dayly to be baptised. For John did bothe preache and baptise there.

The texte. ¶ The next day John seeth Jesus cumming vnto him, and saieth: Behold the lambe of God, whiche taketh away the sinnes of the worlde.

And

And hitherto he did so beare witnesse of Jesus, that he did neyther name hym, nor poynte hym with hys fynger, when he stoode emong the multitude, because he would not styre vp the enuie of the Phariseis against hym: And also because he would set on fier the mindes of simple folkes the more to haue a desyre to know him, whom the sayd John being so notable a mā, had so highly commended in his preaching, and for as muche as at that tyme many of the people did make diligent serche to knowe, who shoulde be that great man, to whose dignitie, euen John beeing in all mens iudgement taken for an excellēt persone, did so much geue place to. Jesus therfore came thither agayn the day folowing, and did not then kepe hymselfe close emong the multitude, but went to John seuerally and alone, partely for good maner sake to salute his cosin, partely to knowledge his baptiser, but specially to geue him occasion to testifye more playnely and liuely of Christ emong the people, lest he being yet not knowen should seme to goe to John for that purpose, that other did: that is to saye, to be baptised or taughte, or els to confesse his sinnes, for in that he was baptised of John, was to geue vs exaumple of humilitie: but because no body shoulde suspecte that he had nede of baptisme, or that he had any spot in hym, whiche the water of Jordane could washe away, he separating himselfe from the multitude wente to John aparte. John being warned by the holy ghoste what he shoulde doe, beholding Jesus cumming towardes hym, turned himselfe to the people, and poynted Jesus to them with his fynger: that after they knewe him by sight, they shoulde accustome themselues both to lyke hym and loue him the better, and should rather folow hym then John himselfe, yea and rather couet to be baptised of hym then of John. For the purenesse of Jesus mynde being ful of the holy ghost did shine in his very iyes and countenaunce: And did shew it selfe furth both in his goyng and all other behauiours of hys bodye: as of the contrarye parte, a furyouse mynde and ouerwhelmed with vices, dooeth expresse it selfe in the very countenaunce of the bodye. Beholde (sayth John) this is he whom many of you did see me baptise, wheras in dede the water of Jordane did not purifye him, but he did rather halowe it. For he alone and none other is free from al kinde and spotte of sinne. And verely he is that most pure lambe, whome God (accordyng to Esaies prophecie) had chosen and appoynted to bee a sacrifice moste acceptable to hym, for to purge the sinnes of the whole worlde, whiche was defiled with all maner of vices. This is he whome the lambe in Moses lawe did signifye, whose vnharmeful bloud defended the children of Israel from the reuenging swoord of the Angel. This lambe (I saye) is so fer from being subiect to any kynde of sinne, that he alone is hable to take away all the sinnes of the whole worlde. He is so well beloued of God, that he onely may turne his wrath into mercie: he is also so gentle and so desirous of mans saluacion, that he is redy to suffer paynes for the sinnes of all men, and to take vpon hym our euils, because he woulde bestowe vpon vs his good thynges.

John seeth Jesus cūming.

Behold the lambe of God which taketh awaye the sines of the worlde.

The texte.

This is he of whome I sayd, after me cummeth a man, which wēnt before me: for he was before me, and I knew him not, but that he shoulde be declared to Israell, therfore am I come baptising with water.

Yea thys is very he of whome I haue tolde you diuers tymes, thoughe it were sumwhat derkely, that one should come after me, who going before me in dignitie, and power, did ouerreche me: for because although he semed to come

I knew him not.

after me both in byrth of hys manhed, in the tyme of hys preaching, and also in auctoritie, yet in godly gyftes he was far before me. In so much that I myselfe did not certainly knowe at the fyrst howe great he was, or what he was. For he is so great that I (whome ye haue in suche reuerence) am no maner of way to be compared vnto him. He is the lorde and auctour of all health. I am none other but his seruaunte and goer before, neyther is my baptisme or preaching any other thing but an introduccio͂ to the heauenly doctrine and vertue, whiche he shall bryng vnto you. Neyther yet am I sent for any other purpose by the commaundemente of God, but to preache repentaunce of your former sinnes, to shewe you that the kyngdome of heauen is at hande, and to washe you with water, to thintent that after he should be shewed to me of his father by sure tokens, he might at his coming be the better conceiued in your mindes, being already prepared with these principles. His conuersacyon and life was simple and pure, and beyng in no poyncte notable emong men, he ioyned hymselfe to the multitude as one of the common sorte of the people, and came to be baptised as though he had bene subiect to sinne.

The texte. ¶ And John bare recorde, saying: I sawe the spirite descende from heauen lyke vnto a doue, and abode vpon him. And I knew him not.

Therfore I coulde not knowe surely by the disposicion of hys body, nor by mans coniecture that he was the onely sonne of God, and that moste pure lambe whiche through faythe shoulde put awaye all the sinnes of the worlde, but that I was taught by a notable sygne from heauen that thys was he, to whome I was appoynted to bee the goer before. And what this sygne was, John did openly declare to the multitude. When Christe (sayeth he) willynge to shewe to the worlde an exaumple of humilitie, and ioynyng hymselfe to the company of sinners, came to be baptised, the father of heauen did honour hym with an heauenly token. For I my selfe sawe the holy ghost cummyng downe vpon his head in the likenesse of a doue and there remaynyng. Until that time I did not certaynly knowe hym, whose goer before I was: by reason that his corporall estate, did hyde hys celestial excellencie.

I sawe the spirite descende from heauen. &c.

The texte. But he that sent me to baptise in water, the same sayed vnto me: Upon whom thou shalt see the spirite descende, and tary stil on him, the same is he which baptiseth with the holy goste: and I sawe, and bare recorde that he is the sonne of God.

For as yet the tyme was not come in the whiche the father of heauen woulde haue him to be openly knowe͂ to the people. Therfore when I knew by the inspiracion of the sayde father that Messias was alreadye come, then to take awaye the errour and mistakyng of hys persone, or leste mannes coniecture should haue any doubt therin, he, by whose commaundement I toke vpon me the office to baptise you with water, taught me by a sure token: by the shewing wherof I might assuredly knowe who he was, that shoulde baptise you with an effectuall baptisme, and should by the holy gost, wherwith he was replenished, freely geue to all them that trusted in hym, remyssyon of all theyr synnes. For before Jesus came to me to be baptised, the father of heauen did aduertise me before hande, saying: By thys token thou shalt surely know my sonne. Emonges many whom thou shalt wash with water, vpo͂ whomsoeuer thou shalt see the holy ghost in the lykenesse of a doue descending, and remaynyng,

be

be wel assured, that the same is he which hath power to baptise with the holy gost. For man washeth wt water, but he onely by his heauenly power, taketh away sinnes, and geueth righteousnesse. I saw this token according to the fathers promyse in hym whan he was baptised. And for thys cause, he gaue me grace to see him, that you also through my preaching, should know the autour of your saluacō. Wherfore like as heretofore I haue witnessed, so doe I now also openly testifie, that this is the sonne of god, from whence, as frō the heauenly fountayn, ye must require all thynges whiche perteyne to righteousnes and eternall felicitie. For I will suffer you no longer to suspecte greater thinges of me then I deserue, nor yet to be ignoraunte of hym, whome to knowe is saluacion. By these manier of witnesses, John did often commend Jesus (beyng as yet vnknowen) to the multitude, and gaue ouer his owne auctoritie to him as to his better: to the entent that from that time furth, the people should leaue hym and cleaue to the gouernaunce of Jesu: Goddes prouydence in the meane tyme procuring this, to thentent that they both might be to vs an holsome exaumple of a true preacher of the Ghospell. For truely John neyther with the entisemente of so great renoume beeing willingly offered vnto hym, was so much corrupt that he would take vpon hym an other mannes praise, nor yet so afrayed of the enuie of the Priestes and Phariseis, (whose ambicyous enuie, and enuious ambicyon woulde suffer no bodye to bee exalted but themselfe) that therefore he dyd ceasse to speake of the glory of Chryst: neyther did he regarde his owne commoditie, but what was expedient for the people: hereby teachyng how a preacher of the ghospel ought to haue a constaunt and sure stayed mynde, yea, euen to the auenturyng of hys lyfe, not onely agaynste excesse & couetousnes, but also against al ambicion. And as for Jesus Christ, when he came as one of the common sorte of the people to be baptised, and also when he behaued himselfe amongest Johns disciples, as if he had bene one of them, wheras he was lorde of all, he taught vs how we must come to true glorye, by great humilitie and modestie of mynde, and that none is mete to be a mayster, vnlesse he haue played the parte of a good scoller, neyther that anye ought to take rashely in hande the office of preachyng, excepte he hath bene all manier of wayes well tryed and approued: and in manier appointed therunto of God.

Upon whō thou shalte see the spirit descend &c.

I saw and bare recorde that this is the sonne of God.

The next day after, John stode agayn, and two of his discsiples, and he beheld Jesus as he walked by and sayeth: Beholde the lambe of God. And the two disciples heard him speake, and they folowed Jesus.

The texte.

Now to thentent that Johns most excellent purenes and honestie might more clerely appere, he thought it not inough to turne thaffeccions of ye people from him to Christ, but he laboureth also to despatch from himselfe his owne peculier disciples whome he had, and to put them to Christ. For the day after these thinges, which I haue already rehearsed vnto you, were doen in the presence of the people, John stoode there agayne, and twoo of hys discyples with hym. And Jesus walked vp and downe not farre from thence (whiche thyng in dede was doen to signifie a misterye thereby.) For John was a fygure of Moses lawe, and Christe was the auctour of the profession of the ghospell. Therefore the law, whiche was now come to the vttermost poynt, stayed, as though it coulde goe no further, but shoulde ceasse by and by, and giue place to Christ at hys comming, and commit his disciples to hym, but neuerthelesse in the meane while constauntly bearing witnesse of Christ: and as it were deliuering the Sinagogue to the true spouse, to be his churche. Christe walketh vp and downe to declare that he should alway growe greater and greater, and euery where gathereth disciples to heare hys heauenly doctrine. Therefore whiles John stoode and behelde Jesus as he walked, knowyng righte well that the sayde Jesus dyd desyre and long for the saluacyon of mankynde, and also did couet to geat disciples mete for hys heauenly doctryne, John turning him to the twoo disciples whiche stoode by hym, beeyng theyr maister, because he would put them to Jesu, that was a better maister then hymselfe, he poynted him to them with his finger, as he was walking, and sayde: Beholde yonder is the lambe of God of whome I haue so often testyfyed, who alone doeth take away all the sinnes of the whole worlde. I haue prepared you for him, whosoeuer desyreth true and effectuall baptisme, whosoeuer loueth true innocēcie, and whosoeuer coueteth true and perfit health, must nedes commit himself to his rule and ordre. For they that were the true obseruers of Moses lawe, (as the lawe it selfe doeth witnesse) did profit and goe forwarde thereby to the perfeccion of the ghospell, that is to say, from fayth to fayth: wheras the Phariseis through their peruerse and ouerthwart loue of the lawe, did persecute him whō the law had cōmended to thē. Now Johns disciples made their maister no aunswere, but geuing credite to his worde, they left the sayd John that was the goer before the ghospell, and folowed Jesus the auctour of the euangelicall health. And they sayde neuer a woorde, but folowed hym, beeyng set on fyer with the loue of hys hye doctrine, the hope wherof they had conceyued by the testimonie of John. But they dare not be bolde to moue anye communicacion to him with whome they had not bene acquaynted.

He behelde Jesus as he walked. &c.

Behold the lambe of god. &c.

And yͤ two disciples heard him.

The texte.

And Jesus turned about, and saw them folow him, and sayeth vnto them: what seke you? They said vnto him: Rabbi (which is to say, if one enterprete it, Maister) where dwellest thou? He sayeth vnto them: Come and see. They came and saw where he dwelte, and abode with him that daye, for it was about the tenth houre.

Therefore Jesus perceiuing for what purpose they did folow him, to declare how ready he woulde be to mete and ioyne with them whiche with pure mindes doe thirste and couet the doctrine of the ghospel: he (I say) not tarying for theyr calling vpon hym, of hys owne good wil doeth encourage and alure their bashefulnes, & turning himselfe towarde them, did beholde them as they folowed him, not yͭ he was ignoraunt whom they folowed, or of what minde they folowed him, but because he would shewe to other theyr woorthye and mete affecciō for the gospel. He speaketh to them and asketh what they woulde haue, to the intent that theyr desyre beeing knowen, might also kindle and styre vp the myndes of other. But they furthwith declared themselues to bee verye desyrous to learne of him, euē by yͤ very name they called him by, saying: Rabbi (which worde in the Siryans tongue is as much to say as Maister) where is your abyding? And vndoubtedly in that they called him Maister, they confesse themselues to be his disciples. And whereas they enquire of him, where his dwelling place is, by that they doe declare, that they haue a will to learne of him certayn secret thinges more familiarly, which (peraduēture) he would not speake openly before euery body. Here now our lorde Jesus taking pleasure in theyr deuoute feruentnesse to learne, maketh no excuse by reason of the nyghnesse of the night, nor commaundeth them to come againe the day folowing,

What seke ye?

Rabbi, where dwellest thou?

neyther

neyther yet signifyeth to them where his house is, in case they woulde at theyr conuenyence leysure visite hym: But he ientlye and courteously requireth them to come talke with him at his lodgeing, saying: Come ye and se. For he perceiued that any delay shoulde haue bene paynful to theyr earneste desyre. They reioycing in that aunswer, beyng euen suche as they woulde haue wished for, came thither, and did not onely see the litle house, where then Jesus had hys abidyng, but also taried with him all that day: and were so enflamed with his holy communicacion, that not onelye they reioyced in theyr owne behalfe, but mocioned and procured other also to come to the company of that felicitie. And when they came to Jesus house, it was almost the tẽth houre of the day, that is to say, nye vpon the goyng downe of the sunne. For there is no tyme nor place vnfit or vnconueniente for to learne those thynges whiche pertayne to euerlasting welthe. And the presence of the preacher of the ghospell oughte alwaye to bee in a redinesse: For suche an one oughte he to be that taketh vpon hym to teache Christen philosophie and wisedome, whiche is onely the philosophie that can no skill of any pryde or statelynesse.

Cum and se.

They came. And abode with him that daye.

The texte.

One of the two which heard John speake and folowed him, was Andrew, Simon Peters brother. The same found his brother Simon first, & sayeth vnto him. we haue found Messias (which is by interpretacion anoynted) and brought him to Jesus. And Jesus beheld him, and sayd: Thou art Simon the sonne of Jonas, thou shalte bee called Cephas, which is by interpretacion a stone.

As concerning these two, whiche had folowed Jesus by the counsayl of John, the one of them was Andrew, Simon Peters elder brother: to whiche Peter, although he were the younger, yet for the excellẽt feruencie of his faith, Jesus afterwarde did promise him the keyes of the kyngdome of heauen: and committed his shepe to be fedde of hym, after he had thryse professed hys loue towardes Jesu. The godly loue of the ghospell hath thys difference from that which man of himselfe is inclined vnto, that if it haue gotten any notable treasure, it hydeth it not, or enuieth other: for manye thynke that they dooe not possesse that thyng, which is common to other aswell as to themselues: but thys godly loue reioyceth that the commoditie therof shoulde be common to many. Andrew being much comforted with so great felicitie, for asmuche as by the report of John, but much more by the familiar communicacion of Jesu hymselfe, he found it true that Jesus was ẏ heauenly Lambe, which onely should take away the sinnes of the world, that he was the sonne of GOD, the onely redemer of mankynde: and that also he was Christe whiche was promised of the Prophetes, and looked for so manye hundred yeres beefore: the sayde Andrew (I say) as soone as he had found Simon Peter his brother, whose presence he desyred greatlye, for thys purpose, that Peter whome he knewe dyd looke for Christe with greate feruencie, myghte be made partaker of the felicitie of that assured knowledge whiche Andrewe hym selfe had of Christe: We haue founde (sayeth he) that Messias, whome the Prophetes had promysed shoulde bee redemer of the worlde. And Messias in the Sirians tounge is as muche to say as Christe, that is to vnderstande anoynted: because that anoynting perteineth to kynges and priestes. But Christe was the onelye anoynted of God, to hym onely all power was geuen both in heauen and yearth, and he onely was ẏ priest eternally after Melchisedechs ordre, which hath reconciled God to mankynde with the sacrifice of hys bodye. Symon beeing glad of so

We haue foũd Messias. &c.

 pleasaunt

And brought hi to Jesus.

pleasaunte and welcome a message, and not satisfyed onely to haue hearde it, ioyfully preaseth hymselfe also to see Jesu. Andrew who had already proued the gentlenes and graciousnesse of Jesu, furthwith broughte Simon to hym. And when Jesus behelde Peter, he did not onely vewe his face, wherin neuerthelesse did shine a purenes of hert, but he rather loked vpon his minde which was endued with doouelyke simplicitie: and thereby apte to receyue the grace of the ghospell. The sayde Jesus takyng pleasure in hys pure affeccion, dooeth tell the name of Peters father (by that declaryng how nothyng was hydden from hym) and therewithall prayseth the godly simplicitie of Peters minde, gathering an argument thereof, by the propertie of hys fathers name: and by the darke sence of the chaungeing of Peters owne name, he telleth before that in time to come, there shall be in hym stablenesse of inuyncible faythe. For Jonas is asmuch to saye, as a dooue or grace. Simon, by interpretacion, signifieth obedient, for out of the obedience of Moses law, is had some furtheraunce to the fayth of the gospell. Therefore after that Jesus had loked vpon hym, he doeth lyke both hys present simplicitie, and also doeth sum what open, as you woulde saye darkely, his stedfastnesse to come, saying: Thou arte that Simon the sonne of Joanna, right aptly agreyng both to thyne owne name, and thy fathers: But hereafter when this fayth shall haue gathered strength, that it may be able to stand stable and vnshaken against al temptacions of the deuill, thou shalte be called Cephas, whiche in Greke is as muche to saye as Peter, in Latine, *saxum*, and in Englishe a stone. And this was the firste instruccion and principle of Christes church: this was also the first beginning of the schole of the ghospell.

And Jesus behelde him. &c.

Thou art Simon the sonne of Joanna. &c.

Thou shalt be called Cephas. &c.

The texte. The day folowing, Jesus would goe into Galile, and found Philip, and saieth vnto him: folow me. Philip was of Bethsaida, the citie of Andrew and Peter. Philip founde Nathanael and saieth vnto him: We haue found him of whom Moses in the law and in the prophetes did write. Jesus the sonne of Joseph of Nazareth. And Nathanael said vnto him: Can there any good thing come out of Nazareth? Philip sayeth to him: Come & see.

The day after, it pleased Jesus to goe into Galile, whiche was least set by of al the prouinces of Jewrie, because no man of any great renoume or fame, had at any tyme come from thence: and yet neuerthelesse Esay dyd prophecie before that the light of the ghospell should first appeare and haue hys begynning about ye place. Also the diuine counsayl thought it good so to be, because he woulde beginne his churche of meane persones, vntaught and vnlearned, borne and come out of a countrey that was barayne, and of no regarde. For both Peter and Andrew, whiche without calling folowed Christe, were men of Galile: and that the one brother did perswade and drawe the other to Jesu, was a fortunate pronosticacion of the churche nowe newly beginning, whiche consisteth in brotherly charitie and mutual concorde. Therfore when Jesus shoulde goe his way into Galile, hauing alreadie two disciples of Galile to wayte vpon hym, because he myghte come sumwhat the better accompanied, he taketh to hym two other also of the same countrey, and of lyke nobilitie. For Jesus founde one called Philip borne in Bethsaida a citie of Galile, whiche is nye vnto the lake of Genazareth being the countrey of Andrew and Simon, to whome the name of Peter was added. Furthermore in that they were all of one countrey, it betokeneth the concorde and agreement of the ghospell:

He founde Philip.

ghospell: And that the diuersities of all maner of people, should be ioyned and brought together into one churche, as it wer into one citie. Philip semed to haue met with Christe by chaunce, but the very thyng in dede was doen altogether by the prouidence of God, whiche had eternallye decreed and appoynted, whome he woulde haue to be ye first rulers and beginners of his churche. Therefore Jesus sayed to Philip when he met with him: folow me. He taried nothyng at all, but by and by folowed Jesus, of whome alredy he had knowen many thinges, both by the witnesse of John, and also by the common rumour of the people. The woord of the speaker was of so great effect, and the mind of the hearer was ready of hys owne good will. It chaunced verely, that as Andrew had allured and drawen hys brother Simon, so Philip nowe reioysing that he was in the seruice of Jesu, when he had found Nathanell, whome he knew to be wonderfully desyrous of Messias cummyng, for whiche cause he was woont very diligentlye to marke and obserue in the prophecies of the lawe and the Prophetes, from whence and when the same Messias shoulde come, Philip (I say) because he would make Nathanaell partaker of that ioye wherin he did reioyce withall his hert, sayeth vnto hym: We haue found that true Messias of whome Moses hath written, that there should a Prophet rise out of the kinred of Israel, & of whome the prophecies of the Prophetes hath vttered and declared so many thynges: Thys is Jesus the sonne of Joseph of Nazareth, for at that time euery man toke Jesus to be Josephs sonne, and he was better knowen by that name then by the name of Marie hys mother. Moreouer he was called emong the cōmon sorte a Nazarean, not that he was borne there, for Bethleem was halowed with hys birth and infancie, but because he was conuersaunt and brought vp there of a childe, with his parentes. When Nathanael hearde this, truely he lyketh wel the most ioyfull tydinges: but he is offēded with ye doubt, wherwith he was secretly troubled, through the prophecie, whiche (as euery man knew) doeth promise that Christ shoulde come furth out of Bethleem: therfore he desyring to be taught more certainly, sayeth vnto Philip: Can any good thing come out of Nazareth? of the whiche towne the prophecies of the Prophetes hath made no mencion? When Philip himselfe being yet vntaught, and hauing no ferther knowledge but hys plaine simple faith, could not discusse this hard matier, he aduiseth and allureth Nathanaell to goe to Jesu the fountayn it selfe, not doubtyng but that he woulde beleue as soone as he had seene and heard him. If you doubt (sayeth he) to credite me, come your selfe and see.

Folowe me &c.

Philip found Nathanael.

We haue found him. &c. Jesus ye sonne of Joseph &c.

Can there any good thinge come out of Nazareth?

Philip sayeth: come & see.

The texte.

Jesus sawe Nathanael cumming to him and sayeth of him: beholde a right Israelite, in whome is no guile. Nathanael saieth vnto him: Whence knowest thou me: Jesus aunswered, and said vnto him: Before that Philip called the, when thou wast vnder the figge tree, I saw the. Nathanael aunswered and saide vnto him: Rabbi, thou art euen the very sonne of God, thou art the king of Israel.

And Jesus who as yet was of no fame or renowne by working any miracles, sumwhat to open his godlye power by the knowlage he had of secrete thinges, whē he beheld Nathanael cūmyng toward hym, turned to his dysciples, before Philip gaue hym any warning of hym, & before he named hym, and shewed Nathanaell to them, saying: Behold a verye Israelite in dede, in whome there is no guile. In these wordes Jesus did both prayse the true meaning beliefe of Nathanael, and also his pure desyre to haue knowlage, where-

Beholde a right Israelite. &c.

as they which vntruely doe boast themselues to be Israelites, are wont to be busy and curious of a desyre they haue to lay matters to mennes charge. Nathanaell perceiuing that Jesus shewed by these wordes, how that he knewe well inough the communicacion which was betwene Philip and him concerning Jesus hymselfe, & meruaylyng how this came to his knowledge, for as yet he toke Jesus to be none other but má, sayth vnto him: how knowest thou me? But Jesus yet declaring more euidently how he knew the thoughtes of men, were they neuer so secret, sayth: before Philip called the when thou wast vnder the figtree, I had already sene the. The cõmunicació was but betwene them two, and there was no witnes by, that could make any relacion thereof. The place was expressed, and the figtree was noted and spoken of by ÿ way in a mistery, as a thing priuie and of counsel to his firste fault (that is to saye, of hys vnbeliefe) whiche faute they must nedes leaue, that will knowe Christ. It was manifest by these argumentes that Jesus knewe the matter of theyr whole communicacyon, wherof neuerthelesse he maketh no great rehersal, lest he should seme to vpbraide hym with his lacke of fayth, which was shamfast, and asked the question of a good symple mynde. Assone as Nathanaell hearde these thinges, who was perswaded, that the secretes of the hearte was open to god onely, and that the thing which he heard was more than man could do, nowe beeyng nothyng offended with the doubte concernyng the name of the place of Christes birth, he gaue his verdit of hym, saying: maister. Thou arte the very sonne of god, by whom the father hath determined to deliuer his people. Thou art that king of Israel whiche was long a goe promised by the prophecies of the Prophetes.

Nathanael sayeth vnto him. &c.

Rabbi thou art euen the very sonne of God. &c.

The texte.

Jesus aunswered and said vnto him: because I sayde vnto thee, I saw thee vnder the figtree, thou beleuest. Thou shalt see greater thinges than these. And he sayeth vnto him: Verely, verely, I say vnto you, herafter shall ye see heauen open, and the aungels of god ascending and descending ouer the sonne of man.

Jesus gladly enbracing the mannes so ready and chereful fayth, and his so euangelicall profession, doeth stablishe also the opynyon that Nathanaell had of him. And now more euidently declaring his godly nature, sayth: Thou hast hereby conceiued a beliefe that I am the very Messias & king of Israel, which was promised, because I tolde thee howe I sawe thee euen then when thou waste with Philip vnder the figtree, and therefore thou hast a very good opinion of me: In tyme to come thou shalt see more apparaunte sygnes, whereby thyne opinion of me may encrease. And foorthewithall Jesus turned hym to his other disciples, (of whome as yet, neuer a one did iudge of hym according to hys dignitie) and he sayde vnto them. Take thys for a suretie, herafter ye shall see the heauens open and the aungels of God ascendyng and descendyng ouer the sonne of manne. By thys derke saying, our Lorde Jesus did styrre vp the fayth of his disciples, which although it were simple and vncorrupted, yet was it not fully enstructed, and besyde that far from the perfect knowledge of the excellencie of Christ: He did styrre vp their faith (I say) to the lookyng for of greater miracles, and therby to haue higher knowledge. For althoughe the disciples did fantasie, as it were in a dreame, some thing to be in Christ passing mannes nature, whereat they marueiled: neuerthelesse they dyd not as yet vtterly beleue that the fulnesse of the Godhead was in hym. Nathanaell dyd confesse the selfesame thinges whiche Peter dyd after confesse: But because hys meanyng

Thou shalt se greater thinges the these. &c.

Verely verely. &c. ye shall se the heauens open.

meaning was not lyke Peters, he had not therfore lyke aunswere that Peter had, whiche was: Upon this stone I will buylde my churche. And to thee wyl I geue the keyes of the kingdō of heauen. And in very dede for because some that were very mē, are called the sonnes of god in holy scripture, for their great holines, and other besides Christ also did many times se before, thinges which shoulde folowe, by the inspiracyon of the holy ghoste: therfore it is not to bee marueiled at, if Christe knewe without relacion of any other, what was doen secretly betwene the two disciples. Furthermore in that he called hym kyng of Israell, intending thereby to honour Jesus, as it were with an hye and glory- ous tytle, it declareth that euen as yet he dreamed of a worldelye kyngdome. And to haue a kingdome in thys worlde is but a very base & an earthly thing: But it is a thyng of far more honour to bee kyng of all the whole worlde, and also of aungels. This thing mente Christe when he sayde that the aungels as ministers diligent to doe seruice, should ascende, and descende ouer the sonne of man. And although the disciples did not yet vnderstande at that tyme this say- ing of Jesu, neuerthelesse he dyd hyde it and layed it vp in theyr myndes, as a seede whiche shoulde bryng foorthe fruicte in due tyme: For afterwarde we knew how the aungels dyd often knowledge hym to bee kyng of all thynges by theyr obedient seruice, as whan Gabriel brought tidinges of his concepci- on, when they song at hys natiuitie: Glory be to god that is aboue: when at di- uerse tymes they appearing to Joseph, did procure the safegarde of the childe, when they did hym seruice after he was tempted of the deuyll, when they dyd coumfort hym in his conflict at the tyme he swet water and bloud: and whiles they did often appeare in the tyme of hys resurreccion: Agayne also, when in all mens sight he was taken vp into heauen, the aungels wer present, as suerties of the promise of his returne. And that in dede shalbe doen most specially, whē he shal come in the cloudes with the maiestie of his father, and with the whole hoste and company of aungels, to iudge bothe quicke and dead: and to deliuer a kingdome to god the father.

¶ The .ii Chapter.

And the third day there was a mariage in Cana a citie of Galile: and the mother of Jesus was there: and Jesus was called and his disciples vnto the mariage. And when the wine fayled, the mother of Jesus saith vnto him: they haue no wine. Jesus sayth vnto her: wo- man what haue I to doe with thee? myne houre is not yet come.

The texte.

AND Jesus had not taryed long in Galile, but thorowe working of a miracle he begā to declare ye Johns wit- nes of him was not vntrue. In dede Jesus was better knowen in Galile then in other countreys of Jewrie, but yet they had no notable opiniō of him, when as at ye time also euen his brethren and kinsfolkes had no right iudgement of him. Therfore the third day after he came to Galile, there was a solemne mariage made in Ca- na, which is a towne of ye countrey. Jesus mother was biddē to this wedding, because she was of alyaūce to thē. And by this occasiō Jesus hīselfe also was biddē, & his fowe disciples wt hī, which he had gathe- red

The mo- ther of Je- sus was there &c.

red together a litle before. Now then when ẏ feast was at the hottest, and the bridegrome for lacke of wyne was lyke to be abashed, as if he had made but a nygardely feast: And besides that it was to be feared leste hys geastes carefulnesse for lacke of wyne shoulde make the feaste the lesse cherefull: Marie the mother of Jesu of a certain womanly carefulnes desyring to haue this discōmoditie remedied, seing that already by manye tokens and also by the witnesses of John she was not ignorant of the power of her sonne, she is bold to cal vpō him, saying: Sonne, they haue no wine. In that she dare speake to him, it declared her motherly auctoritie: And in that she dooeth not prescribe nor appoynte any thyng to him, what she would haue doen, it sheweth her reuerence towarde her sonne. But Jesus intendyng nowe to take in hande the heauenly busines of the ghospell, whereof he would haue hys father to be the onely auctour, suffereth not mans auctoritie to be mixte therewith. For he dyd not myracles for this purpose to please the affeccions of hys kynsfolkes, but to cause his spiritual doctrine to be the better beleued through corporal sygnes and tokens, amonges the vnfaythfull people of that countrey. Therfore he aunswereth his mother sumwhat roughly, not that he did not loue her entierely being suche a one as she was, consyderynge he loued all mankynde so muche, but to thentent ẏ he would kepe his auctoritie of working miracles fre from worldly affeccions, and to cause the whole glory therof to be ascribed to the power of God. For this was a thing expediente for mans saluacion, whiche Jesus dyd greatly thyrst for and couet. Therfore not vtterly denying hys mother, but declaring that she had litle to doe with ẏ busines he went about, he aunswereth her: woman what haue I to doe with the? I haue a time appoynted me of my father, when and after what sorte I should worke the saluacion of mankind, that time is not yet come. Hitherto I haue shewed my self obedient to thy wil, from hens forth I must doe all thinges according to my fathers will, and not after mans prescript and appoyntmente. In other thinges thou hast bene my mother, herafter I wil take thee but as a woman, as often as I am occupied about my fathers businesse. Whensoeuer his glorie shal be to be serued, I shal not nede thy calling vpon. I wil doe of mine own good wil, ẏ which ẏ thing it selfe shal require. I haue a time appoynted me of my father. So before ẏ time also, whē he was but a childe, he tolde his mother of ẏ she did interrupt hym, when he was disputing in ẏ tēple. And of the like thing againe he warned her, whē she bad out cal him furth to her, whiles he was preaching emōg ẏ people.

They haue no wine.

Jesus saith &c.

Woman what haue I to doe with thee?

The texte. His mother sayeth vnto the ministers. Whatsoeuer he sayeth vnto you doe it. And there were standing there sixe waterpottes of stone, after ẏ maner of the purifying of ẏ Jewes, conteyning two or thre firkins a piece. Jesus sayth vnto them: fill the waterpottes with water. And they filled them vp to the brimme. And he sayeth vnto them: drawe out nowe and beare vnto the gouernour of the feast. And they bare it.

But Marie the mother of Jesu, beyng neither offended with her sonnes aunswere, although it were sumwat roughe, nor in the meane tyme mystrustyng either his goodnes or hys power, maketh no aunswere agayn, but calleth the seruaun:es of the house to her, and secretly in theyr eares sayeth thus vnto thē: Doe ye, whatsoeuer he shall bid you doe. Undoubtedly the godly pitifull carefulnes of his mother, did procure that, lest ẏ seruauntes lacke of belefe, or their vnready seruice, should be a let wherby that whiche lacked at the feast should not be amended. But how and what time ẏ thing should be dooen, she holding her peace leaueth it secretly to hir sonnes wil and appointment. These thinges

Whatsoeuer he saieth vnto you, doe it.

were

wer not doen by chaunce, but Jesus deferred the miracle for þ nonest, because the lacke of wine should be the better perceiued of euery body, and shoulde be well sene to bee geuen for necessitie, and not for any vayne boasting or glorye: For so our Lord wrought all hys miracles, that he semed not to doe them for thaffection of any worldly praise, but to succour & relieue men of their euilles and griefes: he did them so temperatly & in so due ordre, that they could not be don more faithfully nor with more trueth. Therfore now whiles the geastes taried and were carefull for lacke of wine, Jesus perceyuynge the tyme to bee come that he should be knowen to his own, commaundeth the seruauntes to fyll with water sixe pottes of stone, which stode there for this purpose, that if any, according to þ custome of the Jewes, would clense himself with washing, he might haue plentie of water ready, forasmuche as that countrey was very drye, & in fewe places well watered with fountaynes & running riuers. Thys truely did cause the miracle also to be rather beleued, because þ vse of those waterpottes was a solemne thyng emong the Jewes. And the sayd pottes neuer receyued any other licour but water. Moreouer the greatnesse of þ vessels setfoorth the beleft of the miracle, for they contained two or three firkens a piece, so that they could not easily bee remoued out of theyr place. The seruaūtes did obey him and filled the waterpottes with water, as they were commaūded euen to the brimme. Whē that was doen, because he would haue mo witnesses of the miracle, he commaunded them to drawe out of the waterpottes and to offer that whiche they had drawen, to hym that was the chiefe ruler & had the ordreyng of the feast. And this Jesus did, partely because the ruler was sober, for he that hath the charge committed to hym to see all thinges wel furnished, is euer wont to abstayn from wyne, whiles other folkes doe drinke: And partely because he being well skilled in tast, and hauing a fyne iudgement therein, myght more trewely geue verdite of the wyne thē the rest of þ geastes, whose tastes myght seme to bee dulled with drynking of muche wyne before.

Fil the water pottes with water

And they filled them vp to þ brime.

The texte.

¶ When the ruler of the feaste had tasted the water that was turned into wyne, & knew not whence it was (but the ministers which drew the water knew) he calleth the brydegrome and sayeth vnto hym. Euery man at the beginning doeth set furthe good wine, & when men be drunke, then that whiche is wurse: but thou hast kept the good wyne vntill now. This beginning of miracles did Jesus in Cana of Galile, and shewed his glorie: and his disciples beleued on hym.

But as soone as the ruler of the feast had tasted of the wine, that was turned out of water, & knew not where they drewe it, suspecting the faute to be in the seruauntes, that cōtrary to the custome of other, they deferred to bring in such wine until the latter end of the feast, he calleth the bridgrome to hym, desyring to know of him by what occasion þ fault chaunsed. Others (sayeth he) which make a solemne feast, at the beginning thereof, bryng to the table of the beste sortes of wine, afterward whē their geastes being already drunke haue their mouthes out of tast, & powre in drinke vntemperatly, thē they bring & serue of the wurst sort. But thou cōtrariwise hast reserued vnto the end of þ feast, this wine which is better & more pleasaunt than any þ was serued yet. And by this occasiō þ miracle of þ thing þ was doē, spred abrod litle by litle emonges many. And afterward by examining the seruauntes of this thing, it was knowen that the water was not onely turned into wyne, but also into very good wine. And as for the waterpottes they had no mistrust, but that they were onely dedicate and ordeyned for water. The seruauntes put water to water, and filled them vp to the brimme, & after they had drawen of the same which they powred into the vessels, they offered it to the gouernour of þ feast, who was sobre. The bridgrome knoweth well inough that there was no such wine prouyded nor prepared. They wente to the waterpots and found them ful of þ selfesame good wyne. With this dede our Lorde Jesus began the working and setting foorth of his miracles in Cana a towne of Galile, intending by litle and litle to shew furth tokens of his godly power to the worlde. For first of all this thing was doen in a matter not very weightie & also priuatly, yea & almost to please his mother and kinsfolkes withal: whiche had him in lesse admiracion because they were his familiars & of his kinne. And this miracle was not much noted of very manye, but afterwarde it grewe to bee hadde in greatter credite with more: yet in the meane while þ fayth of his disciples þ were present was stablished concerning Jesu, who hauing promised greater thinges, perfourmed that whiche he had promised. And besides that, this miracle (wherby he framed as it were a beginning to þ rest that he should do afterward) was not in vain. For firste of all he woulde honour the mariage with his presence, knowing beforehand that in tyme to come there should be some which would condemne it as an vnpure & filthye thing, whereas an honourable mariage and vndefiled bed, is a thyng most acceptable to God. Moreouer Jesus dyd as it were shadowe vnto vs by a certayn figure, that thing, whiche he then chiefely went aboute. For now was the tyme come þ in steade of the vnsauery & waterishe lettre of Moses lawe, we should drinke the pleasaunt wyne of the spirite of the gospel, by reasō that Christ turned into our more welth that thing which was without strength & vnprofitable. For the law was not only vnsauery to þ Jewes without Christ, but also hurtfull & deadly. They which haue not beleued in the ghospel, doe stil drinke of the water of Moses law, but they, which haue beleued Christe doe happely waxe warme, & growe liuely toward the loue of heauenly lyfe, through the moyst & swete licour of his heauenly doctrine. And this was not doen before that Christ had ioyned vnto him the churche hys spouse. Also the mother of Jesu was present there, representing the forme of the sinagogue, whose autoritie is diminished, yet she telleth the lacke of the wyne, but she her selfe doeth not remedy it. Neuertheles she was for our behoufe mother vnto him, which doth reioyce and commforte our mindes with the swete wine of his spirite. The names of the places also do agree to the mistery of þ thing. For Cana of Galile betokeneth possessiō of a ready passage frō one place to an other. For now was þ original beginnīg of a new people gathered together, which should remoue from the letter of the lawe, to the spirite of the ghospell, from the world, to heauen.

The begin-
ning of mi-
racles did
Jesus. &c.

The texte. ¶ After this he went downe to Capernaum, he and his mother, and his brethren, and his disciples: and there continued not many dayes.

After Jesus by thys miracle had begonne to declare his mightie power emonges his kinsfolkes in a towne of smal renoume, he went downe to Capernaum. That citie is in the selfesame Galile of the Gentiles, all ryottouse and swelling in pryde, by reason of the plentie of richesse therin: beyng also nye vnto the lake of Genazareth and in the coastes of zabulon and Neptalim. But according to the wisedome of the ghospel, that thing which is highely estemed in the world, is abiect, and litle set by afore God. Jesus mother with his brethren

thren and disciples went down thither with him, but they taryed there very fewe dayes. Neyther was there any miracle doen in that place. But this benefit semed to be doen in the meane time, for his mothers & kinsfolkes pleasure: whō now he would no longer cary about with him, forasmuch as he would take in hand greater thynges, because that worldly affeccion and loue should chalenge vnto it no parte of those thinges whiche were doen for the glorye of the heauenly father.

And the Iewes Easter was euen at hande: and Iesus went vp to Hierusalem, and found sitting in the tēple those that solde oxen & shepe, & doues, & chaungers of money. And when he had made as it were a scourge of small coardes, he droue them al out of the tēple, with the shepe and oxen, and powred out the chaungyers money, and ouerthrewe the tables. And sayd vnto thē that solde dooues: haue these thinges hence, and make not my fathers house a house of marchaundies. And his disciples remembred it that is written: the zele of thine house hath euen eaten me.

The texte.

Therfore Iesus leauyng his kynsfolkes behynde at Capernaum, seeketh time and place mete to declare openly hys power and auctoritie, which he had receiued of his heauenly father, & not of men. For euen then the most high and solemne feast of the Iewes was at hand, which is called Easter, and after the Hebrewe tounge, is as much to say as a passing ouer. They did kepe this day as an holy feast euery yere in the remembraunce of the olde story: because their elders had safelye passed ouer oute of Egipte: when they wente into the lande whiche God had promised them. But now that thing whiche they did honour but in figure, was doen in dede by Christ, ẏ is to say, he now brought to passe that men hauing forsaken the darkenes of errours, and cloude of sinne, should be remoued, and brought, through the fayth of the gospel, to innocencie, light and immortalitie: forasmuch therfore as at that time there was at Ierusalem a great number of people which out of al the partes of Sirya did assēble there againste that feastful day, Iesus wente thither nowe going vp towardes hys fathers busines, wheras before he went down to Capernaū to obey & please his kinsfolkes withal. And furthwith he goeth into the temple, which place is wont to be oftē gone to of a religiouse minde, to serue god therin: And verelye Christ was the maister of true religion, who when he entered into the temple which was ordeyned for deuout religion & wurshipping of god, founde there thapparaunce not of a tēple, but rather of a market place. For he founde verye many there which in ẏ holy place did exercise themselues about filthie, yea & sinful gaine, & so turned into robbery that which was ordeined to geue occasiō of godly religion. For to thintēt that straungiers might haue somewhat to offer, they solde to them of an hye pryce, shepe, oxen dooues, & other suche lyke thinges, whiche (according to the custome of ẏ Iewes) were woonte to be offered or geuen to the priestes: but in the meane while ẏ sellers bargained with the priestes and leuites that the sayd priestes & leuites should sel agayne to thē by a lesse pryce, the selfesame beastes that the priestes had receyued of them which had offered, whiche thing the sellers did, because they myghte sell those beastes agayn to other straungiers with a double gaine. So it was brought to passe that by powling the straungers, the filthie gayne whiche rose double by selling one thing twyse, shoulde be deuyded betwene the merchauntes and the ministers of the temple. And to haue more quicke and readye marchaundise, ther was presente, according to the custome of their cōmon market, chaungers of money and bankers, such as did chaunge the greater coynes for

Iesus went vp to Ierusalem, &c.

And found those that sold oxen.

money

money of smaller coyne, or golde for siluer, or els did exchaunge strange coyne for coyne of that place. And thereby also they had shamefull gayne, litle dyffferyng from vsurie. Jesus then declaryng by hys very acte how great a pestilence corrupt desyre of lucre is to the church, and howe far al they ought to be from thys disease, which professe themselues rulers of religyon of the gospell, made him (as it were) a scourge of smal cordes, as though he would driue dogges out of goddes temple. And both with great indignacion and auctoritie, he droue them all out of the temple, displacyng and throwyng downe bothe the merchauntes and their wares: And did not onely put out the men, but also the shepe, and oxen, that there shoulde remayne behynde no suche filthie baggage.

Yea and besydes that, he scattered abrode the chaungers money vpon the ground, and ouerthrew also their boardes, teaching how these thinges ought vtterly to be troden vnder foote of the wurshippers of true religiō. Moreouer as if he had bene moued with indignacion therat, he sayd to them which sould the dooues: haue these thinges hence: and make not my fathers house an house of marchaundise. And hys disciples when they sawe Jesus, beyng at all other times quiete and meke, here now how earnestly he chased out those which did vnsemely vse and defyle the godly religion of the temple with theyr fowle and sinnefull gayne, the disciples, I say, remembred the prophecie whiche is in the three score and eyght psalme. The zele of thy house hath euen eaten me.

The texte.

Then aunswered the Jewes and sayd vnto him: what token shewest thou vnto vs, seeing that thou doest these thinges? Jesus aunswered and sayed vnto them: destroy this tēple, and in three daies I will reare it vp.

But as for the Jewes when they had hearde that he namyng his fathers house, did as it were by a certayne peculier and singular way, declare himselfe to be the sonne of god, and saw hym also so hyely take vpon hym openlye and in apparaunce to be so very angrye with them, whiche semed to further bothe the priestes profite, & also the religiouse seruice of god, they crie out vpon hym and saye: If god be thy father, and if thou wilt reuenge the contempte and iniurie of thy father, doe sōe miracle yͭ we may perceyue thou doest these thinges by the auctoritie of thy father. If thou doest these thinges by thyne owne auctoritie it is presumpcion: And if thou dost them by goddes autoritie, what token shewest thou that we may beleue thee? But Jesus knowing yͭ they would slaunder him in case he had wrought any miracle to shew himselfe therby, seeyng he neuer yet did any miracle but onely to succoure them that lacked helpe in theyr nede, to thintente yͭ the same thyng whiche was a proufe of hys godly power, should be also a benefit & helpe vnto the necessitie of man, he promised thē a tokē vnder a parable, which tokē if he had thē opēly declared, they would not haue beleued, in so much as they did not beleue it whē it was doē in dede. The tokē was cōcernyng his death & resurrectiō. The same was also signified by Jonas, which tokē Jesus had promised after he had doen many miracles, & also at such time as they required him to shew sū tokē yͭ should cū frō heauē. But now he promiseth (although more darkely) yͤ selfesame token to thē, who as yet were but ignoraūt: The tēple wherin they were at that time, occasioned him to say as he did: of the which tēple yͤ Jewes dyd boast thēselues beyond measure. Breake down this temple, sayth he, & in three dayes I wil set it vp agayn. This parable not so much as his Apostles did vnderstand. But at lēgth whē they had knowē & sene his resurrectiō, they perceiued the meaning of his

Destroy this temple, and in three dayes. &c

saying

saying, by theffect of the thing it selfe: For Jesus ment it by the temple of hys owne body, whiche they through their malice should pul downe, by putting it to death: & he by his godly power, should raise it vp again within thre daies. The Jewes thought thys saying not onely to fonde and without reason, but also vngodly and wicked. For it was an vngodly thyng to commaund a temple of so great religion to bee broken: and to set vp agayne within three dayes so laboriouse a building, semed to be a saying contrarye to all reason.

The texte.

Then sayde the Jewes: xlvi. yeres was this temple a building, and wilt thou reare it vp in three dayes? But he spake of the temple of hys bodye. Assone therefore as he was risen from deathe agayn, his disciples remembred that he had thus sayd: And they beleued the scripture and the woordes whiche Jesus had sayde.

And as they vnderstode the thing, so they answered accordingly, saying: Men labored very sore ỹ space of. xlvi. yeres after that the Babilonians had brought Jewry into captiuitie to repayre this temple, and wilt thou set it vp again in thre daies? Our lord Jesus made no aunswer to that obieccion, knowing that he should haue doen no good, in case he had made playne his darke saying, whē not so much as his owne disciples, yea, after they were instructed by his doing of so many miracles, & his so manifolde preachinges, could abide to heare hys death spoken of, nor beleue the mistery of his resurreccion. Yet this saying did cleue and remayne still, as a certayne sede in the myndes of the hearers: but it brought furth sundry fruites in soondry persones. For the Jewes kepyng the same still in theyr remembraunce, did lay thys saying to hys charge before the wicked priestes, as a cryme worthye of deathe. The disciples in as muche as at that time they coulde not vnderstande it, yet bearing it in theyr mindes, dyd meruayl what it shoulde meane vntyl the tyme that after hys resurreccion the holy ghost taught them how Christ by the name of the temple, ment his own bodye that was muche more holy then the temple, whiche the Jewes dydde honour so religiously: for so muche as the fulnesse of the godheade dyd dwell therin. And yet emongeste them it was sacrilege to defile and violate that temple of stone: but they were nothing afrayed synfully to throw downe the most holy temple of hys moste holy and precious bodye. Howbeit Jesus the verye Salomon who had builded this temple for his owne selfe, of the virgin Marie, did restore it agayne within three dayes after they had pulled it downe, according to the prophecies of the prophetes. Therfore the disciples conferring the scryptures with Jesus saying at thys tyme, dyd perceyue thys hys resurreccion to be the greatest token wherby he declared to the Jewes his godhed. For albeit we haue red that some men haue risen againe from death to life, yet no man did raise vp himselfe to life but onely our lord Jesus. For he onely had power in himselfe to leaue his life and to reuiue it agayn, when he would. And so by these principles & beginninges, Jesus did stiere vp al the Jewes mindes to loke for greater thinges in hym against theyr hye feast, which was nowe at hande.

But he spake of the temple of his bodye.

And they beleued the scripture. &c.

The texte.

When he was in Jerusalē at Ester, in the feast day, many beleued on his name whē they saw his miracles which he did: but Jesus did not commit himselfe vnto them because he knew al men, & neded not that any mā should testify of him: for he knew what was in mā.

But after ỹ he had taried at Jerusalem certayn dayes of the feaste of Ester, & by his miracles and doctrine had, as it were, sowen some sedes of the faythe

of the

of the ghospel, many being moued rather with the miracles whiche he did the with his woordes, did credite his saying: and beleued him to bee the sonne of god, whome he preached himselfe to be. For the Jewes be not so much moued with reason as with the sight of miracles: but Jesus then shewyng to vs the very forme and fashion of a teacher of the gospel, to whose wisedome it apperteyneth not euen at the firste to commit to the myndes of ignoraunte persones all the misteries of his hye doctrine, whose gẽtlenesse it behoueth to beare with, and to suffer them that be yet but weake and vnperfit vntill they may attayne to hier thinges: Jesus, I say, because he knewe theyr fayth was yet but wauering and vnperfite, and theyr myndes not hable to receyue the mysteryes of the wisedome of the gospel, he dyd not auenture himselfe emong the common sort, lest the peoples affeccions should be sodainly altered, where by some commocion were like to rise. For there were many that were sore vexed with this auctoritie of Jesus, specially they whiche dyd suppose that hys doctryne and glory shoulde hinder theyr lucre and auctoritie. The enuie of the Phariseis and Scribes had not yet brast foorth into open slaundering of hym, but neuerthelesse they kepte enuie and malice close in theyr heartes, deceitfullye sekyng occasion to hurte hym. And therfore because at this time Jesus coulde dooe litle good emong them, lest he should geue euil persones occasyon of greater euyll, he withdrewe himselfe from them, forasmuch as he knew the secret thoughtes of them all, neither neded he to bee tolde any thyng of any manne. For he, who was ignoraunte in nothing, knewe euen of hymselfe the verye secrecie of euery man there. Neyther yet in the meane whyle dyd Jesus make any prouisyon to saue himselfe, who willyngly came of veraye purpose to suffer deathe for the saluacion of the world, but he toke away from theyr malice occasyon wherby they shoulde els haue sinned.

¶ The .iii. Chapter.

The texte. ¶ There was a man of the phariseis named Nicodemus a ruler of the Jewes. The same came to Jesus by night and said vnto him: Rabbi, we know that thou art a teacher come from god, for no man coulde doe suche miracles, as thou doest, except god were with him.

Mongest many whiche had conceiued some good opinion of Jesu by seing him do his miracles, there was a certain man called Nicodemus, who was of yͤ phariseis secte: and one of the noumber of them whiche were taken emong the Jewes for chiefe rulers. Thys Nicodemus knowing right wel that there were many of his ordre and secte, whiche did enuie Jesu, and lay in waite to doe hym displeasure, went vnto Jesu, but it was in the night tyme: declaring by that dede how he was as yet but weake & wauering in hys loue toward Jesu: whome although heretofore he had in great admiracion, neuertheles he woulde not for hys sake sustayne anye losse of hys own renoume & glory emong men: nor yet for his loue would he be brought to be hated & enuied of his own cumpany: but this came rather of feare then of vngodlines, and surely more of worldly shamefastnes, then of frowardnesse: and of trueth this maner of shamefastnes hath so great power in some folkes myndes, that they whiche can litle regarde bothe theyr

The same came to Jesu by nighte &c.

goodes

goodes and their lyfe, cannot ouercome this kinde of affeccion, which is specially graffed in those hertes that be naturally disposed to gentlenes. For he which was the chiefest emong the rulers of the Jewes, was ashamed to bee taken for poore Jesus disciple. And he who was placed in ẏ hiest seate of the Synagogue, feared to be put out of that place. But Jesus the moste milde and gentle teacher, who doeth not breake the broused reede, nor quenche the smokyng flaxe, did not repel or refuse the saied Nicodemus, that came to salute hym, though he were both fearfull and came out of due tyme, but doeth curteously receiue hym who was doubtlesse a weake spirited manne, but yet without malyce, and for that cause worthy to be promoted lytle by lytle, to higher thinges. Now byanby Nicodemus declaring how much he had profited by seyng Jesus doe his miracles, maketh suite to gette his good will with this preface. Maister, saieth he, we doe already euidently perceiue this thy doctrine not to be suche as the Phariseis is, for the thyng it selfe dooeth shewe that thine autoritie of preaching is geuen the not of man but of God. For no manne coulde doe these miracles, which thou doest except God were present with hym and did helpe hym. Nicodemus dyd set forth this opinion concernyng Jesus, as an hye and great estimacion, howbeit it was farre vnder his dignitie: for Nicodemus supposed him to be none other, but summe Prophete whom God dyd fauour, and was present with in the doing of his miracles, as though he had not wrought them by his owne power.

The texte. Jesus answered and sayed vnto him: verily verily I saye vnto the: except a manne bee borne frõ aboue, he cannot see the kyngdome of God. Nicodemus sayeth vnto hym: howe can a man be borne, when he is olde? can he entre into his mothers wombe and be borne againe?

But Jesus doeth neither reproue Nicodemus vnperfite opinion cõcerning him, neither doeth he forthwith boast of his owne greatnes: but with gentle and frẽdly behauiour, litle by litle bringeth him that is so apte, & easy to bee taught, vnto further knowledge of more secrete misteries of the euãgelicall doctrine. The Jewes which had as yet drũke but only of ẏ water of Moses lawe, whiche had knowen nothyng els but the baptisme of John, neither had they yet tasted the wyne of the euangelicall doctrine, nor had been baptysed by the spirite and fyer: The Jewes (I say) vnderstode all thynges carnally, and for that cause were very rude & vnfit for the Philosophie of the gospel, whiche is all spiritual. Therfore our lorde did not cast him in the teeth with his ignoraunce, nor with his halting minde on both sides, in that he did partely apply himselfe to the worlde, & partely to God, nor yet spake that thing to him which afterwarde he required of his disciples, when they were come to more knowledge, saying to them: whosoeuer shalbe ashamed of me afore men, I will be also ashamed of hym before my father. Our lorde, I say, did lay none of these forsaied thynges to his charge, but by his darke sayinges he causeth Nicodemus to vtter his ignorãuce, to the entent that litle by litle he may instruct him, and bring him from carnal affeccion to spirituall vnderstanding. Nicodemus (sayth he) take this for a very suertie, except a man be borne again new, & as it were chaũged into a new man, he cãnot see the kingdome of God: So very new is this doctrine which thou desirest to learne of me. Forasmuche as Nicodemus thought that saying to be to no purpose, he aunswereth in dede ignorauntly and grossely, but neuerthelesse simply and plainly, saying: how is it possible that a man beyng already of so many yeres

Jesus answered. &c.

as I am, can be borne again? Canne it any waye be brought to passe that he should entre into his mothers wombe, and come thence again and so be borne a newe?

The texte. Jesus answereth: verily verily I saye vnto the, except a man be borne of water and of the spirite, he cannot entre into the kyngdome of God. That whiche is borne of the flesh is flesh, and that whiche is borne of the spirite is spirite.

Jesus beyng not offended euen with this so grosse an aunswere, vouchesaueth gentelly to enterprete and declare what it is to be borne a new, or from aboue. Nicodemus (sayth he) the thing that I haue saied to the is most true. He that hath a will and desire to be hable to receiue the euangelical doctrine, must be borne again: but the maner of byrthe that I speake of, is after another sorte: for it is not carnall but spirituall, and it doeth not consist in multiplying of bodyes by generacion, but in turnyng of sowles into a new forme: neither by this byrth be we made again the children of mē, but ẏ children of God. Therfore be wel assured (as I toulde you euē now) that excepte a man be borne again by water & the holy gost, & of a carnall mā become spirituall, he cannot entre into the kingdom of God which is altogether spiritual. Lyke is borne of the lyke. That which is borne of the flesh, is none other thyng thē flesh: but that which is borne of the spirite is spirite. And verily as much difference as is betwene the flesh, & the spirite, betwene ẏ body & God, so much is this generaciō (wherof I speake) more excellent then that which bringeth forth one body out of an other. They which be borne after ẏ flesh, doe sauer none other thing but the flesh, nor beleue any thing to be, but ẏ which they fele and perceiue wͭ their senses. But those thinges which be not seen, be moste excellent, and of greatest strength, where as the flesh is weake and impotente.

Except a mā be borne of water and of the spirite.

That whiche is borne of fleshe. &c.

The texte. Merueyle not thou that I sayed to the, ye must be borne from aboue: The wynde bloweth where it listeth, and thou hearest the sounde therof, but canst not tell whence it cummeth or whyther it goeth. So is euery one that is borne of the spirite.

Wherfore seyng that there be two sundry wayes how to be borne: there is no cause why thou shouldest meruaile that the same veray man, which is once borne naturally after the flesh, wherby he might be the child of a man, should be borne again of the spirite inuisible, that therby he maye be the childe of God, who is a spirite, & also might be made apte for the kyngdom of heauen whiche is spirituall and not carnal. But if thou doest not yet vnderstand me, take vnto the a similitude of suche thynges as be sumwhat agreable to spirituall thynges, and yet may be perceiued with our bodily senses. God in very dede is a moste sincere and pure spirite, and very far of, from all bodily senses: but this ayre, wherby we be cōserued in life, & wherof we fele so great strength and profit, is called a spirite or wynde, bycause in cōparison of our bodies it is right subtile and fyne: but this kinde of spirite the wynde, is not stayed at mannes wil and pleasure, but of his owne violence is caryed whyther soeuer he list: spreading it selfe ouer all thynges, and putting into corporall thynges a meruaillous force and strength. Sumtyme it bryngeth lyfe, sumtime death: it is otherwhyle calme and still, and otherwhile more boysteous & violent: sumtyme it bloweth out of the East, sumtime out of ẏ West, sumtime out of one part of the world, sumtime out of another, shewing himselfe by theffect therof: & so thou hearest the soūd of it whē thou seest no body at all, nor any thyng whiche thou canst catche or lay hand vpon: thou perceyuest

Meruaile not thou that I sayd to thee, ye must be borne from aboue.

The winde bloweth. &c.

nest that it is present, yet doest thou not see it when it cummeth, nor to what place it conueyeth it selfe when it goeth from thee. This spiritual birth is of lyke sorte. The spirite of God doth rauishe & transforme the myndes of men by secrete inspiraciōs: Therfore there is felt an vneffable strength & efficacie, and yet the thyng whiche is doen is not perceyued with our iyes. And they whiche be thus borne again, be not now led with a worldly & carnal spirite, but with the spirite of God, whiche geueth life to all thinges and gouerneth thesame.

So is euery one that is borne of the spirite.

Nicodemus answered and sayed vnto him: How can these thinges be? Jesus answered and sayed vnto hym: Art thou a maister in Israel and knowest not these thinges?

The texte.

Nicodemus being as yet rude and grosse, did not repugne against Jesus, but not perceyuing the meanyng of his wordes, and desirouse also to haue those thynges, which he had heard, more plainly declared, sayeth to Jesus: By what meanes can these thinges be brought to passe that a man of bodily substaunce should be turned into a spirite by a newe byrthe, and of God bee borne godlyke? Nowe Jesus to declare that those thinges which pertaine to the heauenly doctrine are not perceiued with mans reason, but rather are cōprehended with fayth, and shewyng lykewyse that the philosophiers of the world being proude of their naturall wytte, were vnapte to be taught these thinges, yea & the Phariseis also whiche stoutly professed the litterall sence of the lawe, when in dede they knewe not the spiritual meanyng therof: but to declare therfore that this his doctrine is thesame wisedom which the father of heauen would hyde from worldly persones, & open to them which as touchyng the world, are simple witted, & taken for fooles: Jesus (I say) maketh this answer to Nicodemus saying: thou art taken for a maister in Israel, and professest thy selfe to be a teacher of the people, & art thou ignoraunt in these thinges which thou oughtest most chiefly to knowe? how farre of then are the common sorte of people from spirituall doctrine, if thou being so great a teacher of the people, doest not vnderstād these thinges? but in the meane while it shal profit thee to beleue that thing which thou canst not vnderstād. Faith shall cause the to feele and perceiue these thinges although thou seest thē not: for if thy witte cannot serue thee, to come to the full knowledge of the nature and violence of this worldly ayre, when thou felest it with thy sences, howe shalt thou attaine to the knowledge of these thinges which are farre hier and further of from al bodily senses? For truly in as much as they be godly, they doe farre passe and surmounte the capacitie of mennes myndes, except theyr myndes be inspired with the holy ghoste.

Howe can these thinges be?

Art thou a maister in Israel? &c.

Verily verily we speake as we doe knowe, and testifie that we haue seen, and ye receyue not our witnes. If I haue toulde you yearthly thinges, and ye beleue not, how shall ye beleue yf I tell you of heauenly thynges?

The texte.

But thou mayest surely and safely beleue me whiche doe not onely by inspiracion feele these thynges that be heauenly, or haue only heard them after such sorte as the Prophetes did (of whose numbre thou takest me to be one) but we speake thinges wherof we haue had full proufe & sure knowledge, yea & we beare witnes to you in earthe of ẏ thing which we haue seen in heauen. But ye which be not yet borne again by the spirite, doe not beleue these spirituall thinges. Ye beleue a man when he beareth witnes of those thinges which he hath seen wᵗ his bodely iyes, & yet ye doe not credit him, who being

We speake as we doe knowe. &c.

heauenly himselfe, hath seen heauenly thinges with his spirituall iyes. As heauenly thinges be of more certaintie then earthly thinges: so they be more assuredly perceyued of hym which hath heauenly iyes. Verily our Lord Jesus spake these thynges couertly and darkely, signifying that he was naturally God, although he caryed about a mortall body: and to shewe also that this witnes which Nicodemus did attribute to hym as an hye thing (that is to say that he was sent from God) was farre vnder Jesus dignitie, after his sorte of meanyng whiche he spake it: for Nicodemus as yet iudged no higher thing of Jesu, but that he was sent from God as we reade other Prophetes haue been, and in suche wyse as John also was sent from God. But the sonne of God was after an higher sorte sent from God, who alwaie had been with God the father, before he was sent: yea and euē then was with the father as touching his godhead: by reason wherof, he neuer departed from the father. And for because those thinges which hertofore Jesus had spoken cōcernyng how to be borne a new by water & spirite, might appere to grosse or rude for the highnes of this misterie, that is to say how Gods nature & mans should be vnited together in one person, that the same person should lyue in earth a very mortall man, and be so immortall God still remaynyng with his father in heauen: Therfore (I say) Jesus spake further, saying: If you, by reasō of your carnal and fleshly minde, doe not beleue me speakyng to you as yet but of earthly thinges, how will ye beleue me, if I shal tel you those thinges that be altogether heauenly? which neuertheles both I my selfe haue seen, & knowen more assuredly then ye knowe these thynges which ye see with your bodily iyes.

The texte. And no man ascendeth vp to heauen, but he that came downe from heauen, euen the sonne of manne whiche is in heauen. And as Moses lifted vp the serpente in the wildernes, euen so must the sunne of manne be lifte vp: that whosoeuer beleueth in hym, perysshe not but haue eternall lyfe.

For who emong eyther menne or angels was euer able to ascende vp to heauen, there to beholde celestiall thynges, and presently to looke vpon the diuine nature as it is in dede? No mā at al ascendeth vp into this heauen, but the sonne of man, who came downe from heauen into the earth: and the very same doeth yet still remaine in heauen, beyng neuer seperate from the perfite beholding of the godhead, albeit in the meane while he semeth here in earth, to be base & litle regarded. But thus it was thought mete to ye determinaciō of God, to declare his glory to ye world by worldly reproche, & lowe estate: to thintent yt by the very same way, men after they haue forsakē false glory: should make haste to the true and eternall glory. And if any manne aske what necessitie compelled the sonne of God to come downe from heauen, & to lyue here in earth as a poore abiecte persō: truly none other thing was cause therof, but the moste hye and excellent loue of God the father toward mankynd, for whose saluaciō he hath geuen his only begotten sonne to suffer death, yea and suche a death as is moste shameful after the worldes estimaciō, his will was to bestow & geue one for the saluaciō of al men. Nicodemus (sayth he) let not this thyng seme to thee to be suddayne and straunge, this is the very thyng which Moses by a figure did signifie should come, when, at such time as the people did perishe thorow the vehement inuasion of serpentes, he did hang vp a brasen serpent vpon a stake: that whosoeuer had loked therupon, should be safe from the deadly biting of the serpētes. Therfore as that brasen

No manne ascēdeth vp to heauen.

As Moses lyfted vp ye serpent.

sen serpent hauing in dede the likenes of a venemous beaste, but yet beyng so voyde of all venome, that it did also helpe others whiche were poysoned, was hanged vp in the desert, that all men might see it, for their safetie: so muste the sonne of man be exalted, to thintent that all, which thorowe faith shall lifte vp theyr iyes vnto hym, maye be deliuered frō the deadly poyson of synne, that not onely the people of Israel, but generally what manne soeuer with a pure herte putteth his full truste in hym, should not perishe, as subiect to sinne which bringeth euerlastyng death: but thorow the death of one innocent, shoulde obtayne eternall lyfe. Trulye our lorde Jesus by this maner of darke sayinges opened to Nicodemus the misterie of his manhed, and of redemyng the worlde by the crosse: albeit he was not yet able to receyue and vnderstande these thynges. In the meane while declaryng therewithall, howe great difference was betwene them whiche did reade the lawe after a carnall sence, considerynq nothyng but the plaine story therof, and them, whiche by inspiracion of the holye ghoste (of whom heretofore we haue spoken) did perceyue the mistical sence that lieth hid, couered ouer with the texte. But neuertheles our lorde Jesus did then, as it wer, sowe sedes of fayth into Nicodemus minde: that hereafter he might perceiue this thyng to haue been doen not by casualtie or chaunce, but by the appoyntment of God: and so the good seede beyng receyued into apte grounde, might bryng furth in due tyme, the fruite of faith, not only in Nicodemus hert, whiche did heare these thynges, but also in all theyr myndes, vnto whom these thynges should be declared by his reporte.

The texte.

For God so loued the worlde, that he gaue his onely begotten sonne, that whosoeuer beleueth in hym, should not perishe, but haue euerlastyng life. For God sent not his sonne into the worlde, to condemne the worlde, but that the worlde thorow him might be saued. He that beleueth in hym is not condemned. But he that beleueth not is condemned alreadye, because he hath not beleued in the name of the onely begotten sonne of god.

He gaue his onelye begotten sonne.

For who would haue beleued the charitie of God to haue been so greate towardes the worlde beyng rebell to hym, and giltie of so many great faultes, that not onely he did not reuenge the vngraciouse actes that had been committed therin, but also sent downe his onely sonne from heauen into earth, and deliuered hym to suffre death: yea euen the moste shamefull death of the crosse, to thintente that what man soeuer would beleue in him, wer he Jewe, Grecian, or neuer so barbarouse, should not perishe, but obtaine eternall lyfe, thorowe the fayth of the ghospel. For albeit that in tyme to come the father should iudge the vniuersall worlde by his sonne at his last cummyng, yet at this tyme, whiche is appoynted for mercie, God hath not sente his sonne to condemne the worlde for the wicked dedes therof, but by his death to geue free saluacion to the worlde thorow faith. And leste any body perishyng wilfully, should haue wherby to excuse their owne malice, there is geuen to al folkes an easie entrie to saluacion. For satisfaccion of the faultes committed before, is not required: neither yet obseruacion of the law nor circumcision: only he that beleueth in hym shall not be condemned: forasmuche as he hath embraced that thing, by the whiche eternal saluacion is geuen to all folkes, be thei neuer so muche burdened with synnes, so that the same person after he hath professed the ghospell, dooe abstayne from the euil dedes of his former life, and laboure to go forward, to perfect godlines according to the doctrine of him, whose name he hath professed: but whosoeuer contemnyng so great charitie of God towardes hym, and putting from himselfe the saluacion that was freely offred hym, doeth not beleue the ghospell: he

He that beleueth on him is not condemned

Because he hath not beleued.

hath no nede to be iudged of any body, forasmuche as he doeth openly condēne himselfe, and reiectyng the thyng, wherby he mighte attaine eternall lyfe, maketh hymselfe giltye of eternall payne. God hath offred saluacion to all folkes by his onely begottē sonne, and y thorow faithe, to thyntent we maie knowlege and wurshyp hym as the auctour of saluacion, and put the hope of all oure felicitie in hym. Whosoeuer refuseth thus to do and despiseth the goodnes of god beyng so readie to be had, and dishonoreth his sonne, whom the father woulde haue to be honored, and also estemeth as nothyng his death that he suffred for vs, that person (I saye) doeth declare himselfe euen in very dede to be woorthy of euerlastyng punishement. For who perceyueth not hym to perishe of good right, and thorow his owne faute, whiche willingly & wittyngly doeth embrace that thing, by the which he perisheth, and resisteth that thyng, wherby he might haue recouered health?

The texte. And this is the condemnacion, that light is come into the worlde, and men loued darkenes more then lighte, because their dedes were euill: for euery man that euill dooeth, hateth the light, neither cummeth he to the light lest his dedes should be reproued: but he that dooeth trueth, cūmeth to the light that his dedes maye be knowē how that they are wrought in god.

Errour and synnes be the darkenes of myndes, and synnes doe ingender euerlastyng death. The sonne of God is the lighte of the worlde: for the lighte is trueth, to beleue him is euerlastyng health. Therefore when thorowe the bountifull goodnes of God, light came into the worlde, whiche was blynded thorowe lacke of knowledge of the trueth, and with innumerable vices, to thintent that the trueth beyng knowen, it should be conuerted and saued: yet men loued theyr owne darkenes, more then the lyght that was sente from heauen. If the sicke man perishe, whiche hideth his disease from the phisician, because he would not be holpen, dooeth not he geue iudgemente of hymselfe that he perisheth thorowe his owne faute? So menne that were altogether geuen to the worlde, did refuse the light when it was offred them, because their workes were euill. For as he whiche committeth a shamefull acte, dooeth loue the darke nighte, and shunneth the light of the sunne, leste his dedes should be knowen, so thei whiche know themselues giltie, hate the light of the euangelical trueth, by the whiche all foule and naughtie doinges are bewrayed, because thei might be amended: for he cannot be holpen that loueth his disease. The sinner must mislyke himself, that he may please God. But he whose workes be good, loueth the light of the sunne, that he maye be commended for his well doyng. So he that hath a good cōscience, or at least he whiche desyreth to be healed, and doeth not dissemble or coloure his synnes: (for this is also a kynde of trueth to knowlege the euill that is in thee, and to couet the good thyng which thou lackest) he, I saye, doeth willyngly offre hymselfe to the light of the gospell, that his workes maye be made manyfest: and those dedes which be good maye be praysed, bycause they procede not from the spirite of the worlde, but from God: and those whiche be euill maye be corrected and amended. But they whiche doe presumpteously attribute to themselues perfit righteousnes by the obseruacion of the lawe, when inwardly their myndes swimme in vices, they also which sette their felicitie in the defenses of worldly wisedome, and in the commodities of this worlde, eyther they lyue in great darkenes in case they belieue this in their herte, or els they liue in greatter darkenes, yf they being blinded with their

Men loued darkenes more then light.

Because their workes were euill.

For euerye man y euill doth hateth the light.

their naughtie affeccions, doe stifly vphold and mainteine that thyng, which they perceyue to be euill, and obstinately refuse that thyng which they see to be helthfull. Our lorde Jesus dyd (as it were) lay vp in store certain seedes of suche like misteries, in Nicodemus harte. And verily this is that Nicodemus, which afterwarde did defende and aunswer for Jesu, against the false surmises of the Phariseis by meane of his autoritie, saying, howe no manne ought to be condẽned, but vpō due profe of his actes. This is he also which dyd honour his buriall with his seruice, when he was dead.

After these thinges came Jesus and his disciples into the lande of Jewry, & there he taried with them, and baptised, and John also baptised in Enon besides Salim, because there was muche water there: and they came & were baptised, for Jhon was not yet cast in pryson. And there arose a question betwene Johns disciples and the Jewes about purifying. And they came vnto John, & sayed vnto him: Rabbi, he that was with the beyonde Jordan (to whom thou barest witnes) beholde thesame baptiseth, and all men come to hym. The texte.

Jesus then, after he had laied these foundacions of the glory of the ghospel in Galile, and Jerusalem, to thintent he might more and more be knowen abrode, went into the lande of Jewry, which countrey had his proper name of Judas the autor of that tribe, of the which Jesus lineally descended. And there he taried a lytle whyle with his disciples, beginnyng his euangelicall preaching with thesame principles wherwith John had begun. For he dyd allure them to penaunce, & did baptise them. And at that tyme also John dyd stil baptise, for Herode had not yet put him in prisō. But now he did not baptise in Jordan as he was wounte to doe, but in a place lesse notable, whiche was called Enon, not farre from Salim, (whiche signifieth in the Syrians tongue, guishyng streames of water) by the reason wherof, there was plẽtie of water to baptise the people withal. Many did come to that place, & were baptised of John: Sum went to Jesus, and were baptised of his disciples. And by this occasiō certain of Johns disciples did enuy Jesu, forasmuch as concernyng he himselfe was lately baptised of John: & had behaued himselfe as though he had been his disciple, & also had been cōmẽded & set furth to the people by his witnes, he would now sodainly make himselfe equall to him: yea & moreouer preferre himselfe before hym, in that his disciples did take vpon them the thyng, which hitherto none but John had doen. And first of al they laboured to withdraw the people frō the baptisme of Jesus disciples, & went about to perswade them that Johns baptisme was of more effecte, in washyng awaye of synnes, then the baptisme of Jesu. When they coulde not perswade the people to beleue this, they wente to John, makyng their complaynt to him, thinking that he would be miscontented therwith, and by sum meanes stay this their griefe & grudge. But this worldly affecciō of Johns disciples, did ẏ more set furth Christes glory, & caused John to testifie more manifestly of Christ. And they doe cōplaine of the matter ẘ these woordes. Maister (say they) he that was lately ẘ you, when you did baptise besydes Jordan, & was baptised of you himselfe, yea & euen he whom ye did cōmend with your witnes emonges the multitude, when he was vnknowẽ to al folkes, now taketh vpon him to doe as you did, that is to say, to baptise opẽly: and all menne runne on heapes to him, by which thyng it must nedes come to passe, that by hym thyne autoritie shall be darkened. Johns disciples spake

He taried with them and baptised, and John also baptised. &c

There was muche water. &c.

And there arose a question. &c.

And they came vnto John.

All men come to him.

these thynges of a certaine carnall affeccion, desiryng to haue their maisters glory and renoume to be dayly increased, and for this cause they dyd enuy Christe, whose autoritie semed to hynder Iohns estimacion.

The texte.

Iohn aunswered and sayed: A man can receyue nothyng excepte it be geuen hym from heauen. Ye your selues are witnesses, howe that I sayed: I am not Christe, but am sente before hym. He that hath the bryde, is the bridegrome, but the frende of the bridegrome which standeth, and heareth hym, reioyseth greatly, because of the bridegromes voyce. This my ioy therfore is fulfilled: he must encrease, but I must decrease.

When Iohn had heard these thinges, he did so goe about to remedie the euill desyre of his disciples, that he dyd not onely shewe himselfe not to take greuously that the dayly increase of Iesus glory should darken his, but also did greatly reioyce therat. He shewed that he had fully accomplyshed the office that he was charged withall, & that now Christes tyme was come, who should performe thinges far more excellent. Therfore he answereth on this wise. Why will ye glory in me, of a carnall and worldly affeccion? doe ye desyre that I should make my selfe greater then I am? Man can haue nothyng, except it be geuen hym from aboue. For these thinges be not doen by mannes helpe and strength, but by the autoritie of God: that office which he hath assigned to me, according to my habilitie, thesame haue I perfourmed faythfully. I haue doen the office of a goer before: I haue allured and prouoked men to penaunce, warnyng them that the kyngdome of heauen was at hande. With the baptisme of water I haue prepared many to the baptisme of the spirite and fier: I haue shewed you whom ye ought to folowe from henceforth, & of whom ye must aske perfecte health. If ye regard myne autoritie, why doe ye not geue credite to my wordes? your selfes can beare recorde, that I haue diuerse times openly confessed my selfe not to be Christe, whom many toke me to be: neyther y I was sente for any other purpose but that I going before, should make redy the waye for him against he came. I am his seruaunt, he is Lord of all thynges. But if he now begin to be knowen to the worlde, & that his fame and renoume doeth derken myne, I reioyce that my witnes was true. For I did only wish & desire, that my seruice myght growe to that ende and effecte. For as the bryde is his by right, whiche is the very bridegrome in dede, and yet he whiche is not the bridegrome but onely his frende, doeth not enuy the bridegromes felicitie, nor taketh his spouse from him, but reioyseth on his behalfe, whom he loueth in his herte: and holdyng his peace standeth by him, & also with great ioy of mynde heareth the voice of the bridegrome whiles he talketh with his spouse: so I, who haue wished for nothing more, then that he should be knowen to be so great a man, as of trueth he is, & that I should be no more taken for a greater man than I am in dede, doe greatly reioyce, in that I perceiue this matter to haue so good successe. Of right he must encreace, which hitherto hath been reputed to be much lesse, then he is in dede. And it is mete that I should decrease, who haue alwaye be taken to be greater then I was. Thus it is expedient for mans saluacion, both that myne estimacion should be darkened, and his glory should dayly growe greater: and that my disciples should leaue me, & goe to him: in comparison of whose power, myne is but weake and of none effecte. And my baptisme is as farre underneth his, as fire is of more might then water.

A man can receyue nothig excepte it be. &c.

Ye your selues are witnesses. &c.

I am not Christ, but am sent before hym.

He y hathe the bryde is the brydegrome.

The texte.

He that cummeth from on hye, is aboue all. He that is of the yearth, is yearthly, and speaketh of the yearth. He that cummeth from heauen is aboue al, and what he hath seen & heard,

that

that he testifieth, & no mã receiueth his testimonie. He that hath receiued his testimonie, hath set to his seale, that God is true: for he whom God hath sent speaketh the woordes of God.

It is mete that yearthly thinges should geue place to heauenly, worldely to Godly, vnperfite to thynges perfite. He that cummeth from the earth, is earthly, and speaketh thinges that be earthly and base. For what other thing can man speake but thynges pertaynyng to man: but he whiche is come from heauẽ excelleth al men, be they neuer so great. We haue receyued but a small knowledge of heauenly thinges, & as we are able, so we testifie: but he doeth beare witnes moste faithfully emoung men, of that thyng whiche he hath seen and heard in heauen with his father. And men haue me in admiracion, who am muche his inferiour, but no man almoste receiueth his witnes: they doe require me that am but a seruaunt, to beare recorde of hym. And they refuse the witnes that he beareth of his father. And in dede yf any bodie doe not trust me, he doeth but mistrust a man: yf any doe not beleue hym, whiche is the only sonne, as the father hath witnessed with his owne voice, that person maketh God a lier. The Jewes doe wurship the father, and they contemne and dishonor his sonne whom he sent: howbeit euery reproche & iniury doen to the sonne redoũdeth to the father. Therfore whosoeuer receiueth the witnes of the sonne, he geuing credit to the sonne, doeth certainly affirme God to be true, whiche speaketh in the sonne. For the sonne which is sent from the father, speaketh not the woordes of a mã, but the woordes of God. God hath spoken bothe by the Prophetes, and also hath made euery man partaker of his spirite, accordyng as they haue been able to receyue it. But God hath geuen his spirite to this his onely sonne, not after any certaine measure, but he hath powred vpõ him, the whole fulnes of his spirite, so that the father hath nothyng, but the sonne hath the same.

What he hath seen, & heard that he testifieth

The father loueth the sonne, and hath geuen all thynges into his hande. He that beleueth on the sonne hath euerlastyng lyfe. He that beleueth not the sonne, shall not see lyfe, but the wrath of God abideth on hym.

The texte.

And whatsoeuer the incredulitie of men would take from the sonne, the father imputeth it to be taken from himselfe: for the father loueth his only sõne most intierly, and hath put in his hande, the whole summe of all thynges, not depriuing himselfe of his owne power, but maketh that vertue and power which he hath, common to both. And what thing soeuer God hath willed to geue and bestowe vpon mankynde, his pleasure was to geue it by his sonne. And verily he offreth to all men no small or meane thyng, for he offreth euerlastyng lyfe, but by hym whiche is the only fountayne of eternall lyfe: howbeit that person maketh hymselfe vnapte to receyue this so excellent a gyfte, whiche refuseth to take it. And surely he refuseth it, whiche doeth not beleue that the sonne can geue and perfourme that whiche he promiseth. Moreouer he doeth charge the father with vntrueth, as who sayeth he should promise by his sonne vaine & vntrue thinges. Therfore the rewarde of belefe is great: and the punishment of vnbelefe is fierce and terrible. For of trueth, whosoeuer putteth his hope and trust in the sonne, hath already the sonne, and whoso hath the sonne, hath eternall lyfe. Contrariwyse he that trusteth not in the sonne, forasmuch as he hath, as it were closed vp his owne iyes, that he cannot behold the light, he shall not see lyfe, because this lyght is the lyfe of men: but he continewyng in his sinnes, remaineth bounde, and gyltie of the vengeaunce and wrath of God, that is to say, euerlastyng death.

The father loueth the sonne, &c.

He that beleueth not the sonne shall not see lyfe.

¶ The

The.iiii.Chapter.

The texte. As soone as the Lorde knewe howe the Phariseis had heard that Jesus made and baptysed moe disciples then John (though that Jesus himselfe baptised not, but his disciples) he leaft Jewry, and departed agayne into Galile.

AND so John with these woordes corrected the vnmesurable loue and affecion of his disciples toward hymselfe, and their euill and wicked opinion concernyng Jesus: secretely prouokyng them, that they should leaue him, and now folowe Jesus, of whom all men ought to aske al thynges. Therfore when Jesus (frõ whom nothyng at all was hid) dyd perceiue the like thing to haue chaunced to him, which is wonte to happen emongest men, that is to saye, that enuy foloweth prayse and renoume, and also that now already the Phariseis tooke in euyll parte, that he should allure and drawe to hym many disciples, and that more people had recourse to his baptisme thẽ to Johns, although in dede not Jesus himselfe, but his disciples did baptise. (Euen thẽ declaring ẏ to preache the gospel was a more excellent office, then to baptise.) And the Phariseis were so muche the more greued & displeased, because his disciples dyd take so muche vpon them as they scantly would haue suffred John to haue doen, to whom they dyd attribute very muche: Jesus, I saye, partly because he would not prouoke, sharpen, and stiere vp theyr enuy, in case he should haue longer taried there and therby should seme to haue contemned them, partly because at that tyme he would as it were shewe before, that in the tyme to come, after the Jewes had refused and repelled the grace of the ghospell, it should be brought and geuen to the Gentiles, he leaueth Jewry, hauyng begunne there already the principles of the euangelicall doctrine, and prepareth hymselfe to returne into Galile, from whence he came.

The texte. For it was so that he must nedes goe through Samaria: then came he to a citie of Samaria (which is called Sichar) besydes the possession that Jacob gaue to his sonne Joseph. And there was Jacobs well. Jesus then beyng wery of this iourney, sate downe on the well. And it was about the sixte houre. And there came a woman of Samaria to drawe water. Jesus sayeth vnto her: Geue me drinke. For his disciples were gon awaye vnto the towne to bye meate. Then sayeth the woman of Samaria vnto hym: howe is it, that thou beyng a Jewe, askest drinke of me which am a Samaritane? for the Jewes medle not wt the Samaritanes. Jesus aunswered & sayed vnto her, if thou knewest the gifte of God, & who is it that sayeth to the, geue me drink, thou wouldest haue asked of him, & he would haue geuen the water of life.

But in the meane while his waye was to goe through Samaria, whiche countrey the Gentiles did in old time enhabite, after they had expulsed ẏ Israelites from thence, and brought thither straungers assẽbled out of diuerse places to dwel there. The Samaritanes being at last taught of God by many troubles & afflictions, did partely embrace the religion of the Jewes, for they began to wurship one God, although after a contrary sorte, & also they referred their petigrew vnto Jacob, Abrahams sonnes sonne, because he the sayed Jacob dwelled in times past emõges the Caldeis. The Samaritanes did receiue Moses bokes only, but the Prophetes they did not allowe. And that people toke their name of the mount Samor. Therfore the Jewes dyd beare cruell and common hatred agaynst them, remembryng howe once they wonne theyr countrey by violence, and had put the inhabitauntes therof out of theyr dwellyng places. And also forbecause of theyr contrary rites and customes, in most parte of thinges. For they had so receyued Moses lawe, ẏ yet there did remayne many tokẽs of their old supersticiõ. Therfore whẽ Jesus

For it was so that he must nedes go thorowe Samaria.

Than he came to a citie. &c.

sus was cum to a citie of Samaria called Sichar, and he lacked meate (for the
disciples dyd so muche attende vpon theyr maister, that they had made no prouision for any vitels) Jesus himselfe went not into the myddes of the citie, because he would not geue a iuste occasion to the Jewes to laie to his charge, that
hauyng forsaken the Israelites, he dyd goe to the heathen and wicked Gẽtiles,
as afterwarde in great despite they called hym Samaritane, and a man possessed with a deuill, but he suffered his disciples to go into the citie to bye meate.
He himselfe taryed there alone, partly to looke for and abide the returne of his
disciples, and partely because he would not be absente when occasion shoulde
serue him to do a miracle. For he knewe afore what should happen after: and
there was that porcion of ground whiche Jacob had geuen to Joseph his sõne
to possesse. The place was holy and famous emõges the Samaritanes for the
memoriall of the olde storie, because Leui and Simeon hadde reuenged in that
place the vilanye of the rauishyng of Dina with a great slaughter and destruccion of the inhabitauntes there. There was also a wel very notable emong the
people, euen for because Jacob had digged it, in whom, as I sayde before, the
Samaritanes do glory as in theyr first progenitour & auctour of their linage.
Then Jesus beyng weary of his long iourney, whiche he had goen all on fote,
and not on horse backe or in a wagon (euen then geuing vs an exaumple what
maner a man a preacher of the gospel ought to be) sat hym downe there, as the
place serued nigh vnto the well, and (as it were) refreshed hymselfe with the
ayre therof. And it was then about sixe of the clocke after the Jewes computa-
cion, when the sonne alreadye drawyng towarde nonetyde, dooeth with heate
double the paynfulnes of Jesus labour. And by these tokens Jesus didde declare hymselfe to be a very man in dede, subiecte euen to the selfe same passions
wherunto the bodyes of other men be subiect. In the meane whyle in came a
certain woman of Samaria thither to drawe water out of the same well, nighe
vnto whiche Jesus did sit. To whom Jesus, because furthwith he woulde my-
nister to her matter of communicacion, & would go about to bring her to saluacion vpon the occasion of that thing whiche she did herselfe, saieth in this maner: Womã geue me drinke. And it chaunced well ẏ the Apostles in the meane
while wer absent, because Jesus would speake certayne secrete thynges to her,
which if he had spoken in presẽce of others, it might haue been thought a point
of lightnes. In the whiche thyng certes the Lorde Jesus shewed and gaue to
the teachers of the gospel an example of sobre behaueour and gentlenes, who
doeth so litle disdayn to talke with a sinful woman, & one that had naughtely &
vnchastely misused her body with diuerse, that also by the meanes of his being
with her alone, he did prouide for the bashefulnes of the vnchast woman. The
woman perceiuing by Jesus tõgue & apparell also that he was a Jewe, & knowyng right well how muche the Jewes are wont to abhorre the cumpanye of
the Samaritanes, insomuche that they thought themselues also to be defiled
when they do eyther mete or speake with any of them, she hauyng great meruayle that he of his owne good will called to her, and asked drynke of her, aunswereth in this wyse: How commeth this to passe, that thou beyng a Jewe (as
I maye well contecture by thy speache and garment) doest contrarie to the custome of the Jewes, aske drinke of me that am a Samaritane, consyderyng
that ye Jewes are wont to abhorre to haue any thyng to do with the Samaritanes, accomptyng it a thyng detestable to haue any familiaritie or conuersacion

And it was about the sixt houre.

His disciples were goen awaie vnto the toun to bye meate.

sacion with vs. But Jesus who did not so muche thirste for that kynde of water (albeit as concernyng his manhed he was a thirst in dede) as he did couete the health of the soules, litle by litle doeth allure the poore woman to the knowledge of the grace of the ghospell: aunswerying her after this sorte by a darke saying: to the entent he might the more kindle in her a desire to learne. If thou diddest knowe, saieth he, how excellent that gifte is whiche now God doeth offre vnto you, and in case thou knewest hym also whiche at this presente asketh water to drinke of thee, thou wouldest rather aske drinke of hym, and he coulde geue vnto thee ferre better water then this is, that is to saye, the water of lyfe.

The texte. The woman saieth vnto him: Sir thou hast nothyng to drawe with, and the wel is diepe, from whence then hast thou that water of lyfe? Arte thou greater thē our father Jacob, which gaue vs the well, and he himselfe dranke therof, and his children, and his cattell? Jesus aunswered and saied vnto her: Whosoeuer drynketh of this water, shall thirste againe: but whosoeuer drinketh of the water that I shall geue hym, shall neuer be more athirste: But the water that I shall geue hym shall be in hym a well of water springing vp into euerlastyng lyfe. The woman sayeth vnto hym: Sir geue me of that water that I thirste not, neither come hither to drawe.

Forasmuche as this was spoken of the spirite whiche the beleuers in the ghospell should receiue, it is no meruaill thoughe a poore selie woman of Samaria did not vnderstand it, seing that Nicodemus beyng both a Jewe and a maister could not perceiue that thing, whiche Jesus had spoken sumwhat more plainly, concernyng being borne agayne from aboue, yea and yet did he aunswere more grossely then this woman. For he sayed: can a man when he is olde enter again into his mothers wombe, and so be borne a newe? But this woman after she had conceiued a certayn great high thyng of this saying of Jesus, (If thou knewest the gifte of God, and if thou knewest who he were, and he coulde geue thee water of life,) she was not miscontēt that he semed litle to regarde Jacobs well, whiche she had in great reuerence, neither yet did she mocke the bolde sayinges of him, whiche was to her both a straunger vnknowen, and also a Jewe, but she desyryng to learne what this was whiche he did so set furth as a thyng straunge and notable, in token of honour calleth him Lord, as who saieth, she had alreadie conceiued no small opinion of him. But in the meane while this exaumple of the woman of Samaria was thus deuised and brought to passe by the ordynaunce of gods counsel, to rebuke and declare thereby the peruerse frowardnes of the Jewes, whiche were so ferre from shewyng themselues easie to be taught of our lord Jesus, that thei did wiekedly despise his benefites, and finde fault with his holsome doctrine, wheras this poore woman hauing a desyre to be taught, did curteously and gently aunswere to al thynges, insomuche that she tarying styll in the heate, and hauyng forgotten the thyng for whiche she came, gaue hede to his wordes, who was to her both vnknowen & a straunger, and of whome as yet she had heard no notable reporte. Sir, saieth she, thou doest promise vnto me water farre more excellēt then this. but thou hast no vessell wherewith to drawe the same, and the well is diepe. Therfore, how shouldest thou come by this liuely water, which thou doest promise? Art thou greater thē our father Jacob, whome ye Jewes also haue in reuerence? He gaue this well vnto vs as a notable gift, & did so muche set by this water, that he himself was wont to drinke therof with al his familie, and also his cattel. Jesus perceyuing that the woman was apt to be taught, which did not suspect hym to be a southsayer or an enchaunter, but some notable great man whom she thought worthy

The woman saieth vnto hym. &c.

to

to be compared with Jacob (a man highly estemed of her) Jesus, I say, doeth not disdeyne to allure her by litle and litle to haue him in higher and greatter estimacion, shewyng how the water wherof he did speake is spirituall, whiche should not refreshe beastes, but soules. Whoso drynketh (sayeth he) of this water whiche the Patriarche Jacob gaue vnto you, dooeth but onely for a shorte time slake the bodily thirst, whiche within a while after will returne agayne. But to thintente that thou maiest vnderstande howe muche this gyfte of God (wherof I haue spoken) is more excellent then the gift of Jacob, & how muche the water (which I promise) is better then this water which floweth furth oute of the veines of the yearth: if any man drinke of this water which I shall geue him (if he desyre it,) he shall not thirste eternally, neyther shall any thirste euer after put hym in any ieoperdye, nor yet shall he nede from tyme to tyme anye where els to aske water, but after he hath once drunken this water, it shall remayne in hym which hath drancke it, and shall bryng furth in thesame a fountaine perpetually springing vp euen vnto life euerlastyng. Jesus spake these thynges by a darke similitude, knowyng that the woman was not yet hable to receyue the misterie of faith, by the whiche the holy ghost is geuen, who beyng once receyued, neuer failleth, but doeth styll goe forwarde whilest it bryngeth man vp to eternall life. But the simplicitie of this woman was so great, that whereas the Jewes are wont ouerthwartly and wrongfully to interprete suche maner of parables, she not vnderstanding what he saied, but yet both beleuing and louyng hym, sayed: Lord I praye the geue me parte of this water, that I be not compelled by beyng often and sundrie times a thirst, to go vnto this wel, and drawe therof. Albeit this aunswere was grosse, yet neuertheles it did declare that her mynde was enclined and readie to beleue.

¶ Jesus saicth vnto her, goe call thy husbande and come hither. The woman aunswered and sayed vnto hym: I haue no husbande. Jesus sayed vnto her, thou hast well saied: I haue no husbande, for thou hast had fiue husbandes, and he whom thou now hast is not thy husbād. In that sayedst thou truely. *The text*

Therfore because she had alreadie conceyued no small opinion of Jesus, he doeth inuite and moue her further with greater tokens and proues of his godhead to thynke yet more highly of hym. Jesus then, as though he woulde not open so secrete a matter to her, vnles her husbande wer present, commaundeth her to call her husbande, and bryngyng hym with her, to returne agayn to hym byandby. When the woman had heard this, thinkyng that she spake but to a man, and by the reason of womanly shamefastnes, desiryng to dissemble & hide her vicious liuyng, and with deniall of matrimonie to kepe secret her aduoutrie, she saieth: Sir I haue no husbande. Here Jesus both declaryng his godhed and gentely reprouyng the womans lyfe, saieth vnto her: In that thou sayest thou hast no husbande, thou hast tolde the trueth, for although thou hast had fyue husbandes to satisfy thy filthy luste, yet neuer a one of them was lawfull, yea and euen very he whom thou now hast, is not thy lawfull husbande. Therefore in this poynte thou hast spoken nothyng but trueth.

The woman sayeth vnto hym: sir I perceyue that thou arte a Prophete. Our fathers wurshipped in this mountaine, and ye saye that in Hierusalem is the place where menne oughte to wurshippe. Jesus sayeth vnto her: woman beleue me, the houre commeth when ye shall neither in this mountayne, nor yet at Hierusalem wurshippe the father. Ye wurshippe ye wotte not what, we knowe what we wurshippe, for saluacion cummeth of the Jewes. But the houre cummeth, and nowe it is, when the true wurshippers shall wurshyppe the *The text.*

father

father in spirite, and in the trueth: For suche the father also requireth to wurship hym. God is a spirite, and they that wurship him must wurship hym in spirite and in the trueth.

The woman when she perceyued the rebukeful synnes of her life, committed at home, not to be hidden from Jesu, beyng a straungier and also a Jewe, who could not know by the reporte of menne, that thing whiche he did disclose, she shrynketh not awaye from hym, as one confounded with shame, neither is she with anger moued to answer him agayn spitefully, but so muche the more she is inflamed to haue hym in great admiracion: wheras if Jesus had spoken any suche thyng vnto the Phariseis, they would haue cried out & saied: he is an enchaunter & possessed with a deuill. But what aunswere made this godly sinner the Samaritane? Sir saieth she (as I perceiue) thou arte a prophete. The feith of the woman was come to this poynte. At the firste she calleth him but a Jewe: and meruaileth that he did no more earnestly obserue the Jewes religion, because that contrarie to the custome of other Jewes he did aske drynke of a Samaritane. Anon after she calleth him Lorde. Here nowe she attributeth vnto him the name of a Prophete, because euen of himself he knew the secretes of other. And at last she desyryng to learne certayne higher thynges of this prophete, ceassed to speake of lowe and meane matters, and propoundeth to him a question, (as a thyng) to her thynkyng, impossible to be assoyled concernyng the waie and maner how to wurship God, because in this poynt the Jewes and the Samaritanes did very muche disagree. For albeit bothe those kyndes of people did wurship one god, yet the Jewes had an opinion that God should be wurshipped in no place but onely at Jerusalem in the temple, as though God did no where els heare the desires of them that did praye. Cōtrariwyse the Samaritanes with like superstician (but after another sorte) denyed that God should be wurshipped in any place but in the mounte Garizim, because that place was appoynted by Moses where the Patriarkes should blesse the people that kepte the commaundementes of God. And forasmuche as both these nacions, beyng wel pleased with their owne seuerall rites and customes, did the one of them contemne the religion of the other, the woman desyred to learne of Jesus (as of a Prophete not ignoraunt in suche thynges) whiche of those two nacions had the holyest waye in seruyng of God, as one that would folow that waye whiche she should knowe to be best.

Sir I perceiue that thou art a prophete.

our fathers wurshipped in this mountayne.

Therfore she sayeth: Our elders wer wont to wurship God in this mount, and they thinke it not lawfull to wurship hym in any other place, where as you Jewes contrariewyse accoumpt it abhominable to do sacrifices in high places & groues, & that it is not lawfull to wurship God any other where then at Hierusalem in the temple: wherof they do glorie, as though God were shut vp in a house builded with mans hand. Because this question of the womā did appertaine to the learnyng of true godlynes, Jesus openeth & declareth to her howe that after the true and spirituall wurshippyng of god should be sette foorth by the doctrine of the ghospel, the supersticious religion of the goddes and deuils of the Gentiles should be vtterly extinguished: yea and also that the maner of the Samaritanes wurshyppyng of God, should be abolyshed, whiche had no suche iudgement of god as they ought to haue: but toke hym to be as a certain special deuell, and did mixe the wurshippyng of hym with the wurshippyng of deuils, mingling and confounding together the wicked superstición of the Gētiles with the wurshyppyng of God, as a man should put fyer to water: and folowing

And ye saie that in Jerusalem is the place where men oughte to wurship.

folowing the saird Gentiles exaumple, did their sacrifices in hye groues and
mountaines. And furthermore he shewed her that the Jewes religion which
(as the time required) had been hitherto grosse and carnal: and did rather represent certain shadowes of true godlines thē very godlines it selfe, should
encreace vnto more perfeccion, & that God being afterward more fully knowen through the sonne and the holy gost, should be wurshipped not onely in
Jurie, but through the whole worlde: yea & that in more holy temples then
the temple of Hierusalē was, that is to say, in the pure myndes of mē which
God had dedicate vnto himselfe with his spirite, and is not nowe to be pacified with the sauoure of burt offreynges of beastes, but with holy prayers,
godly desires, and chaste affeccions. But before Jesus would open this misterie of the godlines of the gospel: he speaketh first of feith, without which
none is mete to be a hearer of the euangelicall doctryne, neyther fitte to be a
wurshipper of Christes religion: for faith only doeth purifie the hertes and
maketh them apt to be put in trust with the secretes of heauenly wysedome.
Woman (sayth he) beleue me (if thou take me for a Prophete in dede) the time
is come now, when both the vnpure wurshippyng of the Samaritanes shalbe abolyshed: and also the carnall religion of the Jewes shall be turned into
better, neither shal ye herafter wurship the father in this mountayne (who is
not only the God of this mountayne, but also of the whole worlde) ne yet at
Jerusalem: but wheresoeuer shalbe the congregacion of good & godly people, there shall hereafter be Jerusalem. In the meane whyle, we Jewes
doe excell you in this behalfe, that we wurship God whom we know by the
lawe, & whom we doe confesse to be the Lord of all thinges & all people: nor
we doe not defile the wurshipping of him, who is only to be honoured, with
the wurshipping of other Gods. You wurship you cannot tell what, supposing God to be no bodies God but the Jewes & your owne, yea and ye take
hym to be suche a one as would suffer hymselfe to be matched with deuyls:
wheras all godly honoure is due to hym alone. The lawe hath taught the
Jewes these thynges. And by Gods commaundement there was a temple
builded at Jerusalem to wurship one God therin, which should be a fygure
of the spirituall temple. There were priestes ordayned, & also rytes and ceremonies of sacrifices as it were with certain shadowes betokening the holynes of the gospell. Therfore the Jewes doe excell you herin, that both we
haue a better iudgemet of God then you haue, & also that we doe not pollute
or defile ye wurshipping of him with any prophane wurshippinges of other
Gods: And moreouer we doe excell you in that we doe wurshippe hym in a
place appointed of God himselfe, & with rytes & ceremonies of his owne teaching. Howbeit in ye meane while this our religion although it be not perfit,
yet it is (as it were) a step or furtheraūce toward perfit honouryng of God.
Therfore eternall health came firste of the Jewes, to whom the Prophetes
haue promised Messias to come, whiche by the meanes of the lawe haue the
fygures and shadowes of the religion of the gospell. Now the tyme is come
that the false religion of the Gentiles must geue place, and that both the carnall wurshipping must geue glace to the spirituall wurshipping of God, and
also the shadowes of the lawe to the light of the gospel. For now I tell you
the tyme is at hande, yea it is alreadie presente, when true wurshippers,
shall wurshippe the father not in temples, not with beastes, nor with bodily
thynges

Ye wurship ye wot not what, we know what we wurshippe. &c.

thynges, but in the spirite: not with shadowes, but with trueth. For God seyng he is a spirite, is not delyted with the purenes of the body, nor with the walles of the temple, neyther yet to haue beastes offered in sacrifices, but he loueth spiritual wurshippers, of whom he may be wurshipped according to the spirite and trueth. For there hath been hitherto enough attributed to the shadowes and figures of Moses lawe: Hereafter wheresoeuer there shalbe a mynde pure from synne through the faith of the ghospel, there shalbe a worthy tēple for God. Wheresoeuer there shalbe heauenly desiers, pure praiers, and holy thoughtes, there shalbe sacrifices wherwith God is pleased.

The texte.

The woman sayeth unto hym: I wote that Messias shall come, which is called Christe. When he is come, he wyll tell vs all thynges. Jesus sayeth vnto her: I that speake vnto the am he. And immediately came his disciples, and merueyled that he talked with the woman, yet no manne sayed: what meanest thou? Or why talkest thou with her? The woman then left her waterpot, and went her waye vnto the citie, and sayeth vnto the men. Come see a man whiche tolde me all thynges that euer I dyd. Is not he Christe? Then they wente out of the citie and came vnto hym.

The simple and pacient belefe of this woman of Samaria dyd so muche profite by the forsaid communicacion of Jesu, that she nowe supposeth hym (whom first she had called a Jewe, then a Lorde, and after a Prophete) to be Messias himselfe. For the Samaritanes also by the promyse of Moses, dyd loke for that excellent Prophete to aryse & come of the Jewes. Therfore she aunswered after this sorte: I knowe that Messias shall come whom the Jewes doe loke for, of whom already there is a rumoure emong the Jewes. Therfore when he shall come, he shall declare vnto vs all these thynges whiche thou haste spoken concernyng the newe maner of the wurshippyng of God, neither shall he suffre vs to be ignoraunte in any thyng. Jesus perceyuyng the belefe of the woman apte to be taught, and suche feruente desyre to knowe the trueth, as he had not founde the like among his countrey men the Jewes, he vouchesalueth therfore to opē and declare vnto her who he was. Thou lokest (sayeth he) for Messias to come, be thou assured he is come, and euen nowe thou seest hym, for I that doe talke with the am he in dede. And as soone as these thynges were spoken, his disciples returnyng from the toune came thyther, and before they came at hym, perceyued that he talked with a woman of Samaria, and dyd meruaile at his so great gentlenes. yet no manne durst aske hym what thyng he required of the woman, or for what cause he had talked with her. But the woman beyng amased with the saying of the Lorde Jesus, did aunswer nothing at all: but leauing her waterpotte at the well (for nowe the thirsting for that water was clearely gon and forgotten, after she had tasted of the water which Christe had promised) she maketh haste towardes the citie, and of a synful Samaritane sodenly became a messenger, & as it were an Apostle in that she doeth declare this thing openly to all folkes, to thintent that the knowledge of many should cōfirme her feith: Come, saieth she, and see a manne to be meruailed at, & one that knoweth all secretes, who although he be a straunger and one that I neuer sawe before, yet hath he tolde me all the secretes that I haue doen, it is possible that the same is Messias. Trust not my woordes, proue the thyng your selues and ye shall fynde me no lyar.

I knowe ꝧ Messias shall come, whiche is called Christe.

Jesus sayeth vnto her: I that speake vnto the am he.

In the meane while his disciples prayed him, saying: Maister eate. He sayed unto them: I haue meate to eate that you knowe not of. Therfore sayed the disciples emongest themselues: hath any man broughte him oughte to eate? Jesus sayeth unto them: my meate is to do the wyll of hym that hath sent me, and to finishe his worke. Saye not ye there are yet fower monethes and than cummeth haruest? Beholde I saye unto you, lifte up your iyes and looke on the regions for they are all white alredy unto haruest, and he that reapeth receyueth rewarde, and gathereth fruite unto life eternall, that bothe he that soweth and he that reapeth might reioyce together. And herein is the saying true that one soweth and another reapeth. I sende you to reape that, wheron you bestowed no labour. Other men laboured and ye are entred into theyr labours.

The texte.

Whiles the woman did bruite abrode this rumour emonges the citizens of Sychar, in the meane tyme Jesus disciples supposyng hym to bee payned with houngre, moued hym to take suche meates as they had brought. But Jesus euery where takyng occasion to drawe men up from the care of bodilye thinges, to the desire of spirituall thynges: lyke as he had allured and drawen the woman to the knowlage of the fayth of the ghospell by his speakyng of the water, so by the occasion of meates he prouoketh his disciples that were as yet but ignoraunt, to be diligent in preachyng the ghospel: yea and peraduenture at that time he did not so muche thyrste for the water of the well, and although he did so, yet did he more desyre and thirst for mans saluacion: neuertheles the affeccion of the woman whiche came to drawe water, gaue him occasion of this godly cõmunicacion: In lyke maner although he was then hungrie in that he was a very man, he was muche more hungrie to saue mankynde, for which cause he descended from heauen. Therfore he sayed unto his disciples whiche moued hym to take his bodilye refeccion: I haue other meate to eate (sayeth he) and suche meate as I delite more in, then in that whiche you bryng me. His disciples meruailyng what this saying mente, and yet not bolde to aske their maister, for reuerence they bare unto hym, leste he shoulde bee any thyng offended therewith, talked thus emong themselues: what meaneth he by this? hath any other body whiles we were absent brought him any meate? But Jesus because he would nowe imprint in theyr myndes the thynge whiche he had spoken before darkely, sayeth nowe openly: I passe very litle (sayeth he) upõ this bodely meate. There is an other kynde of meate which I do specially care for: that is to saye, to accomplishe that thyng for whiche cause my heauenly father hath sent me hither. This is my houngre, this is my thirst, to go about the thyng which he hath cõmaunded me. Both the time prouoketh, & the promptenes of mens mindes to the faith of the ghospell, do also require the diligence of preachers. If you whiche doe so muche care for the welth and commoditie of ye bodies, know that haruest is at hande fower monethes after that seede tyme is past, how muche more ought we to regarde the tyme of our spirituall harueste? And as when the corne beginneth to grow yealowe, it dooeth (as it were) require a syckle, and the diligence of reapers: so yf you wyll lyfte up your iyes and behold the corne that groweth in mens mindes, yea euen in them emonges the Samaritanes and Heathen, which make haste to the doctrine of the ghospell, ye shall perceyue the regions and countreyes on euery syde to be as it wer reapyng rype to the haruest of the ghospell, and to require our labour and dilygence. But yf the hope of yearthly fruite dooeth soone prouoke the reaper to his labour, howe muche more ought we to be forwarde to gather this harueste

I haue meate to eate that ye know not. &c.

Jesus saith unto them: my meate is to do the will of hym that hathe sent me.

Say not ye there are yet.iiii.monethes and than cummeth haruest?

to our father, whiche bothe shall obteyne for the reaper a ryghte large rewarde in heauen, and shall gather for God, not wheate into the barnes, but the soules of men into euerlastyng lyfe. And so it shall come to passe that bothe the sower and the reaper shall reioyce together. For that thyng happeneth to you whiche is woont to be spoken, in a common prouerbe, one soweth and another reapeth: there is more payne and laboure aboute the tilling and sowing then in the haruest and reapyng. The grounde muste be plowed, the cloddes muste be broken with the harowe, the fielde must be dunged, the sede muste bee sowen, couered with earth, attended and kept, the cokle also muste be weeded out, but after whē the corne is ripe, there is not so great a do about the reapyng therof: and the fruite beyng ripe and ready doth mitigate the tediousnesse of the laboure, but in this spirituall haruest it happeneth muche otherwyse then in the bodily haruest: for there (accordyng to the common prouerbe) as often as the fruite and commoditie of the haruest, cūmeth to another then to hym that soweth, the reaper in dede reioyceth but the sower is grieuously vexed. In this spirituall haruest it is otherwyse, for both the sower and the reaper reioyseth, and neyther of them lacketh theyr fruite and commoditie. I haue sent you to reape the corne, in sowyng wherof ye bestowed no labour. The prophetes haue tilled the groūd with their trauaile, and haue with theyr doctrine prepared to the ghospell, the world beyng as at that time vntractable: ye nowe succede and entre vpon their labour, and goe about a thyng prepared to your hāde, by reason that the world nowe applyeth it selfe to receyue willyngly heauenly doctrine, and men goeth about to prease into the kyngdome of heauen, in maner by violence.

And herein is the saying true that one soweth and an other reapeth.

The texte.

¶ Many of the Samaritanes of that citie beleued on hym for the saying of the woman, whiche testifyed that he tolde her all that euer she dyd. So whē the Samaritanes were come vnto hym, they besought hym that he woulde tary with them, and he abode there two dayes. And many menne beleued because of his owne woordes, and sayed vnto the woman. Now we beleue, not because of thy saying, for we haue heard him our selues, and knowe that this is euen Christe, the sauiour of the worlde.

Whiles our Lorde with these sayinges doeth exhorte his disciples towardes the buisines of the ghospell, the thing it selfe doeth declare that to be true which he had spoken of the corne waxing white and rype towardes the haruest. For in the citie many Samaritanes dyd beleue that Messias was come: whereas that woman had testified nothyng els of Jesu, but that he had opened and declared vnto her the secrete shamefull deedes of her life time. As yet they had neyther heard him speake, nor seen him doe any miracle. So readye was, yea euen their beliefe which semed to be farre from the promisses of the Prophetes. Therfore a multitude of the Samaritanes came renning out of the citie to see him, whom the foresayed woman had so earnestly commended and sette furthe vnto them. Neither doeth his presence diminishe their opinion of hym, neither be they offended with his homely and course apparell, ne yet with his slendre trayne of his simple and vnlearned disciples: whereas the Jewes after that they had seen so many of his miracles, hearde so many of his sermons, and receyued so many commodities and benefites at his hande, did eyther falselye accuse hym, openly rebuke hym, or els chased him awaye with castyng stones at hym. In conclusion the Samaritanes vpon a womans reporte and witnesse, goe foorth to mete with a manne whiche was not of theyr owne nacion, whome as yet they had neuer heard speake, of whom they had neuer seen any notable thyng doen, and yet do they require and desire him to bee contented to take a lodging in theyr citie. But what did moste gentle Jesus? he knew the enuie of the Jewes, he knewe what hatered they bare to the Samaritanes, and yet the tyme was not come that the ghospell should be taken from them beeyng reiected for theyr inuincible lacke of beliefe, and shoulde be preached to the Gentiles. Therfore he so tempered the matter, that he neyther gaue by apparaunt profe, any occasion to his owne countrey men the Jewes to complaine that they were despised of him, and the Samaritanes preferred before thẽ: consideryng the Prophecie promised that Messias should come to them: neither yet would he vtterly disapointe the godly beliefe of the Samaritanes. For in that he went through Samaria, he did euen of very necessitie. And at theyr request, to tary there but two dayes, was good maner and gentlenes, wherewith no manne of right coulde fynde faulte. And nowe when they had heard Jesus, many moe there dyd beleue, and theyr beliefe was stablished, which vpon the reporte of one woman, had conceyued a notable opinion of Jesu. And nowe they beare a full witnesse of Jesu: and suche a testimonie as was ryght semyng for a very true Jewe, saying to the woman: Thou haste reported lesse of him then the thing requireth. For we nowe doe beleue hym to be Messias, not by the perswasiõ of thy woordes, but we our selfes doe assuredly knowe by his woonderful communicacion that he is the very true Messias which was loked for of the Jewes: who shall bryng saluacion not only to them but to the whole worlde. With this so cherefull, and so full a witnesse, the Samaritanes did both declare theyr owne beliefe, and therewithall reproued the wicked vnbelefe of the Jewes.

And he abode there ii. dayes.

The texte.

After two dayes he departed thence, and wente awaye into Galile. For Jesus hymselfe testified that a Prophete hath none honour in his owne countrey. Than assone as he was come into Galile, the Galileans receyued hym, when they had seen all thynges that he did at Jerusalem at the daye of the feast, for they went also vnto the feast daye.

Therfore Jesus because he would geue no occasion to the Jewes of greater hatred and enuy: wrought no miracle emong the Samaritanes neyther tourned he in to them but by the waye, and at theyr desire, nor yet dyd not he lodge emong them lenger then two dayes, but forthwith he maketh an ende of his purposed iourney, and so goeth forth on his waye into Galile. Moreouer albeit his owne countrey lay in his waye here in this iourney, yet would he not turne into it: not that he did despise it, but that by reasõ of the contempte and lacke of belefe of his owne countreymenne, to whom he was knowen and also of kindered, as concerning his mãhood, he had no hope that the gospell should bring forth any fruite there, and than his preaching should haue doubled the faulte of theyr vnbelefe. For by this meanes theyr faulte was the lesse in not beleuing Jesus doctrine. And whẽ our Lord was asked the questiõ why he did not goe to his owne nacion to shewe of what power he was: in his aunswer he vsed that auncient prouerbe whiche the common people vseth, that is to saye: a Prophete is no where contemned but in hys owne countrey and emong his owne kinsfolkes. For such are the affecciõs of men, that familiaritie bringeth contempt. And they esteme many thinges for none other cause, but that they come frõ farre & straunge countreys. Furthermore forasmuche as in Galile by reason of Johns testimonie and the miracle which Jesus hymselfe had doen there of late, a ryght honest brute and fame was spred of him, they of Galile receiued him when he came thither, specially because at Jerusalem they had seen hym dryue the byers & sellers out of the Temple, and other thynges which he had doen there with great authoritie in the presence of the people: for at that tyme they also of Galile were assembled at Jerusalem to kepe the holy and feastfull day. All these thynges verily doe condemne the incredulitie of the Phariseis, and betoken that the grace of the ghospell shall remoue from them to the Gentiles. The Samaritanes doe beleue at the reporte of one symple woman: They doe in maner force hym beyng a straunger to lodge with them: They confesse hym to bee Messias and the redemer of the worlde, when as yet he had not vouchsaued to worke any myracle emong them. The people of Galile (beyng but a grosse naciõ and vnlearned in the lawe) who neuer had any Prophete emong them, after they had seen his miracles, began to beleue. They of Jerusalem both priestes, Phariseis, and Scribes, which seemed to kepe moste perfectly the religion of the Jewes, and also were excellently learned in the lawe: did obstinately fynde faulte both with Jesus doinges and sayinges. Therfore the more iust and religious euery man thought himselfe to be, so muche the farther was he from the godlines of the ghospell: and agayne the further of he semed in mannes iudgement from the knowledge of the Prophetes and the lawe, whiche dyd promyse Christe, and the more contrariouse to the Jewes religion, so muche the nerer he was vnto Christe: whom the lawe had promysed to come, and more apte to receyue the doctryne of the ghospell.

The texte. So Jesus came agayne into Cana of Galile, where he turned the water into wyne. And there was a certayne ruler whose sonne was sicke at Capernaum: as the same heard that Jesus was come out of Jewry into Galile, he went vnto him, and besought hym that he would come downe and heale his sonne, for he was euen at the poynte of death. Then sayed Jesus vnto him: excepte ye see signes and woonders ye will not beleue. The ruler sayeth vnto him: Sir come downe or euer that my sonne die. Jesus sayed vnto him: Goe thy waye, thy sonne liueth. The man beleued the woorde that Jesus had spoken vnto him. And he went his waye, and as he was nowe goyng downe, the seruauntes met hym, and tolde him saying: thy sonne liueth. Then required he of them the houre when he began to amende. And they sayed vnto hym. Yesterdaye at the seuenth houre the feuer lefte hym. So the father knewe that it was the same houre in the which Jesus sayed vnto hym: Thy sonne liueth. And he beleued and al his housholde. This is agayne the seconde miracle, that Jesus dyd when he was come out of Jewry into Galile.

Therfore Jesus beyng entred into Galile, wente againe to Cana a towne of the saied Galile: where not long before he had turned water into wyne. That miracle at the first being knowen but to a few, when afterward it was commonly bruted abrode: caused the people to haue some good opinion of Jesu, but yet not suche as was wurthy for his dignitie, for very fewe dyd beleue that he was Messias, & many toke him to be but a prophete. Therfore Jesus went againe to Cana not to get any prayse for the miracle which he had doen there, but now at this time to reape some corne of that sede which he had sowen secretly: for this was the thing that he thirsted for & coueted, that is to say, the faith of men wurthy of the ghospell: and here againe an occasion rose to lay to ye Jewes charge their vnbelefe: for at that time there was in Galile a certayne a certaine ruler which was the Emperours deputie in prophane and tempo-rall causes, who was neither Jewe nor Samaritane, but an heathen manne, and clene contrary from the Jewes, religion: he had a sonne whom he loued entierly, whiche lay very sore sicke and in great daunger of life in the citie of Capernaum: when he heard that Jesus had left Jewry and was come into Galile, he leauing his sonne at home, departed out of the citie of Capernaum & came to Jesus, requiring him very earnestly to go with him to Capernaū and heale his sonne, because the vehemencie of his disease was such, that the sicke man could not be caried to Jesus: for he was euē at the poynte of death when the forsayed ruler departed from hym. Nowe Jesus declaring ye faith of this ruler to be as yet vnperfit, in that he dyd not rather beleue that his sōne could be healed vnles Jesus himselfe had gon thither, as though he cal-led vpon a physician, or els as though Jesus could not restore euen the dead vnto life: but Jesus rather rebuking the incredulitie of certain Jewes, which would not beleue, after they had seen his miracles, sayeth vnto the ruler: I doe alowe their beleke (sayeth he) whiche doe credit my woorde alone, with-out confirmacion of miracles: ye beleue not me vnles you see tokens and mi-racles. The ruler was so myndful of his sonnes perill and ieopardy, that he made no answer to this saying of our Lorde Jesus, because he thought such cōmunicacion was but a wasting of time, wheras the disease required a pre-sent remedie. Therfore he requireth him more importunately to make haste to come to Capernaum, before his sonne were dead, as though he shoulde come in vayne in case he dyd come after he had geuen vp the ghost, whereas it was as easie to Jesu to call againe the lyfe after it was once past, as to kepe the same in the body when it was ready to go out therof. Therfore Jesus without rebuking the rulers fayth, sheweth by the dede it selfe, that he can doe much more then the ruler trusted that he could doe: I nede not (sayth he) for this cause go to Capernaum. Go thy waie, thy sonne whom thou diddest leaue at the poynte of death, is now aliue and in helth. The rulers faith was somewhat stayed by this saying, for he (trusting to Jesus woorde) maketh haste homewarde. And as he was goyng thyther, his seruauntes mette with hym to bryng the father good tidinges of his childe: that is to saye, that he whiche was a litle before at poynte of death was sodeinly recouered: & that he should not trouble Jesus, of whose helpe they had no nede: for they sup-posed that the childe had recouered his health but by hap, as men that were ignorāūt what was doen betwene the ruler and Jesus. In this poynt verily the rulers lacke of full trust, being mixte with some hope, caused the miracle to be better beleued. For the ruler desirouse to knowe the trueth certaynly whether his sonne was restored to helth againe by chaunce, or by the power of Jesu, enquired of his seruaūtes at what houre his sonne began to amend. yesterday (say they) at the seuenth houre, that was about one of the clocke at after none, the feuer sodeinly lefte hym, and by and by your sonne was whole. The father knewe that euen at that very houre Jesus sayed vnto hym, go home, thy sonne lyueth: and than he was well assured that his sonne was re-uiued not by chaunce, but through the power of Jesus. And though this mi-racle was wrought vpon an heathen man, yet muche fruite came therof: for not only the ruler himselfe beleued that Christ was Messias, but also by his perswasiō and exaumple his whole housholde beleued the same, which must

The ruler sayeth vnto hym.

Jesus sayeth vnto hym: goe thy waye, thy sonne lyueth.

Then he enquired of them the houre whe he began to amende.

So the father knewe &c.

And he beleued, and al his housholde.

nedes haue muche people in it, considering that he was ryche, and a manne of high autoritie, wheras Jesus after he had wrought many miracles amongst his owne countreymẽ and kinsfolkes, had muche a doe to wyn a fewe to the gospell. This is the second miracle that Jesus wrought when he was come out of Jewry into Galile, to the entent that he myght confirme agayne the former miracle whiche he had wrought in Cana, with doyng an other that was greater then it, and by the example of a prophane and heathen manne, might prouoke his owne countreymen vnto fayth: and did euen than by that occasion, as it were, pronosticate and signifie, bothe that the Jewes should be repelled for theyr incredulitie, and the Gentiles through faith receyued to the grace of the ghospell.

This is the seconde miracle.

¶ The .v. Chapter.

The texte.

¶ After this was there a feast daye of the Jewes, and Jesus went vp to Jerusalem. And there is at Jerusalem by the slaughter house, a poole (which is called in the Hebrue toungue Bethsaida,) hauing fyue porches, in which lay a great multitude of sicke folke, of blynd, halt, and withered, waiting for the mouyng of the water. For an Angell wente downe at a certain season into the poole, and stired the water: whosoeuer then first (after the stirring of the water) stepped in, was made whole, whatsoeuer disease he had.

After that Jesus had in this wyse begunne his matters among the Samaritanes, and the people of Galile, he goeth again to Jerusalem, euen about the feast of Penthechost, intendyng there by reason of the great resorte of people, to declare & setforth his autoritie to many, and to reproue ŷ Phariseis of their infidelitie, (whiche swelled in pryde through false perswasion of holines and knowledge) whom nowe the Samaritanes & heathen did so muche excell. At Jerusalm verily there was a poole or a certayne depe lake of water, whiche the Grekes calleth *probatica*, takyng that name of cattell, because the priestes were wonte there to washe the sacrifices that were to be offered: and of a lyke reason it is called in Hebrue Bethsaida, as a mã would say, a slaughter house, or an house of cattel. This lake hath fiue porches ouer it. In these porches lay a great numbre of men that were sicke of diuerse bodily diseases: and besydes that, there was a great multitude of folkes that were blynde, that halted, and were lame, abiding and lokyng for the mouyng of the water: for the Angell of the Lorde went downe at certaine times into the poole, and therwithall the water was moued: who so than (after the Angell had stiered the water) stepped first into the poole, he was made whole, were he sicke, or whatsoeuer bodily mayme he had. And euen at that tyme was this a figure of baptisme, wherby the filthines and diseases of our soules (be they neuer so deadly) are washed away at once, so often as the office of the baptiser & Gods operacion from aboue, be concurrant with the element of the water. There is no doubte but by this occasion muche people at that time were in that place, either of such as were gathered together there, to beholde and see what was doen, or els of them whiche dyd attende vpon the sicke folkes that lay in the fyue porches.

And there is at Jerusale by the slaughter house, a poole. &c.

And a certayne man was there, whiche had been diseased .xxxviii. yere: when Jesus sawe hym lye, and knewe that he nowe long time had been diseased, he sayeth unto hym: wylt thou be made whole? The sicke man aunswered him: Syr I haue no man, when the water is troubled, to put me into the poole, but in the meane time while I am aboute to come, an other steppeth downe before me. Jesus sayeth unto him: ryse, take vp thy bedde, and walke. And immediately the man was made whole, and toke vp his bed and walked.

The texte.

And because the miracle myght be the more notable, Jesus did chose out from among all the sicke folke, one whiche was of them all furthest frõ hope of recouery, whose disease was dangerouse and almoste incurable, and had also holden hym a long tyme: finally the saied manne moste of all lacked the helpe and succour of other men, & was so poore, that he was not able to prouide any man, by whom he might at due tyme be caryed downe into the water. Nor any one of the multitude was cured but only he, whose chaũce was first to goe downe into the water. This mans great misery must nedes setforth the greatnes of the miracle, and the same mans faith helped muche to the example of other. For the palsie had vexed him .xxx. yeres together: to teache vs that there is no disease of the soule so deadly and of so long cõtinuaunce, but that baptisme and faith in Jesu, may easily take it awaye. Therfore when that moste mercifull Jesus had beholden this sicke mã of the palsey, whom euery body pitied, lying withall his membres looce & shakyng by reason of that disease: & also perceyued that sickenes so muche the more to be dispayred of, for that it had holden already the miserable creature thirtie yeres together: Jesus, I saye, beeyng moued with mercy, sayed vnto hym: wilt thou be made whole? wyllyng to declare hereby to the standers by, the fayth & sufferaunce of that man, & also to make them besydes this, perceyue the violence of that disease, declaryng therby, howe no man can be cured of the vyces of the soule, vnles he hate his owne sickenes, & haue a desyre to be made whole. For it is not to be doubted but that he desired health, whiche so many yeres had lyen besydes that poole with a constante hope of health, and being so ofte disapointed, ceased not from his hope nor dispaired. Therfore the sicke man of the palsey, made no aunswer to Jesus question, and yet conceyuing some good hope vpon his so cherefull demaunde, sheweth that he lacketh no will, nor that he mistrusteth for all the greatnesse and long continuaunce of his disease, but that he should be healed, in case he were brought into ẏ poole: howbeit (he sayth) he lacketh a man to helpe to beare hym, who myght in due season cary hym into the poole, assone as the water should be stirred. For when other perceiued that ẏ poole was stirred, euery man made haste for himselfe to entre first & so to obteine alone the benefite of helth: but as for the sayed sicke man, being slowe by reason of his disease, & lackyng one to beare hym, dyd but in vayne crepe forth towarde the lake, forasmuche as an other had gon into it before hym. Truely the sickemannes meaning in this his saying was lowely and shamefastly, to desire Jesus that he beyng a man of strength, & piteouse as it semed by his woordes, would when time were, cary him downe into the poole: whiche thing he durst not requyre of hym opẽly: but yet after he had disclosed his necessitie, he shewed what hindred his helth, for the sicke man knew not Jesus. But Jesus being well pleased with the mans pacient sufferaũce, whiche did not as the moste parte of suche miserable creatures are wont to doe, that is to say, cry out, wishe himselfe dead, and curse the daye he was borne in: neyther was he offended with Jesus askyng

Whan Jesus sawe him lye. &c.

He sayed unto hym: wylte thou bee made whole?

Sir I haue no man. &c.

kyng him whether he would be made whole or no, and therfore did not saye or make any clamour that Jesus had him in derision: our Lord being in likewyse moued with his so constant hope to recouer his helth, and in conclusion willing to shewe, both that they which were healed by the mouyng of the foresayd poole, were cured by his power, ⁊ that it was an easy ⁊ ready thing for hym, euen only with a becke to take awaye all diseases, both of body and soule, he saied vnto the sicke man: ryse, take vp thy couche, and goe thy waye. And the woorde was no soner spoken, but the man was healed, ⁊ so healed, that not only he was clerely deliuered frō his disease, who els should haue been fainte and feble, like as they are wont to be, which are cured by phisike: but this man (I saye) was so throughly healed, ẏ without any stay of mans helpe, he rose vp vpon his fete, caried awaye his bed vpon his shoulders, ⁊ so beyng strong inough to beare his owne bed, did walke forth, and bare it home in all mennes sight, as a remembraunce of his long continued disease.

The texte. And the same daye was the Sabboth. The Jewes therfore sayed vnto him that was made whole: It is the Sabboth daye, it is not lawfull for the to carry thy bed. He answered them: he that made me whole saied vnto me, take vp thy bed and walke. Then asked they him: what man is that whiche saied vnto the, take vp thy bed and walke? He that was healed wist not who it was; for Jesus had gotten himselfe awaye, because that there was prease of people in that place.

And the same daye was the Sabboth. &c.

And it was the Sabboth daye whan the sicke man of the palsey dyd these thinges, wherat the Phariseis toke occasion to finde faulte with him: which Phariseis did superstitiously mainteine suche thinges of the lawe, as were carnall ⁊ geuen but for a time: and contēned those thinges which were chiefe and should still continue: amonges thē it was counted a wicked dede to doe any busines on the Sabboth daye, but to deceyue their neyghbour vpon the Sabboth daye, they toke it but for a trifle. They would haue it seme an vngodly thing that a poore sicke mā should cary away his bed vpon the Sabboth daye, but to grudge and enuy his helth, they thought it no faulte. They knew this man which was sicke of the palsey well inough, ⁊ that he had lyen sicke many yeres. They did well perceiue that he was nowe strong, and had no tokē or apparaunce of his disease in him. Of so great a miracle, they ought both to haue glorified God, and to haue reioysed in his behalfe which was cured, vnles they had been very wicked against god, ⁊ enuiouse toward their neighbour. Therfore these, like peruerters of true religion, fall in hand and chide with him, which caried awaye his couche. This is the Sabboth daye (say they) which ought to be kept with rest ⁊ quiet. It is not lawfull for the to cary awaye thy couche: he not dissemblyng the benefite that he had receyued, ⁊ to deliuer hymselfe from their enuy of that faulte, by the autoritie of Jesu, shewyng that he which coulde doe so great a thyng with his woorde, semed to be greater than either man or the Sabboth daye, the poore man (I say) maketh this answer to ẏ spitefull Jewes: he that made me whole with his very woorde only, commaunded me to cary awaye my couche ⁊ walke. When they heard this (wheras they ought by reason of the miracle to haue beleued it) they did not only enuy him that was cured, but also wēt about to deuise matter against him by whom he was cured: who is ẏ man (saye they) whiche badde thee cary awaye thy couche and walke? for they would haue burdened him with the faulte of breaking ẏ Sabboth day, as they had doen many tymes before. Nowe he that was healed, knewe not Jesus by name,

Tha asked they hym what man is that. &c.

but only

but onely by sight: howbeit at that tyme he coulde not shewe hym vnto them, because that Jesus after he had spoken to the sicke man of the palsey, immediately withdrewe hymselfe from the multitude: partely lest his presence shoulde more prouoke the Jewes enuy, and partly that he beeyng absente, the miracle should be the better knowen by the reporte of hym whiche had felte the benefite of health.

The texte.

Afterwarde Jesus found him in the temple, and sayde vnto hym: behold, thou arte made whole, synne no more, lest a wurse thyng happen vnto thee. The man departed and tolde the Jewes that it was Jesus whiche had made hym whole. And therfore the Jewes dyd persecute Jesus, and sought the meanes to slea hym, because he had doen these thinges on the Sabboth daye.

But after the miracle was made manifest and euidently proued, Jesus willyng that the autour therof also should be knowen, when he met with the man vpon whome he had bestowed that benefite of health, he sayed vnto hym: beholde, thou hast obteyned health, and art deliuered from the bodelye sickenes whiche came to the, by reason that thy soule was sicke, I haue cured thee of bothe those diseases. Take thou good hede hereafter that thou fall not agayne into thyne olde former synnes, and therby cause thy selfe to haue some wourse disease. Therfore after the man that was made whole knewe that this was he whiche before had commaunded him to carrye awaye his couche, and whiche nowe also hauyng testified himself to be the authour of health, did monish and warne hym to beware leste he shoulde fall agayne into some sorer and wurse disease, by committing and renewyng synne: also perceyuyng that his name was Jesus, the sayed manne went to the maliciouse and slaunderous Jewes, and tolde them howe it was Jesus whom he might thanke for his health, thinkyng that it should be profitable for manye, to haue hym knowen to all menne, whiche with a woorde could so helpe a desperate disease. And here nowe againe the Jewes peruerse and damnable frowardnes, sheweth it selfe: for wheras the Samaritanes had honourably receyued Jesus, by the reporte of one woman, whereas the people of Galilee beeyng euill spoken of commonlye among the Jewes, for theyr basenes & ignoraunce of the lawe, had geuen credite to Christ: when a great ruler also beyng a gentile, and an heathen man with all his familie and housholde for one onely miracle had confessed Jesus to be the sauioure of the worlde, yet the citizens of Jerusalem beyng proude as well of the noblenesse of theyr citie, as also of the wholy religion of theyr temple, and in lykewise auauntyng themselues to bee menne exactely learned in the lawe, picked quarels to Jesus, of suche purposed malice, that albeit the benefite of healthe was so euident that it coulde not be denayed, and so holy that it coulde not be found faulte with, (for what thyng is more holy then freely to geue healthe of body to a manne miserablye afflicted?) yet dooe they laye to Christes charge as a faulte, that without regard of the Sabboth daye he hath commaunded hym to carye awaye his couche, as who saye man had be made for the Sabboth daye, and not rather the Sabboth daye ordeyned for manne, or as though the ceremonies of Moses lawe oughte not euerye where to geue place to more holye preceptes and dueties. But what great blyndnes was this, to disdayne Jesus because he hadde healed a piteouse creature vpon the Sabboth daye? when they whiche thoughte themselues moste precyse kepers and obseruers of the lawe, were not afrayed to helpe vp theyr asse beyng fallen into the ditche

The man departed & tolde the Jewes that it was Jesus.

Because he doeth these thynges on the sabboth daye.

vpon the Sabboth daye. They falsly say that in helpyng the manne, God was offended, without whose helpe the man coulde not be cured, but in helpyng vp the asse they thought not the religion of the Sabboth day to be broken. This is the ouerthwart and disordered religion of the Jewes, imbracyng outwarde apparaunce of religion, and therby subuertyng the very perfeccion of true religion: stiffely obseruing the shadowes of the lawe, and with obstinate mindes persecutyng hym who was the cause that the lawe was wrytten. For they did not onely slaunder Jesus but also persecuted him, because he had doen an holy and good dede vpon the Sabboth daye.

The texte. And Jesus aunswered them: My father worketh hytherto, and I worke. Therfore the Jewes sought the more to kyll hym, not onely because he had broken the Sabboth, but sayed also that God was his father, and made hymselfe equall with God.

But Jesus, to shewe that he was maister of the Sabboth day and not bonde, the verye auctor, and not subiecte to it, therewithall declareth that the thyng wherof the Jewes slaundred hym, beyng sonne to the father of heauen, and one that did worke whatsoeuer he did by his fathers auctoritie, dyd also redounde to his fathers dishonour: Jesus (I saye) went about to represse and put awaie the Jewes false reporte of him with these wordes. My heauenly father (saieth he) whose religiouse wurshippers ye would seme to bee, who also made the sabboth daye for you, when after he had made the whole worlde in sixe daies, he rested the seuenth daye and wroughte not: he (I saye) did not so bynde hymself to rest and quiet, but that he maye worke whatsoeuer he wyll as oftē as it pleaseth him. For althoughe the sabboth daye dooeth yet stil endure, neuerthelesse he ceasseth not from his works wherby he gouerneth all thynges whiche he hath made, wherby also he causeth from tyme to tyme by procreacion, one thyng to succede of another: and finally wherby he restoreth thynges decayed. Therfore lyke as he doeth not cease dayly to do good both to men & all other thinges that he hath create (notwithstanding the religion and obseruaunce of the Sabboth day, wherin as scripture saieth, he ceassed from the creacion of thynges) so I, who am his sonne, hauyng both power and exaumple of hym to worke suche thinges as perteineth to mans saluacion, am not letted by the religious obseruacion of the Sabboth day, but I maye perfourme those thynges whiche my father hath commaunded me. But yf ye blame me for breaking of the Sabboth daye, by the same meanes ye condemne also my father, who geueth me both exaumple and autoritie to do these thynges. But yf ye thynke hym faultlesse and glorifie hym for restoryng health to a desperate creature: wherfore do ye laye to my charge the fault of breaking the Sabboth daie, and do not rather acknowledge the vertue and power whiche is greater than the keping of the Sabboth daie. I haue restored lyfe to a miserable man. And you craftely go about to procure my death for doyng so good a dede. These moste sacred wordes which Jesus spake, dyd so litle asswage the fury of the Jewes, that they were thereby the more sharpened and vehemently styrred against hym, sekyng occasion to putte him to death, because that nowe he dyd not only breake the Sabboth daie, but also dyd (as they sayed) wrongfullye take god to be his owne father: makyng himselfe equall with god both in his woorkes and auctoritie to do whatsoeuer he would.

Therefore the Jewes soughte the more to kill hym.

The texte. ¶ Than answered Jesus, and sayed vnto them. Verely, verely, I say vnto you: the sonne canne do nothyng of hymselfe, but that he seeth the father doe. For what soeuer he doeth that doeth the sonne also. For the father loueth the sonne, and sheweth hym all thynges that

hymselfe

hymselfe doeth, and he will shewe hym greater workes then these, bycause you shoulde meruayle. For lykewyse as the father rayseth vp the dead and quickeneth them, euen so the sonne quickeneth whom he wil. Neyther iudgeth the father any man, but hath cōmitted all iudgemente vnto the sonne, because that all men would honour the sonne, euen as they honour the father. He that honoureth not the sonne, thesame honoureth not the father, whiche hath sent hym.

But after our Lord Jesus had perceiued their malice, he procedeth further with them, and openeth more manifestely vnto them his power which he had receiued of God the father: therby to make them afearde to procede in theyr wicked crueltie: and doeth so tempre his communicaciō, that other whiles he talketh of certaine hye thinges, to signifie vnto thē couertly his diuine nature whiche was all one betwene God the father ⁊ hym: And other whiles againe in his communicacion he bringeth in lower thinges, to testifie his mãhed therby: that if the affinitie which was betwene him and them in that he was mã, would not stirre them to loue, at the leaste the maiestie of his godly power should let them from their wicked rashenesse: but yet he doeth so chalenge to hymselfe lyke power with his father, that neuertheles he attributeth to him the preeminence of autoritie. And he spake on this wyse: ye meruayle that I haue taken vpon me to be of equall power with my father in his workyng. This I doe assuredly promyse you, the sonne whiche doeth wholy depēde of the father can doe nothyng of hymselfe: forasmuche as he is not of hymselfe, but doeth that whiche he seeth his father doe. They haue both one will and one power: but the autoritie resteth in the father, from whence procedeth to the sonne whatsoeuer the sōne is, or may doe. Therfore whatsoeuer ẏ father doeth, thesame in likewise worketh the sonne by the equalitie of power communicate to him through his eternall natiuitie. Among men oftentymes children be vnlike in maners to theyr parentes, neyther is the fathers wyll and the sonnes all one, nor yet theyr power like: but in this case the thing is farre otherwyse. For the father loueth his sonne intierly, and hath begotten hym moste like to hymselfe, pouryng into hym egall power of workyng, and sheweth vnto the sonne howe to doe all thynges whiche he doeth himselfe. The exaumple cummeth from hym, but the workyng is common to both: he hath create the world, and he also gouerneth the world, yea euen vpon the Sabboth dayes. He hath made man, and it is he also that preserueth man vpon the Sabboth dayes. Therfore whosoeuer doeth slaundre the workes of the sonne, doeth iniurie to the father. These thynges whiche ye see me doe on the Sabboth daye, I doe them by the fathers autoritie, ⁊ at his appoyntment: but yf ye thinke it a thyng to be meruayled at and aboue mans power, to restore helth with a woorde to a man sicke of the palsey, the father (at whose commaundement the sonne doeth all thynges whiche he doeth) wyll declare that he hath shewed to his sonne greater workes than these, because ye may the more maruaile. For it is a thyng of farre greater power to raise the dead to life, than to restore helth to the sicke, yet the father hath geuen this power also to the sonne, and he hath geuen him it as his owne for euer: that as the father with his only becke rayseth the dead and calleth them agayne to lyfe, so the sonne also by that selfe power may call agayne to lyfe, whom he lust: for whatsoeuer the father doeth, he doeth it by the sonne: whatsoeuer the sonne doeth, he doeth it after the will of the father: and the father ⁊ the sonne haue both one wyll, lyke as they haue both one power. The moste hye and chiefe

The sonne can doe nothyng of himselfe. ⁊c

For the father loueth the sōne. ⁊c

chiefe autoritie of God is to iudge the worlde. For he is king and Lorde of all thynges. And yet hath he made his sonne partaker with hym of this whole power, vnto whom he hath geuē al power to iudge whatsoeuer is in heauē, in yearth & vnder the earth. Like as the father hath create all thynges by his sonne, gouerneth al thinges by his sonne, and hath restored al thinges by his sonne, so he iudgeth nothing but by his sonne: to the entent that eyther of thē may glorifie and honour the other. The father is knowen by his sonne, by whom he worketh: the sonne on the other partie declareth the maiestie of his father, from whence he hath whatsoeuer he worketh: so that eyther of them beyng knowen by the other, all men may honour the sonne as they doe the father. For it is mete that they which be egall in power and will, should be also felowes in honour. Thinke not that ye can haue the father mercifull vnto you, if ye be alienate & fallen from the sonne. Whosoeuer honoreth the father working in the sonne, he honoreth also the sonne working by the power of the father. And whosoeuer doeth not honour the sonne, which is moste intierly beloued and moste lyke to the father, that person doeth dishonour the father who sent the sonne to thintent he might through hym be honoured: for euery thyng is common betwene them, be it honour or dishonour. He that mistrusteth the sonne, mistrusteth also the father which sent hym into the worlde, by whose wyll and appoyntmente, he doeth all thynges that he doeth: and by whom also the father speaketh vnto the worlde. Lyke as the faithfull shall haue great reward, so the vnfaythfull shall haue no small punishmente.

Neyther iudgeth the father any man.

He that honoureth not the sonne. &c.

The texte.

Verily verily I saye vnto you: he that heareth my woorde & beleueth on him that sente me, hath euerlasting life: and shall not come into damnacion, but is scaped from death vnto life.

For this I tell you for certayne, whoso heareth my woorde and beleueth hym whiche both sent me, and speaketh in me, that persone hath alreadye euerlasting life. For whosoeuer is iustified from his sinnes, and lyueth to God thorowe righteousnes, he hath God and also life eternall: neyther shall he nede to feare the damnacion of eternall death, whiche is redie to receyue the vnfaithfull, yea rather which doeth alreadie possesse the vnfaithfull, but the true beleuer beyng clensed from his olde sinne by faith, passeth thorowe frō death to lyfe. For it is a greater thyng to rayse a soule that is dead by sinne, from death to life, than to restore a dead body to life: but the father hath geuen power to the sonne to doe both these thynges.

The texte.

Verily verily I saye vnto you, the houre shall come, and nowe it is, when the dead shall heare the voyce of the sonne of God. And they that heare, shall lyue. For as the father hath lyfe in hymselfe, so lykewyse hath he geuen to the sonne to haue lyfe in hymselfe, and hath geuen hym power also to iudge, because he is the sonne of manne. Maruayle not at this, for the houre shall come in the whiche all that are in the graues, shall heare his voyce, and shal come forth, they that haue doen good vnto the resurreccion of lyfe, and they that haue doen euil vnto the resurreccion of damnacion.

Be ye well assured of this, the tyme is now at hande, yea it is alreadie presente, that euen the dead also shall heare the voice of the sonne of God: and whoso heareth it, shal liue: for they being as it were raysed out of their slepe shall come forth out of their graues, and shall declare vnto you (beeyng astonished therwith) that they liue in very dede. In like maner also ỷ dead soules doe liue againe, if they will heare the voice of the sonne of God: but he doeth

not

not heare it, whiche heareth it without fayth.

In tyme to come all dead bodyes shall ryse agayne at the voyce of the sonne of God, now hauyng shewed a likelyhoode of the resurreccion to come by raysing of a fewe from death to lyfe: a greater matter is in hãde, to rayse vp soules from death to lyfe at his worde and call. As nothyng is more preciouse than lyfe, so nothyng is more godlike than to geue lyfe, or to restore thesame. There is no cause why any man should mistrust the power of the sonne, yf he beleue in the power of the father. No man doubteth but God is the fountaine of all life, from whence all liuing thinges eyther in heauen or earth, haue theyr lyfe: but as the father hath life in himselfe to geue it or restore it to whom he list, so hath he also geuen to his sonne to haue in himselfe yͤ fountaine of all lyfe. And besides that, hath geuen him power to iudge both quicke and dead. For by the sentence of the sayed sonne, whiche cannot be eschewed, they that haue obeyed his doctryne, shall go from hence to eternall lyfe: and contrarye, they that woulde not obey it, shall be appoynted and iudged to eternall punishment. Meruayle not that so great power is geuen to a man, consideryng that thesame is the sonne of God. The selfe thyng is nowe committed to hym, whiche he alwaye had common betwene hym and the father. Endeuour your selues in the meane tyme that thorowe fayth ye maye be wurthy to haue lyfe. For the tyme shal come that all whiche be dead and buryed, shall heare the almightie voyce of the sonne of God: and furthwith the bodyes shall liue agayne. Then shall they which haue been dead and buried, come out of theyr graues, to be rewarded in sundry sorte, eyther accordyng to theyr beliefe or vnbeliefe: for they whiche haue doen good workes in this lyfe shall than lyue agayne, to enherite immortall lyfe: on the other syde, those whiche haue doen euill here, shall lyue agayne to suffre paines of eternall death. And lyke as fayth is the well and fountayne of all goodnes, so is infidelitie the spryng of all euill.

The time shall come and nowe it is. &c.

For as the father hath life in hym selfe. &c.

Maruail not at this. &c.

I can of myne owne selfe do nothyng. As I heare I iudge, and my iudgemente is iuste, because I seke not myne owne will, but the wyll of the father, whiche hath sent me. If I should beare witnes of my self, my witnes were not true. There is another that beareth witnes of me, and I am sure that the witnes whiche he beareth of me is true.

The texte.

Neither is there cause why any man should slaundre the iudgement of the sonne, as though it were not indifferent. If the fathers iudgement cannot bee but indifferent, no more can the sonnes iudgement (whiche is all one with the fathers) be but in like maner indifferent. For the sonne iudgeth none otherwise but as the father hath appoynted and prescribed vnto him. Whoso feareth the fathers iudgement, ought also to feare the sonnes iudgemẽt. I can do nothing of my selfe. As I heare of my father, so I iudge, and therfore my iudgement is iust, because I haue no other will, but that whiche is my fathers, so that in no wyse there can be a corrupt will, wherof maye procede a corrupte iudgemente. Among men small credite is geuen to him whiche beareth witnes of himselfe, and he is counted arrogant and proude whiche by his owne reporte, attributeth great thynges to hymselfe. If I alone be myne owne witnes, then let my witnes be taken emong you to be but vayne and vntrue: but there is one which hath borne witnes of me, that is to saye John, to whom ye dooe attribute very muche in other thynges: but here nowe as vnstedfast men, ye dooe not credite him, wheras I knowe his witnes to be true, forasmuche as he hath not vttered it of hymselfe, but by the inspiracion of my father.

I can of mine owne selfe do nothyng.

yf I should beare wytnesse of my selfe.

Ye cannot deny but that Johns recorde and witnes is muche set by amonges you: your selues haue sent graue men vnto him, that by trustie men you might knowe of him (as of a moste true auctor) whether he were Messias or no. He did not take vpon hym that false prayse, whiche ye would haue attributed vnto hym, but confessed the trueth, openly testifying himselfe not to be the manne that he was taken for, but sayed that I was the Messias whiche shoulde take awaye the sinnes of the worlde, and geue lyfe to thesame.

The texte.

Ye sent vnto John, and he bare witnes vnto the trueth, but I receiue not the recorde of man. Neuerthelesse this thing I saye that ye maye be safe. He was a burning and a shining light, and ye would for a season haue reioyced in his light: but I haue greater witnes then the witnes of John, for the workes whiche the father hath geuen me to finishe, thesame workes that I do, beare witnes of me, that the father hath sent me. And the father himself which hath sent me, hath borne witnes of me. Ye haue not heard his voyce at any tyme, nor seen his shape, his woorde haue ye not abydyng in you: for whom he hath sent, hym ye beleue not.

But I receyue not the recorde of man. &c.

At the least his witnes (whom ye did so muche exteeme, that ye dyd beleue hym to be Messias) ought to haue been regarded among you, specially seyng it was not procured on my behalfe, but brought to light by your owne selues. I as concernyng my selfe haue no nede to bee commended by mannes witnes, but I do reporte vnto you Jhons witnes of me: not because I (who care nothyng for worldly glory) would be the more made of among you: but to thintent that you, whiche so muche regarde Johns auctoritie, shoulde credite me, of whom he hath borne witnes: wherby ye maye eschewe the condemnacion of infidelitie, and thorowe faith obteyne saluacion. John doubtles was a greate man, yet was not he that light whiche was promised to the world, but onlye a burnyng candell tynded at our fyre, and geuyng light by our light. And yet whereas ye ought at his tellyng and declaracion to haue made hast to ẏ true light which doeth alwaie illuminate euery man that cummeth into this world, ye had leauer for a shorte tyme to boast and glory in his lighte, than to embrace the true light which geueth euerlastyng glory, & is neuer darkened nor dyeth.

He was a burnyng & a shynyng light.

John gaue light before the sonne, as one that should immediatelye geue place to thesame and be derkened thorowe the shining of the true light. You woulde haue taken hym for Messias, which denyed hymselfe to be woorthy to vnleuse the latchet of Messias shooes. Why doe you then so litle regarde his witnes that he bare of me, seing in other thynges ye haue had so good an opinion of hym? I do not depende vpon Johns witnes, but yet I woulde wishe that ye woulde geue credite vnto it, that ye do not perishe thorowe infidelitie. And though ye do not beleue his witnes, yet haue I a more certaine testimonye of my selfe, that is to saye my fathers testimonie and witnes, who is greater than John, and whose witnes cannot be reproued.

But I haue greater witnes then the witnesse of John.

There is no recorde more sure than the very dedes that a man doeth: yf ye do perceyue those workes to be worthy for God whiche ye haue seen me dooe, they beare sufficient witnesse of me that I doe nothyng of my selfe, but by hym whiche for your saluacion hath sente me into the worlde, wherfore ye haue no cause whereby to excuse your infidelitie, and diminishe my credence, as who sayeth I alonely were myne owne witnesse, and did declare great thynges of my selfe. Ye haue Johns witnes, whiche among you is muche regarded and taken to be very weightie, howbeit in dede he rather nedeth my witnesse leste he seme to haue borne false witnes. Ye haue the testimonie of my workes, so

For the workes whiche my father hath geuen me to finishe. &c.

that nowe ye nede not to beleue any mannes sayinges when ye looke vpon the dedes themselfe. And if all this dooe not satisfie your vnbeliefe, yet haue ye hearde at Jordane the voice of my father from aboue bearing witnes of me. But yet my father (forasmuche as he is a spirite,) neither hathe voice whiche maye be perceyued with mannes eares, nor fourme or shape that maye bee seen with bodely iyes. For Moses did neyther heare him, nor see hym in the veraye fourme of his owne mere nature as you suppose he did. Onely his sonne hath seen hym, and heard him after that sorte. yet neuertheles he hath made himselfe knowen to your senses, by some kynde of voyce, and thorowe some manner of fourme. He spake to the Prophetes, and by the Prophetes hath spoken to you. He hath spoken to John, and by John to you, but vnto me he hath spoken as he is of his owne very nature, and by me he speaketh vnto you. If ye can make no excuse but that John did beare playne & manifest witnesse, why do ye not beleue hym? If ye thinke that God in very dede did speake, and was seen of Moses and the Prophetes, wherfore do ye not credite those thynges which he hath spoken by them?

Ye haue not hearde his voyce at anye tyme nor seen his shape.

¶ Searche the scriptures, for in them ye thinke ye haue eternall lyfe. And they are they, whiche testifie of me, and yet will ye not come to me that ye mighte haue lyfe. I receyue not prayse of men, but I knowe you that ye haue not the loue of God in you. I am come in my fathers name, and ye receyue me not, if an other come in his owne name him will ye receiue. Howe can ye beleue, whiche receiue honour one of another, and seke not the honour that cummeth of God? Do not thinke that I will accuse you to my father. There is one that accuseth you, euen Moses, in whome ye truste. For had ye beleued Moses, ye would haue beleued me, for he wrote of me, but yf ye beleue not his wrytynges, howe shall ye beleue my woordes?

The texte.

Verely ye beleue that the scriptures are come from God: and albeit you do diligentely occupie your selues in searchyng of them, and put the hope and felicitie of your lyfe in them, yet euen as ye would not beleue John, (to whom in other thynges ye gaue very great credite,) when he bare witnes of me: so you beleue not the very scriptures in that whiche is the chiefe poynte of all: for they promyse life, but through me.

The father doeth there beare witnesses of me, and promiseth that he wil send his sonne, by whom men shall be saued. But as ye haue heard John and not beleued hym, and also the voice of the father and not geuen credite vnto it: so neither the witnesse of the lawe nor of the Prophetes sticketh in your myndes. And although ye haue theyr bookes euer in your handes, and their woordes alwaye in your mouthes, yet doe ye reiecte hym whome those scriptures dooe promyse: and doe not beleue hym whome the father hath sent accordyng to the promyses of the Prophetes: and wheras there is none other entrie into life but by me, who hathe been approued to you by so manye testimonies, yet ye wyll not forsake all thing and come to me, wherby ye maie obtain life withoute difficultie. For the gate and entrie of saluacion is to haue beleued the sonne whō the father sent. There is no cause why I should seke for worldlye glory amonges you by the testimonie of John, or the Prophetes, but I am sory for youre destruccion, whiche through your incredulitie dooe in maner enuye your owne saluacion. And besides that I leaue you no maner of excuse to make for your selfe, if you will not beleue: for I haue brought foorth thus manye witnesses, whiche in other thynges be of veray great auctoritie among you: and onelye in matters concernyng me (for whose cause all thynges wer written and spokẽ,) ye doe not alowe them: ye pretende to wurship and loue God, ye haue the prophetes in reuerence by whom he spake: and yet you do despise him, which was promised of God: and doeth declare himselfe by his workes what he is. This is a playne argument that ye wurship God with counterfaicte holynes, and that ye loue not God in dede, whom the lawe commaundeth you to loue with all the power of your soule, and your strẽgth, inasmuche as ye contemne and regarde not his sonne. Therfore your infidelitie is not for wante of witnesses, but for lacke of true loue towardes God. You loue worldly glory, you loue money, you loue pleasures, and to get these thynges you misuse your selues with false pretence of religion. But ye persecute the sonne of God: because he teacheth those thynges, whiche be contrary to these your wicked desyres, albeit his teachyng agreeth with the will of the father. These thynges declare that ye loue not god with your herte. For he whiche loueth doeth also beleue and obeye: and whoso loueth the father cannot hate his moste entierly beloued sonne. In lyke maner he that loueth the sender, cannot mislyke and contemne the messanger, specially consideryng I couet neither glory, kyngdome, nor richesse among mẽ, but onely the glory of my father. And also I couet that, to thentent you maye be saued. You see workes wurthy for God, and yet I doe not ascribe the worldlye prayse to my selfe, but to my father, who worketh by me. Therfore although ye would seme religiously to wurship my father: yet ye do not receyue me who am come in his name, and doe none other thyng but that whiche he hath prescribed vnto me. And looke howe peruersely you do discredite me, who cummyng in my fathers name do freely offer lyfe and saluacion: euen so fondely shall ye beleue whosoeuer cummeth in his owne name, presumpteously takyng vpon hym the glory of God, and therewith attendeth his owne busines and not Gods, bryngyng suche thynges vnto you as maye leade you into eternal death. If ye loue God, why do ye murmure and crie out agaynst him that seketh his glory? If ye loue euerlastyng lyfe, why do ye reiecte the autour of lyfe? If ye accompte hym wicked whiche chalengeth the glory of God to hymselfe, wherefore then do ye receyue hym whiche doeth presume falsly to take vpon him the glorye of God? what is then more to be sayed, but that ye must nedes confesse your holynes towardes God to be but fayned? ye wurship God with woordes, with outwarde obseruaunces, and ceremonies, but ye hate hym in very dede: ye haue alwaye in your mouth, the temple of the Lord, the temple of the Lord, the temple of the Lorde, but your herte is set vpon rychesse. Ye talke muche of the lawe and the Prophetes, but in your herte ye couet and desire worldly prayse: you bee euer speakyng of these woordes of the lawe, loue thy Lorde God with al thy herte, & thy neighbour as thyselfe, but in your hert remaineth enuy, hatred, and manslaughter. To deserue prayse before God is the true prayse in dede. True godlynes is to geue and ascribe all glory to god. Therfore howe can ye beleue me settyng furth to you none other thyng but gods glory, when you despisyng the true glory which procedeth from god, goe about to seke false glorye and prayse amongst men, one of you flatteryng another, and enuying that God shoulde haue his owne due prayse and glorye? sekyng also vnder a false pretence, to be thought holy before men, and not regardyng the sincere and pure conscience whiche

Ye haue not the loue of god.

whiche

whiche God beholdeth, whiles ye trauaile to get the vile lucre of this worlde, ye lose eternall life. Therfore it is no meruail though God be angrie with you whom ye resiste so stubbernely. Thynke not that I, of any desire to reuenge the contempte ye haue me in, will accuse you to my father. I nede not to bee youre accuser. Moses hymselfe shall accuse you, whose autoritie you amongeste you take to be right holy, & in whō ye put veray great trust, takyng whatsoeuer he wrote as a thyng spoken of Gods owne mouth. But as ye pretended but a feigned reuerence towardes John, whose witnesse concernyng me ye doe not beleue, and as ye doe shew your selfes to regarde the saiynges of the Prophetes but feynedly, in that ye doe nowe persecute hym, whome they haue promised, finally as ye do vntrewly wurship god, whose workes ye doe not acknowlage, whose sonne ye doe hate: So ye doe honour Moses but after a feined sort: whose autoritie ye sette litle by in yͤ thyng, wherein ye ought moste to regarde him. And yet euen veraye he hath written of me, for when youre elders beeyng agreued with the terrible voyce of God, and with the perillous fyer, made intercession that from thenceforth they might no more heare the voyce of God, or proue that dreadfull fyer, God dyd graunte their requeste, and promysed Moses that he would rayse an excellente Prophete lyke vnto hymself, whiche shoulde cumme of your brethren, whose gentle and pleasant voyce not fearyng men with threatenyng, but alluryng theim to saluacion, it shoulde behoue the to heare. But God did threaten punishement to him that would not obey thys Prophetes woordes, saiyng: Truely I will be reuenged of hym whiche wyll not heare the woordes that he shall speake in my name. And agayn he cōmaundeth him to be destroied whiche wyll heare a Prophete cummyng in his owne name, and speakyng suche thinges as God hath not commaunded hym.

Therefore none other shal more accuse you before god, than Moses your frend, whose writinges ye contemne: he hath promysed that I shoulde bee quiete, gentle, and should speake all thynges accordyng to Goddes will. Such a one am I beeyng here presente, and yet ye refuse me: he also commaundeth that persone to be killed, whiche shall cum in his own name and speake of his own spirite. Such a one doe you embrace & make much of, for the hatred ye beare to me, as one that is more agreable to your wicked desires. Therefore you be not onely stubberne agaynst me, but also agaynst Moses hymselfe, whose promyses you do not credite. For truely yf ye beleued Moses, ye would credite me also, whom he hath promysed, and whose saiyng he hath commaunded to bee beleued. Therfore it is no meruaile though ye beleue not my woordes whom ye doe openly contemne as one that is but a meane simple person, when ye geue no credite to Moses writynges, whose autoritie ye woulde seme to haue in so great estimacion, and of whom ye haue so notable an opinion. With these saiynges our Lorde Jesus beyng the light and truth, did reproue and disclose the feyned religion of the Jewes, a thyng as muche contrarye to the godlinesse of the ghospell as may bee, to the entent he would make it euidently knowen to all menne, that they through theyr owne faulte and deserte didde perishe, whiche would not be moued with so many recordes and testimonies of hym, nor be allured by his benefites & gentle woordes, nor feared with his threatenynges, neither prouoked to fayth by the desire of eternall life, nor yet turne from theyr infidelitie for feare of hell. But if Jesus hadde spoken these thinges amonge the Samaritanes or the Gentiles, specially causing his woordes the better to be beleued through myracles, they would haue been conuerted to penaunce. But the Scribes and Priestes of Hierusalem make no aunswere to these thynges which they could not reproue: but yet neuertheles they doe stil remaine in theyr murderous thoughtes: & procure his deathe, whiche offreth to them the benefites of eternall life.

The.vi.Chapter.

The texte. After these thinges, Jesus wente his waie ouer the sea of Galile, whiche is the sea of Tiberias: and a great multitude folowed him, because they sawe his myracles, which he did on them that were diseased. And Jesus wente vp into a mountaine, and there he sate with his disciples. And Easter, a feaste of the Jewes was nye.

Owe therfore, to geue place for a tyme to their furie, and to withdrawe hymselfe from amongest those that swelled in pride through an opinion they hadde in their false feyned religion, and in theyr vnexperte knowledge of the lawe, Jesus presented hymselfe to more plaine meanyng men: goyng not now again into Cana, but into that Galile whiche lyeth beyonde the great lake Tiberias, takyng that name of the citie Tyberias, whiche citie Tiberius the Emperoure buylded vpon that ryuers syde. And a great noumbre of folke folowed hym goyng thither partely beeyng moued so to doe of the great minde they hadde to his myracles, because they hadde seen him healpe men of theyr diseases by a rare and straunge power, partelye because that they whiche were sicke of vncurable diseases mighte bee holpen of hym, and partely for that they desired to heare his doctrine. But when he sawe the feruencie of that disordred and confused multitude to bee so great, that forgettyng prouision of vitels, they wente farre into the deserte with him: now to make his disciples mete for the myracle (to whome moste specially he would haue the thing that he should worke to be knowen and imprinted in their hertes, for as yet they were but rude and ignoraunte:) Jesus I saye, gote himselfe secretlye vp into the mountaine, and his disciples with hym: teachyng euen by the same dede, that albeit he whiche professeth hymselfe to be a shepeheard of the people, doe accumpany hymself often with the meane and lowe sorte to profite them, yet it behoueth suche a one to eleuate and lifte vp his mynde to more high thinges, so oft as through holye studie or prayer his mynde is to bee stirred and prouoked to the contemplacion of heauenlye thynges. The people abideth benethe vpon the plaine grounde, and onelye Jesus disciples wente vp with hym, for it behouethe bishops to bee withoute all vile care of temporall thynges: and as menne that haue mounted higher, to contemne those thynges whiche the ignoraunte people setteth muche by. Therfore Jesus beyng sumwhat separate from the people, setteth hym downe on the hyll, accumpanied with his disciples: but so that he might loke vpon the people: for bishops ought not to goe backe from Christe, although the comon people sticke muche to lower thynges.

And in dede aboue all in the hyll is conuenient for men to sitte, that is to saye, in studye of celestiall thynges muste menne take reste, and as for lower and inferiour matters (whiche thynges are to bee handled and gone aboute as charitie, citie, and tyme requireth) men muste rather walke therin, then sitte downe and reste. Nor our mynde ought not so to be delited in the contemplacion of hye thinges, that we fall to be carles of our common flocke: for the solitarinesse of bishops ought to be to thys ende, that they more liuelye and better enstructed, myght repayre againe to looke to the peoples profite. Neyther doeth it beseme them whiche are in Christes stede to leaue counpany for bankettyng, wanton-nesse of bodye, dicyng huntyng, or suche lyke inordinate pleasures: but through quietnes to renewe the mynde (whiche before was muche buisied and weried with more lowe and meane buisinesse.) And to make the same by pure desyres, instant praier, by holy studye and deuoute communication, mete for the offyce and ministerie of the ghospell. Moreouer whylest these thynges were dooen in Galile, Easter was at hande: A feast which the Jewes kepte verai religiously. Wherfore if he had sought for to haue bene noted of theyr religion, it had been more conuenient for hym now at this tyme, to haue been at Hierusalem, but to shewe sum likelihood that in tyme to cum theyr house should bee leaft desolate, after the Jewes wer once becum rebels against God through incredulitie, and also that after the holy ghospell should be openly setfurth, al theyr carnal wur-shippyng of God should ceasse, and there finally the feaste of Easter to be moste specially celebrate, whereas (worldly affeccions renounced and put away) the mynde shoulde be brought vnto the loue of celestiall thynges: vpon these consi-deracions (I saye) Jesus had rather bee among the people of Galile in deserte solitarily, then at Hierusalem in the temple.

When Jesus then lift vp his ieys, and saw a great cumpany cum vnto him, he saieth vnto Philip. Whence shal we bye breade, that these maie eate? This he saied to proue him, for he himself knew what he would do. Philip aunswered him. Two hundred peny worth of bread are not sufficiente for them that euery manne maie take a litle.

The texte.

Nowe then when Jesus had opened his iyes and looked vpon the people, perceiuyng the noumbre to bee exceadyng greate, he so prepared the myndes of his disciples towardes true credence of the myracle, that fyrst he woulde haue the lacke of meate well marked and considered of them, and also that the mul-titude whiche stoode beneath in their sight was innumerable: besydes thys that there was but verye fewe loaues whiche they themselfes with their own handes shoulde take vnto Jesus, and from hym distribute the same among the people. Finallye, howe that there shoulde bee leafte manye baskettes full of broken meate, whiche the same disciples should gather together as fragmentes of the feaste: And all this woulde Jesus haue them to consider, because they should not be ignoraunte in the thyng, neyther afterwarde forget the same. For he knewe that as yet his disciples wer but of smal vnderstandyng and for-getfull. Therefore to proue what mynde Philip was of, and little by little to make hym beleue better the myracle, Jesus sayeth vnto hym: where shall we bye breade that this great noumbre of people maye haue sumwhat to eate? Our Lorde Jesus asked these thinges, not that he was ignorant what store of breade and other vitels they hadde, but partelye (as was sayed euen nowe) to cause his Apostles more aduisedlye to considre the myracle: and partelye also ỷ all men myght knowe howe without care of bodilye sustenaũce the disciples were whiche folowed Christe, and howe well contented with common and homely meate. But Philip, as yet lookyng for no myracle, althoughe he hadde

Where shal we by bread that these maye eate.

FFf.ii. seen

seene Christe before turne water into wyne at the mariage, when he wayed well how lytle money they hadde to succoure theymselfes withall, and further what a great multitude of men there was, he aunswered: Syr, why speake you of byinge breade? I assure you, in case we bestowe twoo hundred pence in bread, yet wyll it not be enough, I meane for to satisfie these menne, which by reason of long abstinence are veray muche an hungred, it wil not so relieue them that euerye one eatyng but a litle, maye escape thereby the peryll of famishyng.

The texte,

One of his disciples. Andrew (Simon Peters brother) saieth vnto him: there is a lad here, whiche hath fiue barly loaues, and twoo fishes: but what are they among so manye? And Jesus saied: make the people sitte downe. There was muche grasse in that place. So the men sate downe in noumbre about fiue thousand. And Jesus toke the bread and whan he had geuen thankes, he gaue to the disciples, and the disciples gaue to them that were set downe, and likewise of the fishes as muche as they would.

When Philyp had spoken thus, Andrewe (brother to Symon Peter) beyng sumwhat wyser, lifted vp hys mynde to some hope of a myracle. Howbeit as yet with no full confidence, for he had seene the water turned into wyne and therefore dyd not altogether mistruste but that the loaues also myght bee multiplied, neuertheles as he thought, none otherwyse then after a moderate porcion, so that of fewer loaues, the lesse bread, and of mo loaues more breade shoulde encrease. Whereas Jesus (of trueth) had no nede at all of anye matter to make breade of, who createth euen of nothyng what he wyll, and when he will. Andrewe therefore sayed, here is a certayne boye that hathe fyue barlye loaues and two fishes, but what can so litle do to so great a multitude, beyng alreadye hungrie?

When Jesus sawe they perceyued the lacke of meate, and pondered what a multitude there was, he entendyng to stiere vp theyr myndes to locke for a myracle, commaunded his Apostles to see the people placed and set downe vpon the grasse, whereof in that place was great plentye. The disciples doe not nowe aunswere againe, and saye: what nedeth it to haue them sette downe when we lacke meate to sette before them? For that whiche we haue in store will not suffice our selfes, but simply they without more a doe obeyed Jesus commaundemente, and caused the people to sitte downe in ordre, as it wer to a feaste. The people also lyke simple playne men, trusted wel, and did obedientely as the Apostles badde them, although they sawe no prouision of meate.

Jesus saieth, make the people sitte downe,

There was that sate downe almost fiue thousand. Jesus therfore toke the fiue barly loaues, and when he (after his customable maner) hadde geuen thankes to the father, he brake theim, and so toke them to his disciples to distribute the same vnto the people, then framyng and fashionyng theim, that by thys corporall similitude they should enure theimselues to playe well the shepeherdes: and beyng ministers of the ghospel, to feede and norishe the soules of Christes flocke with spirituall foode. For he is that very bread, which came down from heauen, to geue eternal lyfe to them that desirously eate thereof. This breade verily do byshops bestowe and ministre vnto the people, but from no where els, then out of Christes handes, and not without rendryng thankes to the father of heauen, of whome we must knowlage our selfes to haue receyued whatsoeuer apperteineth to the saluacion of mankynde.

And Jesus toke the bread,

And vnto whom as to the very auctour, our Lorde Jesus referred all notable thynges whiche he dydde here in this worlde, monishyng vs therewith by the way, that in case we should haue any excellente vertue in vs , we shoulde not chalenge the prayse thereof, but clerelye putte from our selues all the glorye of thesame and geue it vnto God, from whom procedeth al thynges that of right deserue prayse.

Furthermore, Jesus dyd euen here nowe thesame thing by the two fishes, that he had before doen by the fyue loaues, deliueryng it vnto his disciples, and at his wyl and pleasure, the meat did encrease betwene the handes of the dealer of it, so muche in quantitie as he knewe would suffice theim all, yea and also a great deale more, to make the myracle the better to be beleued.

When they had eaten enough, he saieth vnto his disciples: Gather vp the broken meate whiche remaineth, that nothing be loste. And they gathered it together, and filled twelue baskettes with the broken meate of the fiue barlye loaues: whiche broken meate remained vnto them that had eaten . Then these men (when they had seen the myracle that Jesus did) saied. This is of a trueth thesame Prophete, that should cumme into the worlde.

The texte.

Finally, when that great cumpany was well filled with meate, Jesus settyng foorth the certaintie of that dede by an other profe, leste anye manne shoulde fynde faulte and impute the thyng to bee a delusion or a countrefayte thyng, sayed thus to his disciples: Gather vp the broken meate whiche is lefte of the feaste, that nothyng bee loste. And they founde so muche broken meate after euerye one had eaten his fylle, as fylled twelue baskettes: The bountifull goodnes of Jesus augmented that scarcitie and small store of vitayles (that is to wete, of fyue loaues and two fishes) into this so greate plentye, to teache vs by the way that we shoulde not niggardlye do our charitie vnto the poore. But by this his myracle muche more he teacheth howe that it behoueth hym whiche hath taken vpon hym the charge to feede the flocke of Christe, largely to bestowe oute of the ryche treasourye of holy scripture whatsoeuer perteineth to enstructe, to counsayle, to coumforte and encourage theym that nedeth suche foode.

Moreouer, when they whiche had eaten enough at full, were not ignoraunt howe there was at the fyrst founde out but fyue barleye loaues and two fishes , and hadde alreadye seene so manye baskettes full of broken meate remayne, they begonne highlye to reporte of Jesus, saying : Truelye this is thatsame Prophete whiche hath long tyme been looked for, to cumme into the worlde. This is euen the nature of the common people , they dooe sooner feele the benefite of the bely then of the mind. They had seen greater myracles, yet did they neuer geue hym so hye a prayse. Plentye of meate could cause them speake thus.

When Jesus therefore perceiued that they would cum, and take him vp to make him a king, he departed again into a mountaine himselfe alone. And when euen was now cum, his disciples wente downe vnto the sea, and gat vp into a ship, and came ouer the sea vnto Capernaum. And it was now darke, and Jesus was not cum to them.

The texte.

And at this presente, (because as yet they were ignoraunte and grosse, lookyng that Messias shoulde cum to get hymselfe a worldelye kyngdome) they did dyd consulte among theimselfes to take Jesus, and make hym their kyng, well assuryng theimselfes thereof, that in case they myghte haue suche a kyng, they should haue plentye of all thynges, vittayles enough, riches, libertye, and other worldly commodities aboundantly.

But Jesus whiche did couet an other maner of kyngdome, and came to teache vs to contemne riches, pleasures, and worldely glorye, knowyng right well what they entended and wente aboute, dydde nowe agayne secretelye conuey hymselfe to the hyll (from whence he came downe to the people.) From theym that called hym to a kyngdome, he withdrewe hymselfe priuelye alone, so that no manne coulde perceiue his goyng awaye, but of his owne free will he meteth theym that pulleth hym to the crosse, therein geuyng a playne exaumple to them that shoulde hereafter be his deputies. For he can neuer preache the ghospell purelye, that loueth a worldelye kyngdome and pompe, whiche thynges spirituall shepeherdes ought so litle to seeke for, that it behoueth them to refuse those thynges, though they be freelye geuen them. For the kyngdome of the worlde agreeth not with the kyngdome of heauen, no more verilye then darkenesse and light accordeth.

When the disciples had long looked for theyr maister in the hyll, and euenyng was nowe at hande, leste the darke nyght should cum vpon them beeyng in deserte, they wente downe to the lake to rowe ouer vnto the citie Capernaum (for Jesus had there a litle place to repose hymselfe in) well hopyng eyther that he in summe other shyppe should mete them as they wer sailyng ouer the lake, or at the leaste they shoulde fynde hym in the citie. And it was darke already when they prepared theyr passage ouer: neyther dyd Jesus in the meane while cumme to his disciples, beyng long and much looked for of them, knowing wel enough howe much they were agreued with his absence.

But Jesus mynde was through his absence to make his disciples more desyrous of hym, and therewyth also to teache in what great daungier we be in, what great darknes, what worldely trouble hangeth ouer vs, as often as we be disseuered from Jesus. In the meane whyle a matter was prepared for a greater miracle.

The texte. ¶ And the sea arose with a great wind that blew. So when they had rowen about a xxv. or xxx. furlonges, they sawe Jesus walkyng in the sea, and drawyng nighe vnto the shippe, and they wer afraied. But he saieth vnto them: it is I, be not afrayed. Then would they haue receiued him into the shippe, and immediatly the shippe was at the lande whither they went.

The lake was so great that they called it the sea, which the nyght made more terrible. And to make it moe waies daungerous then one, they hadde the windes so outragious agaynste theim, that the lake was exceadyng rough withall: yet neuerthelesse the disciples were so desirous of theyr mayster, that they dydde aduenture to rowe vpon the water. Nowe therefore, when they were farre from the lande and hadde rowed vpon a fyue and twenty, or thyrtie furlonges, being almoste in despaire of theyr liues, oure Lorde Jesus was cumme nighe vnto theym vnlooked for: notwithstandyng the darkenesse they se hym goyng on foote vpon the sea, as thoughe he had troden vpon the harde grounde, to declare hymselfe thereby lorde not onely of the yearth, but of all elementes also. And of trueth the charitie of the ghospell hath iyes and can see euen in the darke, neyther is there anye nyght where Jesus is presente, nor anye

deadly

deadly tempeste whereas he is nygh, that maketh all thinges clere and caulme. But nowe when our Lord was cum nighe vnto the shyppe: the disciples were sodaynly aferde, and because they could not well see and perfectly discerne in the darke, they nowe suspect the thyng to be but as it were a vision in the nyght, a ghoste or suche lyke as the vulgar people beleue many to bee seen of theym that sayle by nyght.

Neuerthelesse, to put theym out of all feare with speakyng vnto theym in his owne propre voyce (whiche they knewe, and were well accustomed therewith) Jesus sayd vnto them: it is I, bee not afraied, signyfiyng therby that such as haue the assistence of our Lorde Jesus, oughte not to bee afrayed of worldly trouble, bee it neuer so great and fierse. All they truelye whiche in simplicitie and plainnes of heart do constātly and faythfullye depende vpon hym, hath hym presente euen to the worldes ende. Now the disciples being boldened at the voyce of theyr maister, were desirous to take hym into the shyppe: for euen they verily were sumwhat afrayed, whose truste and hope yet was bothe weake and vnconstant. But to thintent that our Lord Jesus myght declare to his disciples the whole thing ẏ was doen, to be wrought by his diuine power, and that the storme was not swaged and ceassed by casualtye, the shippe which incontinentelye before was tossed hyther and thyther a ferre of from the shore, did sodainly ariue to the lande, whereunto they entended to goe. The disciples (whose faythe was to be framed and confirmed by all the wayes that could be possible) by these proues and tokens dydde more diligentelye imprinte in theyr myndes this myracle.

The daie folowing when the people (whiche stoode on the other side of the sea) sawe that there was no ship there, saue that one wherin his disciples wer entred, & that Jesus went not in with his disciples into the ship, but that his disciples wer gon awaie alone, howbeit there came other ships from Tiberias vnto that place, where they did eat bread after the Lord had geuen thankes. When the people sawe that Jesus was not there, neyther his disciples, they also tooke shipping and came to Capernaum seeking for Jesus. The texte.

And in dede the people were not altogether ignoraunt of this straunge thing and myracle, for the nexte daie after these thynges were dooen when the multitude whiche remayned styll on the other syde of the water, sawe that none other shyppe was there, saue that one wherein the disciples went ouer, whom when they sawe shootyng on the shore, they were well assured that Jesus wente not with his disciples into the shippe, but that they went awaye alone: The people (I saye) merualled to what place he hadde secretelye withdrawen hymself, forsomuche as notwithstandyng the multitude whom he had fed the day before dyd muche desire and long for hym, yet in the mornyng dydde he no where appeare: But yet supposyng that he woulde not be very long absente from his disciples, whiche were alreadye gon ouer, euen these folkes also were determynyng to rowe ouer the water to proue yf they could fynd hym on the other side. And there was presente at the same tyme certayne shyppes which had cum, not from Capernaum, but from Tyberias, a citie also standyng by the sea syde, nigh vnto the place where they had been fedde, and eaten their fil with. v. barly loaues, wherewith beyng satisfied they gaue thankes to god whiche had sente to his people suche a prophete. Therefore when these shyps were in a readinesse to carrye ouer the people, and Jesus that was muche soughte for, coulde no where bee founde, the people tooke shippyng there to seke Jesus, because he had there a restyng place, and because they also knewe that the Apostles were sailed ouer thyther.

The texte. And when they had found him on the other side of the sea, thei said vnto him: Rabbi, when camest thou hither? Jesus answered them and saide: Verelye, verely, I saie vnto you: ye seke me, not because ye sawe the myracles, but because ye did eat of the loaues, & wer filled. Labour not for meate that peryssheth, but for that whiche endureth vnto euerlasting life, whiche meate the sonne of man shall geue vnto you. For him hath god the father sealed.

When they had founde Jesus here, and sawe that he had passed ouer the lake, and knowyng righte well that there was no shippe to conueigh him ouer, muche meruailyng by what meanes he coulde passe ouer the water, asked of him, saiyng: Maister when camest thou hyther? desiring to gather by the very time howe he hadde passed ouer. For they supposed euen this thing also to bee doen by myracle, lyke as he had the day past fedde a very great multitude. But the feruencie whiche they had the daye before, wherby the other daye they went about to force him to a kingdome euen agaynste his will, was now well cooled. And leste Jesus should seme to auaunte his owne power, he maketh no aunswere to these thynges: to the intente they shoulde be more credibly enfourmed of the myracle by his disciples, and also by euidente proues thereof. But Jesus dyd sore rebuke and earnestely reproue the affeccion of the multitude (as not onely vnconstaunte, but also rude and grosse, and farre vnmete for the doctryne of the ghospell,) because that albeit they hadde seene greatter myracles whiche dyd more proue his diuyne power, yet neuerthelesse one plenteous diner dyd more stirre them, then the desire of eternal saluacion. And they sette more by bodily susteinaunce (wherewith that thyng is now and then and but for a time releued, whiche within a whyle after shall perishe) then they dydde hungre after that meate, without whiche the soule dothe euerlastingly perishe.

Finally, he didde correcte their grosse iudgemente of him: whereby they thought he did worke his miracles, to the intente to deserue therewith, at the rashe peoples hand, a worldly kyngdome: whereas Christe in veraye deede (accordyng as the tyme required) didde shewe sum proufe of his diuine power by certaine miracles, for none other cause surelye but that throughe sensyble and bodilye thinges, he myghte cause more credit to bee geuen vnto his doctrine: whiche promysed those thynges that cannot bee perceiued with bodilye senses. And by this waie also to bring vp those (that were yet rude and weake) by certaine degrees, to the capacitie of more hye thynges. Like as a trustie Maister would wishe, that (if it coulde be) his scholer shoulde foorthwith take and vnderstande his whole science, yet for a time he fourmeth and fashioneth the rude and vnframed wytte wyth certayne prynceples, vntyll he haue broughte hym vp to the perfecte knowlege of his facultie, so that he shal after neede none of those introduccions. And though the teacher dooe not teache the veraye letters and his fyrste rules without werines, yet he doth beare that tediousnesse and weare it awaye with the hope of profityng his scholer, labouryng all the wayes he can, to get him soone out of those course principles. Therefore Jesus to declare here also his godhead, in that he knewe theyr thoughtes, when he sawe the people hadde nowe agayne recourse vnto hym, for the desire of suche myracles whiche shoulde rather fyll the bellye then instructe the mynde: he tooke occasion of the meate that he hadde once geuen them, to teache theym

what

what foode they ought to haue moste desired. The effecte of his saiyng was this. Verely this thing is true (saieth he) whiche I wyll tell you: ye calle me maister, not because ye bee muche desirous of my doctryne whiche is all spirituall, but because ye seeke for worldelye pleasures and small commodities, whiche are more estemed of you then thynges whiche dooe farre excelle them. And at this presente ye dooe seeke me with great affeccion, and yet (i wisse) not so muche for to see myracles, whiche ought in dede to allure you to mynde celestiall thynges, but yesterdayes chere dooeth more prouoke you, then that ye bee enamoured of goddely power. And ye coumpte it a great matter if a manne fede your bodye without your charge. It is but a small matter to feede this bodie, that otherwyse muste needes decaye and bee destroied: neyther shal they that bee desirous of the doctrine of the ghospell, lacke meate. Therfore turne all youre care to gette that foode, whiche where it is taken, dooeth not perishe by disgestion, nor dooeth prolong lyfe of the bodye for a shorte tyme, as the common materiall susteinaunce dooeth, and yet within a while hungre cummeth againe: But gette suche foode (I saye) as tarrieth styll in man, noryshing the soule with spirituall foode: and geueth eternall lyfe thereunto. The sonne of man wil geue you this excellent bread, if he perceiue that you doe long and hungre for it. For certainly God willyng to geue eternall lyfe to mankynde, dydde speciallye appoynt this sonne of manne, geuyng vnto hym power, and with myracles bringing him to greate estimacion, that he shoulde geue spirituall foode to all that desyre eternall life. And also for this purpose he gaue vnto the same, power and auctoritie, and with myracles brought hym to great estimacion. For Jesus came not into the worlde to get vnto himselfe worldelye honour, or to make menne blessed with worldly commodities, but he came rather aboute this buisinesse, that is to wete, to lift vp men from vyle filthy cares, to care and studye for heauenly thynges.

Labour not for ÿ meate which perisheth

¶ Then said they vnto him: what shal we do, that we might worke the worke of God? Jesus answered and said vnto them: this is the worke of God, that ye beleue on him who he hath sent. They said therfore vnto him: what signe shewest thou then, that we maie see and beleue thee? what doest thou worke? our fathers did eat Manna in the deserte as it is written: He gaue them bread from heauen to eate.

The texte.

When as the rude and ignoraunt people (minding altogether their belly) vnderstoode not these thynges, no nor once considered them, they aunswered Jesus on this wise. For so muche as thou councellest vs to woorke a certaine meate, that shoulde still remayne in vs, and bring with it euerlastyng life, what shall we doe therefore, that we maie woorke those thynges which are mete for God, and that we maie deserue eternall lyfe, for whiche causes you saye that you were sent into the worlde? Jesus beeyng nothyng offended with this so grosse an aunswere, procedeth by litle and litle to call them from their fondnesse to more perfite thynges. If ye aske (saieth he) what is the woorke whereby ye maie deserue to haue God, whiche is a spirite and is pleased with spirituall thynges, ye shall vnderstande, that it is no sacrifisyng of beastes, no keepyng of the Sabboth daye, no outwarde washynges, no choyse of meates, no relygion of garmentes, nor other thynges whiche dooeth consiste in corporall ceremonies: but this is the woorke whiche God requireth of you, to beleue his sonne whome he hath sent, and by whome he speaketh vnto you: leste he shoulde

This is the worke of God that ye beleue.

seme

seme to graunt euerlasting life to you that be vnthankeful persones, or rather vnworthy suche a benefite. The people whiche chalenged a wondrefull religion throughe the obseruyng of Moses lawe, made nowe aunswere vnto these thynges, not onely grosly, but also vnkyndelye and wickedlye, and saye: If you take vpon you a speciall auctoritie aboue our elders, whose auctoritie we haue hitherto folowed, shewe sum profe and lesson of thine auctoritie geuen thee of God: that vpon syght therof we maye beleue not thy woordes but thy deedes. For it is no reason that without sum woonderous signe we should beleue the, whiche in wordes takest arrogantly vpon the this auctoritie. Neyther woulde we rashelye haue geuen credence vnto our forefathers, but that throughe a token whiche came from Heauen, they dydde certifye vs of theyr goddelye authoritie. Our auncetours dydde eate Manna in the wildernesse vnder Moses that was theyr guyde. This was of truethe the breade of God, an heauenly foode whiche dydde not putrifie, as it is writen in the Psalme: he gaue them celestiall breade to eate. Therefore by reason of this woondrefull thyng, the people then beyng moued, obeyed Moses. And in case thou canste doe the lyke or els summe greatter thyng, we wyll also beleue the. Nor yet dyd this so grosse, so vnkynde, so wicked an aunswer of the people, make the gentlenes of Jesus weary, from alluryng them to the knowledge of spirituall thynges. For fyrste of all they require sum straunge token, as thoughe they had neuer seene anye myracle before: neyther be they contente with euerye kynde of myracle, but as men that woulde goe before hym in all thynges, they prescribe hym what kynde of myracle they would haue hym doe: and to conclude, amongest so many wonderful doinges that are red to be doen vnto the old auncient Jewes, they picke out that chiefly which apperteineth to fedyng: so muche care had they of theyr bellie.

What signe shewest thou them?

The texte

Then Jesus said vnto them: verely verely, I saye vnto you, Moses gaue you not that bread from heauen, but my father geueth you the true bread from heauen. For the breade of God is he whiche cummeth down from heauen, and geueth life vnto the world.

Therfore Jesus as it wer dissemblyng the ignoraunce of the people, thus little by litle bringeth them to the perceiuyng of spirituall thinges, saiyng: If Moses auctoritie bee therefore weightie and regarded among you, because he gaue you Manna from heauen, and ye honour it as heauenlye foode because it came doun from heauen: God is moste then to be thanked herein, from whome Manne dyd flow, and to whom the glorie and praise of al myracles is due. For neyther Moses could do this thyng of himself (who was nothyng els but Gods ministre) neyther was that bread very heauenly breade in dede, although Dauid that wrote the Psalmes cal it bread of heauē: for it came not from very heauē, but it rained doune out of the ayer, lyke as byrdes liuyng in the ayer are called byrdes of heauen: and truely this Manna was but onely a figure of the heauenlye bread. And euen as god gaue corporall breade to a carnall people by Moses, that serued him in the world: so now my father by his heauenly sonne geueth vnto you, as to a spiritual people, that bread whiche vndoubtedly came from heauen: and doeth not onely fill and saciate the bodyes for a time, but geueth immortalitie of soule to them that will receiue it. That was but materiall breade, and gaue lyfe onely to the bodye for a tyme, and howe great a benefite so euer it was, yet did it profit but the people of one nacion alone: but the bread that I speake of, is neyther corporall, neyther dyd it distyll out of the ayer, but did procede euen from very god hymselfe, and is of suche efficacie, that

it geueth

it geueth lyfe, not to bodyes but to soules, and not to one sorte of people alone, but to þe whole world: As touchyng the autour thereof (in case ye passe muche therupon) well, in stede of Moses in whome ye muche glorye, ye haue God the very auctour of this gyfte: and for the seruaunte of god, ye haue goddes owne sonne. And yf ye regarde the gift, there is as great diuersitie betwene these, as is betwene the bodye and the soule, and as is betwene this life which shal shortly cease, and euerlastyng lyfe in heauen.

¶ Then said thei vnto him: lord, euermore geue vs this bread. And Jesus said vnto them: I am the breade of life. He that cūmeth to me shal not hungre, and he that beleueth on me, shall neuer thyrst. But I said vnto you, that ye also haue sene me, & yet ye beleued me not. The texte.

Whan the Jewes had heard all these thynges, yet wer not they for all that lifte vp to the loue of celestiall thynges: but styll dreamyng vpon matters touchyng the belly, sayde vnto Jesus: Syr geue vs alwaye this breade. They loued the sacietie of meate better then healthe, and soughte rather for a plentifull geuer of meate and drynke, then for a sauiour. Therefore, to take frō thē their dreame of corporall foode, Jesus expresseth more plainelye vnto theym, that he did not speake of bread that is chewed with teeth, and whiche beeyng conueied throughe the throte into the stomake, swageth bodilye hungre for a season, but of heauenly bread, whiche is the woord, of God. Therefore he saith: I am that bread the very geuer of eternall life. He that hungrely lusteth after this breade, and will cumme to me, and suffre it to haue passage into the bowelles of the soule by fayth, shall not feele any grief of hungre, that shall cum to hym after he bee once fullye satisfied, but it shall tarrye stil and abide in hym that hath receyued it, vnto eternall lyfe. And my woorde hath in it a fountaine of spirituall water: whereof the soule drynketh by fayth, and not the bodye: therfore he that beleueth in me, shall not onely be without hungre, but also without thirst eternally. This bread is not receiued by gapyng of the mouthe, but through beliefe of the soule. And therfore I haue spoken these thynges vnto you, to let you knowe, that thoroughe your owne faulte ye shall perishe, in case ye dooe persiste and continue in your infidelitie. My father denieth this breade to no man, and to you of all men it hath been fyrste offered, notwithstandyng ye care more for the bread that shal vtterly cum to naught. Ye haue sene me do greatter thynges then yf I should feede you with Manna: and I promyse vnto you also thinges of greatter felicitie, and for al this ye beleue me not. I am the bread of life

The texte

¶ All that the father geueth me shall cum to me, and he that cummeth to me, I cast not away. For I came doune from heauen, not to do that I will, but þe he will which hath sent me. And this is the fathers will whiche hath sent me, that of all which he hath geuen me, I shall loose nothing, but raise them vp againe at the last day. And this is the wil of him that sent me: that euery one which seeth the sonne and beleueth on him, haue euerlasting life. And I wil rayse him vp at the last day.

And albeit ye do through vnbeliefe loeth this breade, yet for all that my father hath not sent it into this worlde without cause. There shall bee sum folke to whom this breade shall bryng euerlastyng lyfe, althoughe the whole nacion of the Jewes shall reiecte gods sonne: and therefore be euen wicked towardes god because they do contemne the said sonne, whome the father hathe sent to saue the whole worlde. For my father is God not onely of the Jewes, but also of al Gentyles. I haue nothyng in dede of my selfe, but yet whatsoeuer my ner my father hath geuen to me (what kynde of people so euer it bee of) the same shall cum to me by fayth , although it hath nothyng to dooe at all wyth Moses law . And whosoeuer wyll cumme to me, hym will I not reiecte, yea and woulde to God all folke woulde cum vnto me . For my fathers will is (as muche as lyeth in hym) that all men shoulde bee saued by fayth. And for as muche as his wyll and myne is all one, for this ende therfore I descended from heauen: not to doe what I wyll, as it were disagreyng with my father, but to dooe my fathers wyl whiche sente me: from whose wyll myne cannot dissente. And truely my fathers wyll that sente me is this, that what thyng so euer he hath through faith geuen vnto me, no deale thereof dooe perishe, I beeyng the preseruer of the same, leste the worlde shoulde violently drawe vnto death that thyng whiche my father hath ordeined to liue.

For I am cum downe from heaue

Furthermore, although the bodye do dye by the course of mans nature, yet doeth the soule, whiche is the better parte of man, remain still aliue. And to thintente also that the whole man shoulde liue throughe me, my father wylleth thys thyng too, that in the last day I shal restore the dead body also to lyfe . For this is my fathers wyll that sente me, euen by his soonne to geue eternall lyfe vnto all men: and that not through Moses lawe, but by faythe of the ghospell . The father dooeth nothyng but by his sonne. And therfore he that dooeth not acknowlage the soonne, doseth not acknowlage the father: and whoso resisteth the sonne, he also resisteth the father . The father is inuisible, but yet he is seen in his sonne. Therfore whoso seeth the sonne, acknowe-ledgeth hym, and beleueth his woordes, the saide soonne will not suffre hym to perishe , but althoughe he bee deade in bodye, he wyll rayse hym agayne in the laste daye, accordyng to his fathers wylle, that he so maye liue wholly, both in bodie and soule, in the presence of the soonne whome he gaue credite vnto. The father hath geuen this power vnto the soonne , that he maye restore euen the dead vnto life.

This is the wil of him that sēt me,

The texte

The Iewes then murmured at hym because he said: I am the bread of life which came downe from heauen. And they said: Is not this Iesus the sonne of Ioseph whose father and mother we knowe? How is it then that he saieth? I came down from heauē. Iesus aunswered and saied vnto theim. Murmure not among youre selfes. No man can cumme to me, excepte the father whiche sente me drawe hym. And I wil rayse hym vp at the laste daie.

When Iesus had spoken these thinges, the people whiche hytherto thorough hope of meate, coulde metely wel away with his communicacion, now seyng that they sawe their hope of bodilye sustenaunce was taken awaye, they fell to quarellyng with hym, to maligne against him. And also whome they (beeing sufficed with eatyng) woulde haue made king, hiin doe they nowe contemne as a vyle persone. and laie arrogancie to his charge, not openlye as yet, but murmuring emong theimselues , chieflye at that saiyng whiche of all others they oughte to embrace, that is to wete: I am the liuelye breade whiche descended from heauen. They moste coueted and gaped for bodilye foode , and with this saiyng, they thoughte theimselues deluded and mocked, where as in dede a thyng farre more excellent was offred them then they loked for. Certes the infirmitie of his manhed offended theim, whiche they onely looked vpon with bodily iyes , when as they myght bothe of his dooynges and sayinges haue seene the power of god in hym, yf they had had iyes of faythe . Is

not this

not this man (saye they) Joseph the carpenters sonne, whose father and mother we knowe well enough by sight: and to be but poore folkes and of a very meane estate? Furthermore how can he for shame say, that he came doun out of heauen, when as but of late time he was borne here in earth emongest vs, a very man of men as we bee? or what meaneth he by tellyng vs of an other father? And whyles they wer talkyng secretly one to an other of these thynges, Jesus (declaring forthwith that mēs very thoughtes wer not hid frō his knowlage) did make more plain, and also confirme that which he had spokē before, saiyng: there is no cause why ye shoulde murmure among your selfes at these thynges, which I haue spoken vnto you. Your infidelitie is the cause why my woordes sticke not in your myndes. Ye se and se not, you heare and heare not, and whyles ye be present yet are ye absent. Of truth whosoeuer cūmeth to me, shal obteine eternall life, but by fayth muste men cum to me. And faithe cummeth not at all auentures, but it is hadde by the inspiracion of god the father: who, like as he draweth vnto him mens myndes by his sonne, so by breathyng in fayth secretly into mens soules, he draweth them to his sonne in suche wyse, that through the operacion of both ioyntly together, men cum to them both. The father doth not geue this so great a gift, but to them that be willing, and desirouse to haue it. And truely whoso doeth with a redy will and godly diligence desire to bee drawen of my father, he shall obteine euerlastyng life by me. For I (as I tolde you) shall call to lyfe again euen him that is dead, when ẏ day shall cum, wherin the felicitie of the godly and the destruccion of the wicked shalbe finished and fully concluded. He that beleueth me receiueth an excellent greate thyng, but he ought to thanke the father for it, without whom no mā can beleue, and yet for al that they that in the meane season doe not beleue, can not excuse theyr faute by saying that they were not drawen: For the father (so muche as lieth in hym) coueteth to drawe all men. He that is not drawen is in faute himselfe, because he wythdraweth hymselfe from him that els would drawe hym.

The texte

¶ It is written in the prophetes: and they shalbe al taught of god. Euery man therefore that hath heard, and hath learned of the father, cummeth vnto me, not that any man hath seen the father, saue he whiche is of god: the same hath seen the father. Verilye, verilye, I saie vnto you: He that putteth his truste in me, hath euerlasting life.

Thynges of thys worlde are learned by mannes endeuour and studye. This celestiall philosophye is not vnderstande, vnles the secrete inspiracion of the father make mannes harte apte to bee taught. Vndoubtedlye thys is that whiche the prophetes long a go dyd saye shoulde be, thus prophecying before had: And they shall be al taught of god. But the lustes of this world maketh many one vntowardes to be taughte: whiche worldelye desyres whyles they euen droune men in these earthlye thynges, they suffreth hym not to lifte vp theyr myndes to heauenlye thynges. The gyfte is goddes, but the endeuour is yours. A man heareth my wordes with bodily eares in vayne, excepte he heare before the secrete voyce of the father, whiche must inspire the mynde with an insensyble grace of faythe. Therefore whosoeuer fashyon theymselfes to bee apte to receiue this inspiracion, the father dooeth thus drawe theym. And he onely that is so drawen, cummeth finally to me. For god is a spirite, and is neyther hearde nor seen, but to them that bee spirituall. And so to haue seene and haue hearde hym, is saluacion. Many shall see and heare the sonne to theyr peryl and daunger, notwithstandyng that ye do glorye in that god was seene

And they shall bee al taughte of God.

and

and heard to Moses and to the prophetes. There was neuer mortall manne that sawe and hard god, as he is in his own nature and substaunce, that thing is geuen to the sonne of god alone, whiche onely came from God, with whom he was euermore before he came into this worlde. Therfore put clearely out of your myndes the vyle cares of this corporall lyfe, labouryng al that ye can, that through earnest desyre of thynges that be spiritually good, ye may attaine life euerlastyng. I would ye should forget that bread wherewith the bodie is satisfyed, and be ye desirous of that heauenly bread, whiche geueth eternall lyfe. This bread is receiued by fayth, and fayth is to be obteyned of god the father: be ye well assured thereof, that whosoeuer hath affiaunce in me, the same hathe already eternall lyfe, for so muche as he hath the fountaine of immortalitie.

The texte. ¶ I am the bread of life: your fathers did eate Manna in wildernes, and are dead. This is that breade, whiche cummeth down from heauen, that a man maie eate therof and not die. I am that liuing bread, whiche came downe from heauen. If any manne eate of this breade, he shall liue for euer. And the breade that I will geue, is my fleshe, whiche I will geue for the life of the world.

I am that very bread whiche geueth not a bodily and a transitorye life, but the lyfe of the soule, and eternall lyfe. Althoughe ye haue me presente, yet neuerthelesse ye desyre Manna, as a woondrefull thyng. And al beit Manna (whiche youre auncestours didde eate and feede upon for a certaine tyme in the wildernesse) didde cum from heauen (as you suppose) yet it dyd theim no ferther pleasure then wheaten or barlye breade woulde haue dooen. It putte awaye for a whyle the hunger of the bodye, whiche shortelye after woulde returne agayne, and require more meate: but it coulde not geue them immortalitie. For though your forefathers were neuer so happye, yet dyd as manye of them dye as dyd feede of that Manna. This breade (whiche I speake of) descended out of heauen in veraye deede, and it hath receiued of god celestiall strengthe to make hym that eateth of it, to liue in bodye and soule euerlastynglye, and neuer to bee subiecte unto deathe. Ye nede not therefore aske impoortunately any Manna from heauen, when as ye haue very heauenly breade presente and ready prepared for you, whiche geueth eternall lyfe, in case ye wyll receiue it by fayth. For I my selfe am that bread, the grauter of immortall lyfe, who alone came down from heauen, whome you (beeyng offended with the infirmitie of this bodye) take and thynke to be nothyng els but the sonne of Joseph and Marye.

I am the liuing bread.

Truely I am the very woorde of god the father, whiche whoso beleueth shall haue immortall lyfe. If any man wyll conueye and digeste this heauenlye bread into the inwarde partes of the soule, he shalbee quickened and growe into eternall lyfe. And yf you beyng but carnall do not yet understande spirituall thynges, I wyll shew you a more a plain and grosser matter, and a thyng that is more apperteinyng unto the fleshe. Euen thys fleshe whiche you see and loke upon, and whiche I shall bestowe and geue unto deathe for to redeme the lyfe of the whole worlde, is the liuyng breade. Beleue, eate it, and lyue. By thys sayyng our Lord Jesus did sumwhat (after an obscure sorte) open unto them the misterie of his godhed, whereby he was alwaye with God the father, and of his death also: by the whiche he should deliuer and saue the worlde from the tyrannye of deathe. Finallye he did insinuate herein unto them, the priuitie of hys mysticall bodye: whereof he that is not a membre and by fayth annexed there-unto

unto, and so styll cleaue and sticke fast unto it as the braunche dooeth cleaue unto the vyne, he shall not haue life in hym. And Jesus knewe well enough that at that tyme the Jewes dyd not understande his saiynges, but yet for all that he was assured that in tyme to cum it should cum to passe, howe that these sedes (and as ye would say norishmentes of misteryes) beeyng shutte and closed up within the myndes of good men, should growe up and bryng forth plenteouse fruite.

The Jewes therfore strove among theimselfes, saiyng: howe can this felow geue us that flesh of his to eat. Then Jes^s said unto the: verely verely I saie unto you, except ye eat the fleshe of the sonne of man, and drinke his bloud, ye haue no life in you. Whosoever eateth my flesh and drinketh my bloude, hath eternall life, and I will raise him up at the last daie. For my fleshe is meate in dede: and my bloude is drinke in dede. He that eateth my fleshe, and drinketh my bloude, dwelleth in me, and I in hym.

The texte

Therfore whã as these thynges semed to them very incõuenient and to folish to be spokẽ, & durst not talke homely & familiarly with ẏ lord himself, there arose a great discorde in opinions amõg them, diverse of them diversly interpretyng the thyng ẏ was spoken. For even as Nicodemus understode not Jesus when he spake of a newe heavenlye birth, nor the woman of Samaria knewe what Jesus ment in his darke speakyng of the water that should flowe into everlastyng life: so this rude & grosse people cõtẽded how it could be brought to passe, that a mã should geue hys flesh to be eaten of other: and that in suche sorte as it should suffyse al men to perpetual lyfe. For he dyd bid, & inuited all mẽ to eate heauenly bread, & sayd moreouer that his flesh was bread. How shall we (say they) eate the flesh of a livyng mãne? And again, Jesus beeyng not ignoraunte about what matter they contended, dyd not declare unto them by what way & meanes that flesh might be eaten in steade of breade, but here now confirmeth ẏ thyng to be nedeful, & a very necessarie thyng, which they iudged but a vayne thing and a plaine absurditie, and that it could not be doen. Take this for a veray suertye (saieth he) excepte ye receiue me whole, that is to saye, unlesse ye eate the flesh of the sonne of man in steade of breade, and in the place of wyne drinke his bloud, ye shall not haue life in you. On the contrarye syde, whosoever eateth my flesh and drinketh my bloud, hath by eating and drinking therof eternal life. Neyther shall the soule alone liue blessed & most happy by reason of this meat & drinke, but also after the resurreccion of the bodye, the whole man bothe bodye and soule shall haue with me the fruicion of everlastyng lyfe. For like as mans naturall meate beeyng conueyed downe into the stomake, and after it bee digested is conueyed thence throughout all the membres of the bodye, & so turnethe into the substaunce of the bodye, so that then the meate and the man that eateth it, is al one: in lyke maner on the othersyde, he that hath eaten me, shalbe spiritually transformed and turned into me. Furthermore, forsomuche as I am the chefe auctour of the resurreccion I wyl not suffre my membres to be dissevered and pulled awaye from me: but whoso ever is surelye ioyned to me by thys meate and drinke, I shall rayse hym up agayne in the last day: that because the whole man hauyng bothe bodye and soule beleued me, the whole man nowe also maye liue with me everlastynglye. Bodelye meate woorketh not this effecte, neyther yet Manna wherein ye reioyce, but the eatyng of my bodye, and the drinkyng of my bloude, bringeth this thyng to passe. And therefore my flesh is truelye meate, whyche geueth immortalitie, and my bloude is truely drynke,

Excepte ye eat ẏ flesh of of the sonne of manne.

which

which doeth procure eternall life, not only to ẏ body, but to ẏ whole man both body and soule. And as the lyfe of the bodye whiche is nourished with dayly sustenaunce, lest it shoulde perishe before the tyme, is common to all the membres of the body, by reason of the indiuisible felowshippe that all the partes of the bodye hathe togetherwardes, in so muche that though the membres of the bodye be diuerse and sundrye, yet there is but one bodye, because that one soule geueth lyfe to euerye parte of the bodye: so he that eateth my fleshe, and drynketh my bloude, is in suche sorte coupled and ioyned to me, that neither can I be seperate from hym, nor he from me. For I am in hym by my spirite, by whō I wyll geue lyfe to hym. And he is in me as a membre in the bodye, and as the braunche is in the vyne, by suche a participacion as cannot bee dissolued.

The texte, ¶ As the liuing father hath sente me, and I liue for the father: Euen so he that eateth me, shal liue by the meanes of me. This is the bread which came downe from heauen, not as your fathers did eate Manna, and are dead. He that eateth of this breade, shall liue euer. These thinges sayed he in the synagogue as he taught in Capernaum. Many therefore of his disciples (when they had heard this) sayd, this is an hard saiyng: Who can abide the hearing of it?

The father that sent me is the principall fountaine of al life. Whosoeuer is ioyned to hym, is made partaker of life. And therefore as the father is in me, & geueth me life, and also power to geue life vnto other: euen likewyse to him that eateth me (and is so annexed to me, by reason of that misticall eatyng, and drinkyng, that he is made one with me) doe I geue lyfe, not to endure for a shorte tyme, but eternall life. What thyng soeuer is of earthly nature, the same dooeth continue but for a tyme, and is of small efficacie. Manna whiche stylled downe from heauen for you, then beyng vnder Moses tuicion and conductyng, because it was foode pertaynyng to the bodye, it coulde not geue eternall lyfe to your elders: for whereas all men did eat therof, they neuertheles dyed, neyther did any one of so great a numbre remain vndead: yea more part of thē died also in soule, because they prouoked god manye waies, to wrath. But certes this bread, that vndoubtedly came downe from heauen, hath a celestiall vertue in it and geueth eternall lyfe to the eater thereof. The Lorde Jesus did instruct the ignorant and grosse multitude with such wordes: very desirous to stirre them vp from the loue of vysible and corporal thynges, to the loue and desire of heauenly and eternall thynges. And he spake these woordes in the Sinagogue amōgest a great assembly of people exercising the office of a teacher. Howbeit the grosse people was so farre of from the capacitye of these heauenlye mysteries, that a great sorte of his disciples also beyng offēded herewith, wer about to fall from theyr maister, murmuryng amongest themselfes and whisperyng this saiyng: This is an harde cruell saiyng (saye they) concernyng the eatyng of a lyuyng mannes fleshe, and drinkyng his bloude: whose eares can abyde to heare such doctryne?

This is the bread whiche came down from heauen. &c.

The texte. Jesus knew in himself that his disciples murmured at it, & he said vnto them: doeth this offend you? What & if ye shal se the sonne of mā ascēd vp thither where as he was before? It is ẏ spirit that quickeneth, the flesh profiteth nothing. The wordes that I speake vnto you are the spirit & life. But there are sum of you ẏ beleue not. For Jesus knew frō the beginning which thei wer ẏ beleued not, & who should betraie him. And he said: Therefore said I vnto you, that no man can cum vnto me, except it were geuē vnto him of my father

Jesus, vnderstandyng what they murmured at secretly among themselfes, labored to bored to remedie the thing that they were offẽded with, geuing knowledge before hand vnto them that they shoulde see greater thinges with their iyes then that they heard hym at this tyme speake of hymselfe. And he shewed them that the woordes whiche he had spoken as touchyng the eatyng of his fleshe, and to drinke his blood, was no incõueniẽt thing, nor to be abhorred, but a right pleasaunt, graciouse and fruitfull saying: in case it were taken and understande not after their course and grosse intelligence, but after a spirituall sence. Nowe therfore being turned towardes his disciples, whom it had behoued to haue further consydered, and to haue been wyser then the base sorte of people, by reason of the acquaintance and familiaritie whiche they had with Jesus, and also for the myracles which they had seen hym worke: Jesus (I say) loking vpon his disciples, rebuked theyr dulnes in this wyse, saying: Doeth it offend your eares to heare me saye that I am the breade which came out of heauen, to geue lyfe to the worlde? whether is it a greater difficultie (after the grosse vnderstandyng of mannes wit) to haue descended from heauen, or to ascend vp into heauen? What then, yf hereafter ye do see the sonne of man, whom ye nowe see to haue the natural body of a man, ascende into heauen, where he was before he came downe thence, and before he had this mortal bodye? This is doen and graunted by reason of your senses: not that ye shoulde bee alwaye carnall and vnderstand all thinges fleshly, but that ye shoulde leaue the fleshe, and go forwarde to the spirite. The spirit descended from heauen, and was incarnate: the fleshe beeyng now made spirituall, shalbe carryed awaye vp into heauen, leste ye should all waye loue the fleshe, and be carnall, but yet beeing first instructed by the flesh, ye ought to profit and go forward toward heauenly thinges. For the flesh alone & of himselfe, profiteth nothing, it is the spirite that geueth life. For what is bodily substance of men, if the spirit lacke? euen so my woord carnally vnderstand, shall not geue life vnles ye take it as an heauenly thing, and vnderstãd it spiritually. By my fleshe and blood, I meane my doctrine, and so I tearme it, whiche doctrine yf ye do by true faith receiue it desyrously, and effectuously, and than conueigh it into the bowels of your minde, and retaine it there, it will quicken and make your mindes liuely, and cause you and me to be al one: so that ye shal through my spirite, liue euerlastingly: likeas the membres of one bodye lyueth by one common spirite, so long as they do adhere and cleaue fast together. And I shall leaue vnto you my fleshe and blood as a hid secret mystery, and mistical token of this copulacion and felowship: which selfe thing although ye do receiue it, yet will it not profit you vnles ye receyue it spiritually. Therfore do not repugne and refuse my saying (though being still carnal ye do not rightly vnderstande it, nor take it as it ought to be taken) but rather labour for the true vnderstanding therof. For the woordes which I haue spoken vnto you, are not carnall (as you interpretate them) but be spirite, and lyfe: and whye? Verely because they beeing spiritually vnderstand, do conferre and geue lyfe to the soule. He that receiueth these woordes rightly and truely, eateth my fleshe, and drinketh my blood: & being coupled to me, gayneth thereby euerlasting lyfe. But he that willingly refuseth them continueth in death, thorough the synnes of his former lyfe, and doubleth his owne damnacion of eternall death, by reason of infidelitie. And all they refuse this bread when it is offered them, which beleue not my woordes. And I knowe that these thinges are spoken al in vaine to sum folkes: being right wel assured that there be sum

What and yf ye shall see the sõne of man &c.

among you which doeth not credite my woordes, and therefore reiectyng life when it is offered them, they be cause of their owne utter destruccion.

And for that cause our Lorde Jesus spake these thynges, who was ignorant in nothyng, yet he knewe well ynough or euer he spake these woordes, whiche of his disciples woulde geue faith unto hym. And moreouer he coulde tell this also: that euen amongest the twelue Apostles, (whom he so surnamed for honour sake) and whome hee dyd also choose specially to bee aboute hymselfe, as most sure frendes: he knewe (I say) that there should be one of theim whiche woulde betraye hym to the Jewes, that shoulde put hym to death. Therefore, to note them, whiche though they dyd heare all one woorde and saying with the reste, and though also one of the twelue should eate of the same bread and drinke of the same cup, which his felowes shoulde eate and drinke of, yet shoulde not they obtaine lyfe thereby, because they tooke and receiued that heauenlye bread not spirituallye, but carnally, Jesus added more, and sayde: for this cause I tolde you a litle before, that no man coulde cum unto me, except it were geuen him so to do from heauen of my father. To haue heard this my voyce, is nothing: to haue seen and felte this body, is nothyng, except the father of heauen haue geuen withall, the iyes of fayth: with the whiche I am loked upon to the beholders health, and unles he shall geue therwith heauenly eares of the mynde, with the whiche I am heard fruitefully, and to the hearers commoditie.

The texte. From that tyme many of his disciples went backe and forsooke hym, and walked no more with hym. Then sayed Jesus to the twelue: wyll ye also go awaye? Then Symon Peter answered hym: Lorde to whom shall we goe? thou hast the woordes of eternall lyfe, and we beleue and are sure that thou arte Christe the soonne of the lyuing God. Jesus answered them: Haue not I chosen you twelue? and one of you is a deuill: He spake of Judas Iscarioth the sonne of Simon, for he it was that should betraye hym, beeyng one of the twelue.

These woordes of Jesus beyng full of the doctrine of saluacion, dyd not descende doune into theyr myndes, whose mindes were occupied with earthly desyres and couetousnesse: who also understood no heauẽly thinges, besides the grosse and carnall religion (as they used it) of Moses lawe. Therefore after that Jesus had this communicacion among them, the more parte not onely of the common people, but also of his owne disciples, fell awaye from theyr maister, and thereby are made wurse, whereby they myght haue been muche better, in case they had taken all thinges well, and receiued hym accordynglye, and they so muche forsooke hym, that they withdrewe themselfes from his cumpany, and from eating and drinking with hym, as men that by that facte woulde condemne his doctrine. But Jesus to shewe euen now the maner and way how that preachers of the ghospel should behaue themselfes: doeth neyther make to humble and vile suite to haue them tarie styll with hym leste he shoulde seme to dooe the thing that other are wounte to dooe: that is, to shew himselfe to stande in nede of their cumpany: Neyther doeth he speake to the reproche of theyr goyng awaye, leste therein he myght haue been thought to haue more sought his owne prayse and glory, then theyr saluacion: and yet he doeth not utterly put them away from hym, because they myght (perchaunce) afterwarde haue been better aduised: but to declare that through their owne faute they were offended, and so without any occasion geuen thẽ, went awaye: and y his saying shoulde not altogether lacke fruite, although that sum made themselfes

themselfes through infidelitie vnworthie any heauenly gifte. Jesus (I saye) vpon these skylles tourning him to wardes the twelue Apostles, whom he had admitted and taken vnto hym, to be the speciall witnesses and bruters abrode, of all the thinges that he wroughte, did so get out of theim the open confession of theyr beleue, that he neyther retaineth these with flatterye, as thoughe he had gonne about his owne businesse rather then theyrs, neither did he so much feare theym with threatening and chiding, leste they shoulde seeme to folowe Jesus, rather compelled, then (with their owne consent) persuaded. For no man is to be compelled vnto the fayth of the ghospell. And Jesus had leauer men should openly forsake him, then to haue a disciple colourably and faynedly: And therfore whiles other were departing from him, Jesus saieth to the twelue: And will ye also goe away from me? ye maye tarye styl and ye lust, vnlesse ye thinke it more your commoditie to departe. Verely I doe desyre that it might be euery mans lucke to haue this heauenly gyft by me: but it is neither to be geuen to theim that refuse it, for they dooe not deserue it, nor any manne can attaine to cum by it, excepte he be desirouse of it. And yet it is the gift of the father that any man doeth couet and earnestly desyre it.

Will ye also go away &c.

Here nowe doeth Simon Peter, a man alway of a plaine and ardent faith towardes Jesus (representyng in his person the whole churche) and in the name also of other, maketh aunswer cherefully, and with great courage saying: O Lorde, God forbyd that we should forsake the, for considering that we be muche desyrous of eternal saluacion, and also knowe right wel how bare and vnpleasaunt, how colde and vnprofitable those thinges are, which the Phariseis teache, and seing also that we haue hearde John testifying of the, whither els and to what other man should we go from thee? for thou alone speakest the woordes which bring with them euerlasting lyfe.

Thou hast the woordes of eternal life, &c.

Thou that receyuest euery one (that will cum) shalt not driue vs from the, whom thou hast once admitted to thy seruice, neyther do we desyre to chaunge our lorde and maister, for we shoulde change for the wourse, what new maister soeuer we shall choose. For we not only trusting vpon thy woordes beleue thee, but also wee knowe by the very dedes that thou doest and haue certainlye foūde and tried out therby that thou arte verie Christe and the anointed sonne of God: of whom onlye all men ought to hope for eternall health and saluacion.

We are sure that thou arte Christ. &c.

But Jesus did neither shew himselfe muche to wounder at this stoute saying of Peter, wherby Peter did so hielye reporte of Christe, lest he should seme to take pleasure in mens praisyng of him, nor he did not vtterly refuse it, lest he shoulde so haue denied the truth: but exhortyng all men to perseuer in that faithfull confession, which Peter had made in all their names, he did sumwhat disclose that one of those fewe shoulde bee suche one as shoulde not only go from hym, as other disciples had doen, but should also couenaunt with his aduersaries, and betraye him euen to deathe. And his pleasure was to sygnifye that thing couertly, because he would not bewray Judas: lest any man shoulde thinke that Judas beyng with suche a rebuke prouoked, did worthely reuenge hymselfe vpon his maister, and Jesus minde was also to cause euery man with this saying to beware lesse through theyr owne faulte, they fal into so wicked a dede. And he sayeth: what is the cause ye do meruaill that already sum of my disciples are gone awaye from me? haue not I chosen you as moste excellent, out from amongst all other? And yet one of so small a numbre and so specially chosen is a very diuell, and shal accuse and betraie him whose bodie he hath eathen, & whose bloud he hath dronkē carnally, but not spiritually: whom he hath hearde also preache, and seen doe miracles. Therfore do not shrinke from the thing that you haue begonne, as they haue doen, whom ye haue seen go awaye, but perseuer and waxe alwaye better and better, vntill ye maye wurthelye cum to be suche, as can spiritually eate the foode of my heauenly doctrine, and beyng thereby as it were conuerted into me, ye shall obtaine euerlasting lyfe.

The. vij. Chapter.

The texte.

¶ After these thinges, Jesus went about in Galile, for he would not goe about in Jewry because that the Jewes sought to kill hym. The Jewes feast of tabernacles was at hande. His brethren therfore sayed vnto hym: Get the hence, and goe into Jewry, that thy disciples also maye se thy workes that thou doest. For there is no man that doeth any thing in secret, and he hymselfe seketh to be knowen openly. If thou do suche thinges, shewe thy selfe to the worlde. For his brethren beleued not in him.

But after that our Lorde Jesus went about & was muche cōuersaūt in Galile, forsomuch as by reason of his wordes whiche did implie certayne heauenly thynges, and thynges of greater importaunce than mans reason coulde reache, and also through the miracles that he wrought, he gat him self muche enuie amōgst his own disciples, who had him in more contēpte, because he was knowen vnto thē by beyng in house among them: and verely the basenes of the house and parentes that he came of, made their hatred more bitter and vengeable againste hym. For he could not now lyue in Jewry with suretie of his lyfe, because ẏ Jewes had a good while sought wayes to kyll him, yet Jesus went not out of Jewrie for fear of death, or that he had not power to slyde awaye out of the middest of theyr wilie traines as ofte as he list: but shewing himselfe very man, he layed before his disciples as it were an image and portrature of thinges that shoulde folow, to whom it should chaunce, that through the maliciouse infidelitie of the Jewes, he should be cōpelled to go from them to the Gentiles. But the Jewes very feastful hye and solemne day, which is emong the Grekes called Scenopegia (in Englishe the feast of tabernacles) was at hande. And this feast had that name scenopegiam, to call to remembraunce the olde Patriarches, and their wayes: whiche led theyr lyfe in pauillions and tentes, many times remouyng from place to place, euen so at that tyme declaring by a figure what maner of lyfe theirs ought to be, which professe the doctrine of the gospel. And because a great mayn companye of folkes came now against this holy tyme & hye feast out of all Syria, and other countreis whiche border therupon thicke and threfold vnto Hierusalem, for the solemnitie of the temple, the holynes and religion wherof was had in reuerence euen among the heathen people, Jesus kynsfolkes all ignorant and subiect as yet to worldly desyres and affections, hauing affiaunce in the title of theyr kinred, more boldly than was mete, exhorte hym, as if he had ben desyrous of fame and glory, but yet they toke hym to be timorouse, and of lesse audacitie than behoued hym, and for that cause they moue him that if he thought himselfe well inough ayded and durst trust therto, that he would not lurke and hide himselfe amongst the aliens of Galile, but woulde

His brethren therfore sayed vnto hym.

woorke

woorke and perfourme at Hierusalem, in the full syght and euen in the middest of the people that was resorted thither, those thinges whiche he had so hiely spoken of hymselfe. The great day and solemne feast (saye they) is at hande: leaue Galile therfore, whereas thou hast so long tyme kept thy selfe close, and go into Jurie the most florishing part of the whole kingdom, & so bring thyselfe to Hierusalem the chiefe citie, and head place of all the Jewish nacion, thou maiest there get many disciples if they all once looke vpon thy doynges. No man that would be extemed, doeth those thinges priuely & in corners, wherby he maye get a name amongst men. If thou be cum from heauen in dede, and canst do so great thinges as thou sayest thou canst, do so that thou mayst be knowen to the world. But let no mā meruail at this carnal, presumptuouse, & very vngodly saying of the lorde Jesus kinsfolkes. For of truth at that time, they that were his nye kinsmen (and therfore called his brethren) & knit to him by a straight familiaritie, did not beleue on him: of whō, sum for all that, being afterward of the numbre of his Apostles, did most constantely setfurth Christes glory in theyr preachinges.

There is no man that doeth any thyng in secrete. &c.

For his brethre beleued not in hym.

¶ Then Jesus sayd vnto them: My tyme is not yet cum, but your tyme is alwaye readie. The worlde cannot hate you, but me it hateth, because I testifie of it, that the workes therof be euill. Go ye vp vnto this feast, I will not go vp yet vnto this feast, for my tyme is not yet full cum. Whan he had sayd these woordes vnto them, he abode styll in Galile. But as soone as his brethren were cum, then went he also vp vnto the feast, not openly but as it were priuely. Then sought hym the Jewes at the feaste, and sayd, where is he? And muche murmuring was there of hym among the people. For sum sayed: he is good: other sayed nay, but he deceiueth the people. Howbeit, no man spake openly of him, for fear of the Jewes.

The texte.

Jesus therfore according to his singular modestie & gentilnes, did blame the boldnesse of his familiar frendes easely, and with greate softnesse, signifying that carnal kinred hath no intresse in that he did concerning the saluacion of mankinde, but that all suche businesse (because it is heauenly) is to be moderate by thauctoritie of the father of heauen: he declared also that he neyther feared death, which he was ready willingly to suffer for the saluacion of mankind, nor that he desired the glorie of this world, the hatred wherof he did prouoke towardes himselfe by speaking trueth, & thīges cōtrary to mens worldly affeccions: and in consideracion hereof, Jesus sayed: My tyme is not yet cum. Whan that shall exhorte me, then shall not nede your aduertisementes.

My time is not yet cum &c.

It dependeth of the father of heauens determinacion, & not of mans deuise how & whan it behoueth me to be knowen to the world. I that came at the fathers pleasure and arbitremente, haue my tyme. But your tyme (whiche beyng led with worldly affeccions, seketh for the glorye of this world, & woulde haue me according to the iudgement of the worlde to glory) is alway ready, ye may safely go whither ye list, whan as the world loueth you as men cōformable therunto. I do not seke glorye at the worldes hande with this affeccion & loue that ye hunte about for it, for I seke my fathers glory, and go about the saluacion of man. It is so vnlike & far of, that I should (by any kynde of flattery) get glory and prayse in the world, that I do rather bring the hatred of the world vpō me by dissentinge from the lustes and carnall pleasures therof, & by testifying openly ẏ the woorkes of it are euel, not withstanding that the world selfe putteth forged godlynesse and false felicitie in such workes as be but carnall and worldly. The Jewes haue theyr feastfull dayes whiche now of late

The worlde cannot hate you.

time God abhorreth. For they offre vnthankfull sacrifices and odiouse to God, seying in the meane tyme they haue their handes all bloudie, and in the selfsame daies which they would should be thought pure and holye, they go about the death of innocentes. There is one true feastfull daye which I must celebrate spiritually, wherewith the father is pleased and delited. That day is not yet cū, but when it shal cū I shal willingly go mete with it. You that are yet stil carnal and worldly wise, get you vp to this solēne feast. I intend not to go with you to this greate feast that is now nie at hande, for because my time is not yet fullye accomplished. With these woordes our lorde Jesus sent awaye from hym his natural kynsmen, being alwaye wont to set asyde the regarde and affection towardes theim, as often as the busynes of the gospel was to be gone in hand withall, whiche matter because he woulde it shoulde be wholly ascribed to his fathers wil & arbitremēt, he would not suffre it to be polluted wt any worldly thing. Thus did he restraine & stint the autoritie of his mother at the mariage, and again he was euil apaied, and in maner thought scorne and disdayned that he should be called out by his mother & kynsfolkes from talking of the gospel, & after that he had made his abode a while with his nye frendes at Capernaū, he left them and set in hande to preache: furthermore hanging vpon the crosse he called his mother woman, as though he had knowen no mother in ye businesse. Yea and also beyng a child but of .xii. yeres old, he semed to disdayne that by theyr autoritie he shoulde be called from his fathers affaires. Now therfore they supposyng that for feare of the Jewes Jesus woulde not cum to the hye and solemne feast, wēt thither alone. And they going vp to Hierusalem, Jesus taried still in Galile: so tempering al his doinges and with moderacion duelye bestowing thē, that somtime he proued himself to be verye man, lest he shoulde not haue semed to be man, and sum other time he shewed great likelihood of his godlye power, lest men should beleue that he was but man only. But after that his brethren were departed and gon towardes the feast, then did he himself go after: so that the matter is plain, he did not so muche refrain going to ye solemne meting for feare of the Jewes, as he did to eschewe the coumpany of his kinsmen, whom being as yet carnall, he would not haue to be associate wt hym in the gospels cause, or to haue anye medlyng therwith. But he came to Hierusalem, not to auaunt himself, but as it were by stelth and priuely, & as a man would say, to cause them the more earnestlye to loke for his cūmyng: and when his time were, to cum abrode and declare himselfe to the brode worlde with more fruite. For he knewe the Phariseis mindes, how that they had been a great while about in their conuenticles and secrete counsels to fynde sum occasion vpon the holy daye to attache and apprehende him. Now therfore when he was of trueth cum to Hierusalem, but as yet he went not abrode into the common resorte and assemblie of people as he was wont to doe, the Jewes marked him and layed spyal for him whether he went to the keping of the holy day or no, and forasmuche as they desyred to se him, they enquired one of an other where he was. And euen nowe alredy many sundry tales went of him amonge the people, as if he had been absent, because all men had not one opinion nor were not lyke affected towardes Jesus. For of suretie manye of the homely sort of the people whiche had been present at his miracles workyng, & had heard him preache, who also had had experience of his gentlenes by being in his cumpany, said that Jesus was a good man, and one not mete to be euil

I will not go vp to this feast. &c

entreated

entreated and cruelly hādled. Of the cōtrarye side, the Priestes and Phariseis, whom the prayse and renoume which was of Jesus had vexed a great while, denyed that he was a good man, who lyke a sedicious felowe did allure the people to hym and turne thē from hauing the Priestes, Scribes, & Phariseis in reuerēce. Uerely these sayinges were by secrete whisperinges sperpled abrode concernyng Jesus, whereas no man durst in ỳ meane while opēly make any good reporte of hym: Howbeit there was many whiche had a good opinion of hym: For they feared the head men of the Jewes, of whome they knewe Jesus to be muche hated, because he semed with his wordes and dedes to diminishe theyr auctoritie. Moreouer, as touchynge the kepinge of hym selfe out of the waye, he so did of very mekenes and modestie, lest he should be thought wittingly and willingly to haue prouoked the malice of the Phariseis, who soughte for nothinge els but matter and occasion to put him to deathe. That he did go abrode, was doen for theyr cause whō he knewe shoulde bee furthered to saluacion by his doctrine: whereas he was not ignoraunt ỳ the Phariseis & Scribes would growe more heady and fierce through that he should saye and doe for the saluacion of the worlde. For the Lorde beynge moste desirous of mans saluacion, coueted that yf it mighte be possible, his doctrine should worke saluacion in al men: but yet so muche was not to be geuen to the frowardnes of certaine, that the doctrine of the gospel was to be withdrawen and kept from the good simple people.

Howbeit no mā spake openly of hym. &c.

For feare of the Jewes.

The texte.

Now whan half the feast was done, Jesus went vp into the temple, and taught. And the Jewes merualled, saying: how knoweth he the scriptures, seing that he neuer learned? Jesus aunswered and saied: My doctrine is not mine, but his that sente me. If any man will be obedient to his will, he shall knowe of my doctrine, whether it be of god, or whether I speake of my self. He that speaketh of himselfe, seketh his owne prayse; but he that seketh his prayse that sent him, the same is true, and no vnrightousnes is in hym.

Therfore when as the highe an solemne feast was halfe doen, Jesus went openly in the syght of all men into the temple, and there taught the people not pharisaicall ordinaunces or ceremonies of the lawe, whiche should anon after cease, but the philosophy and wisdom of the ghospell. But when the Jewes could picke no quarell against his doctrine, yet they deuise and studie to brynge him out of credence & to diminishe his autoritie amōge the people, meruailinge how that he, being not learned and vnlettred (for in dede he was neuer brought vp in pharisaicall doctrine, in the reading and profession whereof they swelled for pride) should cū by those sayinges, whiche he alledged and brought out of holy scripture, with great wisdom, & to muche purpose: in maner appeaching him as one that had a deuill to teache hym, or that he had cū by the knowledge of that learning (whiche he learned of no man) by sum other magical arte and deuillishe witchecraft. The Jewes therfore in consyderaciō hereof, sayed: how doeth this felowe, a Carpēter himself, & a Carpenters sonne, read & vnderstād sciences, when as he neuer learned thē? Uerely Jesus, to shewe vs an exaūple of sobrietie and gentle behauiour, very courteously and with muche lenitie put awaye and confuted their so sinfull and wicked suspicion, declaring plainlye ỳ his doctrine came neyther of man nor deuill, but euen of God whom they also did worship: & whose glorye and honor they ought of duetie to fauour, yf they woulde be taken for true godly men, and as for himself, he told them plainly, that he did neyther chalenge to himselfe the doctrine which they woondred at,

How knoweth he the scripture?

nor the honour and prayse which they did enuie: but that altogether came of the father of heauen, whose businesse he did. He told them furthermore that forasmuche as they had taken vpon them the perfite knowledge of the lawe which God gaue vnto thẽ, and did disdainfullie lothe other as vnlearned and very ideotes, it were indifferentlye doen that in case they had the very true knowledge of scripture, they shoulde embrace and acknowledge the doctrine whiche proceded from the same, from whom the law came: vnlesse they would make men knowe, that enuie, hatred, desyre of their owne glory, loue of gain and lucre, and suche lyke inordinate and carnall desyres, whiche procedeth of a lende minde, had blinded their iudgement. For God is not (sayeth he) contrary to himselfe, that now he would teache by his sonne a contrary thing to that he gaue in his lawe. Therfore Jesus knowyng all their secretes, made this answer to their secrete murmuring, saying: My doctrine which ye wõder of whome I shoulde haue it, for so muche as I haue learned no letter of any man, is not mine: (for in dede I do bring you no newe learning of mã that differeth from the will of God and thẽ minde of the lawe whiche was geuen you of God) but it is my fathers doctrine which hath sent me into the worlde: that the worlde being seduced with the sundry and manifolde doctrines of men, and blinded with wicked affeccions and naughty desyres, might by me knowe my fathers will: & when it is knowen folowe it, and so by folowyng of it, obtein eternall lyfe. For of trueth his will is this, that they that beleue his sonnes sayinges, by whom he teacheth you and speaketh vnto you, shoulde get thereby euerlasting health. And the cause why many do lesse minde and desyre that thing, is enuie, hatred, ambicion, aduauntage, and other euill desyres and carnall lustes. But if any man would (setting asyde all malice) with a true meaning and a plain simple herte, obey my fathers wil, rather then his own lewde and vngraciouse affeccions, he will soone recognyse my doctrine not to be of man, or any newe and straunge inuencion of the deuill, but to be cũ̃ frõ God: nor that I do speake those thinges which I saye, of mannes reason and witte, but after my fathers minde whose ambassadour I am. Men that be more studiouse of their owne glorye than of Goddes, do preferre newe doctrine of their owne inuenciõ before the doctrine of God, to be made more of in ẏ worlde themselues. For they had rather be taken for authors of mans doctrine, the whole glorye wherof shoulde altogether continually redound to themselfes, then to bee publike preachers of Gods doctrine: and had leauer teache those thinges, which might get to themselfes prayse & aduauntage, then that which should bring glory and honour to God, or saluacion to their neyghbour. But he that seketh not his owne prayse, but his from whom he is sent, speaketh all thinges purely and vncorruptely, neyther is his doctrine in daunger of any errour, or fauty through the lustes of ambicion, of auarice, enuie or hatred.

If any man will be obedient vnto his will.

He that speaketh of himselfe seketh his owne praise

The texte.

Did not Moses geue you a lawe, and yet none of you kepeth the lawe? Why go ye about to kill me? The people aunswered and saied: Thou hast a deuil: who goeth aboute to kill thee? Jesus aunswered, and sayed vnto them: I haue done one worke, and ye all merueil. Moses therfore gaue vnto you the circumcision, not because it is of Moses, but of the father. And yet ye on the Sabboth day circumcise a man. If a man on the Sabboth day receyue circumcision without breaking of the lawe of Moses, disdain ye at me, because I haue made a man euery whit wholle on the Sabboth day? Iudge not after the vtter appearaunce, but iudge with a righteous iudgement.

I teache no other thing then that which God had taught you by his lawe, if a man understand the meaning of the lawe, nor I do nothyng els but that the lawe prescribeth unto me. The autoritie of Moses is an halowed thing, and had in reuerence with you that despise me. And did not he take you a lawe whiche he receiued at Gods hande? Ye take vpon you the right understanding and keping of the lawe, whereas none of you doeth truely obserue the law after the wil of God, who gaue you the lawe: yea rather vnder a coulour and pretence of the lawe, ye go about those thinges whiche he doeth moste deteste and punishe. Ye laye blasphemie vnto my charge because I doe more seke the glory of God then mans prayse. Ye obiect against me the breakyng of the Sabboth daye, who haue saued a man on the Sabboth day, when as the holy religion of the Sabboth doeth not stay you from deuisyng and labouring to destroye an innocent, and not only an innocent, but suche one as hath deserued good at your handes. Is this to magnifie Moses whom ye preferre before me? Is this to honour and reuerence God, whom ye with feyned religion worshippe? Doeth not the law curse him that sheadeth innocentes bloud? Neither doeth it permitte any power or autoritie of putting to death but vpon malefactours, nor vpon them neyther, except they be lawfully conuicted and condẽned. Why than do ye contrary to the lawe trauaill about my death, that being sent of God do preache his wil and pleasure to you according to the intent of the law: that do seke his glorye and not mine owne: that do not effectuously seke a kingdome or riches to myself, but that do frely offre saluacion to all men: that hurte no mã but do good to all men? This saying of Jesus did vexe and trouble the Phariseis mindes for two causes: first because they perceiued well that their craftie inuencions (though they were secretly doen) were not hid from his knowledge, whom they supposed might soone without difficultie haue been made awaye, yf the thing that they went about could haue been kepte secrete from him: Secondarily his woordes pinched their mindes, because he did appeale them of sinnefull transgression of the lawe, in the presence of the people, who would haue been thought moste true obseruers of the law. They laying snares for the innocẽt bloud, feared not the knowledge of God, but they feared to haue their dedes knowen to the people. Therfore to face out the thyng by dissimulaciõ, they let fare as if they thought the multitude did not knowe their wickednes, & so fell to open rebukes and checkes as is the maner of all wicked persons that are taken with the maner in a mischeuouse dede that cã not be excused. Thou hast (say they) the deuill, seyng thou makest the father of heauen very God himselfe, to be auctour of thy doctrine, to auaunt thy selfe thereby. God is true, and thou by the deuils instigacion art vntrue. Who goeth about to deuise thy death? The Lorde Jesus did not brawle with them again with any checking answere to their so furiouse blasphemie, lest he should haue made them more woode by putting to of furie to them, that were already cruel and furiouse: but geuing vs an ensaumple of mildenesse, full gentelly he telleth them the cause why he did the dede, for the whiche they quarelled with hym. And whereas themselfes in very dede were breakers of the lawe in all thinges, yet did they accuse Jesus, as a transgressour of the lawe, because he had healed a man sycke of the Palsey on the Sabboth day.

The people answered and said, thou hast a deuill.

Who goeth about to kill thee?

I (saieth Jesus) did one certain dede on ẏ Sabboth daye, which was neyther euil, sinfull nor yet vnhonest: but wherwith I gaue health to a man that was miserably diseased, which you your selues could not but allowe & commend

mend, in case it had not been doen on the Sab'both day. But they do rather breake the Sabbeth whiche goeth about that thing on the Sabboth, which is sinful and wicked on what daye soeuer it bee doen. The religion of the Sabboth is not so great, but it ought to giue place to those thinges whiche are of more weight and greatter importaunce, and good and godly euery daye whensoeuer they be doen.

If Moses himselfe, whom ye highly esteme and attribute so much vnto, haue geuen you the same exaumple, and hath doen before me like wise as I haue doē: If also the very lawe do teache that worke maye be doen on the Sabboth day without breakyng the lawe of the Sabboth, eyther ye muste nedes absolue and cleare me: or els in case ye condemne me, ye must also cōdemne Moses with me, and the lawe it selfe to, because what soeuer he gaue vnto you, was a lawe. Moses gaue circumcision vnto you, not that circumcision began euen very than whan Moses lawe began, for it was geuen of God to the Patriarches before the lawe was writen: & for that cause circumcision is a greatter matter in religion then the Sabboth daye, because it went before the lawe, and is as it wer, the head of the lawe. But the very same Moses whiche commaunded circumcision, commaunded the Sabboth daye. You do circumcise a man on the Sabboth daye, and ye thinke not that ye violate the Sabboth day therin: because of the dignitie of circūcision, wherunto ye thinke that ẏ religion of the Sabboth ought of right to geue place: like as the Deacons and Priestes doe also in the temple these thinges whiche be pertaining to Goddes seruice, and yet in so doyng they take not themselfes to be breakers of the Sabboth daye, for somuche as they esteme the thyng that they doe, to be of more holynesse then that it should be omitted because of the Sabboth daye.

And ye on the Sabboth day circumcise a man.

Consideryng therefore that ye doe circūcise a man on the Sabbothe daye, leste through he not beynge circumcised he should not be one of you, neyther doe you wene that the Sabboth day is by that worke the wurse kept, I meruaill why than do you like disdainfull men make suche clamour, that by my worke the Sabboth daye is vnkept and broken, who haue healed not one parte alone of mā, but haue preserued and saued the whole manne altogether on the Sabboth daye? Although circumcision were before the lawe, and is after a sorte the very beginning & chiefe parte of the lawe, yet it is not perpetuall. For men were acceptable and dearly beloued of God before there was any circumcisiō, and the time shalbe, when God shall mislyke and refuse the ouerthwarte circūcision of the fleshe, beyng without the inward circumcision of the herte. But to geue health both of body and soule to a mans sily wretched neighbour, as it is a greater acte and a more holy dede than to circumcise a man, so is it alwaye good: before the law, in the tyme of the law, and after the law, because it is of it owne selfe good.

Why than doe ye, in a cause not vnlyke, yea in a much better matter as touching my behalfe, wurship and haue Moses in reuerence, and accuse me as giltye of a greater crime? For I doe not now dispute whiche of vs twayne is greatter then the other. Take Moses still (as he is) for an excellent man, let it be so that I am euen as you suppose me to be, a mean and an abiect person, yet if ye loke well about you, and do consider the matter rightly, either ye ought to cōdemne vs bothe, or to assoyle vs bothe. And ẏ very lawe, of trueth, teacheth vs this, that in geuyng iudgement, ye should loke vpon the matter, and not

the

the persone: and he standeth accursed that through fauouring the riche, oppresseth the poore.

Therfore iudge not after the qualitie of the persone, but lette your iudgemēt be iuste and rightful according to the matter, if ye will truelye obserue Moses lawe. But after these thinges and many suche other were spoken by our Lord Jesus, so gentelly that they had been able to haue pacified neuer so cruell a minde, & when his sayinges also were so trewe that they could not be proued false and confuted of any man, were he neuer so shamelesse, the Phariseis (of truth) ceassed from speakyng, but neuerthelesse they persist and continue in theyr malice without any mitigacion of minde, because he durst in the presence of a multitude, in suche wise laye from himselfe the faulte of breakyng the Sabboth, that he burdened them with a muche greater crime.

Judge not after the utter appearance. &c.

¶ Then sayed sum of them of Hierusalem: is not this he, whom they go about to kil? But lo: he speaketh boldely, and they saye nothing to him. Doe the rewlers knowe in dede, that this is very Christe? Howbeit we knowe this man whence he is, but when Christe cummeth, no man knoweth whence he is. Then cryed Jesus in the temple (as he taught) saying: Ye bothe knowe me, and whence I am ye knowe. And I am not cum of my selfe, but he that sent me is true, whom ye knowe not. But I knowe him, and if I saye that I knowe hym not, I shall be a lyar lyke unto you. But I knowe hym, for I am of hym, and he hath sent me.

The texte.

The Phariseis pride was so great, that they would be thus farre priuileged, that an innocent being accused should rather geue ouer his true cause, then that theyr auctoritie shoulde any thing quayle amongest the people: and rather that Gods prayse and glorye shoulde be nothyng at all spoken upon, than that any parte of their honour shoulde decaye. And yet euen this kynde of men founde many among the people whiche had rather serue this lewde ambicion of theirs, then to obey Gods will. For certain of Hierusalem sayed: Is not this he, whom the Scribes and Phariseis drift is to put to death? and whom men thought did hyde himselfe and durste not cum to the hye feastfull day for feare of them? Lo, he speketh openly in the temple, and uttereth his mind unto them frankely and frely euen to theyr face, yet do they geue hym no aunswer. What meaneth this their sylence? Are our head rulers brought in belefe that this is Messias, and now confesse that thing with silence whiche they did before impugne and denie? Howbeit, it is not lyke to be true that the chefe rewlers should thus thinke, for euen all we knowe whence this man came. His father and mother are knowen well inough to be playne folkes and of a meane sorte, we knowe what countrey man he is, we knowe also his brethren and his other kinsfolkes. But whan Messias cummeth he shall so cum, that no man shall knowe from whence he cummeth. Jesus perceyuing theyr blindnesse to be so great, that where as the prophecie had geuen knowledge beforehande that Messias shoulde cum out of Bethleem, where Jesus was borne, and where all other signes of the prophecies agree with hym to all purposes, yet they beyng blynded with malice, denye that they knowe hym, for no cause els, but because they knowe him, and therfore euen of purpose they make a lye, saying that Christ shoulde cum so, that no man should know from whence he cummeth: and this they forge, because they would not be compelled to recognyse him. Jesus, I say, frō whose knowleage, no not the secretes of men were hidde, to rebuke also this foolish ignorance of the multitude, whiche was corrupt

Then cried Jesus in the temple. &c.

rupt with seing their head men so set and affected, whiche multitude was wilfully ignorant in that thing whiche they might haue knowen, but that theyr lewde minde letted theyr iudgemente, doeth now with a more shrill and loude voice (to thintente he might be heard not onely of them that were nye at hande, but of all the people whiche were within the temple, a place moste conuenient to haue Gods glorye preached and setfurth in) beginne to teache openly who he was, and from whom he was sent: and that no man could be ignorant who he was, but eyther suche one as wilfully would be without knowleage, or els he that of very malice, would not confesse the thing that he knewe: and thus doing, Jesus doeth admonishe vs therwith, to giue place oftentimes to the malice of men, lest it beying more kindled, shoulde do worse and more cruelly, and so prouoke a more sorer iudgemēt of God against them: thus also, after that by all assayes he did all that could be doen for their amendment, he might iustely geue them ouer and leaue them as desperate persones, to theyr owne folly and disease, not ẏ the Glorie of God should be hid & conceled, ne yet the neyghbours health and saluacion neglected for theyr obstinate wickednesse. If therfore (sayeth Jesus) ye do not thinke me to be Messias, whome by the prophecies of your Prophetes ye looke for, bycause ye knowe from whence I came, euen that is the very thing which might teache you that I am he in dede, who haue cum after such sorte, & was borne in that selfe place, out wherof the Prophetes hath tolde before hand ẏ Messias should cum. ye haue heard Johns record of me, ye se my miracles, ye heare me beare witnes to the trueth, studying about none other thing, but Gods glory & your saluaciō. And therfore ye muste nedes knowe me, except ye had leauer wylfully be ignorant in the thing ye knowe. And how can ye say ẏ Messias should so cum that no man can knowe from whence he cummeth, when as the Prophetes pointe and assigne both his stocke and his countrey? These thinges being knowen vnto you, might induce and further you to the vnderstanding of the prophecie: howbeit it is a thing of more force and better it were to knowe from whence I came, than what stocke I am borne of. And in case ye woulde consider me with pure and sincere iyes, ye could not of trueth be ignoraūt therin. Neyther am I so of the worlde, nor do nowe cum out of the worlde, as ye do slaunderously reporte of me, but I cum from him that sente me into ẏ worlde, to the intent it might conuert and be saued. For I am sent from him whom ye knowe not, and for this cause he sent me, that ye also shoulde learne to knowe him by me, as muche as he may of man be knowen. Albeit ye can by no meane yet knowe him except ye applye your selfes through godlines, to deserue that he would geue you knowlage of him. For they knowe him not, ẏ doeth not obey his will: And it is not sufficient to knowe God in woordes, if ye denye him in your dedes. If ye will haue true knowelage of the father, ye must learne it of his sonne. I onely haue truely knowen him, because I proceded from him, and was with him before I came into the worlde, and I was sent into the worlde from him to teache you to knowe him: that throughe your belefe ye might be saued. For I came not of mine owne head as other dooe, sekyng their owne praise rather then Goddes honour, teaching their owne commentes and fantasies and not the doctrine of God. And he that sent me is true: and forbecause I haue it of him whatsoeuer I speake, therfore my sayinges be also true.

And I am not cum of my selfe: but he that sent me is true.

And him ye knowe not.

The texte. ¶ Then they sought to take him but no man layed handes on him, because his houre was

was not yet cum. Many of the people beleued on him, and sayd: Whan Christe cummeth will he do moe miracles then these that this man hath doen?

The seniors and rulers being stirred and sore heated with these woordes, weared more wood and chafed more in their heartes because he toke vnto him suche authoritie before the people and openly rebuked theim of their peruerse wickednes. They had muche a do to holde their handes of him, for now their angre was turned into woodnesse, they now passed nothing of that good aduisement and deliberacion, wherwith they were purposed to make him awaie secretly: But though their will was readye to do that mischieuous deede, yet no mā at that time laide handes vpon him: Christ willing so to haue it, because the time was not yet cum whiche his father had appointed, to worke therin by his death, the saluacion of the worlde. For as he willingly dyed, so coulde not he against his will be taken. It lay in him to stay mennes mindes, were they neuer so fierce, nor no mannes power could preuaile against him, vnlesse it had pleased his exceding charitie towardes man to be crucified for the saluacion of the world: but the priestes, Scribes, Phariseis, and headmen of the people, whom for their holy profession and knowlage of the lawe, it had behoued first of all other to haue acknowlaged Christ, perseuering in their wycked purpose euen of corrupte mindes, many of the comminaltie, and of the vnlearned in the lawe, whiche (as they were of the lesse auctoritie and learning, so they had more good mindes and deuocion) did so beleue our Lorde Jesus woordes and miracles but not yet of trueth fully persuaded that Jesus was Messias, howbeit they were brought to this poinct, that they semed apte to be persuaded: If this man (say they) be not Christ, as the Phariseis thinke he is not, yet it is muche to be meruailed at how he hath so great power in workyng miracles. For yf Messias himselfe shoulde cum, shoulde he do greater thinges then whiche this man doeth?

¶ The Phariseis hearde that the people murmured suche thinges concerning hym. And the Phariseis and hie priestes sente ministers to take hym. Than saied Jesus vnto them: yet am I a litle while with you, then goe I vnto him that sente me, and ye shall not fynde me: whither I goe, thither can ye not cum.

The texte.

But the Phariseis and the seniors, whose part had been to haue allured and inticed the vnlearned multitude vnto Christe, after that they perceiued there was many of the people inclined towardes hym, fel to suche furicus headines ye they were determined euery way without any stoppe, that he ought to dye: whiche was thought would obscure their honour. Suche a pestilence is ambicion when it is coulcured with pretence of religion and doctrine. But in the meane tyme feare of daungier, and neither shame nor pitie stayed theim from manifest doing of that enormitie. Therfore they did hyre priuely the common catchepolles to take Jesus in the sight of the people, and when they had taken hym, to bring him to them as an euill doer. But Jesus that knewe their priuie conspiracie conspired against him, and could not be taken excepte he had liste himselfe, sumwhat openeth vnto them by darke sayinges, that the time should come when as he would voluntarily offre himselfe to death, wheras then they sought his death in vain, and in a maner also gaue them warning to be more glad of him, and wel to vse him whiles they had hym. For the tyme should be that all in vain they shoulde desire him being absent, whom they did persecute beyng present, specially when as they coulde not cum to the place whiche he shoulde should conuey himselfe to. For he went euen to death, whereunto as yet they might not folowe him. He returned again to heauen, & thither was no mortall bodye able to pursue after him. Well, Iesus spake vnto them in this manier: I am yet a litle while with you & then goe I vnto him that sent me. Ye shall then seke me, and not fynde me, and where I shal goe to, ye cannot cum. The Lorde Iesus spake these thinges vnto them couertly, as he was wont to dooe many mo thinges, that they should not vnderstande them before they were put in vre and finished. And the darkenes of speaking maketh a man diligent to seke the matier. And whē the thinges be exibite and dooen, the wordes are more surely beleued. Finally, the thing grue to this point, that it was well knowen to all men, that whatsoeuer our lorde suffered, he suffered it aduisedly and vpon deliberacion, not of casualtie: he suffered it willingly, and not of necessitie. Though these wordes were spoken to all men in generall, yet it did most specially pricke the Phariseis seruauntes, whiche were sent to take Iesus, against whom they perceiued that they coulde nothyng do, except he were willyng. And whiles he toucheth secretly their inwarde conscience, he declareth that he knoweth what thyng soeuer is moste secretely hid in mennes heartes. And therwithall he winneth those hertes vnto him through his gentilnes, whose wicked enterprises he did not disclose vnto the people.

Ye shall seke me and shall not finde me &c.

¶ Then sayd the Iewes among themselues: whither will he goe that we shall not fynde him: will he goe amonge the Gentiles (whiche are scattered abrode) and teache the Gentiles: what maner of saying is this that he sayd, ye shall seke me, and shall not fynde me, and where I am thither can ye not cum.

The texte.

Therfore when as the multitude did not vnderstande this his saying, they reasoned among themselues: what meaneth this that he sayeth, where I goe to, thither can ye not cum? will he priuely steale awaye and goe to sum farre countrey among the heathen people? will he suffre himselfe to forsake this holy lande and holy people to go dwell among wicked & prophane people, whither he thinketh we will neuer folowe him? or will he wander hither and thither like a vagabounde among the Gentiles dwellyng farre awaye, that he cannot be found of vs?

Than sayd the Iewes among themselues whither will he goe? &c.

In the last day, that great day of the feast, Iesus stode and cryed, saying. If any man thirst, let him cum vnto me and drinke. He that beleueth on me (as sayeth the scripture) out of his belly shall flowe riuers of water of lyfe. But this spake he of the spirite which they that beleue on him, should receiue, for the holy ghoste was not yet there, because Iesus was not yet glorified.

The texte.

But when the last day of that feast was cum, whiche was moste solemnely kept with moste great resorte of people, & with great religion, (for when this day was past, euery mā was glad to repayre home againe) Iesus stode vp in the temple as though he also would leaue the coūtrey of Iurye, & doth halow that moste solemne day of that great feast with a notable sermō, and therwith purueyed vitailes of euangelicall faith of the ghospell, for them that should iourney. Nor he did not onely speake openly, but also cryed with a firme and a stayed voyce, therby declaryng that the matier was mete to be heard of all folke. The Phariseis had babished the simple people, with fained and colde religion, and had tangled theyr consciences with mannes ordinaunces. And surely the multitude had nothing els almost in admiracion that Iesus sayd or did,

did but his miracles. But for somuche as they had not dronke of the spirite of the gospell, they toke the lesse spirituall profite at his handes. Therfore Jesus called and allured all menne openly from the barren and colde doctrine of the Phariseis, unto himselfe, promisyng them the spirite, whiche once being receiued, not only they (by his grace) themselues shall attaine to the true & euangelicall doctrine, but shall also by theyr preachyng issue foorth upon other great aboundaunce and efficacie of wysedome: I am (sayth he) the fountaine of helthfull wysedome: whoso thirsteth, let him aske nothing of Moses, the Phariseis, the Scribes, or of the priestes. Let him cum to me, and drinke of this well. And whosoeuer beleueth my wordes; the same drinketh. Therfore whosoeuer beleueth on me, & desyrously drinketh up my wordes, as the scripture biddeth bearing witnesse of me, he shal not weaxe dry throwe infidelitie, but yͤ draught that he dronke of the spirite of God, shall bring foorth in his heart a well that shall runne euermore and plentifully, in suche wyse, that out of his heart shall flowe, not onely small litle streames, but also great & plenteous fluddes, wherwith the drynesse of the Gentiles shalbe watered, & therof shall spring muche fruite of the ghospell. By this parable & far of speakyng, Jesus did meane that fertile and plenteous spirite whiche afterwarde they should receiue that woulde beleue on him: whiche spirite after that the Apostles had receiued, forthwith they begon with great confidence to preache in diuers toungues to the whole worlde yͤ philosophie of the gospel, & to distill into the soules of all that beleued on Christ, the same spirite that they receyued from heauen. For albeit that many at that time had sum smattering and were sum what entered into knowlage of the faith, for all that the verye effectuall and plentifull spirite was not yet cum to any of them, forbecause Jesus was not by his death and resurreccion glorified, nor had not ascended up to heauen to sitte on the fathers right hande, from whence he should sende that spirite to his Apostles. But the misterie of the crosse was to be perfourmed before, whiche thing could not be doen and accomplished, except his glorious maiestie had been kept secret, and as it were dissembled for a season: and they also could not be made able to receyue that diuine spirite, unlesse they had first been framed and fashioned therunto by many miracles, sayinges and doinges. Therfore the Lorde Jesus doeth call and byd all folke to this well of the water of lyfe, yet he compelleth no man againste his wyll, nor he excludeth no man, so that he cum athirst.

If any man thirst, let him cum unto me and drinke.

Many of the people therfore, when they heard this saying, sayed: of a trueth this is a prophete: but other sayd, this is Christ: but sum sayd, shall Christ cum out of Galile? Sayeth not the scripture, that Christe shall cum of the sede of Dauid and out of the toune of Bethleem, where Dauid was? So there was discencion amog the people, because of him. And sum of them woulde haue taken hym, but no man layed handes on hym.

The texte.

When the Lorde Jesus had spoken this, and many mo lyke thynges, though they were not fullye understande, yet they dyd woorke sundrie myndes and affeccions in the multitude of the people: for sum, upon sight of so many miracles, and the great auctoritie of his wordes, sayed: truly this is a very prophete. Again, other that thought more hyghly of him, sayed: yea this is that very Messias, whom the prophetes haue promised in their prophecies. On the contrary syde, other being corrupted with pharisaicall leuen, went about to reproue and confute these mens opinion by the very woordes of the prophetes, whiche tolde before that he shoulde ryse out of the tribe of Juda, and

out.

out of the towne of Bethleem. Christe was thought with moste part of men to be borne in Nazareth, because he was nursed there, and broughte vp with his parentes whiche dwelte there, and also because he begamne his preaching in Galile: and for the moste part had his abode there. But the people of Jerusalē and the Jewes that were of the tribes of Jurie, toke the people of Galile as mēn nigh neighbours vnto the heathen, and were myxte together, but for halfe their countreymen, because they neyther excelled in knowledge of the lawe, nor euer had any prophete in whome they might worthily reioyce. They knewe verily that Messias was promysed to the tribe of Juda, not to men of Galile, and that he shoulde cum of the seede of Dauid, who had his princely palace at Jerusalem. And thus therfore they dyd chalenge vnto them, honour of Christ to cum, whom they themselfes being with malice corrupted nowe at his very cumming did persecute. They say therfore: it is not lyke to be true that this man should be Messias, if you do ponder and straitly examine the prophecies. When Christe shall cum shall he cum to vs oute of Galile? doth not the prophecies manifestly saye that Messias shall come of the sede of Dauid, who was certainly of the trybe of Juda? And furthermore, it also expresseth the tounes name where he shoulde bee borne, that is to say, Bethleem, whiche is the citie of Dauid, that was geuen to Judas for his parte or tribe. Therefore forasmuche as the prophecie dooeth plainlye shewe that he shoulde cum of a kynges stocke, of the moste holye tribe of all Juda, out of a princely toune, howe can it stande and accorde that this man shoulde be Messias, whose parentes be poore and of no estimacion, and cummeth to vs out of a vile toune, of no name, whiche standeth in Galile a countrey of no renowme? After this sorte, the people disputed of Jesus with diuers iudgementes, and there was dissencion among theim for his sake. Yet did not Jesus accumpany himselfe with theim in this disputacion, because they did not dispute with suche simple purenesse of mynde, that they dyd deserue to bee taught: and it was not yet tyme to declare hymselfe howe great and excellent a man he was. For yf they had vprightly and truely desyred to knowe who he was, they themselues might haue learned of Jesus kinsfolkes that he was not borne at Nazareth as more part of theim supposed, but in Bethleem, and that he came of Dauids familie. Nor there was not a fewe that knewe these thinges, but because Jesus dyd not bryng with hym, and shewe vnto them thinges agreable to their lustes, they were more wyllyng to serue theyr owne affeccions, than to receiue and acknowledge hym. For and if their minde had been plain, simple and pure, they might haue learned the thing wherabout they contended, in case they woulde haue asked Jesus hymselfe the question. And there were many of the people so blynded with enuy and hatered, that they conspired among theymselfes to take our Lorde Jesus and laye handes on hym. But the malice of man had no power and strength against hym, who hath all thinges in his power.

The texte. ¶ Than came the ministers to the high priestes and Phariseis. And they sayed vnto them: why haue ye not brought him? The ministers answered: neuer man spake as this man doth. Then answered the phariseis Are ye also deceiued? doeth any of the rulers or of the phariseis beleue on hym? but this common people whiche knowe not the lawe, are accursed.

And therefore the sergeauntes whom the Phariseis had sent as seruauntes of of their mad fury, to attache Jesus, returned againe, with their mindes cleane chaunged, unto the hye priestes and Phariseis, whiche with fierce and cruell myndes, taryed lokyng for theyr seruaũtes to haue brought the apprehended person unto them, to the intẽte that so at last they might haue satisfyed and accomplisshed their hatered upon hym.

But in the meane tyme the prouision of God, whiche farre passeth all worldly mennes crafte and subtiltie, procured such succoure, that whatsoeuer the malicious Phariseis wente about to procure, the same lighted upon theyr own heades and made well for the settyng foorth of Christes glory. The unlearned multitude, the rude ignoraunt people of Galilee, the Samaritanes, the Cananites, and the Heathen people beyng moued with Jesus sayinges & doinges, beleued on hym. Onely the Scribes, Phariseis, seniors, and priestes in whose gouernaunce the open confessiõ and discussion of the whole law and religion was, were not only neuer a deale moued to cum to better aduisement, and to be conuerted: but were made euery way wurse and more woode. It was now cum to this point, that their hiered men the catche polles, a curryshe kynde of people, & readye to be hiered to do all unhappinesse for money, should bothe honestly reporte of Jesus, and also reproue theyr uncurable blyndnesse. These seruauntes had seen no miracles wroughte, they had but onelye hearde hym speake a fewe wordes, yet hauing their myndes cleane altered, and without any regarde to the commaundementes of the Phariseis, they retourned agayne unto them, and brought not Jesus with them: And when they that sent them, asked and quarelled with them, why they did not as they were commaunded, the menne did not saye for their excuse the feare of the multitude, nor feined any other excuse, but frankly and freely confessed that of truth they went purposely to haue taken Jesus, and to haue brought hym with them, but they were through a few of his effectuouse & gracious wordes, so as it were charmed and newely hearted agayne, that they utterlye repined in theyr hartes to do that thyng whiche they had purposed: we neuer (saye they) hearde manne speake as this man doeth. Who can laye violent handes upon suche lyke men? What recorde coulde haue been auouched in the synagoge, which should more haue burdened and pressed, and more openly disclosed the Phariseis obstinate malice? They did all they could to the uttermoste of theyr power to subuert the doctrine of Jesus, but all their endeuoure wente backewarde: for whiles they went about by all the waies they could, utterly to destroy Christ and his doctrine, they stablisshe and set forth both. But as yet still they dissemble the wood furie of their hartes, speakyng to their seruauntes more courteously and more quietly then according to the fury of their thoughtes: howe chaunsed this saye they? Are ye which belong to us, and therfore not to be taken as of the raskall noumbre, also deceiued by him? Do ye not perceyue him to go about to deceiue men with faire promisses, and to sell false ware for good? If he were true, do ye not thynke that suche notable men as doth excell both in learning and auctoritie would approue his sayinges? do ye see any rulers or magistrates, unto whõ the auctoritie of the religion belongeth, or any of the Phariseis, which hath the moste exacte knowledge of the law, perswaded by his wordes? doeth the exaumple of a fewe catifes, a sorte of drudges, moue you? This sorte of people is ignoraunt, & knoweth not the lawe, and therfore are accursed. Well, euen God thus disposed these thinges, to certifie and teache us that nothyng

Doeth any of ye rulers or of the Phariseis beleue on hym?

doeth more obstinately resist true religion, then the malice of them whiche are cloked with the false pretence of religion, nor no man more deadly enemy to ye doctrine of the gospel, then he that wresteth holy scripture to his owne lewde affeccions: neyther are any more desperately wicked, then those, whiche with pretence of holynes, with perswasion of learnyng, with publike auctoritie, be armed against the trueth of the gospell. But in dede, whatsoeuer this worlde deuiseth with all his engyns agaynst the heauenly trueth the successe therof is to the glorie of our lord Jesus Christ. Now than, marke me this well (O wise reader) that there is no where more scarcitie of them, that with theyr hartes fauoureth the christen trueth, than among the ringleaders of religion, and head learned men.

The texte. Nicodemus sayeth vnto them (he that came to Jesus by night, and was one of them) doeth our lawe iudge any man before it heare hym, and knowe what he hath doen? They answered, and sayed vnto him: art thou of Galile? Searche and looke, for out of Galile ariseth no prophete. And euery man went vnto his owne house.

In so great a counsail which was of Phariseis, Scribes, Seniours, and Priestes, there was no man saue onely Nicodemus which would stand in the defence of that innocente lorde, against suche wicked enterprises. This Nicodemus was one of the headmen of the secte of Phariseis, a grosse mā of truth and lesse learned thē other, but he was of a lesse corrupt minde: and it was the same which for feare of the Jewes came to Jesus by night (as I tolde you before) to be better instructed by him through priuate and secrete communicaciō. And by that one metyng, he profited so muche that he toke Jesus for a good man, though he did not fully vnderstande the mistery and spirituall meanynge of his woorde. When this man sawe his felowes with bloud suckyng myndes, tende to the vtter destruccion of Jesus, whome he so fauoured that neuertheless he feared the malice that was armed with auctoritie, he tooke Jesus part warely: And spake those thynges for him whiche might haue been spokē for any malefactour before he had been conuicted: we do (sayeth he) professe a law, which doeth not condemne the euill doer, except he be first heard, and the matters duely discussed, whiche be layed to his charge that is accused. Lette this manne haue at leste this benefite of the lawe, whiche is common for all folke: and the lawe selfe geueth it euen to them that be misdoers. When they had no matter once to open theyr mouthe to speake against this so indifferent and manerly defence, whiche Nicodemus vsed in speakyng for Christ, they do not onely not call themselfes home, & turne to a better mynde, nor yet be pacified and appeased, but without regarding the mannes dignitie and auctoritie they fall in hande to rebuke him, & to his reproche, say thus vnto hym: art thou also nowe become a man of Galile? The common people and the vnlearned are to be holden excused, and maye be forgeuen: but is it not a great shame for thee that art an head man, & a doctor of the lawe, to be the disciple and scholler of this Galile man, whiche is a verye deceiuer of the people? to whom no man ioyneth himselfe, but suche as be moste vile abiectes before manne, and cursed before God? Thou that professest the knowledge of the lawe, and art an open reader and discusser of the same, searche well the scriptures, & throughlye examine them, and if thou fynde any where throughout all the scriptures that either any prophete hath euer cum or euer shall cum out of Galile: beleue then this

Searche & loke, for out of Galile ariseth no prophete.

this felowe to be a prophete. This answere of the Phariseis was not onelye wicked, but also folishe. For Nicodemus had not affirmed him to be a prophete, but sayde: whosoeuer he be, he ought not after our common, or rather publike law, (that is to saye, a lawe which indifferently perteyneth to all men of euery state) to be condemned, except his cause be knowen before. But where malice & hatred is in the heart, & occupieth the powers of the mynde, there is no iudgement. After these thynges wer commoned to and fro from one to an other, the counsell brake vp and was dismist: And so euery mā went home, their wyll to berive Christ of his life, beyng delayed and prologed, but not chaunged. For Jesus tyme was not as yet.

The. viii. Chapter.

Jesus wente into the mount Oliuete, and early in the mornynge he came agayne into the temple, and the people came vnto hym, and he sate downe and taught them. *The texte.*

And so now (when it drewe nere night) Jesus wēt vnto mount Oliuete, where Bethanie was, a pleasaunte lodgeyng for the lorde, consideryng that there was no quiete place in Jerusalem: & herein he taught vs that a secrete place, or some vacaciō, is cōueniēt for preachers of the ghospell: and that the trueth hath no where lesse place, than in riche and welthy cities. Howebeit sometyme the euangelicall wyse preachers shall resorte thither, not to get riches or honoure, but to do good to other: though they do endaungier their liues thereby. Therfore the next daye folowynge, Jesus returned againe to Jerusalem early in the mornynge, and now not stādyng (as he did the daye before) but sate downe, and taught in the temple, with a bolde countenaunce: openly shewyng hymselfe to be nothyng afearde of the Phariseis wicked conspiracies. And all the people came in a great assembly vnto him, partly being brought to haue him in admiracion throughe the miracles and wordes that he had doen and spoken before tyme: and partly to intrappe hym, and to get matter to harme him.

And the Scribes and Phariseis brought vnto hym a woman taken in aduoutrye, and whan they had set her in the middes, they saye vnto hym. Maister this woman was taken in aduoutrie euen as the deede was a doyng. Moses in the lawe commaunded vs that suche shoulde be stoned. But what sayest thou? this they sayde to tempte hym, that they mighte accuse hym. *The texte.*

And for because they had marked in hym a certayn merueilous clemencye & gentle pacience towardes the poore miserable cōmon people, thereat they toke occasiō to accuse him: wheras thei ought ẏ rather to haue loued hym. Moses law had ordeined a sore statute against aduoutrie, that is to saye, that in case any woman were taken vnlawfully vsyng her selfe with any other manne, she should be stoned at the peoples handes. And in the meane while the men pardoning themselfes, were extreme against the women: as though thei should be innocent before god, or auoide eternal paine, if they were not punished by the lawe, though otherwyse they committed greater faultes. The lawe onely punisheth open faultes: It doth not punishe pride, hautenes of mind, nor hatred, but god doth more abhorre these thinges, thē ẏ other, which ẏ law punisheth. Now therfore the Scribes and Phariseis, (that is to wete, men ye knowe well inough, very seuere kepers of iustice, and of very zeale and loue to ẏ lawe fiercely set against malefactours, and open synners, when they themselues are inwardly in their hertes soused and washed with muche more enormious sinnes) brought a woman taken in aduoutrie vnto Jesus, at that time sitting in the temple. They set the woman opẽly in the middes of ẏ people, to thintente that if Christ would haue geuen sentence of condemnacion against her, many of the multitude shoulde haue borne him lesse fauoure, whose fauoure he had gotten, chiefly by reason of his lenitie and gentlenes, but and if he should pardon her and clearely dismisse her, as they thoughte he woulde haue doen, that then they might finde some faulte by him, wherof to accuse hym: whiche was not afrayde to forgeue an aduouterer cõtrary to Moses ordinaunce and lawe: and so then they hope to bring to passe, that (when all should be set on a roare) in steede of the woman, Christ himselfe should be ouerthrowen and euẽ pressed downe with stones. And verely these Phariseis themselues, beyng more wicked synners, accuse the synfull woman before Jesus, as a iudge on this wyse. This woman (saye they) was euen now taken in aduoutrie, euen as the deede was doing, and Moses made vs a law that suche shoulde be stoned. Therfore we bryng her vnto the people to be stoned, excepte thou disagree therunto: what thynkest thou?

And the Scribes & Phariseis brought vnto hym a woman taken in aduoutrie.

The texte. But Jesus stouped downe, and with his fynger, wrote on the grounde. So when they continued askyng him, he lifte himselfe vp and sayed vnto them: Let him that is amonge you without synne, caste the firste stone at her. And againe he stouped downe and wrote on the ground. And assone as they heard this, they went out one by one, beginning at the eldest. And Jesus was left alone, and the woman standyng in the middest. When Jesus had lifte vp himself, and sawe noman but the woman, he saied vnto her: womã where are those thine accusars? hath noman condemned the? She sayd, noman lorde. And Jesus sayed: neyther do I condemne the. Goe and synne no more.

Verely Jesus, who knewe the secretes of their heartes, and was ignoraunt in no manier of thyng were it neuer so priuie, did so elude and disapoynte their malice, by his godly wysedome, that he deliuered the aduoutresse oute of the stonecasters handes, and yet did not clerely absoyle her as faultlesse, leste he should seme to abrogate Moses lawe, whiche was necessarily geuen, to cause men refraine from euil dedes. This, I say, did Jesus, who came not to breake and abrogate the lawe, but to fulfil it: and againe on the other syde, he did not condemne her, because he came not into the worlde to haue sinners loste, but to saue them. For of trueth Jesus doeth euery where so moderate his wordes, as touchyng those ordinaunces whiche the worlde obserueth necessarily, euen to preserue a publike peace, and for a common quietnes, that he neither muche aloweth them nor improueth them, but vpõ occasion therof, geueth monicion that generally all vngraciousnes is to be eschewed, and not onely these dedes whiche worldly prynces lawes do punishe.

For truely there be in goddes iudgement crymes more horrible than these, which yet the lawe doeth not punish, notwithstanding they cannot escape punishment at goddes hande where he taketh on hand to reuenge the doer. Therfore Jesus doeth neither refuse the iudgement, which was cõmitted vnto him, forasmuche as he is iudge ouer all, nor he doth not appoint and cõmit the woman, which was giltie, vnto the men that wer in readinesse to cast stones, neither doeth he cleare the woman of the matter, who in dede had deserued to be punished,

punished: but with silẽce he succoureth her, that was pulled & hurried to pain, to preserue her vnto penaunce: and that she mighte with due repentaunce bee better aduised, and conuerte to healthe and saluacion. He gaue no aunswere by worde of mouthe, but he spake the more by his dede. He knewe the selye giltie woman to bee a sinner, but he also knewe her accusers, whiche woulde haue been thought righteous, to be more sinfull then she was. He did not take away Moses lawe, but he shewed the mercifulnes of Christes newe law, whereof he was thauctor: he informed them that drewe the faultie womã to cruel pain, to loke well vpon thẽselues, and according to gods lawe, to examine their owne conscience duely: & euery one to shewe himself suche a one towardes his neighbour that had offended, as he would haue god to iudge hym. This thyng our Lorde Jesus did for our instruccion, and he bowed downe hymselfe, to signify that a man, al statelinesse and pride layd doune (wherwith any man flattered himself, and of an hault minde despised his neighbour,) should descende doune into himself, and loke wel vpon himself: and being bowed doune, Jesus wrote vpon the grounde, euen to geue vs warnyng that God shall iudge euerye man after the lawe of the gospel: The lawe written in tables, made them by an vntrue righteousnes proude and arrogant. The law written vpon the grounde, maketh euery man through a conscience and knowlage of his owne infirmitie, meke and mercifull vnto his neighbour.

Now whiles the Jewes preaced still vpon him, to knowe his iudgemente (although he had already by his dede pronounced it) he stoode vp, and so tolde them playnly his minde, that wyst not what he meant by his doing, and sayd: He that is among you without synne let him cast the first stone at her. With this saying he did not clearely assoyle the offender, but he pearced their consciences. And euery one of them knowynge himselfe giltie, feared leste Jesus, to whom they sawe wer knowen euen moste hid and secret thynges, should haue published their vngracious actes. When he had thus pricked their conscience, he stouped doune againe, and wrote vpon the grounde, as it wer by that dede payntyng before theyr iyes, what he would haue them to do.

Let hĩ that is among you without sinne cast ÿ firste stone at her.

He noted their arrogancie, whiche toke vpon them to be holy, when as in dede they were more synfull then those whom the lawe extremely punished. For she, whom they had brought foorth to be stoned with the commõ handes of manye, had not kylled her husband: but through the frailtie of the fleshe, had geuen the vse of her body to an other man, and so committed aduoutrie. They beyng full of enuy, hatered, complainyng, couetousnes, ambicion, and deceite, laye in wayte to kyl the lorde of ÿ whole lawe, who alone was free in al thynges, and clerely pure from all synne. Therefore vpon this the lordes answere, euery one knowing himself giltie, & being afrayed lest he shoulde be bewraied and his faultes disclosed, went out of the temple one after another: the seniors, the Phariseis, the Scribes, the Priestes, and other head men goyng before, and the rest folowing them. For they whiche among that sorte wer taken for the very pillers and mainteiners of religion and iustice, were euen sowsed in enormities, and inwardly moste great synners: When these folkes were gone out, of whom neuer one was cleare and without fault, Jesus remained alone, who onely was without fault. And nowe the synful womã found him, which neuer hadde doen synne, a mercifull iudge, wheras she should haue had them cruel murderers, who were themselues giltie of grieuous synnes. Therefore the woman seing their crueltie, stoode alone as a wofull synner before Jesus that was alone: a woman ready to perishe, before a Sauiour: a sinfull creature before the fountaine of all perfection and holynes. She quaked for feare euen of a very conscience, but the clemencie of Jesus, whiche shewed it selfe euen in his countenaunce, put her in good coumfort: and in the meane whyle our lord (as it were a man occupied about an other thyng) wrote vpon the grounde, so that the Jewes (as it well appeared) wente awaye, not as men afraied with the lordes threatnynges, but condemned in their owne consciences.

At lengthe Jesus stoode vppe, and when he sawe that all were goen and the woman all alone and fearefull, he speake curteously vnto her, sayinge: woman wher are thine accusers? hath any man condemned the? She answered: no mā sir. Then Jesus sayed, neither will J that came to saue all men, bee more vnmercifull then they, nor condemne her whom they haue not condemned. The rigour of the lawe doeth punishe, to feare men: the fauourablenesse of the gospell seketh not the deathe of a synner, but rather his amendemente and lyfe. Therfore go thy waye and sinne nomore hereafter. By this example our lorde Jesus taught those that taketh vpon them to be shepherdes ouer the people, and to be teachers of the gospell, howe greate sufferaunce and gentelnesse they ought to vse towardes them, whiche fall into synne by frailtie: for considering that, he in whom was no synne at al, shewed hymself so merciful towardes an opensinner, how great ought the bisshops gentilnes to be towardes offēders? when as they themselues haue many times more nede of Goddes mercy then they, against whose fauttes they be very angry: or in case they be not so synful, certes their life is not without some spotte: at leaste waye truely they maye by the frailtie of man, fall into all kynde of synne.

He said vnto her: woman where are thyne accusers?

Go & synne nomore.

Texte.

¶ Then spake Jesus agayne vnto them, sayinge: J am the light of the worlde. He that foloweth me, doth not walke in darkenesse, but shall haue the light of life. The Phariseis therfore sayed vnto hym: thou bearest recorde of thy selfe, thy recorde is not true. Jesus answered and sayed vnto them: Though J beare recorde of my self, yet my recorde is true, for J knowe whence J cam and whither J go. But ye canne not tell whence J come and whither J go. Ye iudge after the fleshe. J iudge no man. And if J iudge, my iudgement is true. For J am not alone but J go to the father that sent me. Jt is also written in your lawe, that the testimonie of two men is true. J am one that beareth wytnesse of my selfe, and the father that sent me beareth witnesse of me. Then sayed they vnto him, where is thy father? Jesus aunswered, ye neyther knowe me nor yet my father: yf ye had knowen me ye shoulde haue knowen my father also. These wordes spake Jesus in the treasury as he taught in the temple, and no man layed handes on hym, for his houre was not yet come.

Therfore nowe when they whiche complayned of the woman, were sente awaie and euery man brought to the knowledge of his owne synne, and the synner dismyst, Jesus vpon this occasion goeth in hande agayne to make an ende of the sermon whiche he had begun. Synne is darkenes. They that bee true and of plaine meaninge, & studie not to be thoughte other maner of folke then they be, go to the light, and are deliuered out of darkenes, lyke as the synfull woman wente vnto Jesus. And because she did not denye, but confessed the thynge that she had committed, she wente awaye iustifyed. Contrarywyse the heade men and the Phariseis, because they woulde be thoughte righteous, when as in very dede they were vngraciouse, and very wicked, fledde from the lyghte, leste theyr dysease shoulde be knowen, and so they made whole. Therfore Jesus doeth exhorte all folke ỹ whosoeuer is bewrapped in synne, should come to hym, but so that he come penitente: and shoulde rather folowe hym then

then the Phariseis, who being blynde, were guydes of the blynde. And leste any man throughe knowledge of his synnes, shoulde not be bolde to come unto hym, he taught us in the aduoutresse a litle before, howe he rejected no man that desireth to be healed. I am (sayeth he) that to the whole, not to Palestine alone, which the sunne in the firmamente is to all the worlde: as muche to saye,

I am the light of the worlde. &c

I am the light of the worlde. The sunne taken awaye maketh all thinges darke withall. It beareth lighte before all bodyes: I am light to pure soules. It geueth life and likynge to all bodyes: I am lighte more presently to soules. He that walketh in the lighte of the sunne, stumbleth not in the darke: whoso foloweth me and beleueth on my doctrine, shall abide no longer in darkenes of errour and sinne: but beinge purged frō sinne and illumined with the doctrine of the gospell, shall haue the true light which geueth lyfe to the soule. It belongeth to the dead to be hid in darkenes, and the propertie of them that be aliue is to walke and be cōuersant in the light. To haue knowledge of me, is the life of the soule. Contrary, synne, and to bee ignoraunt of me, is eternall death. The Phariseis enuye coulde not broke this magnificence whiche Christe preached of hymselfe, specially forasmuche as they thoughte themselues to be touched couertly, and whatsoeuer did redound unto Jesus commendacion and praise, the same to be a derogacion to theirs. And furthwith therfore they cried out against hym, in the presence of the multitude, fearyng leste the common people would forsake them and folow Christ: and to bryng hym out of credence, they would make him a lyar, and charged hym therwith. Thou (they saye) bearest

Thou bearest recorde of thy selfe.

recorde and speakest stoutly of thy selfe, but no mans owne recorde is to be beleued. It is no true mans parte, but a proude mans fashion, to set forth his owne prayse: wherfore this thyne owne testemonye is not true. To this vengeable checke (whiche yet in dede coulde not so muche hurte his glory, as it mighte hynder the saluacion of that great nombre of people) Jesus made a sharpe aunswere, saying: Trueth it is, amonges men the witnesse of hym whiche bothe maye deceyue and be deceiued, is of small importaunce, and weyeth litle.

I alone am not witnesse to my selfe, who can bring for me Johns recorde, and the witnesse whiche the prophetes bare of me, yea and though there were no mannes recorde of me, who stande in no nede of it. For if I alone shoulde beare witnesse of my selfe, yet could not you (in case ye knewe plainly who I am and whence I came) reproue mine owne recorde. It is expedient that those mennes witnesse be drawen in question and doubted of, which (being nothing els but verye men, and according to mans iudgement make relacion of themselues,) may be deceiued, & also lye if they list: but these thinges hath that way no place in me. For I speake nothing of mine owne head, but the thyng that I say, cummeth of him from whom I was sent: & I haue none other pretēse therein, but to set furth his glory. He cannot lye, and his onely recorde is more holy and uncorrupt then all mennes witnesses. Whosoeuer hath proceded frō him, and speaketh all thinges according to his minde, within a while to returne again unto the same person from whence he came, hath no nede of mans

But ye can not tell whence I am.

witnesse: when as his owne propre actes are in redines to declare who he is. But you being blinded with enuye, of purpose will not knowe the thing that ye might knowe: and because ye iudge peruersly of me through the estimacion that ye haue of those thinges which are in me, & other mortall men indifferently, and comen to both, ye do not perceiue frō whence I came, nor whither I shall go. For this is not seen except mennes myndes (wicked affeccions set aside) do iudge after the spirite, and in ready beleke of myndes, learne by the thynges whiche I do & speake (with cōferryng together the sayinges of the prophetes) to see that it is an heauenly thyng, and no worldly thyng. But you iudge after the fleshe: & why? because ye be corrupted with worldly affection, condemning wickedly to your owne better destructiō, that thing which ye ought to imbrace to eternall saluacion. Your iudgement therfore is corrupte and false, because it cūmeth not of God, but out of worldly and humaine lustes. And in the meane tyme do I iudge no man. For the tyme of iudgement is not yet, but of saluacion. And yet if I should geue iudgement of you my iudgement should be true, because it doeth not swarue and dissent from Gods iudgement. For I shoulde not geue sentence alone, but I and my father who sent me, ioyntelye together should pronounce semblably one thyng, forasmuche as we bothe throughlye will all one. In worldly matters the iudgement of many weyeth more, and is of greater auctoritie then one mannes mynde alone: but yet Goddes iudgement alone, passeth the iudgement of all mankynde. If ye despise my sentence as but mans iudgement, trulye ye cannot contemne the iudgement of God, though he himselfe alone geue iudgement. And yf ye do not despise the iudgement of God, neither can ye reiecte or refuse my iudgement, whiche is consentyng to his in all thynges, except with a common contempte ye do vs bothe at once wrong: bothe him that sendeth, and me that am sent from hym. I speake or do nothyng but that whiche he hath commaunded me.

I iudge no man, and yf I iudge, my iudgemente is true.

Semblably euen amongst menne the recorde of many is more substauncial then of a fewe: & after your lawe there is no recorde, vnlesse it be of two at least, allowed and admitted before a iudge. But yet in dede it is more to be regarded if a man beare recorde of another, then if he beare witnesse of himself. Howbeit it cannot be auoided but among men there be wrong iudgementes, and vntrue recordes: yea and although a thousand men should agre vpō one thyng beyng but men, either forbecause through errour they knewe not the truth, or els because they being corrupte in their affections, do not pronounce & geue sentence accordyng to the true iudgement of reason, but after the leude affections of the heart: Notwithstandyng where euen one alone sayth any thing of hymselfe, incase he do not pronounce the thyng which he reporteth of himselfe, as of his owne heade, but by Gods commaundement, his iudgemente and recorde must nedes be true, because God can neither be deceiued nor corrupt.

I beare no witnesse of my selfe, but by the autoritie of my father, who doeth also himselfe beare witnesse of me: neither do I pronounce any other thing cōcernyng myne owne person, then he hath testified who sent me into the worlde to be a witnesser of the truth, which onely he hath knowē. If ye do putte away my recorde, ye must nedes therin also reiecte his. If ye infringe and repel my iudgement, ye must of force and necessitie contrarie him. We be twaine, but we two haue all but one witnesse and iudgemēt. And there is one of these twaine who if he were alone, yet were his iudgement not to be replied against. And if ye aske when did the father testifie of me, forsoth he bare recorde of me, in your law: whose voyce ye should know, if ye would wt pure heartes vnderstand ÿ which is writtē: he did also testifie of me at Jordane, his recorde of me is to be seen in the very actes and dedes which he doeth by me: and in conclusion whē

tyme

tyme shall be, he shall glorifie me with more euident and clere witnesses. After these thinges wer spokē, the Iewes because they heard the father oftē named, from whom he was sent, and whose auctoritie he laied for his defēce, meruailed if he woulde speake so highly of Ioseph the carpenter, whose sōne he was then commonly thought to be. And in case he ment not of him, they be desirous to get out of him who should be that other father, frō whom he had come, & to whom he should go: Where is (q thei) this thy father, of whom thou speakest suche wonderful thynges. But Iesus somewhat openīng that as yet he was not knowen vnto them, touchyng his diuine nature and Godhead, whē as they supposed him to be but a very man and nought els: and yet for al that they should haue beleued him as a man vnlesse theyr iudgment had been corrupted with carnal affections, yea & his wordes did also implie that neither the father could truly be knowen, but by the sonne, nor the sōne fully knowen except the father wer knowen: for the sonne is not knowen with bodilye iyes but by fayth, nor ẏ father can be shewed to mans sēses, but maye be brought into deuout myndes spiritually. Well, Iesus (I say) maketh answere on this wyse: ye neyther know me, nor yet my father: and so long as ye will not know me, ye can not knowe my father. Geue credence vnto me, & ye shall both know me, and my father. ye saye that ye know me, because ye know my countrey, my dwelling place, my parētes, & brethren: Whē as through these wordes, which they vnderstode not, our lorde Iesus did sore prouoke the pharisei's myndes against him, teaching openly in the temple, yea & where most preace of people was, in a place of the Temple called the treasury (because that offringes and thinges geuen to the Temple were brought thither, and kept there, whiche thinges wholly wer turned to the priestes and Phariseis pleasures, and gaine excessiuely, though the thinges were geuen, and as ye woulde saye were consecrate to God.) Albeit I say that Christe did this, as I haue said, yet no man layde handes on hym: not because they lacked any vngracious wyll, but because God did not suffre them to do it. For the time was not yet come, whē as Christe had appoynted himselfe to suffre, neither would he suffre vntyll he had fully taught that doctrine whiche the father had committed to his ministracion, for the saluacion of man.

¶ Then sayde Iesus agayne vnto them: I go my waye, and ye shall seke me, and shall dye in your synnes. Whither I go, thither can ye not cum. Then sayed the Iewes, wyll he kyll hymselfe, because he sayeth, whither I go, thither can ye not come? And he sayed vnto them, ye are from beneth, I am from aboue. Ye are of this world, I am not of this worlde. I therfore saye vnto you, that ye shal dye in your synnes. For if ye beleue not that I am he, ye shall dye in your synnes. The texte.

Therfore whiles they wer whisht and kept silence, yet cumpassyng in minde full vngracious and murderous thoughtes, Iesus went forth with his talke priuely pricking their cōsciences, that so at leaste wai it might forthinke them, when as they knew that nothing was hid vnto him: a thyng whiche was neuer before geuen to hym that was but a verye man. No mannes wickednesse, (sayeth he) can let the thyng that I do by my fathers commaundement. That thyng once finished, I go to hym that sent me, and then ye shall seke me all in vayne, and in myne absence ye shall desyre me, whom beyng present, you enuy, and do displeasure vnto. Then ye shall know me by the ende and conclusion of the matter, who I am: ye shall wyshe my presence, and not haue it. But you whiche doe nowe persecute the preacher, and setter foorthe of eternall trueth, shall dye in your synne yf ye do persiste and continue in your infidelitie. For he doeth perishe through his owne faulte that obstinately putteth awaye healthe when it is freely offered vnto hym: and he prouoketh and seketh his owne deathe, whoso doeth despyse the fountayne of lyfe. I go not thither, whereas youre wickednes compelleth me, but I do willynglye go thither where as ye cannot folowe me. By this parable our lord Jesus did meane manye thynges: first of all, that of his owne good will he went to his death, furthermore ÿ by his death and resurrection he should be lyfted vp to heauen, whither as no man by any worldly wisedom could be brought. When with this saying ÿ Jewes wer made afeard, and vnderstode not what he ment, they durste not for al that aske the meanyng: but whispered and talked therof secretely among thẽselues saying: What is the matter that this man doethe sundrye tymes threaten vs with his goyng awaye thither, whither we cannot folowe hym? wyll he violently kyll hymselfe, and so withdrawe him from vs? Jesus, whiche knew the very thoughtes of them all, dyd so temper and moderate his aunswere vnto this very grosse muttrynge and sinfull murmuryng, that the thyng whiche he spake shoulde not bee vnderstande, but after his death, resurrection, and ascencion. For they supposyng that Jesus was nothing els but a man, could coniecture none other thyng, but that he shoulde go to his death, and so be delyuered from the grefe of his persecutours, when as his meanyng was that hymselfe (as touchynge his godhede) came from heauen, and that he should anon after ouercome deathe: and returne agayne thither from whence he came. Ye (sayethe he) beynge of this worlde are worldly wise, and speake after the carnall iudgement of the world. I am not of this worlde, and do speake hyer thynges then you can vnderstande, neyther shall ye euer vnderstande them excepte ye leaue your infidelitie, and shew your selues ready to be taught, and therefore I tolde you erwhile and nowe tell you once againe, that vnlesse ye put away your malice ye shall dye in your sinnes. The onely waye to escape the darkenes of synnes, is to receiue the lyght. The onely waye to lyfe, is to knowe him whiche onely delyuereth from deathe by the faythe of the gospell. And in case ye do obstinately refuse to beleue that I am he, by whom the father willeth that all men should obtaine life and saluacion, ye shall thorow your own faulte dye in your synnes.

If ye beleue not that I am he, ye shall dye in your sinnes

The texte.

Then sayed they vnto hym: Who art thou? And Jesus sayeth vnto them: euen the verye same thyng that I speake vnto you. I haue many thynges to saye and to iudge of you. Yea and he that sent me is true, and I speake in the worlde those thinges, whiche I haue hard of hym. Howbeit they vnderstoode not that he spake of his father. Then sayed Jesus vnto them: When ye haue lift vp on hye the sonne of man, then shall ye know that I am he, and that I doe nothyng of my selfe, but as my father hath taughte me, euen so I speake those thynges, & he that sent me, is with me. The father hath not left me alone, for I do alwayes those thynges that please hym.

Neither yet did this saying of the lord Jesus settell downe into the mindes of the Phariseis, so very muche had the inordinate loue of this world blynded theyr myndes, and therefore as though they had neither seen nor hearde anye thing wherby they might knowe who he was, they now maliciously saie vnto Jesus: who art thou? but Jesus knowing before hand that thei would picke some quarell against whatsoeuer answere he should make, which asked him ÿ question of a frowarde mynde, therewith also iudgeyng them to be more fitte to heare what themselues wer, then what he was, maketh them aunswere on this

this wise, sayinge: ye desyre to knowe who I am, wel then, do beleue, but surely ye shall not beleue excepte ye put awaye grosse and worldely affeccions, for els if I do tell you who I am, I shall tell it to your harme. For ye wyll not onely be neuer a deale better therby, but forasmuche as ye be manye wayes euyll, ye shall so muche the more be made wurse. And this that I nowe speake vnto you, shall make your damnacion the greater. I thyrst and couet the saluacion of men and not theyr vtter destruccion. Or els I coulde speake manye thynges of you, and for manye causes condemne you. But it is not so thought good to my father, who sente me into the world, not to cause the euyll to bee wurse, but to thintent that those whiche be euill should forthinke and amende themselues, and be saued. The father that sent me is he that sayth trueth, yf ye beleue hym ye shall be saued. And ye shall beleue hym, yf ye will beleue me: of truethe ye shall without daunger safelye beleue me that speake nothynge vnto you, but what as I haue heard of my father, with whõ I was before I came into the worlde. He hath commaunded me to speake true thynges, & the trueth of suche thynges as do further mẽ to saluacion, and not to damnacion. And yf any man do perishe he shall perishe, thorow his owne faulte, who doeth enuye his owne health that is offered him.

But the blyndnes of the Jewes was so grosse, that although he had so ofte made mencion of his father, from whom he was sent, and to whom he shoulde go, of whom he should haue recorde, and did heare the thynges whiche he did speake, as yet for all that it vnderstood not that he spake of the father of heauen, because they coulde beleue nothynge in hym aboue a manne. For these sayinges were then as seedes closed vp in the memorye of the hearers, to thintente that they shoulde then bring furth frute, when as all thinges shoulde be fully accomplished, whiche the Prophetes had written of Jesu. It was expediente that as yet he shoulde be thought a very man, vntill he had fully finished for ye saluacion of the worlde, that hye sacrifice whiche was to bee offered vpon the alter of the crosse. For it so pleased the father, that by death God shoulde bee glorified. Our lorde Jesus in the meane time meaning this, goeth furth in his communicacion, insinuating couertly that he shoulde afterwarde willinglye be crucified by them, & sayeth thus: When ye shall lyfte vp on hye the sonne of man, euen very then ye shall vnderstande who I am: and after that ye shall thinke me vtterly made awaye, then in conclusion ye shall well knowe my power. For ye shall right well perceiue that the thing is wrought, not as men do thinges, but by my fathers power: after whose pleasure and iudgemente I do what thing soeuer I do practise herein earth, to the saluacion of man. Neither do I speake any thing but accordìng to his minde. And albeit I am sente into the worlde from hym, yet am not I forsaken of hym, he hath not lefte me; but he is alway present with me, and doeth assiste me, and by me, he both worketh and speaketh vnto you, for betwene vs two is a moste hye consente: he is glorified by me, and I againe by hym: but he is the auctor and I the messenger. And I do the office of an embassadour so faythfully, that I alwaye do those thinges whiche he hath commaunded and determined. Moses and Dauid, whom ye haue in great reuerence, spake and did manye thinges according to Gods will, but yet the same did many tymes offend hym with their doynges. I neuer dissent from that whiche is my fathers pleasure.

They vnderstoode not that he spake of his father.

The texte.

As he spake these wordes, manye beleued on hym. Then sayed Jesus to those Jewes whiche beleued on him: If ye continue in my worde, then are ye my very disciples, and ye shall knowe the trueth, and the trueth shal make you free. They aunswered hym: We be Abrahams seed, and were neuer bounde to any man: sayeste thou than, ye shall be made free? Jesus aunswered them: Verely verely I saye vnto you, that whosoeuer committeth sinne, is the seruaunt of sinne. And the seruaunt abideth not in the house for euer, but the sonne abideth euer. If the sonne therfore shall make you free, then are ye free in dede. I know that ye are Abrahams sede, but ye seke meanes to kil me, because my worde hath no place in you. I speake that whiche I haue seen with my father, and ye do that whiche ye haue seen with your father.

If ye cōtinue in my woorde, &c.

When as at that season none did fully vnderstāde these sayinges, yet there was many among the people whiche thought them not vngodly. And diuerse conceyuyng good hope of the thynges whiche Jesus promysed them, beleued hym, but yet not perfitly, for they were still ignoraunte, but as they wer then able to vnderstande the doctrine of the gospell. There was in dede a certayne way prepared to fayth already: although they wer not yet so far forwarde as they should be brought afterwarde. The Lorde Jesus therfore doeth exhorte them to perseuer in the thynge wherin they were metely wel entred, vntill they might atteyne the perfyte knowledge of him. For faith of good men doeth euē deserue those thynges whiche it vnderstādeth not. The malice of the Phariseis waxed alwaye wurse and wurse. He sayeth vnto them: take you no exaumple at these which do wilfully perishe, it is a good beginnyng for you, some deale to beleue my sayinges, from which if other mens infidelitie do not withdrawe you, and if ye will firmely abide in that ye are entred vnto, I which do professe heauenly trueth and no Pharisaicall doctrine, will take you for my very owne proper disciples. And you whiche hitherto haue embraced the shadowes of Moses lawe for truthes, shall in processe of tyme knowe all trueth. And the knowen trueth shall make you free.

And the trueth shall make you free.

But the Jewes not perceiuing that Christe mente of that libertie whiche the gospell teacheth, whiche libertie doth not chaunge any worldly aduauncement, as to deliuer the bodye from the intereste that the maister hath ouer it, but setteth the mynde at libertie from sinne, from leude and worldlye desyres, from the tirannye of the deuil, from feare of death, from bondage of Pharisaicall ordinaunces, from the yoke of carnall obseruyng of the lawe: The Jewes I saye, not vnderstandynge this, make the aunswere disdaynefully: for they wer proude of the nobilitie of theyr carnal aunceters. We, say they, by successiō come of Abraham the Patriarche, and are naturally free men borne, and not onely free but noble gentlemen also, neither did we euer serue any man as bōde men. What libertie therfore doest thou promyse vs as though we were bōde seruauntes, nedefull of manumission? This aunswere declared the Jewes to be grosse, whiche put their affiaunce and glory in carnall thynges, neglectynge spirituall thinges whiche commende vs to God.

They tooke purenes to consiste in washyng of the bodye, of cuppes, and of vessels, though they had theyr soule polluted with sinfull vices. They despised other in comparison of themselues, because they were bodely circumcised, whē as they had an vncircumcised mynde. They thought themselues holy because they caried about with them the lawe written in brode scrolles rounde aboute theyr heade, when as they be holye to God, whiche haue the lawe wrytten in theyr myndes, and expresse the same, not in scrolles, but in theyr dedes. So nowe they wer proude in herte because after the fleshe they came of Abraham,

as

as thoughe it were a great matter to be borne of holy ones, when before God they be noble and famouse, whiche, of whosoeuer they be borne, do expresse the condicions of holy men in their maners. Therefore when Jesus had reproued them for two causes, both because they were ignoraunt in the trueth, and also because they serued as bondemenne: they dissembled the fyrste, and stomaked the lesse weyghty matter: for ignoraunce of the trueth is a fault of the mynde, to be a seruaunte is no euyll thynge of the mynde, but a lacke of worldlye fortune. Nowe therefore oure Lorde Jesus teacheth plainlye what seruitude he ment: You sayeth he, disdayne that I promyse liberty, because in your owne cõceyte ye be free, that is to saye, the naturall free children of Abraham: but there is an other kynde of seruitude muche more vyle and myserable, from which no noblenes of auncesters, be it neuer so greate, can clayme fredome and make a man free. Ye haue not a man to your lorde, from whose bondage ye are to bee made fre, but hereof I do well assure you, whosoeuer sinneth, maketh himself seruaunt to synne, and looseth his fredome: he is verily a naturall borne fremã that is subiect to no dishonestie, nor giltie of sinnefull vilanye. This is the fredome, whereof ye maye worthely reioyce before God. But whosoeuer is addicte to sinne hath the deuill his lorde, and is moued and drawen at his pleasure and arbitremente: although he maye clayme kynne and can bryng his petigrue to moste holy auncesters.

Whosoeuer cõmitteth sinne. &c.

For an other mans holynes taketh not awaye the bondage of them that succede in bloude, but euery man is taken and estemed after his owne dedes: a seruaunt can not make his felowe seruaunt that is also sinfull as he is, partaker of his fredome: but he only maketh men free and setteth at libertie, whiche onely is voyde of all sinne. For albeit a seruaunte do for a tyme certain thinges in the house, yet because he is a seruaunt and no heyre, he hath no perpetuitie or enterest there for euer, but is put out of the house when it pleaseth the maister: but because the sonne is heyre and Lorde of the house, he hath continuall right in the house, nor he hymselfe onely is free in dede without all seruitude, but he may also make other folke free. If ye therfore desire this freedome, there is no cause why ye should loke to haue it of Moses, or from the Patriarkes, or your priestes, whose ministracion was for a while: neyther was any of these vtterly voide of all sinne, nor had autoritie to abolishe or put awaye sinnes, ne yet did any of them knowe the trueth exactely and at full. But if one cleaue fast to the sonne (to whom is geuen the whole & perpetual power of the house) the same, of whatsoeuer stocke he be borne, maye well hope to haue true fredome.

But if the sonne make you free. &c.

Therfore Abraham dyd not begette vs free, Moses did it not, the Priestes did not with their sacrifice make vs free. If the sonne shall make you free from errour and sinne, ye shall be truely and fully free.

You stande muche in your owne conceyte because ye be the sonnes of Abraham. I know that ye be borne of Abraham as touching the flesh, but this honour is but smal, vsual, and cõmon to al Jewes. If ye will algates be thought to be Abrahams posteritie, and children of a moste holy father, nothing degenerate, in your dedes declare you to be his sonnes. For it is yͤ propertie of a very true naturall childe, to resemble and expresse the fashion & maners of his parentes. Abraham did so muche beleue God, that where as there was promised him of God a populouse succession, and great in nũber, to come of his sonne Isaac, he doubted not at one commaundement of God to slea his sonne Isaac.

But

I speake ÿ which I haue sene, &c.

But ye see now how farre ye be of, from the maners of your father, whiche do your endeuour to kill euen me, for no cause els, but that you being blinded with desyres of the flesh and the worlde, do not vnderstande my communication and wordes whiche be spirituall. Abraham not doubtyng of the promyses, did in a thing against nature, beleue the aungel by whome god spake vnto him. To me whom ye se, and by whom god speaketh to you, promising greater thynges then in times paste he did to Abraham, ye do not onelye not geue credence, but also maliciously seke and deuise my death. Do not therfore arrogantly chalenge Abraham to be your father. Euery one is before God ÿ sonne of hym, whose actes and condicions he folowethe. For as the children seeth theyr parentes do at home, so will they do, and growe to be of lyke affection & maners. I proue both by wordes and dedes that I am his sonne from whom I was sente: for I speake that which I haue sene and heard of my father. You lykewyse do the thynges whiche you haue seen your father do.

The texte

¶ They aunswered and sayde vnto hym: Abraham is our father. Jesus sayeth vnto them: If ye were Abrahams children ye would do the dedes of Abraham, but now ye go about to kill me, a man that hath tolde you the trueth, which I haue hearde of God: this did not Abraham. Ye do the dedes of your father. Then sayed they vnto hym, we were not borne of fornicacion, we haue one father, euen god. Jesus saied vnto them: If God wer your father, trulye ye woulde loue me, for I proceded forth and came from God, neyther came I of my selfe, but he sent me. Why doe ye not knowe my speache? Euen because ye cannot abide the hearyng of my worde. Ye are of your father the deuill, and the lustes of your father wyl ye serue. He was a murtherer from the begynning, and abode not in the trueth, because there is no trueth in him: when he speaketh a lye, he speaketh of his owne, for he is a lyar, and the father of the same thing. And because I tell you the trueth, therefore ye beleue me not.

Forsomuche as the Jewes toke this saying of our Lorde Jesus in euill parte, they frame their aunswere in suche sorte, that they go aboute therein to picke out of Jesus wordes some thing spoken to Abrahãs rebuke: which thing if it had been so in dede, they woulde haue prouoked the people to haue stoned Christe: for where as he had openly testified that their dedes were euill, and added further that they did those thinges whiche they had sene theyr father do (neyther did they knowledge any other father then Abraham) they toke it as if by this saying of Jesus, Abraham the Patriarche had been reproued, who had hymselfe been suche one as were the children that came of him. But Jesus spake nothing sore at all against Abraham, but reasoned cōtrary to their saying, prouing that therfore they were not the children of Abraham, because they were moste farre from his wayes, & moste vnlike hym. If ye will, sayeth he, be taken for the true children of Abraham do as your father did: beleue Goddes worde. For he of trueth through notable affiaunce in God, deserued the commẽdaciō of righteousnes, and was called righteouse. Now although ye haue neuer doen boastyng Abraham to be your father, neuertheles your studie and drifte is to kill me, a mā that albeit I were none other but very man, yet were I innocent and one that harme no man, and you therefore woulde slea me, because I tell you the trueth, whiche I do not fayne of myne owne heade, but that trueth whiche I haue hearde of God: insomuche that whosoeuer distrusteth me, the same must nedes distruste God. But Abraham will not acknowledge you for his sonnes whiche goe about a wicked matter, and muche disagreable to his maners. And if it be so that euery one is that mans sonne, whose

Yf ye were Abrahams children, &c.

whose dedes he foloweth, and that your dedes withall are farre vnlike to A-
brahams, you muste nedes haue some other father, whosoeuer he be, whose
naturall disposicion you do resemble, and shewe your selfe lyke in condicions.
The Jewes beyng of trueth more prouoked by these sayinges, nowe (as it
were) gessing to what ende the processe of Jesus wordes tended, and whom
he noted to be their father, aunswere: whom els apointest thou for our father,
that takest awaye our father Abraham?

We be not base gotten, we maye reioyce in that which is common to all the
Jewes, who are not onely the succession of Abraham, but also the sonnes of
God, whiche calleth Israell his first begotten childe. And we are Israelites.
And if thou take away our father Abraham from vs, if thou geue vs another
father then God, the common father of all our nacion, thou art not only iniuri-
ouse and dispiteful to vs, but to the whole nacion of the Jewes. Wheras this
was a wicked and shameles aunswere, (for what coulde be more shameful thē
to boaste themselfes to be the children of God, who knewe themselues giltye
in such great faultes, who also laied in wayt to bring ẏ sonne of God to death)
Jesus replied sharpely to this answer and saied: If God were your father,
that is to witte, if ye were very true and naturall Israelites, ye woulde I am
sure loue me, as a brother ⁊ begotten of the common father of all, and as one
that doeth expressely folowe his fathers behauour and maners, euen as it becummeth a true naturall childe. For I neyther shewe foorth any other thyng
then God the father, nor I do none other mens busynes then my fathers, from
whom I proceaded and came into this world. For I neither speake nor do any
thing of my selfe. I do not apoint my selfe to this embassage but he sente me,
whom ye clayme to be comon father to you all.

If god were your father

And yf ye saye trueth, why do ye not acknowledge his speache, that is the
same fathers sonne, and his very true sonne, who was also with his father before he came into the world, neither speaketh he any thyng but at his fathers
appoyntment? Why can ye so very euill beare my wordes whē as by me, god
speaketh vnto you? If ye beleue God to be true, beneficiall, ⁊ an health gener,
frendely to thē that be godly, and enemy to the wicked, when as ye see nothing
in my sayinges or doynges vnlyke vnto these thinges, why do you not acknowledge the manners and verye nature of youre father? But if ye couet to heare
your fathers name, whome in witte and dedes ye do resēble: ye be neyther bee-
gotten of Abraham, nor of God, but euen of the deuill: ye be his very naturall
children, whose witte and disposicion ye breathe out and shewe likelyhoode of,
and whose will ye obey. For ye haue bothe hated the trueth, and go aboute to
kyll an innocent. This is an exaumple of the deuill your father. For because he
hath been the chiefe auctor of bothe lyes and murder, who by his lying entised
vnto deathe the firste parentes of mankinde, being with none other thing prouoked then throughe enuie of other folkes felicitie. And the same sinfull disease
doth pricke you forwarde to slea one that is innocent, and a beneficiall person.
The deuill enuyed man, that was of a blessed creacion, ye enuie man to be restored vnto the felicitie from whence he fell. He fell from the truethe by hys
pryde. And his fall was suche that there is no hope of his amendemente, but
persistyng in euill, he heapeth sinne vpon sinne, striuing againste Gods veritie
by you at this presente, and doyng the same thyng that in the beginnyng of the
worlde he firste practised, when he drewe the first auctors of mankynde vnto
death.

death. Whoso therfore hateth trueth and loueth lyes, he declareth sufficiently who is his father. Whosoeuer pronounceth a lye, he speaketh of hym that is the fountaine of all lyes. Whatsoeuer that auctor speaketh is a lye, and he speaketh of hymself for he is not onely a lyar, but the father and prince of lyes. As of the contrary syde, God is the fountayne of all truethe, and whosoeuer speaketh the trueth to Gods glory, he speaketh not of hymselfe but of God.

But if you be begotten rather of God the auctour of trueth, then of the deuill the father of lyes, wherfore then (consideryng that I dooe speake vnto you heauenly trueth,) doe not you beeyng the chyldren of Abraham beleue God? why do not ye the children of God, acknowledge and loue Goddes trueth?

The texte

¶ Whiche of you rebuketh me of sinne? If I saye the trueth, why do not ye beleue me? he that is of God heareth goddes woordes. Ye therfore heare them not, because ye are not of God. Then aunswered the Jewes, and sayed vnto hym: Saye we not well that thou art a Samaritane, and hast the deuill? Jesus aunswered: I haue not the deuyll, but I honoure my father, and ye haue dishonored me: I seke not mine owne prayse, there is one that seketh and iudgeth.

If ye fynde any lye in my woordes or any faulte in my proceedyng, geue not credite to my wordes. But which of ye all can burden me with any one faulte? What maner of men ye be, ye your selfes are priuie: but if whatsoeuer be right and true, the same is of God, and neither can ye proue in me any thyng that varieth from right and trueth, why then in not beleuyng me do ye distruste god, specially consideryng that ye boaste your selues to be the children of God? But and if ye did extolle and aduaunce your selues truely, ye would acknowledge the woorde of God, but in case ye do it vntruelye, ye declare your selues to haue a lying father.

He that is of god, heareth Gods wordes.

Whosoeuer is begotten of god, the same doeth (lyke a true naturall chylde) geue eare to his fathers woordes. And that thing well proueth you not to be begotten of God the father, because ye cannot abyde to heare the truethe that cummeth from him. The Jewes beeyng made through these woordes more wood, fall to geuyng cursed woordes in theyr aunswere, wherunto the malice of men beyng with reason concluded is woont to haue refuge, and saieth: Do not we saye right of thee, that where thou wilte be taken for a Jewe, and boastest god to be thy father, thou art a Samaritane, and haste the deuill? whiche selfe thyng, thou doest now declare in dede, and approuest our iudgemente of thee. But what aunswer made moste gentle Jesus vnto this peuishe mad reproche? As touching the reproche in namyng hym a Samaritane although it were commonly taken for a greate rebuke and slaunder, yet because it was naught els but a funnishe checke spoken in a furye, he made no aunswere at all therunto, as though they had but called hym a mushrome, or an oynion, but yet to the bearing hym on hande that he had the deuill, he aunswereth, but in suche sorte that he gaue them no euill language againe, whiche he mighte worthely haue doen, and countermaunded backe againe, theyr lewde saying to themselfes, but auoydeth it courteouslye from hymselfe: teachynge vs by the waye, that as ofte as we haue to do concernyng goddes glory, as ofte as the truethe of the ghospell is to be defended agaynst the wicked, we should be earnest, quicke and sharpe: And as often as we oure selfes be rebuked, that we

shoulde

should shew our selfes ientle and meke. In suche wise that we do not make au=lwere to all thynges, but repell and auoyde those thinges onely from vs, which we cannot concele without hinderaunce of the gospell.

To haue the people vnderstande that Christ did euery thyng in all his pro=cedynges, not by the deuils auctoritie, but God the father beyng aucthour, made muche to the furtheraunce of the ghospell. I haue sayeth Christ, no fami=liaritie with any deuill, nor I doe not therfore boaste my selfe of God beeyng my father, to thintent that I woulde with a lye obtayne myne owne prayse, but that through me my father myght be glorifyed emongst men. And albeit ye doe glorie that ye haue thesame god to your father, yet doe ye me despite, who seke nothyng els but his glory, of whom ye woulde be thought true wur=shippers.

I do not curiously seke myne owne prayse at mennes handes, neyther doth your contumeliouse wordes hurt me, but rather worketh your destruccion. For there is one, who as he is couetous to be glorified amonges men by me, so he wisheth that I agayne should haue glorye by hym: not that eyther he or I haue nede of this glorye, but that so to haue it is expediente for you for the ex=chaunge of death, and that ye maye attayn saluacion. Of trueth, lyke as I doe not muche couet myne owne glory (howbeit in dede my glory is the glory of my father) so am I no reuenger of myne owne rebuke or iniury. But yet for all that thinke not that ye shall be without punishmente for that ye haue slaunde=red me. For there is he that both seketh my prayse and glory, and will reuenge my iniury and contempte, except ye amende.

I seke not myne owne prayse. &c.

Verely verely I say vnto you, if a man kepe my saying, he shall neuer see death. Then saied the Jewes vnto him: Nowe knowe we that thou hast the deuil. Abraham is dead, and the Prophetes, and thou sayst: If a man kepe my saying he shall neuer taste of death. Arte thou greater than our father Abraham whiche is dead? and the Prophetes are dead: who makest thou thy selfe?

The texte.

To glory in names, as ye doe, profiteth nothyng, for in that sorte neyther Abraham, the originall begynnyng of your stocke, nor Moses, nor the Prie=stes, nor the Pharisees, ne God the father, shal do you any good. Be ye well assured hereof, if any man obey my wordes (as I haue sayed ofte) he shall ne=uer see death, onely beleef is the way and entrie to immortalitie. Althoughe the Jewes ought with this so cauline and gentle an aunswere to haue ben appea=sed, and with this so great a rewarde to haue ben allured vnto fayth, yet accor=dyng to theyr rudenesse, dooe they interpretate that thyng whiche was spiritu=ally spoken of life of the soule, to be spoken of bodily lyfe, and that whiche was told them for their instruccion, they sediciously marre and frowardly turne in=to the reproche of the Patriarkes, studyng euerye waie to procure some hatred agaynst our Lord Jesus among the multitude. They aunswere verely in thys manier. We haue also of that thy saying more certayn knowlege that thou art possessed with a deuill wood and frantike, which promisest this thing to them that kepe thy worde, whiche manier of thing our Patriarkes, menne of moste highe prayse, neuer had, vnto whome God himselfe spake. God spake vnto A=braham, as he did also to other Prophetes. They were obedient to Goddes worde, and neuerthelesse they be all deade, and thou promiseste perpetuall lyfe to them that obserue those thinges whiche thou teachest.

What makest thou thy selfe.

With what countenaunce or howe darestе thou bee bolde to promise other that thyng whiche thou haste not thy selfe? Doeste thou promise immortalitie to other, beyng mortall thy selfe? Arte thou greater then oure father Abraham whiche is deade? yea and moreouer the Prophetes also be all dead. They durste promise no suche thyng to any man. How highly doest thou presume of thy selfe? Whome makest thou thy selfe? Thou preferreste thy selfe before the Prophetes, and Abraham, and in promising that thing which is gods, thou makest thy selfe god.

The texte.

¶ Jesus aunswered: if I honour my selfe, my honour is nothyng. It is my father that honoureth me, which ye saye is your God, and yet ye haue not knowen him, but I know hym. And yf I saye I knowe hym not, I shall bee a lyar lyke vnto you, but I knowe hym, and kepe his saying. Your father Abraham was glad to see my daye, and he sawe it and reioysed. Then sayed the Jewes vnto hym: thou arte not yet fiftie yere olde, and haste thou seene Abraham? Jesus sayed vnto them: Verely, verely, I saye vnto you: ere Abraham was borne, I am. Thē toke they vp stones to caste at hym. But Jesus hid himselfe and wente out of the temple.

The Lorde Jesus did so moderate his aunswere vnto these fonde peuyshe reproches, wherewith the Jewes taunted hym, that because they were not yet able to receyue so great a mistery, he dyd of trueth somewhat by insinuacion open that he was greater then the Prophetes, and Abraham hymselfe too: and that he was one that might perfourme by Gods power that thyng which he did promyse, yet he would not appeare arrogant amonges the ignoraunte. But he tempered his sayinges leste he shoulde kyndle more wrathe in them that were moued already, and sayeth: I attribute nothyng vntruely to my selfe. For yf I shoulde after the manner of men seeke for prayse at mannes hande, then were my prayse false and vayne. And in case I were curiouse to seeke for prayse and glory, it were not nedefull to hunte for it amongest men. For it is my father, from whom all true glory cummeth, that glorifyeth me. He that is honoured of hym, the rebukefull wordes of menne doe not dishonoure thesame. And yf ye wyll algates knowe hym that is my father, it is very he whome ye boaste to be both your God and father. Whose chyldrē if ye were in dede, forsothe ye would recognyse his embassadour, and yf ye were true wurshippers of hym, ye would fauour his glory, and not bryng hym in contempte whome he sente into the worlde for your saluacion. But as ye wurshippe hym with false religion, so ye vntruely clayme vnto you the knowledge of hym. He is spiritual, and you sauour and knowe nothyng els but carnall thynges. I who am his very sonne in dede, doe verely knowe hym, which thyng I doe not of arrogancye vntruely chalenge, but I saye that whiche is true: and yf I shoulde saye I knowe hym not, I should be a lyar, and lyke vnto you that professe the knowledge of God whom ye knowe not. I am sent from hym and was with hym before I came into the worlde. Therefore I knowe hym, and what thyng soeuer he hath commaunded me, I doe it. But whosoeuer contemneth my worde contemneth god, in whose name I exercise the commission of his embassage, and that faithfully. And whosoeuer despyseth gods worde, he neither knoweth God nor taketh him as God.

It is my father which honoureth me &c.

Furthermore whereas ye neuer ceasse braggyng of youre father Abraham to whom ye be moste farre vnlike, and that ye procure hatred vnto me, for that I take my selfe to be Abrahams better, verely I do neyther vainly boaste mine owne greatnes, nor diminishe his dignitie. This I will now saye vnto you, that Abraham whome you doe rather wonder at then folowe, how great a man

soeuer

soeuer he was, yet he was glad and thought he should be happy if it myght be his lucke to see my daye. And he sawe that thyng whiche he desired, and that great man greatly ioyed to haue my daye chaunce to hym, and yet you contemne me. Jesus dyd herein and by this straunge saying, signifie that whan Abraham made hymselfe ready to offre in sacrifice his sonne Isaac, he sawe by the spirite of prophecie that our Lord Jesus should be geuen of his father vnto the death of the crosse, for the saluacion of the worlde: and yet should not through that death vtterly perysshe, but within three dayes after reuiue againe to an immortall lyfe. The Jewes not yet vnderstandyng this misterie, doe nowe againe accordyng to theyr carnall iudgement, fall in hand with checking: supposyng Jesus to be no nother thyng then man, nor that he had any beyng before he was borne of Mary. Thou art not yet (say they) fiftie yeres olde, and haste thou seen Abraham that died so many hundred yeres agoe? Finally the Lorde Jesus as a man prouoked with theyr opprobrious woordes, some deale openeth, and as it were vttereth a lytle sparke of his Godhed through whiche he knoweth no tyme nor number of yeres, but was alwaye all one before all course of tyme, lyke as God the father being without the limites of tyme alwaie is that he is. For thus he speaketh vnto Moses. I am that I am: signifyinge an eternalitie, and a nature that cannot chaunge. And in lyke maner the sonne vsing the woordes of his father, sayeth: This I doe assuredly confirme vnto you (though as yet ye wil not beleue it) or euer Abraham was borne, I am. At these woordes as playne blasphemous, because he beyng a mortall man semed to take vpon hym the eternalitie, a thyng for God only conuenient, they coulde not withholde theyr handes, but toke vp stones, and wente in hande to ouerthrowe and presse hym with stones. But Jesus professyng hymselfe to be God, to declare hymselfe to be a very man also, gaue place to their fury, not because he feared theyr forcible violence, whiche he had power to kepe of, but to teache vs by the waye that when time requireth that the trueth of the ghospell should be preached valiantly and boldely, and again, that when we had once executed our duetie, the fury of euill men should not causelesse and in vayne be prouoked and exasperate: for our Lorde Jesus knewe that it coulde not haue been beate into the heades, I will not say of the grosse and ignoraunte multitude, but not of his disciples: and they to be brought to belefe therof, in case he had openly preached himselfe to be both God & man, and the same to be all at once both mortall as touching his manhed, and also immortall as touching his deitie: and as perteyning to the fleshe to be a man borne of a virgin in time, as touchyng diuine power to haue been alwaye before all time God of God. Surely this so secrete a misterie was rather to be at time conueniente perswaded to the worlde by miracles, death, resurreccion, ascendyng to heauen, and by the inspiracion of the holy ghoste, then before due tyme to be brought in, and vttered in open playne woordes to them that would not beleue it. Therfore Jesus withdrewe hymselfe from them, geuyng place to theyr fury, and wente secretly forth of the temple: by that acte declaryng beforehande, that afterwarde the light of the ghospell beyng repelled of the wicked and voluntary blynde Jewes, should be put ouer to the Gentiles, & their house left to them desolate which only thought themselfes the true seruauntes of God, and ob-

Than toke they vp stones to caste at hym.

fekers of true religiō. And so Jesus which is the author of true godlines, wente to an other place.

The .ix. Chapter.

The texte. And as Jesus passed by, he sawe a manne, whiche was blynde from his byrth, and his disciples asked him, saying: Maister who did sinne, this manne, or his father, or mother, that he was borne blynde? Jesus sayed: neyther hath this manne sinned, nor yet his father and mother, but that the workes of God should be shewed.

Therfore our Lorde Jesus did now for a while geue place to the fury of them, whom as yet he sawe incurable, and falleth in hande with miracles to declare his Godly power, whiche he coulde not all this while dryue into theyr headdes by any perswasion of wordes. And loe there fel forthwith a matter in his waye not vnlike those thynges which were doen in the temple. For of trueth much a doe was there with the blynde. But suche as were blynde in soule, not in body, whiche is the moste vnhappy kynde of blyndnesse. And so muche also the wurse, as that although they were more then blynde, yet they thought themselues quicke sighted, so that they were not only miserable, but also vnworthy to be cured. For somuch a miser was not that blynde man whom Jesus sawe as he passed by, whiche man lacked onely bodily sight, and was borne blinde, so that it was a maladie aboue the Phisicions cure, but yet coulde Christe heale it. This man had an inwarde sight, & sawe with iyes of the soule: when Jesus therfore sawe the man, and had compassion on him, much pitying his misery, the disciples which called to their remembraunce that Christe had sayd to the man that was healed of his palsey: Go, and hereafter sinne no more, leste some wurse thing come vpon the, supposing that euery blemishe of the body had come of some faulte of the soule, axed Christe of the blinde man, and sayed: through whose sinne chaunced it that this man should be borne blinde? for where as none coulde sinne or he were borne, whosoeuer is borne with any sickenes or impediment of body, is to be thought punished for some other mans faulte, which thyng should yet seme against equitie, the disciples therfore sayed: Maister whēce came so great euill to this felowe, that he should be borne blinde? whether came it of his owne or of the sinne of his parentes? Jesus aunswered: Neyther did this man through his owne sinne deserue to be borne blinde, who coulde not sinne when as yet he was not: nor his parentes. For as the lawe teacheth, God punysheth not the chyldren for the faultes of theyr parentes, excepte the children folowe the sinnes of theyr parentes. But blyndnesse chaunced to this man vpon a casualtie (and not through any mans sinne) as in the course of mans life, many thinges chaūce to many folke. This mans misery & lacke of sight was not prohibit, but suffered to chaunce vnto hym, because that by hym the mightie power and goodnesse of God, whom the blinde Jewes so obstinately cryeth out vpon, should be declared to mē. The more incurable the disease is, the more famous and commendable shall be the healing of the same.

He sawe a man which was blind.

I must worke the worke of hym that sent me, whyle it is daye. The night cummeth when no manne can worke. As long as I am in the worlde I am the light of the worlde. Assoone as he had thus spoken, he spatte on the grounde, and made clay of the spettell and rubbed the clay on the iyes of the blynde, & sayed vnto hym: Goe washe the in the poole of Siloe, which (by interpretacion) is asmuche to saye as sent. He wente his waye therfore and washed, and came agayne seeyng.

The texte.

For this cause was I sent into the worlde eu͂e to procure the glory of God with suche dedes, as should cause the vnfaythfull to beleue my woordes to be true, and to thintent also that those whiche will beleue, should be cured of their blindnes. I must doe this commaundement diligently while it is daye: for yf menne haue any worke in hande, they be wonte to doe it in the day. The night (perdy) is vnhansome to worke in. Therfore in the meane tyme, whyle present day geueth vs leaue to worke, we may not cease: for the night shall come when as men (all in vaine) would worke and cannot. As long as I am in the worlde, I am the light of the worlde. If men make spede to finishe the worke, which they goe about for some commoditie of this life, before night, how muche more behoueth it euery man to labour, that while they haue me with them, they may go thorowe with the busines of the eternall saluacion. In fauour wherof, whatsoeuer (in the meane season) I doe in this worlde, I doe it for that thing sake, and to further saluacion. For what other thing doe I, then that all folke should, through iyes of faith, see and acknowlege God and his sonne, whom he sent into the worlde: I shall within a while departe hence, than shall those that haue nowe had no will to worke, desyre lyght in vaine. The Lord Jesus did with this saying, couertly notise vnto them that were present, that (al infidelitie set aparte) they should quickely go about to beleue the sonne of God, whom they coulde not long after see bodily. Moreouer, he did insinuate therwithall that those which otherwyse coulde not be brought to beliefe than by hearing him speake, and seeyng him worke miracles, should to none effecte desire to haue him made away, whom they despised beyng present. And at whose light, beyng obiecte to all mennes sight, they shut their iyes. Furthermore he signified likewise, that al suche as of obstinate minde did persist in wilful blindnesse of minde, should, when time were, as menne vnrecouerable and without hope to be amended, be lefte to theyr owne folly vnto eternall destruccion, euen when aduersaunte miserye is imminent and ready to inuade them, whiche calamitie wyll rather cause them perishe than heale them. And ouer all this he dyd ensigne them in tyme to come, a terrible iudgemente, at what season the wicked shall couet to labour aboute businesse of theyr saluacion: And it shall not bee lefull, for that the night will not suffre it, for as muche as they neglected the day in which they myght haue wrought: yet for all this, euery one whyle he is in state of this bodely lyfe, and also after Christes ascencion into heauen, hath this dayes lyght of the Apostles, and of holy scripture, whiche geueth habilitie to doe the thyng that appertayneth to our saluacion: But after the bodye be once dead, than is his daye awaye from hym, nor it cannot worke any thing more: but the rewarde of his foredoen dedes is to be hoped vpon and loked for. These diffuse sayinges our Lord Jesus than had, to quicken and pricke forwarde with feare of the thyng to come, men that were slowe to beleue. But nowe, while the disciples looked for a miracle, Jesus spatte on the grounde,

I am the lyght of the worlde.

 and

and of his spattle and duste mixed together, he made clay, and he anoynted the blinde mans iyes with the clay, euen therby resemblyng his fathers, or rather his owne worke, wherein he made the firste manne of hard clay, mollified with licoure. And to restore that whiche was loste, pertayneth to the same author, which fyrst made the same thynges of nought. And to purifie or make whole agayne, a thyng that is corrupted, is of more power & strength, than to begette a thyng that is not borne. Well but in the meane tyme, the noueltie of this plaster made all theyr myndes attentiue and quietely to geue hede, and well to considre the miracle that should be wrought, and it also proued a stedfast fayth in the blynde man, whiche murmured nothyng at hym that anoynted hym, but simply obeyeth hym that doeth what hymselfe liste, doubtyng nothyng at all of the benefyte, what waye soeuer it should be geuen. The blynde dyd not furthwith receyue his sight, but as soone as he was anoynted with the clay, he is commaunded to goe to the poole Siloe, and there to washe awaye the clay, wherewith his iyes were embrued, to thentente that both the blynde mannes faithfull affiaunce should be of greater fame, for that he made no refusall to doe that he was commaunded, and that the noueltie of that straunge sight, & also the delay whiche was through length of the Journey, should bryng furth moe recordes of the miracle: for the blynde manne sat not farre of from the temple beggyng by the waye syde. And the well Syloe wherof ryseth the poole, is at the foote of the mounte Syon: of whiche water Esay speaketh too and complayneth that that water was contemned, not, that the water geueth to any manne helthe, but because it beareth the figure of holy scripture. Which scriptures of God, whē as without blusteryng of worldely eloquence they issue furth caulmely and smoothely, yet because they bubble out of the priuy hid caues of godly wisedome, they haue heauenly violence to remoue the blyndenesse of mannes mynde, howe long soeuer it hath continued and to open those iyes wherwith God is seen, whom to haue seen is felicitie. For Syloe in the Syrians tongue sygnifieth sent. For one there is euen specially sente from the father, whiche only geueth lyght to mennes myndes, for he is the fountayne. It did represente Christe hymselfe, who euen at this presente tyme also, beyng as it were with a secrete power enclosed in holy scripture, openeth the iyes of the blynde, yf so be that they will acknowledge theyr blyndenesse. He must be made more then blynde that will receyue light of Christe. He that is wyse to the worlde, is very farre of from hope of heauēly wisedome: he that thinketh himselfe well sighted, nor vouchesaueth to haue his iyes closed vp with the clay of Jesus, there is no cause why he should hope for the lyght of the ghospell. Nowe than whan the blynde felowe, a notable knowen manne for his beggyng, and knowen also to bee borne blynde, wente thither as he was commaunded, no doubte but a great croude of people folowed hym as he wente, not without laughyng, to see his iyes blurred with clay: and so twise blynde goyng to a water whiche was of no name through any miracle that euer was doen therin: when they were come to the water, he washeth awaye the clay from his iyes, and returneth home with open iyes and and cleare sight.

The texte. ¶ So the neyghbours and they that had seen hym before howe that he was a beggee, sayed: is not this he that sate and begged? Some sayed this is he: Agayne, other sayed: no, but

but he is lyke hym. He hymselfe sayed, I am euen he. Therfore sayed they vnto hym: howe are thine iyes opened? He aunswered and sayed. The manne that is called Jesus, made clay, and anoynted myne iyes, and sayed vnto me: Goe to the poole Siloe and washe. And whan I went and washed, I receiued my sight. Then sayed they vnto hym: where is he? He sayed, I cannot tell. They brought to the Pharisees, hym that a litle before was blynd, and it was the Sabboth daye, when Jesus made the claye and opened his iyes.

Neighboures therfore and other whiche had knowen hym before (neither coulde he but be well knowen to many, consideryng he was a common beggar) when they knewe his face, but as for his iyes they sawe altered, they sayed: Is not this he whome we sawe sitting before the temple, and begged by the waye syde? Some sayde: It is he. Other contrarie, it is not he, but it is an other like hym. Whyle they disagreed among themselues, the blynde himselfe sayed: Yes verely I am the same beggar, and he that was borne blynde, whome ye haue often seen. And he thus sayed, that his voyce also beyng knowen, should cause the miracle be the better beleued. But we (say they) sawe the blinde: now see we thee see with open iyes. How chaunced it that thyne iyes were shut, and now are open? The man (saieth he) that is called Jesus, made claye, and therwith anoynted mine iyes, and that doen he sayed: goe thy waye to the poole Siloe, and there washe thine iyes. I wẽt my waye, I washed me, and now I see. They than sekyng occasion to pycke a quarell to the Lorde Jesus, to put him to rebuke, because in tempering the claye and anoynting the iyes therwith, he sumwhat laboured on the holy daye, they enquire where he was that did this dede. When the beggar had aunswered that he knew not who it was, for he had not knowen Jesus by sight, but onely by name, they bryng him whiche of a blynde man was brought to his sight, vnto the Pharisees, that by shewyng the thyng playnely before them, he shoulde detecte Jesus that he hadde broken the Sabboth daye. For it was the Sabboth daye whan Jesus opened the blynde mannes iyes.

¶ Then agayne the Phariseis also asked him howe he had receyued his sight. He sayed vnto them: he put claye vpon my iyes and I washed, and do see. Therfore sayed some of the Phariseis: this man is not of God, because he kepeth not the sabboth daye: other sayde, how can a man that is a sinner, do suche miracles? And there was a strife amongst them. They speake to the blynde man agayne: what sayest thou of him, because he hath opened thine iyes? he sayed: he is a prophete.

The texte.

There the Pharisees enquire of the manne once againe howe he came from beyng blinde to haue sight. He casting no perils shewed playnly how the matter was, and sayed: he annointed mine iyes with claye that was tempered with spattle. And vpon his commaundement I washed me in Siloe, and that doen I receyued my sight. Certayne of the Pharisees when they hearde this, sayed: this Jesus is not of God, though he speake of God the father: for if he tooke God for his auctour, he woulde not by doyng suche miracles violate the Sabboth whiche God commaunded to be kepte. It is a detestable thyng to breake the holy Sabboth daye. God medleth not with suche a one. So those maliciously faithlesse because they could not denye so manifest a dede, nor reproue so beneficiall a dede, they borowe and make shift to haue a quarell against him at the holines of the daye. other agayne that were more curable, sayth: if this man were not beloued of God, or detestable before hym for breakyng the Sabboth,

 how

howe coulde he worke these miracles? The matter it selfe sheweth that these thynges are dooen by the ayde of God: Nor this is not nowe the firste miracle that he hath wrought. After this sorte was alteracion and sondrye opinions among them, touchyng Jesus. Therfore the Phariseis, whiche by all assayes, toke occasion to reproue hym, spake yet againe to the blynde: What thinkest thou (saye they) of hym that opened thyne iyes? The thyng that they hunted for was this: that in case he had spoken euill of Jesus (whiche thyng the blynde man knewe was their mynde) they might haue matter to saye againste those whiche had metely good opinion of Jesus: but and he had reported well by hym, they woulde haue been fierce againste the blynde man selfe, and haue caste hym out of the Synagogue. The beggar of trueth simplie and withoute dreade spake out what he thought of Jesus. I take hym (sayeth he) to be a prophete, meanyng by that same, some greate and notable man of whom he had both heard great fame, and had had also experience of his power and strengthe in hymselfe.

The texte.

But the Jewes did not beleue of the man (howe that he had been blinde and receyued his sighte) untyll they called the father and mother of hym that had receyued his syghte. And they asked them, saying: Is this your sonne, whome ye saye was borne blinde? Howe dooeth he now see then? His father and mother aunswered them, and sayed: we knowe that this is our sonne, and that he was borne blynde: By what meanes he nowe seeth we cannot tell, or who hath opened his iyes, cannot we tell: he is olde ynough, aske hym: leat hym aunswer for himselfe. Suche wordes spake his father and mother, because, they feared the Jewes. For the Jewes had conspired already that if any man dyd confesse that he was Christ, he shoulde be excommunicate out of the Synagogue. Therfore sayed his father and mother: he is olde ynoughe aske hym.

There were many Jewes therfore, whiche coulde not be brought in beliefe, that this was the same whiche late before sate beggyng at the doore of the temple, beyng borne blynde, forsomuche as it did euidentlye appeare that he nowe had cleare sight and open iyes. Therfore his father and mother were called for, whiche coulde knowe their sonne euen by some speciall marke. And here nowe the malicious curiositie of the Pharisees set forwarde the beliefe and also the commendacion of the thyng that was doen. Therfore they saye to his parētes: Is this your sonne whome ye were woont to saye was borne blind? And howe chaunced it that nowe he seeth? They (as in dede suche bee timorous as haue small substaunce at home) answere warely: The thing (saye they) whiche we certainly know, we can testify: We knowe that this is our sonne, & that he was borne blind. But of the sight that is geuen him, we neither knowe how it cāme, nor from whom, himselfe shall testifie this thyng more assuredly than we can. He is old ynough, aske him rather then vs, lette him speake for himselfe that he knoweth. His parentes had these sayinges, not as ignoraunt what had befallē vpon their childe, but they had leauer that he alone shoulde come in daunger, than they to endaunger themselues with him: for the Jewes had already conspired, that if any man durste professe Jesus to be Messias, he shoulde bee excōmunicate and caste out of the Synagogue, whiche was taken for a matter among the Jewes of great reproche, wherof it cūmeth that euen among the professers of the gospel, the sharpest kynde of punishment is, that if a man swarue frō his professiō and fal into an haynous cryme, he be remoued from the felowship of other, to the intente that he whiche cannot bee refourmed by wholesome

Is this your sonne. &c.

information,

information, beyng eschewed of other, shoulde be better aduised, and for veray shame amend. But this exaumple of gentle fiercenesse, whiche was fitte to bee exhibite vpon them onely, which through theyr enormities shoulde make themselues detestable and pestilente, the Jewes nowe turne to the establishement of theyr tyranny: lyke as they dyd also abuse all other good ordinaunces to theyr owne gayne and pompe. The darte whiche ought to haue been hurled at the euill sorte, to haue healed them therby, rather than to haue destroyed them, they turne the same weapon agaynst them, whiche professe Christe. The blinde mās parentes fearyng this thyng, layeth vpon theyr sonnes backe, the enuie that shoulde rise of testifying the trueth: he is (saye they) of sufficiente age, ye maye aske him.

Then agayne call they the man that was blinde, and sayed vnto hym: Geue God prayse, we knowe that this man is a sinner. He aunswered. Whether he bee a synner or no, I cannot tell: one thyng I am sure of, that where I was blinde, I nowe see. Then sayed they to hym agayne: what did he to thee? howe opened he thyne iyes? he aunswered them: I tolde you ere while, and ye did heare, wherfore woulde ye heare it agayne? wyll ye also be his disciples?

The texte.

Than he that had been blynde, was called for agayne, to bee his owne witnes and aduocate, and to bee also a publisher of Christes renoume, for it was Christes vse to reuerse and turne the malice of the Pharisees, vnto Gods glorye. For though the dede was more euidente, partelye by the recorde of the parētes, & partely by ẏ acte selfe, than that it could be cloked or denied, yet to turne awaye the prayse of that dede from Christe, whome they hated, they saye: That thou haste sight where before thou waste blinde, do not ascribe it to Jesus: vnto whom thou arte nothyng beholden, but prayse god for this benefite. For we know that this felow Jesus is a sinner, who hath no acquaintaunce with god. The Pharisees did their endeuour to deuide in sundre that whiche coulde not be seperate, that is to wete, the glory of the father from the glorye of the sonne: and they spake colourably, to hyde theyr owne iniquitie with the pretence of hye godlynesse, as thoughe they toke great care leste Goddes honoure shoulde decaye, when as in very dede they sought theyr owne prayse in all thynges, and regarded not the prayse of God. The blynde manne answeryng vnto these sayinges, bothe boldely and aduisedly, sayeth: whether he bee a sinner or no, let other men iudge, it is not my parte to geue sentence therin, one thyng I can truelye testifie, I founde in very dede that I was before blynde, and I nowe see: here nowe, when as no sufficient occasion was geuen to the Pharisees, eyther to rebuke Jesus or to bee cruell agaynste the man, whiche had spoken warelye and with good aduisement, they were turned backe agayne to theyr former interrogatories, driuing driftes on euery syde how to bereue Christ of his praise: what did he to the (saye they) or by what meanes did he open thine iyes, hoping that by a new maner of framing his tale, thei might picke out somewhat wherby they should perswade that this prayse was not due to Christe. Agaynst this impudēt & shamelesse malice of the Phariseis, the beggar beyng now wel boldned, maketh this answere: I tolde you erewhile playnelye as the thyng was doen in dede, once ye haue heard it. To what purpose is it, to repete the same agayne? If ye do enquire of a pure simple minde, well, I haue already opened ẏ matter, and with my recorde, I haue satisfied that whiche was demaunded of me: and yf ye dooe not so aske, it were not indifferentelye dooen, eftesones to

Geue God prayse.

 tell

tell the same. Dooe ye therfore so diligently enquire the maner of the dede, that after the matter be throughly knowen, ye also wil become his disciples, by whō God worketh so great thinges? lyke as I (vpon experience of his power) and many other moe are his disciples.

The texte.

Then rated they him and sayed: be thou his disciple. we are Moses disciples: we are sure that God spake vnto Moses: As for this felowe, we knowe not from whence he is. The man aunswered and sayed vnto them: this is a merueylous thyng that ye wot not whence he is, and yet he hath opened mine iyes. For we are sure that God heareth no sinners, but yf anye man be a wurshipper of God and obedient vnto his wil, him heareth he. Sence the world began, was it not heard, that any man opened the iyes of one, that was borne blynd. If this man were not of god, he could haue doen nothing. They aunswered and sayed vnto hym: thou arte altogether borne in sinne, and doest thou teache vs? And they cast him out.

The Phariseis beeyng sore prouoked with the beggars great affyaunce, made no aunswere, but all to rated him: wishing that thyng to the manne as an extreme euill, whereby themselues might bee made blessed, and through abhominacion putting backe from them that thyng, whiche oughte to haue been moste hartely desyred, sayng for that they were as blynde in soule as the beggar beyng nowe an euangeliste, was before in bodye: the Pharisees (I saye) saye vnto hym: O thou vngracious wretche, bee thou that naughtye felowes disciple. We that are the disciples of Moses, with whome this Jesus is not to bee compared, doe deteste and abhorre suche a maister. For we bee certayn that god spake to Moses, and that whatsoeuer he teacheth vs, he hath it at Goddes hande to teache. But why should we geue eare to this Jesus, seing we knowe not from whence he came? leat him teache and proue vnto vs his authoritie, and perchaunce we will beleue him. The beggars courage and boldenes dyd in the tyme of theyr reasonyng, growe and increase: And thoughe he perceiued that they by all subtill meanes went about to destroye Jesus, yet did he stoutely (setting a syde all perils) pleade Jesus cause, gathering and well prouyng by the miracle that was wroughte in geuyng him his sighte, that it was cleare ynough from whence Jesus came. I meruayle (sayeth he) why ye saye ye knowe not from whence Jesus is, when as it cannot be denayed but that by hym myne iyes be open: with whiche (being shut and withoute sighte) I was borne. Certes this is a thing without controuersie, neither dooe ye thynke the contrary, that God heareth not the desyres of sinners. But if a man wurshippe him deuoutly, and obeyeth his will whome he religiouslye serueth, hym dooeth God heare. But if God by Jesus haue taken from me my blyndnes, albeit the chiefe prayse is to be geuen to god, yet neuertheles it must nedes be that he is a reuerente wurshipper of God, and one that God loueth, at whose desyre and prayer God gaue vnto me so notable a benefite. For it is no common or meane miracle whiche ye see wrought in me. Many wonderous thynges are tolde of, which god lōg agoe did by our elders, but suche as were holy and not sinners. But except this Jesus were come from God, except the power of god were present with him, he coulde of himselfe do nothing at all. It is not of mans strēgth whiche yet we see doen.

We are Moses disciples.

The Phariseis beeyng made extreme woode with this courage and boldnes that the beggar was of (and when there was no hope to bee hadde that the poore felowe would either bee corrupted, or with feare astonished, and so cease

of

of from preaching Christ, fal to extremitie, and to say the vttermost they could. They vpbrayed him with his olde blindnesse, they cast him in the teeth with his beggerlynesse, as though God hadde punished him therwithall for his sinnes, and as though he were borne wicked and vngracious, that commeth into the worlde poore or blind, or other wise bleamished in bodye. Thou (saye they) arte altogether borne in sinne, and teachest thou vs that knowe howe to defende religion and vpholde the profession of the lawe? darest thou here in the presence of so great men teache diuinitie, whiche but a while a go asked almes? neyther did they suffer him to speake any longer. And beyng ashamed to be so put to silence, and haue their mouthes stopped by a poore ignoraunt person: they thrust him out of the Sinagogue as a leude masters leude disciple.

Jesus hearde that they had excommunicated him: and when he had founde hym he saied vnto him: doest thou beleue on the sonne of god? He aunswered and sayed; who is it lord that I might beleue on hym? And Jesus sayed vnto hym: thou hast seen hym, and he it is that talketh with the. And he sayed: Lorde, I beleue, and he wurshypped hym. The texte.

But whome Pharisaicall fiercenes thrusteth out of the Sinagogue, them doeth Christe receiue into his churche. For to bee disseuered from the communion of the wicked, is to be coupled to Christe. And to bee disallowed of them, that stablishyng their owne righteousnesse, speake agaynste the righteousnesse of God, is to bee approued and alowed: and of them to be rebuked, that seking their owne prayse, goe about to darken the prayse of Jesus, is moste hye prayse: and to be detestable to thē that are to be detested, is to be derely beloued of god. Therefore relacion was made vnto Jesus how boldely the man that so muche set foorth his prayse, behaued himselfe towardes the Phariseis. For it was already bruted abrode by the people, that he was caste of and reiect. Therefore as soone as Jesus had met with him, to make this mans fayth more knowen to al men, he sayeth vnto him: howe sayest thou felowe, beleuest thou on the sonne of God? For he had already confessed before the Pharisees, that he whiche did so greate a thyng came playnely from God. Nor Jesus was ignoraunte thereof, but he gatte out the mannes open confession thereof, for other mennes sakes, procuryng thereby a good exaumple for other. But though he that had been blynde, as yet knewe not Jesus by sighte, yet hauyng great affeccion to knowe that mannes face, whome Jesus named the sonne of god, sayeth: lorde who is he, that when I knowe hym, I maye beleue on him? The manne had beleued on Jesus, yea ere he sawe hym: nor this was not the voyce of a faythlesse man, but of one that vehemently desyred to see the auctour of so great a benefite. Jesus therefore with humble woordes, signifying hymselfe to be the personne he spake of, sayeth vnto hym: thou haste already seen hym whome thou desyreste to see, and he it is that talketh with thee, on whome it behoueth thee to beleue.

The man vpon these woordes without any staying at all, confesseth with great promptnes of mynde that he doeth beleue: and euen with that saying, he fell downe at Jesus knee, and wurshipped hym, and so his dede declared what he thought of Jesus.

¶ And Jesus sayed vnto hym: I am come vnto iudgemente into this worlde, that they which see not might see: & that they which see might be made blynde. And some of the Pharisies which were with hym, heard these wordes & sayed vnto hym: are we blynd also? Jesus The texte.

sayed

saued vnto them. If ye were blind ye shoulde haue no synne. But nowe ye saye we see, therfore your sinne remayneth.

Now than, Iesus (to thentent, that by example of this manne he might the more prouoke other mens mindes that wer present) sayeth: I that am the light of the worlde, therfore came into the worlde that the course of thynges mighte be turned vpsyde doune: as muche to say, that the symilitude and sleight of vntrue hollinesse and forged knoweledge, beyng disclosed, these whiche heretofore sawe not, might se: and that they whiche see might be made blynde. With this saying, Iesus noted the naughty peruerse iudgement of the Pharisees, which though they thought that onely they knew what was religion, what was law, and what was righteousnes, yet wer they more foule ouerseen, than any of the mean sorte of people, by reason that worldelye couetousnes had darkened the iudgemente of their mynde, when as that sely poore blinde felowe, simple and vnlearned, likewyse as he had bodily sight frely geuen him, so did he inwardly see so muche in soule, that in knowlage of trueth he excelled euen the very pharisees. Neither did these bytyng wordes so scape all the Phariseis (whiche folowed Iesus of no good minde, but rather to seke on euery syde, occasion to reproue hym) but that the styng of this saying caused some of them to marke it, so that those were not beguiled therwith. These, beyng nothyng altered from their malepert presumpcion, to thintent that they might either force the Lorde to testifie honorably of them, or to haue some matter to accuse him of vnto them that were of the pharisees orde, saye vnto hym: are we than blynde also? But Iesus doeth so aunswere vnto this question, whiche was very wily, capcious, and also presumptuouse, that he declareth them, whiche thoughte themselues men of great sight, to be more than blinde: not in body but in soule, and to bee the more vncurably blynde, because they thought themselues quicke sighted. Verely (sayeth Iesus) yf ye were blynde, and woulde knowledge howe ignorāt in soule ye be, your simplicitie should be pardoned. But nowe, forasmuche as ye be blinde in dede, and yet ye would be praysed among the people for learned men, ye are so very starke blinde that ye cannot be healed. As this blinde manne hath obteyned sight because he knowledged the deformitie of his body, euen so you, because ye be voluntary blynde, as menne blynded through lustes of your fleshe, cannot be cured, but continue in the sinne of infidelitie: whereas the vnlearned whiche firste were ignoraunt of the trueth, vpon the syght of miracles, and by hearyng me preache (all darkenes taken awaye) enbraceth the light of the trueth. He that presumptuously taketh vpon hym to knowe the lawe, and speaketh againste him that is the principall poynte and conclusion of the lawe, is more than blynde, and altogether out of the waye. All men haue liued heretofore vnder shadowes, nor any waye lieth open to the lightwarde, but by fayth of the ghospell. Therefore the common and vulgare people soner receiue sight, because they do not very muche thynke themselues well sighted, and if they be any whit ouerseen, it is rather through rude ignorāūce than malice. But they that whan themselues be twise blinde, yet they professe themselues teachers of the people, that is, guiders of the blynd: suche, I say, be starke blynde, and moste daungerously, without recouery. For neyther they thēselues come to the light, and yet through false opinion, and pretence of learnyng and holinesse, they seduce and bryng other into errour.

I am come in iudgemēt &c.

If ye were blynde ye should haue no sinne.

The

The.x.Chapter.

Verely verely I say vnto you, he that entreth not in by the doore into the shepefolde, but climeth vp some other waye, thesame is a thiefe and murderer. But he that entreth in by the doore is the shepeherde of the shepe, to hym the porter openeth and the shepe heare his voyce, and he calleth his owne shepe by name, and leadeth them out. And whan he hath set forth his owne shepe he goeth before them, & the shepe folowe him: for they knowe his voyce. A straunger will they not folowe, but will flee from hym, for they knowe not the voyce of straungers.

The texte.

AND albeit they were such, yet did they disdain & enuy the Lord Jesus, because he did allure the people vnto hym, and withdrewe them from the obedience of the Phariseis and priestes, whiche sayed persones, because they coulde no longer defende their autoritie by honest meanes, they doe their endeuoure to mayntaine their tiranny with disceites, frayinges, wyles, traynes, thretninges and wicked conspiracies, not attendyng the peoples commoditie, as it had been fitte they should haue doen, cōsidering they professed themselfes teachers, guydes, and shepeherdes of the people, but with the peoples discommoditie sought their owne commoditie: Jesus therfore, who had before tyme by many and diuerse similitudes enuited all men vnto hym, somewhyle callyng hymselfe heauenly breade, wherof he that dyd eate should lyue eternally: Some tyme namyng hymselfe liuely water, wherof whoso did drinke, should conceiue in hymselfe a spryng of water that would gushe out and runne into euerlasting lyfe: some tyme the light of the worlde that lighteneth all mennes mindes: an other time the sonne and ambassadour of God the father, on whom he that did beleue should obtaine eternall saluacion: In this place he doeth thesame thyng by an other parable, entendyng that that thyng should more depely settle in al mennes myndes, which is the chiefe and head poynte of mannes whole saluacion, that is to witte, that no manne can be a directour or shepeherde of people, vnles hymselfe be firste a shepe of Christe, that true shepeherde of all the shepe that are to be placed on the right hande in the last daye. But surely he is not Christes shepe, that is not a membre of Chrste: and he is no membre of Christe that doeth preferre this worlde or his owne honour before Christes glory. But the Phariseis, because they would be shepeherdes without Christe, they were therfore robbers and theues and no shepeherdes though they chalenged as due to themselfes, the name, the hye looke, and solemne grauitie of a shepeherde.

Jesus therfore noting them, sayeth: one thyng I assure you of, whosoeuer entereth into the shepefold, not by the doore, but entereth with force an other waye, as eyther by climyng ouer the enclosures, or by diggyng through the walles, thesame is no shepeherd, but a thefe, & a murtherer. A thefe to catche somewhat by fraude and stealth, a murtherer to kill by violence. But whoso entereth in by the doore, because he deuiseth no guile against the shepe, he is a shepeherde: & to him hauing minde to entre in by the doore, shall he open the doore, whiche onely hath the right to let in. Though the shepe be afearde at the vnknowen voyce of the thefe and murtherer, yet doe they acknowledge and heare this mannes voyce: because it is the true shepeherdes voyce. For albeit the shepe be a seely simple beast, and dependeth of the ayde of other,

yet shepe

yet shepe doe knowe the voyce of the shepeherde, of whom they perceyue releefe: and they quake for feare at the voyce of wulfes, by whom they be put in feare of death. Therfore the shepeherde goyng into the shepefolde by the doore, maketh not the shepe afearde, but is well inough knowen, and on his behalfe knoweth his shepe, so that he can also name euery one of them, and they beyng called doe obey his voyce. For they be called to theyr foode and meate, and not to the fleshe shambles to be killed. And they be called with a frendely and with a knowen voyce: they be not thruste out with violence: and the shepeherde conducteth them, beyng redy and towardes at his call, to pastures: and when they be once brought out of the folde (wherin they were enclosed) and are come abrode into the common fieldes, leste they should runne astray, the true and knowen shepeherde goeth before his flocke: and y flocke foloweth him. For he goeth not all husht and dumme before them, but eftsones entiseth them to folowe hym: and calleth the shepe backe againe in case they be wandered and strayed asyde. And they knowe theyr shepeherdes voice, and therat come into ordre. But they doe not folowe the shepeherde of an other flocke: but loeth him, and flie from him as vnknowen, because they knowe no nother shepeherdes voice but their owne.

The texte. This prouerbe spake Iesus vnto them, but they vnderstode not what thynges they were whiche he spake vnto them. Then sayed Iesus vnto them againe: Verely verely I saye vnto you: I am the doore, of the shepe: all (euen as many as came before me) are theues and murtherers, but the shepe dyd not heare them: I am the doore, by me yf any man entre in, he shall be safe and shall goe in and out, and finde pasture.

With this parable our Lorde Iesus did sore reproue the Phariseis, the Scribes, the priestes, and headmen of the people, whiche had indignacion and disdained that there should be so many whiche had leauer cleaue vnto Iesus than to them that toke themselfes to be the guides of the people. Moreouer they that were very swyne and goates, gaue eare to those mens voyces. But they that were truely shepe, without fraude, simple, and that doeth no harme, did knowlage the voyce of the Lorde Iesus: who was the true shepeherde to whom the father beyng porter, opened the doore, that he might lede his obedient shepe into the pastures of euerlastyng lyfe. But forsomuch as the Phariseis did not vnderstand what this parable ment, Iesus did vouchesafe to make playne the thynges whiche he had spoken darkely, for two skilles, thone, to make them more attētiue, the other, that the matter whiche he vttered by a parable, myght take roote deper in theyr hertes that heard him, he sayeth vnto them: I doe affirme vnto you a moste true thyng. I am the very doore wherof I haue spoken, by which doore the shepe y will be saued must goe in & out. By this doore it behoueth him to goe in, that will entre to the office of a shepeherd, & exercise that funccion, for it is not ynough, at all aduentures (not regarding what waye) to haue entred forceably within the limites, enclosure, & shepefolde of y churche. It is not sufficiēt to haue attained the name & dignitie of a shepeherde, not forcing howe. Howe many soeuer hath been such, that by euil meanes haue rashely runne into the shepefolde of Gods people, not of any minde to feede, but to spoyle, because they haue not entred by me that am y doore, they be no shepeherdes, but theues & murderers, forasmuch as they be gredy of lucre, & in crueltie rigorous & very tirauntes. But yet those swine & goates that loue this worlde, haue geuen eare

eare to all these manier of voyces. But shepe limited and predestinate to the pastures of eternall life, and that are desirous of foode of the gospell, haue not hearde the voyce of these, nor knowen in them any gospellers voyce, because they were not true shepeherdes. For their voyce soundeth nothyng shepeheardlyke. But more lyke the voyce of a robber, and of a rauenous woulfe. I am (I tell you) the dore. There is no healthfull entryng into the churche and kingdō of heauen but by me, whether thou wilt be shepeherde or shepe. If any entre in by me, he shall attain eternall health: and shalbe without all daunger of theues and murderers, but through this shepehearde shall go into the shepefolde safe, and take the fruicion of the blessed quietnes of contemplacion, and shall again go out into the pastures, to practise and put in vre the office of charitie. And there shal no where lacke pastures, but in all places shall be matter to do good vpon, to the intente he maye bothe profit other, and he hymselfe through good dedes repayre home agayne to the shepefolde more fatter and better likyng. Thus now ye haue one token, wherby ye maye discerne a shepe from a goate, a true shepeherde from a false. He that beleueth not on me, & yet maketh himself a shepeheard of the people, of him ought men to beware. And his voice shal thā disclose what manier one he is, if his woordes haue no taste of Goddes glorye, if they sauoure not of the peoples health: but of his owne praise, of gaine, of worldly subtiltie, and of tiranny: let the shepe take hede to themselues and beware of him: for he is a thefe and a murtherer, he is no shepehearde. And he is the more daungerous, because he faineth himselfe to be a shepeheard. And in case the voyce be not a sufficient profe, take hede to theyr dedes.

A thefe cummeth not but for to steale, kyll and to destroye: I am come that they mighte haue lyfe, and that they might haue it more aboundauntly. I am the good shepeherde. A good shepeherde geueth his life for his shepe, an hired seruaunt, and he whiche is not the shepeherd (neither the shepe are his owne) seeth the woulfe comming and leaueth the shepe, and flieth, and the woulfe catcheth and scattereth the shepe. The hired seruaunte flyeth, because he is an hyred seruaunte, and careth not for the shepe. I am the good shepeheard, and know my shepe, and am knowen of myne.

The texte.

The thefe cummeth for none other purpose but to steale, and to get himselfe vile and filthy gaine of the harmes of an other mans flocke. The murderer cūmeth not but to worry and destroye, and to practise tirāny vpon the flocke, vnto the whiche to haue dooen good, had been his parte and duetie. Thre wayes therefore it shalbe lefull to decerne the true shepeheard from the thefe or prayecatcher: If he entre not in by the doore, that is to saye, yf he dooe not acknowlage me by whome onely there is hope of eternall healthe: If he speake not those thynges whiche agreeth with the doctrine of God: thyrdely if his intente be directed any other waye than to those thynges that appartayne to Goddes glory, and saluacion of the people. If none of these faultes can be found in me, but if rather the father of heauen haue opened the doore, if I speake those thinges whiche accordeth with the meanyng of the lawe, & whiche are agreable to the will of the father of heauen, yf I doe no where hunte for lucre or mine own prayse, but obeying my fathers pleasure, thirst after nothyng els but al folkes health, than vnderstande ye that I am the true shepehearde, and acknowlage ye my founder, my voyce, my desyre and study.

I am the good shepeahearde.

They that auaunt themselues to be shepeheardes, goe aboute this, verely euen to get themselues commoditie of your discommodities, who than fare best whan the flocke fareth wurst. I that haue entred in by the doore, came for none

none other thing, but that the diseased shepe should bee healed, the dead should liue, and the quicke shoulde be fatted with all kynde of vertues. He is taken for a good shepehearde which liueth in dede of the reuenewes and yearely profites that come of his shepe, whiche purloyneth nothyng, or nothyng deuoureth. But an euangelicall shepehearde ferre passeth this vpright dealyng. For he doeth not onely not spoyle as the thefe doeth, not onelye not teare in pieces as the praie catcher doeth, but also bestoweth his owne life for to defend his shepe, so farre of it is that he would for any gayne sake, hurt the flocke that he is put in trust withal, or lose that which he hath taken in hand to kepe. Therfore the other sort, that braggue vpon theyr beyng shepherdes, are woulfes & no shepeherdes. But if ye demaunde an exaumple, and a profe of a good shepherde, it is I that am a good shepherde, whiche do not onely my selfe not seke my commoditie of the flockes harme, but I also dooe frely geue of myne own goodes, yea and my lyfe too, to resiste theim that come againste the flocke, to endammage or greue it. I dooe that for my shepe, that one frende will not doe for a nother. He cannot be a shepherde vnlesse he be pure from all singular profite and priuate commoditie, except also he set euen his owne life at naught, whan at any time the flocke standeth in ieopardy. For ther be many thinges that make incursion against the health of the flocke. Therfore he that is a true shepehearde, and in his herte careth for the flocke for none other skill, but because he loueth the flocke, redy to do his commaundemente that gaue him that flocke to be kepte safe, and not to be nye shorne, spoyled, slayn, or worried, he defendeth the health of his shepe, euen with the losse of his owne lyfe.

But contrary, he that is an hierelinge, & hath taken the ouersight of the flocke for his owne aduauntage, yet although he doe rightlye gouerne, and rule the flocke whiles al thinges be caulme and quiet, yet if there hange any ieopardye of life thereupon, that is to wete, if he see the woulfe prease vpon him furyously, he betrayeth the shepe, and leaueth the flocke to the woulfe to be scattered abrode, and so pece meale to be worried, and saueth his owne lyfe by runnyng awaie. And what is the cause? Nothing els but because he is an hired seruaūt, and no shepeherd. True charitie hath no respecte to the rewarde. Whereas consideracion of the reward hath place, there is either no charitie, or vnperfite charitie. And if there be any duetie doen, it is not doen with that good wyll that a true shepehearde would dooe it with all. But where the thyng moste requireth the very naturall shepehearde, there thā is ẏ flocke deceitfully betrayed, whiles the hired shepeherde runneth awaye. And why is that? Because, when that he hath considered the matter after worldly iudgement, he counteth it better that an other mans flocke do perishe, than himselfe to come in perill of life. And yet is this maner of men some deale better than they, whiche playe the woulfes themselues against the flocke, vnder the false title of shepeheardes. For there be they, whiche in tyme of prosperitie doeth right faythfully take hede to theyr flocke, but yet when there is a great daunger, they leaue traiterously the flocke to the woulf to be disperpled abrode and torne in pieces: for he fantasieth thus: In case thei go to wracke, what than? I haue no losse therby. My wage is safe, and though I lose some deale therof, I had rather lose it, than to cope and fight with the woulfe, for another mannes cattell. There shal another flocke be foūd out, whiche I shall bee hyred to haue the ouersight of: thoughe the maister of this flocke loose it.

Neyther

Neyther doeth the death of the flocke greue the hyred mans mynd. So it happeneth that both the owner hath losse of that thing which he entierely loueth, and the flocke cummeth to destruccion, whiche mighte haue bene saued. It is therfore no merueyl, though euangelike shepe knew not the voyce of such like shepeherdes. The shepe be not in faute, but the lewde shepherdes are to blame. Nor it is not to be disdained at, if they whome my father so draweth, do folow me, forsakyng the hyred shepherdes that are but very theues and murderers. For they feele and perceiue that I am all maner of wayes a good shepeherde, euen to spend my lyfe therfore. I know my shepe cōmitted to me of my father, al whose goodes are mine: and on the other syde, the shepe that are drawen by the inspiracion of the father, acknowlageth their shepeherd, loueth him, and foloweth hym, knowing right well that there is no hope of saluacion but by me.

As my father knoweth me, euen so know I also my father, and I geue my lyfe for the shepe, and other shepe I haue, which are not of this folde. Them also must I bring, & they shal heare my voice, and there shal be one folde and one shepeherd. Therfore doeth my father loue me, because I put my life from me, that I might take it againe. No man taketh it from me, but I put it away of my self: I haue power to put it from me, and I haue power to take it againe: this commaundement haue I receiued of my father.

The texte.

The father knoweth me as his owne naturall sonne, obeying his wil in all thynges: and agayne I know the father, who desyreth, that all menne shoulde be saued. At his commaundemēt I bestowe my life for the safetie of my shepe whiche he hathe geuen me to haue them saued: nor any thyng wyll I so dooe, that this worlde (while I am the shepherd) shall haue power to harme them, nor yet the prince of this world the deuil: but to kepe my shepe whol and soūd, I will geue my selfe to death, by that meannes to abate the woulfes violence: and to deliuer my obedient shepe out of his chawes.
Nor it doeth not fully content the fathers wil and my charitie, if I should saue these shepe alone, whiche beyng of the people of Israell, he hath geuen to me to be saued first, but my cure reacheth further than so. There bee also in other nacions shepe scattered and in daungier of snares, of woulfes, theues, and murderers: neyther will I rest vntil I bring these also into the common shepefold. And although they heare not the voice of Moses, or of the prophetes, yet shal they knowe and geue eare to my voyce, I meane suche as be ordayned to saluacion. For the countrey dooeth not exclude from saluacion. Whosoeuer heareth the voyce of the sonne of God, (who is the very true shepeherd) shalbe saued. Hitherto the flocke of God hath bene scattered through the multitude of false shepeherdes. All doeth promise saluacion, and euery one hath his voyce, and one calleth this waye and an other the other waye. In the meane whyle, the flocke being destitute, is scattered here and there, and dyuers wayes perisheth. But so soone as they shall heare me, all they wyll knowe the voyce of the true shepeherde, and they shall come together out of all partes of the worlde. And so shall be made one folde of all, and no moe shepeherdes but one. He that is without this folde cannot be saued. He that dooethe not acknowlage thys shepeherd, shal goe to perdicion. But lest that should happen through my fault, I so throughly play the good shepeherde, that I lose my lyfe clerely. There is no decay in my father, thoughe all thyng that be create doe perysshe, for he hath nede of nothing, but of mere charitie towardes mankynde, he sente hys sonne to saue all menne if it coulde be. And because I am of the same mynde that my

I geue my life for the shepe. &c.

father is of, therfore he doeth derely loue me, as hys owne sonne, and no hired manne, because of myne owne good will I bestowe my lyfe for the health of my fathers flocke, it is so muche more vnlyke that I would, to hurt the flocke withal, seke out myne owne cõmoditie. Amongest men it is a great loue, if one when there is ieopardie towardes and daungier inminente, doeth not priuely steale a waye. I doe more, who with a free good will, geue my selfe to deathe. There be that lyeth in wayte to haue my lyfe, well, theyr malice could not preuaile agaynste me, excepte I were determyned of myne owne free will, to dye for the saluaciõ of mine. These folke of truth are in mind to murther, yet could they not kyl me vnlesse I would my selfe. Therfore they shal not take from me my life, but I will willyngly yelde it vp to redeme my shepe wt my death to euerlasting lyfe. Doe not beleue that I shall willingly geue my selfe vnto death, except I take agayn that willingly left lyfe, euen of myn own power, when I will. Herein consisteth the prayse of a true shepeherde, that of hys free will he offereth himself to death for the flockes helth, when it lieth in his owne power to eschew death if he list. No mans power could take my lyfe from me against my wil, but I geue it willingly for the flockes saluacyon. Other dye when as they would not, & being dead they reuiue not. And though a mā may wickedly kill him selfe, yet cannot he reuiue hys bodye agayne, with the lyfe that is once gone. I haue power to doe both, to sende foorth this lyfe out of the bodye, and to call agayn the same into the very selfe sayd body. In case it seme a thyng incredible vnto you, that any manne shoulde willingly redeme an other mannes lyfe with his owne death, no more to say, but it is so thought to my father that sente me into this worlde, by this waye to worke the feate of mannes saluacion. I willingly and gladly doe obey his commaundement, whose wil and mine are all one, and who hath geuen me power to perfourme my will.

I put my life frō me ẏ I might take it againe.

The texte. There was a discencion therfore agayne among the Iewes for these sayinges, and many of them sayd: He hath a deuil and is madde, why heare ye him? Other sayd: these are not the wordes of him that hath the deuil. Can the deuil opẽ the iyes of the blind? And it was at Ierusalẽ the feast of the dedicacion, and it was winter. And Iesus walked in the temple, euen in Salomons porche. Than came the Iewes rounde about him, and sayde vnto him: How long doest thou make vs doubt? If thou be Christ tell vs playnly.

When Iesus had tolde a long tale of these thinges that were straunge, vnhearde of and far aboue the common capacitie of most men, there fel a newe iar in opinions among the people: for some sayde that, whiche they had already many tymes sayed, whensoeuer he disclosed theyr secrete conspiracies, or if he spake or did any thyng aboue the power of manne: he hath the deuyll (saye they) and is madde. For the wordes whiche he speaketh, lacke common sence. What pleasure is it to heare this felowe? Againe some folke els sayde: these be no suche mans wordes, as is in the deuils daunger. For his woordes, smelleth of the power of God, specially for as muche as his deedes be agreable to his wordes. As his wordes be, suche be his dedes. He speaketh thinges farre passing mans wit, but the same doth thinges, which far excede mans power. Can a mad man, and he that is possessed with a deuil open blinde mens iyes? It is ẏ propertie of deuils to put out ones iyes that seeth, but to geue syght to him that is borne blind, cummeth of the power of God. Forasmuche than as as it is euident that that thyng is doen by hym, hys talke cannot procede of a noysome deuil, whose dedes appereth playne to come from a beneficiall God. The Lorde Jesus maketh no annswere to thys altercacyon, teachyng vs by the way, that the wicked are not alway to be striuen with in wordes: and that by dedes it is rather to bee declared what we can dooe, than by woordes: and sumtimes place is to bee geuen to the furie of the euil sorte, nor the moderate temperaunce of the ghospell, is at any tyme to bee forgotten. After all thys the feastful daye ministred newe matter to sette in hande and dispute with hym agayne. That solemne feaste was than, whiche they call the dedicacyon of the temple, for because the temple was reedefyed and repayred after the exile that was made at Hierusalem by the Persians. Neyther was Jesus absent at this feasteful daye, a newe maker of the law, and of a new temple, that is to say, the churche, chefe deuyser and maister of the woorkes. And it was winter: a full very mete tyme for theyr myndes, whiche throughe loue of the colde lawe, dyd not burne in the loue of the ghospell. Therfore Jesus was not nowe in the inner parte of the temple, but walked in the porche which ioyneth to the temple, that is called Salomons temple, to the intent that the very place shoulde declare that peacemaker to be presente, whiche shoulde reconcyle all thynges in heauen and earth. There walked truely the aucthor of the lawe of the ghospel, Moses lawe being nowe at a poynte to cease. The Jewes therefore, leste he should escape theyr handes, came rounde about him, whyle he was walkyng there, sore moued with many of his sayinges and dooynges: neyther dyd they well agree among themselues, some maliciously fyndyng faulte with al thing, some gathering of hys dedes and wordes, a certain thing to be honored in him aboue mannes power. And they set vpon hym with these woordes: Howe long wilt thou kepe vs in a doubtful mynde, and there with sette the people on a rore? If thou bee that verye Messias, whome we looke for, tell it vs openly without all colour.

Yf thou bee Christ, tel vs playnly.

The texte.

Jesus aunswered them: I tolde you, and ye beleue not. The workes that I doe in my fathers name, they beare witnes of me, but ye beleue not because ye are not of my shepe, as I sayd vnto you. My shepe heare my voyce, and I know them, and they folow me, and I geue vnto them eternal life, and they shal neuer perishe, neyther shal any man plucke them out of my hande. My father whiche gaue them me, is greatter than all, and no man is able to take them out of my fathers hande. I and my father are one.

But although Jesus was not ignoraunt that they dyd demaunde of a peruerse mynde this thing, whiche they had both often tymes hearde, and myght also haue perceiued the same by his doinges, yet he maketh them a gentle aunswere, more desyrous to enstruct them, then to angre them. What nedeth it me (sayth he) so often to speake of my selfe, and tell who I am, namely forasmuch as if I doe openly testifie the trueth, ye call the recorde therof arrogancie. I haue already tolde you (if ye woulde beleue me) who I am: Yea though ye dooe not credite my woordes, yet ye cannot be ignoraunt of the thyng whiche ye desyre to knowe of me.

There is no surer profe than dedes: ye see my doynges, which your selues doe witnesse I doe at my fathers will and not the deuilles, as some doe misreporte. If my actes be worthie to bee imputed to God, beleue that I am sente of God. But ye dooe neyther beleue my dedes nor my woordes: whereof I am not the cause, but your owne corrupte and suspiciouse mynde. They that meane well and playnelye and bee not polluted with the naughtynesse of thys worlde, beleue my woordes, and lyke good shepe knowe the voyce of a good shepeherd: and semblably I knowlage them for my shepe, though after the worlde they be poore sely thinges. But ye therfore doe not knowledge my voyce, because ye are not of the number of my shepe, whose simplicitie is lightely taughte, when as youre myndes be swollen with ambicion, leuened with malice, with enuie corrupted, infected with couetousnes, and with sundrie affeccions of this worlde defyled, from whiche vices, if ye would purge your minde, verely euen you also should heare my voice: neither should you so doe without benefit. For first of al, ye should therby auoide death, which hangeth ouer all rebels agaynst the sonne of God: moreouer ye shall obteyne therby euerlasting life. For of trueth, those my shepe (how simple and vnlerned soeuer they be after the iudgement of the worlde) as long as they doe knowleage me the shepeherde, and all the while they folow me as gyde, doe through my liberalitie, get euerlasting life: when as other that are taken in the worlde for men of great felicitie, goe to euerlastyng death. They be symple shepe, harmelesse, weake, lacking all worldely succour. The world riseth against these with all engiens and force. But the aduersarye shall not haue so greate power, that he shall be hable to take them out of my handes. The world hath auctoritie of phariseis, dignitie of priestes, it hath armed kynges, hye magistrates, iudges, places of iudgement, prisones, cheines, roddes, axes, brodded to prike with, exile, deathes, & whatsoeuer is wont to bring feare, yea euen to stedfast myndes. On the other syde, it hath riches, pleasures, dignities, honours, and what soeuer is wont to corrupt most vncorrupt myndes. The world vseth all these engines to plucke my shepe out of my handes, but I beeyng theyr protector & gouernour, no man shall be hable to take them awaye from me. What thyng soeuer the worlde shal goe about, the same shall be commodiouse to the shepe, and turne to my fathers glorye. We will not fyght agayne with weapons, or with poyson, we will not counter with them and geue rebuke for rebuke, but without suche defence, we shall yet by a new way, haue the victorye.

My father. &c. is greater than al. &c.

That defence alone, whiche my father hath geuen me to defende my shepe withall, is greater and of more force than all the wepons, wherewithall the world shal ryse agaynst me and myne. Neyther will my father forsake me, nor I my shepe. The same thyng that lyeth in me to doe, lyeth also in my father to doe. And because there is no power of the world that can force any thing out of his handes, whiche can doe all thynges with a nodde, neyther can any thyng pull that out of my handes, which he hath taken me to kepe: As there is an exact companionship of power betwene my father and me: so there is a full consent of will. We be throughly one, all one in power, all one in will and will.

The texte.

Then the Iewes agayn toke vp stones to stone him withal. Iesus aunswered them: many good workes haue I shewed you from my father, for which of them doe ye stone me? The Iewes aunswered him saying: For thy good workes sake we stone thee not, but for thy blasphemie, and because that thou being a man, makest thy selfe God.

The Iewes being sore moued with these sayinges, not content with so often namyng hys father, by whose defence he promised so great thynges, tooke vp stones again to stone Iesus. But yet no mā set vpō him, because his time was not as yet come, in whiche he had determined to dye for the saluacyon of mankynde, but he assayeth to assuage & mitigate theyr furie with gentle wordes. The people are accustomed to take vp stones in theyr handes (sayth he) and so openly to punishe euil doers, and common malefactours. I haue doen nought

els

els but bestowed benefites on you of my fathers liberalitie: I haue better enstruct them that erred, I haue comforted them that were in affliccion, I haue fedde ye hungrie, I haue restored the one handed to both, I haue made cleane the leprouse, I haue healed the sicke, I haue driuen away deuils from menne, I haue set them on fote that were diseased of the palsey, and such as had their sinowes shrounken, I haue put awaye feuers, and all diseases and maladies, I haue called the dead to lyfe agayn, & the whole power and auctoritie which my father hath geuē me, hath bene bestowed to succour you, & it hath bene frely employed to your cōmoditie. In al these thinges now which is ye one thing that ye thinke worthy stoning? If he that is good and liberall be stoned, what is to be doen to naughtie folke, & to them that be harmful? The Iewes being brought in conclusion to this poynte, that eyther they muste bring furthe some faulte agaynste hym, or elles acknowlage theyr owne folye, leste they shoulde haue no pretext to hyde theyr furie withall: we (say they) are not wont to stone any man for his good workes sake, but we coūt thee woorthy to bee stoned for an horrible crime, of all other moste greate, euen blasphemye: And in thys thyng we folowe the auctoritie of the lawe, which commaundeth such should be ouerthrowen with stones. Who can suffer any longer, that thou being a man, makest thy selfe God, hauyng eftsones god thy father in thy mouthe, as though we al were not the children of god, and as though thou were by some newe and peculiar waye, Gods sonne, that thou and thy father may be partteners in all thynges? Is not this to take a certayn godhead vpon thee? But forasmuche as there is but one God, what manne soeuer (therefore) taketh vpon him to be felow with god in power, is iniurious to Gods maiestie, & a rebel.

Iesus aunswered them: Is it not written in your law, I sayd ye are Gods? If ye cal the Gods, vnto whome the worde of God was spoken (and the scripture cannot be broken concerning him, whome the father hath sanctified; and sent vnto the worlde) doe ye say that I blaspheme, because I sayd, I am the sonne of god? If I do not the workes of my father beleue me not: but if I doe, and if ye beleue not me, beleue the workes: that ye may knowe and beleue that the father is in me, and I in him. The texte.

The Lorde Iesus dooeth with suche moderacion make aunswere vnto thys faulte which was layed to his charge, that he clearelye auoyded from him the sinne of blasphemie; and that also he did not, with any terrible woordes more engreue theyr frowardnes, and yet he did with great sobrietie defend that his due, whiche he ought not to denye, because he woulde not haue it vnknowen to vs: You (sayth he) lay blasphemie to my charge, because I name God to be my father. Is there not a greatter thing than that writtē in your lawe, euen in the Psalmes? I haue sayd ye are al gods, & sonnes of him that is hie. If god himselfe geue prayse of the dignitie of his name to them, vnto whome the woorde of God was spoken, not onely calling them the children of God, but gods too, and yet was not the maiestie of one god harmed, nor that thing can be vntrue whiche is declared in holye scripture, howe can ye stretche to me the faulte of blasphemie, that doe say, I am the sonne of God, whome the father hath only sanctified & sent vnto the world, that by the sonne al should obteine holynesse? If cōmunicacion had betwene God and man, make of men gods, and the chyldren of God, is it not a thing to be borne with, if I say that I am gods sonne,

 whiche

whiche am the woorde of God it selfe, and who was with god before I came into the worlde, and am he that hath coumpany with him in all thinges. It is no presumpteouse thyng that I take vpon me in my woordes, a thyng verely that beseemeth many other, by the auethoritie of scripture. But it were more conuenient to iudge by the selfe dedes, what name I ought to haue.

If my dedes dooe not proue me to be aboue a man, if they haue not the proofe of godly power, beleue not that I am the sonne of God, and that God & I agree throughly in al poyntes. But if ye see God the father shew furth his power in me, though algates ye will geue no faithe to my wordes, yet at least beleue the dedes that ye see with your iyes, and take me for arrogant if I doe not perfourme more in dedes, than I take vpon me in woordes. If ye would consider those thinges with pure simple mindes, it should come to passe that ye would geue faythto my wordes too, and doubte no more, but that the father is in me, and I in the father, that bothe we, the one and the other, are sociate & adherent together naturally & vnseparably, whiles he woorketh by me, whatsoeuer he will, and I doe no where swarue or alter from his exaumple & commaundemente: In so muche that he whiche beleueth on hym, beleueth on me, and whosoeuer speaketh agaynst hym, speaketh agaynst me.

The texte. Agayn they went about to take him, and he escaped out of theyr handes, and went away agayn beyond Iordane into the place where Iohn before had baptised, & there he abode. And many resorted vnto him, and sayde: Iohn did no miracle, but all thinges that Iohn spake of this man, were true. And many beleued on him there.

When the Iewes had hearde these sayinges, being therwith more an angred, wherwith in dede they ought to haue bene refourmed, they goe about to lay handes on hym, and so to accomplishe that thyng whiche they had already often attempted in vayne. But Iesus escaped oute of theyr handes, declaryng therby, that he was wel willyng to suffer, when time should come. Therfore when Iesus had taught there sufficientlye, he geueth place for a tyme to theyr vncurable fury, and wēt ouer agaiñ beyond Iordane, to the very place where Iohn begun first to baptise, (for as we haue sayd, he afterward chaunged his place, and baptised at the water of Sichem.) Here now Iesus abode in the deserte, as one that had lothed or extremely hated the sinnefull wickednes of the cities. And many came also thither vnto him, out of places ỹ ioyned nye therevnto, whose myndes the fame that was bruted of Iesus, the sermons and miracles ỹ were heard and sene, did inflame. And of truth, the very place brought them furthwith in mynde to compare Iesus, who had alreadye shewed some tryall & profe of himselfe, wt Iohn, whome they had knowen before. And whā they remembred that Iohn had bene in highe auctoritie, and yet had dooen no thing els but preached the baptisme of penaunce, and without dooyng anye miracles had gotten himselfe so greate estimacyon among the multitude, that he was thought to be Christ: And on the other side, when Iesus had by shewing furth so many miracles, declared a power greater then mans strengthe, ỹ he had so often put the Scribes and Phariseis to silēce, with his prudent and piththie aunswers: Finally, that Iohn himselfe had so often testifyed so highly of Iesus, confessing openly that himselfe was not worthie to leuse the latchet of of his shoe: The Jewes (I say) consideryng all these thinges, had thys saying among themselues. John (say they) when as he wroughte no miracle, was in credite with the Jewes. Much more therfore ought faith to be geuen to this man, that with so wõderful seldome sene miracles, gathereth or winneth faith to his wordes. And albeit Johns recorde of this man were heretofore litle beleued, yet now the matter selfe declareth that his recorde was true, for so much as this saide Jesus hath accomplished mo thinges than John promised of the mans behalfe. And so now therfore, partely for Johns relations sake, (whose reporte had no slender auctoritie among the Jewes,) partly through his own wordes that were ful of godly wisedome, and partly for his dedes sake which did beare witnes of his diuyne power, many beleued that Jesus was verye Messias, whiles yet the Phariseis, the Scribes, and the Priestes, did styl continue and persiste in theyr frowarde malyce.

The xi. Chapter.

A certayn man was sicke named Lazarus of Bethania, the towne of Mary, and her sister Martha: It was that Marie which anointed Jesus with oyntment, and wiped his fete with her heare, whose brother Lazarus was sicke. Therfore his sisters sent unto him, saying: Lord beholde, he whome thou louest is sicke. Whan Jesus hearde that, he sayde: this infirmitie is not unto deathe, but for the prayse of God, that the sonne of God mighte bee praysed by reason of it. The texte.

AND furthwith occasion is offered, whereby Christes glory and his fathers shoulde highly be renowmed, & withal the malice of the phariseis should be prouoked to murther. For while he made his abode at Jordane, it chaũced that a certain mã called Lazarus, lay sicke in the towne Bethania. This was both the sicke mãs and the twoo sisters Marie and Marthaes countrey. Furthermore, Mary was she, that (to ẏ notable profe of loue towardes Jesus) with a precious oyntmente anointed his head sitting at the feast, and with her heare wiped his fete, which she had washed with teares. Wherof came a great amitie betwene the Lorde Jesus and this familie. Therfore whẽ Lazarus was through greuous sickenesse in perill, his sisters (trusting vpon the acquayntaunce that they had with Jesus) sendeth to shewe him of his frendes dysease, doubtyng not but that he would of his merueylouse gẽtlenes towardes all folke, helpe his frende being in daunger. Behold (say they) he whome thou louest is sicke. For they thought it inough to signifie the thing to him that loued the manne, and therefore they made not further intercession. To whome Jesus made answere: this sickenes is not vnto death. God hath suffered it to fall vpon hym, that by that occasion, God and his sonne shoulde be glorifyed, with putting awaye the sickenesse by theyr godly power.

Jesus loued Martha and her sister, and Lazarus. When he hearde therfore that he was sicke, he abode two dayes still in the same place where he was: then after that, he sayde to his disciples: Let vs go into Jewrie again. His disciples sayd vnto him: Maister, ẏ Jewes lately sought to stone thee, and wilt thou goe thither agayn? Jesus aunswered: Are there The texte.

not twelue houres of the day? If a man walke in the day he stumbleth not: because he seeth the light of this worlde: but if a man walke in the night, he stumbleth because there is no light in hym.

Jesus verely loued Martha and Mary, and theyr brother Lazarus too, & yet suffered he him to fall into sickenes, and also to dye: lest we shoulde thinke it an vnsemely thing, if at any tyme good folke and right holy menne bee punyshed with miseries of this world: god, as it were dissembling, either bicause so it is expedient for them that suffer, or els because it so helpeth to set furth the glory of God, not that God doeth through mans harme procure hys owne glory, but that for mans sake, he is wont to turne the euels, which chaunseth vs after the lawe of mans state and condicion, or by casualtie, to our saluacyon, or to hys owne glory. He knewe right well his frendes sickenes: yea, before it was tolde him. But yet was it fit, that his disciples mindes should be prepared and made redy for the great miracle that was to come. Therfore after report was made to Jesus of his frendes disease, he did not furthwith goe thence, but taried still two dayes in that same place, verayly not neglecting the daunger of hys frendes, but looking for a more large matter to worke a miracle of, wherwithal he himselfe, who should sone after dye, might lift vp the mindes of his disciples, weake and feble as yet, to the hope of the resurrection.

But his disciples kepyng silence for feare, because he of late escaping the handes of the Jewes, was thought to be more safe in the deserte, Jesus sayd vnto them: Let vs go into Jewrie again. Whē the disciples heard Jewry named, remembryng howe vengeable and cruell the Phariseis hatred was towardes him, and how often they had taken vp stones to cast at him, how oftē they endeuored themselues to apprehende hym: the disciples (I saye) stoode in dreade not onely of theyr maisters harme, but also of theyr owne. For as yet they had not receiued the holy ghost, and bare a certayne worldely affeccion towardes Jesus, themselues lykewise through feblenes lothyng death. Therefore dissuading him from goyng agayne into Jewrie, they say: Sir haue you forgotten how that there a while agoe the Jewes would haue stoned you, vnlesse ye had secretely withdrawen youre selfe? And will you goe thither agayne puttyng your selfe in open daunger? But Jesus did coumforte theyr fearefulnesse by a parable, signifying that nothing is to be dredde of them that cleaue to Christ: who is the light of the worlde. For the night hath vayn feares. The daye knoweth no suche terrours. Hathe not the daye (sayeth Christe) twelue houres? The night shall not come before his tyme. In the meane tyme, whosoeuer walketh in the daye, stumbleth not: for why, the sunne maketh him to see and to eschewe stumblyng. But the sunne beeynge taken awaye, whosoeuer walketh in the night, stumbleth, because he lacketh light. I am the light of the worlde, it is right mete that you be guided by me, and folow my conductyng, and not to goe before the lighte. Be not afrayde before the tyme. So long as I geue light vnto you, there is no ieopardie. The night shall come, whē you beeing disseuered from me, shall bee troubled.

The texte. ¶ This sayd he, and after he sayd vnto them: our frende Lazarus sleapeth, but I goe to wake him out of slepe. Then sayd his disciples: Lord if he slepe he shal doe well inough.

Howbeit,

The texte.

Howbeit Jesus spake of hys death, but they thought that he had spoken of the naturall slepe. Then sayd Jesus vnto the playnly: Lazarus is dead, and I am glad for your sakes, that I was not there, because ye may beleue: neuertheles let vs goe vnto him.

When Jesus had with this saying mitigate the Apostles feare, he sheweth the cause of his goyng furth on his iourney, saying: Our frende Lazarus sleapeth, I therfore go hence to wake him. When as the disciples that were troubled with feare supposed that Jesus dyd not speake of very deathe, but of the common slepe, they aunswer: Sir if he slepe, there is no cause why you should goe thither, for slepe in sicke folke is woont to bee a token of recouery of health. The disciples wer loth to go into Jewry again, and therfore to the vttermost of theyr power, they doe auoyde the causes of going thither. But Jesus did by litle and litle prepare the myndes of his, earnestly to consyder and beholde the miracle to come. For he had therfore leauer say fyrst he was aslepe then dead, to the entente he might after the vsage of holye scripture, shewe the hope of the resurreccion. For they be rather aslepe then dead, whiche reste to lyue agayne. Neyther is it so easy for any of vs to awake hym that sleapeth, as it is for the Lorde to call the dead to lyfe. Therefore the discyples not vnderstandyng the thyng that he spake of sleape, and waking out of sleape, to let them know that no hidde thyng was vnknowen to him, he sayth vnto them more playnly: Lazarus is dead, nor he added not the thing that was than more stoute to be spoken, as concerning the raysing him vp agayn. For he woulde rather that to be signifyed than expressed, and hys mynde was rather to doe the thyng, than promyse it, euery where makyng readye for vs an exaumple of modestye and temperaunce. And because he aunswered them that tolde hym his frende was sicke, that that sickenes was not deadly, but chaunced to the entente that Goddes glorye and hys sonnes also shoulde bee set furthe by it: a lyke thyng sheweth he to his disciples, saying: I am glad that I was not there while my frẽde was sicke and dyed, and for youre cause I reioyce, that youre truste whiche I perceyue to bee weake as yet, may bee strengthed and confirmed with a more euident miracle. For if the sicke man had mended and recouered healthe (I being present) it might haue bene thought a casualtie: in case I had at hys sisters requestes raysed hym that had bene newly dead, the Pharisees whiche fynde faulte with all thynges, mighte haue layed for them that it had bene a lacking of senses, or but a swounyng, & no death, for that sumtimes happeneth in some diseases, that the bodies lying a long time in swoune, come to lyfe agayn. Now for asmuche as it is a very death in dede, there shal be a more plenteouse matter of beliefe. Therfore let vs go to him. The going thither pleased not the disciples for feare of the Jewes, which feare stacke sore in theyr myndes, and yet coulde they not improue the godly and weightie cause of that iourney.

Lazarus is dead and I am glad for your sakes. &c.

And albeit Jesus was not ignoraunt what thing troubled the myndes of his disciples, and though also he swaged theyr dreade by reason that he sayed he shoulde goe to Bethania and not to Hierusalem, yet neuerthelesse the nyenesse of the place that they feared, made also theyr timorouse myndes afrayd.

The texte.

Then sayed Thomas, which is called Didimus, vnto the disciples: let vs also go that we may die with hym. Then went Jesus, and foũd that he had lien in his graue fower daies already. Bethanie was nye vnto Hierusalem, about fiftene furlonges of, and many of the Jewes came to Martha and Marie, to coumforte them ouer theyr brother.

The disciples being carefull and pensyfe,(and yet durste they not refuse to do their maisters commaundement,) Thomas whome the Grekes cal Didimus, and in Latine is named geminus (a twinne) being more timorouse than the rest, sayeth vnto his felowes: let vs also goe,(if it be certaynly thus) to dye with him, for as muche as his determinate mynde is, to bring bothe himselfe and his, into a manyfeste peril of lyfe, wheras he may so deuise that bothe shall be in safetie. Jesus than went furth with hys disciples to Bethania, & founde that Lazarus had lyen in hys graue fower dayes alreadye. Uerily Bethania was about fiftene furlonges of from Hierusalem, and thereof came the discyples feare, and thereupon also arose occasion that caused the miracle haue more witnesses and lokers vpon. For the nighnes of the place caused many to come thither out of Hierusalem, euen of fauoure they beare to Marie and Martha, and of neyghbourlye duetie to coumforte them in the deathe of theyr brother, Whiche kinde of office and duetie was wont to be doen to riche folke, euen for honour sake.

The texte.

Martha assone as she hearde that Jesus was cumming, went and met him: but Marie sate stil in the house: Then sayde Martha vnto Jesus: Lorde if thou hadste bene here, my brother had not dyed: neuerthelesse now I know that whatsoeuer thou askest of god, god will geue it the. Jesus sayth vnto her: thy brother shall rise agayne. Martha sayeth vnto him: I knowe that he shall rise agayne in the resurreccion at the last day.

Martha that diligently bestirred her, wente about all thinges with diligence: when one had tolde her that Jesus was come nyghe at hande; she with spede went out to mete hym. Marie kept still the house: Martha therefore when she was within the sight of Jesus (vpon ryght good hope that she had conceiued of her brother to be called to life again) with a doleful voice, she sayd vnto him: lord if thou hadst bene here, my brother had not bene dead, for thou couldeste soone haue healed him with a worde. Although in dede the thing is not yet euen at this present vtterly without hope. For I know that what thyng soeuer thou askest of God, he will deny the nothing, although thou wouldest aske life in hym that is dead and buried. These sayinges were spoken of Martha with a minde that neither did vtterly despayre, nor yet fully beleue. Therfore to confirme her beliefe, Jesus sayed vnto her: be of good coumforte, thy brother shal ryse agayne. Neither did this promise satisfye Marthaes minde, who (because she had but a sely piteouse hope of her brothers rysing agayne) coulde not but feare the matter. She was afrayd verilye, that lyke as he aunswered the messengers, saying that the sickenes was not deathlyke, and with that doubtefull aunswere beguiled them, so was there nowe lykewise some mistery in his wordes that should disapoynt and deceiue her hope: I knowe (sayeth she) that my brother shal ryse agayne: but that shall bee in the laste daye when we shall all ryse agayne, for some Jewes, namely they that were of the Phariseis secte, beleued that there should bee a generall resurreccyon.

The texte.

Jesus sayeth vnto her: I am the resurreccion and the lyfe: he that beleueth on me, yea though he were dead, yet shal he liue, and whosoeuer liueth and beleueth on me, shall neuer dye: Beleuest thou this? She sayde vnto him: ye Lorde. I beleue that thou arte Christ the sonne of God, whiche should come into this worlde.

Jesus therefore to further the womans affiaunce and opinion of hym, by litle and litle to greater thynges, and that he might declare himselfe to be very he, he, that not onely could obteyn by prayer, of God, lyfe to the dead (a thing that is redde ofte to bee dooen of other holy men) but to be the very fountayne selfe and authour of lyfe, both already geuen and to bee geuen to all thynges, nor that any death is to be feared of them, that putteth theyr confidence and hope in him, forasmuche as thoughe deathe chaunce, it can nothyng hurte hym that cleaueth fast to the fountayne of all lyfe: Jesus (I saye) vpon these consideracions, aunswereth Martha on thys wise: Thou beleueste Martha that with my prayers I may obtayne of my father, lyfe for thy brother whiche is deade: thou beleueste that thy brother shall bee restored to lyfe agayne (as other shall be) in the last day. Yea but thou must beleue this also: that they which shal ryse in the last daye, shall haue lyfe by me, nor that any man hath lyfe at all, but by my gifte, neyther is any restored to lyfe agayne but by me, not onely touchyng death of body, which is not muche to be feared, but as concernyng the death of the soule also, whiche is most of all to be feared. And the soule that liueth, liueth by me. And the reuiuing soule, reuiueth by me, for I am the very fountayne of resurreccion and lyfe. He that cleueth to me by fayth, although he bee dead in bodye, yet shall he lyue. And take not thys saying to be onely spoken of thy brother, but generally, what man or woman soeuer hath faythful affiaũce in me, he shall not dye euerlastingly, although his body lyuelesse lye at rest for a tyme. Martha, beleuest thou the thyng that I saye? Martha beeyng at thys tyme altogether myndeful to haue her brother reuiued againe, geueth no very apte aunswere to Jesus saying, but yet she did confesse generally how hiely she iudged of him, saying: Lorde I doe beleue. I beleue that thou arte Messias, the sonne of the liuing God, who beeing promised of the Prophetes, and many hundreth yeres looked for, art come into the worlde.

And assone as he had so sayd, she went her waye and called Marie her sister secretly, saying: The maister is come and calleth for the: assone as she heard that, she arose quickly and came vnto him. Jesus was not yet come into the towne, but was in that place where Martha met him. The Jewes then, which were with her in the house, and comforted her, when they sawe Marie that she rose vp hastely, wente out and folowed her, saying: She goeth vnto the graue to wepe there. The texte.

Martha vpon these wordes being commaunded to returne home agayne, and to call her sister Marie, (her lamentable mourning already aswaged) doth nowe leaue Jesus, and goeth al chearefull and full of good hope home to her sister: and calleth her secretly out of the throng of suche as were sette rounde about her, and priuely telleth her in her eare the ioyfull thyng, saying: The master is come and calleth for the. Assone as Marie knew that Jesus was come, and saw her sister chearefull and of good coumfort, she her selfe also conceiued some good hope, although Jesus semed to haue come alredy to late, on whome therfore they dyd not often call by messenger, because they thoughte it inoughe if he once knewe his frendes perill, committyng all other thynges to hys arbitrement. And so Marie, supposing that his cũming was not for nought, without delaye, rose vp to goe mete him before he should entre into the house. And so it was expedient for the better bestowing of that miracle ẏ was to be shewed. For fitte it was that many Phariseis shoulde be present, which although they came of very duetie for priuate frendeship sake to se Marie, yet dyd they hate Jesus. These surely woulde not haue folowed Marie, in case they had knowẽ howe that she went to mete Jesus. But therefore the Jewes that were with Marie in the house to coumfort hir, when they saw that with so great hast she arose vp and wente furth of the house, they folowed hir: suspectyng that vpon a soden pangue and brunte of heuynesse, she woulde haue goen to the graue, and there to wepe hir belly full, to saciate her sorowful harte with teares.

The texte. Then when Marie was come where Jesus was, and sawe him, she fell downe at his feete, and sayth vnto him: Lord if thou haddst bene here, my brother had not bene dead. When Jesus therfore sawe her wepe, and the Jewes also weping which came with her, he groned in the spirit, and was troubled in himselfe, and sayd: where haue ye laied him? They sayd vnto him: Lorde come and see. And Jesus wept. Then sayed the Jewes, behold how he loued hym: and some of them sayde: Could not he whiche opened the iyes of the blinde, haue made also that this man shoulde not haue dyed?

So than Marie went furth and founde Jesus as yet vnentred within the walles of the towne: but abode in that place where as Martha had late before met him. For he taried there for Marie, whome he commaunded to be called to hym, chosyng a place fitte to worke the miracle in: because the graue was not far from that place, as the maner was than to make the dead mens sepulchres nye the hye wayes. When Marie was come thither, assone as euer she sawe Jesus (as in dede she was very woefull) she fell downe at his feete & spake weping, the same thing that hir syster had sayde: Lord (sayth she) if thou haddest bene here in due time, my brother had not bene dead, and we had bene without this miserable weping and waylyng. But Jesus, seeing Marie altogether in heuinesse, & the Jewes lykewise that folowed her, weppyng withall, he dyd not reason and stande in disputacion with her, as he dyd with her sister Martha, with whome he talked aparte (the people being remoued asyde) neyther dooeth he promyse any thyng, when as nowe was place and tyme to performe in dede, that whiche he had promysed Martha: but Jesus (I say) firste of al groned in the spirite, and was troubled in himself, euen to shew the truth of his manhoode, ready anon after to bryng furth a sygne of hys diuine power and Godhead. They were no fayned affections, that he was of so lothsome a mynde, and in himselfe so troubled, but there was good skill why he tooke vnto hym those mocyons of mynde, whiche came not of the infirmitie of nature, but by the consente of reason: neyther was it al one cause why other wept and why Jesus was troubled. They bewayled the death of the body of a certayn worldely and naturall affeccyon, Jesus rather misslyked and lothed mennes sinnes, wherby so many soules shoulde peryshe: he was dysquyeted through the inuincible dyffydence of the Jewes, who wepte for theyr frendes bodelye death, when as them selues (as touchyng the soulle) were subiecte to eternall deathe, and yet dyd they not wepe for themselues. Jesus desyred that all men should reuiue from this deathe, and had indignacion that hys doctryne, miracles and deathe, should be loste in many one. Therefore, after that by horriblenes of spirite, and by trouble of mynde, in countenaunce, iyes, and in the whole habite of his bodye, he had geuen a manifest profe of hys manhoode (teachyng also by the waye that it behoueth not to yelde and bee subdued to suche affeccions, or to be called awaye from thynges of vertue) the turmoyle of his mind beeyng refrayned and stayed, Jesus sayde: where haue ye layed hym? not that he was ignoraunt therof, but to remoue all suspicion of disceyt from the myracle. His kinsfolkes aunswereth: Lorde, come and see.

That

That aunswere proued that the graue was not far of. And nowe as if at the sight of the graue his sorow had ben renued, Jesus wept. Groning and trouble went before, a token of sorow that with force entred into hys mynde. Teares are as it were the bloud of a minde already wounded and ouercome. But these teares came not from a mind that was ouercome, for they were not bestowed vpon Lazarus that was dead, but they were for vs, that we should beleue him to be very man, and also learne how death of the soule is to bee pitied and lamented, whiche yet men doe not in suche sorte abhorre and bewaile. But the Jewes supposing that Jesus was in suche moode for nought elles, but for the death of hys frende, with whome he was acquaynted, behold (say they) how enterely he loued Lazarus, for whom being dead he wepeth in such sort, and yet were they nothing of kinne. And some there were that would haue layed to his charge and rebuke, his teares, wherwith he testifyed no meane or common loue towardes Lazarus, sayng: Dyd not thys felowe of late geue sight to the blinde beggar wt whō he had no acquaintaunce? Why than made he not that his great frende should not die? In case he had no wil to doe it, why dooeth he nowe signifye with teares, loue that cummeth out of season? If he could not doe the thing that is more easie to be doē, how did he that feat which is of more difficultie to be dooen? The phisicion manye tymes saueth the sicke mans lyfe. There was neuer mā before gaue sight to him ÿ was borne blind.

Jesus wept

¶ Jesus therfore againe groned in himselfe, and came to the graue: It was a caue and a stone was layed on it. Jesus sayed, take ye away the stone. Martha the sister of him that was dead said, vnto him: Lord, by this time he stinketh, for he hath bene dead fower daies. Jesus sayth vnto her: Saied I not vnto thee, that if thou didst beleue thou shouldest se the glory of God: then they toke away the stone from the place where he that had bene dead, was layed.

The texte.

But Jesus nowe being nye to the graue, to declare playnly how horrible is the state of a manne that hath alreadye lyen long in synne, and with howe great repentaunce, howe many teares are nedeful, that throughe Gods mercy he may penitentely returne to the lyfe of innocentie, dyd grone agayne, and fared euill with hymselfe, exemplyfying in hymselfe verely the thyng whiche ought to be exhibite in vs if we will eftsones repente vs of the euilles and returne from the same, wherin we haue long tyme nusseled our selues. Nowe than they were come to the graue. It was verelye a caue, whose mouthe was closed with a stone layed vpon it. And that made much to the beliefe of the miracle, and to exclude the suspicyon of inchauntment and delusion, and because the beliefe therof should be more certayne and sure if the thyng were dooen by the handes of hys frendes, and not with Jesus owne handes or hys disciples (for those frendes suspect no fraude or illusion,) Jesus than turned him to thē and sayed, take awaye the stone. The playne meanyng of Martha, sister to the dead man, did also set furth & made a more certentie of the miracle. For she now forgetting what Jesus had promised her, did through the wepyng and heuinesse that she sawe Jesus in, come agayne into her olde mynde and affeccyon, and conceiued almost a certayn diffidence. Verely she feared lest (the stone beeyng taken awaye) the styncke of the deade bodye shoulde offende theyr noses that stode by, not considering that he which in the general resurreccion should rayse all mens bodies already many hundreth yeres before turned into duste,

coulde

coulde rayse a dead bodye euen newlye putrifyed: She (I tell you) thus thyn-king, sayd: Lord, by this tyme he stinketh. For he hath bene dead fower dayes. Jesus therefore did with a litle rebuke, styrre vp the vnconstaunt, and wauering womans fayth, saying: hast thou forgotten how I tolde thee euen now, that if thou diddest beleue, it shoulde come to passe that by thy brothers death god should be glorifyed. Al they therefore depending and staying in the expectacion, and vpon hope of a newe woonderfull miracle, the stone by the Lorde Jesus commaundement was remoued.

The texte. ¶ And Jesus lift vp his iyes and sayed: Father I thanke thee, that thou hast heard me. Howbeit I know that thou hearest me alwayes, but because of the people which stand by I sayde it, that they may beleue that thou hast sent me: and when he thus had spoken, he cryed with a loude voyce: Lazarus come furth. And he that was dead came furth bounde hande and foote with graue clothes, and his face was bound with a napkin. Jesus sayd vnto them: Leuse him and let him goe.

And furthwith all theyr myndes and iyes pawsing as men in doubte, our Lord Jesus lifting vp his iyes, to teache vs therby ye whatsoeuer great thing we dooe, we ought to referre it to God as authour thereof, and withall, to declare vnto the standers by, that himselfe should by goddes power doe it, what thing so euer he should doe, saide: father, I thanke the because thou hast heard my desyre, not because that it is an vncouth or a timeduring thing to me: for I knowe that forasmuche as thy will and myne is all one, thou dooeste alwaye heare me if I aske any thing of the. For neither do I wil any thing ye thou willest not, but thys prayer I make because of the people that stande by: to thentent that whē they haue sene the miracle, they may beleue that I doe al thinges in earth after thy will, and that also I am sent into the worlde to set furthe the glory of thy name amongest men. When he had spoken thus to hys father, he calleth out the dead man by name, saying: Lazarus come furth. He could euen with a becke alone haue made hym that was buryed reuyue and come out of the graue: but this great sterne voyce, was a token of great power, wherwith the sinfull soule that is far of from the syghte of God, beeyng buried in darkenesse of sinne, and rotten with filthinesse of enorme crymes, maye ryse agayne, and come furth into the light of trueth. And without delay, he that was dead and buryed, came out byanby at the voyce of him that called vpon him before all theyr iyes And he came foorth before them, hys body sounde and whole of trueth, but he came with all ye clothes vpon hym that he was buried in, that al they might know him to be the same man whome they buried in such apparell thre dayes before. For as corses were wont to be doen withall, his feete were tyed with lystes: and his handes bounde with sepulchre bandes, hys face also bound with a napkin. And nowe than was thys a wunder, the dead corse dyd not quiuer and styrre litle ⁊ litle, ⁊ so shewe likelihod of life returning again as for the more parte it happeneth in them, whome we rede to be raysed to life by good and holy men, but thys man that had bene dead fower daies space, came sodaynly to lyfe agayn at the commaundement of a woorde. And to make the miracle seme greater, he, both tied ⁊ harde fast bounden, sodeinly cūmeth furth abrod out of ye depe secret place of a caue. Than (lest any thyng shoulde wante to the full perfecte beliefe of the miracle,) Jesus sayde to the mannes frendes: leuse him ⁊ let hym goe, that hys mouyng and lustie quicke pace maye declare

that

that the manne doth not onely liue but hath also his health. Jesus could haue made the bandes to haue lewsed of theyr owne accorde: but sith with theyr seruice they had throughly the doing of al thinges, by al wayes and proues they both excluded suspicion of forgeyng the thynge, and confirmed the certayntie of the miracle. The twoe sisters aduertised Jesus, than beyng absent, of theyr brothers sickenesse by other men. And in the absence of Jesus the man dyed, he was buried, he was kept till he stonke withall. He was mourned for, with solemne recourse of muche people. The sisters theimselues tolde Jesus of hys death, they shewed him the graue: when he had muche people waityng vpon hym, the stone is taken away with other mens handes, and with other mennes handes, was he lewsed that came foorth of the graue. Here is nothyng left to the vnfaithfull that they coulde lay for their excuse. Neither did Jesus, when he had wrought so notable a miracle, speake any stoute word of himself. He did not checke & reproue the people because their accustomed maner was to slaundre, & fynd faulte with his miracles: he requireth no thanke of Lazarus or of his systers.

Then many of the Jewes which came to Marye, and had seen the thynges which Jesus did, beleued on hym: but sum of them went their waies to the Phariseis, and tolde theim what Jesus had doen. Then gathered the hie priestes and Phariseis a counsell, and said: what doe we? for this man dooeth many miracles: if we let him escape thus, al men will beleue on hym: and the Romaynes shall come and take away bothe oure towne and the people. The texte.

Therefore, many that came of frendly duetie to Martha and Marie, Lazarus sisters, when they had seene so notable a miracle, they beleued ẏ Jesus was Messias, and stacke to his doctrine, the power wherof they sawe before theyr face to bee so greate and effectuall. And truely some of them returnyng home to Hierusalem, shewed to the Phariseis the thinges that Jesus had dooen a litle of Bethania. Therfore, when thys great acte beyng so exceadyng wonderous was hearde of ẏ Bishops and Phariseis, who for the euident declaracion of gods power, ought to haue wurshipped Jesus, and to haue bene ioyous on Gods behalfe, they being styrred with the prickes of enuie, cannot now forbeare any longer, but (to cause the thyng seme more lawefully dooen) they call a wicked counsayl, wherein they consult emong theimselues, by what way and meanes they maye resiste suche great daungiers. For albeit that the respect of priuate wealth, & sickenes of soule set thē on a woodnes against Jesus that was beneficiall towardes al men, yet wil they that thys matier do apperteyn vnto the health & preseruacion of all the people. What is your aduyce (say they) to be dooen? This manne dooeth many wonderful thynges, and excedeth himself daily in doing of miracles. If we suffer him to goe on as he hath begun, it will come to passe, that lyke as now many of the people doeth thinke hiely of hym, so within a whyle al wil take him for Messias. Whiche thyng yf it hap to be, and the brute therof cum to the Romaines (that is to wit) that the nacion of the Jewes hath forsaken the emperour and are fallen to a new king of theyr owne, whiche Romaynes do well knowe that of late a certayn kynge hath been loked for of the Jewes whiche shoulde set the nacion at libertie, the Romaines will make cruell warre against vs: And so with al the prophane

Gentiles shall kepe with force thys holy place , and with mannes slaughter make hauocke and destroy the whole flocke of the Jewes.

The texte. And one of them named Caiphas, being the hie priest the same yere, said vnto them: ye perceiue nothing at all, nor consider that it is expedient for vs that one man die for the people, and not that all the people perishe. This spake he not of himselfe, but being highe priest the same yere, he prophecied that Jesus should dye for the people, & not for the people only, but that he should gather together in one, ye children of god that wer scattered abrod.

Whereas this their aduice, vnder the pretence of a publike health, tended to the destruccion of Jesus Christ, thautour of all health, yet was it thoughte vnto Cayphas to slender a deuice and to weake a counsell. He was the bishop of that yeare. For that dignitie, as thoughe within a whyle it shoulde fayle for altogether, had ceassed to be a continuall roume: but beyng a benefice sette to sale, it was fined for euery yere to the prynces. Therfore he that professed him selfe chiefe prelate of religion, being more wicked then all other, blameth the cowardship of them that with deliberate counsell, did further debate the matter, whether Jesus were to be put to death or nay: whereas it, (thought he) all other thynges set aparte, was to be dooen incontinently and with spede. You (sayeth he) that sitte deliberatyng whether thys felow that doeth suche thynges, is to be put to execucyon or no, seme not to wey the matter as it is: nor ye consider not howe it is profitable and expedyent for euery man, that thys one should dye for the people, rather than that he being saued, al the people should perishe. This saying came not of the byshops owne mynde, that was vngracious and full of murder, but by reason of the office of priestehode, whiche he than bare, the spirite of prophecie dyd bryng foorthe a godly prophecie by the mouth of a wicked man: which sayd prophecie did geue foreknowledge how it should come to passe, that Jesus should by his death redeme & saue the Jewes: not onelye to bryng thys to effecte, that suche of the Jewes as dydde beleue shoulde be saued alone, but that those also among the Gentiles whiche lyued in diuers countreys dispersed through the whole worlde (but to thys ende appoynted that they shoulde once be made the children of God through fayth of the ghospell,) might be counite together, and that the man of Jude, the manne of Ethiope, the Greke, the Scithian, and the Britan, should ioyne together in felowship of a common vniuersall churche.

The texte. Then from that day furth, they toke counsel together for to put him to death. Jesus therfore walked no more openly among the Jewes, but went his way thence into a countrey nighe to a wildernesse, into a citie whiche is called Ephraim, and there continued with his disciples.

Now therfore, the Phariseis being stablished with this voyce of the wicked bishop, doe in theyr hertes certaynly determine (which thyng they often before attēpted as occasion serued) to rid Jesus out of the way, by all meanes possible, as though therby they well prouided for the preseruacion of the common weale: and agayne, leste theyr vngracious act shoulde be the lesse sinfull, they coulour their impietie: supposing they had now found out matter to stiere and prouoke al the people likewise, openly and by the lawe, to put Jesus to death, as a hurtefull man to the whole nacyon of the Jewes: neyther neded they (as they thought) any fault or any new cause to lay to hys charge. Jesus therfore, from

from whom nothyng was hid, although the rumoure of the people did not aduertise him of the Phariseis and priestes pretenced malyce, shewyng himselfe a very man, al ẏ while he was in Jury came not abrode, leste he should increase their fury. But he conueied himselfe a farre of, from the bondes of the citie of Jerusalem, the killer of Prophetes, ⁊ went to the citie of Ephraim: wherunto the deserte was nye, signifying by that dede, that the wicked Jewes should forgoe their Synagogue: and a newe people (that should not sticke to the vnfrutefull workes of Moses lawe, but to the fayth of the gospell) should be gathered together, and a churche made of them: whiche people should also (as the significacion of the Hebrue woorde betokeneth) grow of a small beginnyng into an exceadyng great thing: for Ephraim, to the Hebrues, signifieth encreasing. Jesus therfore tarryed here with his fewe disciples, whiche though they were wofully afearde of themselfes also, yet durst they not forsake their Lorde.

And the Jewes Easter was nye at hande, and many went out of the countrey vp to Jerusalem before the easter, to purifie themselfes. Then sought they for Jesus, and spake among themselfes as they stode in the temple: what thinke ye, seyng he cummeth not to the feast daye? The hye priestes and Phariseis had geuen a commaundement that if any man knewe where he were, he should shewe it, that they myght take hym. The texte.

Now the very time was come, sothly apoynted of the father, when Christ should be offered vp in sacrifice for the saluacion of mankinde. For that most religiouse day of the Jewes was at hande, which they call phase, that is to wete, a passing ouer: (in English Easter) by that name calling to their remēbraunce that dede, which was, that long before ẏ tyme the bloud of a lambe, striken on the postes, did saue the Hebrues from the swoorde of the Aungell that kylled the Egypcians: and those only houses passed ouer that had their postes marked with the lambes bloud. Now therfore before the feast which was verie nie, many went out of diuerse coastes of Palestine to Jerusalem, there being purified with ceremonies of their law, to solemnise ẏ most holy feast. And to let vs know that nothing is more vnreligiouse than Jewish religion, which consisteth in visible thinges: ⁊ sith also ẏ while they take great hede with much vaine deuociō leste they ouerslip any thing that was prescribed them of Moses, or that was added to by the Phariseis: they be not loth to doe that thing on the moste sacred daye, whiche is of al thinges most wicked, that is to wete, to shead ẏ bloud of an innocent mā. Therfore, whē there was a great throng of people together, ⁊ many of thē knewe Jesus, whose maner was to be present at suche feastes, they wondered ẏ he was not there present: and standing in the temple, they talked one to an other what should be the cause that contrary to his customable maner, Jesus was absent frō so solemne ⁊ high a feast. From which solemnitie would not he yet altogether absent himselfe, but to thentente he myght come more loked for, he deferred his cumming vntill such time as he thought best. Furthermore the bishops and Phariseis suspecting him sumwhere to hide himselfe for feare, they traueyled ⁊ gaue a commaundemēt yea with an autoritie also, that if any mā knew where he were in secrete, that they should shew it that he might be apprehēded. With these approued holy customes, the bishops and Phariseis, that were guides ⁊ maisters of religion, prepared themselfes to the feastful day, but in the meane while they vnwares procured the saluacion of the worlde.

LL.i.

¶ The.xii.Chapter.

The texte. Then Jesus sixe dayes before Easter, came to Bethanie, where Lazarus had been dead whom he raysed from death. There they made him a supper, and Martha serued, but Lazarus was one of them that sate at the table with hym.

Esus therfore knowyng that they had concluded vpon his death, and that the tyme also was nigh, when as he had determined willingly to be offred in sacrifice, an vnspotted lambe for the saluatiō of the worlde, he would no longer kepe hymselfe in secrete, but as one offreyng hymselfe to be a sacrifice, the seuenth daye before the feast of Easter, in whiche daye the Jewes were wount at a solemne supper, as it were, to taste before hand the pascall lambe, he retourned againe to Bethania: both to call to remembraunce the lately doen miracle, and also to imprinte the hope of the resurreccion in the myndes of his disciples, whom he knewe should be with his death excedyngly troubled in mynde: For there dwelt Lazarus whom he had a fewe dayes before raysed from death to lyfe. And the place was more notable for beeyng nigh to Jerusalem. There therfore a supper was made readie for Jesus. Martha serued him at supper: But Lazarus was one of the numbre that sate at supper with him, to make it more certain to them all, that it was no vision nor gost whiche lately was seen to goe out of the graue home to his house, forasmuche as he had nowe liued after his death many dayes, and had also, both commoned and eaten with other.

The texte. Then toke Mary a pounde of oyntmente, called Nardus, perfite and precious, and anoynted Jesus feete, and wiped his feete with her heare, and the house was filled with the odour of the oyntment.

There did Mary, (who with a siguler loue, loued the Lorde Jesus ardently,) come to the feast, as wel for many other causes, as for the late benefite shewed vpon her brother: and shedde vpon Jesus head sitting at the table, a great quantitie of very precious oyntmente, whiche was made of the beste kynde of Nardus, to the mountenaunce of a pounde: Insomuche that the whole house was filled with the sauour of the oyntmente. And yet was the womans (suche loue as hath not been heard) not herewith content, but annointed his fete with oyntmente, and washed them with teares, and wiped them with her heer: not that she thought Jesus did delite in suche delicacies, whose moderate sobrietie she knew, but great feruēcie of loue caused her doe as her minde gaue her, without stay of herselfe: for truely she knew not nor cōsidered what she did: but yet through doing honor, she gaue aduertisemēt before hand of Jesus death & buriall, & was a figure of the churche, whiche should embrace with godly honor, the lord whom the Synagogue despised.

The texte: Than sayed one of the disciples, euen Judas Iscarioth Symons sonne, which afterward betraied him, why was not this oyntmente solde for thre hundred pence & geuen to the poore? This he sayed not that he cared for the poore, but because he was a thefe, and had the bagge, and bare that whiche was geuen.

The disciples thought much at the bestowing of this oyntmente as a thing

wastfully

wastfully spente, but specially Judas Iscarioth was moued withall: to whom as to the wurst of them al, the purse was committed, to thintent that the wurst man should be the disposer & laier out of the naughtiest thyng: he was wonte, as the maner of thē that hath the handelyng of money is, which is common to many, to steale priuily somewhat therof to himselfe: nor with a single pure minde depending of the maistership & autoritie that Jesus had ouer him, but euen than making prouision for himselfe, wherwith he might liue, after he were departed out of Jesus felowship. He therfore, repining against Mary sayed: to what purpose is it to loose so precious a thing? For neither is our Lord & maister delighted in suche nyce thinges, neither is this sumptuousnes seming for our feast. And in case this woman had been determined to bestowe so precious a thing, when it had been geuen, it might haue been solde and the price therof geuen to the poore. This (ye wote well) had been more godly and more seming for our maister and vs too. Albeit in dede the other Apostles also did speake these thynges of a simplicitie, and mente none euill therin, yet had Judas a farre vnlike mynde, though his woordes were like vnto theirs: for he had no care of the poore mens cause, but he kept the purse: and the thing whiche frendes sente of their free good will, dyd he full vniustly kepe, & therof priuily stole somewhat, euen than shewyng some profe of hymselfe, howe vnfit he is for the ministracion of Gods woorde, whose mynde the inordinate desire of money doth possesse.

Than sayed Jesus, let her alone: against the daye of my buriyng hath she kept this: for the poore alwayes shall ye haue with you, but me haue ye not alwaye. Muche people of the Jewes therfore had knowledge that he was there. And they came, not for Jesus sake onely, but that they might see Lazarus also whom he raised from death: but the hye priestes helde a councell that they myght put Lazarus to death also, because that for his sake many of the Jewes went awaye, and beleued on Christe. *The texte.*

But Jesus did so apease his disciples murmuryng, that yet he did not openly disclose the malice of Judas, & in suche wise he toke Maries part, that he signified, howe of his owne voluntarie wil, he should dye. For our Lord Jesus most coueted to haue all folke induced to beleue: not that by compulsion of man, but by his owne good aduisement, he should suffre death for the saluaciō of man, euen as he would and when he would. Grudge ye not (sayeth he) at this womans obsequiousnesse & benefite towardes me. This coste is not lost, but this honor is doen and bestowed against the time of my buriyng, which honor this woman doth now preuenting the thing, for than shall ther lacke wherwith to anoynte. You do iudge well of me, that beyng aliue I haue alwaie refused suche plesante thinges, yet I will that my death and burial be cumly and honorable: doe not haue enuy at this my honor, which is bestowed on me, that shall shortely departe hence.
Ye shall haue alway with you ready at your hand, great plenty of these common sorte of poore men, whose nede ye maye succour: ye shall haue me but a while. And because many of Jerusalem came much to Bethania by reason of the nyenesse, and bycause of Lazarus, in that he was a notable & a ryche man, and therby knowen to many, (but yet was he the more knowen through the fame of the late doen miracle:) it was not vnknowen abrode that Jesus was at Bethania. And anon verie many came thither out of the citie thicke and threfolde, partely to see Jesus (whose fame and renowne, the myracle that

was so notable, dyd muche encrease,) partly also they came to see Lazarus, whom they hearde to be raysed from death to lyfe. The curiositie that is naturally geuen to man, caused them thus to doe. Moreouer, enuy and despite against Jesus had so blinded the myndes of the priestes and the Phariseis, that it did not suffice their malice to put Jesus to death, but they fel in deuice also howe to make Lazarus away, against whom they coulde lay no colour or likelyhood of any fault. They had cast out of theyr Synagogue ẏ blinde man, because he did boldly defende Jesus glory among thē, nowe their enuy was growen to suche malice, that they were in mynde to kyll Lazarus, a mā of great estimacion and power, of whom they were neuer by any woorde or dede prouoked and offended, and against whom they coulde not imagine any thing: and kill him would they for nothing els, but because many Jewes being moued with so manifest a myracle, did fall awaye from the Phariseis conspiracie, and beleued in Jesus.

The texte.

On the nexte daye muche people that were come to the feast, when they heard that Jesus should come to Jerusalem, toke braunches of palme trees and went forth to mete him and cried Hosanna: blissed is he that in the name of the Lorde cummeth kyng of Israel. And Jesus got a yong asse, and sat theron as it is written: feare not daughter of Sion, beholde thy kyng cummeth sittyng on an asses colte.

But the daye folowyng when as a great route of men (which were assembled at Jerusalē because of the feastfull day,) had knowledge that he would leaue Bethania and come to Jerusalem, to doe him honor came they to mete him with braunches cut of from the palme trees, wherwith they strawed the waie that he should goe by. For of this tree were theyr garlandes made that gate victorie, and it was a tree perteynyng to triumphes, alwaie grene, long and hye, hard to be climed vpon: but of a pleasante swete frute, and by a certayne peculiar power of nature it riseth vp against the weight and burden that is layed vpon it. And that saying whiche is written in the Psalmes, Osanna, prayse and honor be to him that being loked for of vs, cummeth in the name of the Lorde, was cried vp aloude, like as the people is wonte to publishe and witnes a common ioy. Jesus also (euer before this tyme bearyng a full lowe sayle, and a contemner of worldely glory,) was than contente to come to Jerusalē with a newe solemne portely shewe. For after he had gotten vnto him an asse, he rode vpō her, wheras before he was wount to walke his iourneyes on foote, partly to teache his howe vaine is the honor of this worlde, partly to ratifie that whiche Esay prophecied of him, for it is written. Feare not daughter of Sion, beholde thy kyng cummeth to thee, meke & gentle, sitting vpon the colte of an asse. Suche a pompe certainly becummeth well the kyng of the spirituall Jerusalem, whiche is the churche.

The texte.

¶ These thinges vnderstode not his disciples at the first, but whan Jesus was glorified, then remembred they that suche thynges were written of hym, and that suche thynges they had doen vnto him. The people that was with him when he called Lazarus out of his graue, and raysed him from death, bare recorde. Therfore mette him the people also because they hearde that he had doen suche a miracle.

The apostles verily at that season vnderstode not these thinges, supposyng thē to be doen by casualtie, but after that Jesus through death, through his resurreccion, & by sending downe the holy gost was glorified, than cōferring the thing that was doen wt the wordes of ẏ Prophetes, they wel perceiued, that the wordes whiche the people cried out a loude, & also the thing that he

thus

thus cummyng did, was written of hym. For there were some whiche loked for suche a kyng as worldly kinges be. Christes pleasure was to haue those mens expectacion derided, declaring that the kyngdome of the ghospell doeth not consist and stande in the aide and defenses of this worlde, but in mekenes, and heauenly doctryne. This great and notable affection that was in the people, came of those mens stirryng and prouocacion, which had of late been presente a litle before at Bethania, when the Lord raysed Lazarus out of his graue, and so they made relacion of that thyng whiche they sawe with theyr iyes, to other. And therof came it that suche a preace of people came foorth to mete Jesus, because they had learned of them that sawe it, how that this wonderous miracle, suche one as had neuer been hearde of since the beginnyng of the worlde, was wrought by hym. And accordyng as the thyng broughte with it in open apparaunce, a certain godly power, so had he suche honour geuen vnto him, as was neuer geuen to any prophete.

The pharisees therfore sayed among themselues: perceyue ye howe we preuayle nothyng? Beholde al the whole world goeth after him. There were certayne Grekes amonges them that came to wurship at the feast, thesame came therfore to Philip (whiche was of Bethsaida a citie in Galile) and desired him saying: Sir we woulde faine see Jesus. Philip came and tolde Andrewe. And agayne Andrewe and Philip tolde Jesus. The texte.

That thing droue the myndes of the priestes and phariseis almost into desperacion: neyther do they repent them of theyr wicked enterprise, but there was a spitefull mutteryng emong them, and they sayed: ye perceiue that with all our crafty policies and deuices against him, we go nothyng forwarde in oure purpose, but ẏ more we do resist, the more doeth his autoritie florishe, & the more earnestly doeth the people fauour hym. Before this he had but fewe disciples, beholde nowe the whole world falleth from vs to hym, in somuche that nowe it is sumwhat daungerous for vs, openly to arest him. The vngraciouse phariseis had this communicacion, to thintent thei might thereby stirre and prouoke eche one another to set on, and sodainly to come vpon the lord Jesus, with more succour and greater guiles: wherfore thei did not atchieue and accomplishe this mischieuous acte, before they had the graund consent of the Phariseis, the scribes, the priestes and the auncient rewlers, the people also (as in dede theyr mynde is vnconstant) beyng inflamed with thesame fury and wicked mynde, yea and with Pilate the viceroyes auctoritie: neyther yet withoute deceytfull craft brought in withall by Judas the traytour. The people notwithstanding did that tyme so fauour Jesus, that the Gentiles also whiche for religion sake came to Jerusalem there to praye, muche desired to see Jesus. The reuerence of that temple was so great, that out of farre countreies many went thither of deuocion to serue god, and for religion sake. Uerily from that tyme, a certayne likelyhood of a thyng to be, was shewed, that is to wit, that the Gentiles being before Idolaters, should haue recourse & come to be of Christes churche (wherof that temple at Jerusalem bare the figure) and should louingly embrace Jesus with due religion, whome the Phariseis rejected. These folke therfore beyng very desirous to see Jesus, of whom they had heard so wonderful thinges, yet they were bashefull, and with shamefastnesse letted to approche vnto hym: for in dede they coueted not only as he passed by lightly to se him in the throng, but also to salute him, and to heare hym speake nere hande: these persones, I saye, do come to Philip, to whom (by reason of nighnesse of countrey, for he was borne in Bethsaida a citie in Galilee of the Gentiles) they were knowen: and their cummyng to hym was, that he would make them waye in to Jesus. For they gaue knowledge that they were very desirous to se Jesus. Philip brake the matter to Andrewe, they being cōpanions of one citie. For Andrewe was of a greater auctoritie with the lorde, because he was fyrst of all called. They both therfore wente to Jesus, and declared vnto him that certayne folke there was, not Jewes, but Gentiles, whiche out of measure desyred to se him, if he woulde vouchesafe to admitte them.

The texte. And Jesus aunswered them, saying: The houre is come that the sonne of manne must be glorified. Verely, verely, I saye vnto you, excepte the wheate corne fall into the grounde and dye, it bideth alone: If it dye it bryngeth furth muche fruite. He that loueth his lyfe shall destroye it, and he that hateth his lyfe in this world, shall kepe it vnto lyfe eternall.

But when Jesus was certified by his disciples that the heathen also longed to see him, when as so leudly he was contemned of the Phariseis, and priestes, vpon this occasion he began to open his death to his disciples, and what great fruite it should bring, not onely to the Jewes, but to al the worlde: for because in like maner as the miracle of raysing vp Lazarus, alone did drawe and prouoke not onely many Jewes, but also Gentiles to his loue: so shoulde his death and resurreccion moue and drawe all the countreyes of the whole worlde. Than Jesus gaue aunswer to his disciples that shewed him the godly minde and affeccion of the heathen, and sayed: ye dyd heare the Jewes saie with a loude voice: blessed is he that cummeth in the name of the Lorde. Ye see the Gentiles drawe to me with lyke desyre, and why? Because now the tyme is nygh, that whan the Phariseis beleueth that the sonne of man shall bee vtterlye extincte, than shall he bee most glorified with all nacions of the worlde. It is a newe kinde of glory, and by a newe waye must it be gotten. I beyng aliue, haue drawen fewe to me: but when I am dead, my fame shalbe spred abrode, and drawe mo than my bodily presence hath doen. ye be loth to heare of death, yet take that for moste sure, vnlesse the wheat corne be caste into the grounde, and beyng buryed there, doe rotte and dye, it shall bring furth no fruite, but it only alone abideth safe: But if it be dead and lye buried in the grounde, it sprouteth vp againe with muche gayne of fruite, yealdyng for one corne an hundreth, and nowe the corne standing ioyfully vpon the grounde, garnisheth the fieldes abrode in many places, and with a plenteous encreasse enricheth the countreye. The thing that is commodious to many is the more to be coueted, and the saluacion of many is to be redemed with the death of a fewe. So to bestowe life is no perishemente, but auauntage, and this is not to loose the lyfe, but to kepe it. For the soule doeth not perishe whiche departeth from the bodye, nor the bodye dooeth not altogether go to destruccion, that in tyme to come shal liue more blessedlye, and be immortall. Therfore whosoeuer loueth his life in this worlde, whyle he euill kepeth it he loseth it. Contrary, whosoeuer hateth his life in this worlde, and for the furtheraunce of the ghospel casteth it into perils, and betaketh it to death, he doeth not loose lyfe whiche he so bestoweth, but kepeth it: and for a mortall, a shorte, and a wretched lyfe, shal receyue at the time of resurreccion, an eternal and blessed lyfe. In lyke maner, he that kepeth the wheat corne, looseth it, that euen els of it selfe would perishe, but he that soweth and burieth it in the ground, in conclusion well saueth it, within a whyle after to receiue the same agayne with auantage: whiche he thought he had loste.

Excepte the wheat corne fall into the ground and dye.

If

If any man minister vnto me, let him folowe me: and where I am, there shall also my minister be: if any minister vnto me, him will my father honour. Nowe is my soule troubled, and what shall I saye? Father deliuer me from this houre, but therfore came I vnto this houre. Father glorifie thy name. The texte.

There is therfore no cause why my death should trouble you: whiche death ones shalbe folowed, to thintent that you, whiche shalbe folowers of death, may be partakers both of glory & immortalitie. I as the autour of the ghospels businesse, doe bestowe my life willingly for the saluacion of the world, and my fathers glory. you shall be ministers of the same businesse, reporting and publishing abrode through the whole world with your preaching, those thinges that I haue both wrought and taught. Thesame thing that the Byshoppes and Phariseis doe now with great craft deuise against me, shal the wicked execute vpon you, whiche vngraciouse persones loueth the worlde more than God: and whiles ful folishly they kepe this life, they loose euerlasting life, and cast themselfes headling into euerlasting death. If one professe himselfe my disciple or minister, it behoueth thesame to folowe me theyr maister and Lord. For it is mete that the seruaunte be not pulled away from his Lord, neither in prosperouse thinges nor aduersant. Whom I haue partakers and companiõs in afflictions and aduersitie, them will not I disseuer from the felowshyp of felicitie: but wheresoeuer I become, there shall also my seruaunt be. And though the worlde reiecte me neuer so muche, yet shall my father enhaunce me to glory. And in case any manne behaue hymselfe as a faithfull seruaunt to me, hym (in recompence of transitorie harmes, and for ignominie wherwith he liueth in rebuke among men) my father shal bewtifie and honour with eternall felicitie, & true glory. For my father shall acknowledge not me only, but the ministers also of his only sonne, and shall vouchesafe like reward vpon thẽ, whom he hath knowen to suffre suche like thinges as his sayed sonne did suffre: Affliccion had here, hath of treuth his anguishe and paine, by reason of the infirmitie of mans body. But the saluacion of many well considered, the felicitie of euerlasting life well pondered, whiche are redemed and recouered with a short torment, ought to conuince this quiueryng feare of mans nature. And if in time to come, ye feale that nature irketh and repineth against the dreadfull tormentes and deathes, wherewith ye be menaced and threatned, doe not vtterly sterte awaye as men discomfeited & clearly ouercome, but let valiauntnes of mynde alwaye depending of the father of heauens ayde, vanquish in you the feblenes and cowardnesse of mans nature. But euen nowe also I fele myne owne soule troubled in my selfe, because the daye of my death is nye. I see a sore greuouse tempest imminent and hang ouer me. What shall I saye, or whither shall I turne me? shall I yelde to the infirmitie of the body, which abhorreth death? Shal I flee to the succours of the worlde? or shall I for the loue of mine owne life neglect the life of the whole worlde? no not so. I will accommodate and applye my selfe to my fathers will. My naturall infirmitie, beyng sore incumbred with the horriblenesse of death, shall say vnto him: Father, if it may be, kepe me safe from this instant perill of death. But charitie, whiche muche desireth mans saluacion, furthwith putteth to this saying: yet rather for all that (sayeth she) (in case it be fit and expedient so to be) let the coueted death come, when as after the will of the spirite, whiche doeth no where disagree with thyne, I haue willyngly and wittingly offered my selfe to death. Nowe bryng thou it to passe, that my death and resurreccion maye cause thy name to be notable and famouse in al countreys of the worlde, that when thou art once knowen, the people honoring thee, may attayne to eternall saluacion.

The texte.

Than came a voyce from heauen, saying: I haue both glorified it, and will glorifie it againe. The people therfore that stode by and heard it, sayed that it thundred: other sayd an aungell spake to hym. Iesus aunswered, and sayed. This voice came not because of me, but for your sakes. Nowe is the iudgemente of this worlde, nowe shall the prince of this worlde be cast out. And I if I were lifte vp from the earth, will drawe all men vnto me. This he sayed signifying what death he should dye.

After our Lord Iesus had thus prayed, with his iyes lift vp into heauen, the voice of the father came from heauen saying: I haue glorified my name, and will after this more excellently set it forth. For alredy his name through so many miracles was waxed great and muche knowen among menne by his sonne, but moste chiefly by raysing Lazarus from death to lyfe. And soone after would he augment the glory of his name in all ye nacions of the worlde by the crosse, by the resurreccion, and by the ascendyng vp into heauen, by sending downe of the holy ghost, and by the preaching of his Apostles. Moreouer the route of people whiche stode not farre of, when they heard the voice that came downe from heauen, because they toke lytle hede, neyther was it euident to them vnto whom that voice did appartayne, that cumpany of people (I say) agreed not in their opinions of the thyng. For some did interpretate the voice that they thought they heard to be a thūder, for the voice came out of the cloudes. Some againe did interpretate the thyng more fauourably, saying some angell did speake vnto hym. But Iesus to make them take more hede, & also to put awaye from him all suspicion of prayse, sayeth: this voice which is neither noise of thundres nor voice of angell, but the voice of my father which hath heard my prayers, came not for me who knowe in my selfe my fathers minde, but it is come for you, that ye maye vnderstand that my father & I doe agre, and that whatsoeuer I doe, he being the authour, I doe it for your saluacion sake. You haue hearde what my father hath promised as touching my death. Nowe shortly must Satan be wrestled withal for good & all, who is the prince or rather tiranne of this world, & through sinne hath hitherto kept al thē in death, which loue this world. Nowe is the cause of the whole world drawen into iudgemente, but falshood beyng reproued, trueth shall come to light: And whiles the prince of the world, the authour of death, thinketh himselfe a conquerour, he shall through death be put from his tiranny. For all men shalbe pardoned theyr sinnes through faythe of the gospell. Sinne once take away, the tirantes force & strength is qualled, who is valiant & mighty in no other weapon saue sinne onely. And as he that shall thinke himselfe to haue the victory shal sodainly be expelled his kingdom: so I that shalbe thought vtterly made away, after I be lifted vp frō the earth, wil drawe all thinges on euery side vnto me, of right chalengyng that thyng vnto me, which hitherto he hath kept in possession by tyrāny. Furthermore in that Christe sayed: When I shalbe lift vp from the earth (because the saying was doubtfull, & yet right fitte to expresse ye thing,) he would signifie what kinde of death he should dye. For they that are hanged vp vpon a crosse, hang vp on hye that all men may see thē a farre of: And he gaue them withall a priuey warning of the old story, which sheweth that a brasen serpent beyng a fi-

gure

gure of Christe, and set vp vpon a hie pole, did geue to all them that behelde it, though it were a farre of, presente helpe against the mortall woundes of serpentes.

The texte.

The people answered hym. We haue heard out of the lawe that Christe bideth euer, and howe sayest thou, the sonne of man must be lift vp? who is that sonne of man? Then Jesus sayd vnto them: yet a litle while is the light with you. Walke while ye haue light, leste the darknes come on you. He that walketh also in the darke, woteth not whither he goeth: while ye haue light, beleue on the light, that ye may be the chyldren of the lyght.

And yet were there some in that assembly of people, which did coniecte (because of the forespeakyng of death) that he had spoken of the tormente of the crosse. And therupon they stode in argument, that he was not Messias which published that himselfe should dye: whereas scripture geueth to Messias, power, and a kyngdome eternall. For thus writeth Daniel: His power is an euerlasting power, which shal not be taken away: and his kingdome shal remaine for euer. And again Micheas the Prophete speaketh thus: His outgoing hath been from the beginning, and from euerlasting. Also Esai sayeth: And there shalbe no ende of his peace. Yea and moreouer the prophecie of the psalmes doeth promise hym a perpetuall priesthood, saying: Thou art a priest for euer after the order of Melchisedeck. Than say they therfore: We knowe by the lawe, that when Messias shall come, he shall abyde & continue for euer. What meaneth it therfore that thou sayest, it shall come to passe that the sonne of man shall be lift vp from the earth? but and if to be lift vp from the earth be to dye, and yf thou wilt haue the sonne of man (so often as thou speakest of him) to be taken for thee thy selfe, eyther shalt thou not dye, or els that sonne of man is not Messias, if the prophecie saye trueth.

Well, because these sayinges were spoken of malice: Jesus made no aunswere to them. Verely, he myght haue aunswered that he was not only man, but also God, & that he should of trueth die, as concerning his natural mans body, but yet so that it should soone rise againe, nor yet should that death let the perpetuitie of his kingdome, because it should not be worldly, but a spirituall kyngdome. But neyther did they vnderstande these misteries, nor yet was there oportunitie to declare them openly. He doeth onely councell them that (setting aparte all blyndenesses of harte) they would cease theyr crying out on the trueth that was come to light, specially seyng that it should within a whyle be taken awaye. Not that the light of the ghospell should euer be throughly abolished, but that they should not after this heare of his owne mouthe his doctrine, nor see hym worke any myracles, whiche myght geue them sight to see theyr foly, and repente them of it: yet a lytle while (sayeth he) is the lyght with you. Wherfore, while ye haue this lyght, walke ye, and amende sith there is good cause, leste the lyght being sodainly taken awaye, darke night come on you, and than ye desyre all in vayne, the thing that is taken from you, which nowe being offered vnto you, ye doe contemne. Who so foloweth the blinde affections of his owne minde, walketh in darkenesse, and knoweth not whither he goeth: and whiles he beleueth that he doeth wel and godly, he falleth into death. I am the lyght of the worlde: whoso beleueth in me, shall not erre or swarue from the trueth. The children of darkenesse flyeth from the light, while you therfore haue light, beleue on the light, that ye maye be seen the children of light. He that beleueth, seeth, who so beleueth not, the same hauyng syght, is blinde.

The texte. These thynges spake Jesus, and departed and hid hymselfe from them. But though he had doen so many miracles before them, yet beleued not they on him, that the saying of the Prophete Esaias might be fulfilled, whiche he spake: Lorde who shall beleue our saying? and to whom is the arme of the Lorde declared?

Jesus spake no more to them at that time, leste he should the more prouoke the fury of them, whom he knewe to be very prone vnto all mischiefe, but he went thence, and hidde himselfe from them, and so would he through his absence and with silence asswage their cruell woodnes, and therewithall admonishing vs by the way, that (according to his exaumple) as often as we haue to doe with wilful persones, and that there is no hope to doe them good, we than ought to geue place for a time, leste not only we doe them no good at al, but also make other the wurse. For what is more to be lamented, than the myndes of those Jewes? For where as our Lorde Jesus, through so many, so cleare, and so woonderfull miracles wrought before their iyes, ought to haue brought them moste surely to haue beleued his sayinges, yet dyd they stande stifly in their vnbeliefe, no doubte but euen blinded with enuy, hatred, ambicion, auarice, and other vngraciouse concupiscence of the mynde. And euen so Esai long ago dyd prophecie that some suche should be, saying: Lord who hath beleued our woordes, and to whom is the arme of the Lord opened? Verily, therfore they did not see the power of God in Jesus his doynges, because beyng blynded with their malice, they did not beleue.

The texte. Therfore coulde they not beleue, because that Esaias sayeth agayne. He hath blynded their iyes, and hath hardened theyr harte, that they should not see with theyr iyes, and leste they should vnderstande with their harte, and shoulde be conuerted, and I shoulde heale them. Suche thinges sayed Esaias, when he sawe his glorye and spake of hym.

Yea and they did not beleue, because they would not caste awaye theyr naughtie desires. And this also did Esai speake of before: He hath (sayth Esai) blinded their iyes, & hardened their hartes, that they should not see with their iyes, and vnderstand with their hartes, and should be conuerted, and I shoud heale them. For they seeyng did not see, and vnderstanding did not vnderstand. And contrarye to their owne saluacion, they made all they could against him, at whose hand alone, saluaciō was to be hoped for. These thiges tolde Esai long ago, who beeyng spiritually inspired, sawe with the iyes of prophecie, the glory of the sonne of God, whiche (in tyme to come) he should haue beyng a very man. And he prophecied that he sawe, and the thing which he prophecied should be, haue we seen doen.

The texte. Neuerthelesse among the chiefe rulers also, many beleued on him, but (because of the Pharriseis) they would not be knowen of it, leste they should be excommunicate, for they loued the prayse of men, more then the prayse of God.

yet for al this, these mens vnbelefe did not exclude the saluaciō of other that did beleue: for many gaue faith to Jesus, not only of ye vulgar people, but of the nobles also. But neuerthelesse, the men of wurship durst not confesse the faith openly, for feare of the Phariseis, whiche had made a decre, ye whosoeuer did confesse himselfe to be a disciple of Jesus, should be excōmunicate & thrust out of ye Synagogue. Ouer this, those whiche haue preeminēce in the worlde, ignominie irketh them much. For as yet theyr faith was not stable & perfite, but notwithstanding that, it was for that time, a good begining of an euāgelicall minde, to thinke well of Jesus: though feare & shamefastnesse letted thē to shewe it furth. Enuy stopped some, couetousnes letted other, & othersome other some did ambicion hinder, why they did not with an whole harte cleaue to Christ, for whose sake all thynges are to be contemned. But because the holye ghoste, whiche corroborateth a man towardes the ghospell, was not yet geuen: many beleued fearfully: as yet settyng more by mans glorie than Goddes. To be hiely placed in the synagogue was honorable among men, but to be reiecte out of the wicked mens synagogue for Christes sake, is honour & prayse before God. But feare and infirmitie in men that be of nature weake, soone obteineth forgeuenesse. Howbeit, those whiche were so blynded with euill desyres, that with a wicked conscience they spake agaynst Christe, turned awaye the people from hym, layed snares for hym, and ouer that craftely sought his death, it is nedefull (I saye) that those perishe, because they would not bee saued.

Jesus cried and sayed: he that beleueth on me, beleueth not on me, but on hym that sent me: and he that seeth me, seeth hym that sent me. I am come a light into the worlde, that whosoeuer beleueth on me, should not abide in darkenesse. The texte.

Another tyme agayne, Jesus goyng abrode in the sight of the Jewes, now when their fury ought to haue been well appeased, the more to moue them all to beleue, and to leaue them no excuse at al that through theyr owne wilful malice would perishe, declaryng what great profite should come to them that beleued, and how great destruccion to them that did persiste in theyr vnbeliefe, Jesus (I saye) cryed and sayd: all you do professe that ye beleue on God. But forasmuche than as I am come from god, nor saye or do any thyng, vnlesse he beyng the auctour, whosoeuer beleueth on me, beleueth not on me, ẏ do nothing of my self, but on him that sent me into the worlde. The worlde is full of darkenesse, of errour and sinnes. And therfore dyd I descend into the world from my father, that is the fountayne of al light, as a beame from the sũne: that errours beyng remoued, and synnes taken awaye, I should be the lighte of the worlde. Truely by faythe are the iyes of the blynde opened, that they maye see lighte, and no more fall in darkenesse. All my doctrine, miracles, and what thyng soeuer I haue doen or shall do, to this hath respecte, that he whiche beleueth on me, and putteth his whole affiaunce in me, doeth not abyde in darkenesse: but beyng lightned with knowledge of trueth, and pourged from al sinnes of their old lyfe, maye through leadyng of the light, and by godlinesse of the ghospel, procede to euerlastyng lyfe.

And if any man heare my wordes and beleue not, I iudge hym not: for I came not to iudge the worlde, but to saue the world. He that refuseth me, & receyueth not my wordes, hath one that iudgeth him. The worde that I haue spoken, the same shal iudge him in the last daye. The texte.

But if a man heare my wordes and obey them not, that hearing doeth so not profite him, that for his vnbelefe he shal haue a more sory ende: not that I shall iudge him. For I came not to condemne the worlde for the sinnefull enormities therof, but to saue it, beyng once purged by fayth. But neyther yet shall ẏ man escape terrible iudgemente, whiche when he hath hearde my wordes, casteth thẽ awaye and contemneth thẽ. Verily at this present, I omitte nothyng, wherby I may drawe al folke to eternal saluaciõ, nor any man shal be loste through my faulte. But whosoeuer shall contemne saluacion, when it is offred hym, this selfe sayed worde whiche I now speake, shall condemne hym: and shall in the laste daye rebuke him, because he did perishe through his owne wilfull malice. I (for my parte) haue inuited menne with promising them rewardes, I

haue

haue feared them by threatnyng them with punishementes, I haue allured the with benefites, I haue prouoked them with miracles: I repell no bodye from saluacion, I set open a ready waye for euery man and woman to life. What excuse therfore in the laste daye shall he pretende, that beyng so many wayes prouoked to belefe, doeth continue still in his blindnesse.

The texte. For I haue not spoken of my selfe, but the father whiche sent me, he gaue me a commaundemente what I should saye, and what I shoulde speake. And I knowe that his commaundemente is lyfe euerlastyng: whatsoeuer I speake therfore, euen as the father bad me so I speake.

If ye be wurshippers of God (as ye thinke your selues to be) in case ye haue the lawe in reuerence, ye cannot contemne my woordes. For I do not speake of myne owne heade, as they be woont to do, whiche dooe feine what they liste to theyr owne prayse and aduauntage, nor I do not teache thynges repugnaunte to the law, but I do perfourme in dede, those thynges whiche the lawe did shadow in figures, and prophecied should come. Furthermore, my father who is þ auctour of the lawe, and from whom I came hither, hath prescribed me what I shall saye and do. Therfore consideryng that I do obeye his commaundementes in all thynges, how can ye honour hym, when as ye do cōtemne his ambassadour? And truely, the thing whiche he hath geuen me in commaundement, he hath onely commaunded it of loue towardes you, that you throughe beleuyng the thinges, whiche I shewe vnto you, maye obtayne euerlastyng lyfe. Lyke as my father thirsteth the saluacion of all, and seketh no mans damnacion: so beeely do I desyre to haue all saued, and wyll suffre none to perishe, as muche as in me lyeth verily. Wherfore because I am well assured, that whatsoeuer he hath willed me to saye, doeth perteyne to your saluacion, therefore doe I leaue naught vnspoken that he hath assigned me to saye vnto you. As touchyng this good will of God the father towardes you, and myne also, which throughly agreeth with my fathers wil and minde, see there be no defaulte on your behalfe, wilfully sekyng your owne damnacion, when as ye maie attaine to eternal saluacion.

The.xiii.Chapter.

The texte. Before the feast of Easter, when Iesus knewe that his houre was come that he should departe out of this worlde vnto the father, when he loued his whiche were in the worlde, vnto the ende he loued them.

Ur Lorde Iesus, didde with these kynde of woordes, exhorte þ wicked people to prouide for theyr owne saluaciō, and to leaue their vngracious purpose, consideryng he had leafte nothyng vnassayed, whereby they might be recouered and brought to a better minde and emendmente. Nowe then was no more a doe, but to enstructe his discyples (whom he had speciallye chosen, whome he should shortely leaue behinde him, and whome he knewe would be muche discoumfited with the deathe of theyr maister) against the storme that was imminente and nye at hand, and throughly to pull oute out of theyr myndes those Pestilences whiche corrupteth the sinceritie of the ghospell that is to saye, enuie, hatred, pride, ambicion, and graffe in them affeccions contrary to these, declaryng therein the tokens of perfite charitie, whose example and steppes they should folow in louing eche other mutually, shewing also the mannier of suche mekenesse and humilitie as hath not been hearde of, wherby one shoulde preuente an other semblealy with mutuall benefites. Therfore the daye before Easter whiche the Hebrues (as was sayed before) did call Phase, that is to saye, a passeouer, forasmuche as oure Lorde Jesus from whom nothyng was hid, knewe the tyme nowe to bee at hande, when as hymselfe, aunsweryng to the name of that feastefull daye, shoulde passe out of this worlde, and go agayn to his father, from whēce he came: seyng he had alwaies loued his Apostles, whom he had specially chosē to hymselfe as his familiares and frendes, whiche shoulde not yet depart out of the worlde, but shoulde haue a great and long battayle with the world, he didde declare his continuall loue and charitie towardes them. Neyther the storme of his death, beeyng nowe at hande, did put awaye the zele and affeccion whiche he bare towardes them, but at his veray departyng from them, he did speciallye shewe tokens of a certayne rare loue, not that he had fayntly loued them before, but because those thinges whiche he shoulde printe into theyr myndes, at his goyng from them, mighte more diepely remayne in memorie.

¶ And when supper was ended, after that the deuill had put in the harte of Judas Iscarioth Simons sonne to betraye hym, Jesus knowyng that the father had geuen al thynges into his handes, and that he was come from God, and went to God, he rose from supper and layed aside his vpper garmentes, & when he had taken a towell, he girded hymselfe. After that he powred water into a basin, and began to washe the disciples feete, and to wype them with the towell wherwith he was girded. The texte.

Therefore after that laste and misticall supper was prepared, in the whiche the holy memoriall of his body and bloude beeing geuen, he leafte vnto vs by waye of couenaunte a continuall remembraunce of himselfe, and purposed to make a league of frendeshyp that should neuer by any meanes dye betwene vs, although he knewe wel ynough that Judas Iscarioth by the suggestion of the deuill, already went about to betraie him, that he might be taken of the Jewes: whiche mynde of Judas, the pestilence of couetousnesse had so possessed, that he coulde not be called backe from his vngraciouse wicked dede, for all the greate gentilnesse and mildnesse of his maister towardes him: and seyng Jesus knewe also that his father woulde suffer none of those thynges to perishe whiche he had deliuered him to kepe, and was well assured that himselfe should shortelye go to his father, from whence he came, yet because he would vtterlye pull oute of his disciples mindes, all ambiciouse desire, he riseth from supper, meat being already set vpon the table, and laying asyde his vpper garmentes, whereby he might in euery condicion shewe the similitude of a seruaunte, he tooke a towell and girded himself with it, furthwith he himselfe powred water into the basen, and takyng vpon hym the moste vile and abiect office after the worldes estimacion, he began to washe his disciples feete. The Hebrues in dede did accustomably bestow this manier of seruice vpon their geastes and frēdes, but yet this thyng that Christe did was not onely an exaumple of perfit humblenesse, but also had in it a figure of a misticall meanyng: that is to saye, howe that they

which

whiche should prepare themselues to the office of preaching the ghospell, and would be partakers of yͤ table of the lord, ought to be moste pure from al earthly affeccions, notwithstanding none should attein this puritie, vnlesse our lord Jesus with his goodnesse should wipe awaye all the filthinesse of our infirmitie, who onely was without all spot, and who also beyng veray man was after suche a sorte conuersaunt among men, that he trained forth the whole course of his life without any spot of carnalitie.

The texte.

Than came he to Simon Peter, and Peter sayed vnto him: Lord doest thou washe my feete? Jesus aunswered and sayed vnto hym: what I do, thou wotest not now, but thou shalt knowe hereafter. Peter sayeth vnto hym: Thou shalt neuer washe my feete. Jesus aunswered hym: Yf I washe the not, thou hast no parte with me.

Therefore when the lorde of all thinges that are in heauen and earth, knowyng all thynges before, and hauyng al thynges geuen hym of his father, in his apparell beyng girded after a sorte of a seruaunt, naked and carrying the basin, came to Symon Peter, and kneled before hym to washe his feete. Peter was horribly afearde at this rare and straunge exaumple of humilitie, on the on side knowledgyng his owne infirmitie, on the other syde considerying yͤ maiestie of the Lorde, whiche he had somewhat perceyued by his myracles, and meruelouse doctryne, although he had not yet fully knowen hym to be god, nor as yet seene hym ryse agayne, neyther ascende into heauen, sitte on the ryghte hande of the father, nor wurshipped through the whole worlde, with godly honours: but this thyng beyng knowen after, did the more commend his exaumple of so notable humilitie. Peter therefore refusing to be washed of his maister vpon the selfsame consideració that John baptiste was lothe to take vpon him to baptise Christe, sayed: Lord what a thyng is this whiche thou goest aboute? wilte thou washe my feete? I knowe who I am, and who thou arte: and furthwith to Peters refusall, Jesus aunswered. Suffer me to do that thyng whiche I do, for it is no trifle, nor doen in vain: thou doest not yet vnderstād what this thyng meaneth, but hereafter thou shalt. And than thou shalt wel perceyue the thyng whiche I do, to haue been nedefull for thee. Peter was not stayed with this manier of aunswer, because he vnderstoode it not, but made a further deniall, saying: I will neuer suffer so great a man as thou arte, to washe suche an ones feete as I am. But our Lorde to put awaye this earnest refusal, although it came of loue, as it were, to dryue out one naile with another, by threatninges forced Peter to cōsent, seing he was not otherwise easie to be taught as yet, saying: Peter, why doest thou stryue with me? If I washe thee not, thou canste not be partaker with me. Eyther thou shalte be washed, or thou shalt be remoued from the felowshyp of my boorde and league. He muste be pure and cleane, whom I will admit into my company. And Jesus spake this, not of washyng the fete of the bodye, but concernyng the folowyng of his so notable humilitie, and pureenesse of mynde, whiche oughte to bee excellent in those persones that professe the doctrine of the gospell, and take vpon thē the cure of Christes flock.

Lord doest thou washe my feete?

If I washe yͤ not, thou hast no part with me.

The texte.

¶ Symon Peter sayeth vnto hym: Lord not my feete onely, but also the handes and the heade. Jesus sayeth vnto hym: He that is washed, nedeth not saue to washe his feete, but is cleane euery whitte. And ye are cleane, but not all. For he knewe who it was that shoulde betraye hym. Therefore he sayed, ye are not all cleane.

And

And although Peter that loued the Lorde feruently, vnderstode not than what Jesus sayinges meante, yet because it is greuouse to a louer to heare any mencion made of diuorcement or departure, as soone as he heard that he should be separate from the coumpanie of hym, whom he entierly loued, sodaynly he became more vehement in admitting him to washe his feete, then he was before in refusing the same, and sayed: Lord rather then I would be put from thee, I doe not only suffre the to washe my feete (seeyng it pleaseth the so to doe) but also my handes and my head. To this the Lord aunswered: he that is once washed, hath no nede to be washed again, for the rest of his body beyng cleane, there remayneth nothing to be washed, but his feete: which eftsones by treadyng on the grounde, gathereth some filthinesse.

Truely our Lorde Jesus did signifie by this parable, that it is not sufficient for him that is a preacher of the gospell to haue that cōmon puritie which baptisme and the profession of Christes fayth geueth to al folkes, except his feete, that is to say, the affections of his minde, be often purged from all impuritie of this worlde, from the whiche neuerthelesse no man can be pure, vnlesse he study to washe awaye many tymes, through the mercy of Christe, the infeccion that he hath taken by the cumpanie of men.

Therfore (sayeth he) I will not washe againe the reste of your body but onely your feete, for ye be cleane: but not euery one of you. In this exception our Lord Jesus did touche the conscience of Judas Iscarioth, for he knewe well inough who should betray him to the Jewes. The gentlenesse of Jesus was so great, that although he knewe him, yet would he not bewray him to other, nor rejecte him from hauyng his feete washed, neyther would he put him backe from his holy Supper, nor yet from the communion of his body and bloud: he doeth only touche his conscience, who knewe himselfe wel ynough, that he might repent & emende himselfe, after he should perceiue that he was not vnknowen to the Lorde, whom he was determined to betray. Therfore was he the cause why Jesus sayd, verily ye are cleane, but not all.

The texte.

So after he had washed their feete, and receyued his clothes, and was set downe, he saied vnto them againe: Wote ye what I haue doen to you? ye call me maister and Lorde, and ye saye well, for so am I. If I then your Lorde & maister haue washed your feete, ye also ought to wash one an others feete. For I haue geuē you an exaumple that you should doe as I haue doen to you. Verily verily I saye vnto you, the seruaunt is not greater then his maister, neyther the messenger greater then he that sent him. Yf ye vnderstand these thinges, happy are ye if ye doe them. I speake not of you al, I knowe whom I haue chose, but that the scripture may be fulfilled, he that eateth bread with me, hath lifte vp his hele against me. Nowe tell I you before it come, that when it is come to passe, ye might beleue that I am he.

When Jesus had finished this kinde of seruice towardes his twelue Apostles, he put on againe his garmentes, & sate downe to sup with them, but in the meane while he doeth once againe put into their myndes the exaumple of lowelines which he had shewed thē, leste they should forget the thing which was necessary for thē, for he sayth: doe ye not vnderstād what is mēt by that I haue washed all your feete? ye call me maister & Lorde, and there is good cause why ye should so doe, for doubtlesse I am the same that ye call me: and seyng I haue washed your feete, that am in very dede your maister & Lorde, you that are brethren and seruauntes together, shall muche lesse grudge eche

one

For I haue geuē you an example.

one to serue an other continually. For I that am so farre aboue you, haue therfore geuē you this example, that you should not be lothe to doe the lyke among you that be felowes, whiche I haue doen to my disciples & seruauntes, and that one brother, should be ashamed to take vpon him the pryde of a tyraunt ouer his brother, and likewise a seruaunt ouer his companion, seyng I, that maye worthyly take vpon me the preeminence of this dignitie, haue humbled my selfe to washe your fete. Neyther is there cause why any manne should say, the thyng that I doe is to vyle, abiecte and seruile. The greater a man is, the more it behoueth him to humble himselfe. The pestilence of ambicion doeth crepe in, euen emong euangelicall vertues. When ye shall doe myracles through my name, when ye shal prophecie, than ought ye chiefly to remember that thing whiche I haue doen this day vnto you: ye may not defend the autoritie of the gospel with high lookes, with pryde, nor with violence, by other meanes shall that be attayned. That thing verily cannot be denied, which is certainly knowē by naturall reason, that is to say, howe there is no seruaunte greater then his maister, nor the messenger that is sent to doe any other mans businesse, is greater then he that sendeth him: ye knowe me to be your maister, and hereafter ye shall knowe it better: ye are my messengers, and I am the authour of your Message. Therfore it were a shame for you to be puft vp with pryde, or to be fierce and cruel against the flocke that is committed vnto you, or also among your selfes, considering ye haue found me so meke and curteous a Lord and maister. Because nowe ye vnderstande this, if ye doe it hereafter, ye shalbe blessed after my doctrine, which I so often repeate vnto you, leste it should any waye be forgotten. But all you shall not obtayne this blessing. In dede I haue chosen you all to the honourable roumth and office of an apostle. But all you shall not aunswere to the worthynesse of this office. Blessed shall they be which shall vse the Apostles office after myne example. But there is among you that shall so lytle folowe this myne example towarde his brethren and companions (with whom he hathe heretofore been felowe like) that he shall lift vp his head against me, whiche am so great a Lord and suche a maister. But it was long agon prophecied in the Psalme, that this thing should be, where as it is thus sayed: he that shal eate my bread, shall lyfte vp his hele against me. I doe nowe shewe you before it come to passe, that this thyng shall be, because when ye shall see that doen whiche scripture hath spoken of before, ye maye beleue that I am he of whom it hath prophecied, and that nothing is doen against me by chaunce or aduenture, but all this matter is moderate according to Gods determinacion. And like as he that foloweth mine example is happy: so shal he be vnhappy (whosoeuer he be) that had rather folowe that trayters doing that myne. For he shall haue in time to come many folowers of his naughtinesse, which shall set more by money then by the glory of myne name: and pretendyng the honour of the Apostles name, shall traiterously misuse the office of an Apostle, and shall deface thapostles office.

Now I tel you before it come.

The texte.

Verily, verily, I saye vnto you: He that receyueth whomsoeuer I sende, receyueth me: and he that receyueth me, receyueth him that sent me.

But the greater the dignitie of this office is, so muche the greuouser is the faulte to abuse the honour of that profession thorowe playing the traytour: for this I tell you assuredly, who soeuer receiueth him that I send, receyueth ceiueth me, and whosoeuer receiueth me, receiueth hym that sente me: for as I being my fathers messenger, do nothyng but accordyng to his wil, so you that be my messengers and Apostles, yf you faythfullye put in execucion the thyng ẏ I haue commaunded you, shall bee so receiued of godlye folkes, as though I spake in you: lyke as my father speaketh in me, who teache none other thyng but that whiche he hath limyted.

The texte.

¶ Whan Jesus had thus saied, he was troubled in the spirite and testified and saied: Verely verely I saie unto you, that one of you shall betraye me. Then the disciples loked one on an other, doubtyng of whom he spake. There was one of Jesus disciples, whiche leaned on him (euen he whome Jesus loued.) To him beckened Symon Peter therefore, that he should aske who it was, of whom he spake. He then when he leaned on Jesus brest saied unto him: Lorde who is it? Jesus aunswered: He it is to whom I geue a soppe. And he wette the breade and gaue it to Judas Iscarioth Simons sonne. And after the soppe, Satan entred into him.

When Jesus comfortyng his Apostles myndes had spoken these wordes, furthwith, because he woulde make theim the more afrayed to folowe the traytours exaumple, and to the entente he woulde more vehementelye proueke the traytoure to amende, he was troubled in spirite as one greuouslye vexed for the destruccion of hym, whiche thorowe his owne malice, wente aboute to procure to himselfe euerlasting death: and dooeth againe witnesse euen by othe, that the thyng whiche he spake beefore shall verilye come to passe. Forsoothe, I tell you yet once again (saieth he) that one of you, whiche beeyng but a fewe doeth here sit downe with me at one table, shall betraye me. This saiyng so often repeted did awake the disciples myndes, whiche els had bene ful heuye and pensife for the foresaid departure of their Maister. And euerye mans conscience (sauyng Judas) did coumforte hymselfe, because onelye one was noted to bee the betrayer. But this addicion (of you) did trouble theim, neyther didde they doubte but the thyng shoulde at some tyme come to passe, whiche our Lorde saied should bee, and yet no man could suspecte of an other so detestable a dede, forasmuche as they thought all other to be of theyr minde, sauyng that euerye man mistrusted the fragilitie of mannes nature. Onely Judas knowyng hymselfe giltye neyther shrinketh thereat, nor was ashamed, nor yet dreadfull to bee presente at that holye repaste: and besides that, in the meane whyle coulde abyde the syghte of his maister, to whome he knewe the whole purpose of his minde to bee manifestelp knowen. So pestilent a thyng was couetousnesse, and so it liked hym to abuse the gentlenes of his maister, beeyng alreadye well knowen unto him. Therfore the reste of the disciples beyng heuy and careful, dydde beholde one an other, to see if they coulde perceiue any token by countenaunce, by whome Jesus had spoken this: as they whiche (withoute doubte) woulde furthwith haue been fierce agaynst him that had determined so wicked a deede. Here truelye was Simon Peters mynde set on fyer, who loued our Lorde no man more, but hitherto (for ẏ more parte) the boldenes which he had by reason of his loue towardes his maister, had euill successe. He hadde heard our Lorde saye before: Go backe from me Sathan, thou sauorest not those thynges that appertaine to God: and euen nowe he hearde hym saye. Thou shalt haue no parte with me. Therfore when Peter dyd greatly desyre to be deliuered from this doubtefull care, and to knowe assuredlye who he was that went about so great a mischiefe, as one that would not haue suffred hym to haue sitte emong them at that feaste, yet durste not he hymselfe be busie to aske Jesus who was

One of you shall betray me.

that traytour, whom he aduertised them of: but he beckened to a certayne disciple, to demaunde of Jesus, who was the manne he spake of: whiche disciple the Lorde loued intierly, and vsed familyarly, and at that same tyme he leaned vpon the lordes breste, by reason of whiche kynde dealing and familiar handeling of hym, the manne dyd mourne, and was halfe deade, because the lordes death was at hande: but the Lord dyd coumforte and recreate him.

Therfore that disciple as he was then leanyng vpon Jesus breste, saied secretly vnto hym: Lorde who is he that shall dare enterprise suche a mischeuous dede? Jesus aunswered hym saiyng: He it is to whome I shall geue a dipte soppe. And when he hadde dipped the breade in the brothe, he gaue the soppe to Judas Iscarioth, Simons sonne. The vnhappye traitour was neyther ashamed therewithall, nor wente about to amende hymselfe, but with a shamelesse countenaunce settyng at noughte the Lordes knoweledge, and despisyng his greate gentylnesse, he tooke a token of frendshyppe at the Lordes hande, whome he woulde anone after betraye for a litle money. And after he had receiued that litle morsell, the deuill dyd fully possesse his minde, and of a wicked man, made hym vncurable.

The texte,

Than said Jesus vnto him. That thou doest do quickely. That wist no man at the table for what entent he spake vnto him. Some of them thought because Judas hadde the bag, that Jesus had saied vnto him, bye those thinges that we haue nede of against the feaste, or that he shoulde geue some thing to the poore. Assone then as he had receiued the soppe, he went immediatly out, and it it was nyght.

Now when Jesus sawe that the purposed malice of Judas woulde neyther bee chaunged with shame nor feare (for he was almoste bewrayed allready, and should haue bene in daunger, yf Jesus hadde disclosed hym) he therefore sent hym awaye from the feaste, and suffred hym to dooe that vngraciouse dede, whiche he already had committed in full wyll, and purpose of mynde. The thyng which thou goest about (saieth he) doe it quickly. Judas knowyng himselfe giltye, dyd onelye vnderstande that saiyng: none of the reste that sate at the table, perceiued wherefore Jesus had spoken this. For as goodnesse is nothyng mistrustfull, none of them coulde suspecte this, that he, to whome Jesus had shewed so manye tokens of loue, whome he semed in a manner to preferre before ẏ reste, in that he had the kepyng of his moneye, who also sate righte nere vnto hym, in that feaste, to whome euen nowe our Lorde gaue a dypped soppe: no man (I saye) dyd mistruste that he durste enterprise so haynous a dede, as to betraye hym to death. And whereas Jesus had saide, the thyng which thou dooeste, dooe it quickelye, some, because they knewe Judas kepte the purse, dyd take it, that the Lord had admonished hym to bye some such thinges as should be nedeful to the solemnisacion of that feastful day, or that he should distribute somewhat to the poore.

That he shoulde geue some what to ẏ poore.

For Jesus was often wounte to commaunde hym to doe this, thereby instructyng and prouokyng vs to be liberall to poore folke. When Judas hadde receiued the soppe, and made as thoughe he hadde not vnderstande the Lordes saiyng, he went furthewith out of the parlour, where they supped. For it becamenot hym to be any longer presente in the coumpany of holy folkes, whiche had geuen hymselfe to the deuil, and shewed hymselfe to Jesus so often vncurable. And it was nyght, a tyme betokenyng his mynde that was blynded

with

with the darkenesse of couetise, whiche shoulde withdrawe hymselfe from the lyght and make suche haste to doe the worke of the prince of darkenes, that not so muche as the vndue season of tyme coulde moue hym to delaye his purposed wicked dede. He lacked no euyll will before, but then Jesus hadde geuen hym no power, to the intente that here also it myght bee euidently perceiued, how that no man coulde preuaile any thyng agaynste hym excepte he woulde geue licence to his vngracious wyll, to accomplishe in dede that thyng whiche he had determined in his mynde.

¶ Therefore when he was gone out, Jesus saied: Nowe is the sonne of man glorified, and God is glorified by him. If God bee glorified by him, God shall also glorifie him by himselfe, and shall streightwaye glorifie him. Litle chyldren, yet a litle while am I with you, ye shall seke me, as I saied vnto the Jewes, whither I go thither can ye not cumme, Also to you I saie nowe, a newe commaundemente geue I vnto you, that ye loue together as I haue loued you, that euen so ye loue one an other. By this shall all men knowe that ye are my disciples, yf ye haue loue one to an other. The texte.

When he therfore was departed whiche had made hymselfe vnwoorthye to bee in coumpanye, Jesus beganne to speake manye thynges to his disciples, whiche should partely coumforte and stablishe them, and partly arme them against the storme that was at hande, vtterlye printyng in theyr myndes those thynges, whiche at the fyrste beyng ignoraunt, and afterwarde dulled with sorowe and sleape, they coulde not fully perceiue, but yet they shoulde afterward vnderstande the same. And fyrste of all he shewed his death to be at hand, which although in the iudgemente of the worlde, it shoulde seme full of reproche, yet should it set furth both his fathers glorye and his owne. Nowe (sayeth he) this thyng is specially in hande, for the whiche ye haue hearde me praye: For nowe the tyme is come that the soonne of manne whiche hath semed hytherto poore, and as an abiecte, shoulde after a newe sorte, become notable among men: and that his fathers glorye shoulde likewise be set foorth by him. For as he sought not his owne glory, but thorowe his infirmitie sette forth his fathers glorye: so in lyke manier the father (which is the true fountayne of all true glory) shall glorifye his soonne before men, not by Aungels, nor Archaungels, nor yet anye other creature, but by hymselfe, declaryng to the worlde howe the fathers and the sonnes glorye is all one, to the entente menne so maye knowe on euerye syde theyr mutuall woorkes, not that they canne wynne any thyng by it, but that men by knowyng the glory of them bothe, myght obteine true glorye. In tyme to come, verily he shall throughly glorifie his sonne in his laste cumming before all the company of heauen, and in the meane whyle also, he shall furth with glorifie hym by his owne death (whiche shall bee of more force them al mans power) and anone after by his resurreccion and ascencion. Wherfore my children let not my death discoumforte you, whiche although it seme to come for wante of strength, yet shall it bee of more power then my lyfe.

Though it shall seme to be shamefull and vyle, yet shall it sette foorth bothe my glory and my fathers: yea and though it shall seme an vtter abolishyng of me, yet shall it bryng saluacion, bothe to you and to the whole worlde: lette these thynges comforte the heauinesse of your myndes. For it is expedient for you that this mortall bodye of myne bee withdrawen from your syght, and nowe the tyme is euen at hand for it to bee dooen. In the meane whyle vse my coum-

parte as one that shall goe shortelye from you, and printe well in your hertes those thynges that I commaunde you, or els as I haue tolde the Jewes, ye shall seke mem vayne when I am gone hence. For within a while I goe away, and that to suche a place whither at this tyme ye cannot folowe me. Therefore nowe there is no more to do, but take my departure paciently, and fasten well in your myndes, both my doctrine and the remembraunce of me. This is the thyng that shall make you happye rather then the syghte of this mortall bodye.

A new commaundement geue I vnto you, that ye loue together:

There bee many precepres of Moses lawe: I nowe at my departure commaunde you one, and that a newe precepte, that lyke as I haue loued you, so one of you loue an other: I haue vsed no tyranny againste you, I haue not coueted praise, or lucre, nor haue gotten any worldelye commoditie by you. I haue loued youre welthe, yea and that freelye, and I haue loued you euen vnto the death, for I will willingly bestowe this life for you. In like manner loue you one an other. Other mens disciples are knowen by their names, apparel, and by the obseruing of certaine ordinaunces of menne: ye haue learned none of these thinges. By this onely signe menne shall knowe that ye bee my verie disciples in dede, if ye haue suche mutuall loue among youre selues, as I haue effectuously shewed to you all: this is a rare thing among menne, but yet is it the fruite whereby the good tree is knowen.

The texte.

¶ Simon Peter saied vnto him: Lorde whither goest thou? Jesus aunswered him: Whither I goe thou canste not folowe me nowe, but thou shalte folowe me afterwardes. Peter saied vnto him: Lorde why cannot I folowe the nowe? I will ieoperde my life for thy sake. Jesus aunswered him: Wilte thou ieoperde thy life for my sake? Verely verely I saye vnto thee: the cocke shall not crowe till thou haue denied me thrise.

Peter whiche was all set on fier with the loue of his maister (althoughe he tooke his death grieuously,) yet because he hadde said vnto him, go after me Satan, he durste no more moue and moleste him, concerning that matter, but this thing troubled Peters minde, who loued him so well, that he coulde haue no leaue to folowe him, when he shoulde departe from his frendes. For it is a great comforte if a manne loue one vnfainedlye, to folowe him in all chaunces wheresoeuer he shall become. Therefore Peter asketh: Lorde whether goest thou that I maie not folowe thee? To this Jesus aunswereth: Thou maiest not presentely folow me thither as I goe, but hereafter thou shalte. Peter not vnderstanding as yet to what purpose Jesus spake these woordes, wheras he mente it of his owne deathe, whiche they were not yet apte to beare well: Lorde (saieth he) why maie not I folowe thee? what perilles woulde I refuse for thee, whiche am readie to die for thee? His loue beeing verai earnest in dede, neuerthelesse as yet but worldly, nor throughlye knowen to himselfe, caused hym thus to speake beyonde his power. Jesus therefore to thentent he would frame his successoure litle by litle, and vtterly pull out of his disciples mindes confidence in mannes power, like as before he hadde somewhat remoued and put backe thesame, at suche time as Peter didde boldelye aduise him not to die, and againe he rebuked the saied Peter, when he had rashelye caste himselfe into the water, and furthwith beganne to doubte: yea and but a while a gooe also he was controlled, for so muche as when he woulde not haue obeyed hym at suche time as he wente aboute to washe his feete: euen so nowe he is taught not to truste in his owne strength, nor credite hys owne affeccions, but distrustyng hymself, to depende vpon the helpe of Christe: what saieste thou Peter (sayeth Jesus) howe stoute thynges of thy selfe doest thou promise vs to doe?

wylte

wilte thou bestowe thy life for me? nay but veray experience shall teache thee howe true the saying is whiche I speake euen nowe, and coulde not bee beleued of thee (that is to saye) whither I goe thou canste not folowe me, the profe therof is at hande. For this be thou well assured of, that this nyght before the cocke shall crowe (that is to saye, at the firste cocke crowyng) thou shalte haue denied me thrise: muche lesse shalte thou bee hable to saue my lyfe with thyne. With these woordes our Lorde did restrayne Peters stoute saying, although it came of great loue, and therewithal warned other, that in perylles they shoulde not truste in theyr owne strengthe: but whensoeuer they broughte to passe any suche thyng, they should knowelege it to come of the power & gyfte of God. At these thynges Peter helde his peace, as one that was not yet all free from carefulnesse, concernyng the betraying whiche Jesus had made mencion of.

Before the cocke crow &c.

¶ The.xiiii.Chapter.

¶ And he saied unto his disciples: let not your herte be troubled, ye beleue in God, beleue also in me. In my fathers house are many mansions. If it wer not so I would haue tolde you. I goe to prepare a place for you. And yf I go to prepare a place for you, I wyll come againe and receiue you euen unto my selfe, that where I am, there may ye bee also, and whither I goe ye knowe, and the way ye knowe.

The texte.

When as at this saying (whiche sygnifyed that a certayne straunge and outragious tempeste was imminente and hanged ouer theim, whiche storme shoulde also driue Peter that was moste manerly, to so greate errour, that he shoulde thrise the same nyghte denye the Lorde) when as (I say) the disciples were therewith stricken, euen to the hertes, and after Peters exaumple euerye one stood in dreade of himselfe, Jesus beeyng a maister of moste gentlenes, dyd with moste fayre and pleasaunt wordes comforte his troubled and sorowfull disciples, saiyng: All these thynges shall be doubtles whiche I haue tolde you of beforehande. But yet there is no cause why ye should therewith be herteless or dismayed, cruell thynges shall bee dooen againste me, and the lyke shall after be dooen againste you, nor I am not ignoraunte howe greate the infirmitie of mans nature is. But notwithstanding, if you will put youre whole affyaunce in God and me, ye shall not neede to feare anye violence of wicked men: God is almighty, and he alone maye doe more than all they that fearcelye stryuen againste us. And verilye euen by Moyses lawe you truste to hym, and in case ye do truely truste to hym, it also behoueth you to trust to me. I through him, and you through me, shal haue victory, yf distrustyng your owne proper ayde & defenses, ye wyll fyxe all youre affiaunce and hope upon me. Nor deathe it selfe shall be able to dysceuer us: lyke as ye shall at a tyme bee partakers of afflictions, so shall you bee of croune and glorye. I wyll fyrste shewe the waye and exaumple howe to fyghte and to gette victorye, by me shall boldnes bee geuen unto you, and felowshyppe of glorye. Onely trust unto me. Nowe than:

In my fathers house be many dwellynges readye for them that haue vertorye: for neyther are rewardes prepared for me alone, neyther shall Peter alone folowe me, but all those that cleaueth vnto me by charitie and fayth of the ghospel, shall bee recompensed seuerallye, and haue euerye one his rewarde prepared for hym. For vnlesse I knewe certaynly that dwellyng places were alreadye prepared for you, which are to receiue you that shall in a whyle bee taken oute of the hurly burly of this worlde into the felicitie of euerlastyng lyfe, I woulde nowe beforehande haue admonished you. That I doe therefore goe before to my father, is to thentente I maye there prepare a place for you also, whome I wyll not suffre to be dissociate from me.

In my fathers house bee manye mansions. &c.

And nowe because I knowe it to be certayne, that in my fathers kyngdome euery manne hath his mansion in a readinesse for hym: you haue no neede to bee carefull of beyng recompensed, it onelye lyeth you vpon hande to fyght manfully. And though I dyd go farre awaye to prepare a place for you, yet is there no cause for all that why ye shoulde in the meane while thynke your selfe succourlesse, for I shall come agayne vnto you for to receyue you wholye vnto me, neuer after to departe from me. For than wheresoeuer I am, there shall you also bee: there is no matter why to distruste your cummyng thyther where as I nowe goe to before you, and in very dede ye do knowe whither I do go, and the waye thyther. By this darke parable our Lorde dyd geue them some littell knowledge that he shoulde go to his father, but none other wyse than by death of the crosse. The thyng that was gone to, was worthye to be desired and well liked, but the way to it was thought worthy to be misliked and not to be beloued. The disciples coulde not but knowe this, hearyng the Lorde so often speakyng thereof, but pensifenes and obliuiousnesse made theym ignoraunte in the thyng that they knewe.

The texte.

Thomas saieth vnto him: Lord we knowe not whether thou goest. And howe is it possible for vs to know the waie? Jesus saieth vnto him: I am the waie, and the trueth, and the life. No man cummeth vnto the father, but by me. If ye had knowen me, ye hadde knowen my father also, and nowe ye knowe him, and haue seen him.

And so therfore Thomas being very desirouse to knowe certainely whyther our Lorde woulde goe, sayeth: Lorde when we knowe not whether thou goest, how can we knowe the waye thither? but rather where thou sayeste we knowe both, we be in dede ignoraunte in both: with this blunte (althoughe vehemente) saiyng, Thomas dyd in a maner force oure Lorde to tell more playnely, whyther he woulde goe thence: whiche thyng all they dydde (for a space) euen long to knowe. Of trueth Jesus enstructyng, framyng, and fashyoning his, litle by litle, doeth in dede teache the thyng that they wishe to knowe: but he doeth it as yet couertly, to thentente that the thing might more depely be fixed in their mindes, whiche they shoulde haue muche a doe, and long tyme, to learne. That is to saye, that after he hadde lefte his mortalitie, he shoulde retourne agayne to his father, from whence he came before he was incarnate: but withall he teacheth that the waye vnto the father, is open vnto no manne, but by the sonne, whiche onelye shoulde open the waye to heauen, whiche onely shoulde instructe mennes fayth with heauenly knowledge, and shoulde bee the onelye fountayne of immortalitie: to whome whosoeuer dydde firmely sticke, the same shoulde bee

without

without feare of death: Thomas (sayeth he) howe happeneth this, that thou deniest the to knowe the waye, vnlesse thou as yet (percase) knowest me not at all? For verely I am the way, the truth & life. I sayed euen nowe yͭ I doe goe agayne to my father, and onely do open for all folke the way vnto hym: and because he is come to by dedes fit and semyng for god, ye haue the proufe of good life in me: and also because no man without me cummeth to the father, ye haue learned of me the truth. And yf the feare of death do in the meane tyme trouble youre myndes, knowe well that ye bee sure of immortalitye, forasmuche as I am lyfe: dooe ye onelye folowe thyther as I goe beefore, beleue and kepe in minde that whiche I haue taughte you, hope assuredly for the thyng which I promise. If ye aske whither I goe, I goe to my father, yf ye desyre to knowe the waye whereby ye maye come thither, I say to you, no man cummeth to the father but by me: wherefore you knowe bothe aswell whyther I dooe goe, as what waye the iourneye lyeth, excepte (paraduenture) ye bee vtterlye ignoraunte who I am: verely yf ye hadde knowen me, ye hadde also knowen my father, yea (to say trueth) ye haue already some waye knowen my father, whome ye thynke to bee vnknowen vnto you, nor ye haue not onelye knowen hym by the determinacion of the lawe, but ye haue also seen hym doubtlesse. Our Lord Jesus dyd with this obscure saiyng sumdeale aduertise his disciples, that hys father, of trueth, was inuisible, and not onely inuisible to the bodilye iyes: but also that the mynde of it owne propre nature coulde not see and perceiue what he is, yet notwithstanding but that he had beene seene after a sorte in his sonne, as whyle they see hym in his soonne rewlyng the wyndes and the sea, forcyng deuils to obeye, putting awaie with a woorde sicknesses and diseases, were they neuer so incurable, and with a woorde raysing the deade to life. But the vnlearned Apostles didde not as yet vnderstande these hye misteries, and yet for all that euen as though they had in very dede vnderstand that which the Lorde spake vnto them, they euen leap and skip of greate affeccion to see the father: Imaginyng that the father mighte bee seene in suche sorte as they sawe his sonne, such was there simplicitie as yet: albeit neyther sawe they the sonne throughly, whiche behelde hym with bodily iyes alone.

I am the waye yͭ truth and life

No manne cummeth to the father but by me. &c.

¶ Philip saieth vnto him: lord shewe vs the father, and it suffiseth vs. Jesus saieth vnto him: haue I been so long time with you, and yet hast thou not knowen me? Philip, he that hath sene me, hath seen my father. And howe saiest thou than, shewe vs the father? beleuest thou not that I am in the father, and the father in me? The wordes that I speake vnto you, I speake not of my selfe, but the father that dwelleth in me is he that dooeth the workes. beleue me that I am in the father, and the father in me. Or els beleue me for the workes sake

The texte.

Philip therfore, beyng more desirous to learne then the reste, speaketh thus: lorde (ꝙ he) thou tellest vs that the father is seene of vs, but woulde God thou wouldest graunte that it myghte bee lawfull for vs to see and looke vpon thy father: then were oure desyres satisfyed, and we woulde wishe no more, nor desire ought els. In deede we haue hearde muche speakyng of him, we lacke onely the sight of hym. Our lorde doth controull and correct Philips request, that was so very rude and foolishe, saiyng: Philip, haue I been so long tyme wyth the, and yet thou knowest me not? It is not the syght of my face that thou knowest me by, but the ryght vnderstandyng of my power, vertue, and trueth, maketh the to knowe me.

This my mighty trueth and true power, is not seen with bodilye iyes, but the minde and soule seeth it. Therefore when as I am the verye Image of my father, in all thynges lyke vnto hym, and that by my deedes and woordes thou oughtest already to haue knowen me, (and verilye to haue knowen is to haue seen) howe dareste thou bee so bolde, with what countenaunce sayeste thou to me, shewe vs the father? as though he that hath seene me hath not seene my father. I meane not that my father is none other than I, but that betwene vs two is no vnlikenes, or any thyng vncommon as touchyng the higher and our diuyne nature. In case thou canste not vnderstande what I saye by naturall reason, he seeth also (I tel you) that beleueth. Thou hast heard me speake, thou hast seen me do myracles, and therein surely thou haste seen and heard of my father: doest thou not yet beleue that by an inseparable copulacion of nature, wil, and power, my father is in me, and I in my father?

He yͭ hath seen me, hath seen yͤ father.

What thing soeuer I speake, I speake it of his mynde: what thyng soeuer I dooe, I dooe it after his mynde: I am therefore alwaye in hym (by reason of suche a coniunccion of nature and wyll, as cannot be vnioyned and disseuered) and he alwaye in me, speakyng by me: and by me declaryng with miracles, his power. Neyther doe I speake any thing of my selfe, whiche same thing he speaketh not by me: neither dooe I any thing of my selfe, whiche he by me ioyntelye, doeth not worke: howe therefore doest thou separate them that be inseparable? and with seueral sight desireste to see them seuerally? beleueste thou that the one being knowen, the other can be vnknowen? doth the reste of you also yet not beleue yͭ al thynges cummeth of my father which are spoken and doen by me? and that there is no separacion betwixt vs two? It had behoued you to haue credited me, so oft teachyng this thing: and if ye mistrusted my woordes, yet truely the diuine woorkes and deedes surmounting mannes power, oughte to haue caused you to beleue, that what thing soeuer procedeth frō me, is of my father: yf my father himselfe should speake vnto you, he would speake none other thing than I doe: or if he would worke by himself, he would worke none other thing than I do worke: we haue one minde, one will, one power and nature.

The texte, Verely, verely, I saie vnto you: he that beleueth on me, the worke that I doe, the same shall he do also: and greater workes then these shall he do, because I goe vnto my father. And whatsoeuer ye aske in my name, that will I dooe: that the father maie bee glorified by the sonne, If ye shall aske any thing in my name, I wil dooe it. If ye loue me, kepe my commaundementes. And I wil pray the father, and he shal geue you an other coumforter, that he maye bide with you for euer, euen the spirite of trueth, whom the world cannot receiue, because the world seeth him not, neyther knoweth him: but you knowe him, for he dwelleth with you, and shalbe in you.

Therefore beleue this, retaine this, haue this surely fixte in youre hertes: whiche thyng yf you doe in dede, the withdrawyng of the syghte of this bodye, shalbee no harme vnto you: ye shall better see me beeyng absente with the iyes of faythe: and the same thing whiche ye nowe see my father dooe by me, whiche doe faste cleaue vnto him all manner of wayes, shall I dooe by you, if you will cleaue to me by fayth and charitie: yea and I shall also more euidently extende foorth the mightie power of my godheade, after that I shall remoue awaye from you this my manhead: yea and moreouer whoso euer dooeth ioyne himselfe to me by true christen fayth (like as I am naturally alwaie ioyned, and neuer disseuered from the company of my father) the same persone shall also dooe

greater

greater thynges, than I doe, so often as the glorye of God requireth a miracle. For as my father worketh nowe by me, so shall I worke by you.

And because it is so expediente for the saluacion of manne that I doe goe againe to my father, ye shall succede me, and by course enter into my roume concernyng the ministracion of the ghospell. Nor this thyng shal onelye bee doen, but what thing soeuer elles ye shall aske of my father in my name, whiche shal appertayne vnto the prayse and glorye of my fathers name and myne, that same shall I doe: to the ende that by you also I maie bee glorified emong men, as my father hath beene hitherto glorified by his soonne. Let not my departure therefore trouble you, whiche shall tourne to your greate commoditie and prefermente. Than moste of all shall I bee youre ayde in al affayres and purposes, whiche make for true health, when as I shall take awaye from you this sielye body. Onely aske the thing that you couete, my father shall heare your desires, and I beeing a continuall presente aduocate vnto him, will bring to passe that what soeuer ye shall aske, shall bee obteined: for as he denieth me nothing, whiche dooe no manner of thing that redoundeth not to his glorye: so will I denye you nothyng, so long as ye doe that whiche shall setforth the honoure of my naime: Forsooth my spirite shall put into your myndes what you ought to aske. Thus to be greued with my going hence, is no proufe of christen charitie, for so men are dismaied when a frende remoueth whome they shall soone after forget. If ye loue me truely, as I dooe loue my father, declare your charitie towardes me in very dede: ye shall soothly and certainelye declare it, if ye dooe kepe my commaundementes. So shall it come to passe, that as my father loueth me and denieth me nothyng: In like wise shall he also loue you, obeying my preceptes, whiche be the veray commaundementes of my father. Thus it is nedefull for the saluacion of the worlde, that I doe absente my selfe from you.

What soeuer ye aske in my name.

And yet going awaie I wyll not leaue you desolate, and altogether without coumforte. But rather if ye abide firmelie in my loue, and kepe my commaundementes, I shall obteine of my father by praier after my returne againe vnto him, that he which denieth me nothing, shall sende you an other coumforter: whiche after he be once sente, shall not goe awaie from you, as I nowe do, concerning this manner of corporall presence. I am pulled awaie from you, but he shall continue with you for euer. He shall bee the spirite of me, and my father, whiche shall make you of carnall folke spirituall: and he shall tourne this worldelye affeccion whiche ye nowe beare towardes me, into an heauenlye loue: he shall also with secrete inspiracions, putte in you the treweth of all thinges, whiche ye nowe vnderstande as it were but by a dreame and throughe a cloude. This speciall pledge of me shall bee peculiar and propre vnto you. For I haue all this while exhibite my selfe generallye and in common to euill and good: leste anye mighte make excuse that he was not inuited to saluacion. But this worlde whiche coueteth muche, and gapeth for goodes that bee of the worlde, and deceitfull, cannot receiue that spirite, beecause he is heauenlye and true. And why can it not? because it hath grosse iyes, whiche deliteth and loueth not but grosse and earthlye thynges, it seethe not hym nor knoweth hym: for he withoute noyse beyng all whisshed and still, casteth in hymselfe to the secrete senses of the mynde, if he fynde anye where a conueniente place to reste in. But truelye you, in case that the delusions and deceytfull thynges of this worlde beeyng despysed, ye wyll folowe thynges that be good in dede, and liue well: you (I saie) shall then knowe hym, because he will not onely come vnto you, as I am come, one that may bee seen, but he shal also abyde continually with you: nor he shall not in suche sorte be conuersaunte emong you as the aduocate is with his client, but he shall inhabyte hymselfe in the secrete inner partes of your soules, and shall ioyne hymselfe as it were glued to your spirite, that he maye become one spirite in all folkes: and because he shalbe as it were bred and planted in your hertes, he shal accumpany and assist you in all thynges, and the meane tyme shall not bee long ere this coumforter that shalbe in the steade of me, and my vicegerente, shall come vnto you. Wherefore there is no cause why your hertes should be discoumforted or afeard, good children, whom I haue perfeitly begotten, and sumwhat framed with the heauenly doctryne of gods woorde, and do nourische you beeyng as yet but vnperfite, and not fully taught vntill ye growe vnto the strength of the ghospell.

¶ I will not leaue you coumfortlesse, but will come to you: yet a litle while, and the world seeth me no more, but ye see me. For I liue and ye shall liue. That daye shall ye knowe that I am in my father and you in me, and I in you. He that hathe my commaundementes & kepeth the, the same is he that loueth me. And he that loueth me shalbe loued of my father, and I will loue him and will shewe mine own selfe to him.

The texte.

Although I goe hence for a tyme, and shal no longer liue a manne with men, yet wyl I not leaue you in the meane tyme fatherlesse, and without comfortable succoure at my hande: for I will cumme to you agayne, before I returne to my father: and I wyll shewe my selfe before your iyes, and bee seene of you with a very bodye in dede, but than not mortal, to the entente that I maye aduaunce and bryng you from loue of the fleshe, to the spirite: for it were no great matter yf I should geue this my bodye to you alwaye to looke thereupon, because euen the wicked dooe also beholde it to theyr damnacion: within a whyle therfore I shal be out of the worldes syghte: for death and the graue shall take me a waye frō the syght of worldly folkes. Neuerthelesse I wyll see you again, and presente my selfe vnto you aliue, for this kynde of deathe shall not alienate vs in sundre, nor kepe me out of youre syghte, for I shall liue agayne, yea after that I bee deade: and I shall not onelye liue, but therewithall bryng to you lyfe euerlastyng: and notwithstandyng the tyme of myne absence, I beeyng aliue shall fynde you aliue, and I will so spende my life for you, that you shall be in health and safegarde. Then shall you vnderstande more fully, that as nothyng can pull my father from me, nor me from my father: so am I bothe to you and you agayne to me, ioyned by mutuall charitie together, that death can not disioyne vs: let your onely care be, that by youre owne faulte ye bee not vncoupled and let lewse. The obseruyng of my commaundementes shal trye true charytie: nor he loueth not in herte, that neglecteth the preceptes of his Lorde. It is not sufficiente to haue accepted my commaundementes, vnlesse a manne retayne them in mynde. Nor it is not inoughe to remembre theym, excepte they bee kept: he that doth accomplische and kepe these, is he that truelye loueth me. For to bee tormented in mynde for my departure, is no proufe of veraye trewe loue. I that truely do loue my father: do kepe all his commaundementes, and will kepe theym vnto death of the crosse. And there is no cause why my commaundementes of sufferyng iniurye pacientelye, of bearyng the crosse quietely, shoulde muche putte you in feare, as seuere and grieuous commaundementes: and why? for charitie shall sweten and make them all easie, and there shall not

lacke

lacke coumforte at my hande, for surely whoso loueth me, he shalbe bothe loued of my father, and I also wyll loue hym, and neuer leaue him succourlesse, but will see hym againe, and will openlye shewe my selfe vnto hym to bee looked vpon: to make it more certain that I doe not vtterly perishe by suffryng deathe of the crosse. Nowe I geue my selfe to bee seen of all folke, but than no manne shall see me, excepte he abyde constantly in frendeshyppe. Of trueth our Lorde Jesus spake these thynges sum what darkelye, not onely signifiyng that he beeyng reuiued agayne would often after his death come among his frendes to bee seen, but that he would also by the holy ghoste his spirite, secretely place and wynde himselfe into theyr myndes, and that finally he woulde come in the glorye of his father, in the open sight of all folke.

¶ Judas saieth vnto him, not Judas Iscarioth: lorde what is done that thou wilt shewe thy selfe vnto vs and not vnto the worlde? Jesus aunswered and said: if a manne loue me he will kepe my saiynges, and my father will loue him, and we will come vnto hym and dwell with him. He that loueth me not, kepeth not my sayinges. And the worde which ye heare is not mine, but the fathers whiche sent me. These thinges haue I spoken vnto you beyng yet present with you, but the comforter whiche is the holy ghost whome my father will send in my name, he shall teache you al thinges, and bring al thinges to your remembraunce, whatsoeuer I haue sayed vnto you. Peace I leaue with you: my peace I geue vnto you. Not as the worlde geueth geue I vnto you. Let not your hertes be greued, neyther feare: ye haue hearde how I sayd vnto you. I goe and I come againe vnto you: If ye loued me, ye woulde verily reioyce because I sayd: I goe vnto the father. For the father, is greater than I. The texte.

Now than where as Judas, not he verely that is called Iscarioth which was absente at this sermon, but the other Judas whose surname was Lebbeus, did not fully vnderstande our lordes saiyng: but beyng throughe sorowe and feare very sore troubled, dyd suppose that our Lorde shoulde in suche wyse appeare to his frendes, as terrible spirites & phantastical sightes, shewe themselfes many tymes in the darkenesse of the nyght: or as certain visions appeare in dreames rather to the feare of men, then to mennes coumforte. This Judas therfore, saith: Lorde what hath chaunced that when now thou maieste be seen of all folke, thou shalte not than appeare to the worlde, but onely to vs?

And howe canste thou be one that maye be seen of vs, yf thou be such one as other cannot see? But Jesus because he knewe that his disciples were not yet able to vnderstande the misterie howe that the same bodye, whiche hadde been deade and buried, but nowe made spirituall, and hable to dooe as it lyste, shoulde ryse agayne: Jesus I saye, knowyng this, dyd not playnely answere to the thyng that was asked, but turned his saiyng to that thyng whiche was more necessarye to bee imprinted in theyr heartes, whereby they shoulde nowe bee prepared spirituallye to haue his presence: for as muche as that presence whiche shoulde bee exhibited vnto theim after his resurreccion, coulde not long endure with theim. Therefore Jesus sayed: I will not presente my selfe to the worlde, because it loueth me not, neyther dothe it kepe my commaundementes. If one loue me truely, he wyll not testifie his loue with sorowe, but by kepyng my commaundementes, and hym wyll I loue semblablye: and whome I shall loue, hym wyll my father loue, and we shall neuer bee pulled awaye from hym: nor I wyll not onelye see hym agayne that hath my commaundementes in remembraunce, but therewithall my father and I wyll by the spirite, whiche is common to vs both, come vnto hym: and we will not only come, forthwith to departe againe, but we will dwell with him, and neuer go a way from him. That which is doen after the spirite is both perpetuall and effectuall: bodilye ioynyng together muste nedes haue an ende, euen for because ye shoulde sette at naught transitorye thynges, and inure your selfes to loue eternall thinges: and where ye as yet cannot come to vs, we will come to you inuisible, but effectually to dwell in the temple of your hertes. We be three in deede, but so ioyned and conuerte together, that he whiche loueth one, muste loue all: and he that hath one of vs lacketh none of vs. Only on your behalfe let charitie be presente, and that couenaunte kepte, whiche I made with you of late. That shal so couple you and vs together, that neyther life nor deathe can vncouple vs. If membres maie bee disseuered from the heade, we maie be disseuered. There bee many whiche boaste themselfes to loue God the father, and seme to obserue the commaundementes of the lawe, but none dooeth truelye loue God, yf he hate and contemne his sonne: and he verelye contemneth the soonne, who soeuer kepeth not my commaundemente, who soeuer neglecteth my preceptes, he neglecteth withall the preceptes of God: for in good sooth the thyng that I haue taught you, is not so my peculiar doctrine that the same is not my fathers: but is rather my fathers than myne, from whome cummeth whatsoeuer I can or doe teache, doyng nothyng but by his autoritie, from whom I was sente into the worlde, to teache these matters whiche I dooe teache. But nowe these thynges haue I spoken accordyng to youre capacitie, as yet a mortall manne, beeyng conuersaunte among mortall menne: soone hereafter I wyll repayre to see you againe, for certayne dayes space: and beeyng immortall, wyll kepe cumpany with menne mortall, to the entente I maye coumforte, teache, and geue you my counsell.

Neyther is it vnawares to me, that ye shal not fully vnderstande these thinges, whiche I nowe speake, and shall speake anone after my deathe, because ye be yet styll carnall and rude: notwithstandyng they are not spoken all in vayne, for after that I shall take away this body from you: an other comforter shall come to you, yf ye aske hym (of God) in my name: a comforter (I saye) not bodily as ye se me to to be, but that holy spirite which doeth sanctify spirites and mindes, whome my father shall sende you in my roume yf you require hym in my name. Ye shall not after this neede my corporall presence, whiche for a season was geuen in consideracion of mens grossenes, to the entente that they myght by degrees and orderlye go forwarde to more perfeite thynges, for that spirite, in asmuche as he is myne and my fathers, shall putte you in remembraunce of all the thynges, whiche I nowe speake vnto you that bee as yet ignoraunte, and of small capacitie: and besides that obliuious. And he also shall make you vnderstande these thynges whiche ye hadde not vnderstande before, neyther will he suffre you to forget anye thyng or to lacke knowelege of anye thing that perteineth to saluacion. Of menne obliuious he shall make you of good remembraunce, of slowe witted, easie to bee taughte, of sleapishe sluggardes, vigilante and watchefull, of sorowfull men cherefull, of yearthly folke heauenly. Onelye perseuer you in charitie, hauing in remembraunce my commaundementes.

There is no cause why that ye shoulde in the meane while feare the troublesumnesse of this worlde, whiche ye shall see ryse agaynste me, and in tyme to come againste you also: let it suffise you that at my departure, I shall leaue

peace

peace vnto you, and geue you my peace. No worldelye storme can destroye and vndoe hym that hath my peace . The worlde also hath his kynde of peace whiche it besto weth vpon them whome it loueth , but this is a peace not to be trusted on. My peace whiche I doe geue you, doeth make frendeshyppe betwene God and you: and who can hurte hym whiche hath God his protectour and gouernour: The peace whiche I do leaue vnto you ioynyng you together among your selfes by mutuall concord, shall make your felowship strong and inuincible, agaynst all that the worlde or Satan, prince of the world, can doe. What meaneth it than that my goyng hence, whiche shall bee veray commodious vnto you, doth so muche feare you: Let not your hertes therefore bee troubled nor stricken in feare, ye haue heard me saye alreadye, and (that ye shoulde the more credite me) I eftsones tell you, that of trueth I goe hence. for a tyme: but I wyll anone returne againe vnto you . And in the meane tyme I will bryng to effecte that I shall fynde you at my returne safe and in health. This blusterous storme of cruell persecucion shall for this one tyme be executed vpon me onelye. And soone after I am come againe to my father, I wyll bee presente with you agayne throughe the spirite that is the comforter. And by hym my father shall also bee with you, and we shall neuer bee separate from you, vntyll you be fully placed with vs in the kyngdome of heauen. Ye are sorowfull because I goe my waye, but & if ye did rightly loue me, forsooth ye woulde reioyce, both for your owne sake and mine: for I wyll not playe the runagate and gooe euerye where, but I will returne agayne to my father to obteyne for you more excellent giftes at his hand, for because my father is greatter then I am: and from him it commeth, what thyng soeuer I doe departe with you. If ye stande in dread of any harme to wardes me, and are sorowefull for my cause, it were more semyng ye should be ioyfull on my behalfe, that am remoued and taken a waye from these euils of the world, and goe to my fathers coumpany: and yf ye be sory for your selfes, my departure shall bring to you muche profite.

Peace I leaue vnto you.

And nowe haue I shewed you before it come, that when it is come to passe, ye might beleue. Hereafter will I not talke many woordes with you: for the prince of this worlde cummeth and hath nothing in me. But that the world may know that I loue the father, and as the father gaue me commaundemente, euen so doe I. Arise leate vs goe hence.

The texte.

I knowe that I speake this to them that neyther greatlye take hede, nor vnderstande the same, but I do therefore repete, and often inculcate and bryng in the same, that after the dede shal effectuously verifie ye thing that I haue spoken, ye may than therewith beleue all the rest to be true, which I haue tolde aforehande shoulde folowe: after this I beyng a mortall man shall not speake many thynges with the that be mortall: for the time is at hande when I shalbe taken away from you in body. Verye Satan the prynce of this worlde is presente by his minysters ready to set vpon me, with his full myght & force vtterlye to caste awaye and to extinguishe me. But at his hande is no ieopardie, for he hath no right nor autoritie ouer me , and when he moste trusteth to haue the ouerhande and victorye, than shall he bee vanquished and ouerthrowen: he hath no ryghte but vpon theim whiche bee in synne, and because the worlde is in bondage to synne, he maye playe the tyraunte ouer them that make the worlde theyr God: for in dede I am neyther forced to dye, nor for any faulte do I dye, but I suffre, throughe my deathe to redeme those that bee ioyned to me by faythe, as

The prince of this worlde cummeth & hath nothing in me.

membres

membres to the bodye, from the tyrannye of sinne and deathe : and my father hath commaunded me thus to doe, whiche his commaundemente I dooe accordyng to his minde: wherefore we haue nowe already sitte here long inough. Because I doe my fathers commaundemente willingly, it is tyme to goe mete death, whiche is at hande. Arise therefore and goe we hence. Our Lorde Jesus seeyng his disciples many wayes dismayed, partely with sorowe because that they sawe that theyr Lordes death was nye, whom they loued somewhat worldly, but yet moste vehementelye: partelye for feare of harmes whiche they thoughte did hang ouer hym beeyng once abrode: and he also seeyng them heauye of slepe whiche both the nyght prouoked, and also sorowe of mynde augmented, and theyr sittyng made theym of more sluggishe mynde: he commaundeth theym to ryse, that so at the least, dulnesse beeyng auoided, they myghte bee made more pregnaunte and quickewitted to those thynges whiche he shoulde saye vnto them, and therewithall he monished thē a farre of, and darkely, that nowe is the tyme to eleuate theyr myndes from yearthly affeccions to heauenly thynges, from bodily thynges to spirituall thynges, from mortall thynges to immortall, from thynges transitorye to eternall thynges, he woulde haue that also imprinted in theyr myndes, that he knewe before, and was willyng to suffre what thyng soeuer he shoulde suffre, his father also willyng the same: from whose wyll his did neuer varye. His will was that his Apostles, so farre as mannes weakenesse coulde beare, should be witnesses and seers of his passion, and therefore in this sermon he maketh oftentymes mencion of his departure, litle by litle, thereby to inure them to sufferaunce, but mixyng withal many coumfortes to mitigate the bitter payne of sorowe, saiyng that in very dede he muste departe: but so that within a while he shoulde come to them agayne: that he should go to his father, that thence he should sende him an other coumforter whiche should finishe that he had begoonne, and also that he and his father ioyntly together, should come and dwell with them. He sayed furthermore that this persecucion shoulde not vtterlye deuour and consume them: and after all this he had them thence to an other place, because the place where they wer than, was open & in syght: and for because that they had hearde that the prynce of the world was euen than presente, they stoode in a generall feare of themself, and therfore he brought them to an other place wheras they wer more in safetie, to thyntente they myght with more bolde hertes geue eare to other thynges.

Arise let vs go hence.

In conclusion he telleth them aforehande, that at the length they shoulde folowe hym thyther, whether he nowe goeth before them: well nowe he hath recourse agayne to that saiyng whiche algates muste sitte inwardely and abyde in theyr heartes: in whiche saiyng he counsaileth them to perseuer in charitye, and obseruyng his commaundementes, leste throughe theyr owne faulte, they shoulde disseuer theymselfes from the felowshippe of the father, the sonne and the holy ghoste, from whiche Judas had already forceably dissociate himselfe. But he aduiseth theym to sticke to theyr couenaunte by obeying the saiynges of theyr Lorde, and to thuttermoste of theyr power to folowe his doynges.

And trueth it is that this coulde not be doen, vnlesse they dyd perseuer in the spirituall felowshippe of the soonne, and yet in the meane tyme not to truste to theimselfes, or any thyng at all to presume vpon theyr owne proper strength, for they shoulde neuer bee able to dooe oughte at anye tyme, but by the benefite and free gyfte of Godde, from whome floweth and issueth oute to all folke, what thyng soeuer setteth forwarde true health, and maketh to saluacion, and that they myght the better vnderstande this, and retaine it in memory, he declareth the matter by a similitude, taken and brought in of a plaine knowen thing, that is the vyne and the braunches thereof.

¶ The.xv.Chapter:

I am the true vine, and my father is the husbande man. Euery braunche that beareth no fruite in me, he will take awaye. And euery braunche that beareth fruite, he wyll pourge that it maie bring foorth more fruite, *The texte,*

To thintent, saieth he, that ye maie vtterly vnderstand how cleane voyde of all perill ye be, yf ye wyll continue stil to be of my felowship, and what great daunger it is for you, yf ye fallyng from the couenaunte that I haue made with you, bee disseuered from me: remembre this that I am the true vyne, ye bee the braunches, and my father is the housbandman. I am the roote or stocke of the vyne, ye are my membres as braunches sprong out of the stocke. My father hath planted me, that is to saye, he hath begotten me. The stocke came foorth from hym, and ye out of the stocke. The thanke of the whole benefite redoundeth to my father, as the fountaine therof, whiche doth geue vnto you by me, and his spirite, whatsoeuer he geueth you. And the sappe of the stocke whiche geueth vnto the braunches both lyfe and strength to bring forth fruite, is the spirite that is common bothe to my father and to me. Lyke as the spirite knitteth me to my father, so doth it also ioyne you to me. Therefore what braunche soeuer cleaueth to me, and liuyng by my spirite, bringeth forth fruite woorthy for the stocke, thesame shall my father purge, cuttyng awaye the superfluous desyres thereof, that it maye bring forth more plenteous and kindly fruite. But whoso cleaueth to me by ye profession of faith, and bringeth foorth no fruite of euangelicall charitie, my father shall cutte him of from the vyne, as a cumberous and vnprofitable membre. For that braunche which hath no fruite, but onely leaues, serueth to no purpose in the vyne.

Nowe are ye cleane through the woordes whiche I haue spoken vnto you: byde in me, and I in you. As the braunche cannot beare fruite of it selfe excepte it bide in the vine: no more can ye excepte ye bide in me. I am the vine, ye are the braunches: he that abydeth in me and I in him, thesame bringeth forth muche fruite. For without me can ye do nothing: if a man bide not in me, he is cast foorthe as a braunche, and is withered: and men gather them and caste them into the fier, and they burne. If ye byde in me, and my wordes abide in you, aske what ye will, and it shalbe doen for you. Herin is my father glorified, that ye beare muche fruite, and becum my disciples. *The texte.*

Now already ye be braunches somewhat purged and made cleane through beleuyng my woorde: but yet ye muste hereafter bee more purged, that ye maye bring forth more plentye of fruit. At this tyme it is inough for you to bee grafted in the stocke, from whence through fayth ye maye receyue life: laboure dilygently to abyde in me, & I will in lyke manner dwelle in you, so long as you depende vpon me. For as the braunche if it be pulled of frō his vine, cannot it selfe bring foorth the fruite, because it taketh all his sap of the stocke: no more can ye bryng forth the fruite of any good worke, excepte ye cleaue to me by faythe and charitie: from whence muste come to you whatsoeuer furthereth to trewe and

eternall

eternall saluacion. Wherefore neyther Moses nor any of the Prophetes is the vyne, but I am the onelye vyne, to the whiche all they muste cleaue that wyll bryng foorth the fruite of saluacion. Ye be the braunches of this vyne, wherein ye are frely grafted, freely pourged, but ye maye fall from thence through your owne faute. Wherefore ye muste earnestely take hede that ye maye bee alwaies ioyned to me. For whosoeuer continueth stil ioyned to me, hauyng me likewyse ioyned to hym, and liuyng by my spirite, that persone throughe my fathers inspiracion, bringeth forth fruite plenteously, gaynyng for himselfe eternall saluacion, and causing God, for whose sake al thinges bee doen, to bee glorified amonges men. And his glorie is my glorie: by whome it hathe pleased him liberally to geue al that he geueth menne, to the atteinyng of eternall saluacion. Therfore remembre this well, that without me ye can doe nothyng that good is. But if anye braunche dooe through his owne faulte pull hymselfe backe againe from me, he not onely bringeth foorth no fruite at all, but like as an vnprofitable braunche, when it is cut of with a shreadyng hooke, withereth, and afterwarde beeyng gathered vp with other twigges that bee shred of, is caste into the fyer to burne: so thesame braunche destitute of my moysture & spirite, dyeth spirituallye althoughe he liue bodilye. And beeyng after this like seperate withoute recouerie from the vyne, is caste into euerlastyng fyer, there to burne for euer to his great tormente: for so muche as he woulde not abyde styll in the vyne, & so bryng forth fruite of eternall felicitie. And ye shall abyde in me, yf my woorde abyde in you, if ye kepe in mynde the thinges whiche ye beleue, and execute in dede that whiche ye remembre. If ye wyll do this, ye neede not feare any worldelye stormes, for thoughe I bee not still presente with you in bodye, yet both my father and I will heare you. And yf ye do rightly aske all such thinges as ye would haue, ye shal obtayne your asking. But like as of your selfes ye are not able to bryng foorth fruite: euen so ye ought not presumptuously to attribute to your selfes the prayse of your good dedes, for as I haue not sought mine owne glorye but my fathers, of whome I haue all my being and power: so shall ye referre all the thanke and commendacion of your good deedes to my father and me. When menne shall perceiue you to bryng foorth muche euangelical fruite, then is my father glorified among theim: for what prayse soeuer I shall gette by you, thesame shall redounde to my fathers glorye: whome ye shall cause to be praysed among menne, by shewyng your selfes the ryght disciples of his sonne, not that we neede worldely praise, but because so it is expedient for the saluacion of mankynde, which thyng we do thriste for and couete. It cummeth of charitie and not of ambicion that my father thus desireth to bee glorified amonges men.

Yf ye byde in me &c, aske what ye wyl and it shall bee geuen you.

The texte

¶ As the father hath loued me, euen so haue I also loued you. Continue ye in my loue: If ye kepe my commaundementes, ye shall byde in my loue euen as I haue kept my fathers commaundementes, and haue byden in his loue. These thinges haue I spoken vnto you, that my ioye might remaine vnto you, and that your ioye might bee full.

I haue loued you whiche are my braunches, euen as my father hath loued me, that am the stocke. Be carefull to kepe this so great a benefite freelye geuen you, lesse ye lease it through your negligence, and ye shall not lease it: Lyke as I alwaies procuring my fathers glorye, haue continewed euen to the death in my loue towardes hym: so will ye perseuer in your loue towardes me.

Wherin

wherin ye shall perseuer not by the obseruing of the Phariseis or phylosophers preceptes, but by keping of my commaundementes: so that neither any flattery or feare of the world may separate you from thē, no more then it doeth me, which do constantly to the death, kepe my fathers commaūdementes, being neuer disseuered frō the loue of hym, but by very deedes declaring my selfe to requite his loue with lyke loue. wherfore as it shall be my fathers glory, to haue so naturall a sonne, and so worthy for hym, no lesse shall it be for both our honours that I may haue you my disciples obseruers of my woordes, and folowers of my doinges. Albeit these things be sumwhat painful & tedious, yet do I therfore vse so long cōmunicacion therin, to thintent that as I haue not labored for the ioye of this worlde, but herein do reioyce that for obeying my fathers cōmaundemēt I am beloued of him, no more should you seke comfort of the worlde, but reioyce in this my kynde of ioye, whensoeuer ye folowing my steppes shall be afflicted: and let that ioy remayne in you euer increasyng into greater, and better, vntill it cum perfitly to the perpetuall felicitie of immortall life. One of you charitably to loue an other, shalbe a great cumforte to you, euen in the myddest of all your troubles, when ye be at the wurste.

¶ This is my commaundemēt, that ye loue together as I haue loued you. Greater loue hath no man than this, that a man bestowe his life for his frendes: ye are my frendes yf ye do what socuer I commaund you. Hence furth call I you not seruauntes, for the seruaunt knoweth not what hys Lorde doth, but you haue I called frendes, for all thynges that I haue heard of my father, haue I opened to you. The texte,

There be diuerse preceptes of the Phariseis, and Moses hath also manye, but this one precept is my very owne whiche includeth all thinges that I do teache, and shall make pleasaunt all aduersities whiche shall happen, that is to say, that ye beare such loue one to an other, as I haue borne towardes you. I doe testifie my loue not with woordes onely, but also with deedes: and that loue not to be after the commune sorte, but excellent: and the greatest that any man lyuing can haue, for there can bee no greater token of loue amonge men, than a man to bestowe his lyfe for his frendes sake, for euery man setteth by his lyfe aboue all thinges. Many perchaunce myght bee found that coulde bee content to bestowe money or labour for an other mans sake, but the person is rare to bee found out, whiche will bestowe his lyfe for his frendes sake. I doe more then all this, whiche bestowe my lyfe for mine enemies, so they will becum my frendes. And in the meane while I call them my frendes in the waye of honour, whom I haue good right to call my seruauntes. Neuertheles I will not take you for my seruauntes, but for my frendes: yf ye wyll as cherefully and gladly perfourme these thinges that I commaunde you, as I doe willingly obey my fathers commaundement. They that are vnder Moses lawe, be rightfully called seruauntes: because they depend vpon diuerse rules prescribed vnto them, and rather for feare then for loue doe the thing that is apointed them. But as for you (whom I haue called from the bondage of the law, vnto the libertie of the gospell) from hencefoorth I will no more call seruauntes but frendes, as them whome mutuall loue and not necessitie doeth ioyne vnto me. For the seruaunte perceiueth not his Lordes intent, but onely dooeth that he is bydden, lokyng for no greate rewarde yf he dooe it, and well assured to bee punished yf he dooe it not, besydes that for euerye sundrie doyng must be had a sundry commaundement, as goe, cum agayne, doe this,

Cōtinue ye in my loue. &c.

eschewe that. For the maister telleth not his owne counsell to his seruauntes, whiche are therfore euil to be trusted, because they rather feare then loue hym. The cause wherfore I haue called you my frendes, is for that I once haue opened vnto you all the purpose of my minde, to thintent there should be no nede herafter of mennes preceptes contrary to myne. Whatsoeuer my father hath willed me to shewe you, therof I haue made you partakers, as my trusty frendes. Those thinges whiche I haue taught you, be out of all doubte: for I haue taught you none other, saue what I haue hearde of my father. My preceptes be his preceptes, by kepyng wherof he shall count you his frendes in stede of seruauntes.

The texte ¶ Ye haue not chosen me, but I haue chosen you, and ordeined you to goe, and bryngé foorth fruite, and your fruite shall remayne, that whatsoeuer ye aske of the father in my name, he maye geue it you.

And because ye maye the better vnderstand how great the honor of this my gentlenes towardes you is, consider how that ye haue neyther prouoked me with your seruice doing, to my frendship, that of duetie I ought to loue you again: nor yet haue you willyngly cum to my frendshippe, that for gẽtlenes sake, I should requite you with lyke loue: but when ye wer in bondage of the lawe, and farre of from the fauour of God, then did I of myne owne voluntarye wil chose you from among al the reste, without your desert. And for this purpose haue I chosen you, that ye should more and more increase in goodnes, beeyng grafted in me thorow mutuall loue, whiche ye coulde not haue towardes me, except I had first loued you. As the braunche is alwaye norished by the moysture of the vine, and spredeth it self in many braunches, so must you lykewise plentifully bring forth fruite of the ghospell throughout the whole world, and so do good to other that your self loose no fruite therby. For the common vyne bringeth foorth fruite, but for other, and that suche as soone decayeth: wherfore the braunches therof be fruitefull but for a tyme, because they growe in a vine that soone fadeth. Contrarywise you, because ye cleaue to an immortal stocke, shall bryng forth fruite that neuer shall perishe, but continue se̅inde to your eternall saluacion. And ye haue no cause in the meane while to say it is a great payne to trauayle about the worlde to teache the Gentiles, to suffer the dispites of wicked people. What wages, what ayde, what rewarde is apointed for vs? passe not vpon these worldely defenses. Let this stand you in stede of all rewardes and helpes, that whatsoeuer ye shall rightly aske my father in my name, he shall geue it you. What thinge is more easy then to aske? And what is it that he is not able to geue? Furthermore what is the thyng that he will not geue for my sake?

The texte. This commaunde I you that ye loue together. Yf the world hate you, ye knowe that it hated me before it hated you. If ye were of the worlde, the worlde woulde loue his own. Howbeit because ye are not of the world, but I haue chosen you out of the worlde, therfore the world hateth you. Remember the word that I sayed vnto you, the seruaunt is not greater then the lord. If they haue persecuted me, they wil also persecute you. If they haue kept my saying, they will kepe yours also.

Besides this, my commaundementes be not tedious, for what is more pleasaunt then one to loue an other? Who bee so weake but mutuall loue maye make them strong? what thyng is so greuous but mutuall charitie can make it delectable? Neither let this trouble you, that whiles you and I bee frendes and

and one of you charitablie doe agree with an other, ye shall be at discorde and strife with the worlde, but rather the selfe same thyng ought to coumfort your myndes, for so muche as by thys token ye shall well perceiue your selfes to bee my very disciples and frendes, that is to saye, contrary to the worlde, whyche is all sette vpon malice: whereas you are apointed for heauen, disdayne not to suffer that in the world which I haue suffered before you. The worlde hateth me also not for my deserte, but because I reproue and disclose the euill dedes therof, teachyng thynges whiche do not agree with theyr worldly affeccions. The worlde knoweth menne of his secte, and them doeth it loue and exalte, as lyke loueth lyke: and as an euyll itche coueteth an handsume scratcher. Therfore be they vnhappy whom this worlde flattereth and fauoreth, for that declareth them to bee farre from the fauour of God, whiche is that onely thyng that maketh e man happie in dede. Whan the worlde hateth you, remember myne exaumple and reioyce in your owne behalfe that ye haue no felowshyp with the worlde, but do cleaue faste vnto me. For this shall ye perceiue by the hatred the worlde beareth you, howe that ye be myne. In case ye were of the world, if ye loued worldly thinges, and taught according to worldly desyres, then the worlde woulde knowe you and loue you as hys owne, but because ye folowe not the wayes of the fleshe, but of the spirite, and couete not worldly goodes but heauenly, therefore the worlde hateth you: not that ye deserue it, but for that ye be vnlyke to the same whiche is euill & wicked. In tymes paste when ye thoughte perfitte righteousnes to consiste in the grosse ceremonyes of Moses lawe, and setting your mindes on transytorie thinges, had no loue to heauenly thinges, the worlde did then well lyke you: but after that I had once called you from this secte to the euangelicall and heauenly doctrine, and graffed you in me as braunches in the stocke, the worlde beganne to hate you, and that onely because ye bee myne. yet of trueth for no cause elles shall ye bee blessed, then for that ye be mine. Meruayle nothing at all though your innocencie shall not defende you from the hatred of the worlde. Remember howe I haue tolde you, the seruauntes state is no better then his lordes. For neither coulde my innocencie, which is greater then yours, defende me from the malice of the worlde, neyther were they afearde to despise my doctrine, nor yet for all my benefites would they waxe gentle, and call themselfes backe from theyr cruell purposes. That thing whiche they durst enterpryse against me, who am your Lorde and Maister, muche more boldely will they do it to you. Seing they haue deuised so many snares to bring me euen to the most reprocheful death, and haue so often spitefully railed vpon me, they wil also persecute you my disciples, nay but rather me in you. If they will obey my woordes they wil also obey vnto yours: but lyke as they haue not well borne my doctrine, no more wil they yours, because ye shal teache the selfe same thinges, that I teache.

But all these thinges will they doe vnto you for my names sake, because they haue not knowen him that sent me. If I had not cum and spoke vnto them, they should haue had no synne, but nowe haue they nothing to cloke theyr sinne withall. He that hateth me, hateth my father. If I had not doen among them the workes which none other man did, they should haue had no sinne. But now haue they bothe seen, and heard, not onely me, but also my father. But this happeneth that the saying might be fulfilled that is written in theyr lawe. They hated me without a cause.

The texte.

And whatsoeuer despite they shall doe against you, I will thinke it doen to

 me: for

me: for all thynges that they shall do agaynste you, they shall doe it for the hatred they beare to me: when they curse you, they shal curse me: when thei reiecte you, they shal reiecte me: when they beate you, they shall beate me. For whatsoeuer displeasure is doen to the membres, the same redoundeth to the head. And they would doe the lyke to me, if they had me present with them. Now because they cannot shewe their crueltie to me, they wil shewe it to you. But as all the iniurie that is dooen to you toucheth me: In lyke maner whatsoeuer is committed against my name, tourneth to my fathers dishonour also: whom if they did rightlye knowe, as they thynke they doe, they woulde neuer so shamfully haue handled his sonne. They arrogantlye pretende loue towardes God, and yet they bee wickedly minded against his sonne. They aske saluacion of God, and goe aboute to destroye his sonne. They boaste themselues to be kepers of Gods commaundementes, and doe reiecte the preceptes whiche his sonne geueth by the auctoritie of his father. They glorie in their knowledge of the lawe, and doe not receiue the knowledge of hym, whom the lawe setteth forth. They worship the sender and persecute hym whome he hath sente. Therefore they knowe not God, whome they boaste themselfes to knowe. And yet thys ignoraunce shall not excuse them in the daye of punishemente. They be ignoraunte in dede, but why? because they woulde not learne. And therfore woulde they not learne, because they loued more theyr owne glorye, then the glorye of god. They did set more by their owne aduauntage, then to winne saluacion by the gospell. Wherefore that thynge whiche my father hath ordeyned for theyr saluacion, haue they through their owne stubbernesse, heaped vp to theyr eternall damnacion. For verily I am come and was sente for this purpose, if it mighte be, to saue all men. If I the sonne of God, and greatest persone that could be sent, had not come my selfe, and declared vnto them all suche thinges as might haue brought them to a better minde: if I had not also doen these thinges whiche had been inough to haue forced euen stonye hertes to faythe and beleefe, surely theyr destruccion shoulde haue been the more easie, as giltlesse of this infidelitie, the addicion wherof, shall make the burden of theyr eternall damnacion the heauyer. But nowe sith I haue leafte nothing vndoen wherby they might be saued, and they againe with obstinate malice haue resisted him whiche frely offereth saluacion, they can alledge no excuse for theyr incredulitie. If one hate a straunger, it maie bee thought sumwhat woorthie of pardon because he hateth him whom he neuer sawe, but me they haue bothe seene and hearde. They haue seene me doe good to all folkes, and haue hearde me speake thinges woorthy for God. Neuerthelesse they hate me for those thinges, for whiche they ought to loue me. But whoso hateth me, must nedes hate my father, by whose auctoritie I speake that I speake, by whose power I do all that I do. And I haue not onelye spoken by wordes, but also by my dedes: yet were they so blinded, that they did neither beleue my woordes nor dedes. And this selfe thing shall make their damnacion more greuouse, in that they haue so stubbernely abused the goodnesse of God, being alwaye so ready for them. If I had not doen suche miracles among them as neuer any of the Prophetes afore me did, whether a man consider the noumber or greatnesse of them, and that not to make them afeard or astonished therewith, but to helpe them that were afflicted, If I had not doen al this, I say, they should not haue been giltie of this moste greuouse sinne: but nowe they haue both heard and seene,

But nowe haue they nothing to cloke theyr sinne withall.

seene, and so muche the more haue hated not only me that haue both spoken and doen, but also my father whiche hath spoken by me, and set furth his power by me. They neuer sawe Moses and yet hym they doe extreme hylye, they beleue the Prophetes whom they neuer hearde, but they turne cleane awaye from me whom they haue presentely seene before theyr iyes, whom they haue hearde speake, of whose benefites they haue so manye wayes had the profe. And not herewith satisfyed, they take my lyfe from me. In the meane while they pretende a reuerente loue to God the father, whereas whoso truely loueth the father cannot hate his sonne. Howbeit these thinges happen not by chaunce, for the very same thing that these men doe, the Psalmes whiche they haue and reade, did long agon prophecie should cum to passe, that is to saye, that in stede of thankes, they shoulde recompence good turnes with euill will. For thus spake I there, by the mouthe of the Prophete: let them not reioyce and triumphe ouer me, whiche vniustely are myne enemies & hate me without cause. If a man being prouoked, hate an other, it maye bee suffered: if one hate a straunger, it maye sumwhat be pardoned: but who can forgeue him that hateth one whom he bothe knoweth and hath found beneficiall.

But when the comforter is cum, whom I will sende vnto you from the father (euen the spirite of trueth, whiche procedeth of the father) he shall testifie of me. And ye shall beare witnesse also, because ye haue been with me from the beginning. *The texte.*

Neuerthelesse the incredulitie of these persones shall not make their fruite vneffectuall whiche will cleaue to me. For when I shall haue accomplished al that my father hath geuen me in commaundement, and after that the comforter is come, whom proceding from my father, I will sende you accordyng to my promisse, whiche is the holy goste (beyng the inspirer and teacher of all trueth) he shall declare all that euer I haue sayd and doen, wherby bothe my goodnesse and their obstinate blindnesse shall euidently appeare. He shall shewe how there hath been nothing doen against me, but the same hath been prophecied before in their owne bookes whiche they reade and yet vnderstande not: ye also whiche are now but weake, then being made strong through the inspiracion of my spirite, shall testifie of me before all menne, for so muche as ye haue seene in ordre what I haue doen, and hearde what I haue sayed: lyke as I haue tolde you thinges certaine, euen the very whiche I haue seene and heard of my father, neyther shall the holye goste put any thing but trueth in youre mindes, for so muche as he procedeth from my father: so shall ye beare witnesse of thinges not doubtefull, but suche as be throughly tryed by all your senses. And there will be sum whiche will not beleue you, but yet muste not the saluacion of other be loste, bycause of them whiche wilfully perishe through theyr owne faulte.

The.xvi.Chapter.

These thinges haue I sayd vnto you, because ye shoulde not be offended. They shall excommunicate you: yea the tyme shall cum that whosoeuer kylleth you, will thinke that he doeth God seruice. And suche thinges will they doe vnto you, because they haue not knowen the father, nor yet me. But these thinges haue I tolde you, that when the tyme is cum ye may remember then that I tolde you. *The texte.*

T shal not be seming that euerye daunger should withdrawe folke frō the open cōfessiō of the gospels trueth, which the world, of trueth, shal spurne against with all deuices, but it shall neuer bee able to put it to vtter silēce and conuince that trueth, which staieth it selfe vpō God the auctour thereof. Ye see what thynges the woorlde goeth about to doe against me, for publyshyng my fathers trueth. And it is nedeful ẏ ye prepare your mīdes paciently to suffer the lyke. I doe therfore tel you ẏ these thinges shall cum, lest ye suppose the professiō of the ghospell to bee all pleasaūt and delicate, and than you to be ẏ sorer dismaied whē the same thinges chaūceth to you at vnwares, & otherwise than you loke for. For the euils which a man foreseeth, against whiche he stifly bendeth his mynde ere they cū in place, lesse grieueth. I will not deceiue you, neither in the displeasures whiche muste nedes be suffered for ẏ gospels sake, neyther as touchyng ẏ rewardes which tarieth for them ẏ valiantly doe theyr duetie and office. To you that beginne to preache the ghospell shall this thing fyrste happen. They that are thoughte to vnderstand the highe poyntes of religion, and to kepe the perfeccion, and do teache and professe the knowledge of the law, shall caste you out of their Synagogues as wicked & coursed people, a thing amōg them of moste reproch, and herewith will they not afterwarde be contented, but they will cum to imprisonment and to strokes. And at length the thyng will growe to this ende, ẏ whosoeuer kylleth you, shall thynke himself therein to offre a thākefull sacrifice to God. They shall colour out their wickednesse with pretense of godlinesse, & shall accuse & condemne as giltie of impietie, the teachers of true godlinesse: and so it shall cum to passe, that not onely ye muste suffer harde & greuouse thinges, but ye shall bee punished as vngodly persons & malefactours. But care ye not what the worlde iudgeth of you, let my exaumple comforte you, remembring that ye suffre these thinges with me, and for my fathers sake and myne. The iniurie is ours, we haue the wrong, and it shal be our parte, bothe to ayde you in youre conflicte, to rewarde you hauing the victorie, to resiste them and also punishe their obstinacie: thinke ye nothing at all of vengeaunce, for they shall not thus handle you because ye be theues or transgressours, or any waye els woorthie suche ciuill intreating, but because they doe not yet perfectly knowe neyther me nor my father. The ignoraunce wherwith their crueltie is mingled, shall cause my father to take compassion vpō them, nor I would not ye should so muche desyre their punishmente, as to haue them saued by doctrine: for the zeale of religiō shal sette or prouoke many against you, rather through errour of iudgement, than of ciuill wil. These folke shall repent themselfes and amend, after that my father be knowen to the worlde by you, and assone as men shall through youre preachyng vnderstande my doctrine, and knowe what is the power of the holy goste. I knowe ye bee sory for my departure hence, and sorow is not to be added vpon sorow, but I thought mete to forewarne you hereof, that when these discommodities falleth vpon you, ye maye the more paciently and with lesse hertebreake beare them, calling to your remembraūce how I had tolde you before, ẏ these thinges shoulde folowe: and that after myne exaumple, ye should suffer of the wicked, of suche as be ignoraunte of the trueth, and euen for my fathers sake and myne; but be ye suffised with a

stayed

stayed conscience in the trueth, and passe not what menne iudge of you, or rather folow my doctrine, and iudge your selfe blessed, when for my names sake menne doe persecute you, when they speake all euil of you, and belie you. They shall put you out of their Synagogues, but that selfe thing shall proue your names to be registred in heauen.

These thinges sayd I not vnto you at the beginning, because I was present with you. But now I go my waie to him that sente me, and none of you asketh me whither I goe: but because I haue sayed suche thinges vnto you, your hertes are full of sorow. Neuerthelesse I tell you the trueth. It is expediēt for you that I goe awaye. For yf I goe not awaye, that comforter will not cum vnto you, but if I departe I will sende hym vnto you. And when he is cum, he will rebuke the world of sinne, and of righteousnesse, and of iudgement: of sinne, because they beleue not on me: of rightuousnesse because I go to my father, and ye shall see me no more. Of iudgement because the prince of this world is iudged alreadye. *The texte.*

I knewe all these thynges shoulde happen you. Neuerthelesse when I firste tooke you to me, I spake nothing of them, not to deceiue you thereby, but because the time serued not than, as in dede all thinges are not fyt for al times. This my bodily presence hath for a season nourished and strengthned your weakenesse, but now forasmuche as the tyme of my departure from you is at hande, it is nedeful ȳ ye be openly admonished what ye shall suffer, to the entent ye maye by litle & litle enure your selfes to be content to lacke the comforte of my corporall presence, and after ye haue sequestred worldly affection, to take vnto you more fyrme and manlyke boldenesse of herte, and not to be childishe and lyke vnto babes that hang on their mothers lap, all afraied, if it chaunce them at any tyme to be pulled away out of their parentes syght. I would not pamper and disceyue you with vaine hope, nor yet an other tyme discourage you: ye haue been serued according to your infirmitie, and as tyme required. I haue been your comforter, aduocate, and defender. Now I must departe hēce, & though I do so, for your cause chiefly to strengthen you in greater thinges, after this my body bee withdrawen out of your sight, yet my talke therof dooeth put you in suche feare that none doeth aske, or so much as thinke whither I goe, where as in dede ye ought rather to reioice, than in mind to be troubled with my departure, seing I goe to my father, from whom I came: not that I shall hereafter be vtterly absent from you, but in an other sorte present with you. Nor I was not ignoraunt what would haue been more pleasaunt to your affections: ye had rather haue the continuall fruicion of this my conuersacion among you, but I had leauer speake to you of thinges that do profite, then which doth delyte you, & would leauer haue you vpō knowelage of the trueth to be in heauinesse for a time, than not to procede to the sure constancie ȳ shoulde be fitte for the storme to cum. And for this cause I do open vnto you what shall chaunce hereafter. Verily thus I must leue you, and after that I be taken away from you, ye shall suffer many thinges: & that ye may be the more apte to beare the same more paciently, it is expedient for you, that I be had out of your syght. For vnlesse by takyng from you the sight of the fleshe, ye waxe spirituall, that comforter the spirite which shall make you strong, and not to be vanquished, shal not cum vnto you. And because I haue prepared you for him, he shall perfourme & finish that which I haue begonne in you. Finally through that spirite I shall alwaye continue with you, yea and that more presently after I be gone, than I am nowe in this kynde of presence. For the purpose of my

It is expedient for you that I goe awaye.

For if I goe not away the cōforter wil not cum vnto you.

cumming was not to dwell still with you in the worlde, but the cause why I did abase my selfe to your state and infirmitie, was to enhaunce you to heauen. It hath so semed good to my fathers wysedome as processe of tyme shoulde serue, to aduaunce you litle by litle, and by certaine degrees, to thinges of perfection: and it is but reason that ye on your behalfes do accommodate your myndes and good willes to my fathers order and disposiciō of thinges: ye shall haue al thing of our gifte, but your parte is to endeuoure your selfe to be mete to receiue our benefite, for if ye should alway cōtinue thus affect as ye be now, that heauenly comforter wil not cum to you, as yet vnable to receiue his giftes. But if I goe my waye, and that you not regarding this corporall presence, will frame your myndes to hier giftes, whiche that spirite shall geue you, then shall my father sende hym vnto you, neuer to forsake you nor to leue you succourlesse, whether you lyue or dye. Nor he shall be no frutelesse spirite, but when he cummeth he shall worke more by you, than I nowe doe: not that but our power is all one, but because to appointe to euery busynes his tyme, is a thing expedient for mannes saluacion. I haue reproued the worlde, the same thing shall he doe more fully and more plainly: for he shall sore charge the world, that excepte it do forthinke and amende it selfe, geuyng faithe to the ghospell, it shall be without all excuse: for in dede lyke as the infirmitie of our fleshe offendeth the worlde, euen so doeth it seme to minister matter why the sayed world maie pretende an excuse of his infidelitie. They haue seen this outward man very hungrie and a thurst, they haue seen me poore, and had in contempt, within a while they shall se me sore afflicted, taken of mine enemies, al to beate and turryed, and in conclusion die. But when all thinges be finished that the flesh hath here to do, & that they shall se this body after it be dead, liue againe, and ascend vp into heauen, and shall se the holye ghoste sent, and make you sodainly vnfearefull preachers of my name; and shall also perceiue wonderfull power, vertue, and strength, shewed by calling vpon my name, as deuils to go sodainly out of men, the halte & lame to be restored to their lymmes, the sycke to be healed, the dead to lyue againe, and moreouer euery thing to cū to passe whiche the Prophetes had prophecied shoulde folowe and be: than (I say) no maner of excuse shal be left to the wicked and miscreantes: for than the worlde shall be adiudged and condēned of thre pointes, and can not be excused: firste of synne, after of rightuousnesse, and thirdly of Iudgemēt: he shal rebuke the worlde of the greatest and suche a synne as doeth include in it all other sinnes, (a synne inexcusable) and why? because seing they perceiued the prophecies of Gods owne Prophetes take effect, many thousandes professe my name, they that beleued in me (after they had receiued the holy goste) speake straunge languages, much noted for their miracles, forsake the superstition of Moses lawe, imbrace the holy gospel, detest theyr forefathers Idolatrie, and yet worshippe the father of heauen in true godlynesse of life, nothing regarding worldly commodities, but haue their myndes wholye sette vpon heauenlye thinges: the worlde, I saye, perceiuing this, what excuse shall it make for his lacke of belefe? If there shalbe no lacke on my fathers behalfe that hath sent me, nor of myne whiche was sent to haue had all men saued, and yf the holy ghoste shall omit nothing, whome both we shall sende, neyther ye whome that heauenly spirite shall vse as his instrumentes, what resteth but that al may vnderstand howe that they perishe in the synne of vnbelefe? And whan they shall

see the

see the prophane Gentiles to haue the synnes of their olde former lyfe washed away, and themselues endued with innocencie, thorowe baptisme and professi= on of my name, it shalbe manifeste that wittingly and willingly they abyde still in their filthines, and adde synne vpon synne.

And the worlde also shall bee reproued of falsely vsurped righteousnes, for nowe they sum waie pretende the kepyng of the lawe, they sumwhat glo= ry in obseruing the ordinaunces of their progenitors, they pretende religion whiche their forefathers gaue them, the feastes, the sabboth dayes, the pray= ers, the woorkes of mercie, their wayes of honouring God, and suche other lyke whiche hath the pretence of righteousnesse: but after that they shall see the wonderfull power of that spirite, not to bee geuen but to those that haue pro= fessed my name, and that it shall bee their chaunce whiche were Idolatres to haue it without kepyng of the lawe, what than shall they say thereby, whiche challenge to themselfes righteousnes by kepyng of the lawe? All in vaine do they glorye before menne in a false righteousnes, whiche haue refused hym by whome onely true righteousnesse cummeth. And all this to bee true shall then be more open to the worlde, whan that spirite shall declare me not to bee dead, whom they had fastened to the crosse, and had buried, but that I dyd returne agayne to my father, (from whom I came,) to lyue with hym: and than being inuisyble & withdrawen out of mens syght, to do greater thinges by you being inspired with my spirite, than I dyd beeing with you lyuyng in the worlde. Thus it shall cum to passe, that through these thinges the vn= righteousnes of them shall be rebuked, which haue put their hope of righte= ousnesse other where than in me: and the iustice of God made more notable, whiche faithfully hath perfourmed the thing which many yeares agoe he pro= mised to mankynde by his Apostles, and Prophetes: and within a while the thing shalbe put in vre and take effect, for I shall not long be conuersaunt among you in this visible bodie, but shall dye and goe to my father. And yet ye shall perceyue me to be one that liueth, and hath power, and that shall ac= complishe all that I haue promised.

and of righ= teousnes &c.

Moreouer the worlde also shal be rebuked and reproued of iudgement, be= cause that (by seing men euery where through penaunce conuerte from synne to innocencie of lyfe, leaue the grosse ceremonies of Moses lawe, and turne to godlynesse of the ghospell, the nacions of the whole worlde forsake theyr wurshipping of diuels and images, and falle to the true wurshypping of God the father, the sonne, and the holy ghost) it shall manifestly appere the prince of the worlde (who hath heretofore by synne practised tirannie) to be already with his owne weapons vanquished, put out of the waye, and iudged as one that hath procured my death, by whom innocencie, libertie of the gospell, and immortalitie is recouered, employed, and geuen. Than shall it well appere to haue been a triumphe, whiche semed to be a thing of shame and reproche, and that to haue been a victory whiche was imputed and counted for an ouer= throwe and an vtter destruccion: for whan deuils shall eche where be cast out of the temples, and shall crye out at the signe of the crosse, when they shall leaue the bodyes whiche they had of long tyme possessed at naming of me, shall not that openly proue theyr prince to be iudged and condemned? Shall it not bee apparante and a clere matter that they also be woorthely iudged and con= demned whiche had leuer folow hym being alreadye vanquished and iudged

Of iudge= ment, because the prince of this world is iudged al= ready.

to eter=

to eternall deathe, than me, whom as a conquerour, and to all folke the verye auctour of innocencie and of life, God shall carrye vp and auaunce to the felowship of his kyngdome.

The texte. ¶ I haue yet many thinges to saye vnto you, but ye cannot beare them awaye nowe. Howbeit when he is cum whiche is the spirite of trueth, he will leade you into al trueth: he wil not speake of hym selfe, but whatsoeuer he shall heare, that shall he speake, and he wil shewe you thinges to cum. He shall glorifie me, for he shall receyue of myne and shall shewe vnto you. All thinges that the father hathe are myne. Therefore sayed I vnto you, that he shall take of myne and shewe vnto you.

I coulde tell you many mo thinges, but the tyme serueth not, nor your weakenesse wyll not as yet beare them: and since I haue not yet altogether gone thorow with this mine ambassade, I do therfore reserue them to the cummyng of the holy ghoste: he beyng once come, shall fynde you more apte to receyue a more full knowledge, euen when the busynesse of my deathe, resurrecion, and ascencion shall be dispatched and fynished. This spirite that I speake of shall be no lying or worldely spirite, but my very spirite, that is to saye, the spirite of trueth, he shall teache you all trueth, whiche ye are not nowe able to receiue at ful. He also shall speake vnto you, but (that shall be) by secrete inspirations. He shall not with mouing the ayer touche your bodely eares, but by a priuey secrete vertue shall moue the inwarde myndes: neyther shall he speake thynges of vncertaintye, but in lyke maner as I haue spoken nothyng whiche I haue not heard of my father, so shall he inspire nothyng into your hertes, but that he hearde of my father and me: and he shall not onely open vnto you all trueth of thynges paste, but also he shall foreshewe you thynges to cumme ere they happen, so often as nede shall require: for he is not alone only almighty, but hathe withall knowleage of all thinges.

He shall by you make the glory of my name be knowen to all men, lyke as I by my deathe and resurreccion shall make my fathers glory notable and famouse: for as what thing soeuer I doe, redoundeth to my fathers praise and glory, of whome I haue my being, and of him haue receiued all that I haue: euen so shall it growe to my honour and praise, whatsoeuer he shall worke by you. He shall mocion you to nothing contrary to those thinges, whiche I (receiuing them of my father,) haue taught you. All thinges is common betwene vs, all thinges procede from my father: but whosoeuer is his, is mine, nor any thing is my fathers or mine, whiche is not common to the spirite. Therefore by the sayde spirite shall I speake to you, as my father hathe spoken to you by me: he that beleueth me, beleueth my father, and he that beleueth the spirite, beleueth vs both.

The texte. ¶ After a while ye shall not see me, and againe after a while, ye shall see me: for I go to the father. Then sayed sum of his disciples betwene themselues: what is this that he sayeth vnto vs, after a while ye shal not see me, and againe after a while ye shall see me, and that I go to the father? They sayed therefore, what is this that he sayeth after a whyle? we cannot tell what he sayeth: Iesus perceiuing that they woulde aske hym, sayed vnto them: Ye enquire of this betwene your selues, because I sayed after a while ye shall not see me: and againe after a while ye shall see me: Verily verily I saye vnto you, ye shall wepe and lament, but contrarywyse the worlde shall reioyce, ye shall sorowe, but your sorowe shall be turned into ioy.

Now than being corroborate and stablished with many thinges, be ye bold and take good hearte vnto you againste the storme that hangeth ouer you, al

bradiin aduersitie saue your selues to the prosperitie which shall folowe: within a whyle ye shall lacke the syght of me, but ye shall be without it no longe time: for within a shorte space after, I shall be presented to your syght agayne, that so ye may litle by litle be brought in vre to wante the sight of this body, which is not moste commodiouse for you. For I returne to my father, to thentent that after I cease to be seen of you, I maye endue you with greater giftes.

But not withstanding all this, so great sorowe did possesse the disciples mindes at that time, that they neyther vnderstood nor coulde kepe in memorie thinges that were often repeted and reiterate: for whereas our lord Jesus did declare in these wordes not very obscurely, ÿ by death and buryall he should be absent out of his disciples sight, yet none otherwyse but that within thre dayes after he would appeare vnto them againe, euen in the selfsame bodye, but now immortall: & so after he had for a fewe dayes space confirmed and stayed the mindes of his disciples, to conuaye hymselfe again into heauē. And to thentent that hauing his bodely sight withdrawen from them which letted them to be spirituall, they mighte deserue that heauenly spirite, and after that to looke no more for their lordes bodely presence, saue onely when at the laste daye he shall once for all shewe hymselfe to the whole worlde for to iudge the quicke and the dead: all this, I saye, notwithstanding, yet did not the disciples perceiue the thing that was spoken, but sayde mutteryng among themselues: what meaneth this saying: after a litle while and ye shall not see me, and again there shalbe a litle time that ye shal se me, for I go to the father? How shall we se hym that hath himselfe awaye to go to his father? Or what meaneth this litle while wherein he shall restraine vs from seing of hym, and againe after a litle while, when as he shall permit vs to see him? This is a darke saying and we vnderstande not what he speaketh.

Than Jesus perceiuing that their mindes was to aske him what he ment by his saying, preuented their demaunde and question: to declare (as his custome was) that he knewe the moste secret thoughtes of mē: and againe he saith: this that I sayde, (after a litle whyle the sight of me shalbe taken frō you, and againe after a litle while it shalbe restored newly vnto you, because it is not expedient that I shoulde alwaye tarry among you in suche sorte as I now do, but it is more for your profit ÿ I depart hence and go to my father,) doeth trouble you. The thing that I haue sayd is moste true. The tyme is nyghe, when as hauing this our familiar cumpanie disceuered and broken, ye shall with wayling, sorowe, and weping, be in manner consumed, and werye of your lyues, as men destitute of all succoure. Contrarie, the worlde shal ioye, praunce and triumphe as a conquerour, but within a litle tyme the course of thinges shall be chaunged: for the worldes ioye shall be turned into sorowe, & your sorow into ioye and gladnesse. The cause is that as my death shall greue and make you pensife, but it shall make the Jewes gladde, so my resurrection shall make you ioyouse, and contrarie it shall vexe and trouble the Jewes. Wherfore beare you well and boldly this shorte sorowe, thorowe hope of the ioye that shall folowe soone after.

What is this that he sayeth vnto vs after a while.

¶ A woman when she trauayleth hath sorowe because her houre is come, but assone as she is deliuered of the childe, she remembreth nomore the anguishe, for ioye that a man is borne into the worlde. And ye now therfore haue sorow: but I will see you againe, and your hertes shall reioyce, and your ioye shall no man take from you. And in that daye shal ye aske me no question.

The texte.

In like

In lyke manner as a woman greate with childe suffereth sore greuous paynes in the tyme of her trauayle, but yet she beareth oute those painefull throwes with a stout good herte, because she knoweth they shall not long endure, and soone after there foloweth vpō the byrth of the childe, ioyous pleasure: for as sone as she hath brought foorthe the childe that she laboured of in trauayle, her pleasure in beyng a mother of a newe childe is so great, that she forgetteth the dolourouse payne whiche she sustained in her trauailes: yea to saye sothe, she ioyeth muche that she hath boughte long comforte with a shorte dolour. In the same wyse shall you also for a litle time that draweth fast on, be sore vexed in minde, yea and ye be nowe already in great sorowe, yet so that within a fewe dayes hereafter when I being a conquerour of death, shal present my selfe alyue againe vnto you, your hertes shal be replenished with great ioye, because him, whome ye did bewayle and mourne for being dead, ye shall than se aliue and made immortall, neuer after to dye. The sorowfull mourning shall be shorte, but the ioyeful mirth shall be perpetuall: for death ouerpasseth, but immortalitie remayneth for euer.

The texte

¶ Verily, verily, I saye vnto you: whatsoeuer ye shal aske the father in my name, he wyll geue it you. Hitherto haue ye asked nothyng in my name. Aske and ye shall receyue, that your ioye maye bee full. These thinges haue I spoken vnto you by prouerbes. The tyme wyll cum when I shall no more speake vnto you by prouerbes, but I shall shewe you plainly from my father. And that daye shall ye aske in my name. And I saye not vnto you that I wyll speake vnto my father for you, for the father hymselfe loueth you, because ye haue loued me, and haue beleued that I came out from God. I went out from the father, and came into the worlde, agayne I leaue the worlde, and go to the father.

There be nowe many thinges whiche your herte lepeth for desyre to question with me of. Than shall your mindes and also your iyes bee so fully content and satisfied, that ye shall wene no mo questions are to bee demaunded: for great excelling ioye shall shake of and vtterly put awaye all griefe of minde, neyther shall you wyshe or require any thing els, considering ye shall se and perceiue more giuen you than you loked for, or durst be bolde to desyre. I assure you, after I be taken from you vp into heauen, ye shall wante nothing, for what can bee more easie than to aske of a father? whatsoeuer verely ye shall aske of him in my name, it shall be geuen you. What nede you any other ayde? The father alone maye do all thinges, and he will deny my frendes and them that aske in my name, nothing: hitherto my bodely presence hath letted you to aske any thing in my name worthie the same: for as yet ye do not wholy depende of heauenly ayde, but as being led by worldly affection ye do depende vpon this bodie: hereafter lyfting vp your hertes to heauen make your peticion where ye knowe me to be a present aduocate, and ye shall obtaine whatsoeuer ye aske, that your ioye, which shall after this heuines wherein you be now, come vnto you by reason that ye shall se me againe, maye than be full and perpetuall, for than shall be no chaunge of sorowe and ioye, by hauing or not hauing of me after the infirmitie of the body, but trusting to heauenly succour that is alwaye ready for you, hauing alwaye the spirite a present coumforter and counceler, ye maye enioye a continuall gladnes of conscience, thankyng and praysyng God bothe in prosperitie and also in aduersitie.

Whatsoeuer ye shall aske my father in my name, he shall geue it you.

This nowe by the waye haue I sumwhat obscurely and prouerbially spoken vnto you, as yet not fully vnderstanding what I doe saye, for it behoued so to geue place and beare with your infirmitie, that you also maye learne to cō descend and agree to the imbecillitie, and weakenesse of other: but the time shall come whan hauing this mortall body remoued hence, I shall cōmen with you (than being more stabliched and stronger, and also sorowe set a syde more attent) of my father manifestly, without closynge vp the matter in parables, for now by reason ẏ your minde is vnsteadie, weake, and carefull, the thing which is plainly and openly spoken, is to you as it were a parable. At length I shal euen by my spirite declare and open vnto you, the very certaintie of my fathers wyll, for it becummeth not you to be ignoraunt of my fathers wyll: verely I shall than speake vnto you whishtlie and without wordes, but I shall speake assured and manifeste thinges, if so bee ye aske them: yea and than also the holy ghoste shall incense you, what to aske, and howe to aske in my name, whiche incase ye so do, surely though it were a great matter, and a thing of difficultie, yet shall the father for my sake not deny it you askyng it.

And I doe not nowe speake this as if ye shall obtaine your requeste by my mediacion, in suche sorte as men doe sumtime at a kinges hande ẏ is but a mā, obtaine their requeste at the desyre and suite of sum one that is in fauour with the kyng, whiche peticion the kyng woulde not els haue graunted, but that he was content to geue it for his sake whiche did commende & set forward the suters supplicacion: but as for my father, although he loueth to bee asked of by his sonne, by whome his will hath beene to graunte all thynges to menne, yet that notwithstandynge he wyll otherwise consente to your desyres, not onlye for the loue that he beareth towardes his sonne, but whiche he hath also towardes you: for he loueth not his sonne so that he loueth not you, but whomsoeuer the sonne loueth, those the father loueth also. Therefore he loueth you, not for your workes sake, but for that ye loue me semblablie, and beleue that I am cum out from hym, for this is to loue the father, euen to loue his sōne: and to beleue the father is euen to beleue the sonne. He of trueth dooeth not beleue whiche denyeth the sonne to haue cum from the father, and not to haue sayed and doen all thyng euen by the fathers auctoritie.

I was already with the father, before I came into the worlde, euen for to cary you vp, takyng vnto me this mortall body ẏ ye se, but for your cause came I into the worlde, euen for to cary you vp into heauen. Now than the thynges beyng once doen, whiche the father gaue me in commaundemente, I doe euen for your sake, leaue the world as touchyng bodily presence, and returne again vnto the father: and truely whatsoeuer is or shalbe doen here, it is and shall bee doen to bryng you to saluacion.

His disciples sayde vnto hym: lo, nowe talkeste thou plainly and speakeste no prouerbe. Nowe are we sure that thou knowest all thynges, and nedest not that any man should aske the any question: Therfore beleue we that thou camest from god. Iesus aunswered them: Nowe ye do beleue: beholde the houre draweth nye, and is already cum, that ye shalbe scattered euery mā to his owne, and shall leaue me alone. And yet am I not alone, for the father is with me. These wordes haue I spoken vnto you, that in me ye might haue peace. For in the worlde shall ye haue tribulacion, but be of good chere. I haue ouercum the world. *The texte.*

The disciples beynge boldened with these sayinges, begunne sumwhat to stande in their owne conceite, and as though they had of theyr owne strength beene able to abide and beare their lordes death that was at hande, they answere on this wyse: loke (saye they) euen now at this present doest thou fullfill

the

the selfe thynge whiche thou promisedst afterwarde to doe: for nowe withoute any darkenes of parables, thou speakeste plainly out, what thou wilte do: neyther nedeth it to aske the any further question. For thou knowest all thynges, and with thy good wordes hast deliuered our hertes from sorowe, so that we nede no further communicacion: & why? we nothinge doubte, but that through hope of thy ioye to come, wee shall boldly and paciently suffre the thynge that is imminent and cumming towardes vs: and we do therfore finallye and verily beleue that thou art cum out from god, because thou seest throughly the very botome and secretie of our hertes. And than the Lord Jesus, whose maner was euery where sharply to controll, and restraine whatsoeuer humayne and worldely arrogancie, ambicion, or selfe affiance, he perceiued to arise in his disciples heartes, ẏ they mighte plainely learne to distruste their owne strength and vertue, whereby they myghte dooe nothyng, and wholly to depende vpon the hande of God the father: The Lorde Jesus (I saye) dyd thus abate and acoole that arrogancie (whiche was suche) that thoughe they yet vnderstoode not what he sayed, thoughe they had no true beleke, and as yet were not meete for the stormes that wer cummyng vpon thē, for all that they tooke on hande the thing that was to be asked of God by prayer. And he aunswereth them after this sorte: What dooe I heare? the thynge whyche I promyse to geue you hereafter whan ye shalbe made stronge, and be stated by my doctrine, and by the inspiracion of the holy ghost, ye now proudely take on hande before due time: as if ye might do at least sumwhat by the helpe and assistence of mās owne power and vertue: when as rather the tyme is full nyghe that ye shall declare howe strengthelesse ye are of your selfes. For ye shall not onely bee vnable to go through the instante tempeste, but leauing me alone in the handes of the sergeauntes & catchpolles, whiche shall violently drawe me to the deathe of the crosse, ye shall run awaye eche one a sere waye, through feare so amased, that ye shall not one beare cūpany with another to your succoure and comforte, whyles euery one shall feare other, leste by any others telling he mighte be bewrayed and come in daunger, albeit in dede I nede not your aide and helpe: I shall of trueth be forsaken of all my frendes: but yet shall I not be desolate, because the father shall neuer leaue me. Therefore I do speake these thynges vnto you, that distrusting your owne strength, ye maye reste and staye your selfe in me. The worlde shall make greate commociō, and fiercely rise againste you, as it doeth agaynst me, but bee bolde and shrynke not, remēbryng that I haue conquered the worlde: ye shall take exaumple at me, and shall trust to be holpen by me, ye shall also haue victorie, but through me, beyng of youre owne nature very weake: and yet when tyme and occasion shall require, ye shalbe throughe my spirite stronge and vnuanquished.

Now ye beleue, &c,

The.xvii.Chapter.

The texte.

¶ These wordes spake Jesus, and lift vp his iyes to heauen, and sayed: father, the houre is cum, glorifie thy sonne, that thy sonne also may glorifie the. As thou hast geuē him power ouer all fleshe, that he should geue eternall lyfe to as many as thou hast geuen him. This is life eternall, that they might know thee, the only true god, and Jesus Christ whom thou hast sente.

After

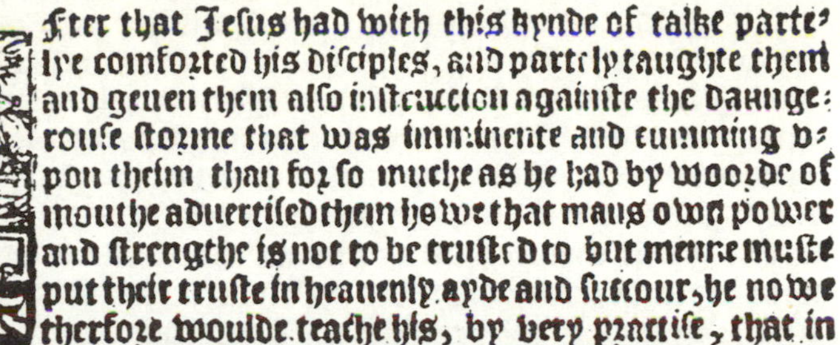

Fter that Jesus had with this kynde of talke partely comforted his disciples, and partely taughte them and geuen them also instruccion againste the daungerouse storme that was imminente and cumming vpon them than for so muche as he had by woorde of mouthe aduertised them howe that mans owne power and strengthe is not to be trusted to but menne muste put their truste in heauenly ayde and succour, he nowe therfore woulde teache his, by very practise, that in worldely afflictions, whiche percase myghte sodeinly falle vpon them, they shoulde looke to none other for succour, but vnto the father of heauen, vpon whome oughte all they wholly to depende, that bee desyrouse to bee strong inough and able to beare persecucion. Therfore, lyfting vp his iyes to heauen, to thentente he so might euen by the very semblance & behauiour of body teache whither the minde shoulde bee directed, and wherupon fixed, he spake on this wise: father (sayed he) nowe the tyme is cum whiche I haue alway longed for. Glorifie thy sonne amãg men by death and resurreccion, that thy sonne on his behalfe maye glorifie the amongest all men, and so the one to be knowen by the other: For so it is expediente for the saluacion of all mankynd, that the worlde knowe the sonne by thee, and the father again by the sonne. And for this cause hath it pleased thee to geue vnto the sonne power ouer all mankynde vniuersally: And for none other ende haste thou geuen this power, but that all folke shoulde be saued. And being deliuered from death, should attein to euerlasting lyfe. For it hath liked the, that what thing soeuer thou grauntest and geuest to men, thou geuest and grãtest it by me: through whose death thou geuest to all that will, eternall lyfe. Furthermore, the very originall fountain of eternal life is, that (both the one and the other setting forth eche others honour and name) men by fayth know vs both: that is to saye, thee, whiche art the onely true god, not only of the Jewes but of al the people of the whole world, from whom procedeth whatsoeuer is any where good, and to knowe him also whom thou hast sent into the worlde, for the saluacion of mankynde, Jesus Christ, by whom thou geuest whatsoeuer it pleaseth thy goodnes to geue to men: and this thou doest that they should rendre thankes to vs both, to thee as to the chiefe autor of al thinges, to me who at thy wil and pleasure, am about willingly and gladly to finishe vp this busines that I am appointed to. For he cannot cum to saluacion whiche honoureth the father, in case he despise the sonne, nor yet he that hath the sonne in reuerence, if so be he contẽne and neglecte the father: for asmuche as the praise and glorye of the one, is the praise and glory of the other.

I haue glorified thee on the earth. I haue finished the worke, whiche thou gauest me to do. And now glorifie thou me, o father, with thine owne selfe, with the glorie which I had with the ere the world was. I haue declared thy name vnto the men, which thou gauest me out of the worlde. Thine they were, and thou gauest them me, & they haue kept thy worde. Nowe haue they knowen, that all thinges whatsoeuer thou hast geuen me, are of the. For I haue geuen vnto them the wordes whiche thou gauest me, and they haue receiued them, and haue knowen surelye, that I came oute from the: and they haue beleued that thou diddeste sende me. *The texte.*

I haue hitherto renoumed thy name by miracles, and with my doctrine

here

here in the worlde, and haue goen abont and doen thy commaundement being forwarde and readie to prosecute and accomplishe that which remaineth to be doen. I haue not sought myne owne glory, but thine: yea I haue abased and caste downe my selfe into extreme contempte, to thentente I might blase and honorably set furth thy name amōg men. For thy glory is alwaye whole, substanciall, and sounde in it selfe, without decaye, nor thou haste no nede of mās prayse, but it standeth them on hande that thou be knowen vnto theym. And now my father, bring thou it to passe, that on the other parte, the worlde may semblably knowe and perceiue that I am fully and wholy receyued into that same glorie whiche I had with the, before the worlde was made. By reason of the frayle mortalitie and brittlenes of the bodie, men impute me to be very base, and exteme me very courselye, but they vilely exteme the. Thy glory as of it selfe it hath neyther beginning nor endyng, so can it neither encrease nor decrease. Nor the infirmitie of this bodie that I haue put vpon me, doeth not impouerishe or lessen my glorie, whiche I haue alwaye had beyng euermore borne of the, but thou haste made the worlde by me, to haue folke that shoulde knowe, that shoulde haue in admiracion, and shoulde loue thy power, wisdō, and goodnesse: and nowe agayne is the time that thy goodnesse muste restore by me, that whiche hath been fourmed and made. It shall verelye be restored, if the worlde knowe howe great thy loue is towardes mankinde, whiche to saue, thou haste geuen thy only sonne vnto death: howe great thy power is that hath conquered the deuill and vanquished his tyrannie: how great is thy wisdome that hath with suche wonderfull deuice, conuerted the worlde vnto thee which was alienate from thee. The thing is begun, and the foundacion of this worke is layed.

I haue made thy name knowen vnto them, whom (being through thy godly inspiracion exempte and priuileged from the worlde) thou haste geuen and committed vnto me. They could not haue beene taken out and separate from the world, they could not haue been grafted in me, vnles thy liberall free goodnesse, had inspired their minde. Thyne they were, whom thou createdst, thine they were whom thou haste appointed to this businesse, and geuen them to me to be taught and infourmed.

Neither hath thy bounteousnes nor my laboure and diligence been bestowed vpon them in vaine. They haue beleued my doctrine, wherin I haue taught them thee, and not onely geuen credence vnto it, but they haue hitherto stande stedfastly in faythe, obeying my wordes. For it is well knowen and persuaded vnto them, that the Iewes would not beleue, that whatsoeuer I haue taught, whatsoeuer I haue doen, it hath proceded from the as the auctor: and hath been doen through thy power and vertue.

For I haue taught them none other thing than that I haue learned of the, who also haue al my being and whatsoeuer I am, of thee, and whatsoeuer is thine is also mine. Therfore my worde (whiche the Phariseis haue contemned,) haue they receiued as cum from the, and beleuing thesame haue certainly knowen that I proceded from the, and of the am sent into this worlde. They haue thus muche profited, that they be perswaded howe that I am Messyas, whiche haue been so many hundreth yeares looked for: whome thou haste sente into the worlde, for the saluacion of all that faithfully beleue. And nowe because I do leaue theim as touching companiship of body, I do on my be-

halfe

halfe agayne commende them to thy goodnesse to be kepte and preserued, that they decaye not, but alwaye profit more and more and waxe better. Thei knowe whom they ought to thanke for theyr saluacion. They knowe of whome to bee succoured, and whome to leane to. They doe depende vpon thee.

I praye for them, I praye not for the worlde, but for them whiche thou hast geuen me, for they are thyne. And all mine are thyne, and thine are myne, and I am glorifyed in them. And nowe I am not in the worlde, and they are in the worlde, and I come to thee. Holye father, kepe thorowe thyne owne name, them whiche thou hast geuen me, that they also maye be one as we are. Whyles I was with them in the worlde, I kepte them in thy name. Those that thou gauest me haue I kepte, and none of them is loste, but that loste chylde, that the scripture might be fulfylled.

The texte.

Therefore I praye for them whome beyng withdrawen out of the worlde, thou wouldest shoulde be thine: and my prayer is that thy goodnes would stablyshe and make the thyng perpetually theyr owne, which thou haste begun in them. I do not nowe praye for the worlde, which being blynded in euyl desyres, doeth stubbernly oppugne and reclayme agaynste my doctrine, hauyng enuie at theyr owne saluacion, when it is freely offred them: I praye for them whom thou hast committed to my tuicion, because thei be not of this worlde but thine, and agaynst the malyce of the deuill, they cannot be in sauetie but by thy continuall ayde. I therefore, o father, commende them to thee, that it maye please thee to let them be alwaye thyne, lyke as I am perpetually thyne for euer.

And therfore are they myne, because they bee thyne: For betwene vs are all thynges common. For whatsoeuer is myne, thesame is also thyne: And whatsoeuer is thine, thesame is also myne. And like as thou arte honoured and glorifyed by my doctryne among menne, so am I glorifyed by the beliefe of these, whiche sticke vnto me constauntly: when as the Phariseis and the scribes stāde obstinately in the denial therof. For these shall after a sorte succede me in offyce, and come into my roume, and after that I be takē away out of this world, they shall make bothe thy name and myne to be of famouse memorye, throughout all the worlde. I haue played the preachers parte, and doen my function and office therein, wherein these shall succede me, and come to lyke offyce.

And nowe am I not in the worlde, whiche I do furthwith leaue, and goe out of it, but yet these abyde styll in the worlde in my steade, to disperse abrode throughout all nacions of the worlde, that whiche they haue learned of me. But I (leauyng them behynde me) come whole to thee. O holy father, kepe and preserue them in preachyng of thy name, whome thou gauest me to teache: and so kepe them that they maye preache and teache those thynges, which thou haste wylled me to preache, and whiche thynges I haue taughte obeying thy wyll in all thynges. And this do, that as I neuer went from thy commaundementes, but in all thynges haue agreed and consented to thy wyll, so bothe the doctrine of these, and also theyr lyfe, do neuer dissent frō myne. For so shall our name be truely glorifyed by them, yf as we agreyng within our selues do bothe the one and the other glorifie eche other: so euen these neuer dissentyng from vs, doe make our name famouse all the worlde thorowe. For whatsoeuer they haue taught and doen, because it shall be perceyued to haue come from vs, it shall therfore redound and be referred to the prayse and glorie of our name. As long as I lyued in theyr company familiarly, as a man with men, I was diligente to kepe them as thyne, and as men that thou haste put me in truste withall, eue

with

with bodely seruice, and doynges also, and I haue reteyned and continued the hitherto in league with vs. So manye as thou gauest me, haue I faythfullye kepte safe, and neuer one of this couente or felowship hath perished except one: whiche (though he lyued in my companye) yet was he none of myne, but borne to damnacion, whiche hymselfe through his owne faulte willinglye called for, and occasioned to fall vpon hym. For I omitted nothyng that should haue reuoked him, and haue brought him to better mynde. And this thyng truely dyd not happē by casualtie, but holy scripture dyd long tyme before shewe it should come to passe, that a familiar and a companion of householde, shoulde betraye to death his owne lorde and Maister. Notwithstandyng, throughe thy godlye deuise and diuine prouidence, it is come to effecte, and purpose, that also this mannes death and damnacion, shall be profitable and do good to the publique healthe and saluacion of the whole worlde, synce that by hym is procured the thyng, without whiche saluacion coulde not be had, and sithe also an example is gotten thereby, whiche ought to counsayle and admonishe euery man to abyde constantly, and to perceyuer in the thyng that he hath once begunne, and taken in hande: leste he by his owne folie turne to his owne vtter destruccion and cause of his owne damnacion, that thyng whiche (by the mere bountie, and free goodnes of God) was geuen hym, to obteyne thereby eternall health and saluacion.

The texte.

Nowe come I to thee, and these wordes speake I in the world, that they might haue my ioye full in them. I haue geuen them thy worde, and the world hath hated them, because they are not of the worlde, euen as I also am not of the worlde. I desyre not that thou shouldeste take them out of the worlde: But that thou kepe them from euill. They are not of the worlde, as I also am not of the worlde. Sanctifie them thorow thy trueth. Thy worde is the trueth. As thou dyddest sende me into the worlde, euen so haue I also sent them into the worlde: and for theyr sakes sanctifie I my selfe, that they also might be sanctified thorowe the trueth.

But nowe, lyke as these matters are dooen by thy eternall wisedome and iudgement, euen accordyng as thou wouldest haue it, so I now after I haue finished the thynges that thou commaundedst me, do leaue the worlde and come to thee. But I that shall go hence, do in the meane while speake these thynges vnto thee, not that I am any thyng doubtfull of thy wyll, but that I maye by this prayer comforte and stablishe my disciples: to the entent they maye vnderstand how that thou wilt care and prouide for them, after that they shall wante the presence and sight of my body, and that they maye also put awaye sorowfull pensiuenesse, for that they knowe howe that I shall lyue agayne: and so theyr ioye to be soone renued agayne, when they haue sene me risen from death to life: and in conclusion, after they haue seene me taken vp into heauen, and they to haue receiued that heauēly spirite, the holy ghost, one that shalbe both in steade of thee and me, they maye conceyue and receyue no temporall or vnperfite ioye, whiche maye ryse by the sight of my body, when it is brought to them agayne: but to haue a perpetuall and a perfite ioye whiche oure spirite shall alwaye infuse in them, dwelling in theyr hartes: to the entent that nowe they shoulde depende of nothyng els than of a good affiaunce in vs, and in the vprightnes of conscience. The worlde shall stire vp sore stormes of grieuous persecuciō agaynste them, because my doctrine agreeth not with the affeccions and carnall desyres of this worlde. For men, of trueth, be desyrouse of, and gape for earthlye and transitory thinges, and I teache heauenly thinges. This doctrine which I had of the, I haue taught it them: and these fewe haue well liked it and enbraced the same, the worlde setting nought by it. And because these loue my doctrine, the worlde hateth thē, as forsakers of the worlde, & runnagates to vs: & the worlde hath none other grounde thus to doe, but because they stick vnto vs, & renounce the worlde. This worlde hath his baites & enticementes that seme pleasaunt for a time: it hath also his dreadfull thinges, and threatninges, wherwith it doth discourage & weaken euen a right stronge and bold herte. Herewith he mayntaineth and defendeth his faccion, & fighteth against our religion. Therfore equitie would, & no lesse becummeth our bounteousnesse, that those whiche hath forsaken the worlde to come to vs, and haue cōmit and credite themselfes wholy to vs, and altogether depend vpon vs, we should care and prouide for: to thentent the worlde may knowe that they be in more safetie which betaketh themselfes to our succoure and mayntenaūce, than those that leaneth to the ayde & helpe of the worlde. The simple, playne true hart, which they beare towardes vs, and the trust that they haue in vs, deserueth heauēly fauour, & the hatred which the worlde beareth towardes them for our sake, prouoketh our beneuolence and good will towardes thē. For the worlde doth not therfore hate them, because they be theues or murderers, rauishers, or deceyuers with false bying & sellyng, but because they be cleare and pure from the enormities of this worlde: as ambicion, couetousnes, malice, pharisaicall fraude, from idolatrie, from vnclenesse and other sinnes wherwith the worlde is euery where infect. Furthermore as the worlde hateth me bicause I haue obeyed thy will, so doeth it also hate them, because they doe mislyke and contemne the doctrine of the Phariseis, and set nought by the folishe wisedome of the worlde: but in a simple and true meaning fayth, obey my lawes and tradicions. And the worlde doeth not onely hate me but also my name, and is lothe to haue me spokē of: yea for my cause it hateth them whosoeuer they be, that wyll neglecte mans doctryne, and folowe the plaine pure doctrine of the gospel, euen because it doeth muche disagre with the lustes and desires of them whiche withal affeccion and pleasure doe enbrace thinges of this worlde. I nowe that haue diligently doen my duetie and office, am separate from the felowship of the worlde, for so it is mete to be: But I would not as yet haue them cumpanions with me, for the time is not yet that they also should be taken cleane out of the worlde, vntill they likewise haue with diligence executed the office that is commit vnto them. This I only pray for, that they liuing in the worlde, be not polluted with the vices of the worlde, and that they fall not away from vs, and turne backewarde into the faccions and vnstable opinions of the worlde: For they beyng so many wayes assauted, cannot shumme and eschue that, without thy helpe. They stycke to me, they be my braūches, and my membres. Thus the matter stādeth, that as I am diuers and not agreable to the worlde because I stycke to the: euen so these also are vnlike to the worlde, & misliked, because they cleaue and stycke to me. As I haue kept me safe and pure from the filthy polluciōs of the worlde, so kepe thou these cleane and impolluted from all contagious infeccions of the worlde. That shall take effecte, yf by thy ayde and helpe they perseuer in the trueth. The wisedome of the worlde hath muche falsehood mixte withall: Moses lawe is wrapped in shadowes

I desire not that thou shouldest take them. &c.

 of thinges:

of thinges: but thy woorde whiche I haue taught is pure trueth, it hath no disceite, it is cleare and easie without smoke & shadowes. This trueth haue I taught purely & sincerely, that there nedeth not nowe so many interpretacions or translacions, so many Pharisaical ordinaũces, or so many laboured Philosophical sophemes and subtyll sentences. Only my doctrine is playne and easie to be vnderstand of all folke, if so be that fayth be had: And than it shall be a sufficient doctrine to euerlastyng felicitie.

Lyke as I beyng thy Apostle, and messenger, and sente from thee into the worlde, haue doen thy busines faithfully, and haue not been corrupted with contagiousnes of the worlde, but rather haue drawẽ the worlde to my purenesse, euen so doe I send these into the worlde in my steade, to teache purely & sincerely that whiche they haue heard of me, not studying their owne gaine and prayse, but folowyng thy will, to the intent that by their testimonie, many maye be drawen to vs, and be separate from the worlde, whiche is altogether sinfull. And because these may be pourged from synne, and so perseuer pure in preachyng the trueth of the gospel, I doe offer my selfe a sacrifice to thee. For he cannot purely preache my doctrine to the worlde, that is subiect to worldly affeccions.

The texte. Neuerthelesse, I pray not for them alone, but for them also, whiche shall beleue on me thorowe theyr preachyng: that they all may be one, as thou father art in me, and I in thee, and that they also may be one in vs: that the worlde may beleue that thou hast sent me. And the glory whiche thou gauest me, I haue geuen them: that they may be one as we also are one, I in them, and thou in me, that they may be made perfecte in one, & that the worlde may knowe that thou haste sente me, and haste loued them, as thou hast loued me. Father I will that they whiche thou haste geuen me, be with me where I am, that they may see my glory, which thou haste geuen me; For thou louedst me before the makyng of the worlde.

Nor I doe not onely pray for these whiche are fewe in numbre, but for all that shall through my doctrine preached of these, renounce the worlde, & put their whole affiaunce in me. For it shal so come to passe, that as I sticking to thy woordes, am not pulled away from thee, & like as these, sticking to my preceptes shal not be pulled away from me, but as braũches shal liue in vs, and as our membres shalbe quickened and made liuely with the spirite: euen so other (which shall sticke to these mens woordes, which beyng receyued at my handes they shall teache to the worlde) beyng graffed in me, maye be ioyned to thee by me, so that the whole body maye cleaue ioyntly together, thou beyng the roote and I the stocke, the spirite beyng distribute thorowe out al the membres: and both these braunches, and the other that shall be brought to the fayth by these, beyng dispersed thorowe out the whole worlde farre & neare. I can do nothing without thee, these coulde do nothing without me: The same thing that I receyued of thee, haue I poured into them by the spirite whiche is common to all, that as thou extendest foorth thy power and strength in me, and I inseparably do cleaue vnto the: euen so bothe we maye extende foorth our power in these cleauing vnto vs, and will not be disseuered, to thintent that ẏ worlde being prouoked with these mẽs vniforme doctrine, miracles, and honest chaste maners, maye beleue that I am come from thee: & that whatsoeuer I haue doen, may redound to the glory of thy name: and that the worlde also may vnderstande and perceyue our spirite to bee in these persones, shewyng foorth and bryngyng to light his force and power,

The glorye which thou gauest me I haue geuen them.

by

by miracles and other divers prouses. For as I haue not chalenged to my selfe the prayse and glorie whiche the miracles that I haue wroughte haue gotten me amongest men, but I haue translate, surrendred, and put it ouer to thee (o father) whome I haue confessed to be the auctor thereof: so the glorie whiche these shall prepare by theyr great actes for the tyme to come, shall be altogether ours: because they shall do nothyng in theyr owne name, but shall referre all thynges to the commendacion and glory of our name. And so therfore the world shall perceyue suche a concorde betwene them and me, as is betwene thee and me. I wil worke in them by my spirite, as thou hast set abroche thy trueth in me. And so it wyll come to passe, that they also, as membres of one bodye, cleauing to one heade, and quickened with one spirite, maye by mutuall concorde sticke together among themselues: that on all parties, there maye be a consummate and a very perfite concorde in heauen and in yearth.

The discencion in opinions doeth take awaye the beliefe of doctrine. If they agreyng one with another shall teache thesame that I haue taughte, yf lyke agre with doctrine, doubtles the world shall perceyue it is no worldlye or humayne doctrine, but to be come from whome thou sendeste into the worlde. It shall also vnderstande that they be beloued of thee, obeying thy will, as I am beloued of thee, one that no where declineth or swarueth from thy mynde and purpose.

Father my desyre is, that as these whom beyng disseuered from the world thou haste geuen to me, shall be folowers of myne afflictions and crosse, so they maye be partakers with me of glorie: that like as they haue bene beholders of my base and meane state, and witnesses of my payne and tormentes: so they maye likewyse see and beholde the glorye, whiche thou shalte giue me after I haue passed thorowe these euils and haue finished my whole passion, that also they maye learne by afflictions to go to the eternall ioye, and by reproche and ignominie, to go to immortall glorye. For it is no newe glory whiche thou shalt geue me, nor newe charitie wherwith thou louest me: but therfore thou shewest tokens and argumentes among menne, of thy loue towardes me, to the intente that those whiche wyll be myne, shoulde by lyke waye and meane cumpasse and seke for thy loue: and by lyke dedes laboure to be promoted vnto the glorye of heauen. They whome thou hast vouchesafed to loue, and shalt alowe them as wurthy thy glorye, haue been loued of the before the creacion of the worlde.

The texte.

O righteouse father, the worlde also hath not knowen the, but I haue knowen the, and these haue knowen that thou haste sent me, and I haue declared vnto them thy name, and wil declare it, that the loue wherwith thou haste loued me, maye be in them, and I in them.

O righteouse father, nothyng hath been ouerslipt or omitted of me, whereby thou shouldest haue been brought to be knowen of all folke, but the worlde beyng for the more parte blynded in the sinne & faultes therof, would not know thee, because it would not beleue me, whiles I taught thee vnto the worlde. But I beyng pure from the worlde, haue knowen thee, and haue taughte thee beyng knowen vnto me. Neyther hath my preachyng been altogether in vaine. They, whome thou specially diddest chose for that purpose, haue knowen thee by me: they knewe that I came from thee, although the Phariseis with open clamoure sayeth, that I came from Beelzebub the prince of deuils. But as thy goodnes had sent me to haue saued all folke, if it could by any waye haue been brought to passe, so thy righteousnesse will not suffre the desires of the faythful to be frustrate and voyde, for the infidelitie of some that be vnfaythfull.

The learned, the potentates, the chiefe heades of religion, haue contemned thy doctrine, but these rude, ignoraunt, meke and vnlearned persones, haue by me receyued the knowleage of thy name: and I shall cause it to be more and more knowen vnto them, that thou mayest with thesame great charitable loue wherwith thou embracest me, lykewise embrace them: and so they beeyng more fully taught by my spirite, maye on theyr behalfe agayne bothe loue vs, and one of them by mutuall gentlenes, nourishe, cherishe, and defende eche one the other. For so shall they be strong agaynst all the troublesome hurlyburlies of this worlde, and shall persist vnuanquished.

The. xviii. Chapter.

The texte. When Jesus had spoken these wordes, he went foorth with his disciples ouer the brooke Cedron, where was a gardeyne, into the which he entred and his disciples. Judas also which betrayed hym, knewe the place: for Jesus oft tymes resorted thither with his disciples. Judas then after he had receyued a bande of men, and ministers of the hye priestes and Phariseis, came thither with lanternes, and fyrebrandes, and weapons. And Jesus knowyng all thynges that shoulde come vpon hym, went foorth, and sayed vnto them: whom seke ye? They aunswered hym: Jesus of Nazareth. Jesus sayeth vnto them: I am he. Judas also whiche betrayed hym stoode with them. Assone then as he had sayed vnto them, I am he, they wente backewarde and fell to the grounde.

With this kynde of talke, our Lorde Jesus did confirme, stablishe, and bolden the hertes of his, and after he had so doen, and commēded his flocke to his father, he departed thence of his owne voluntary wyll, to go mete them, that shoulde apprehende hym: therein declaryng playnly to his disciples, that he woulde willynglye and gladly suffer, whatsoeuer payne shoulde be put vnto hym: for it was midnight, and except it had been a well knowen place, he could not haue been taken. Therfore he departed out of that place whereas he had thus spoken to his disciples. And when he was goen ouer the brooke whiche the Hebrewes call Cedron, because many Cedre trees growe there, he and his disciples wayting on hym, wente into a gardeyne: not ignoraunt that Judas woulde come thither with a bande of harneysed men to attache hym, because Judas that betrayed hym, knewe full well that our Lorde Jesus was wonte often to gette hymselfe secretely thither, late in the night with his disciples, to praye. They tooke the night tyme for this cause, leste the company that Jesus had with him, shoulde make resistence, and let them to take hym.

For Judas that was of a disciple become a traytoure, and of a cumpanion to hym that was a redemer made a capitaine of theuishe souldiers, came into the gardeyne (where the lorde beyng with his disciples, prayed) with the bād of men whiche he had taken vnto hym by the appoyntmente of the Bishoppes and Phariseis, with whome he had couenaunted to betraye Jesus, and bryng hym into theyr handes: And verily they brought with them, fierbrandes and lanternes, by meanes whereof he might be discerned and knowen in the night. Nor they came not withoute swerdes and staues agaynste the force and violence of Christes disciples, yf percase any would haue profered to defende their lorde. Howbeit Jesus knowyng all thynges that were wroughte and dooen agaynste gaynst him, to teache playnly that hymselfe wittingly and willingly did suffer al that he suffered, not tarying for theyr cumming, went forward to mete them as they were cumming towardes him, and of his owne mynde unforced, asked them whom they sought: leste for lacke of knowledge, they myght haue layed handes upon some of his disciples. And when they had answered hym, Jesus of Nazareth, he sayed boldely unto them: I am very he whom ye seke. There was then also Judas Iscarioth present, and his bande of mē with him: whiche Judas had a litle before betrayed Jesus with a kysse under a false pretended frendeship, ere the Lord had spoken these woordes. yet did Jesus neither in the meane time bewray him, of whom he was betrayed, nor spake any rough & rebukefull woordes against the souldiers that were hyred to attache him: because he would styll euen tyll all were fully ended, shewe his disciples exaumple of gentlenesse and modeste mekenesse. But as soone as Jesus had sayed unto them: I am he, the bande of men beyng soore afrayed went backwardes and fell to the grounde, not able to sustayne and abyde the violence of the Lordes voice.

Then asked he them agayne: whom seke ye? They sayed: Jesus of Nazareth. Jesus answered: I haue tolde you that I am he. If ye seke me therfore, let these goe their way, that the saying might be fulfilled which he spake: of them whiche thou gauest me haue I not lost one. The texte.

After that they were come to themselfes againe, and made ready to set upon Jesus the secound time, the Lord asked them once againe, whom they did seke. And when they had nowe answered as before, saying they sought Jesus of Nazareth, he made them a lyke bolde answer, as he had doen before, and sayed: I toulde you euen very nowe, that I am the same manne ye looke for. And if ye seke me, I do lycence you to medle only with me: suffer ye therfore these to go theyr waye, against whom I geue you no interest at this present. The cause why Jesus did thus, was to declare by a manifest tokē, that he could not haue been apprehended, except he had permitted himselfe to be taken, in that he had once with one woorde put backe and cast downe to the grounde, both a desperate and an armed multitude of souldiers, and Judas selfe too, that shameles traitour. Moreouer lyke as he gaue thē leaue to take himselfe, so on the other syde he restrayned them from hauyng power ouer his disciples: because he had tolde beforehande, that the fiercenesse of that storme, should for that presente time light upon his owne head alone, and as for the rest, although they were somewhat ouerthrowen & deiect, yet should they be safe without hurte untill he should see them agayne: herein declaring hymselfe to play the parte of a good shepeherde, which redemeth the health of his flocke with the losse of his owne life.

Then Symon Peter hauing a swerde, drewe it, and smote the hye priestes seruaunt, and cut of his right eare. The seruauntes name was Malchus. Therfore Jesus sayeth unto Peter: The texte. Put up thy swerde into thy sheathe: shall not I drinke of the cup which my father hath geuen me? Then the cumpany and the captayne and ministers of the Jewes, tooke Jesus & bounde hym, and led hym away to Annas firste, for he was father in lawe to Cayphas, whiche was the hye priest the same yere. Cayphas was he whiche gaue councell to the Jewes, that it was expedient that one man should dye for the people.

Nowe then Symon Peter whiche bore a notable ardente loue towardes his Lord, because he had made a great bragg ue of himselfe, no lesse then that he would be content to dye to saue his Lordes lyfe, seing the armed band of men to lay hand vpon Jeſus, forgat what the Lorde had ſayed vnto hym. And ſo beyng in a ſodayne rage, drewe out a ſwerde, not taryng to bee commaunded of his Lorde to doe it, & ſtroke the Byſhops ſeruaunt whoſe name was Malchus, but the ſtroke light not as he would haue had it: he onely ſtroke of the felowes right eare, euen accordyng as the Lorde did ſtaye his hande, to the entent he ſhould geue but a ſmall wounde. Howbeit Jeſus did forthwith of his owne gentleneſſe heale the man agayne. And in dede yͤ Lorde ſuffered him that ſhould be a ruler of his churche, to fall (of a godly zeale truely) into this errour, for that he might afterward more ſurely and more effectuouſly put awaye all deſire to doe vengeaunce, and ſhake of altogether priuate reuenging and vſe of weapons, ſince he had ones rebuked him whiche as yet hauing no contrary commaundement, did of very deuocion, and of a godly affeccion, goe aboute to defende his moſte vertuouſe godly Lorde againſt the wicked. So then Jeſus verily put awaye by his diuine power, the force of the men of warre from Peter, but yet withall he chideth Peter as a diſciple, when he ſeeth hym hotely ſet to fyght out the matter, and ſayth: Peter, what doeſt thou? Haſt thou forgotten what thou haſt heard of late whiles thou diddeſt exhorte me not to dye? that is to witte, howe thou waſt called Satan, and commaunded to folowe behynde. To what purpoſe is thy ſwerde drawen, becauſe thou wouldeſt hynder my death, whiche I goe to ſuffer willingly, and apoynted ſo to doe by my father?

It becummeth the to folowe, and not to repell my croſſe. Therfore put thy ſwerde into thy ſheath. Matters of the ghoſpel are not ſo to be defended. If thou wilt ſuccede me as my vicar, thou muſt fight with no other ſwerd than of Gods woorde, whiche cutteth away ſinnes, and ſaueth the men. Shal not I drinke of this cuppe of death, whiche my father hath geuen me to drinke? How ſhall it come to paſſe all we to be one, accordyng as I prayed to my father, excepte that like as I doe obey the fathers will euen to the very death, ſo you lykewyſe obey my commaundementes?

The diſciples beyng with this ſaying reſtrayned and ſtayed from fightyng, the meinie of warre and their capitayne, with the miniſters alſo whome the Byſhops and Phariſeis ſent to augment the numbre, layed their wicked hãdes vpon Jeſus, and led hym faſt bounde as a malefactour, firſt to Byſhop Annas, Caiphas father in law. Caiphas verily was the hye Byſhop of that yere, therfore thei led Jeſus from Annas houſe to Caiphas, of whom it was ſpoken before, that whiles other were perplexed and in doubt what was to be doen with Jeſus, he beyng (for the office ſake that he bare) inſpired wyth the ſpirite of prophecie, coũſailed that in any caſe Jeſus ſhould finally ſuffre death, becauſe it was ſo expedient for all folke that the helth & ſaluacion of the people ſhould be recouered and redemed with the death of one man. Jeſus therfore was led vnto Caiphas father in lawe, firſt to fede his iyes with a ſight that was wiſhed & longed for: alſo that he might be examined in this mans houſe, if they could finde any lykelyhode of any faulte in him. For although they had ſuche bloudſuckyng hertes, as could haue been contente to haue murthered their owne parẽtes, yet for feare of the people, & of the lieutenant Pilate, they ſtudied to pretend ſome colour of iuſtice, but Gods prouidence turned the wicked ſubtil crafte of man, into the glory of his ſonne. For whyleſt he is thus taken, thus led from Annas to Caiphas, from Caiphas to Pilate, from Pilate to Herode, and backe againe from Herode to Pilate, whiles he is examined of many, and of many matters accused, he made them all witnesses and confessours of his innocencie, yea they that were his enemies. And verily there is no more certaine testimonie of innocencie, then that which cometh forth out of an enemy. How litle equitie did they shewe mete for a Byshop? They bought the betraying of an innocent with money, they arested and toke a naked man without armour, with a bande of armed men hyred for that purpose: they bounde hym that made no resistence, but that he had onely shewed great lykelyhood howe great his power was, in case he would haue vsed it, and willingly gaue himselfe vnto them: they led him not to a iudge, but to an enemy, as men auaunting themselfes of theyr praye, and there finally sought they for a faulte to be layed against hym, when as the equitie euen of prophane lawes, will no man to be arested except first a man be moste hated for his naughtines, and so burdened with a faulte.

The texte. And Simon Peter folowed Jesus, and so did an other disciple that was knowen vnto the hye prieste, and went in with Jesus into the palace of the hye prieste. But Peter stode at the doore without. Then wente out that other disciple whiche was knowen vnto the hye prieste, and spake to the damsell that kept the doore, and brought in Peter. Then sayed the damsell that kept the doore vnto Peter: art not thou also one of this mans disciples? he sayed: I am not. The seruauntes and the ministers stode there, whiche had made a fyre of coles, for it was colde, and they warmed themselues. Peter also stode among them and warmed hym.

Nowe then when Jesus was brought thither, that is, to Cayphas, Symon Peter, notwithstandyng that he was forbid fightyng, neuerthelesse hauing yet some confidence in his owne strength, folowed Jesus, and a certaine other disciple with him: euen the same that a lytle before leaned on Jesus breast at supper tyme. This disciple because he was knowen to the Byshop, was bolde in trust of that knowledge, to go into the palace with Jesus. Peter because he was not knowen, durst not folowe them into the palace, but taryed at the doore without, in the meane tyme muche swaruyng from that bolde saying: I will venter my lyfe for the. And yet some manlinesse remayned in him for all that. For it came of loue that he durst styll folowe vnto the doore, seeyng the reste of his felowes scatter themselues abrode eche one a sere waye: but in that he durst not go in, was a feare, and dyd pronosticate that he should soone after deny his Lorde. Howbeit that other disciple perceyuyng that Peter folowed not, spake to the damsell that kepte the doore, to take in him which stode at the doore without. And when the mayde had let him in she behelde Peter, and thought she should knowe hym: bothe because she had seen him in Jesus cumpany, and specially because he was commaunded to be brought in of him, whom she knewe to bee Jesus disciple. And therfore she sayed vnto Peter: Art not thou also this mannes disciple, whiche is nowe taken and brought in hyther? At this voice of a woman of small reputacion, whiche yet pretended no kynde of crueltie or thyng to be feared, seeyng she compared Peter with him whom she did not appeache nor violently handle, and knewe hym to be Jesus disciple, and so named Jesus vnto him, calling him in suche sorte a manne, as though she had rather pitied him then disdayned him: Peter, I say, for all this sodainly forgetting al thinges whiche Jesus had so ofte repeted vnto him, and forgetting also his

Peter stode at the doore without.

owne

owne stoute promisse, denyed that he was Jesus disciple. And euen this is the firste profession of them that be desirouse to mortife themselfes in princes houses, verily to deny Christe, that is to saye, the truth. And whan Peter was thus gotten in, he wente and stode among the Byshoppes officers and seruauntes which were standyng by the fyre syde to warme themselfes, because it was colde that late tyme of the nyght . And Peter warmed hym with them, trustyng that he so myght kepe hymselfe secrete, and in the meane tyme see what should become of Jesus in conclusiō, and what issue this matter should drawe to, for as yet Peter had not putte awaye all hope that hys Lorde should escape death although he was so striken with feare, that he did not once thinke of that the Lorde had euen newly before told him would be, that is to wete, that Peters selfe for al he was a bolde promiser, would forsweare his Lorde and maister.

The texte.

The hye priest then asked Jesus of disciples and of his doctrine. Jesus aunswered hym: I spake openly in the worlde. I euer taught in the Synagogue and in the Temple where all the Jewes resorte, and in secrete haue I sayed nothyng . Why askest thou me? Aske them which heard me what I haue sayed vnto them. Behold they can tell what I sayed. When he had thus spoken, one of the ministers whiche stoode by, smote Jesus on the face, saying. Aunswerest thou the hye priest so? Jesus answered him: If I haue euill spoken, beare witnes of the euill: but if I haue well spoken, why smytest thou me?

Nowe the Bishop Cayphas to shewe some semblaunce of rightfull iudgement, but yet his entent was to gather somewhat of Jesus sūdry answeres, that he myght charge hym withall as a manne faultye, and therfore he questioned with Jesus of his disciples, what maner of men they were, whence he had them, and to what purpose he had gathered suche a cumpanye together, yea and also what he secretly taught them: Howbeit Jesus knowyng that he dyd not demaunde these questions of a ryght iudgelyke mynde to knowe the truth, but deceytfully to hunte out some thyng in hym woorthy blame, and to gette occasion withall howe to harme his disciples, whom he would yet should be in safegarde, Jesus, I say, knowyng this made no answere to the Byshoppes wylie and traiterouse interrogacions, but banysheth the testimony of hymselfe and his, and sendeth them to the common reporte, and also to the recorde of his enemies, a profe of moste certaintie for the innocent, and sayth vnto the Byshop: Why askest thou me what I haue taught my disciples secretly or in hugger mugger? My doctryne hathe not been sediciouse nor secrete. I haue spoken openly to the brode worlde. That whiche I haue taught, I haue alwaye taught it in your Synagogues. I haue taught in the temple vpon the holy dayes, in place and tyme moste notable and famouse, whither Jewes on euery syde out of all partes of Syria resorte. And I haue spoken nothyng in priuitie or corners, whiche same thing I durst not teache openly. Full oftē hath the people and Phariseis too, heard me. Why then doest thou nowe aske me of suche maner of doctrine as should be taught by stelth and very priuely? But rather aske them, that haue heard me teache openly. Their recorde shall be of more certaintye which hath with me no familiar acquaintaunce, yea of whom some do hate me. Let euen them that be mine enemies reporte what I haue taught: for many knowe it, and it shalbe easie to fynde witnesses of my doctrine. Whan Jesus had spokē these thynges, teachyng thereby that the trueth is to be answered for, boldely in

I euer taught in the Synagogue.

dede,

dede, but without tauntes or rebukes, one of the bishoppes ministers that by chaunce stoode nerte him, a man not vnlyke his lord and maister, willing to defende his bishops dignitie agaynst the franke and liberal speache of Jesus, after suche lyke sorte as Peter would haue defended his maisters lyfe against the force of the souldiers, not tarrying for any commaundement of his lorde, gaue Jesus a blow vpon the cheke, and suche a checkeful rebuke as was fit for suche a byshop, and suche a felow his seruaunt, saying: Aunswerest thou the byshop so? Our Lorde Jesus might bothe haue destroyed this wicked byshop, and also haue letted this blowgeuer, but that he would shewe by exaumple to his, howe ferre out of course and how peruerse the iudgementes of the world be. For our Lorde Jesus whiche behaued himselfe moost mekely agaynst all iniuries, beyng no where so sharpe as against them that vnder the pretence of religion barke and worke againste true religion, tooke not the blowe without replying in woordes, whiche yet endured the crosse and made no wordes therat. The bishoppes sate in auctoritie, Jesus beyng bounde was examined: here loe was a face of iudgement. And of trueth before a temporall iudge beyng but an Heathen, he that is accused shall be heard to saye for hymselfe. Here now before a bishop, a blow was geuen for makyng one aunswere, and the blowe too was geuen hym that afterwarde should be iudge of the quicke and the dead.
And so in dede Jesus aunswered, in dede frankely, but yet mildly and coldely, saying: I speake before a iudge, and I aunswere hym beyng required. In this case before Gentiles also is the matter hādled with good reasons, and not with strokes. If I haue sayed any thyng amisse tell me howe: but if I haue spoken nothing euill, why doest thou beyng a iudges officer, here in tyme of iudgemēt, the iudge holdyng his peace, beate me without consultyng the thyng that I saye?

And Annas sent hym bound vnto Caiphas the hie priest. Symon Peter stoode and warmed hymselfe, then sayed they vnto hym: Art not thou also one of his disciples? He denyed it and sayed: I am not. One of the seruauntes of the hye priestes, his cosin whose eare Peter smote of, sayed vnto hym: Did not I see the in the garden with hym? Peter therfore denied it againe, and immediately the cocke crewe. Then they led Jesus from Caiphas into the hall of iudgemente. It was in the mornyng, and they themselues wente not into the iudgement hall, leste they shoulde be defiled, but that they mighte eate the Passouer.

The texte.

Verily Annas, although vpon malice he reioysed that Jesus was vnder warde, and had in hold, neuertheles because he could trye out nothyng of him, whereby he might by any colour be proued giltye: he sendeth hym euen bound as he was to bishop Caiphas his sonne in lawe. But in the meane time whilest these thynges were in handlyng, Peter vewyng all thynges a farre of, whiche as I begun to tell, stoode in the throng of the ministers, warmyng hym at the fyre syde, and among these some there were which by certayn tokens somewhat knew Peter, and sayed vnto hym: Arte not thou one of this mannes disciples whome the byshop thus handleth? Peter seeyng so cruell a syght, whiche made hym also sore afrayed, once agayne denyed that he was Jesus disciple. For he nowe perceyued by the byshops interogatyues, howe that they were in deuyse to attache Jesus disciples: also Peter thought by this deniall to bee safe from daunger, lyke as he had shifted hymselfe from her that kepte the doore, but to make him know the better, how he could nothing do of his owne propre strēgth beyng disseuered from the felowshyp of his Lorde, there stoode among other in

that

that throng of the ministers, a certayn kinsman of him that had a litle before in the garden first auentured to laye handes vpon Jesus, and had his eare strikẽ of by Peter. This felow was by the iudgement of god brought in as an instrument, vnder pretence to auenge his cosen Malchus harme, but in very dede it was to correcte the rashe confidence that Peter had in hymselfe. For the sayed felow beyng not content with Peters only one denial (for his fighting though it were doen in the darke, made him to be wel knowẽ) sayeth vnto Peter: What (sayeth he) doest thou denye thy selfe to be one of his disciples? Did not I euen right nowe see the with mine iyes in the garden with Jesus? Peter beyng with this saying vtterly blancke and sore astonished, wished himselfe accursed yf euer he knewe Jesus. And anon the cocke crewe. Neyther did Peter by this token, whiche oure Lorde had tolde hym of before, come to hymselfe agayne, neyther woulde haue been well aduised, except our Lorde had recouered hym, and brought him to himselfe agayne by his effectuall lokyng vpon Peter: and had also by inwarde inspiracion prouoked teares of penaunce in hym.

So many wayes was he that should be a speciall minister vnder Christ of the holy churche, to be taught how in al thinges to mistrust his owne strength, and to depende of his lordes onely ayde and succour. Now therefore after that Jesus had been all the nighte long till the mornyng early, in examinacion before Caiphas, nor no faulte coulde be founde in hym, wherefore he oughte to be called for, and to bee arrained vpon lyfe and death, they haue him out of bishop Caiphas house, and leade hym to Pilate the lorde presidente, to thentente they might charge hym, and discharge themselues of the hatred that they should be in for sheading of innocent bloude. And euen being bounde as he stoode, Jesus was led by the hyred souldiers into the presidentes iudgemente hall. Howbeit the Jewes themselues went not into the house of iudgement, leste they shoulde be polluted, in asmuche as the paschall lambe muste be eaten of them: to the eatyng wherof they woulde go pure and cleane, but of a naughtie peruerse religion be ye sure, consideryng that they thoughte themselues to be contaminate and suspended with the harmelesse house of the president, because he was a Gẽtile and no Jewe, when as themselues by many craftes went about and deuised a mans death, that had doen nothing amisse, yea that had many waies doen well and deserued muche good at theyr handes.

The texte. Pylate then went out vnto them and sayed: what accusacion bryng ye against this mãe They aunswered and sayed vnto hym. If he were not an euill doer, we woulde not haue deliuered hym vnto thee. Then sayed Pilate vnto them: Take ye hym, and iudge hym after your owne lawe. The Jewes therfore sayed vnto hym: It is not lawfull for vs to putte any man to death, that the wordes of Jesus might be fulfilled whiche he spake, signifying what death he should dye.

Therfore Pilate after he sawe the vncouth and that newe maner of iudgement, as a man to be in captiuitie and boundẽ ere he were examined and hearde of the iudge, and to see a band of harnessed men, he commeth forth abrode hymself to be polluted with suche mens communicacion, as thought thẽselues pure and vnpolluted. And verily he came out to appease & asswage, yf it were possible, the furye of the Jewes, and so to quite the innocente. Ye sende (sayeth he) this manne vnto me to be putte to death. But it is not the maner of Rome to put any man to execucion, except hym that is proued giltie of a faulte worthy death. What crime therfore do ye laye to this mannes charge? The Jewes

aunswered,

aunswered: the autoritie of Byshops, and Phariseis is inough for your discharge. If this man were not a malefactour we coulde not of our profession haue committed hym to your handes. Pilate suspectyng, as the trueth was, them to haue some priuate grudge towardes hym about the supersticion and the superfluous religion, and vayne deuocion of the lawe, sayeth vnto them: If it be any matter that appertey neth not to my counte and office, as for exaumple, if case the Sabboth day be broken, if any swynes fleshe be eaten, or percase some rashe & liberall woordes hath been spoken against Moses, the Prohetes, the Temple, or your God: loe, nowe if any suche scape haue been, whiche your owne lawe commaunded to be punished, though yet there be no suche thing prohibite by the lawe of Rome, your selfes take the mā vnto you and iudge hym after your lawe. I am sette here in the Emperours name to rule & play the Judge. If he hath committed any faulte against the Emperours lawes, worthy death, bryng him to me, and after he be conuicte by the lawe, & lawfully cast, I shall cause him to be put to execucion. But I will not intermeddle & perplexe my selfe in doubtfull matters of your lawe. Verily, though the Jewes would (they forced not howe) haue had him made away, yet for all that they pretende reliousnesse of very feare, leste the iudge should forthwith haue punished thē, because they would haue kylled an harmelesse and an vncondemned person. But at thesame tyme they sought effectually a newe kynde of punishement for him, such one as was then among the Jewes moste spytefull and opprobrious. It is not, say they, lawefull for vs to put any man to death. The shamelesse people spake these woordes whiche had slayne so many Prophetes: flatteryng themselfes as cleane frō murder, notwithstandyng they did so many wayes persecute an innocente to death: or els they thus did, as if the hangman which with his handes fasteneth the man to the crosse, were a sole murderer. They were in herte murderers, they were murderers in theyr tongues, with theyr money, they hyred one trayterously to betray hym, they hyred a sorte of warryers, they hyred false witnesses, they forged false haynouse crymes against him. They prouoke & prycke forwarde the iudge, and with threatning make hym afearde, & yet impute themselues pure & fre from murder, and also worthy to eate the Pascall Lambe, for no cause els, but that they dyd stay and refrayne themselues from goyng into the iudgement hall. Well these thinges truely were doen to make it appeare euidente that there is nothyng wurse or more haynouse then false and peruerse religion, and that thesame thyng also should be brought to effecte, which Jesus sayed should come to passe, signifying by a parable what death he shoulde dye, whan he spake these woordes: At suche tyme as I shall be lyfte vp on hye from the grounde, I shall drawe all thynges vnto me: by the force of which woordes, he would that we should take it for a certaintie that not only the selfe death was determinately limited vnto him, but also a choice and seuerall kynde of death.

Then Pilate entred into the iudgement hall againe, and called Jesus, and sayed vnto him: Art thou the kyng of Jewes? Jesus answered: sayest thou that of thy selfe, or did other tell it thee of me? Pilate answered. Am I a Jew? Thine owne nacion & hye priestes hath deliuered thee vnto me. What hast thou doen? Jesus answered. My kingdome is not of this worlde: If my kyngdome were of this worlde, then would my ministers surely fight, that I should not be deliuered vnto the Jewes: but nowe is my kyngdome not from hence. *The texte.*

Wherfore then after that Pilate vnderstanding by the woordes which the

Jewes

Jewes had spoken of a matter (I knowe not what) amonges other thinges to be obiecte against Jesus, concerning a kingdome that he should goe about desirously (and yet there appeared no likelyhood at all in Jesus that shoulde cause any manne to thynke hym fauty therein) Pilate, I saye, after this, went once againe into the iudgement halle, and lefte the people standyng without. And so called for Jesus secretly asyde, that quietly and without all ruffle, he might boult out and gather of hym (which in countenaunce appeared no lesse then both vertuouse and wise) what the matter was, and saied vnto him: Art thou that king of the Jewes whom they are reported to looke for? This one thyng did Pilate diligently searche out, because the other matters touched not the weale publique: but this faulte, to call himselfe a kyng, semed to concerne both the Emperours Maiestie, and a common peace and tranquillitie. And truly Pilate made this searche and enquirie not that he did take it to be true, but to get some matter of him that was accused, wherwith he might reproue ẏ Jewes of falsehood. Howbeit though Jesus knew wel inough the Jewes to haue falsely appeached hym that he should be desirous of a kyngdome to the Emperours losse, or in despite of his highnesse, yet to the entent he myght open and disclose the malice of the Jewes, and commende the reasonablenesse & equitie muche better in Pilate then in the Byshops and Phariseis, though he were but a Gentyle, and set naught by the Jewes religion: for this skill, I saye, Jesus made hym aunswere, saying: Whether thinkest thou of thine owne cōiecture, that I am desyrouse of a kingdome, or haue the Jewes accused me herof to thee? Pilate both to declare his owne innocēcie & the malice of the Jewes too, sayeth: I doe not cōiecture this of mine owne head, neyther doe I see in thee any thyng agreable thereunto. It is a Jewes tale of a king to come. Thinkest thou me to be a Jewe? Thy quarelling cōtrey folkes and the Byshops, committed thee into my handes, seking all the meanes they can to haue thee put to death, but because it is not the fashion of Rome to putte any vncondemned person to death, if therfore thou haste not trāsgressed in ẏ trayterous desire of a kingdom, then what faute beside haste thou made? Because Pilate asked him of these thynges simply, and meaning good fayth, entending to deliuer the innocente, Jesus did vouchesafe to aunswere hym by a rydle & prouerbially: teaching that it was an other maner of kingdom wherof the Prophetes had spoken, a farre more excellent kingdom then is the kingdom of this worlde, whiche consisteth in mans lawes, in the ayde of mē, which haue no power, but vpō bodies. Howbeit he signified this kingdom to be an heauēly kingdom, which could not couet ẏ kingdom of the worlde, but contemne it: and should not harme it, but auaunce it into a better kinde. My kingdom, sayth Christ, is no suche kingdom as ẏ Emperours is, his kingdom is terrestriall, but mine is celestial. And for ẏ cause am I affeccionate to nothing that can harme the Emperours maiestie. If my kingdom were of this world, the world should not handle me as it doth, vnreuenged. For euen I, be ye sure, should haue (as other kynges hath) a garde of harnessed men. I should haue squiers for the body, & suche as should onely attende vpon myne owne persone: I should haue plentie of well appoynted men, and lacke no ayde or succoure that would fight for me, that it should not be in the Jewes power to doe the thyng they goe about against me vnrequited.

My kyngdome is not of this worlde. &c.

At this presente I haue fewe disciples, and those that I haue bee vnapte to

warre,

warre, weake and poore, I my selfe beyng vnarmed and no warryer, euen one that seketh to the helpe of other, because my kyngdome is not of this worlde.

The texte.

¶ Pilate therfore sayed vnto hym: Arte thou a kyng then? Jesus aunswered: thou sayest that I am a king. For this cause was I borne, and for this cause came I into the world that I should beare witnes vnto the trueth. And all that are of the trueth, heare my voyce. Pilate sayde vnto hym: What thyng is trueth? And when he had sayed this, he wente oute agayne vnto the Jewes, and sayeth vnto them: I fynde in hym no cause at all: ye haue a custome that I should delyuer you one loose at Easter, wyll ye that I loose vnto you the king of the Jewes? Then cryed they all agayne, saying: Not hym but Barrabas, the same Barrabas was a murtherer.

Forasmuche as Pylate beyng a laye man and a Gentile did not fully vnderstande this mistye and darke saying, albeit he heard that Jesus dyd not vtterly renounce and denye the name of a kyng, but dyd put a difference of kingdomes, Pilate therfore sayed vnto hym: Is it then true that thou arte somewhere a kyng whatsoeuer kynde of kyngdome it be, and thou not perteynyng to vs? Here now Jesus beyng earnestly asked of the iudge whether he were any waye a kyng, or naye, confesseth the trueth with great temperaunce and modestye, with muche sobrietie and good aduisemente, aunswerynge thus: Thou sayest I am a kyng, for whosoeuer asketh a question, with lyke numbre of wordes, the pronunciacion onely chaunged, affirmeth the thyng. And Jesus sayed further: It is not my parte to denye any trueth, namely consyderyng that for this cause I was borne, and came into the worlde, that I should deceyue no mā with any lye, but that I shoulde beare witnes vnto the trueth.

He that hath a simple meke mynde not blynded with the lustes and desires of this worlde, acknowlegeth, lyketh well, and heareth my voyce. But Pilate hauyng no further intelligence of that whiche was spoken, then that he supposed the thyng to be no matter for hym to know, and as yet Christe had made Pilate no apte aunswere, therewith either to sette the Jewes at a quiet or to dispatche them thence, after he had asked of Jesus what was that trueth wherof he spake, and was come into the worlde to beare witnes therof: Pilate, I saye, wente oute agayne vnto the Jewes, not tarrying for an aunswere of the thing, that he questioned of. What nedeth many wordes, sayeth Pilate: I haue examined the man, and can fynde no faulte in hym worthy death. Nor I am not here president and chiefe iustice vnder the Emperour, because I shoulde with my sentence condemne the innocente, but in case he be noysome to you, and that ye thynke him fautye (which I fynde not) yet it standeth with equitie and good indifferencie, that if ye wyl not spare and forbeare hym as an innocent, at leastwaye in the honor of this holy feast and for religion sake, pardon hym his life as an offender. And in dede it is here a custome amonges you that in this feast of Phase (whiche is of you moste highly solemnised and kept moste holye of all feastes,) I should at your request pardon and set at libertie some one offender. Therfore ye shall haue free eleccion to chose the one of twayne, eyther Barrabas that arrant theefe and notable robber, a disturber of the publique peace, or this Jesus, a man in my iudgement fautlesse, whome some folke sayeth is the kyng of Jewes. It were beste surely that this man, yea though he haue done amysse, should fele and enioye the graciouse fauour and priuiledge of youre solemne feast.

For this cause was I borne. &c

Wyll

Wyll ye therfore that I forgeue this persone for your sakes? for of trueth the president did not looke for so great outragiousnes in the Jewes, that they woulde preferre a felowe openly knowē full of mischiefe, and a valiaunt tanke these, before Jesus a man moste meke and innocent. But the Jewes with a whole consent and with a great lowde voyce, cryed all of them: We will not haue Jesus geuen vs, but Barrabas.

The.xix.Chapter.

The texte. Then Pylate toke Jesus therfore and scourged hym. And the souldiers wound a croune of thornes, and put it on his head. And they did on him a purple garment, and came vnto him, and sayed: Hayle kyng of the Jewes: and they smote hym on the face. Pilate wente furth agayne and sayde vnto them: Behold I bryng hym furthe to you, that ye maye knowe that I fynde no faulte in hym. Then came Jesus furth wearing a croune of thorne, and a robe of purple, and he sayeth vnto them: Beholde the man.

After that Pilate, the Emperours Lieutenaunt, had also by occasion sente Jesus to Herode, leauyng nothyng vndoen eyther to shifte and ridde his handes of hym that was accused, or els to dimisse and sette hym looce as an innocent: when the lorde president (I saye) had thus assayed all wayes, and sawe he coulde do no good with the furiouse folkes of the Jewes, he than commaunded Jesus to be scourged, as the maner was at Rome, whiche feat he dyd to assuage theyr furie, and to saue the innocentes lyfe. This doen, the souldiers that were in the inner courte, of whome the Jewes had hyred a numbre to serue theyr tyrannye, dyd of theyr owne inuēcion adde muche cruel fearcenesse to that vncouth solemne piece of his passion: for when he had bene so scourged and beaten, to mocke hym withall, they putte vpon him a purple garment, and wounde a croune of thorne, and put it on his head, geuyng hym a reede in his hande in stede of a scepter, and byanby castyng hym in the tethe with a kyngdome that he shoulde be desyrous of, who (God wott) was to see to, an homely, a base, and a contempte persone, they came and kneled vnto him, saying: Hayle king of Jewes. And they spitted vpon his face, and buffeted hym, he beyng Lorde of all thynges and behauing hymselfe moste pacientely and moste coldly in al theyr kynde of mockage, for to teache vs lenitye and pacience in aduersitie: vs (I saye) that haue hautye and verye fierce myndes, though yet in dede we be thinges of nought. Sothe it is, that Pilate suffered Jesus thus to be delt withall, because he would with this the mans affliccion, haue appeased the malice of the Jewes: for when the people hathe for a while raged agaynste whom they be stirred, theyr fury ceaseth sodainly, namely, if scornyng be added to the calamitie, and make hym that suffereth, lamentable, where before he was hated.

Hayle king of the Jewes.

Therfore Pilate the presidente wente furthe vnto them agayne: for to proue yf he coulde mitigate the fiercenes of the meane multitude, and sayeth: Lo, I bryng out the manne vnto you, that ye maye looke your fyll vpon hym, and perceyue howe he hath bene handled for your pleasure, not withstandyng

that

that I can finde no faulte in him. And so therwith Jesus (at Pilates cōmaundement) cummeth furth as he was appareled, bounde, scourged and beate, bespitted, crowned with a crowne of thorne, and wearyng the purple garment. And Pilate presented hym, saying: Beholde the man is here.

When the hye Priestes and ministers sawe hym, they cryed, saying: Crucifie hym, crucifie hym. Pilate sayeth unto them: Take ye hym, and crucifie hym, for I fynde no cause in hym. The Jewes aunswered hym: We haue a lawe, and by our lawe he ought to dye, because he made hymselfe the sonne of God. When Pilate heard that saying, he was the more afeard, and went agayne into the iudgemente hall, and sayeth unto Jesus: whence art thou? but Jesus gaue him no aunswere. The texte.

With this sight therefore, whiche had been ynough to haue tamed the crueltie (had it been neuer so great) of wild and rude barbarouse people, the myndes yet of the Jewes were not onely not mollified, but were therewith more set on fyre to finish the thing that they had so farre proceded in. For the bishops were now afeard, leste if he, which had been so horribly & so cruelly tormented, should now haue been let looce, that then the affeccion and mynde of the people, that were already sette on a roare, being once turned on the other side, the grudge of their extreme great crueltie, might light upon their owne heades. The bishops therfore & their seruauntes, with a great stier and shoue cryed woodly out, crucifie him, crucifie hym: Pilate perceyuing that there was no hope of pitie to be gotten at their handes by fayre intreatie, he goeth aboute to restrayne and bridle in their fury with feare, & sayth: I am a minister of lawe and iustice, and not a reuenger of other folkes malice: and by lawfull processe to punishe trangressours of the lawe, am I autorisate: I am no butcherly murderer, no bloudshedder of innocētie. This that hath been doen, was to serue and satisfie your hatred. I will no more be fierce against him that is no noysome persone. And yf he shall algates be crucified, I wyll not haue this my courte of iudgemente distayned & polluted with the bloud of an innocente. Upon your owne perill haue ye the man awaye: and yf it semeth good, doe ye crucifie him. I am not wounte to crucifie any but wicked doers. In this man I finde no crime that deserueth the crosse. For there is no likelihode in him of that trayterouse dede which is layed to his charge, concerning the kingdome. Nor it is not ynough to accuse a man of a fault, except it be proued to be a matter of certaintie, that is obiected, by sure euidence: specially if it be a cause that concerneth life and death. This whole matter is by no lawful processe hādled, but ruffeled out sediciously. When the Jewes heard Pilate the iudge so frendely and diligently withall, take Jesus parte and defende him, & utterly thinking it not mete that any waye Jesus should escape, they falsely surmised a cryme whiche might seme to the iudge that was not learned in theyr lawe, a greuouse faulte, saying: Although he had doen none offence against the Emperours lawes, yet haue we a lawe geuen us of God: which the Emperour also hath left unto us: And by the force of this lawe he hath well deserued to dye, because he hath made himselfe the sonne of God, and takyng upon him the godhead, he did commit blasphemie against God. After that Pilate had heard this, hauyng no ready aunswere to make them, he led Jesus againe into the iudgement hall, & went in himselfe, and talked againe with Jesus, beyng very desyrouse to learne of hym what a thyng that was wherewith they charged hym, and howe it might bee refelled and auoyded. Therfore, first of all Pilate asketh hym whence he was, to the entent that after he had knowen of what progenie he came, he might haue confuted that, whereas they sayed he was desirouse to be taken for the sonne of God: though in dede among the Gentiles it was both written in Poetes fables, and commonly beleued, that some were taken for halfe goddes, as folkes borne of God and manne. But verily Jesus knowyng that Pilate did assaye all these wayes finally to saue his lyfe, and was not ignoraunte that yet Pilate shoulde afterwarde (when all meanes had bene proued) geue place to the obstinate furye of the Jewes, Jesus (I saye) woulde make no aunswere at all vnto the presidente, leste he should be thought to haue made any meane howe to get oute of theyr handes because he would not seme to be compelled to death. And that hitherto he made aunswere, was because he would haue recorde of his innocēcie, but his pleasure was to dye willingly and gladly.

The texte.

¶ Then sayed Pylate vnto hym: Speakest thou not vnto me? knowest thou not that I haue power to crucifie thee, and haue power to loose thee? Jesus aunswered. Thou couldeste haue no power at all agaynst me, except it were geuen the from aboue: therfore he that delyuered me vnto thee, hath the more synne. And frō thence furthe sought Pilate meanes to loose hym, but the Jewes cryed, saying: If thou let hym go, thou arte not Ceasars frende, for whosoeuer maketh hymselfe a kyng, is agaynst Ceasar. When Pilate heard that saying, he broughte Jesus furth & satte down to geue sentence in a place that is called the pauemēt, but in the Hebrue tōgue Gabatha. It was the preparyng daye of Easter, about the sixt houre. And he sayth vnto the Jewes. Behold your kyng They cryed, awaye with him, awaye with hym, crucifye hym. Pilate sayeth vnto them: Shall I crucifye your kyng ? The hye priestes aunswered: We haue no kyng but Ceasar. Then delyuered he hym vnto them to bee crucifyed.

Pylate meruaylyng at the mans silence standyng in hasarde of his lyfe, consideryng he had the iudge so muche his frende that he dyd prouoke hym to aunswere, saied: Why doest not thou that arte in ieoperdye of lyfe make me an aunswere? knowest thou not that I haue power and auctoritie ouer thee, whyther thou shalt lyue or dye? for I am the presidente and chiefe iustice of this region. And it dependeth vpon my will and pleasure, whether thou shalte be crucified, or quitte and let loose. Unto these woordes Jesus made no suche aunswere as the presidente loked for, whiche presidente desyred to be instructed for the defence of Jesus cause, intendyng to bee in steade of a iudge, an aduocate on the defendauntes syde. But because that waye it shoulde somewhat haue appeared that Jesus hadde not bene willyng to haue dyed, he aunswered no suche lyke thyng: But his aunswere was onelye concernyng the power whiche Pylate dyd arrogantelye attribute to hymselfe: signyfying that it was neyther in Pylates power to sette hym at libertie (seyng that the power whiche he had shoulde condescende to the furie of the Jewes,) nor that Pilate hymselfe shoulde be able to doe oughte agaynst hym, excepte he woulde of his owne voluntary wyll, suffer it: of trueth thou hast (sayeth Jesus) power accordyng to mannes lawes, but thou couldest haue no power on me, vnlesse it hadde been permitted thee of him, whose power passeth all mannes power. And in dede thou fauourest innocencie, but yet the naughtines of other ouercummeth thee, and leadeth thee from the righte trade. Wherfore the people of the Jewes, which be the auctours of this my passion and deathe, and that with theyr violence.

lence constrayneth the iudge to condemne an innocent persone, sume more greuously. When Pilate heard this, and thereby perceyued bothe the modestie and the cleares of him, that was accused, and that also the malice of the Jewes, yea and his owne indifferencie too, was not vnknowen to the same, & the more Pilate fauoured him, because he sawe that the manne was nothing moued or disquieted, no not with the peryll of death that he stode in: when Pilate cōsidered all this, he wrought al maner waies, that at leaste by some meanes, he might cleare and sette Jesus at libertie. The Jewes perceyuyng the same, and that the presidente made light of the cryme whiche fyrste was layed against hym concernyng Moses lawe, and that he ceased not to doe all that he coulde, to dimisse Jesus, they fall in hand againe with the first fault, whiche to be neglecte they declare to be daungerous to the iudge hymselfe, and saye therfore. Though it doe not appertayne vnto the that he hath offended against our God, certaynly wheras he hath offended against the Emperoure, thou haste to doe withall.

Whosoeuer maketh clayme to a kingdome without the Emperours commaundement, offendeth in the cryme of lease maiestie, & committeth hye treason: But this felowe maketh himselfe a king, if thou therfore doe let looce & acquite him, thou which fauourest his enemy, art not ẏ Emperours frende. After that Pilate had heard the Bishops and Phariseis, that were conspired together against Jesus, & the mayne multitude withal, cry out these wordes aloude, although he was not ignoraunt that they went about a false matter, yet because he sawe well that the malice whiche the priestes and Phariseis bare towarde Jesus could not be appeased, and sawe also that the headmen, and the common people were wunderfully consentyng to the sayed grudge, and malice, and all they with one agremēt bente to take away this one mans life: furthermore when Pilate perceiued also Jesus to be (in dede) nothyng fawtie at al, but symple & a poore innocent man, that made no shifte for himselfe, and lykewise thought in the meane tyme, howe that vnder Emperours many had been in daungerouse hasarde of very enuy, without any iust cause: And thought too, of himselfe, that he alreadye had sufficiently traueiled against the whole conspiracie agreed vpon betwene the noble menne, and the commons, in the defence of one poore mannes innocencie: Pilate (I tell you) vpon these skilles, determined with hymselfe to condescende and satisfie theyr malice, but in suche sorte that in condemning Jesus, he thought withal to get him his pardon and deliueraunce: and begynnyng to speake firste of his owne innocēcie, deriued the grudge of the wicked facte vnto the Jewes, and layed it vpon theyr heades. Nowe than was Jesus therfore brought forth as giltie, when as in condemnyng of hym no kynde of lawfull iudgement was vsed: Pilate sate downe in the place of lawful iudgemēt on hye, to geue sentence, & he sate in a high place to be seen of all folke, and of the height it is called of the Hebrewes Gabatha: the Grekes verily call it *Lithostrotos*, because it was paued. For so it behoueth Jesus condemnacion to be solemne, & publike, leste his innocēcie should be hidde from any man. For so to be condemned was to be quitte and cleared. Jesus was deliuered vp to the crosse, but the iudge gaue sentence vpon the Jewes. And nowe the tyme drewe nye, that accordyng to the maner of the solemne feaste, innocente bloude should be offered in sacrifice for the saluacion of the worlde, for it was the Sabboth

Whoso maketh hymselfe a kyng is against Ceasar.

It was the preparyng daye of Easter aboute the sixte houre.

euen, nowe called good fryday, whiche falleth in the Easter feast, aboute the first houre. And therfore the Jewes called more vrgently vpō the matter, vnwittingly doyng therby seruice to the thyng that God appoynted: that is, to haue this sacrifice made in conueniente tyme and due season. And so than Pilate nowe by reason of his Judiciall garment playnly seen and perceyued of the people, shewed vnto them out of the Judgemēt place the accused person, to thentente that euen by the sight of hym and his facion, it myght appeare howe vnconueniently the cryme of any cruel autoritie that he should be desirouse of, for his priuate commoditie, was layed against him: who beyng so vexed & troubled, shewed such great quietnes of minde, & so great mildnes, Pilate (I saye) shewed them this person, and sayed: Beholde your kyng. But the Jewes whiche thirsted for nothing els but innocent bloud, cryed: away with hym, away with hym: Crucifie hym. The infamous and reprochefull death pleased well the Jewes, trusting it would come to passe, that ẏ shame and reproche of the crosse, would make the name of Jesus odious and detestable, and that there should no manne come after, whiche should professe his name beyng in suche wyse made awaye. Pilate deriding their obstinate madnesse, sayeth: what (q̄ he) shall I doe so great a vilanie vnto your kyng as to nayle hym vnto the Crosse?

This dishonor shal redound to the shame & slaunder of all the people whiche haue brought theyr king to the crosse. This voyce of Pilate, although it dyd Jesus no good, yet it disclosed the malice of the Jewes, and forced them to confesse openly, & to knowledge a seruitude, which they hated. The Jewes had desyred and looked for many hundred yeares their Messias, that is to wete, a kyng promised of the Prophetes. As for the Emperours kyngdome (wherwith they were sore pressed and ouerlayed) they had spitefully hated: yet that not withstanding, being through enuy and hatred waxed wylde, and euen woode, they renounce openly in the face of the worlde, theyr Messias: and acknowlege the Emperour for theyr soueraygne Lorde: We haue (saye they) no kyng but the Emperour. The luste to reuēge was so great, that vnconstrayned they adiudged themselues to perpetuall bondage, that they might therby vtterly extinguish Jesus, the autor of libertie. Pilate therfore seyng all that he went aboute, disapoynted: committed Jesus vnto them to be crucified at theyr ordre and libertie.

The texte. And they tooke Jesus and led hym awaye, and he bare his crosse, and wente furth into a place whiche is called the place of dead mennes sculles: but in Hebrue Golgotha, where they crucified him: and two other with hym, on euery syde one, and Jesus in the myddes. And Pilate wrote a tytle, and put it on the crosse. The wrytyng was, Jesus of Nazareth kyng of the Jewes. This tytle read many of the Jewes, for the place where Jesus was crucified was nye to the citie, and it was written in Hebrue, and Greke and Latyne. Then sayed the hye priestes and Jewes vnto Pilate: wryte not kyng of the Jewes, but that he sayed, I am kyng of the Jewes. Pilate aunswered: What I haue wrytten that haue I wrytten.

The Jewes tooke the deliuerye of Jesus beyng brought out of the place of iudgement, and led him to the place of execucion, which was without the citie, that the place might also aunswer to the figure: For the sacrifice wherwith the testamēt was consecrate, was offered without the host. Jesus wēt

thither

thither, hauyng yet his garmentes on, to thentent he might be the more shame to them that fauoured hym: and he goeth full mekely bearynge his crosse hymselfe. For the Jewes prouided that, leste there shoulde lacke any despyte or reproche. Furthermore, a vyle and a diffamed place was also chosen and appoynted, wherein the maner was to put wyked malefactours to execucion, a place perdye detestable and violated with dead bodyes, whose bones laye scattered here and there all abrode: euen a place that shewed it selfe to what purpose it was dedicate, and of the thyng it had the common name geuen it. For in the Hebrue toung it was called Golgatha, in the Greke toung *Cranii topos*, in the Latyn toung *Caluarie locus*, in Englyshe, a place of dead mens sculles: and leste he shoulde not be putte to shame ynoughe, the Jewes procured this also, that other two (whiche were openly knowen to be wycked theues) shoulde be crucified with Jesus together, to thentēte that of the felowshippe of them that were sore offenders, he might lykewyse be thought and taken for an offender: and lyke as they had all one commune punyshemente, so to seme to haue all one commune faulte. But to thentente it might vtterly appere that he was a companyon of theyrs, the Jewes dyd so ordre and place the crosses, that Jesus honge in the myddes, hauyng a thefe hangyng on eyther hande of hym, howbeit the fountayne of all purenes coulde not be polluted with any fylthynes of manne, yea, the fountaine of all glorie is magnified and renowned with mens reproche. The crosse being afore odyouse, and a thyng of reproche, was made by hym a triumphant signe, wherunto the worlde boweth downe the heade, which aungels do wurshyppe, and deuyls feare it. Jesus being then condemned, founde one whome of a thefe he made a citizen of paradyse: so muche vnlykelyhoode was it, that the felowship of punishement shoulde defile hym. And verely, leste there shoulde wante any kynde or apparaunce of iuste and condigne punishmente, euery one had (as the manner was) his title and stile geuen vnto hym, which did describe and declare both the person and the fault. Now then, when Pilate had geuen to the other their titles accordyng to their deseruing, he commaunded that to the crosse of Jesus the Lorde, shoulde bee fastened this title and superscripcion, *Iesus of Nazareth the king of the Jewes*, euen for this cause truely, that by the very selfe inscripcion, he mighte cause bothe the malyce of the Jewes, and the innocencie of hym that was crucified, to be recorded: howbeit this title was not conuenient for him, in respect of the Jewes accusacion: and yet accordyng to that whiche himselfe confessed to the presydent, it was a title moste semyng for hym. For truely *Iudeus* doeth signifie to the Hebrues, confessing. And doubtles he was and is in very dede, a kyng and a setter of all them at libertie, whiche professeth his name: vnto whome he geueth felowship of the kyngdome of heauen. And to bryng the Bishoppes and the Phariseis into more hatred thereby, Pilate prouided this title to bee writē in thre sundry languages, in Hebrue, in Greke, and in Latine: whereof the first was their owne countrey speache, and the other two tounges (by reason of the great occupying that they had with the Grekes, and the Romaines) was so brought in among them, that some Jewes also knewe the Greke and the Latine toung. Therfore it was prouided by the president, that no man neither resiaunt there and the same countreyman, nor straunger and resorter thyther, shoulde be ignoraunt of the title. This title thus wrytten, being odiouse vnto the Phariseis, by reason that the place was muche haunted, and greate was

The wrytyng was, Jesus of Nazareth &c.

the resorte and confluence there, because that Golgatha, the mounte of caluery, was nyghe vnto the citie, and laye full in theyr syght that by casualtie passed by that waye: many Jewes therefore read (J saye) this superscripcion: and sum knewe well the name of Jesus of Nazareth. And howe litle he desyred any worldly kyngdome, many had true knowledge, whiche had seen hym hyde hymselfe when he shoulde haue been drawen by force to a kyngdome. That very kyng whiche was promysed by the prophetes, and whome the Jewes call Messias, was of very truthe loked for among all the Jewes. And althoughe Pilate was ouersene herein, yet vnawares he gaue hym that tytle which dyd moste demonstrate & notise to all folke, who he was that hong vpon the crosse. For of very trueth that selfe kynge of kynges honge there crucifyed, whiche by his deathe, dyd vanquishe the tiramnye of the deuyll. Thou oughtest to call it rather the token and banner of victorie, than a crosse. Thoughe all thynge semed full of shame and rebuke to the byshops, scribes, and to the Phariseis, yet this intitleing and superscripcion did greue theyr myndes, because it was more honorablye set out than they woulde haue had it. So great was the desyre of the wycked, to abolysh a name to the which onely, all glory of the whole world ought to be geuen. And therefore they treate and common with the president of chaungeing the title, and that it should not be written, the king of the Jewes, but that he dyd vsurpe and vniustly take vpon hym that name. But the presydent notwithstandyng that euen then vnawares he dyd pronosticate what should folow, that is to wete, that the profession of that healthfull name (whiche the Jewes falsely denyed) should departe thence to the redy beleuyng Gentiles, that is to saye, to the true Jewes in dede: yet (J saye) this notwithstanding, and that also heretofore he did condescende and folowe theyr malyce, the presydente woulde not alter and chaunge the title, but sayeth: that J haue wrytten, J haue wrytten. For because it was in verie deed to the commoditie and profit of all folke that Christe shoulde be put to death, and agayne also, it was for all mennes weale that his name should be of most fame and renoume thorowe the whole worlde, by the profession whereof, saluacion shoulde bee brought to all folke.

The texte. Than the souldiers when they had crucified Jesus, they toke hys garmentes and made fower partes, to euery souldier a parte, and also his coate. The coate was without seame, wrought vpon throughout. They sayed therfore among themselues, let vs not diuide it, but cast lottes for it, who shall haue it. That the scrypture myght be fulfylled, saying: They parted my rayment among them, and for my coate dyd they caste lottes. And the souldiers dyd suche thynges in dede. There stoode by the crosse of Jesus, his mother, and his mothers sister, Mary the wife of Cleophas, and Mary Magdalene: when Jesus therfore sawe his mother, and the disciple standyng, whome he loued, he sayeth vnto his mother: Woman, beholde thy sonne. Than sayed he to the disciple: Beholde thy mother; and from that houre the disciple toke her for his owne.

Nowe therefore when the Lorde Jesus was nayled (as the maner was) all naked vnto the crosse, and the foresayed superscripcion aboue his heade, the souldiers that crucified hym (accordyng to the vsage) parted among them Jesus garmentes. For this thyng came to them as amendes and reward for theyr paynes taking. And forasmuche as they were fower in nombre, they so deuided the resydue of his garmentes saue his coate (by cause they were made of soundrye pieces and sowed together) that euery manne had hys parte porcionately.

cionately. But than his coate or iacket, a garmēt verely whiche was more inner and nere his bodye, no sewed garment, but so wouen from thouer hem to the lower, that beyng leusyd or rypte, it woulde haue been good for nothinge and nought wourth. Therfore yͤ souldiers thought good that it shoulde bee kept whole vncut, and that sum one of them shoulde haue the whole iacket to whose lotte it should chaunce. But not withstandynge that the souldiers dyd these thinges of a prophane mynde, and of a worldlye purpose, yet vnawares they fulfylled in their so doyng, the prophecies of the Prophetes, that hereby also he might haue bene knowen to bee he, of whome the holy ghoste had spoken in the Psalmes thus: they haue deuyded myne apparel amonge thẽ, and caste lottes vpon my garmentes. And these thinges perdye, the souldiers did whiles yet the Lord honge vpon the crosse alyue. But there stoode by yͤ crosse of Jesus, Mary his mother, associate with her syster Marye, the daughter of Cleophas, and Marie Magdalene. Therefore Jesus lokynge from yͤ crosse vpon his mother, and castynge his iye withall vpon the disciple whom he loued more familiarly than the reste, to thentente that as (his clothes beyng distributed) he lefte no worldly substaunce behynde him, so he woulde leaue vpō earthe no worldly or mannes affeccion: Jesus (I saye) turned towardes his mother and sayed: Woman beholde that thy sonne, poyntynge with a nod of his head, and with a wincke of his iye, to the disciple. And turning furthwith to the disciple, sayeth: Beholde thy mother. And verily from that tyme, the sayd disciple bore a very sōnes mynde and affecciō toward the mother of Jesus, and toke the whole charge and care of her.

After these thinges, Jesus knowyng that all thinges were now perfourmed, that the scripture myght be fulfilled, he sayeth: I thirst. So there stoode a vessell by ful of vinegre; therfore they filled a sponge with vinegre, and wounde it about wͭ Isope, & putte it to his mouthe. Assone as Jesus receyued of the vynegre, he sayd: it is finished, & bowed his heade, and gaue vp the ghoste. — The texte.

When these thinges were doen, and Jesus knew that nothing wanted perteyning to a lawfull sacrifice, yet to bryng therunto and to accomplyshe the Prophetes saying where he sayeth: They gaue me gall to eate, and when I was thirstye they gaue me vinegre to drinke, he cried from the crosse: I am athirst. For of trueth suche as dye in this kynde of death, are wonte to be sore greued with vehement thirst, by reason that through the woundes of yͤ body, the bloude is exhaust and cleane drawē out. And euen this now too, did much proue and declare him to be a very man, & to be oute of doubte, punyshed to his great payne. Now thā a vessel full of vinegre stoode there at hād, which was wont to be reached vp & geuen to thē that were athirste to make them the sooner dye. The souldiers therfore fylled a sponge with vinegre, & woūde it about with ysope, and helde it to his mouthe. But as sone as Jesus had tasted yͤ vinegre, he saied: It is finished, signifying that the sacrifice was righteley doen and accomplyshed accordynge to his fathers wyll, and byanby he bowed his heade and gaue vp the ghoste.

The Jewes therfore bicause it was the preparing of the Sabbothe, that the bodies should not remayne on the crosse on the Sabboth day, for the Sabboth day was an hye day, besought Pylate that their legges might be brokē, and that they might bee taken downe. Then came the souldiers and brake the legges of the first and of yͤ other which — The texte.

was crucified with him, but whan they came to Jesus, and sawe that he was dead alrea-dy, they brake not his legges, but one of þ souldiers with a speare thrust him into þ syde, and furthwith came there out bloud & water. And he that sawe it bare recorde, & his re-corde is true, & he knoweth that he sayeth true þ ye myght beleue also: for these thinges were doen, that the scripture should be fulfilled. Ye shall not breake a bone of him, and a-gayne another scripture sayeth: They shall looke on hym whome they pearced.

But it is a sporte and a wonder withall to heare now againe in this case the peruerse religion of the Jewes so farre out of course and mysordred: The Jewes vpon a myscheuous malice, and by wicked meanes, brought with vio-lence vnto the crosse an innocent, and one that had bene beneficiall vnto them, beyng nothing abashed with the relygion of the feastfull daye, to do so cruel and so vngraciouse a dede, but they were very supersticiouse, and made muche a do about taking the bodies of frō the crosse. They came vnto Pilate, and be-sought him þ by his commaundement, the legges of them which were crucifi-ed, might be broken, to thentent they might the sooner be deade: and then their corpses be taken downe, and had out of the waye, leste beyng sene, they shoulde violate and breake the feastfull daye. That daye was a solemne greate daye, whiche (of the great apareylyng and fournature of holy adournmētes and dy-uine seruice) is called of the Grekes, *Parasceue*, that is to saye, a preparacion. And their holy and solemne Sabbothe daye was nye at hande, vpon whyche daye to worke was a detestable thing. For at this season the men beeynge (ye wote well) very precise in their relygion, after they had finisshed and accom-plysshed so horrybie an acte, as thoughe the thinge, had been well doen, they bente their myndes to celebrate the sacrifice that was to be offered by Moy-ses lawe, solennely and purely, not knowyng that the very true Easter lambe was already offered vp in sacrifice.

Suche a poyson and so pestiferouse a thing is holynesse that consisteth in outwarde and bodily thinges, and hath not holynes and godlynes of herte and mynde, ioyned and annexed vnto it. Nowe therfore Pilate grauntyng them their request, the souldiers brake bothe the theues legges, whome they found yet aliue. And then when they were come to Jesus, because they saw him alreadye deade, and therefore thought it a vayne and superfluous thynge to breake his legges, they lefte them whole vnbroken. For to this ende and pur-pose were the legges broken, that those whiche hung vpon the crosse, shoulde the sooner gyue vp the ghoste. But among the souldiers stoode a certaine man whiche (for the more certeintie of the Lorde Jesus death) opened his syde with a speare, and immediatly out of the wounde there gusshed forth bloude and water, in a great misterye declaryng that his death shoulde washe and cleanse vs from synne, and the same also geue to vs euerlastinge lyfe and saluacion. For baptisme standeth in water, and with water are we baptised. And þ lyfe of a manne is in the bloude. But it is againste the course of nature for water to runne out of a bodye that is wounded. Howbeit he that sawe the thing with his iyes, testified, and beareth witnes hereof: And we knowe his recorde to bee true. And leste any of you shoulde stande in doubte whether ye maye or no beleue the thing, whiche els mighte seme incredible, I assure you that Jesus himselfe knewe that witnes, to tell trueth.

One of the souldiers thrust him into þ syde, and furth wt came there out water and bloude.

And althoughe these thinges semed to be doen by chaunce or casualtie, that is to saye, that in stede of breakyng his legges, as the others were, his chaunce

was

was to haue his side thruste thorowe, yet for all that were they doen by the foresight and prouidence of God, and as his diuine councell disposed, that in this pointe also, the effecte and conclusion of the thing, myght aunswere and agre with the prophecies of the Prophetes. For among other rites and customes wherwith Moses teacheth in *Exodus*, that the paske or passouer ought to be obserued and celebrate, he had prescribed euē that thing specially by name, that is to wete, that lambe which was sacrifised, should be so slaine, that no bone of it should be broken: euen thereby notyng and declaryng, that Jesus was the very true phase or passeouer, the figure whereof that Mosaicall lambe did beare, & resembled thesame. For the bloud of this true lambe Jesus, saueth them that beleue in hym from death. And the spirituall eatyng of this lambe, conueyeth vs beeyng made free from the seruitude of Egypte, that is to saye, from the sinfull lustes of the worlde, and from the tyranny of sinne, into an heauenly region. And againe, the holy ghoste speaketh thus by Zacharye: They shall see hym whom they pearsed. For he shall once come with thesame body wherwith he hong on the crosse, though it be alreadye a gloryouse body, yet shall he shewe the printe of the wounde to all folke, and he shall shewe the vnfaythfull, to theyr rebuke, the fountayne that was open all in vayne to them, that would not beleue: with the flowyng and streames wherof, they might haue been cured.

After this Joseph of Aramathia, which was a disciple of Jesus, but secretely for feare of the Jewes, besought Pilate that he might take downe the body of Jesus. And Pilate gaue hym licence: he came therefore and tooke downe the body of Jesus. And then came also Nicodemus, which at the begynning came to Jesus by night, and brought of myrrhe and aloes mengled together, aboute an hundred pounde weyght. Then tooke they the body of Jesus, and wounde it in lynnen clothes with odours, as the maner of the Jewes is to bury. And in the place where he was crucified there was a gardeyne, and in the gardeyne a newe sepulchre, wherin was neuer man layed. There layed they Jesus therfore, because of the preparyng of the Sabboth of the Jewes, for the sepulchre was nye at hande.

The

And so nowe his death beyng already certayne, and himselfe founde dead by the experience of many, it behoued furthermore that his buryall should many wayes confyrme the belefe of the resurreccion. And as Christe would (perdie) his whole life to be base and of a lowe porte, so he would that his buriall should be honorable, and of a great maiestie, not intendyng therby to teache vs to be carefull of a sepulchre, but to thentent that those thinges once accomplyshed, whiche concerned the abasyng of hymselfe and the whole ministery thereof, he might make a waye to the honour and prayse of his resurreccion. And in very dede the honour whiche is geuen to a manne alyue, is not without either suspicion or daunger, but the honour whiche voluntarily we geue to the dead, is a sure wytnes of prowes, goodnes, and vertue. Nowe therfore Joseph beyng a manne of honour and of great power, & substaunce, an Aramathian borne, which sayed Joseph was a disciple of Jesus, but not openly knowen so to be for feare of the Jewes, which had made a lawe that whosoeuer did openly confesse himselfe to be Jesus disciple, thesame person should be caste out of the Synagoge: Joseph (I saye) came vnto Pilate to whom he was well knowen, and desyreth licence of hym, to take downe Jesus body from the crosse: when Pilate had tried whether that he were dead or not, he was content withal. Therfore Joseph went his way to the crosse, and toke downe the dead corps. In the meane season, as one to helpe furthe with those thinges and doynges, that pertayne to the funerals: euen Nicodemus also, cummeth thither, a man among the Phariseis of a notable estimacion and dignitie: and he also being a secrete disciple of Jesus, which had before that tyme come to Jesus in the night, because he myght so beste auoyde the displeasure and grudge of the Phariseis, as was before rehersed. These menne knowyng that death commonly maketh an ende of hatred, trustyng vpon the presidentes fauour, enterprysed hiely to honoure the dead, with whom (whiles he liued) they durst not talke openly. Nicodemus (of trueth) brought with him an oyntment of myrrhe & aloes mingled together aboute an hundred pounde weyght, so muche as was sufficient to sweten the bodye, and honorably to preserue it from corrupcion. They now therfore ioyntely together with one common seruice, anointed Jesus body being takē downe, on euery parte with pleasaunte and swete sauerye spices, and when they had well imbrued the corps with the odours, thei woūd it in linnen clothes, that the oyntmēt should not runne of from the body. For the maner of the Jewes is, after this sorte to bury, leste the bodies should corrupte and putrefie. And verily they did this honour to the Lord Jesus as to a wurthy mā, and one that was throughly good: and againe, they thus honoured him to thentent no man should thynke that he dyed for any cryme or faulte. For as yet, they had no hyer opinion of hym, but that he was an innocent good man and loued of god, whose name and memory ought to haue this honour doen vnto it, that is to saye, to be remembred as one that was enuied for his vertue euen to the death, a thyng that vsually hapneth in maner to moste beste menne. Moreouer this preparacion and great a doe was euen there finished, leste any man myght supect that the body had been chaunged. And agayne the Lord was buried then in a garden, nye to the place of the crosse. In the garden was a new sepulchre lately made out of an harde thicke stone, wherin was neuer man layed. And albeit these thinges were supposed to be doen by casualtie, yet they made much for the fayth of the resurreccion. For the sepulchre could not seme to be digged vp with vndermynyng, because it was cutte out of an whole sounde vnholowe rocke of stone, nor none other could be thought to haue risen out of it, in whiche he only was layed. But yet Joseph and Nicodeme did not this in respecte of his resurrecciō, for in dede they had no hope that he should rise againe, but they were moued thus to doe with a Jewishe deuocion, for religion sake of the feastfull day. For in dede it was the Jewes Easter day euen, and therfore the Sabboth prouoked and setforwarde this dede. In which Sabboth day it was not lawful for them to worke. Wherfore leste the body should be vnburied, or the buriall be to slender, and with to small honour doen, they ryd the thyng out of hande, and layed hym in the sepulchre that was nexte vnto them. Also furthermore, euen the diligence of the Jewes, serued for the belefe of his resurreccion that should be. For after that the Jewes had obteined of Pilate kepers for the sepulchre, & had procured that it should be watched and attended vpon, leste any body should secretly steale awaye the dead corps, they not contente therewith, close vp the mouthe of the sepulchre, with a great stone, and seale it, when they hadde so doen: so that on euery side the malice of the Jewes, succeded and came to the glory of Christ, whose name they went about vtterly to destroy and abolish.

The.xx.Chapter.

The first daye of the Sabbothes came Marye Magdalene early (when it was yet somewhat darke) unto the sepulchre, and sawe the stone taken awaye from the graue. Then she ranne, and came to Symon Peter, and to the other disciple whome Jesus loued, and sayed unto them: They haue taken awaye the lorde out of the graue, and we cannot tell where they haue layed hym. Peter therfore went forth, and that other disciple, and came unto the sepulchre. They ranne bothe together, and the other disciple dyd out runne Peter, and came firste to the sepulchre. And when he had stouped downe, he sawe the linnen clothes lying, yet went he not in.

The texte.

AND verely the residue of the disciples, beeyng stryken partly with feare, and partely with dispayre, neglected the buryng, and rought not for the dead corps. But certayne weomen that were his disciples cared asmuche for it, as did Joseph and Nicodemus, but the religion of the feastefull daye, stayed them from the labouryng aboute preparaciō of swete odours. Howbeit, as soone as Phase Sabboth daye was past (the oyntmentes beyng made ready in the nyghte Mary Magdalene came earlye when it was yet somewhat darke unto the sepulchre, the morowe after the Sabboth daye. And when she sawe the stone (wherewith the entrie of the sepulchre was closed up) remoued thence, and the sepulchre to be open, the woman supposed nothyng els but that the deade corps hadde been taken awaye in the night, to the intent it might haue been more semely and accordyngly buried. For the body was layed there for a time, as of purpose, that it might soone after be adourned and set foorth with the due and full solemnitie of buryng. For in dede the hope of his resurreccion fell awaye from all the disciples, they were so muche astonied with the certaintie of his death.

Therfore Marie ere she had loked into the graue, retyred backe agayne, and ran to Simon Peter, with whom was euen that disciple whome Jesus loued, and she sayeth: Our lord is taken awaye out of the sepulchre, and I know not whither they haue caryed him that toke him awaye. They both beyng styrred with that voyce, went foorth. Surely they had small hope, yet hadde they a great affeccion, and desyre towardes theyr maister, whom they so muche loued. And therfore they ranne both out together to the graue, but that disciple which was so beloued of Jesus, outranne Peter, and came first to the sepulchre. And when he founde the doore open, he wente not in, but stouped downe and looked into the graue, whether it were emptie or no. And he sawe well there was no dead corps, but the linnen clothes lefte imbrued with swete odoriferous ointementes, wherwith the body had bene wrapped, and also the napkyn that Jesus head had bene bound in, not the linnen clothes and it lying together, but wrapt up and layed aside by it selfe, so that it was easy to perceyue, that the body was not taken awaye by theues, whiche woulde haue rather purloyned the whole corps as it laye, wrapped and wounde up with the swete smellyng spices, with the linnen clothes, and the fine kercher: though it had not bene for the value therof, at least they would so haue doen, because thei should haue lacked laisure to haue separate the oyntmentes and swete spices from the bodye, seeyng they cleaued as fast therunto as byrdelime woulde haue doen, and because also they

They haue take awaye the lord. &c.

should not haue had sufficient tyme to folde vp and couche euery thyng hande-somely and seuerally in his place. This (suche as it was) was in dede the fyrste comforte and hope that was geuen to them of his resurreccion.

The texte. Then came Simon Peter folowyng hym, and went into the sepulchre, and sawe the linnen clothes lye, and the napkyn that was about his head, not lying with the linnen clothes, but wrapped together in a place by it self. Then wente in also the other disciple whiche came first to the sepulchre, and he sawe and beleued. For as yet they knewe not the scripture, that he shoulde ryse agayne from death.

Now than anon after cummeth Peter also, who after that he was certified of the thing by John, as he was slower in running, so was he both bolder and more diligent in trying out the trueth of the thyng. For not beyng content with lokyng into the graue, he also went into it. The other disciple a loker in as wel as he, (whiche yet durst not by hymselfe alone go in, howbeit in dede his companion beyng with hym, tooke parte of the feare awaye) nowe folowed Peter into the sepulchre. And so nowe they sawe certaynly at very hande the thing to be true, (whiche the one of them had seen as it had been a shadowe, or a glymmering sight therof,) that no corse or dead corps was any where in that place: but in dede they sawe the clothes wherin the body had been wrapped, in suche sorte pulled of, and laied aside, that it appeared to be doen not of theues in hast, sleyghtly and shuffled vp, but quietly and layserly. Howbeit as yet they did not beleue that he was risen agayn to lyfe, they onely beleued that to be true, which Marie had tolde them: Verelye that the corps was taken awaye out of the sepulchre. For although they had heard Jesus saye that he would rise againe, yet did not the saying sticke inwardly in theyr mindes, and though some hope therof were in theyr hertes, yet that whiche had already place in theyr myndes, the feare and tumulte of the crosse and his passion, draue it out of theyr myndes. For they did not fully vnderstand as yet, the saying of the Prophet, which had prophecied that certaynly Jesus should suffer death, and rise againe the thirde daye from death to lyfe.

The texte. Then the disciples went away agayne vnto theyr owne home. Marie stode without at the sepulchre, weping: So as she wepte, she bowed hirselfe into the sepulchre, and seeth two angels clothed in white sitting the one at the heade, and the other at the feete, where they had layed the body of Jesus. They saye vnto her: Woman why wepest thou? She sayeth vnto them: For they haue taken awaye my Lorde, and I wote not where they haue layed hym.

Therefore the two disciples departed thence, and wente backe again to the place from whence they came. But Marie of a certain excedyng loue and wonderfull desire that she had to the lorde, coulde not be drawen from the sepulchre: sekyng hym that was now deade, whome she had loued beyng aliue, and was desirouse to shew gentilnes, and to do seruice vpon the dead bodye, forsomuche as she now could not haue the fruicion of his liuely body: and she stoode without nye vnto the doore of the graue, and did nought els but all to wepe, & loke about her, if she coulde haue any hope or lykelyhoode to finde the bodye. Nowe than as she was weping, and in dede durst not go into the graue, she turned her head aside and loked into the graue, and she sawe two angels, goodly to looke too, both of good semblaunce and in pleasaunt white apparell, sittyng in seuerall places, the one at the head and the other at the feete of the place, where the dead

dead corps was laied. And in very dede this pleasaūte, this cherefull and peaceable sight, did somedeale asswage the extreme feare of the night, and of her carefulnesse. The angels also to comforte her sorowfull pensifenesse, of theyr owne accorde and gentlenes speake unto the wepyng woman and saye: O woman, what is it thou wepest for? She than beyng all rauyshed, and as one drounke with a certayne vehemencie of loue, sayeth: They haue taken awaye my lorde, and I know not where they haue laied hym. She calleth him her lorde, and she also loueth hym being dead, hauing yet no hope of the resurreccion. She was onely herewithall grieued, that is, because she coulde not haue the sighte of his bodye.

Whan she had thus sayed, she turned herselfe backe, and sawe Jesus standyng, and knew not that it was Jesus. Jesus sayeth unto her: Woman, why wepest thou? whome sekest thou? She supposyng it had been a gardiner, sayeth unto hym: Sir, if thou haue borne hym hence, tell me where thou hast layed hym, and I wyl fetche hym. Jesus sayeth unto her: Mary. She turned herselfe and sayed unto hym: Rabboni, which is to saye, Maister. Jesus sayeth unto her: Touche me not, for I am not yet ascended to my father, but go unto my brethren, and saie unto them. I ascende unto my father and your father, and to my God and your God. **The texte.**

Whiles she speaketh thus, she coniectured by the semblaunce of the angels, that some man stode behinde at her backe, and not tarying for the angels aunswer, she cast her iye aside, and incontinently she sawe Jesus standyng, whom y angels had wurshipped, but yet Marie knewe not that it was Jesus. For he did appere in the forme of a poore simple man, lest he being sodainly seen in his owne forme and shape, should haue muche astonished the woman. Therfore to bolden her withall, he calleth & speaketh gently unto her with the same later wordes that the angels did, saying: Woman, why wepest thou? whome sekest thou loking about the hither and thither? She suspecting him to be a gardiner, the workeman and keper of the ground, wherein the sepulchre was, (for it was in a garden) with a womanly simplicitie sayed unto hym: Sir, if thou hast taken him away, tel me where thou hast hid him, that I maie go fetche him thece. For she supposed that some frend for feare of the Jewes, had procured the body to be secretly caryed awaye, leste it shoulde come into the Jewes handes, and should be otherwyse handled than she woulde it shoulde be. Jesus therfore beyng delited in the great desyre of the woman, doeth now with a knowen familier voyce, speake unto her, and calleth her Marie. At this knowen voyce, the woman sodainly turnyng herselfe (for euen at this very presente she had bowed downe herselfe agayne towardes the angels, so muche was she by sodayne mocions of mynde stered to loke this waye and that waye) the woman I saie, knewe Jesus, and rauished with a sodayne ioye, she a disciple, speaketh to the master, and calleth hym Rabboni, whiche worde in the Syrians tonge, signifieth, Master: And withal she falleth flatte downe to the grounde, and would haue kissed his feete, hauyng yet in remembraunce theyr olde familiaritie. But Jesus knowyng that as yet she thought no great excellente thyng of hym, although she loued him sincerely and ardently, did prohibite her to touche his bodye. For Marie sawe well that he was aliue agayne, but she thought y he was reuiued for none other cause, but as he did before, to liue familiarlye with his frendes, beyng now a man aliue, where as before he was dead: and ignoraunt she was that he now caryed about with hym an immortall body, which was to be handled with muche greater reuerence, whiche bodye the Lorde did neuer exhibite or present to the wicked, nor suffered it to be handled of euerye man, to thentent he might litle by litle, altogether withdrawe them from the loue of the bodye. Touche me not (sayeth he) it is thesame bodye whiche hong vpon the crosse, but it is nowe beautified and adourned with the glory of immortalitie. But truely thine affeccion is yet somedeale carnall, because I haue not yet ascended vp to my father, whiche thyng once doen, I shall sende vnto you the spirite that is the comforter, and he shall make you perfite and wurthy to haue the spirituall felowship of me.

In the meane time content thy selfe with that thou hast seen me and heard me speake, and specially now go thou to my brethren, whiche are throughe my death comforteles, and foorthwith make them partakers with thee, of the ioye and comforte whiche thou haste receyued by the sight of me: and vpon these my wordes shewe them that to this ende I am rysen from death to lyfe, euen that after I haue taried a certayne dayes among them, I maye leaue the worlde, and ascende vp to my father, who is also your father, and thesame is both your god and mine, common to bothe. Let them therfore put away earthly affeccions and rectifie their mindes, applying thesame to spiritual and heauenly thinges.

The texte. Mary Magdalene came and tolde the disciples, that she had sene the lorde, and that he had spoken suche thynges vnto her. Thesame daye at night, whiche was the firste daye of the sabbothes, when the dores were shut (where the disciples were assembled together for feare of the Iewes) came Iesus and stoode in the middes, and sayeth vnto them: Peace bee vnto you. And when he had so sayed, he shewed vnto them his handes and his syde. Then were the disciples glad when they sawe the lorde.

Now than Mary did as he bad her, and returnyng againe to the disciples, shewed them that she had seen the lorde, and tolde them the thynges whiche he had commaunded to be made relacion of in his name: and this was doen that they should take right great comforte of that he nowe called them his brethren, and prepare also theyr myndes to the loue and desyre of eternall and heauenly thynges, forasmuche as the preset vse of his body should not endure long with them. After that with these and certayne other apparicions the lord Iesus had litle by litle lift vp theyr myndes to quicknesse of spirite, and to the hope of the resurreccion already past, the selfe same daye that was the morowe after the sabboth daye whiche next folowed the sabboth of Easter, when it was nighte, and the disciples secretelye gathered together, whiche for feare of the Iewes durste not assemble together in the daye tyme, Iesus went in to them whan the doores were shut, and standyng in the middes in the sight of them all, to take awaye al feare from them, he saluted them amiably and full gentlye, saying with a voyce well knowen vnto them: Peace with you. And lest they shoulde suspect it to be a ghost or another bodye, he sheweth vnto them the printe of the nayles in his handes, and the scarre of the wounde whiche the souldier hadde made in his side with a speare. With this salutacion and sight, the fayth of his disciples was confirmed, the sorowe take awaye, and theyr myndes muche recreate and made ioyouse. For Iesus had promised them before that thus it shoulde be, that within a shorte tyme he woulde see them agayne, and after they hadde seen hym, and theyr sorowe put awaye, that he would make their hertes gladde and merye. And therewithal he tolde them this also should folow, that in the world they should haue sorow and heuinesse, but in hym they shoulde haue peace and quietnesse.

Then

Then sayed Jesus to them agayne: Peace be vnto you. As my father sent me, euen so sende I you also. And when he had sayed these woordes, he brethed on them, and sayeth vnto them: Whosoeuers sinnes ye remit, they are remitted vnto thē, and whosoeuers synnes ye retayne, they are retayned. But Thomas one of the twelue (which is called Didimus) was not with them when Jesus came. The other disciples therfore sayed vnto hym: We haue seen the lord. But he sayed vnto them: Excepte I see in his handes the printe of the nayles, and thruste my hande into his syde, I wyll not beleue. The texte.

Therfore to confirme the Apostles in theyr ioye and coumforte the more, he once agayne saluteth them with good lucke of peace, saying: Peace with you. And at the same tyme withal, he hiely auctoriseth them, and commaundeth thē to preache the thinges whiche they had seen, and sayeth: As my father sent me, so do I sende you. I haue truely and faithfully glorifyed my fathers name, and you agreyng amōg your selues, shal with lyke trueth and faithfulnesse preache my fathers name and mine. Prepare your mindes to this fūction and office: for asmuche as I nowe that I haue doen diligently the thyng that I had in commission to do, go agayne to my father, and from thence I shall sende vnto you more plentie and more power of the holy ghost. In the meane while shall I also make you partakers of the holy ghost accordyng to your capacitie: and euen as he was thus speakyng, he brethed on them and gaue them the spirite, with auctoritie to forgeue all men theyr sinnes that woulde be ioyned to hym by profession of the ghospel and by baptisme, and that woulde forthinke their former life, and be eftsones amended where they haue erred. Whosoeuers synnes ye remit (sayeth he) they are remitted vnto them, and whosoeuers ye retayne, they shall abide subiecte to theyr synnes. When these thinges were doen, the residue of the disciples were assembled together, Thomas onely except, that than was absent: whiche name Thomas signifieth in the Greke tongue Didimus, and in the Latin *Geminus*, in Englyshe doubtefull. For he was one of the twelue whō the lorde did specially and peculiarly choose to the office of preachyng the gospell. Therfore after that he was come in to them, the disciples that could scant stande for ioye, shewed openly vnto him that they had seen the lorde. Thomas supposyng them to be deceyued and illuded by some vision or spirite, denyed to beleue vnles he might see hym with his owne iyes: and not to beleue his owne iyes as sufficient witnesse, except he might see withall the printe of the nailes euen freshe in his handes, yea and with putting his owne handes into Jesus side perceyue by felyng, the wounde that the speare made. And trulye, this incredulitie of the Apostle, by the dispensacion of God as he shall dispose, didde myche good to the confirmacion and stablishement of our fayth.

¶ And after eyght dayes, agayne his disciples were within, and Thomas with them. Then came Jesus when the doores were shut, and stoode in the middes, and sayed: Peace be vnto you. After that sayed he to Thomas: Bryng thy fynger hither and see my handes, and reache hither thy hande, and thrust it into my syde, and be not faythlesse but beleuyng. Thomas aunswered, and sayed: My Lorde, and my God. Jesus sayeth vnto hym: Thomas because thou haste sene me, thou haste beleued, blessed are they that haue not sene and yet haue beleued. And many other thinges truly did Jesus in the presēce of his disciples, which are not written in this boke. These are written that ye might beleue, that Jesus is Christe the sonne of God, and that (in beleuyng) ye might haue life thorowe his name. The texte.

Therfore eyght dayes after, when the Apostles met together agayne, by stealthe, and at this tyme with the reste, Thomas was in coumpanye, whiche

hither-

hitherto woulde not beleue that Christe was rysen: the Lorde came in to them where they were, the gates beyng hard faste shut, and standyng in the middes of them, he saluted them after his vsuall and well knowen maner and facion, saying: Peace with you. And turnyng hym byandby to Thomas, whose vnbelefe he knewe, that was ignoraunt in nothyng: whiche lacke of beliefe, because Jesus knewe it came not as the phariseis infidelitie did, that is, of malice, but of mans infirmitie, he vouchedsafe to heale it. He sayeth thus to hym: Thomas (sayeth he) forasmuche as it dooeth not suffise the to haue hearde of many (that I was rysen to lyfe agayne) whiche hath seen me and hearde me, except thy senses mighte feale and perceyue thesame, bring hither thy finger and feele the woundes of the nayles, and see that I truelye carye the very true markes therof. Put thy hande into my syde and handle the wounde whiche the speare made, and hereafter be not vnfaythful, and harde of belefe in other matters: but after thou haste nowe seen this thing proued certainly true, whiche yet semed to thee incredible, see thou geue fayth to my promises, howe incredible soeuer they seme to the common sence and iudgement of men. After that Thomas had seen and felte, knowyng bothe the face and accustomed voyce of the Lorde, he than conceyued a full fayth, and spake aloude: My Lorde and my God. For as he was more harde of belefe, so no body did more clearlye confesse Jesus to be God and man, for because the handlyng of the body which late before hong dead vpon the crosse, witnessed that he whiche was rysen to lyfe agayne, was a very man in dede: and the knowleage of hidde secrete thynges, proued well his godhead.

So than of trueth, Jesus did well accepte and embrace Thomas his confession, but yet withall he did reproue his hardnesse of belefe, saying: Thomas because thou hast seen me, hearde me, and handled me, thou beleuest: but blessed shall they be, whiche though they see not, will yet beleue. Verely the Lorde Jesus declared vnto his disciples, his diuine power and godheade by many other tokens whiche are not written in this booke, but some thynges are reported and declared by other Euangelistes, and some thynges also were reported and tolde by worde of mouthe: and euen they were the tellers therof, which bothe sawe and hearde the thynges themselues. For to set out and write all thynges (whiche woulde haue bene a worke that for the greatnes it coulde not haue been measured) was not cared for, but yet it was thoughte necessarye to write of some thinges, that thereby ye mought come to the beliefe, that Jesus was the sonne of God. Whiche thyng yf ye do in dede, ye shall haue that full blisse, and beatitude whiche our Lorde Jesus promised to them that when they see not, beleue. For lyke as he suffered death and liueth immortal, so shall ye also by profession of his name in true faythe, obtayne eternall lyfe.

The

The. xxi. Chapter.

¶ Afterwarde did Jesus shewe himselfe againe at the sea of Tiberias. And on this wyse shewed he hymselfe. There were together Symon Peter and Thomas (whiche is called Didimus) and Nathanael of Cana in Galile, and the sonnes of zebedei, and two other of his disciples. — The texte.

Nd verely, to confirme more and more the faythe of his disciples, Jesus oft times appeared vnto them, and talked with them, sometyme also eate meate in theyr company: leste any suspicion shoulde setle in theyr myndes that it was but a delusion or some ghoste, whiche they had sene, neyther was he therwhiles continuallye, for all that, present in their company as he was wont before his death, nor so familiarly handled himself among them: nor yet was seen of all menne, because he hadde sayed before that he would appere to his and not to the world, nor to his neyther, but euen when he list. For nowe immortalitie shewed a certaine semblaunce full of maiestie, that was to be had in reuerence, to thentent that their faith beyng full stayed and establyshed, he might withdrawe from them altogether the sight of the body, and spirituallye to be now amongst his. And so now therefore he appered and shewed himselfe againe to his disciples, at ẏ depe lake called Tyberias. And he presented himselfe vnto them on this wyse. The disciples, which before ẏ tyme kept thẽselues secrete in Hierusalem, to be in sauetie out of the Phariseis daunger, repayred againe into Galile, ⁊ there was a good sorte of thẽ together, euen no fewer thã Simon Peter and Thomas, called Didimus, also Nathanael of Cana a citie of Galile, where Jesus turned water into wine. And besides these, ẏ two sonnes of zebedei John ⁊ James ẏ greater, ⁊ with these was two other disciples.

¶ Symon Peter saieth vnto them: I wyll go a fisshyng. They saye vnto him: We also wyl go with the. They went theyr waye, and entred into a shippe immediatlye, and that night caught they nothing. But when the mornyng was nowe come, Jesus stoode on the shore, neuerthelesse the disciples knewe not that it was Jesus. Jesus sayeth vnto them: Children haue ye any meate? They aunswered him: no. And he saieth vnto them: Cast out the net on the right hande, and ye shal fynde. — The texte.

Nowe than, because they lacked theyr Lordes helpe, by whom they were woonte to be fedde of the mere fre bounteousnes of frendes, Peter wente in hande againe with his olde facultie, to get his lyuinge with his owne handes: lest he should be burdenouse to any man, or to be fed by any others lyberalitie in idlenesse. For then he might not preache, and he thoughte it was no right that he whiche serued not the ghospell, should lyue of the ghospell. Therfore in the twie lyght, because they shoulde haue goen abrode vpon theyr peryll in the daye, Peter saieth: I go a fishyng. The reste than saied vnto him: We also wyll go a fishing with the. And so goyng foorth a doores togetherwarde, they entred into the shippe. And they fished all that night in vayne. For they gate neuer one fishe, to the intente that waye shoulde be made for a miracle, and therwith as in a misterie to be signified, that the labour of an Euangelist is all in vayne, vnles Christe do prosper the mannes endeuour.

But now when it waxed daye, Jesus stoode on the shore, but the dysciples knewe not it was he, partely for the distaunce that was betwene him ⁊ them, and partely because it was scant daye: also partely because the Lorde woulde not furthwith be knowen. Therfore Jesus spake vnto them from the shore, saying: Children haue ye any meate? They than, forasmuche as they knewe not the Lorde by his voyce, but supposed him to be some other manne whiche came to the sea to bye fyshe, made aunswere that they had none that they could selle him, because they had taken nothing. Jesus than to declare litle and lytle who he was, sayed vnto them: Caste out the nette on the righte syde of the shyppe, and ye shall fynde that ye coulde not hytherto.

The texte. They caste out their nette, and anon they were not hable to drawe it, for the multitude of fishes. Then sayed the disciple whom Jesus loued, vnto Peter: It is the Lord. Whē Simon Peter heard ỷ it was the Lord, he girded his coate vnto him (for he was naked,) and sprang into the sea. The other disciples came by shyppe, for they wer not farre from lande, but as it were two hundred cubites, and they drew the nette with fishes.

They dyd as he bad them, for through werynesse of their vaine laboure, and of a great desire to take some fyshe, they conceiued some hope: byanby so great a multitude of fyshes was taken, that the net was laden withall, and coulde vnneth be drawen vp to the boate: And wete ye well, this was euen a resemblaunce of the multitude of men, whiche afterwarde by the preachynge of the apostles, should be brought and ioyned to the churche out of the whole world of what language or countrey soeuer they were. By the noueltie of the thing, that disciple whome Jesus loued, was moued to be more attentyfe and to marke the thing, and so knewe Jesus. And incontinently aduertysed Peter (who was altogether busye aboute drawynge vp the nette) that it was the Lorde, whiche standyng on the shore commaunded to looce and caste oute the nette. Peter, beyng alway one man and lyke himselfe, did forget both the nette and the fishe, and toke his shyrte (for before he was naked) and coulde not abyde but sprang into the sea, and so came he first of all to the Lord. The other disciples came to him by shyp, for they were not very farre of the shore, but as it were two hundred cubites, and they altogetherward drewe the nette full and laden with fyshe.

The texte. Assone as they were come to lande, they sawe hotte coales and fishe layde theron, and breade. Jesus saieth vnto them: bryng of the fyshe whiche ye haue now caught. Symon Peter went vp and drewe the nette to lande ful of great fyshes: an hundred and thre and fiftie. And for all there were so many yet was not the nette broken.

And when they wer come to lande, they sawe vpon the bancke hotte coales and fishe layed theron, and breade withall. Therfore Jesus commaunded thē also, to bryng of their fyshes whiche they now caught. Than Peter returned againe to the shippe, and drewe the nette to land full of great fishes: in noumbre an hundred and thre and fyftie. This also made it seme the greater a myracle, that when there was so great a multitude and that of great fishes, yet was not the nette broken in sundre with the weight therof. The thynge dyd represent the humble churche, and as to the worlde weake and narrowe, yet suche a thing as shall embrace all the nacions of the worlde, the Lorde Jesus beyng the head and chefe gouernour therof.

The texte. Jesus saieth vnto them: come and dyne. And none of the disciples durste aske hym: what art thou? for they knewe that it was the Lord. Jesus than came, and tooke breade and gaue them, & fyshe lykewyse. This is now the third tyme that Jesus appered to his disciples, after ỷ he was raysed againe frō death. So whē they had dyned, Jesus saieth vnto unto Symon Peter: Symon Joanna louest thou me more than these? He sayed unto hym: Yea Lord, thou knowest that I loue thee. He sayeth unto hym: Fede my lambes.

Furthermore, to shewe a more certeintie that he was verye manne and no ghoste, he therfore approuyng the veritie of his body by beyng sene with mēs iyes, heard with their eares, and handled with handes, would also eate meate with them. He therfore inuited his disciples to the dyner which was there ready for thē. The disciples sate downe, but all whusht and spake no wordes: for the maiestie of the immortall bodye toke from them their accustomed boldnes. In dede they knewe hym to be the Lorde, but nowe he appeared after a more high and gloriouse sorte, as one of great noblenesse and excellencie. Therfore none durste aske hym, who arte thou? and yet of the very thynge it selfe, they knewe hym to be the Lorde, although the shewe and semblaunce of his bodye was chaūged. Jesus therfore came to the feast, and as his maner was, brake bread with his owne handes, and gaue it to them, and fishe likewise: by exaūple and dede teaching his, whome he had specially chosen to bee shepeherdes of the churche, to fede his euangelicall flocke with holy doctrine. But yet suche as hymselfe had taught them. And this is now the thirde time that Jesus appeared (certayne spaces betwene) to his disciples, for he was not in theyr company continually. After dyner was doen, the lorde Jesus, in maner declaryng by worde of mouthe the thyng, whiche in his facte he signified, committed his shepe to Peter that he should feede thē: but he first thrise required loue of him, to the entent he mighte powre into the mindes of his disciples, that no man is a fitte shepeherde of an euangelicall flocke, excepte he whiche beareth suche loue towardes them that he is put in truste withall to kepe, as Christe shewed himselfe to haue towardes his, for whom he bestowed his lyfe. And he specially spake to Peter, utterly to put awaye the remembraunce of his denying Christ, and to notise that he should haue the hiest and chiefe place in the ministerie of the gospel, that did passe other in excellency of charitie towardes the flocke of the Lorde. And therfore, by hym, whom Jesus knewe to be of a more feruente minde then the reste, he would expresse to all the Apostles and their successours, a proufe of a true and a perfite shepeherde. And in dede Peter is wount at other tymes also to be as a mouthe of the Apostles, and by hym the Lorde woulde haue it knowen and to be hearde what the other also would openly confesse: For because, by the expressed voice of this man, the publique confession of the whole churche dyd but a late tyme before, deserue a promise of the keyes of the kyngdome of heauen. And in the same wyse also, he than woulde that by this mannes voyce, open confession should be made of moste hye charitable loue towardes hym: to the entente that by this one man, the reste shoulde knowe what maner of men ought to be curates of the lordes flocke. Simon Joanna (sayeth Jesus) louest thou me more than these? The Lorde dyd not aske these thinges as ignoraunte that he was muche loued of Peter, but he woulde haue inwardelye fastened in the hertes of his disciples, that moste hye charitie towardes Jesus, is nedefull to him that shoulde take cure of the Lordes flocke, for the whiche the Lorde himselfe suffered death upon the crosse.

Jesus than came and toke bread &c.

But Peter nowe being come to more circumspection than he was wount to be of, made no aunswere concernyng howe muche the other loued the lord, because he knewe not fully other mennes minds: for his owne parte and conscience,

science, he maketh aunswere, whereof he is bolde to make the Lorde hymselfe witnesse. Howe muche any other loueth thee, (sayeth he) I knowe not: Lorde I loue thee, and thou askest me, that knowest I doe loue thee. Thou that knowest the secretes of mennes myndes, art not ignoraunte that I loue thee. Than sayeth Jesus: If thou louest me as thou openly sayest, fede my lambes which I loue moste dearely, and for whom I haue spente my lyfe: and shewe thy selfe suche towardes them, as I haue shewed my self towardes you. This shall be a prouse of a perfite loue towardes me.

The texte. He sayeth to hym agayne the seconde tyme: Symon Joanna, louest thou me? He sayeth vnto hym: Yea Lorde, thou knowest that I loue thee. He sayeth vnto hym: Feede my shepe. He sayeth vnto hym the thyrde tyme: Symon Joanna, loueste thou me? and he sayed vnto hym: Lorde, thou knowest all thyng, thou knowest that I loue thee. Jesus sayeth vnto him: Feede my shepe.

The Lorde Jesus asketh hym agayne euen with like many wordes: Si-mon Joanna, louest thou me? Peter aunswereth him euen with lyke noum-bre of wordes: Lorde I loue thee. Thy selfe knowest that I loue thee. Than sayeth Jesus agayne: if thou louest me in dede, feede my shepe, whyche are deare to me. The lorde asked Peter the thyrde tyme: Symon Joanna, louest thou me? The lordes askyng so often repeted, caste Peter in a scruple and in a sorowe. For although he knewe in his owne conscience, that he loued the Lord exceadyngly, yet because he had thryse denyed the Lorde after he had so stoute-ly promysed the contrary, it caused hym also to distruste hymselfe. For Peters fall into the deniall of his lorde, turned hym to good, and furthered his salua-cion, whiche falle taughte hym humble sobriete, and caused hym to learne a newe lesson, that is, not to put to muche truste and affiaunce in hymselfe, suche a pestilence to euangelicall godlynesse, as none canne be more perniciouse and deadely then it. Therfore he aunswereth sincerely of trueth, but timerouslye and very lowlye withall, and where before he trusted to hymselfe, he now put-teth all his affiaunce in hym, to whom onely truste and affiaunce oughte to be geuen, saying: Lord, why askest thou me so often, seing thou knowest al thing? Thy self knowest that I loue thee. Than sayed Jesus: therfore feede my shepe, and vpon them declare howe muche thou settest by me.

Thou shalte take an exaumple of a good shepeherde of me. I haue spente my lyfe for my shepe, thou lykewyse shalte playe the faythfull shepeherde of my shepe, euen to the losse of lyfe and heade. The shepe be myne whom I haue re-demed with my bloud, & now returning againe to my father, I cōmit & betake them to thy fedyng. Thou therfore shalt playe the shepeherde & not the lorde, & thou shalt fede to saue, & not kyll or pull of theyr skyn to their vtter vndoyng. Yf I be thrise deare and welbeloued of the, they shal be dearely beloued of the, whom I loue exceding well. The lord Jesus would haue these thinges wyth so greate diligence powred into the myndes of his disciples, because he knewe there would rise men, that should, not for the loue of Jesus, but for theyr own commodities sake, take cure of christen people, or rather inuade and with vio-lence take cure vpon hande: which maner of persons woulde in stede of shepe-herdes, playe the tyrauntes, and robbe altogether. Moreouer the lorde didde vouchesafe to declare also what the thre tymes repeted confession of loue, did meane. He that for the health and safetie of the lordes flocke, contemneth his ryches, careth not for worldlye honoure, and neglecteth his owne affeccions, sheweth greate lykelyhoode, of trueth, that he hath a pure sincere loue: but he

that

that for sauyng the flocke, letteth not to auenture his lyfe, that manne (ye wote well) hath (so doyng) geuen a most sure lesson of perfite loue and charitie.

The texte.

Uerely, verely, I saye vnto thee, when then thou wast young, thou gyrdedst thy selfe, and walkedst whyther thou wouldest: but when thou arte olde, thou shalt stretche forth thy handes, and an other shall gyrde thee, and leade thee whether thou wouldest not. That spake he signifying by what death he should glorifie god.

The Lorde nowe willyng somewhat to open that Peter in tyme to come, should do that thyng, sayed: Peter, I do well assure thee therof, thou shalt whē tyme is, perfourme and accomplishe the thyng whiche thou nowe sayest and cōfessest. For truely it is no delicate profession. For when thou wast young, and in bodily strength more able to suffre laborouse and greuouse thynges, thou waste more dayntely occupied and liued more at ease. For thou vngirdedst or gyrdedst thy selfe at thyne owne wyll and pleasure, and walkedst at libertie whither thou wouldest. But when thou arte olde and than in bodily strengthe more weaker, thou shalt be more hardely entreated, thou than beyng in hearte and will more strong. For thou shalt stretche furthe thy handes, and another shall gyrde thee, and leade thee whither thou wouldest not. By this riddle or parable, Jesus signified by what kynde of death Peter shoulde once glorifie God. For because, beyng very aged, he was led to the crosse, whiche though he suffred gladlye for the excellente loue that he bare towardes his Lorde, yet the weakenesse of mannes nature lothed it.

The texte.

¶ And when he had spoken this, he sayeth vnto hym: Folowe me. Peter turned aboute and sawe the disciple whom Jesus loued, folowyng, (whiche also leaned on his breast at supper, and sayed: Lorde, whiche is he that betrayeth thee?) When Peter therfore sawe hym, he sayeth to Jesus: Lorde, what shall he here do? Jesus sayeth vnto hym: If I wyl haue him to tarrye tyll I come, what is that to thee? folowe thou me. Then went this saying abrode among the brethren, that the disciple should not dye. Yet Jesus sayed not vnto hym, he shal not dye, but yf I wyll that he tary tyll I come, what is that to thee?

When Jesus had sayed thus, he begunne to walke, and sayed to Peter, folowe me: so once agayne prouokyng and inuityng hym to the folowyng of his charitie and death: When Peter turned and loked aboute hym, he seeth euen that disciple whome Jesus loued, and that leaned on the Lordes breast at his laste supper, whilest he asked of him who should betraye hym. Forasmuche as Peter did entierly loue this disciple, and knewe that he was alwaye better beloued of the lord then the rest, and than sawe the same vnbidden folow, nexte vnto Peter, Peter asked the lorde what should become of that mā. For he nowe knewe already of his owne death, and he desyreth to knowe whether that he shoulde haue this man a companion to dye with hym.

Folow thou me.

For he thoughte that to be a gloriouse thing vnto hym, and a great token of the Lordes loue towardes hym, that he might dye after the exaumple of Jesus. But Jesus to correct this vnnecessarie care that Peter hadde of an other mannes death, sayed: If I will haue hym tary tyll I come, what is that to thee? He is myne, and after mine aduise wyll I ordeyne and determyne for hym that shalbe for the beste. Care and prepare thou for that whiche appertayneth to thy selfe, that is to saye, that thou folowe me. And than vpon the occasion of this saying, there arose a bruite among the disciples that Jesus his welbeloued disciple shoulde dye no violent death, but should liue styll vntyll the Lord shall come agayne to iudge the quicke and the deade, (which they all thought than should be sone after.) Albeit the Lorde did not saye, he shall

not

not dye, but to make dull, abate, and repulse Peters curiositie, and ouermuche diligence, he denied it to perteyne vnto hym, though hys wyll and pleasure had been, that the man shoulde styll lyue vnto his laste cummyng.

The texte.

Thesame disciple is he, whiche testifieth of these thynges, and wrote thesame thynges. And we knowe that hys testimony is true. There are also many other thynges whiche Jesus did, the whiche yf thei shoulde be written euery one, I suppose the worlde coulde not conteine the bookes that shoulde be written.

And in dede this is thatsame disciple that witnesseth these thynges thus to bee dooen, and that wrote thesame, to the entente they maye more truely, and more farre abrode bee scattered and dispersed to the knowledge of all folke. And we haue knowen that his testimonie is true. For he wrote not other mennes hearynges, but at whiche hymselfe was presente. Nor he hath not made mencion of all the thinges whiche Jesus sayed and did. For if a manne shoulde goe about to tell them, euery thyng by it selfe, an vnmeasurable sorte of bokes shoulde bee made therof. But so muche is written as suffiseth to the obteyning of saluacion. Therfore the rest is, that beleuyng these, and stickyng to the steppes and wayes of Jesus, we labour diligently to get the rewarde of immortall lyfe.

Thus endeth the Paraphrase vpon the Ghospell of S. John.